Friends of the

CONSTITUTION

———•———

Writings of the "Other" Federalists
1787–1788

Edited by

Colleen A. Sheehan and Gary L. McDowell

LIBERTY FUND

Indianapolis

This book is published by Liberty Fund, Inc., a foundation established to encourage study of the ideal of a society of free and responsible individuals.

The cuneiform inscription that serves as our logo and as the design motif for our endpapers is the earliest-known written appearance of the word "freedom" (*amagi*), or "liberty." It is taken from a clay document written about 2300 B.C. in the Sumerian city-state of Lagash.

Library of Congress Cataloging-in-Publication Data
Friends of the Constitution : writings of the "other" Federalists,
1787–1788 / edited by Colleen A. Sheehan and Gary L. McDowell.
p. cm.
Includes bibliographical references and index.
ISBN 0-86597-154-4 (cloth). —ISBN 0-86597-155-2 (pbk.)
1. Constitutional history—United States—Sources.
2. United States—Politics and government—1783–1789—Sources.
I. Sheehan, Colleen A. II. McDowell, Gary L., 1949– .
KF4515.F75 1998
342.73'029—dc21   97-3497

98 99 00 01 02 C 5 4 3 2 1
98 99 00 01 02 P 5 4 3 2 1

LIBERTY FUND, INC.
8335 Allison Pointe Trail, Suite 300
Indianapolis, IN 46250-1687

To our teachers

William B. Allen, Morton J. Frisch, Harry V. Jaffa,

Ralph Lerner, and Robert A. Rutland

CONTENTS

The Necessity of Union

Energetic but Limited Government

Popular Government and Civic Virtue

CONTENTS

PREFACE

THERE HAS perhaps never been a political act of greater historical consequence than the creation of the American republic. The significance of the act derives not only from the subsequent development of the nation into a major presence in the world but also, and more important, from the purpose of the Founding. It was not hyperbole when "Publius" introduced *The Federalist* by noting that a monumental task seemed to have been reserved to the people of America. That task was to demonstrate "whether societies of men are really capable or not of establishing good government from reflection and choice, or whether they are forever destined to depend for their political constitutions on accident and force."[1] From the Declaration of Independence through the Federal Convention of 1787 and the struggle over ratification of the Constitution, Americans knew that the eyes of the world were upon them. What the American Founding symbolizes is the importance of principle in the ordering of man's political life. Its purpose was nothing less than to demonstrate that mankind is capable of self-government. Alexis de Tocqueville put it best when he remarked, "I saw in America more than America."

There are two influential perspectives in American political thinking that denigrate the role of principle in politics. The first, and perhaps the dominant one today, insists that political life is adequately explained by resort to economics, sociology, or psychology. The other perspective claims that all political and human life can be explained by deconstructionist philosophy. These academic approaches are, we believe, too narrow in their treatment of things political. Certainly human behavior is influenced by such factors as economic interest, social status, ethnicity, and relations of power.

---

1. *The Federalist,* No. 1, in Alexander Hamilton, James Madison, and John Jay, *The Federalist Papers,* ed. Clinton Rossiter (New York, 1961).

But while it is *influenced* by these forces, it is not *controlled* by them. To view a political phenomenon of such depth and consequence as the American Founding only through the lens of social science analysis or deconstructionist hermeneutics is to see it in a fragmented and distorted way. To reduce all human behavior to self-interest, or fear, or some other subrational or quasi-rational force, is to fail to consider the capacity of the human soul and the possibility of justice. It is to miss even a glimpse of Tocqueville's vista.

A great many of the essays, letters, and pamphlets reproduced in this volume cannot be understood if one is limited by a materialistic or otherwise reductionist reading. Some of the Federalist writers, in fact, attempt to capture the reader's spirit by entwining it with the spirit of the Founding. We should not presume that the pages they left behind were meant only to persuade and inspire their contemporaries and not to influence future generations of Americans as well. But in order to grasp their entreaty at all, we today must rediscover the openness to historical questions and human motivations that they took for granted. The need for this openness among contemporary readers is perhaps best expressed by Charles Warren:

> In recent years there has been a tendency to interpret all history in terms of economics and sociology and geography—of soil, of debased currency, of land monopoly, of taxation, of class antagonism, of frontier against seacoast, and the like—and to attribute the actions of peoples to such general materialistic causes. This may be a wise reaction from the old manner of writing history almost exclusively in terms of wars, politics, dynasties, and religions. But its fundamental defect is, that it ignores the circumstance that the actions of men are frequently based quite as much on sentiment and belief as on facts and conditions. It leaves out the souls of men and their response to the inspiration of great leaders. It forgets that there are such motives as patriotism, pride in country, unselfish devotion to the public welfare, desire for independence, inherited sentiments, and convictions of right and justice. The historian who omits to take these facts into consideration is a poor observer of human nature. No one can write true history who leaves out of account the fact that a man may have an inner zeal for principles, beliefs, and ideals.[2]

2. Charles Warren, *The Making of the Constitution* (Boston: Little, Brown & Company, 1928), 3.

While economic and social considerations played their normal role in determining which side of the Founding debate individuals would take, lingering over them does not expose the fact that for most of the Founding generation the debate stemmed from a more fundamental concern: What form of government would best secure the private rights and public happiness of the people? The deepest concern of both Anti-Federalists and Federalists was to fashion the best practicable, if not the best, regime.

This volume is intended to encourage a broader and deeper understanding of the debate over the Constitution and the founding of the American republic. Further, it is designed to invite the reader to engage the questions of political philosophy via the route of thinking about our own polity. This approach of coming to philosophic questions via politics, and not vice-versa, is, we believe, of crucial importance. By employing this method we adopt the approach of the Founders themselves. Education in the politics of the American Founding, for example, provides a pathway to education in political philosophy in a way that does not neglect the political considerations at the heart of *political* philosophy—considerations that were vitally important to the Founders. The converse approach of treating politics solely by way of theory allows students to bypass political concerns and questions rather than think through them. It encourages them to substitute mere abstraction for genuine political understanding. The approach we encourage here stands in sharp contrast to this method. Indeed, it is intended to combat the belief that one can draw philosophic conclusions about constitutional politics without knowing anything about the politics of the Constitution.

Accordingly, this volume is designed to feature primary texts of the "other" Federalists and to encourage readers to pay serious attention to the words and views of the authors themselves. In this way the collection is a source book of primary material. By introducing the reader to the divergent opinions between the supporters and opponents of the Constitution, as well as among the supporters themselves, we have made some of the implicit, more philosophic questions explicit. As such the volume is not simply a historical source book but an introductory reader in the philosophic politics of the American Founding as well.

This collection is intended as a companion volume to *The Federalist* and Anti-Federalist writings. It is meant to be a representative rather than a comprehensive collection. These essays have not been chosen to achieve proportion by section of the country or simply because of the repetition or impact of a particular argument though we have endeavored not to neglect any geographic section or influential argument. Rather our primary concern in selection has been to include the most distinctive and richest of the "other" Federalists' essays and to reveal as fully as possible the principles, the range of arguments, as well as the color and flavor of the debate. Read in conjunction with the writings of the Anti-Federalists this volume is intended to give the reader a sense of the controversy that surrounded our national birth; read with *The Federalist* this collection offers the reader a fuller view of the dimensions of Federalist thought. Added to the conveyable editions of *The Federalist* and Anti-Federalist writings currently available, this portable one-volume sampler of "other" Federalist writings makes accessible to students and citizen-readers a broader view of American Founding thought.

The idea for this collection was originally conceived by Professor Herbert Storing, who initially appended a collection of Federalist writings to his essay that now serves as the introduction to this volume. Many of Professor Storing's selections are retained here though we have made substantial additions as well as deletions to his preliminary list. Such additions as selections from "An Essay on the Means of Promoting Federal Sentiments in the United States" by a "Foreign Spectator" were made because they add significantly to our understanding of the principles being explicated during the public debates of 1787 and 1788. Deletions were made to compact the edition and to highlight the more politically and philosophically penetrating essays.

As Professor Storing's introduction shows, the "other" Federalists, from James Wilson and John Dickinson to the more obscure and anonymous penmen, waged the frontline battle in the public defense of the Constitution of 1787. Though often mingled with personal invective and spirited denunciations, the "other" Federalist papers contained herein present the reader with many thoughtful, and sometimes profound, discussions regarding the necessities and the nature of politics, the character of republican government, and the influence of constitutions and laws on the manners and spirit of a people. In studying these essays, the reader is asked to consider the question of the Federalists' purpose. In addition to their general goal of attaining ratification of the proposed Constitution, what were they trying to achieve and why? And how did they think they could best attain their ends? Where did the "other" Federalists agree and disagree? In understanding the politics of the American Founding, can we understand better the philosophic underpinnings of the American republic?

Unlike "Publius" the "other" Federalists did not speak with one voice. But even though the numerous authors took on as many journalistic identities, the question remains whether there is a single body of thought that can be classified as the Federalist viewpoint. Certainly the Federalists agreed on the need for a firmer union and for an energetic but limited government. Further they concurred—not only among themselves but also with the Anti-Federalists—on the wisdom of establishing a representative rather than a direct democracy. Disagreements were present, however, about the proper task of the representative and even about the sovereign authority of the constitutional union though the latter difference of opinion is much less pronounced. And surely there was disagreement among the Federalists regarding the role of government in the formation of the character of the citizenry.

There has been much scholarly controversy in recent years about the American Founders' conception of republican government, particularly in respect to their understanding of the purpose and philosophic character of the polity they created. Did the Founders believe that the ultimate purpose of republicanism was the formation of a virtuous citizenry? Or did they believe that the idea of free, limited government sets parameters not only to governmental powers but reduces the ends of political association as well, thereby precluding the idea of civic education? Furthermore, if republican government depends in some way on a virtuous citizenry, then who—the national government? the state governments? or the private sector?—bears the responsibility for promoting it? If, on the other hand, the idea of free government severs the connection between ethics and politics, then what legitimizes the ultimate authority in the polity?

Human nature is such that on virtually any given issue there will be some disagreement, however small the minority may be. This is certainly true when applied to the issues raised during the ratification of the Constitution, including among the Federalists themselves. Nonetheless among reasonable human beings association implies that they have something in common, be it merely a shared usefulness or a union for some higher purpose. The Federalists were united in support of the document drafted in Philadelphia—they were Friends of the Constitution. We are naturally led to ask then, what made them friends? What was the basis for their friendship? Was it mere utility and self-interest that drew them together, or is there prevalent in their writings a shared, more noble vision that inspired their political association? What was it, in sum, that made them together see in America more than America?

Colleen A. Sheehan
Villanova University

Gary L. McDowell
Institute of United States Studies,
University of London

ACKNOWLEDGMENTS

Herbert Storing was once described as a man of simple republican virtue. We can think of no description that could better fit him, nor one that would have pleased him more. As a scholar he was possessed of a powerful and penetrating mind; as a teacher, he was patient and demanding and always there to help; but, most of all, he was a man of principle. His entire professional life, as Joseph Cropsey has remarked, was preoccupied by his attempt to unfold the "genesis and meaning of the American regime." Yet he left no major book. His teaching on those matters lies scattered in essays and articles that range from a study of the administrative theories of Herbert Simon to the political thought of Frederick Douglass; it is embedded also in all the doctoral dissertations he supervised during his twenty-one years at the University of Chicago; and, most important, it is impressed on that generation of students whose lives he touched and transformed.

When he began to think about collecting the documents of the American Founding he intended to include the "other" Federalist papers along with the Anti-Federalist writings. Unfortunately for us, he was not able to pursue the original scheme. When Professor Storing died suddenly on 7 September 1977 at the age of forty-nine, it seemed appropriate to some of us to make an effort to fulfill his original plan. This collection is a modest attempt to do so. We are indebted to Joseph Bessette, Murray Dry, David Nichols, Jeffrey Poelvoorde, and Ralph Rossum for their encouragement and support throughout this project.

We have been aided throughout by a good many people who gave freely of their time, their experience, and their expertise. William B. Allen, Steven R. Boyd, Charles F. Hobson, John P. Kaminski, Charles H. Schoenleber, and Robert A. Rutland provided us with sure and safe passage through the forest of early American historical documents. Their suggestions and their assistance have made this a far better collection than it would have been without their help. We owe a special thanks to John Kaminski for generously making available to us the collections of the Documentary History of the Ratification of the Constitution Project.

The staffs of the libraries of the Pennsylvania Historical Society, the Maryland Historical Society, the New York Historical Society, the Connecticut Historical Society, the State Historical Society of Wisconsin, the State Library of Virginia, Forbes Library, Colonial Williamsburg Foundation, Villanova University, Dickinson College, the Library of Congress, and the American Antiquarian Society were unfailingly helpful. Their generous assistance in locating materials and exploring the identification of many of the authors presented in this volume have made this a better collection than it would have been without them.

This project enlisted an army of assistants. William A. Smith, David R. Greco, Susan Walker, Donna Bartenfelder, Suzanne Fish, Ruth Homolasch, William McConnell, Laura Maziarz, David Razenback, John Roberto, Marta Rubin, Amy Unger, Victoria Kuhn, and Wendy Lehman lent helping hands at various stages of the undertaking. Jamie Gold, Assistant for Academic Programs of the Heritage Foundation, and Gregory Schaller, of the Graduate Program in Political Science at Temple University, made substantial contributions to this work and were indispensable to the project's completion. Mr. Gold's and Mr. Schaller's scholarly care and tireless dedication to the task at hand revealed an even deeper dedication to the purpose of the Founding. With characteristic aplomb and good humor, they made for us a pleasant experience out of what could have been a most onerous task.

This project was handsomely funded by the Office of Academic Affairs and the Graduate School of Arts and Sciences of Villanova University, the Faculty Committee on Research and Development of Dickinson College, the Institute of United States Studies of the University of London, and the Bradley Residents Scholars Program of the Heritage Foundation. For the financial support given us, and the moral support shown us by our spouses, John Doody and Brenda McDowell, and by our friends and colleagues at Dickinson, Institute of United States Studies, Villanova, and Heritage, we are deeply grateful.

EDITORS' NOTE

I<small>N EVERY INSTANCE</small>, the pieces contained herein are presented in their entirety. While every essay in a particular series may not be included, those that are true to the original publication are reproduced here. Brackets are used to signify editorial insertions, which include the addition of missing or illegible text, and where necessary for clarity, the addition of first or full names. Missing text that has not been replaced is indicated by empty brackets [ ]. When necessary, obvious printer's errors and grammatical infelicities (such as a subject-verb disagreement) have been corrected without notation. Generally eighteenth-century spelling and punctuation have been preserved.

Reference notes by the authors have been kept in the main text and are signified by their original symbols; editorial notes are indicated by a number. Editorial notation has been kept to a minimum.

We have relied heavily on the original newspaper and pamphlet versions of the essays. We have also drawn materials from the series edited by Merrill Jensen, John Kaminski, and Gaspare Saladino, *Documentary History of the Ratification of the Constitution* (Madison: State Historical Society of Wisconsin, 1976), referred to herein as *DH* and then followed by volume number and page number; Jonathan Elliot's *Debates;* Paul Leicester Ford's *Pamphlets on the Constitution of the United States* and *Essays on the Constitution of the United States;* W. B. Allen's *George Washington: A Collection* and *Works of Fisher Ames: As Published by Seth Ames;* James Madison's *Notes of Debates in the Federal Convention of 1787;* and J. Franklin Jameson's *Dictionary of United States History, 1492–1899.*

In order to establish the context of the ratification debates, this volume includes citations to the Anti-Federalist writings contained in Herbert Storing's *The Complete Anti-Federalist* (Chicago: University of Chicago Press, 1981). For example, a reference to the criticism of the proposed judicial power by the Anti-Federalist "Brutus" will be indicated as follows: Storing, 2:9.

The first number indicates in which of the seven volumes of *The Complete Anti-Federalist* the essays by "Brutus" appear (volume 2); the second number indicates the place of the essays within the particular volume (for example, the essays by "Brutus" are in the ninth selection in volume 2).

Because this work is designed for classroom use, wherever possible we have also made cross-references to the selection of Anti-Federalist writings designed for students' use by W. B. Allen and Gordon Lloyd, eds., entitled *The Essential Antifederalist* (University Press of America, 1985). Herein it will be cited as Allen, followed by the appropriate page numbers.

Whenever applicable, in both Herbert Storing's essay and the writings herein, the footnotes contain internal cross-references (*Friends* and page number) to provide further information or to refer the reader to the "other" Federalist Paper's place in this volume.

INTRODUCTION

Herbert J. Storing

"The 'Other' Federalist Papers: A Preliminary Sketch"

The wise CONSTITUTION let's truly revere,
It points out the course for our EMPIRE to steer,
For oceans of bliss do they hoist the broad sail,
And *peace* is the current, and *plenty* the gale.
> Our Freedom we've won, and the prize let's maintain,
> Our hearts are all right—
> Unite, Boys, Unite,
> And our EMPIRE in glory shall ever remain.

—The Grand Constitution: Or,
The Palladium of Columbia. A New Federal Song
(*New Hampshire Recorder*, 23 October 1787)

To an even greater extent than the Anti-Federalists, the "other" Federalist writings stand in the shadow cast by the towering *Federalist* papers. The neglect they have suffered is not altogether undeserved. Taken as a whole, they tend to be rather shallow and routine. That can of course be said of most wide samples of political writing, but it is striking how much of the Federalist effort was directed to mere explication of the Constitution or to criticizing the opposition. Neither of these will concern us much here; but

This essay first appeared in the *Political Science Reviewer* 6 (fall 1976): 215–47, and is reprinted by permission.
Where appropriate, page references will be given to reprints in Paul Leicester Ford, *Pamphlets on the Constitution of the United States* (Brooklyn, 1888); Paul Leicester Ford, *Essays on the Constitution of the United States* (Brooklyn, 1892); or John Back McMaster and Frederick Stone, *Pennsylvania and the Federal Constitution* (Philadelphia, 1888). These will be cited *FP*, *FE*, and *M/S*, respectively.

it is worth reporting that nearly half of the one hundred or so essays and pamphlets that form the basis of the present review are mainly criticisms of specific Anti-Federalist writings. It is hardly too much to say that among the "front line" debaters, the Anti-Federalists criticized the Constitution and the Federalists criticized the Anti-Federalists.

There is nothing in the Federalist writings comparable to the range and depth of *The Federalist;* nor are there the intriguing glimpses of an alternative American polity that emerge from the writings of the Anti-Federalists.[1] Yet these "other" Federalist writings carried the main burden of the public defense of the proposed Constitution in 1787 and 1788; many of them are quite substantial; several of them were vastly more influential than *The Federalist.* Considering the writings of such men as Wilson, Dickinson, Coxe, Sherman, Ellsworth, Noah and Peletiah Webster, Hanson, Jay, Iredell, and the many still-anonymous Federalist writers enables us to fill in our picture of the debate over the Constitution, to see more fully the diversity of Federalist views, and to identify some major themes or issues. What follows is based on a wide though not exhaustive survey of Federalist essays, pamphlets, and published speeches appearing in 1787 and 1788, with the main emphasis on the more penetrating writers and the more fundamental issues. It is meant to be suggestive rather than definitive.

It may be helpful to begin with a sketch of a typical Federalist essay, assuming that it was not merely attacking one of the Anti-Federalists. Our author would be likely to begin with an account of the precarious state of the American Union, emphasizing the economic stagnation, loss of credit, and dangers to commerce and safety caused by American weakness. Looking inward, he would probably refer to Shays' Rebellion and warn of the likelihood of increased domestic turmoil unless the governing capacity of the Union is strengthened. He would show the defects of the government under the Articles of Confederation, a government incapable of enforcing its resolves. He would describe in fulsome terms the Constitutional Convention under the leadership of the venerable Franklin and the virtuous Washington.

---

1. See Herbert J. Storing, *What the Anti-Federalists Were For* (Chicago: University of Chicago Press, 1981). This is also the introduction to Herbert J. Storing, ed., *The Complete Anti-Federalist,* 7 vols. (Chicago: University of Chicago Press, 1981).

All America agrees that the government of the Union requires additional powers; and the new general government will possess only the powers specifically granted to it, which are no more than are required to deal with national concerns. The much criticized powers of sword and purse, to which our author would give considerable attention, are indispensable to any government worthy of the name and are as well guarded as possible. All power can of course be abused, but the solution is to be found not in withholding necessary power but in a well constructed government. Contrary to a common Anti-Federal claim, the states will not be destroyed by the new Constitution; they remain the organs of government for most domestic matters, and they are vital to the operation of the general government itself. The new government, deriving from the pure source of all political authority, the people, will secure all of the advantages of monarchy, aristocracy, and democracy, while avoiding their disadvantages. Our author would show at length why the representatives of the people will continue true to their trust; and he would explain the rational apportionment of power among the parts of the general government, together with the carefully devised scheme of checks and balances, all designed to reinforce governmental responsibility and secure wise government. He would deny, again probably at some length, that a bill of rights is necessary, contending that a good Constitution, such as the one proposed, is the proper "bill of rights" for a free people. In conclusion he would return to the theme of Union and strongly urge that the alternative facing Americans is either acceptance of the new Constitution or the destruction of the Union. To insist on amendments prior to ratification or to call for a second convention is equivalent to rejecting the Constitution altogether. There is no likelihood that future deliberation would display anything like the spirit of patriotism and mutual concession achieved in Philadelphia in the summer of 1787. Having successfully defended their liberties against one of the foremost powers of the world, having freely established governments designed to secure those liberties, having through a convention of their wisest leaders devised and improved their Union, the American people now have it in their power to conclude a political founding unique in the annals of human history. They can give an example to mankind of an excellent constitution adopted by open deliberation and free choice.

Union

The precarious state of the American Union is the first article in the Federalist defense of the Constitution. Relaxing after their great public act of independence, Americans allowed selfish, partial interests to emerge, threatening the objects for which the Revolution had been fought. During the war, John Jay wrote, Americans worshipped their Union as the pagans worshipped their tutelar deities. "That union was the child of wisdom—heaven blessed it, and it wrought out our political salvation."[2] During those times, "a sense of the common danger united every heroic, every patriotic soul in the great cause of liberty." Selfishness itself was stilled.[3] So prevalent was this view that Americans made the "amiable mistake" of thinking that they were unlike other men and could do without coercive government. The ineffective Articles of Confederation were the result. "It was an honest and solemn covenant among our infant States, and virtue and common danger supplied its defects."[4] When the danger disappeared, however, "a sense of security loosened the bands of union." "The spirit of private gain expelled the spirit of public good, and men became more intent on the means of enriching and aggrandizing themselves, than of enriching and aggrandizing their country."[5] Americans need to resolve anew to "cling to Union as the political Rock of our Salvation,"[6] and they need to face the fact that their Union requires a real government.

The Anti-Federalists admitted the inadequacy of the Articles of Confederation, but they thought that the new Constitution would sacrifice the states to a great national government. Responding to this claim that the Constitution was a "consolidation" rather than a strengthened federal government, the Federalists made two main arguments. First, they showed that

2. A Citizen of New York [John Jay], An Address to the People of the State of New York, New York, 1788 (*FP,* 70; *Friends,* 138).

3. A Federalist, Philadelphia *Independent Gazetteer,* 25 October 1787 (*M/S,* 165; *Friends,* 36).

4. A Citizen of Pennsylvania, *Pennsylvania Packet,* 12 October 1787 (*M/S,* 106).

5. A Citizen of New York [John Jay] (*FP,* 70–71; *Friends,* 139).

6. Fabius [John Dickinson], Letters of Fabius, Wilmington, Delaware, 1788 (*FP,* 167; *Friends,* 59).

the states were indispensable participants in the new general government itself. State qualifications for electors were to be the qualifications for the electors of the House of Representatives; states were to choose the members of the Senate and were to be parties in the choosing of the President. In these and other ways, the Federalists repeatedly contended, the states would be so involved in the actual constitution of the general government that it could not exist without them. The second and more fundamental defense, however, was that, despite the increase in the powers of the general government, the new Constitution leaves with the states the whole responsibility of internal government except for those few areas that concern the Union as a whole. The standard argument here is one that is very familiar to Americans today. It describes the American system as dividing the powers of government between the general government, which concerns itself with matters that affect the Union as a whole, and the state governments, which concern themselves with those matters purely domestic. According to Peletiah Webster, "the Constitution does not suffer the federal powers to controul in the least, or so much as to interfere in the internal policy, jurisdiction, or municipal rights of any particular State: except where great and manifest national purposes and interests make that controul necessary."[7] Nor did the problem of drawing a line between state and federal jurisdictions seem so difficult: "the objects of federal government will be so obvious that there will be no great danger of any interference."[8]

These arguments did not satisfy the Anti-Federalists, and with good reason. State participation in filling the offices of the general government would mean little if the states were not secured an independent and significant

7. A Citizen of Philadelphia [Peletiah Webster], "The Weakness of Brutus Exposed," 8 November 1787 (*FP,* 128; *Friends,* 191). See also Peletiah Webster, Remarks on the Address of Sixteen Members of the Assembly of Pennsylvania, Philadelphia, 1787 (*M/S,* 99); and A Citizen of America [Noah Webster], An Examination into the Leading Principles of the Federal Constitution, Philadelphia, 1787 (*FP,* 46–48; *Friends,* 389–90).

8. A Citizen of New Haven [Roger Sherman], *New Haven Gazette,* 4 and 25 December 1787 (*FE,* 239; *Friends,* 269). For a detailed discussion, see A Freeman [Tench Coxe], *Pennsylvania Gazette,* 23 and 30 January and 6 February 1788 (*Friends,* 88–101); and A Native of Virginia, Observations upon the Proposed Plan of Federal Government, Petersburg, 1788, in M. Hamilton, *The Writings of James Monroe,* vol. 1.

sphere of power. And even granting the (doubtful) proposition that a clear line could now be drawn between the general concerns of the Union and the particular concerns of the states, the principle of distinction clearly implies a radical and, over time, almost complete subordination of the states. Some Federalists were happy to draw precisely that conclusion and only feared that federal supremacy would not occur soon or decisively enough. But most were at least equivocal , and it is that equivocation that we must examine.

One side of the Federalist view had been displayed by James Wilson in his 8 June speech in the Constitutional Convention, when he said, "Among the first sentiments expressed in the first Congress, one was that Virginia is no more. That Massachusetts is no [more], that Pennsylvania is no more, etc. We are now one nation of brethren. We must bury all local interests and distinctions." This language continued for some time, Wilson said; but "no sooner were the States Governments formed than their jealousy and ambition began to display themselves. Each endeavored to cut a slice from the common loaf, to add to its own morsel, till at length the confederation became frittered down to the impotent condition in which it now stands."[9] Wilson here suggests that the Union is prior to the states in principle and even historically; the state governments, he says, were formed after the first Congress. "Indulge no narrow prejudices to the disadvantage of your brethren of the other states," another Federalist wrote, following this same line of thought: "consider the people of all the thirteen states, as a band of brethren, speaking the same language, professing the same religion, inhabiting one undivided country, and designed by heaven to be one people."[10] In an interesting Federalist speech from Maryland, intended to be delivered to the ratifying convention but only published in July 1788, the historical and legal priority of the Union is asserted quite explicitly. Responding to the

9. Max Farrand, ed., *The Records of the Federal Convention*, 4 vols. (New Haven:Yale University Press, 1937), 1:116.

10. Civis [David Ramsay], An Address to the Freemen of South Carolina on the Subject of the Federal Constitution Principles, Charleston *Columbian Herald*, 4 February 1788 (*FP,* 379; *Friends,* 456).

tyrannical impositions of the King and Parliament, this Federalist explained, the colonists united and appointed the first of the continental congresses which resisted British encroachments, determined upon separation, and prosecuted the war of independence. The state governments were instituted only later. "It is to be remembered, that congress existed before the [state] legislatures, and that it exercised all the powers, which are conferred by these articles [of confederation], and perhaps greater."[11]

The priority of the Union to the states, which was later to be so eloquently and profoundly argued by Lincoln, may, I think, be said to be the "true" or "best" Federalist position. Yet what is surprising is that the Federalists did not make the Marylander's argument more often; usually they conceded the historical and legal priority of the states. Indeed in the same speech of 8 June in which he urged the primacy of Union, James Wilson made another argument which denied it. "Federal liberty," he said, "is to States, what civil liberty, is to private individuals. And States are not more unwilling to purchase it, by the necessary concession of their political sovereignty, than the savage is to purchase Civil liberty by the surrender of the personal sovereignty, which he enjoys in a State of nature."[12] This "federal liberty" view was prominent in Wilson's defense of the Constitution in Pennsylvania, and it was very widespread among Federalist writers. Wilson explained to his fellow Pennsylvanians that as civil liberty is that portion of natural liberty resigned by men to government, so federal liberty consists in the aggregate of the civil liberty which is surrendered by each state to the national government; "and the same principles that operate in the establishment of a single society, with respect to the rights reserved or resigned by the individuals that compose it, will justly apply in the case of a confederation of distinct and independent States."[13] The federal and the state governments

11. Anonymous, Speech to Have Been Delivered in the Maryland Convention, Baltimore *Maryland Journal,* 25 and 29 July, and 1 and 8 August 1788. See also Philo-Publius [William Duer], New York *Daily Advertiser,* 1 December 1787 (*Friends,* 109–12).

12. Farrand, *Records,* 1:166.

13. James Wilson, Speech in Pennsylvania Convention, 24 November 1787. This quotation is from Dallas's version of Wilson's speech (*DH,* 2:347); Cf. Lloyd's version (*Friends,* 82). See also Civis [David Ramsay] (*FP,* 373; *Friends,* 450).

are not (as was often said) coordinate sovereignties, another Federalist insisted: "The general government is *fœderal*, or an union of *sovereignties*, for *special* purposes. The state governments are *social*, or an association of *individuals*, for all the purposes of society and government."[14] Many Federalists claimed that a bill of rights was unnecessary under the new Constitution because the federal government was an association of states, not of individuals.

There are two implications of the federal liberty/civil liberty analogy that are problematical from the Federalist viewpoint. First, it seems to demand that the states in a federal system have equal votes, as individuals do in civil society, regardless of their different strength and wealth. William Paterson had made this point in the Constitutional Convention: "there was no more reason that a great individual State contributing much, should have more votes than a small one contributing little, than that a rich individual citizen should have more votes than an indigent one."[15] In the Convention Wilson had opposed an equal representation of the states and insisted rather on representation according to population, but he never gave Paterson a satisfactory reply. Some Federalists were more consistent and defended the equal representation of the states in the Senate as not merely a compromise (as Wilson regarded it) but a principled recognition of the "federal" character of the American Union.

A second and more fundamental implication of the "federal liberty" view is that the states are the crucial parties to, and presumably therefore ultimately the judges of, the general government. With independence from the Crown, most of the Federalists seemed to think, the colonies also became independent of one another (as Luther Martin, later a prominent Anti-Federalist, had urged so forcefully in the Philadelphia Convention). The states then determined on and were of course the parties of a new union. As one thoughtful Pennsylvanian put it, since the center of the Union had been the Crown, "the act of independence dissolved the political ties that had formerly existed among the states. . . ." However the former colonies

14. A Pennsylvanian, *Pennsylvania Gazette*, 27 February 1788.
15. Farrand, *Records*, 1:178.

did not wish to continue "distinct bodies of people." "The remains of our ancient governments kept us in the form of thirteen political bodies, and from a variety of just and prudent considerations we determined to enter into an indissoluble and perpetual *union*." The expression "We the people of the United States" means "We the People of the *Several* States," to whom reference was necessary because the new Constitution implied changes in the various state constitutions. Had the framers meant to refer to the American people at large, they would have said, "We the People *of America*," which is the term "constantly used in speaking of us *as a nation*." "Had the fœderal convention meant to exclude the idea of '*union*,' that is, of *several and separate* sovereignties joining in a confederacy, they would have said, we, *the people of America;* the union necessarily involves the idea of component states, which complete consolidations exclude. But the severality of the states is frequently recognized in the most distinct manner in the course of the constitution."[16] "The Constitution now before the public," a Federalist from New Hampshire wrote, "is not a compact between individuals, but between several sovereign and independent political societies already formed and organized."[17] A view of this kind is the basis for the rather typical description of the Constitution by Roger Sherman: "The Powers vested in the federal government are clearly defined, so that each state still retains its sovereignty in what concerns its own internal government, and a right to exercise every power of a sovereign state not particularly delegated to the government of the United States."[18] But does not this view of the Constitution as a compact among states lead straight to the Virginia and Kentucky Resolutions and beyond? Is the authentic legacy of the Federalists expressed not by Lincoln but by Calhoun?

It must be acknowledged of course that no view of the American Union that is true to history and the play of principle in the American Founding

16. A Freeman [Tench Coxe], *Pennsylvania Gazette*, 23 January 1788 (*Friends*, 89–91).

17. Alfredus [Samuel Tenny], Exeter, New Hampshire *Freeman's Oracle*, 18 January 1788 (*Friends*, 252). *Cf.* the discussion of ratification in *The Federalist*, No. 39, and John Marshall's Opinion in *McCulloch v. Maryland* 4 Wheat. 316 (1819).

18. A Citizen of New Haven [Roger Sherman], *New Haven Gazette*, 4 December 1787 (*FE*, 238; *Friends*, 267).

can avoid ambiguity. Moreover the Federalists had the usual motive of the political debater to take as much as he can of his opponent's ground. Nevertheless it is striking how widely the Federalists adopted the view of the Union as a coming together of sovereign states. Yet that is not the end of the matter, for it still somehow misses the way most of the Federalists really understood the American Union. Can their widespread acknowledgment of the origin of the Union in state sovereignty be reconciled with their deeper view of the Union as the basic, defining political association of this American nation?

At least a hint of such a reconciliation may be found in the Federalist essays of John Dickinson, writing as "Fabius." One of the Old Republicans, Dickinson pressed the need for "humility and benevolence" to take the place of "pride and overweening selfishness" if successful free government was to be established. He presents a standard account of the origins of civil society, in which each individual gives up some share of his rights in order to secure the rest. In a confederation a similar principle operates; but Dickinson emphasizes that men are the materials of confederation as well as of simple government; the purpose of a confederation is to promote the happiness of individuals. "Herein there is a progression, not a contradiction. As *man*, he becomes a citizen; as a citizen, he becomes a federalist. The generation of one, is not the destruction of the other. He carries into society his naked rights: These thereby improved, he carries still forward into confederation."[19]

Dickinson's argument was not widely imitated, the way Wilson's "federal liberty" idea was, but it nevertheless conveys, I think, a good deal of the spirit of the Federalist view of Union. The movement from man to citizen to federalist is a moral progression. Civil society is entered into to secure private rights; this requires a moderation of the pride and overweening selfishness of man in his natural state, which Dickinson sees as not only a means

---

19. Fabius [John Dickinson] (*FP,* 177; *Friends,* 68). The ordinary use of the word "federalist" had at this time an ambiguity that should be noted. It referred to the principle of "federalism" (or "confederalism"), but it also referred to the *agencies* of the federation. When a man said he was "federal" in disposition, he meant he was inclined to strengthen and support the general government. This was the usage that entitled the Federalists to their name.

to but as a benefit of civil society. The same kind of observation applies to the next stage. "Federalist" here means a member of a wider association concerned with a wider and thereby somehow higher public good. Thus a Boston Federalist complained that the American people had become "destitute of FEDERAL FEATURES and HABITS—the several *State Constitutions are local, partial, and selfish. . . .*" The new Constitution, on the other hand, is well designed "to form us to a *national spirit,* and to diffuse those generous *federal* sentiments, without which we never can be a happy and flourishing people."[20]

There are repeated references by the Federalists to American nationality as something intrinsically worth preserving and superior to the claims of statehood. The line of thought here is that as civil society not only secures the rights of the natural man but improves him, so the government of the Union does not merely secure the states (admitting them to be the parties) but improves or perfects them. And Dickinson makes clear, what many Federalists do not, that even in a confederation the true parties are men. States may be the formal parties—and in this sense the narrower view of American Union may be correct—but an association of states is justified ultimately not in terms of "state" interest but as a broader or higher association of human beings. The new Constitution will "diffuse a *national spirit,* and inspire every man with sentiments of dignity, when he reflects that he is not merely the individual of a State, but a CITIZEN OF AMERICA."[21] This view of the American Union explains both the Federalists' claim that the significance of the states will be increased, not destroyed, by a stronger Union and their very widespread association of the states with narrow selfishness and the Union with a morally more elevated benevolence and public spirit. Thus in appealing to the "mothers, wives, daughters and sisters of America" to use their influence in behalf of the Constitution, a Boston Federalist said "*your hearts are naturally federal,* prone to friendship, pity, love and generosity."[22]

20. A Federalist, *Boston Gazette,* 3 December 1787.
21. Convention, Boston *Massachusetts Centinel,* 13 October 1787 (*Friends,* 355). See also Philodemos, Boston *American Herald,* 12 May 1788 (*Friends,* 32–35).
22. Anonymous, *Boston Gazette,* 26 November 1787.

It is not inconsistent with this view that most of the Federalists described the specific objects of Union in terms of fairly narrow calculations of self interest. There are a few exceptions, as when the writer just quoted defends the Constitution as providing the civil order that is necessary "for the promotion of piety and every moral virtue."[23] In the main, however, the objects of Union are described in terms like those of Roger Sherman: "The great end of the federal government is to protect the several states in their enjoyment of those rights ["the civil and domestic rights of the people"] against foreign invasion, and to preserve peace and a beneficial intercourse among themselves, and to regulate and protect our commerce with foreign nations."[24] In a word, a perfected Union will make us "respectable as a nation abroad, and rich as individuals at home."[25]

Wealth and national security are good in themselves—they are the primary goods of Union—but they are also means to moral improvement. The aim of securing national prosperity, reluctantly accepted by the Anti-Federalists, was much more enthusiastically embraced by the Federalists, partly because of what they took to be its beneficial moral consequences. The love of wealth, properly regulated, fosters industry. "Industry is most favourable to the moral virtue of the world; it is therefore wisely ordered by the Author of Nature, that the blessings of this world should be acquired by our own application in some business useful to society. . . ."[26] Similarly with "national respectability," Federalist writers saw advantages going beyond mere national security. They often displayed a rather aggressive pride in the greater significance to be enjoyed by Americans under the new Constitution. Under it Americans can achieve "a distinguished rank among the nations of the earth."[27] Indeed "a mighty empire may be formed upon this

23. Ibid. See also James Wilson's Speech in Pennsylvania Convention, 24 November 1787 (*Friends*, 82–83).

24. A Citizen of New Haven [Roger Sherman] (*FE*, 238; *Friends*, 267). See also A Landholder [Oliver Ellsworth], Hartford *Connecticut Courant*, 5 November 1787 (*FE*, 146–47; *Friends*, 292).

25. State Soldier (possibly Charlottesville lawyer George Nicholas), *Virginia Independent Chronicle*, 6 February 1788 (*Friends*, 120).

26. A Landholder [Oliver Ellsworth] (*FE*, 200; *Friends*, 484).

27. Pennsylvania Farmer, Philadelphia *Independent Gazetteer*, 27 September 1787 (*M/S*, 129; *Friends*, 25).

basis, which shall make its enemies tremble."[28] Anti-Federalists were not mistaken in seeing among the defenders of the Constitution a desire that Americans should play a vigorous part on the world stage. Some, at least, of the moral ascent the Federalists saw in the movement from citizen to federalist depended on looking beyond the petty business of the states to greater scenes of national significance, empire, and glory.

The Federalist writings abound with elements of this line of reasoning, from man to citizen to federalist; and it does help to reconcile their view of the historical and even legal primacy of the states on the one hand, and the ultimate primacy of the Union on the other hand. The reasoning is, however, mostly implicit—even Dickinson is cryptic. Perhaps what is involved is less a matter of reasoning than the expression of a strong moral sentiment. What is very clear, however, is the conclusion: "Hear then ye people of the United States! reason dictates, every feeling of the heart entreats, and Heaven commands, *be federal and happy forever.*"[29]

Government

If Union is the frame of the Federalist argument, energetic government is the heart. The Federalists' crucial task, as they saw it, was not to show the desirability of Union, or the ends of Union, or even the need for a Union-wide government. That was common ground. The real task was to make Americans understand what their commitment to Union and to freedom itself implies in the way of government. "If you would be free and happy a power must be created to protect your persons and property; otherwise you are slaves to all mankind."[30] Government is "the foundation of all human happiness"; "there is no way more likely to lose one's liberty in the end than being too niggardly of it in the beginning."[31] To acknowledge the need for a *government* is to acknowledge the need for power and compulsion. "A government capable of controling the whole, and bringing its force to

28. Anonymous, Northampton, Massachusetts *Hampshire Gazette*, 17 October 1788.
29. Anonymous, *Boston Gazette*, 26 November 1787.
30. A Landholder [Oliver Ellsworth] (*FE*, 191).
31. State Soldier (*Friends*, 120 and 114).

a point, is one of the prerequisites for national liberty."[32] Such a government inevitably displays a somewhat harsh aspect. "Were we to view only the gaols and dungeons, the gallows and pillories, the chains and wheel-barrows, of any state, we might be induced to think the government severe; but when we turn our attention to the murderers and parricides, and robberies and burglaries, the piracies and thefts, which merit these punishments, our idea of cruelty vanishes at once, and we admire the justice, and perhaps clemency, of that government which before shocked us as too severe."[33]

Of course power can be abused, but would anyone choose a lame horse, lest a sound one should run away with him? The tiresome Anti-Federal complaints about possible abuses of the powers under the Constitution and the absence of a bill of rights overlook that this government will be in the hands of representatives chosen by the people. Defense of the Constitution as providing a responsible government through the instrument of representation is a prominent, though as we shall see somewhat superficial, aspect of Federalist writing. James Wilson, for example, contended that the ancients had no proper idea of representation; and even in Great Britain the principle of representation was confined to a narrow corner. To America has been left "the glory and happiness of forming a government where representation shall at once supply the basis and the cement of the superstructure. For representation, Sir, is the true chain between the people and those to whom they entrust the administration of the government: and though it may consist of many links, its strength and brightness should never be impaired."[34] This view pervades Wilson's thinking and that of many other Federalists. Echoing the Revolutionary slogan of "no taxation without representation," representation here is seen as the necessary and almost the sufficient condition of good government. In a properly arranged system, the representatives *are* the people. "The distinction between the powers of the *people* and of their *Representatives* in the Legislature, is as absurd in *theory*, as it

32. A Landholder [Oliver Ellsworth] (*FE*, 147; *Friends*, 292).

33. Peletiah Webster, Remarks (*M/S*, 103).

34. James Wilson, Speech in Pennsylvania Convention, 24 November 1787. This quotation is from Dallas's version of Wilson's speech (*DH*, 2:344); *Cf.* Lloyd's version (*Friends*, 77). See also *The Federalist*, No. 63.

proves pernicious in *practice."*[35] The question, then, is not the power of
the legislature but "how are Congress formed? how far have you a control
over them? Decide this, and then all the questions about their power may
be dismissed for the amusement of those politicians whose business it is
to catch flies. . . ."[36] The representatives under the proposed Constitution
will be chosen by the people and will be bound to them by considerations
of honor and gratitude as well as self-interest. Every member of congress
is liable to all the operations of the laws he himself passes and "this circumstance alone, is a sufficient security."[37] Roger Sherman sums up this
traditional view: "The greatest security that a people can have for the enjoyment of their rights and liberties, is that no laws can be made to bind
them nor any taxes imposed upon them, without their consent by representatives of their own chusing, who will participate with them in the public
burthens and benefits; this was the great point contended for in our controversy with Great Britain, and this will be fully secured to us by the new
constitution."[38]

To the extent that they relied upon representation, these Federalists writers joined most of their Anti-Federalist opponents in defending what is ba-
sically a *simple* form of government, a government in which the representatives are elected by the people, responsible to the people, and presumed
to be fundamentally identical to the people with regard to their interests
and opinions. At this level the dispute is between the Federalists' heavy reliance on the mechanism of representation and the Anti-Federalists' insis-
tence that genuine responsibility can be found only in the smaller, more
homogeneous states. So long as the issue is phrased in this way, the Anti-
Federalists seem to have the better of it. But the deeper Federalist argument
sees representation as something much more than a device for mirroring
popular opinions and interests.

35. America [Noah Webster], New York *Daily Advertiser,* 31 December 1787 (*Friends,* 171).
36. A Countryman [Roger Sherman], *New Haven Gazette,* 22 November 1787 (*FE,* 220;
Friends, 181–82).
37. America [Noah Webster] (*Friends,* 173).
38. A Citizen of New Haven [Roger Sherman] (*FE,* 237; *Friends,* 266–67). See also A
Countryman [Roger Sherman] (*FE,* 219–20; *Friends,* 180–81).

The notion of simple representative government has several clear difficulties, a consideration of which shows the weakness of the Federalists' argument at one level and its power at a deeper one. First is the issue of the fidelity of representatives. The Federalists rely heavily on two arguments, both of which are open to question. It is said that since under the new Constitution the representatives will be chosen by the people in open and free elections, they can also be displaced by the people if they should violate their trust. The Federalists do not in fact spend very much time considering the practical effectiveness of this electoral check, but their opponents point out with a great deal of plausibility, that the actual capacity of the people to supervise and control their representatives through the electoral machinery, especially in the very large-scale American republic, will be very limited. Representatives will inevitably be chosen from among a relatively small group of widely known men, and their activities as rulers will be largely obscure to the mass of the electors. Moreover the argument that the representatives are subject to the laws along with their constituents and therefore have identical interests is clearly an over-simplification. Even granting (what the Anti-Federalists did not grant) that there will not grow up a separate class of rulers, it is still clear that any group of representatives will have certain interests distinct from those of their constituents, another tendency certain to be magnified in the new, large federal government. To take the simplest case, the representatives will indeed have to share the cost of the government, but obviously they benefit from those expenditures in a way that the ordinary citizen does not. If a relationship of responsibility or identity of interests between representative and constituent is the central principle of the new government, as some of the Federalists did in fact contend, then it was not difficult for the Anti-Federalists to show the tenuousness of the connection.

This argument was met by other Federalists who, tacitly conceding that the chain of representation is not enough, showed that the Constitution provides additional and very effective safeguards, based solidly on interest, to secure the fidelity of representatives. These are the familiar checks and balances. "The perfection of political science consists chiefly in providing mutual checks amongst the several departments of power, preserving at the same time, the dependance of the greatest on the people."[39] In fact a very considerable part of the Federalist writings was addressed to this issue. The structure and working of the proposed Constitution were explained in detail in order to show how well devised were the internal arrangements and how difficult and unlikely would be major breaches of trust by the representatives.[40]

There is still a deeper problem with simple representative government seen as a mirror of society. Granting that such a government is responsive and safe, is it likely to be stable and competent? Many Federalists thought not and tried to show that the Constitution provides for "responsible" government in the broader (and now common) as well as in the narrower sense. Noah Webster elaborates well this line of reasoning.[41] He describes a chain of ideas about government followed by sober second thoughts, leading to the principle of a bicameral legislature (his immediate concern, writing as he was in Pennsylvania with its unicameral state legislature). Unanimous consent is the basis of all law, Webster begins; but experience shows that civil society is impossible unless the opinions of a majority are allowed to give law to the whole. Similarly, at first sight it seems reasonable for all members of a society to meet together to decide on legislation; but it soon becomes evident that this is neither practical nor desirable, and a scheme of representation is substituted. Again in the government thus established it seems very natural at first that all the representatives should be collected into one body; but on reflection the benefits of a more complex legislative arrangement are perceived. A second body can protect against sudden and violent passions and against being led astray by one extraordinary man; it can also instill qualities of wisdom and experience into governmental deliberations. The mutual checks of a complex government can provide, then, not only fidelity but also stability, prudence, and wisdom. Federalist descriptions of the Constitution to this effect abound. One further example

39. Aristides [Alexander Contee Hanson], Remarks on the Proposed Plan of a Federal Government, Annapolis, Maryland, 1788 (*FP,* 222). See also Anonymous, Speech to Have Been Delivered. . . .

40. See Fabius [John Dickinson] (*FP,*168–74; *Friends,* 59–65); Aristides [Alexander Contee Hanson] (*FP,* 222).

41. A Citizen of America [Noah Webster] (*FP,* 30–32; *Friends,* 374–76).

will suffice here. The President, through the use of his veto and his veto messages, it was explained, will provide a useful channel of communication between those who make and those who execute the law. "Many things look fair in theory which in practice are impossible. If lawmakers, in every instance, before their final decree, had the opinion of those who are to execute them, it would prevent a thousand absurd ordinances, which are solemnly made, only to be repealed, and lessen the dignity of legislation in the eyes of mankind."[42]

In arrangements like these lies the great strength of the new Constitution. Carefully framed in the light of experience in the states, it provides all of the qualities desirable in government: "fidelity, or firm attachments to the good of the people—wisdom to discern what is for the public good—and dispatch in business, or speedy execution of the measures determined upon."[43]

The basis of these arrangements is of course a written constitution. The document framed in 1787 was the completion—and was seen, more or less clearly, by Federalists to be the completion—of the development of constitutional government in the United States since the Revolution. Constitutional government embraces and transcends the principle of representation. Establishing a constitution as supreme law is the act (the only act) of the sovereign people. The Constitution may be amended, a wise feature pointed out by many Federalists, but even amendment does not involve recourse to the original popular source but is an exercise of constitutional authority. Election, the essence of "representative" government as traditionally understood, becomes merely a method of choosing, not a method of authorizing. The legislature is a body of constitutional officers, not a microcosm of the sovereign people. The legislators, like other officers of government, derive their authority from the Constitution, not from their election. There is, thus, contrary to the view expressed by Noah Webster, a crucial distinction between the power of the people (as an original matter) and the power of their representatives.[44] This is the basis of the whole system

42. A Landholder [Oliver Ellsworth] (*FE,* 158; *Friends,* 302).
43. A Citizen, New York *Daily Advertiser,* 6 February 1788.
44. America [Noah Webster] (*Friends,* 171).

of checks and balances as well as of the doctrine, accepted by most Federalists, that acts of the legislature contrary to the Constitution are void. "When the powers to be exercised, under a certain system, are in themselves consistent with the people's liberties, are legally defined, guarded, and ascertained, and ample provision made for bringing to condign punishment all such as shall overstep the limitations of law,—it is hard to conceive of a greater security for the rights of the people."[45]

Not all Federalists grasped the significance of constitutional government. As we have seen, there is still in many cases a heavy reliance on traditional notions of representation. There are occasional statements like that of Noah Webster, who disputed the claim for a bill of rights by contending that "the very attempt to establish a permanent, unalterable Constitution, is an act of consummate arrogance." He argued that susceptibility of the representatives to their acts as legislators is alone "a sufficient security."[46] Most Federalists saw the proposed Constitution, however, not merely as a set of agencies of popular consent, but also as the legal foundation for a government limited in its powers and in its interior arrangements. If all these arrangements "can not keep the public decision within the bounds of wisdom, natural fitness, right and convenience, it will be hard to find any efforts of human wisdom that can do it."[47]

Popular Government

We must now look deeper into the Federalist understanding of popular government. While most Federalists saw that the Constitution was meant to provide a complex and not a simple representative government, they insisted

---

45. Atticus, Boston *Independent Chronicle,* 22 November 1787 (*Friends,* 338). Most but not all the Federalists seem to have assumed that the courts would regard such acts as void. See also Aristides [Alexander Contee Hanson] (*FP,* 234); Fabius [John Dickinson] (*FP,* 182–84; *Friends,* 218–19); A Citizen of America [Noah Webster] (*FP,* 50; *Friends,* 392); and James Wilson's extremely influential explanation of the limited powers delegated to the general government in contrast to the broad powers enjoyed by the state governments in his early and widely distributed "State House Speech" of 6 October 1787 (*Friends,* 102–3).

46. America [Noah Webster] (*Friends,* 172–73).

47. Peletiah Webster, Remarks (*M/S,* 96).

on its fundamentally popular character. Whatever their other disagreements, most Federalists would have accepted this striking description by James Wilson:

> of what description is the constitution before us? In its principles, Sir, it is purely democratical; varying indeed, in its form, in order to admit all the advantages, and to exclude all the disadvantages which are incidental to the known and established constitutions of government. But when we take an extensive and accurate view of the streams of power that appear through this great and comprehensive plan, when we contemplate the variety of their directions, the force and dignity of their currents, when we behold them intersecting, embracing, and surrounding the vast possessions and interests of the continent, and when we see them distributing on all hands beauty, energy and riches, still, however numerous and wise their courses, however diversified and remote the blessings they diffuse, we shall be able to trace them to one great and noble source. THE PEOPLE.[48]

It is doubtless true that the emphasis placed by the Federalists on the popular character of the new Constitution was in part a response to Anti-Federalist criticism. Yet I think it is a distortion to picture them as an elite cleverly scrambling to retain control in a new democratic age. Their sincerity is manifest. Again and again they contend that this new government derives, as all legitimate government must, from the great source of political authority, the people. There must be, Wilson said, in every government one supreme sovereign power from which there is no appeal. "That the supreme power . . . should be vested in the people, is in my judgment the great panacea of human politics. It is a power paramount to every constitution, inalienable in its nature, and indefinite in its extent."[49] Madison himself, the great teacher of the danger of majority faction, had urged in Philadelphia that "the people were in fact, the fountain of all power, and by resorting to them, all difficulties were got over."[50] Even "Caesar," usually cited as strongly critical of the people, while doubting their majesty and political

48. James Wilson, Speech in Pennsylvania Convention, 24 November 1787. This quotation is from Dallas's version of Wilson's speech (*DH*, 2:349); *Cf.* Lloyd's version (*Friends*, 87).
49. Ibid. This quotation is from Dallas's version of Wilson's speech (*DH*, 2:348–49); *Cf.* Lloyd's version (*Friends*, 86).
50. Farrand, *Records*, 2:476.

wisdom, never denied their right to accept or reject a proffered government.[51] Under the Constitution the power of the people is not only the ultimate authority but it pervades the whole system. This government will secure the freedom and promote the happiness of America, Dickinson said, "by giving *the will of the people* a decisive influence over the whole, and over all the parts."[52]

The disagreement among the Federalists concerned not the truth but the sufficiency of the principle of popular sovereignty. In the days of struggle against the King, it had seemed to many that if only the people could grasp the government, the political problem would be solved; the means, as we have seen, is an adequate system of representation. But as popular rule is achieved, it becomes clear to everyone (what was always clear to some) that popular government is problematic because, among other reasons, "the people" is not homogeneous. Old problems of injustice, oppression, and tyranny emerge out of conflicts within "the people."

A traditional way of viewing this problem is that even a "democratic" society tends to divide into the natural elements of one/few/many, which are more or less in conflict with one another. This view was perhaps expressed most fully among the Americans by John Adams in his *Defence of the Constitutions of Government of the United States.* In the Constitutional Convention it found expression in statements by such men as Gouverneur Morris and Alexander Hamilton. It is frequently expressed by the Anti-Federalists and helps to explain their admiration for the British government, despite their preference for the simple, small republic. Among Federalist writers this view is rather rare. They generally saw the Constitution as providing a new kind of complex government, an arrangement of constitutional powers rather than of social orders.

The different branches in the new government were not intended to "balance" one class against another, the way British branches are. "The sole intention of it is to produce wise and mature deliberation."[53] Our senate, Noah Webster explained, is not a different order of men; "but the same reasons,

---

51. Caesar, New York *Daily Advertiser,* 17 October 1787 (*FE,* 287–88; *Friends,* 323–24).
52. Fabius [John Dickinson] (*FP,* 173–74; *Friends,* 65).
53. A Citizen, *Carlisle Gazette,* 24 October 1787.

the same necessity for distinct branches of the legislature exists in all governments." In the United States "we have all the advantages of checks and balance, without the danger, which may arise from a superior and independent order of men."[54] This is a constant Federalist theme. The Constitution "unites in its different parts all the advantages, without any of the disadvantages, of the three well-known forms of government, and yet it preserves the attributes of a republic."[55] Thus the Anti-Federalist "Centinel" was several times attacked for his claim that the Constitution was designed to secure something like the mixed regime described by Adams; on the contrary, it was said, the new government is in every sense a popular government, one that secures the advantages without the disadvantages of the traditional mixed regimes.[56]

There are, however, significant traces of this older view in some Federalist writing, which should be noted before we return to the main line of argument. Especially interesting are the essays of a Boston writer "Atticus" whose topic is party and republican governments.[57] "Atticus" presents a version of the traditional view of government as representing and mediating between the basic elements of society. He begins by criticizing monarchy (it is not necessary for effective government) and parties (no violent party man can be a good citizen); but it turns out that parties are inevitable and useful and that their management does require a strong monarchical element. Two parties tend to emerge in all nondespotic governments. A democratic party, consisting of small property owners and debtors, tends towards levelism and democratic turbulence; an aristocratic party, consisting of large property owners, especially moneyed men, tends towards rigid aristocracy. Properly blended, "Atticus" argues in somewhat deceptively modern-sounding terms, parties give life to politics; they keep alive attention to public measures; they produce attendance and care in elections; and they keep

54. A Citizen of America [Noah Webster] (*FP,* 34–35; *Friends,* 378). See also the good discussion of the difference between the American "second house" and the British House of Lords by A Democratic Federalist, Philadelphia *Independent Gazetteer,* 26 November 1787 (*Friends,* 350–53).

55. One of the Four Thousand, Philadelphia *Independent Gazetteer,* 15 October 1787 (*M/S,* 116; *Friends,* 318).

56. See A Citizen, *Carlisle Gazette,* 24 October 1787; Peletiah Webster, Remarks (*M/S,* 95).

57. See Atticus (*Friends,* 328–44).

any one interest from swallowing the rest. However a third party is necessary to balance the democratic and aristocratic elements; and that must be found, after all, in the monarchical principle. This principle is represented in the American governments in the executive and judicial departments, supported by that class of the population dependent upon salaries, the natural supporters of monarchy. "Atticus" here is describing the American governments in general, and it is not always clear how he connects these principles to the new Constitution; but we have seen enough for our purpose.

Most of the Federalists, to repeat once more, did not see the Constitution as a mixing of social orders. The only American "order" is the people. That is decisive. Yet the "people" is not homogeneous and, according to the Anti-Federalists, will become less so if the relatively small republics of the states are submerged into a huge national aggregation. In the large commercial republic to be formed under the Constitution, the population will shatter into contending groups, with the inevitable emergence of a de facto aristocracy which will eventually control the government and the whole society. Thoughtful Federalists acknowledged the problem. The singularity of the order of "the people" in principle must rest on fact.

But what is wanted is not the petty, static homogeneity of the small, self-sufficient, and presumably public-spirited republic but what might be called the dynamic homogenizing tendency of the great commercial republic. The problem is not to prevent division or inequality but to prevent permanent division and inequality. The old defenders of popular government have looked to the wrong principle. "*Virtue,* patriotism, or love of country, never was and never will be, till men's natures are changed, a fixed, permanent, principle and support of government," Noah Webster insisted. Rather "an equality of property, with a necessity of alienation, constantly operating to destroy combinations of powerful families, is the very *soul of a republic*— While this continues, the people will inevitably possess both *power* and *freedom;* when this is lost, power departs, liberty expires, and a commonwealth will inevitably assume some other form."[58] Differences in wealth can be great, so long as they cannot become permanent. Fortunately the circum-

58. A Citizen of America [Noah Webster] (*FP,* 59; *Friends,* 400–401).

stances of America foster such fluidity. Opportunities are great, commerce is vigorous. There is no need to squabble over a limited pie and little likelihood that a small class can permanently control the wealth and therefore the government of the country. Besides the abundant wealth of America, the system depends on an unqualified acceptance of a modern commercial society. The old vestiges of feudal tenure and the old idea of the landed interest as somehow unique and superior must be firmly abandoned. Eliminate primogeniture, destroy entailment, "leave real estates to revolve from hand to hand, as time and accident may direct; and no family influence can be acquired and established for a series of generations—no man can obtain dominion over a large territory—the laborious and saving, who are generally the best citizens, will possess each his share of property and power, and thus the balance of wealth and power will continue where it is, in the *body of the people.*"[59] One Federalist went so far as to argue that the states should provide for equality in descent without will of females as well as males and in the most remote collateral branches. "By these means, poverty and extreme riches would be avoided, and a republican spirit would be given to our laws, not only without a violation of private rights but consistently with the principle of justice and sound policy."[60]

The elimination of primogeniture and entail and the consequent tendency for large estates to be broken up was not a uniquely Federalist policy and is indeed most often associated with Jefferson and the small agrarian republic. The Federalists, however, were pressing in a different and on the whole more consistent direction. There was among Federalists little of that holding back from the modern commercial world that provides one strand of Jefferson's and the Anti-Federalists' thought. There were about as many "Farmers" and "Countrymen" among the Federalists as among the Anti-Federalists; and the defenders of the Constitution typically deny that there is any antagonism between the landed and the commercial interest, often contending that commerce is but the handmaiden of agriculture. At bottom, however, the Federalists affirm the fundamentally commercial character of agriculture itself. Thus Oliver Ellsworth writing as "A Landholder" de-

59. Ibid. (*Friends*, 400).
60. A Freeman [Tench Coxe], *Pennsylvania Gazette*, 30 January 1788 (*Friends*, 94).

scribed himself as a former merchant, now retired (thanks to industry and economy) to a farming life. Throughout his essays, Ellsworth quietly but persistently presses the claim of commerce, on which the prosperity of agriculture itself depends. "It may be assumed as a fixed truth that the prosperity and riches of the farmer must depend on the prosperity, and good national regulation of trade." He warns against the "artful men" who "tell you let trade take care of itself, and excite your jealousy against the merchant because his business leads him to wear a gayer coat, than your economy directs."[61] The United States will continue to be a country where the vast bulk of the people labor on the land; yet it will be a country in which the basic interest is commerce. The country will contain substantial differences of wealth, but old combinations will tend always to be broken up and new ones built.

Webster lays down two other conditions of free republican government, which are discussed at length by the Federalists but which can be passed over here, as well-known and clear-cut views: the possession of information by the people and free and popular elections. "In a country like ours, abounding in free men all of one rank, where property is equally diffused, where estates are held in fee simple, the press free, and the means of information common, tyranny cannot reasonably find admission under any form of government; but its admission is next to impossible under one where the people are the source of all power, and elect either mediately by their representatives, or immediately by themselves the whole of their rulers."[62] These three conditions, then, are the essential bulwarks of republican freedom: a diffusion or fluidity of property, free press, and free and popular elections.[63]

61. A Landholder [Oliver Ellsworth] (*FE,* 140; *Friends,* 287).

62. Civis [David Ramsay] (*FP,* 379; *Friends,* 456). Ellsworth wrote that the American governments are safe from monarchy or aristocracy "so long as the present descent of landed estates last and the mass of the people have, as at present, a tolerable education. . . ." A Landholder [Oliver Ellsworth] (*FE,* 166). See also A Citizen of America (*FP,* 60–61, *Friends,* 402); Foreign Spectator (*Friends,* 408–9; 433–40).

63. A good deal of Federalist energy was devoted to showing that the press and elections would be free. This involved defending the Constitution against two major Anti-Federalist criticisms: That there was no guarantee of freedom of the press and that the provision of Article I, Section 4(1) permitting Congress to regulate the times, places, and manner of federal elections was a source of danger to free elections.

The main concern of the arguments examined thus far is still the traditional (in the American context) fear that an aristocracy will tend to control the government and the society to the disadvantage of the mass of the people. The Anti-Federalists remained unpersuaded that the people would remain their own masters in the vast commercial empire to be established under the Constitution. Many of the Federalists, on the other hand, doubted that this was the main problem (though because of the reflexive character of Federalist writing, it is the one they spend most of their time dealing with). On the whole the Federalists inclined to the view that more was to be feared in American government from licentious democracy than from aristocratic oppression.[64] This view had been expressed by Edmund Randolph when he initiated the deliberations of the Constitutional Convention; and it is a persistent Federalist theme, though perhaps not so prominent as the Federalists' antidemocratic reputation might suggest.

"Many plausible things may be said in favor of pure democracy—many in favor of uniting the representatives of the people in one single house—but uniform experience proves both to be inconsistent with the peace of society, and the rights of freemen."[65] Dickinson himself, for all of his emphasis on the will of the people, describes the two main problems of American government as the turbulence of the states and the licentiousness of the people.[66] It is perhaps not accidental, however, that Dickinson, like most of the Federalist writers, discusses the problem of the turbulence of the states at considerable length, while only glancingly considering the problem of the licentiousness of the people or its solution.[67]

One answer to popular excess is that the government itself should be strong and independent enough to resist foolish or unjust popular impulses. The American governments have been "too feeble and too popular," "A State Soldier" said forthrightly. "The more independent a government is therefore of the people, under proper restraints, the more likely it is to produce . . .

64. See Cato, Poughkeepsie *Country Journal*, 12 December 1787 (*Friends*, 347–48); Caesar (*FE*, 288; *Friends*, 324); A Foreign Spectator (*Friends*, 408 and passim).

65. A Citizen of America [Noah Webster] (*FP*, 34; *Friends*, 378).

66. Fabius [John Dickinson] (*FP*, 200; *Friends*, 487).

67. Fabius [John Dickinson] (*FP*, 120; *Friends*, 201 and 488).

justice; and the more substantial and efficient under such restraints, the better calculated to protect both the persons and property of mankind."[68] One of the characteristics of constitutional government is that it restrains the people as well as the government. If a constitutional government is strong it is, in principle and practice, independent of immediate popular impulses. This describes precisely the government under the new Constitution. We have come almost full circle back to the need for effective government. The Constitution provides a government with the vigor, competence, and independence that can resist popular licentiousness and secure individual liberty.

This is, however, not sufficient. The Federalists emphatically concede that the government under the Constitution is and must be firmly (if not simply or directly) tied to and dependent on the popular will. The government under the Constitution, Dickinson explained, is *balanced* by the power from which it proceeds.[69] "Publius" would insist on a different formulation that would stress the absence of any direct agency by the people in the government. Nevertheless all Federalists must concede that in a popular government security from popular excess cannot finally be found in a strong, independent governmental force, or even in a supreme constitution. The soundness and health of the popular regime must depend finally on the health of its primary element.

Here the Anti-Federalists bring to bear their powerful argument that the civic virtue of the populace can be fostered only in a small republic.[70] The aggregate selfishness encouraged by the great commercial republic will destroy those qualities of moderation and public-spiritedness on which republican government depends. Many of the Federalists simply did not meet this objection. Wilson, for example, seems willing simply to trust in the vigor, good sense, and patriotism of the American people, without troubling himself very much about the extent to which the trust is justified. "[T]he citizens of the United States can never be wretched beyond retrieve, unless

68. State Soldier, 6 February 1788, 19 March 1788 (*Friends*, 367).

69. Fabius [John Dickinson] (*FP*, 183; *Friends*, 218).

70. This is fully elaborated by Storing in the introduction to *What the Anti-Federalists Were For.*

they are wanting to themselves."[71] More thoughtful Federalists, James Madison among them, saw that the problem was the likelihood that the people very frequently *would* be "wanting to themselves."[72]

Madison rejects the traditional solution—that the people must be formed by the small republic into citizens. He opposes this with his now well-known defense of the large republic: "Extend the sphere, and you take in greater variety of parties and interests; you make it less probable that a majority of the whole will have a common motive to invade the rights of other citizens; or if such a common motive exists, it will be more difficult for all who feel it to discover their own strength, and to act in unison with each other." There are bits and pieces of this view of the extended republic in other Federalist writings; but it is nowhere referred to specifically by other Federalist writers, so far as I can discover, and there is little evidence that it was influential or even widely understood.[73] This is not the place to try to solve the still perplexing problem of the influence and the authority (which are not the same) of Madison's famous account of the large republic. It is perhaps not surprising that the great body of Federalists stayed closer to the surface and to traditional views.

On the whole the Federalist view of both the problem and the solution was more conventional than Madison's. "Popular licentiousness" was likely to be the way a typical Federalist described the problem. In this he would betray a less penetrating understanding than Madison who saw that the fundamental problem of popular government is not popular uprisings or disturbances along the lines of Shays' "rebellion" but the unjust use that can be made by the majority of its lawful authority.

In seeking a solution, too, the typical Federalist was likely to look to the traditional principles of civic education and character molding, precisely the principles that Madison found so unreliable, although there is more

---

71. James Wilson, Speech in Pennsylvania Convention, 24 November 1787. This quotation is from Dallas's version of Wilson's speech (*DH*, 2:349); Cf. Lloyd's version (*Friends*, 86).

72. See, for example, *The Federalist*, No. 49.

73. *The Federalist*, No. 10. See also State Soldier, passim; Plain Truth, Philadelphia *Independent Gazetteer* (*M/S*, 193); A Countryman (*FE*, 215); James Wilson (*Friends*, 74); Aristides [Alexander Contee Hanson] (*FP*, 247); Cato (*Friends*, 346); Cassius, *Virginia Independent Chronicle*, 2 April 1788; Fabius [John Dickinson] (*FP*, 203–7; *Friends*, 490–94); Anonymous, Speech to Have Been Delivered. . . .

question here whether the usual view was quite so superficial as it might appear within the Madisonian perspective (or indeed whether Madison himself escaped the traditional reliance). The typical Federalist was likely, in a word, to preach. "Let the Americans be virtuous—let them be firm supporters of Republicanism—let them have confidence in their representatives—then their liberties will be secured to them, and peace and prosperity will ensue."[74] The point could be put rather more favorably by saying that many of the Federalists saw the continuing need for political leadership to form the manners and character of the people. Thus James Wilson, on the occasion of a Fourth of July speech in 1788, instructed the American people in the duties as well as the benefits of American citizenship. Frugality and temperance, industry, a warm and uniform attachment to liberty and the Constitution—these are the duties of citizenship. All the activities of government "spring from the *original* movement of the *people at large.*" The people must provide "a sufficient force and a just direction" to all parts of the government. Especially, the people must choose good representatives, for on that all else depends. "It is the first *connection* in politics: if an *error* is made *here,* it can never be *corrected* in any subsequent process." Each citizen should vote as if his were the vote that would decide the election.[75]

Teaching, and even preaching, are important for the Federalists, more important than a reading of *The Federalist* would suggest.[76] But that teaching of the duties of citizenship rests on the solid ground of the effective government provided by the Constitution. This is, again, the bedrock of the Federalist position. Civic morality is fostered where civic morality is effectively protected. Want of energetic government is followed by disobedience among the governed; that is followed in turn by general licentiousness, typically giving rise to a harsh antirepublican response that is likely to destroy liberty for the sake of order.[77] "Nothing tends more to the honour, establishment, and peace of society, than public decisions, grounded on principles of right,

74. Maecenas, *State Gazette of Georgia,* 6 December 1787.

75. James Wilson, Fourth of July Oration, 1788 (*Friends,* 507–9).

76. See Ralph Lerner, "The Supreme Court as Republican Schoolmaster," in Phillip B. Kurland, ed., *The Supreme Court Review: 1967* (Chicago: University of Chicago Press, 1968), 127–80.

77. Pennsylvania Farmer (*M/S,* 127–28; *Friends,* 23).

natural fitness and prudence; but when the powers of government are *too limited,* such decisions can't be made and enforced; so the mischief goes without a remedy. . . ." When the powers of government are in dispute, "the administration dare not make decisions on the footing of impartial justice and right" but must temporize, with the result that "the *righteous* go off injured and disgusted." Controversy must have "a just, *speedy,* and effectual decision that right may be done before the contention has *time* to grow up into habits of malignity, resentment, ill nature, and ill offices.[78] A good government on an enlarged scale is a far better teacher of justice and patriotism than is the petty republic, with its inherent weakness and turbulence. The excellent government provided by the Constitution will enforce, habituate to, and teach civic virtue while going about its business of providing security, order, and justice between man and man.

"Virtue or good habits are the result of good laws—and from the excellent American Constitution those *habits* will be induced, that shall lead to those *exertions, manufactures* and *enterprises,* which will give a scope to the American genius, and 'find employment for their activity.' "[79] Reject the Constitution, went a typical warning, and "you will possess popular liberty with a vengeance," with the result that "no man's property will be secure, but each one defrauding his neighbour under the sanction of law,—thus subverting every principle of morality and religion." Accept it, and "you will enjoy the blessing of a well balanced government, capable of inspiring credit and respectability abroad, and virtue, confidence, good order and harmony at home."[80]

78. A Citizen of Philadelphia [Peletiah Webster] (*FP,* 119; *Friends,* 184).
79. Convention (*Friends,* 356).
80. Cato (*Friends,* 348).

l

Friends of the Constitution

Benjamin Rush

"Address to the People of the United States"

American Museum, Philadelphia, January 1787

Benjamin Rush (1745–1813) was an early supporter of a strong central government. In addition to writing articles and speaking out in favor of the Constitution, Rush voted for its ratification in the Pennsylvania convention. Rush also served as Treasurer of the U.S. Mint from 1797 to 1813.

There is nothing more common than to confound the terms of *the American revolution* with those of *the late American war.* The American war is over: but this is far from being the case with the American revolution. On the contrary, nothing but the first act of the great drama is closed. It remains yet to establish and perfect our new forms of government; and to prepare the principles, morals, and manners of our citizens, for these forms of government, after they are established and brought to perfection.

The confederation, together with most of our state constitutions, were formed under very unfavourable circumstances. We had just emerged from a corrupted monarchy. Although we understood perfectly the principles of liberty, yet most of us were ignorant of the forms and combinations of power in republics. Add to this, the British army was in the heart of our country, spreading desolation wherever it went: our resentments, of course, were awakened. We detested the British name; and unfortunately refused to copy some things in the administration of justice and power, in the British government, which have made it the admiration and envy of the world. In our opposition to monarchy, we forgot that the temple of tyranny has two doors. We bolted one of them by proper restraints; but we left the other open, by neglecting to guard against the effects of our own ignorance and licentiousness.

Most of the present difficulties of this country arise from the weakness and other defects of our governments.

My business at present shall be only to suggest the defects of the confederation. These consist—1st. In the deficiency of coercive power. 2d. In a defect of exclusive power to issue paper-money, and regulate commerce. 3d. In vesting the sovereign power of the united states in a single legislature: and, 4th. In the too frequent rotation of its members.

A convention is to sit soon for the purpose of devising means of obviating part of the two first defects that have been mentioned. But I wish they may add to their recommendations to each state, to surrender up to congress their power of emitting money. In this way, a uniform currency will be produced, that will facilitate trade, and help to bind the states together. Nor will the states be deprived of large sums of money by this mean when sudden emergencies require it: for they may always borrow them as they did during the war, out of the treasury of congress. Even a loan-office may be better instituted in this way in each state, than in any other.

The two last defects that have been mentioned, are not of less magnitude than the first. Indeed, the single legislature of congress will become more dangerous from an increase of power than ever. To remedy this, let the supreme federal power be divided, like the legislatures of most of our states, into two distinct, independent branches. Let one of them be styled the council of the states, and the other the assembly of the states. Let the first consist of a single delegate—and the second, of two, three, or four delegates, chosen annually by each state. Let the president be chosen annually by the joint ballot of both houses; and let him possess certain powers in conjunction with a privy council, especially the power of appointing most of the officers of the united states. The officers will not only be better when appointed this way, but one of the principal causes of faction will be thereby removed from congress. I apprehend this division of the power of congress will become more necessary, as soon as they are invested with more ample powers of levying and expending public money.

The custom of turning men out of power or office, as soon as they are qualified for it, has been found to be as absurd in practice, as it is virtuous in speculation. It contradicts our habits and opinions in every other transaction of life. Do we dismiss a general—a physician—or even a domestic, as soon as they have acquired knowledge sufficient to be useful to us, for the sake of increasing the number of able generals—skilful physicians—and faithful servants? We do not. Government is a science; and can never be perfect in America, until we encourage men to devote not only three years, but their whole lives to it. I believe the principal reason why so many men of abilities object to serving in congress, is owing to their not thinking it worth while to spend three years in acquiring a profession which their country immediately afterwards forbids them to follow.

There are two errors or prejudices on the subject of government in America, which lead to the most dangerous consequences.

It is often said, that "the sovereign and all other power is seated *in* the people." This idea is unhappily expressed. It should be—"all power is derived *from* the people." They possess it only on the days of their elections. After this, it is the property of their rulers, nor can they exercise or resume it, unless it is abused. It is of importance to circulate this idea, as it leads to order and good government.

The people of America have mistaken the meaning of the word sovereignty: hence each state pretends to be *sovereign*. In Europe, it is applied only to those states which possess the power of making war and peace—of forming treaties, and the like. As this power belongs only to congress, they are the only *sovereign* power in the united states.

We commit a similar mistake in our ideas of the word independent. No individual state, as such, has any claim to independence. She is independent only in a union with her sister states in congress.

To conform the principles, morals, and manners of our citizens to our republican forms of government, it is absolutely necessary that knowledge of every kind, should be disseminated through every part of the united states.

For this purpose, let congress, instead of laying out half a million of dollars, in building a federal town, appropriate only a fourth of that sum, in founding a federal university. In this university, let every thing connected with government, such as history—the law of nature and nations—the civil law—the municipal laws of our country—and the principles of commerce—be taught by competent professors. Let masters be employed, likewise, to teach gunnery—fortification—and every thing connected with defensive and offensive war. Above all, let a professor, of, what is called in the European universities, œconomy, be established in this federal seminary. His business should be to unfold the principles and practice of agriculture and manufactures of all kinds: and to enable him to make his lectures more extensively useful, congress should support a travelling correspondent for him, who should visit all the nations of Europe, and transmit to him, from time to time, all the discoveries and improvements that are made in agriculture and manufactures. To this seminary, young men should be encouraged to repair, after completing their academical studies in the colleges of their respective states. The honours and offices of the united states should, after a while, be confined to persons who had imbibed federal and republican ideas in this university.

For the purpose of diffusing knowledge, as well as extending the living principle of government to every part of the united states—every state—city—county—village—and township in the union, should be tied together by means of the post-office. This is the true non-electric wire of government. It is the only means of conveying heat and light to every individual in the federal commonwealth. Sweden lost her liberties, says the abbe Raynal, because her citizens were so scattered, that they had no means of acting in concert with each other. It should be a constant injunction to the postmasters, to convey newspapers free of all charge for postage. They are not only the vehicles of knowledge and intelligence, but the centinels of the liberties of our country.

The conduct of some of those strangers who have visited our country, since the peace, and who fill the British papers with accounts of our distresses, shews as great a want of good sense, as it does of good nature. They see nothing but the foundations and walls of the temple of liberty, and yet they undertake to judge of the whole fabric.

Our own citizens act a still more absurd part, when they cry out, after the experience of three or four years, that we are not proper materials for republican government. Remember, we assumed these forms of government in a hurry, before we were prepared for them. Let every man exert himself in promoting virtue and knowledge in our country, and we shall soon become good republicans. Look at the steps by which governments have been changed, or rendered stable in Europe. Read the history of Great Britain. Her boasted government has risen out of wars, and rebellions that lasted above sixty years. The united states are travelling peaceably into order and good government. They know no strife—but what arises from the collision of opinions: and in three years they have advanced further in the road to stability and happiness, than most of the nations in Europe have done, in as many centuries.

There is but one path that can lead the united states to destruction, and that is their extent of territory. It was probably to effect this, that Great Britain ceded to us so much waste land. But even this path may be avoided. Let but one new state be exposed to sale at a time; and let the land office be shut up till every part of this new state is settled.

I am extremely sorry to find a passion for retirement so universal among the patriots and heroes of the war. They resemble skilful mariners, who, after exerting themselves to preserve a ship from sinking in a storm, in the middle of the ocean, drop asleep as soon as the waves subside, and leave the care of their lives and property, during the remainder of the voyage, to sailors, without knowledge or experience. Every man in a republic is public property. His time and talents—his youth—his manhood—his old age— nay more, life, all, belong to his country.

PATRIOTS of 1774, 1775, 1776—HEROES of 1778, 1779, 1780! come forward! your country demands your services!—Philosophers and friends to mankind, come forward! your country demands your studies and speculations! Lovers of peace and order, who declined taking part in the late war, come forward! your country forgives your timidity, and demands your influence and advice! Hear her proclaiming, in sighs and groans, in her governments, in her finances, in her trade, in her manufactures, in her morals, and in her manners, "THE REVOLUTION IS NOT OVER!"

The Necessity of Union

BY THE LATE 1780s virtually all Americans agreed that their union needed
to be strengthened. Some, most notably George Washington and Alexander
Hamilton, saw much earlier the necessity of a firm, indissoluble union. In
the years preceding the Constitutional Convention, those who favored
stronger bonds of union and a larger role for the federal government were
often referred to as "federal men" or "federalists." It is no accident or case
of mistaken identity that these men came to be known as "Federalists" when
the battle for ratification of the Constitution was waged, the grumblings
of some "Anti-Federalists" who thought they better deserved the title, notwithstanding. The Federalists of 1787–88 simply retained the appellation
they had acquired in previous years.

The selection following shows that the Federalists generally agreed that
their country was sinking into disunion and anarchy. They concurred about
the need to cement the union and fortify the federal head. Given what they
perceived as a deteriorating economic situation, rise in domestic factions,
and weakness in the face of foreign powers, their first object, of necessity,
was the security of the United States.

But many Federalists also believed that union was necessary to the liberty,
prosperity, and happiness of the American people. Man's nature fits him
for society, John Dickinson claimed, for man needs society to be secure,
security to be free, and freedom to be happy. James Wilson agreed, arguing
that civil society and government are not only necessary for man's security,
but for his perfection and happiness as well. The achievement of these beneficial ends of political society, the Federalists generally believed, requires
a union of "invincible firmness."

The Federalists did not claim that the Constitution was perfect. They
understood that perfection in the human realm was not to be expected and

that in fact prudential compromises had been made in the Philadelphia Convention. Though imperfect, Federalists nonetheless proudly declared that the proposed constitution was the best that could be obtained and perhaps the best that had ever been offered to the world. Despite the view widespread among Anti-Federalists that ratification should await the addition of a bill of rights, Federalists argued that the correction of any defects or omissions in the new plan of government should be made after ratification, through the constitutionally prescribed amendment process. It would be folly to expect more rather than less unity in a second convention, they asserted, and the immense risk that must accompany another convention would threaten the very existence of the United States. George Washington put it bluntly: the choice was between adoption of this Constitution or anarchy.

Cognizant of living in the opening era of a new and free world, Federalist writers and orators often reminded their fellow citizens that the choice they were to make would decide the fate of freedom for generations yet unborn. This is the time of our political probation, Washington declared; "the citizens of America" are "Actors on a most conspicuous Theatre." It was not uncommon to hear from the Federalists self-conscious acknowledgments of the part the United States had been assigned in mankind's struggle for liberty and just government. With Providence the director, the American people the leading actors, and their war-worn soil the stage of the dramatic scenes to unfold, the eyes of the audience of the world were fixed upon them.

The play is not over, the Revolution is not complete, the Federalist chorus rang out. The "temple of liberty" is yet to be secured from licentiousness and injustice, they said. The Federalists must bind themselves, said "Philodemos," "with the restraints of just government." They must conform their spirits to the spirit and cause of the Union—"the political Rock of our Salvation"—so that the fruits of the Revolution may ripen, and that so many sufferings and sacrifices will not have been in vain.

The Federalists maintained that the fears spread by the Anti-Federalists concerning the Constitution's lack of provision for freedom of the press and trial by jury, annihilation of the state governments, and general alarm for the people's liberties were simply unfounded. The Constitution, they said, creates a federal government of expressly delegated, limited powers, reserving to the states and to the people all other powers; it is marked by a myriad of checks and balances to guard against tyranny and protect liberty. Besides, there are limits to what constitutional, parchment arrangements can do. The fundamental question is not what new provisions and arrangements are needed, but whether the American political system is sufficiently founded on the authority of the people. Is the will of the people given a decisive influence in the American polity? Dickinson asked. If the answer is yes then the preservation of liberty depends, finally, on the people themselves.

The American people have been granted the singular opportunity of governing themselves wisely, said John Jay, and on this the "cause of freedom" depended. "In short," wrote a "State Soldier," "as there is nothing in this constitution itself that particularly bargains for a surrender of your liberties, it must be your own faults if you become enslaved." Washington had issued the republican challenge of self-government even earlier during the founding period. As was his wont, his words and deeds were of the nature of a freeman mindful of the society of other equal and free men among whom he dwelled. His commands were of the kind that taught others that *they* must command *themselves*. Whether the American people will retain their liberty and secure prosperity and happiness depends on their choices and conduct, he said, and if they "should not be completely free and happy, the fault will be intirely their own."

Perhaps it was because of Washington's solemn and commanding presence and Franklin's gentle irony and wit that these two men were so beloved by the American people, but more likely it was because the citizens saw in them an uncommon devotion to the cause of a free people—a public spirit that reigned in them almost before there was any public to be spirited about. That Washington and Franklin were Friends of the Constitution carried enormous weight with the American people, as the Federalists who invoked their names well understood.

George Washington

Circular to the States

14 June 1783

———•———

This circular letter was written originally in June 1783. The copy sent to state executives in that year was dated 21 June. Because Washington here addresses issues regarding the strengthening of the central government, it was published again on 15 March 1787 in the Providence *United States Chronicle*. This letter was the first of many attempts by Federalists to align the great leader with the Federalist cause.

———•———

Sir: The great object for which I had the honor to hold an appointment in the Service of my Country, being accomplished, I am now preparing to resign it into the hands of Congress, and to return to that domestic retirement, which, it is well known, I left with the greatest reluctance, a Retirement, for which I have never ceased to sigh through a long and painful absence, and in which (remote from the noise and trouble of the World) I meditate to pass the remainder of life in a state of undisturbed repose; But before I carry this resolution into effect, I think it a duty incumbent on me, to make this my last official communication, to congratulate you on the glorious events which Heaven has been pleased to produce in our favor, to offer my sentiments respecting some important subjects, which appear to me, to be intimately connected with the tranquility of the United States, to take my leave of your Excellency as a public Character, and to give my final blessing to that Country, in whose service I have spent the prime of my life, for whose sake I have consumed so many anxious days and watchfull nights, and whose happiness being extremely dear to me, will always constitute no inconsiderable part of my own.

Impressed with the liveliest sensibility on this pleasing occasion, I will claim the indulgence of dilating the more copiously on the subjects of our mutual felicitation. When we consider the magnitude of the prize we contended for, the doubtful nature of the contest, and the favorable manner in which it has terminated, we shall find the greatest possible reason for gratitude and rejoicing; this is a theme that will afford infinite delight to every benevolent and liberal mind, whether the event in contemplation, be considered as the source of present enjoyment or the parent of future happiness; and we shall have equal occasion to felicitate ourselves on the lot which Providence has assigned us, whether we view it in a natural, a political or moral point of light.

The Citizens of America, placed in the most enviable condition, as the sole Lords and Proprietors of a vast Tract of Continent, comprehending all the various soils and climates of the World, and abounding with all the necessaries and conveniencies of life, are now by the late satisfactory pacification, acknowledged to be possessed of absolute freedom and Independency; They are, from this period, to be considered as the Actors on a most conspicuous Theatre, which seems to be peculiarly designated by Providence for the display of human greatness and felicity; Here, they are not only surrounded with every thing which can contribute to the completion of private and domestic enjoyment, but Heaven has crowned all its other blessings, by giving a fairer oppertunity for political happiness, than any other Nation has ever been favored with. Nothing can illustrate these observations more forcibly, than a recollection of the happy conjuncture of times and circumstances, under which our Republic assumed its rank among the Nations; The foundation of our empire was not laid in the gloomy age of Ignorance and Superstition, but at an Epocha when the rights of mankind were better understood and more clearly defined, than at any former period; the researches of the human mind, after social happiness, have been carried to a great extent; the Treasures of knowledge, acquired through a long succession of years, by the labours of Philosophers, Sages and Legislatures, are laid open for our use, and their collected wisdom may be happily applied in the Establishment of our forms of Government; the free cultivation of Letters, the unbounded extension of Commerce, the progressive refinement of Manners, the growing liberality of sentiment, and above all, the pure and benign light of Revelation, have had a meliorating influence on mankind and increased the blessings of Society. At this auspicious period, the

United States came into existence as a Nation, and if their Citizens should not be completely free and happy, the fault will be intirely their own.

Such is our situation, and such are our prospects: but notwithstanding the cup of blessing is thus reached out to us, notwithstanding happiness is ours, if we have a disposition to seize the occasion and make it our own; yet, it appears to me there is an option still left to the United States of America, that it is in their choice, and depends upon their conduct, whether they will be respectable and prosperous, or contemptable and miserable as a Nation; This is the time of their political probation; this is the moment when the eyes of the whole World are turned upon them; this is the moment to establish or ruin their national Character forever; this is the favorable moment to give such a tone to our Federal Government, as will enable it to answer the ends of its institution; or this may be the ill-fated moment for relaxing the powers of the Union, annihilating the cement of the Confederation, and exposing us to become the sport of European politics, which may play one State against another to prevent their growing importance, and to serve their own interested purposes. For, according to the system of Policy the States shall adopt at this moment, they will stand or fall; and by their confirmation or lapse, it is yet to be decided, whether the Revolution must ultimately be considered as a blessing or a curse: a blessing or a curse, not to the present age alone, for with our fate will the destiny of unborn Millions be involved.

With this conviction of the importance of the present Crisis, silence in me would be a crime; I will therefore speak to your Excellency, the language of freedom and of sincerity, without disguise; I am aware, however, that those who differ from me in political sentiment, may perhaps remark, I am stepping out of the proper line of my duty, and they may possibly ascribe to arrogance or ostentation, what I know is alone the result of the purest intention, but the rectitude of my own heart, which disdains such unworthy motives, the part I have hitherto acted in life, the determination I have formed, of not taking any share in public business hereafter, the ardent desire I feel, and shall continue to manifest, of quietly enjoying in private life, after all the toils of War, the benefits of a wise and liberal Government, will, I flatter myself, sooner or later convince my Countrymen, that I could have no sinister views in delivering with so little reserve, the opinions contained in this Address.

There are four things, which I humbly conceive, are essential to the well being, I may even venture to say, to the existence of the United States as an Independent Power:

1st. An indissoluble Union of the States under one Federal Head.

2dly. A Sacred regard to Public Justice.

3dly. The adoption of a proper Peace Establishment, and

4thly. The prevalence of that pacific and friendly Disposition, among the People of the United States, which will induce them to forget their local prejudices and policies, to make those mutual concessions which are requisite to the general prosperity, and in some instances, to sacrifice their individual advantages to the interest of the Community.

These are the Pillars on which the glorious Fabrick of our Independency and National Character must be supported; Liberty is the Basis, and whoever would dare to sap the foundation, or overturn the Structure, under whatever specious pretexts he may attempt it, will merit the bitterest execration, and the severest punishment which can be inflicted by his injured Country.

On the three first Articles I will make a few observations, leaving the last to the good sense and serious consideration of those immediately concerned.

Under the first head, altho' it may not be necessary or proper for me in this place to enter into a particular disquisition of the principles of the Union, and to take up the great question which has been frequently agitated, whether it be expedient and requisite for the States to delegate a larger proportion of Power to Congress, or not, Yet it will be a part of my duty, and that of every true Patriot, to assert without reserve, and to insist upon the following positions, That unless the States will suffer Congress to exercise those prerogatives, they are undoubtedly invested with by the Constitution, every thing must very rapidly tend to Anarchy and confusion, That it is indispensable to the happiness of the individual States, that there should be lodged somewhere, a Supreme Power to regulate and govern the general concerns of the Confederated Republic, without which the Union cannot be of long duration. That there must be a faithfull and pointed compliance on the part of every State, with the late proposals and demands of Congress, or the most fatal consequences will ensue, That whatever measures have a tendency to dissolve the Union, or contribute to violate or lessen the Sovereign Authority, ought to be considered as hostile to the Liberty and Independency of America, and the Authors of them treated accordingly, and lastly, that unless we can be enabled by the concurrence of the States, to participate of the fruits of the Revolution, and enjoy the essential benefits of Civil Society, under a form of Government so free and uncorrupted, so happily guarded against the danger of oppression, as has been devised and adopted by the Articles of Confederation, it will be a subject of regret, that so much blood and treasure have been lavished for no purpose, that so many sufferings have been encountered without a compensation, and that so many sacrifices have been made in vain. Many other considerations might here be adduced to prove, that without an entire conformity to the Spirit of the Union, we cannot exist as an Independent Power; it will be sufficient for my purpose to mention but one or two which seem to me of the greatest importance. It is only in our united Character as an Empire, that our Independence is acknowledged, that our power can be regarded, or our Credit supported among Foreign Nations. The Treaties of the European Powers with the United States of America, will have no validity on a dissolution of the Union. We shall be left nearly in a state of Nature, or we may find by our own unhappy experience, that there is a natural and necessary progression, from the extreme of anarchy to the extreme of Tyranny; and that arbitrary power is most easily established on the ruins of Liberty abused to licentiousness.

As to the second Article, which respects the performance of Public Justice, Congress have, in their late Address to the United States, almost exhausted the subject, they have explained their Ideas so fully, and have enforced the obligations the States are under, to render compleat justice to all the Public Creditors, with so much dignity and energy, that in my opinion, no real friend to the honor and Independency of America, can hesitate a single moment respecting the propriety of complying with the just and honorable measures proposed; if their Arguments do not produce conviction, I know of nothing that will have greater influence; especially when we recollect that the System referred to, being the result of the collected Wisdom of the Continent, must be esteemed, if not perfect, certainly the least objectionable of any that could be devised; and that if it shall not be carried into immediate execution, a National Bankruptcy, with all its deplorable consequences will take place, before any different Plan can possibly be proposed and adopted, So pressing are the present circumstances! and such is the alternative now offered to the States!

The ability of the Country to discharge the debts which have been incurred in its defence, is not to be doubted; an inclination, I flatter myself, will not be wanting; the path of our duty is plain before us; honesty will be found on every experiment, to be the best and only true policy; let us then as a Nation be just; let us fulfil the public Contracts, which Congress had undoubtedly a right to make for the purpose of carrying on the War, with the same good faith we suppose ourselves bound to perform our private engagements; in the mean time, let an attention to the chearfull performance of their proper business, as Individuals, and as members of Society, be earnestly inculcated on the Citizens of America, then will they strengthen the hands of Government, and be happy under its protection: every one will reap the fruit of his labours; every one will enjoy his own acquisitions without molestation and without danger.

In this state of absolute freedom and perfect security, who will grudge to yield a very little of his property to support the common interest of Society, and insure the protection of Government? Who does not remember, the frequent declarations, at the commencement of the War, that we should be compleatly satisfied, if at the expence of one half, we could defend the remainder of our possessions? Where is the Man to be found, who wishes to remain indebted, for the defence of his own person and property, to the exertions, the bravery, and the blood of others, without making one generous effort to repay the debt of honor and of gratitude? In what part of the Continent shall we find any Man, or body of Men, who would not blush to stand up and propose measures, purposely calculated to rob the Soldier of his Stipend, and the Public Creditor of his due? and were it possible that such a flagrant instance of Injustice could ever happen, would it not excite the general indignation, and tend to bring down, upon the Authors of such measures, the aggravated vengeance of Heaven?

If after all, a spirit of disunion or a temper of obstinacy and perverseness, should manifest itself in any of the States, if such an ungracious disposition should attempt to frustrate all the happy effects that might be expected to flow from the Union, if there should be a refusal to comply with the requisitions for Funds to discharge the annual interest of the public debts, and if that refusal should revive again all those jealousies and produce all those evils, which are now happily removed, Congress, who have in all their Transaction shewn a great degree of magnanimity and justice, will stand justified in the sight of God and Man, and the State alone which puts itself in opposition to the aggregate Wisdom of the Continent, and follows such mistaken and pernicious Councils, will be responsible for all the consequences.

For my own part, conscious of having acted while a Servant of the Public, in a manner I conceived best suited to promote the real interests of my Country; having in consequence of my fixed belief in some measure pledged myself to the Army, that their Country would finally do them compleat and ample Justice; and not wishing to conceal any instance of my official conduct from the eyes of the World, I have thought proper to transmit to your Excellency the inclosed collection of Papers, relative to the half pay and commutation granted by Congress to the Officers of the Army; From these communications, my decided sentiment will be clearly comprehended, together with the conclusive reasons which induced me, at an early period, to recommend the adoption of the measure, in the most earnest and serious manner. As the proceedings of Congress, the Army, and myself are open to all, and contain in my opinion, sufficient information to remove the prejudices and errors which may have been entertained by any; I think it unnecessary to say any thing more, than just to observe, that the Resolutions of Congress, now alluded to, are undoubtedly as absolutely binding upon the United States, as the most solemn Acts of Confederation or Legislation. As to the Idea, which I am informed has in some instances prevailed, that the half pay and commutation are to be regarded merely in the odious light of a Pension, it ought to be exploded forever; that Provision, should be viewed as it really was, a reasonable compensation offered by Congress, at a time when they had nothing else to give, to the Officers of the Army, for services then to be performed. It was the only means to prevent a total dereliction of the Service, It was a part of their hire, I may be allowed to say, it was the price of their blood and of your Independency, it is therefore more than a common debt, it is a debt of honour, it can never be considered as a Pension or gratuity, nor be cancelled until it is fairly discharged.

With regard to a distinction between Officers and Soldiers, it is sufficient that the uniform experience of every Nation of the World, combined with our own, proves the utility and propriety of the discrimination. Rewards in proportion to the aids the public derives from them, are unquestionably due to all its Servants; In some Lines, the Soldiers have perhaps generally had as ample a compensation for their Services, by the large Bounties which have been paid to them, as their Officers will receive in the proposed Commutation, in others, if besides the donation of Lands, the payment of Arrearages of Cloathing and Wages (in which Articles all the component parts of the Army must be put upon the same footing) we take into the estimate, the Bounties many of the Soldiers have received and the gratuity of one Year's full pay, which is promised to all, possibly their situation (every circumstance being duly considered) will not be deemed less eligible than that of the Officers. Should a farther reward, however, be judged equitable, I will venture to assert, no one will enjoy greater satisfaction than myself, on seeing an exemption from Taxes for a limited time, (which has been petitioned for in some instances) or any other adequate immunity or compensation, granted to the brave defenders of their Country's Cause; but neither the adoption or rejection of this proposition will in any manner affect, much less militate against, the Act of Congress, by which they have offered five years full pay, in lieu of the half pay for life, which had been before promised to the Officers of the Army.

Before I conclude the subject of public justice, I cannot omit to mention the obligations this Country is under, to that meritorious Class of veteran Non-commissioned Officers and Privates, who have been discharged for inability, in consequence of the Resolution of Congress of the 23d of April 1782, on an annual pension for life, their peculiar sufferings, their singular merits and claims to that provision need only be known, to interest all the feelings of humanity in their behalf: nothing but a punctual payment of their annual allowance can rescue them from the most complicated misery, and nothing could be a more melancholy and distressing sight, than to behold those who have shed their blood or lost their limbs in the service of their Country, without a shelter, without a friend, and without the means of obtaining any of the necessaries or comforts of Life; compelled to beg their daily bread from door to door! Suffer me to recommend those of this discription, belonging to your State, to the warmest patronage of your Excellency and your Legislature.

It is necessary to say but a few words on the third topic which was proposed, and which regards particularly the defence of the Republic, As there can be little doubt but Congress will recommend a proper Peace Establishment for the United States, in which a due attention will be paid to the importance of placing the Militia of the Union upon a regular and respectable footing; If this should be the case, I would beg leave to urge the great advantage of it in the strongest terms. The Militia of this Country must be considered as the Palladium of our security, and the first effectual resort in case of hostility; It is essential therefore, that the same system should pervade the whole; that the formation and discipline of the Militia of the Continent should be absolutely uniform, and that the same species of Arms, Accoutrements and Military Apparatus, should be introduced in every part of the United States; No one, who has not learned it from experience, can conceive the difficulty, expence, and confusion which result from a contrary system, or the vague Arrangements which have hitherto prevailed.

If in treating of political points, a greater latitude than usual has been taken in the course of this Address, the importance of the Crisis, and the magnitude of the objects in discussion, must be my apology: It is, however, neither my wish or expectation, that the preceding observations should claim any regard, except so far as they shall appear to be dictated by a good intention, consonant to the immutable rules of Justice; calculated to produce a liberal system of policy, and founded on whatever experience may have been acquired by a long and close attention to public business. Here I might speak with the more confidence from my actual observations, and, if it would not swell this Letter (already too prolix) beyond the bounds I had prescribed myself: I could demonstrate to every mind open to conviction, that in less time and with much less expence than has been incurred, the War might have been brought to the same happy conclusion, if the resources of the Continent could have been properly drawn forth, that the distresses and disappointments which have very often occurred, have in too many instances, resulted more from a want of energy, in the Continental Government, than a deficiency of means in the particular States. That the inefficiency of measures, arising from the want of an adequate authority in the Supreme Power, from a partial compliance with the Requisitions of Congress in some of the States, and from a failure of punctuality in others, while it tended to damp the zeal of those which were more willing to exert themselves; served also to accumulate the expences of the War, and to frustrate the best concerted Plans, and that the discouragement occasioned by the complicated difficulties and embarrassments, in which our affairs were, by this means involved, would have long ago produced the dissolution of any Army, less patient, less virtuous and less persevering, than that which I have had the honor to command. But while I mention these things, which are notorious facts, as the defects of our Federal Government, particularly in the prosecution of a War, I beg it may be understood, that as I have ever taken a pleasure in gratefully acknowledging the assistance and support I have derived from every Class of Citizens, so shall I always be happy to do justice to the unparalleled exertion of the individual States, on many interesting occasions.

I have thus freely disclosed what I wished to make known, before I surrendered up my Public trust to those who committed it to me, the task is now accomplished, I now bid adieu to your Excellency as the Chief Magistrate of your State, at the same time I bid a last farewell to the cares of Office, and all the imployments of public life.

It remains then to be my final and only request, that your Excellency will communicate these sentiments to your Legislature at their next meeting, and that they may be considered as the Legacy of One, who has ardently wished, on all occasions, to be useful to his Country, and who, even in the shade of Retirement, will not fail to implore the divine benediction upon it.

I now make it my earnest prayer, that God would have you, and the State over which you preside, in his holy protection, that he would incline the hearts of the Citizens to cultivate a spirit of subordination and obedience to Government, to entertain a brotherly affection and love for one another, for their fellow Citizens of the United States at large, and particularly for their brethren who have served in the Field, and finally, that he would most graciously be pleased to dispose us all, to do Justice, to love mercy, and to demean ourselves with that Charity, humility and pacific temper of mind, which were the Characteristicks of the Divine Author of our blessed Religion, and without an humble imitation of whose example in these things, we can never hope to be a happy Nation.

"A Pennsylvania Farmer"

Essay

Independent Gazetteer, Philadelphia, 27 September 1787

For the *Independent Gazetteer.*

Mr. Oswald: In searching among some old papers a few days ago, I accidentally found a London newspaper, dated in March, 1774, wherein a certain Dean Tucker, after stating several advantages attendent on a separation from the then colonies, now United States of America, proceeds thus: "After a separation from the colonies our influence over them will be much greater than ever it was, since they began to feel their own weight and importance." "The moment a separation takes effect, intestine quarrels will begin;" and "in proportion as their factious republican spirit shall intrigue and cabal, shall split into parties, divide and sub-divide, in the same proportion shall we be called in to become their general umpires and referees."

I stood aghast on perusing this British prophecy, and could not help reflecting how my infatuated countrymen are on the very verge of suffering it to be fulfilled. Already have they in several of the States spurned at the federal government, despised their admonitions, and absolutely refused to comply with their requisitions; nay, they have gone further, and have enacted laws in direct violation of those very requisitions; nor does the present federal constitution give Congress power to enforce a compliance with the most trifling measure they may recommend. Hence, liberty becomes licentiousness (for while causes continue to produce their effects, want of energy in government will be followed by disobedience in the governed). Hence, also, credit, whether foreign or domestic, public or private, hath been abused, and, of course, is reduced to the lowest ebb; Rhode Island faith in particular is become superlatively infamous, even to a proverb. Would to God that censure in this respect were only due to that petty State! Sorry I am to say, several others merit a considerable share of it. Ship-building and commerce no more enrich our country; agriculture is neglected, or what is just the same, our produce, instead of being exported, is suffered to rot in the fields. Britain has dared to retain our frontier posts, whereby she not only deprives us of our fur trade, but is enabled to keep up a number of troops, to take every advantage of any civil broils which may arise in these States; and to close the dismal scene, rebellion, with all its dire concomitants, has actually reared its head in a sister State—such have been the deplorable effects of a weak and impotent government. Perhaps the present situation of America cannot be better described than by comparing her to a ship at sea in a storm, when the mariners tie up the helm and abandon her to the fury of the winds and waves. O, America! arouse! awake from your lethargy! bravely assert the cause of federal unanimity! and save your sinking country! Let it not be said that those men who heroically extirpated tyranny from America, should suffer civil discord to undo all that they have achieved, or to effect more than all the powers of Britain, aided by her blood-thirsty mercenaries, were able to accomplish. Let not posterity say: "Alas, our fathers expended much blood and treasure in erecting the temple of liberty; and when nothing more was wanting but thirteen pillars to support the stately edifice, they supinely neglected this essential part; so has the whole become one mighty heap of ruins, and slavery is entailed on their unhappy offspring." God forbid that this should ever be the case!

Do any of my fellow citizens ask, how may we avert the impending danger? The answer is obvious; let us adopt that federal constitution, which has been earnestly recommended by a convention of patriotic sages, and which, while it gives energy to our government, wisely secures our liberties. This constitution, my friends, is the result of four months' deliberation, in an assembly composed of men whose known integrity, patriotism and abilities justly deserve our confidence; let us also remember that the illustrious WASHINGTON was their President. And shall we, my fellow citizens, render all their measures ineffectual by withholding our concurrence? The preservation of ourselves and our country forbid it. Methinks I hear every hill from St. Croix to the Mississippi reecho the praises of this simple but excellent constitution.

Having once adopted this truly federal form of government, Dean Tucker and all the divines in England may prophecy our downfall if they will, we shall not regard them. Then shall commerce revisit our shores; then shall we take a distinguished rank among the nations of the earth; then shall our husbandmen and mechanics of every denomination enjoy the fruits of their industry; and then, and not till then, shall we be completely happy.

"Monitor"

Essay

Hampshire Gazette, Northampton, 24 October 1787

To the PUBLICK.

My Countrymen, That important period has now arrived in which political life and death, for the last time, is set before you. It is now in your power to chuse whether you will be free and happy, or enslaved and miserable. Various innovations and changes have happened in your political system within the last few years—various amendments have been assayed to no purpose—all attempts hitherto made to establish your independence and happiness, have been blasted, have proved inadequate to the great purposes for which government is instituted, and have issued in disgrace, disappointment and contempt. Government, that bulwark of common defence, has at sundry times, within a few years past, been seen tottering on its basis, being shaken to its very center, by those frequent commotions which have been produced by the hostile invasions of lawless and ambitious men, intending, no doubt, to lay it level with the dust, and introduce anarchy, confusion and every disorder.[1] Harrassed and worn out with tumults and distractions, and weary of so many fruitless endeavours to secure the rights and protect the citizens of the United States, from the wicked assaults and lawless ravages and depredations of unprincipled men, and finding the confederation of the thirteen states unequal to the great ends for which it was adopted, that the power delegated to that august body, the Congress, was insufficient any longer to hold you together, and that a speedy dissolution under the old administration was inevitable, therefore, that the union may

---

1. This is apparently a reference to Shays' Rebellion in particular. The 1786 rebellion, led by Daniel Shays, was an economically motivated uprising in western Massachusetts. The inability of the national government under the Articles of Confederation to deal adequately with such internal convulsions was still very much in the public mind during the drafting and ratification of the Constitution.

be cemented with an invincible firmness; that a federal government may be formed upon a permanent foundation, endowed with energy sufficient to carry into execution every act and resolve necessary to maintain justice and equity, and to support the majesty and dignity as well as the privileges of a free people; and that an effectual barrier may be set to guard your rights against every invasion, foreign and domestic, and to fix you in a lasting peace upon just and righteous principles, accompanied with its concomitants, national glory and felicity. For these invaluable purposes (after every other effort, as I before observed proved abortive) as the dernier resort, you had recourse to a Convention of delegates from the several states, in which the wisdom thereof, as you may reasonably suppose, was collected—the honourable Members were gentlemen of unexceptionable characters, well acquainted with political concerns, and fully possessed with the danger of the present deranged situation of your public affairs—endowed not only with wisdom and knowledge, but firmness and integrity, equal to the arduous task to which they were called, and their well known affection for and to the interest of your country, must heighten your esteem of their qualifications.

From an assembly of such worthy characters, with the illustrious Washington at their head, what may you not expect? yea, and what raised expectations could you have entertained that are not more than gratified in their result, which now lies before you—the result, not of an ordinary sagacity, but of uncommon wisdom—the result, not of a rash, hasty, and premature judgment, but of calm reasoning, cool deliberation, and a fair, candid and impartial discussion, on every article proposed, together with their supposed consequence, good and ill; every objection having been thoroughly examined and weighed; those obstacles arising from the separate interests of the different states duly considered, the plan was adopted not by one or two states only, or a bare majority, but the unanimous consent of twelve. I will not suggest it to be clear of every possible defect, for that is incompatible with the mutable uncertain state of human nature; and so long as men govern, errors and mistakes will happen: But this I aver, that it exceeds your most sanguine rational expectations. Permit me then to enjoin it as an indisp[ut]able duty on you to accept it. It will be your wisdom to comply with it, your safety and interest call for it. I presume your feelings debate it, and what is more, Heaven itself demands it, for your salvation and national existence depend on it. God forbid, that you should be so lost to your duty and interest, at this late hour, as to spurn the last opportunity which an indulgent Providence, 'tis likely, will ever grant you, to save your sinking country from tumbling into ruin. Suffer me to urge it upon you— not to be dictated by sinister motives—renounce all selfish, mean-spirited and contracted views, and fix your eyes upon the general good, and let those generous and liberal sentiments possess your minds, as shall animate you chearfully to lay aside some advantages that respect you individually, when they stand in the way to the common interest, for yourselves are shares in public benefits: and should you discover some inconveniences that will ac-crue to you from your local situation (as undoubtedly you will, the local interests of the different parts of this extended country being necessarily different) you will by no means suffer that consideration to gain the ascen-dency over your reason, so far as to influence you to reject the proposed plan of government; or, mark it, the moment you reject it, you involve your-selves and posterity in ruin. Should you now refuse to embrace this golden opportunity to establish your independency upon such a permanent and unshaken foundation (as it is now in your power to do) as shall preserve inviolable your dear bought privileges, bought at the expence of many in-valuable lives and much precious treasure. You may with propriety apply to yourselves an observation of one of the wisest of men, viz. He that being often reproved hardeneth his neck, shall suddenly be destroyed, and that without remedy;[2] which respects nations as well as individuals, that have been repeatedly reproved by such disasterous events and threatening com-motions, and dangerous violences as have again and again distracted your country, greatly tending to the dissolution of your government; yea, you in vain, when too late, will see your folly, when a melancholy gloom hath overwhelmed you, and your remediless distresses have overtaken you. But should you be so happy as to adopt the proposed plan of government, as I presume you will, (for I am persuaded there is virtue yet remaining among

2. Prv. 29:1.

you, and some vestiges of that zeal for liberty which glowed in every American in times past, which on a fresh occasion like this, will revive and manifest itself) you may with pleasure anticipate those agreeable prospects that are opening upon you—the congratulations of your benevolent allies, which will soon reach your ears—the satisfaction it will yield to the friends of your independence throughout the world, and the joy that will leap in the breast of every well-wisher to your national interest in the union. Your fame shall outlive you—your memory will be sweet to your progeny, and generations yet unborn will feel their souls inspired with gratitude to you for that firmness, integrity and resolution, which has marked your way in obtaining, preserving, and handing down unsullied to them, those inestimable blessings which they shall hold in quiet possession.[3] Let such motives stimulate you to embrace that which alone will disappoint and chagrin your malevolent enemies, rear the hopes of your timorous and chear the drooping spirits of your despairing, friends, and then will you amply compensate the pains taken by the MONITOR.

3. The "love of fame," observes Publius in *The Federalist,* No. 72, is "the ruling passion of the noblest minds." For the best account of the Founders' view of fame, see Douglass Adair, *Fame and the Founding Fathers: Essays by Douglass Adair* (New York: Norton, 1974), 107–23.

"*Common Sense*"

Essay

Massachusetts Gazette, Boston, 11 January 1788

For the MASSACHUSETTS GAZETTE.

MR. ALLEN; Several honest countrymen have wondered that the advantages of the *new constitution* could not be pointed out to them in plain language. For the satisfaction of this class of men, permit me to inform them, through the mechanics of your paper, that one of the greatest excellencies of the proposed constitution is *power,* adequate *power,* to manage the great affairs of the nation, conferred upon the *Congress.*

For the want of this, the United States have, within these six years past almost become bankrupt. The union have been to a very great annual expense to support a Congress without power to manage the important business of the nation. My countrymen, the plain truth is, that Congress have, in fact, made much such a figure as the General Court in this state would do, provided they had power only to recommend, not to make, laws. Reflect a moment upon the confusion this would introduce into the state of Massachusetts. Delegates annually chosen from every town in the state, to set at Boston, for the bigger part of the year, consulting the best interest of the state, and recommending to each town to make such laws as the General Assembly judged for the benefit of the whole; but no one of these laws to take effect till enacted by every town in the State. In such a case, the town of Boston, for instance, might judge it convenient to enact a law to punish these, while some of the neighbouring towns, for certain reasons, might judge it utterly inconvenient for them; and so, if all the towns in the state, except one should see fit to comply with the recommendation of the General Assembly, to make laws to punish theft, it would avail nothing, except this single, and perhaps small, vicious town should see fit to comply with the general recommendation. Does not common sense tell us, that it would be extreme folly to expect thousands annually to maintain such a body of men?—What a goodly figure would our delegates make, returning home from the seat of [the] CONSTITUTION, loaded with good and wholesome recommendations to their constituents! Would not every idle buffoon, in such a nation, find ample materials for sport and ridicule? and would not every man of sense prefer absolute monarchy to such a government as this? Would it not be ordinarily impossible, in the midst of such a variety of sentiment, local prejudices, and private interests, ever to have one law made in the state, unless it were to enact a law, that if any man did not do that which was right in his own eyes he should be hanged?

My countrymen we have tried this mode, and found it every way insufficient to the great exigencies of the nation. Men of penetration have grown weary of such a weak and inefficient system, and wish to lay it aside; and have substituted in its room, a government that shall be as efficacious throughout the union, as this state government is throughout the Massachusetts. What one would think should greatly recommend the new constitution to an inhabitant of this state is, that it is as much like the constitution of this state, as a national government can be like that of a state. It is an elective government, consisting of three branches—legislative, judicial, and executive—having power to do nothing but of a national kind—leaving the several states full power to govern themselves as individual states. This power, which is so dreaded by some, is, therefore, one of the greatest excellencies of the new federal government, and what must center in some head, or the grand American fabrick of liberty, which has cost us so much blood and treasure, tumble to pieces, to the eternal disgrace of this new and free world.

"Philodemos"

Essay

American Herald, Boston, 12 May 1788

To the PEOPLE of the UNITED STATES.

The progress of events is steadily carrying forward the great business of your general government. May the God of our fathers direct this all-important matter to that issue which is *really right!*—The great opportunity for consideration and discussion afforded to the states, who have elected late, appears to have operated in favour of the constitution. In Maryland, all its faults have been pointed out with little ceremony, and the most delicate proceedings of the General Convention have been laid open without reserve. Yet we find there Johnson, Lee, Goldsboroughs, Plater, Hemsley, Carrol, Lloyd, Hanson, McHenry, and other characters, who were early active in the revolution, now decided in favour of the adoption. These gentlemen are not ignorant of liberty and government, nor of the interests of Maryland and the Union, not enemies of the people of America, nor uninterested in her fate. Maryland contains no patriotism, no genius, no virtue, if they be denied to that list of names and many of their respectable colleagues. Does it appear from this choice, that the people of Maryland have been influenced by the active and numerous exertions of their Attorney-General. Do they appear to consider him as having just conceptions of what they deem necessary to welfare and honor, either in their capacity as a separate state, or as a member of the confederacy. Compare the real conduct of the worthy citizens of Maryland with what was asserted to be their sentiments, and it was predicted would be their conduct, by the opponents to the constitution. Mark the dilemma in which the gentlemen in opposition are involved. If their assertion, that Maryland was unfavorable, was true at the time, then has the constitution stood the test of examination, and gained friends on the freest investigation. If, on the other hand, the assertion was not true, then they have passed on [to] you important information not founded on fact, the impressions of which it is now your duty to erase from your minds.

Further discussions of the constitution are daily becoming less necessary for the people; for in almost all the states they have chose[n] their conventions. Yet a constant remembrance of the present condition of our country should be had in mind. The relaxation of government, consequent on a change from monarchy to liberty, and inevitable in the war,—suspension and installment laws, paper mediums, and legal tenders, corrupting those who handled property—ardent spirits, flowing through the land like the brooks and rivers, corrupting the morals and destroying the constitutions of the mass of the people—the interruption given to the education of our youth—the avocations of many from the sober habits of private citizens, to the irregularity and dissipations of the military life—the influx of foreign luxury, unknown in former times—the derangement of all business—these, and many other unfavorable circumstances, were found to exist at the conclusion of the war, or have taken place since that period. How painful to the man of virtue and spirit is this situation! how noble—how extraordinary—is the spectacle we are now exhibiting to the world! A people, exposed from adventitious circumstances to a condition so dangerous and corrupting as that above described, magnanimously binding themselves with the restraints of just government. Let us then not be discouraged by the unworthy measures of some of our fellow citizens, nor let us be prevented from prosecuting the good work by the mistaken, though honest, jealousy and apprehensions of others.

It has been urged to you, that the terms on which we stand with foreign nations are rendered less advantageous than they might be, were we respectable in our general government. Those who have been honored with the charge of your public affairs have long known and felt this unfortunate truth; but a leading member in the British Parliament has lately stated it as a consideration which ought to suspend all arrangements on their part, concerning the intercourse between America and Great Britain. Tho' the late arret of his Most Christian Majesty is exceedingly favorable to the commerce of the United States, particularly in putting us on a footing with his own subjects in all the ports of India belonging to his crown, yet the same difficulty stands in the way of more important advantages. In short, commerce, whereby we are to vend the surplus of our produce to foreign nations, is circumscribed and suspended, by our standing in the light of separate Commonwealths, instead of on a CONFEDERATED REPUBLIC.

The question before you at this time does not involve the permanent acceptance and adoption of the Federal Constitution for ever, or without amendments. You are called seriously to consider the condition of your affairs at home, and the state of your connexions abroad—to reflect what must be the consequences of your continuing longer in the predicament described—and then to determine whether it is not better to cure a great number of these certain and ruinous evils by the adoption of the government proposed, accompanied as it is with opportunities and provisions for amendment. In resolving this momentous question, I do not wish you to be too far influenced by the distracted state of our affairs. If the liberty and safety obtained by the late revolution will be lost or endangered, take care how you proceed. But let us view the government with candor, and let us consider it as it is, bottomed on the state constitutions. It may not be perfect—it certainly is not perfect. I ask its candid and sincere opposers, where is the constitution, or when has existed the country more fortunate in its frame of government, th[a]n America would be under the combined operations of the State and Federal Constitutions? I admit again, that the constitution is not perfect; but shall we hesitate to accept a constitution better than any heretofore enjoyed by any nation, when the alternative is lawful tenders, insurrection and anarchy at home, and contempt abroad? Surely no. Let us then make the trial of the proposed government, understanding on both sides, that every wholesome alteration and amendment may hereafter be adopted, which shall be necessary to preserve the peace, liberty and safety of the people, and establish the dignity and importance of the United States.

Were the honest opponents of the Federal Constitution to place themselves on the shores of France, Great-Britain or Holland, and thence to view with impartiality the situation and character of this country—were they, in addition to the melancholy evils already enumerated, to see the miserable state of our public and private credit in Europe, and the blessings of worse governments there better administered—they would fly to the Federal Constitution, as the first step to the restoration of order and prosperity at home, and honour and dignity abroad.

It cannot be feared, that amendments will be refused or prevented after adoption. The people and the states will have all power, and if they will not then have wisdom and virtue enough to make wholesome amendments, they cannot be expected to form entirely a new and more perfect system.

The United States, under the proposed system, will be defended from religious tyranny, paper tenders, perpetual or even long grants of military revenues to the executive, and from orders of nobility, or even any other anti-republican distinctions. They will have the independency of judges secured, and will always be certain of a concert of the state legislatures and executives against incroachments of the federal legislature or executive; and they will enjoy constitutions founded in every instance upon the great principle, of representation and political obligation being inseparable. They have rejected feudal principles, the foundation of the European tyrannies, from their habits, and do not now retain them in their laws; for the state legislatures have in some instances already reduced their descents to the principles of republicanism, or perfect equality, and all the rest may do the same without controul. With such securities for liberty, who will hazard the dangers with which it is threatened from a continuance of the present system.

"A Federalist"

Essay

Independent Gazetteer, Philadelphia, 25 October 1787

To the Freemen of Pennsylvania.

Friends and Fellow Citizens: Conscious of no other motives than those with which the love of my country inspires me, permit me to request your candid, impartial and unprejudiced attendance, while I address you on business of the utmost importance to every honest American—a business of no less magnitude than the salvation of the United States.

I need hardly tell you, what is universally allowed, that our situation is now more precarious than it ever has been, even at that time when our country was laid waste by the sanguinary armies of Britain and her mercenary allies, and when our coasts were infested with her hostile fleets: then a sense of the common danger united every heroic, every patriotic soul in the great cause of liberty. Even selfishness itself, forgetting every narrow, contracted idea, gave way to that diffusive liberality of sentiment, which was so instrumental in procuring peace and independence to America.

But ever since that memorable epoch, unanimity, the great source of national happiness and glory, has been banished from among us, and discord, with all its cursed attendants, has succeeded in its stead. Such a train of calamities issued from this fatal change as at length aroused the virtuous citizens of the different States from their lethargy, and excited in them a desire of exploring, and of removing the cause. Nor was the former a different task. Our distresses were immediately discovered to be inevitable effects of a weak, a disunited, and a despicable federal government. To effect the latter, delegates were sent by twelve of the States to the late Federal Convention, who, after four months' deliberation, at length agreed upon a plan of government for the United States, which is now submitted to your consideration. Upon this proposed federal constitution I mean not to bestow my useless panegyrics at this time. My slender praise might cast an odium upon what is in itself truly excellent, and needs but a candid reading to be admired. Suspended, as the fate of the United States now is, how immensely base must the wretch be, who strains every nerve to disunite his fellow-citizens, and by a long train of sophistical arguments, strives to establish antifederal sentiments in this State! Yet, however strange it may seem, such there are among us. One antifederal piece signed "Centinel,"[1] which is replete with glaring absurdities and complete nonsense, has been industriously circulated among you, in the newspapers and in hand-bills. The author (I should have said authors)[2] of this illiberal and scandalous performance, remarks that a "frenzy of enthusiasm," not "a rational investigation into its principles, actuated the citizens of Philadelphia in their approbation of the proposed plan" of government. As some drunken men think every person they see is intoxicated, and as an illiterate observer on this earth is apt to believe in the sun's motion, not discerning that its apparent revolution is the effect of his own real motion, so has "Centinel" charged others with neglecting that rational investigation, to which he has paid very little attention. For if he carefully examines the proposed constitution, he will find that he has either ignorantly, or designedly, perverted its plain and simple construction. He seems to think that the citizens of Philadelphia ought to have suspended their judgment till they had known the result of his *rational investigation.* For, says the profound politician, "Those who are competent to the task of developing the principles of government ought to be encouraged to come forward, and thereby the better enable the people to make a proper judgment. For the science of government is so abstruse, that few are able to judge for themselves." He certainly must have forgot that he was addressing American freemen, who enjoy the darling prerogative of thinking for themselves. Such political priestcraft might have answered some purpose in the early ages of ignorance and superstition, when a set of artful and designing monks assumed an absolute control over both the purses and consciences of the people. But thanks to heaven! we live in an

---

1. The letters of the prominent Anti-Federalist Centinel first appeared in the Philadelphia *Independent Gazetteer* and the Philadelphia *Freeman's Journal* between October 1787 and April 1788. See Storing, 2:7; Allen, 93–101.

2. It is generally accepted that Samuel Bryan was the principal author of the Centinel essays. It is quite likely that his father, Judge George Bryan, a prominent Anti-Federalist leader in Pennsylvania, collaborated in the effort. See Storing's introduction to the Centinel essays, Storing, 2:7.

enlightened age, and in a free country, where such pernicious doctrine has long since been treated with deserved contempt.

He begins with enumerating "certain privileges secured to you by the constitution of this Commonwealth," which, notwithstanding his groundless assertions, are not infringed in the smallest degree by the proposed federal constitution, which obliges Congress to guarantee to each State its respective republican form of government. Whatever he may think of the matter, a firm union of all the States is certainly necessary to procure happiness and prosperity to America. In vain do we look up to the constitution or legislature of this State; they cannot alleviate our distresses.

Is it in the power of Pennsylvania to protest her own trade, by entering into commercial treaties with the nations of Europe, and thereby to secure a West India or an European market for her produce? No. Is it in her power to treat with and obtain from Spain a free navigation of the river Mississippi, to which God and nature have given us an undoubted right? The impoverished state of our Western country, where the luxuriant crops of a fertile soil are suffered to rot in the fields, for want of exportation, answers No. Is it in her power to encourage our infant manufactures, to give sustenance to our starving mechanics, to prevent a general bankruptcy, or to raise a revenue, by laying an impost on foreign goods imported into this State? No. All her attempts are liable to be counteracted by any neighboring State; for it is well known that the imposts have been frequently evaded in this State, and always will while Jersey and Delaware open free ports for the reception of foreign wares. So that the exigencies of government must necessarily be provided for by a heavy land tax, which you, my fellow citizens, have groaned under for some years past with surprising patience and resignation. Should some desperate ruffians, as a Shays or a Wyoming Franklin,[3] with an armed banditti at his back, proceed to murder our defenceless

3. The first reference is to Daniel Shays and the 1786 rebellion he led in western Massachusetts. The second and more obscure "ruffian" seems to be a reference to John Franklin of the Susquehanna Company in Connecticut. Franklin led the company in asserting Connecticut's rightful claim to territory also claimed by Pennsylvania. The dispute, known as the Wyoming Controversy (1782), resulted in bloodshed and violence. It was finally settled in 1790 in favor of Pennsylvania. The territory then under question is the present-day county of Luzerne.

inhabitants, has Pennsylvania the means of speedily repelling their ravages? No. Before the necessary steps could be taken for a defence, her towns might be laid in ruins and her fields deluged with the blood of her helpless citizens. And oh! distracting thought! the citizens of the neighboring States would abandon us to our unhappy fate; nor would they deign to shed a tear of pity on our funeral urn. It would be an endless talk to give a detail of all the cases in which the exertions of individual States cannot afford the smallest relief. An idea of thirteen neighboring States being able to exist independent of each other, without a general government, to control, connect and unite the whole, is no less absurd than was the conduct of the limbs, in the fable, which refused to contribute to the support of the belly, and by working its downfall, accelerated their own ruin. Of this every State in the Union is fully convinced, by awful experience, unless we except Rhode Island; for the meridian of which "Centinel" has calculated his Antifederal remarks, which he has had the presumption to address to the freemen of Pennsylvania.

Afraid of investigating the constitution itself, he previously attempts to prejudice you against it by charging the patriotic members of the convention with a design "of lording it over their fellow-creatures" and with "long meditated schemes of power and aggrandizement." Is it possible that the freemen of America would appoint such men as these to so important a trust? No. The public characters of the gentlemen who were chosen by my respectable fellow-citizens in the different States are such as at once justify their conduct in the choice, and contradict the unjust and ungenerous assertion. This defamer has even dared to let fly his shafts at a *Washington* and a *Franklin*, who, he tells you, have been so mean, ignorant and base as to be dupes to the designs of the other members. Is not every man among you fired with resentment against the wretch who could undertake a job thus low, infamous and vile, and who was so prone to slander as wantonly to traduce names dear to every American—names, if not respected and esteemed, at least admired even by their enemies?

After having striven to inflame your passions against these worthy men, he then makes a general objection to different branches in government; here again he advances doctrine which has long since been exploded as dangerous and despotic. That a single legislative body is more liable to encroach upon the liberties of the people than two who hold an useful check upon the proceedings of each other he does not attempt to deny, but asserts that one body will be more responsible to the people than two or more can be; therefore, after this body shall have erred, the people can immediately take vengeance of its members, that is, if I may be indulged with a trite saying, after the steed is stolen lock the stable door. Had he proceeded in the same mode of reasoning, he might have proved that an elective monarchy is the best government, for it is certainly the most responsible, since one man is accountable for every grievance. In truth, my friends, you will easily perceive that this responsibility, which he lays so much stress on, is by no means sufficient to secure your liberties. If you enquire into the effects of sanguinary punishments upon criminals, you will find that instead of reforming they have increased the wickedness of the people.

But the convention, not content with providing punishments for the misdemeanors of government, have done wiser, in endeavoring to prevent these misdemeanors, which was evidently their intention in new modeling the federal government.

He next complains of the too extensive powers of Congress. "It will not be controverted," says he, "that the legislative is the highest delegated power in government, and that all others are subordinate to it." In this I perfectly agree with him, and am apt to believe, that had he paused here one moment, he would not have been so ready to fear an aristocracy in any branch of the new federal government; since the most essential parts of legislation are to be vested in the House of Representatives, the immediate servants of the people, with whom all money bills must originate.

He is ready to allow Congress to pay the debts of the Union; but then, they are to have power to lay and collect duties, imposts, &c., which the new constitution declares shall be uniform throughout the United States; here the word *collect* seems to stick in his stomach. What! says he, will they have power to enforce the payment of taxes? Oh! it is dangerous to invest them with such authority; they ought to call upon us as heretofore, and leave it at our option to comply with their requisitions or not. Such is the reasoning of this advocate for delinquency, the absurdity of whose political creed is self-apparent, and needs no comment. Happy would it be for Pennsylvania, if the different States were obliged to pay their proportions of the foreign and domestic debt; she would not then be struggling under an enormous land tax, to pay much more than her just quota of the public burthens. But, says he, there is a possibility of having standing armies too. This is quite wrong; let Congress have power to make war, crush insurrections, &c., but let them have no troops for these purposes, unless each State shall think proper to furnish its quota of men; or if we vest the power of raising armies in Congress, let them be tied down, and not permitted to raise a single regiment, until an invasion shall have actually taken place, and the enemy shall have ravaged and spread desolation over five or six of the States; it will then be time enough. Indeed I think we ought immediately to disband the troops stationed on the Ohio, and not raise a man for that service before the savages shall have laid our country waste, as far as Susquehanna at least. Why need we trouble ourselves about the inhabitants on the frontiers? Such truly is the substance of his arguments.

He has further discovered that the trial by jury in civil cases is abolished—that the liberty of the press is not provided for—and that the judicial and legislative powers of the respective States will be absorbed by those of the general government.

As to the first of these, it is well known that the cases which come before a jury, are not the same in all the States; that therefore the Convention found themselves unequal to the task of forming a general rule, among so many jarring interests, and left it with Congress to regulate the conduct of the judiciary in all civil cases. It may not be improper here to remark, that Congress can at any time propose amendments to this Constitution, which shall become a part of it when ratified by the legislatures or Conventions of three-fourths of the States.

True, no declaration in favor of the liberty of the press is contained in the new Constitution, neither does it declare that children of freemen are also born free. Both are alike the unalienable birthright of freemen, and equally absurd would it have been, in the Convention, to have meddled with either.

The *ne plus ultra* of the powers of Congress, and of the judiciary of the United States, is expressly fixed—therefore, no danger can arise to the legislative or judicial authority of any State in the union. *Centinel,* in discussing this point, has ransacked his brains, tortured, twisted, and perverted the new plan of government, to support his blundering assertions; especially where he has quoted sect. 4 of the 1st Art. "The times, places, and manner, of holding elections, for senators, and representatives, shall be prescribed, in each State, by the legislature thereof; but the Congress may at any time, by law, make or alter such regulations, except as to the place of choosing senators."

"The plain construction of which," says Centinel, "is, that when the State legislatures drop out of sight, from the necessary operation of this government, then Congress are to provide for the election and appointment of representatives, and senators." O amazing result of *a rational investigation!* I confess he understands the meaning of words much better than I do, if his construction of that section be just. What may Congress "make or alter?" The times, places and manner of holding elections, in the different States. But why is the place of choosing senators excepted? Who are to appoint them? Certainly, the legislatures of the respective States, who are to elect the senators in any place they may think proper, which probably will be, where they meet in their legislative capacity. The existence of every branch of the Federal government depends upon the State legislatures, and both must stand or fall together.

He next attacks the construction of the federal government, says the number of representatives is too few. Others have thought it too many. How was it possible that the Convention, in this, or indeed in any other instance, could please everybody? For my part I am of opinion that the number fixed by the Convention (one for every 30,000) is fully adequate to the task of effectually representing the people; and that a greater number would only clog the wheels, and add to the expenses of government, in which the strictest economy is at all times necessary. That two years is too long a time to continue in office is a mistaken notion; much more inconvenience and expense would be attendant on annual elections throughout this extensive continent. The most strenuous advocates for a parliamentary reform, in Great Britain, never stickled for more than triennial elections, which they deemed fully sufficient to secure the liberties of the people. This body may justly be called the guardians of our liberties, since they are not chosen by the State legislatures, as Congress has hitherto been, but by the freemen at large, in every State. No undue influence can be exercised over them, nor the Senate, for no placemen, or officers of government, can have a seat among them.

He says the senate is constituted on the most unequal principles, since the smallest State in the Union sends as many senators as the largest. Here is a small concession to the smaller States, which proclaims the liberality of sentiment that prevailed in the convention. Let us, my friends, in the larger States, be satisfied with our superior influence in the House of Representatives. As to the senate being composed of the *better sort,* the *well-born,* etc., it is a most illiberal reflection thrown out by this anti-federal demagogue against the freemen of America, who, I trust, will always elect to this important trust men of integrity and abilities. But how is there any danger of this body becoming an aristocracy? In their executive capacity they are checked by the President, and in their legislative capacity are checked by the House of Representatives, and of themselves cannot do a single act. He seems apprehensive that the President may form a coalition with the senate, "whose influence might secure his re-election to office." I cannot conceive how they can exercise any influence in his favor, for both senators and representatives are expressly excluded from being electors.

The only objection he makes to the power of the President is that he can grant pardons and reprieves. This prerogative must be and always is vested somewhere in all free governments; to whom then can it be given with more safety than to this officer, who never can have any interest in exercising it to evil purposes? If he should, he will be liable to impeachment, etc.

Previous to his conclusion he attempts to lull us into security; but his sophistry can never operate so far upon our senses as to make us believe that our situation is not "critically dreadful." The most ignorant among us severely feel the miseries which surround us on all sides. That he may be very well pleased with his present situation, I have not the smallest doubt; for it is notorious that the Antifederal junto in Philadelphia is composed of a few self-interested men, who, in the midst of our distresses, are receiving most enormous sums out of the public treasury, and like ravens are preying upon our very vitals.

"A Foreign Spectator"
[Nicholas Collin]

"An Essay on the Means of Promoting Federal Sentiments in the United States": XXIV, XXV, XXVIII

Independent Gazetteer, Philadelphia, 18, 21, and 28 September 1787

———•———

Although these essays began appearing before the Federal Convention concluded, they continued to appear into October 1787. Unlike many of the writings by the Federalists, which tend to focus on particular Anti-Federalist attacks, these essays take up the whole range of human affairs. As the author puts it, since the stability of republics depends upon "fixed principles and settled habits," it was necessary for him to consider "education, morals, religion, manners, laws, and learning." The complete set of essays is on the microfiche supplement to volume 3 of *The Documentary History of the Ratification of the Constitution.*

Nicholas Collin (1746–1831) was the pastor of the Old Swede's Church on the Delaware River in Philadelphia. A native of Sweden, Collin wrote twenty-nine essays under the general heading "An Essay on the Means of Promoting Federal Sentiments in the United States." A selection of the twenty-nine essays is reprinted in this volume.

———•———

XXIV

In this federal composition it is not proper to draw comparisons. It is generally known which of the states have been most deficient. Pennsylvania has paid nearly the whole, and New-York more than her quota.* The former has however taken the resolution to discount by federal contribution to her own citizens who are creditors of the United States; and this would not grant the impost but on condition of reserving to herself the power of collecting it, and the liberty of paying in paper money. Both these states assume thus

---

* Hamilton's speech, &c.

powers very antifederal; yet what else can be expected from the federal states, when others are so neglectful. How alarming are these facts! do they not plainly say—*the ship will be lost, let every one take care of himself.* If a foreign power should by arms demand payment from the United States, it would not inquire how they have paid their respective quotas; if most convenient, it may take New-York or Philadelphia, and let these cities take satisfaction from New-Hampshire or Carolina as they can. Is it not then shocking, that in this federal anarchy *those states that have been the most generous may be ruined by the most selfish!* Would not this alone be an ample cause of civil war? When the peace establishment is calculated, and the proportion of the national debt to be annually paid is determined; the federal revenue may with tolerable precision be fixed for several years. Accounts of the federal expenditure to be laid at regular intervals of time before the several Legislatures, will fully satisfy the states. When the national finances will allow, there should be at all times a saving of ready money in the federal treasury, or some certain fund, that could immediately be commanded, as a resource against a war, or some unexpected exigency. In time of actual war, and especially of an invasion, the federal government should have very ample powers for levying money; it will not be possible to limit them but in very general terms.

I have thus ventured to draw a general sketch of the necessary federal powers. To set this grand affair in one clear point of view, let us consider: *first, the great interest of the United States*—this is nothing less than independency, with external safety, and internal peace; and on this depends the liberty, property, families, lives, and whatever dearest concerns of the people in general, as I have fully proved: *secondly, the extent of the union*—this requires *a center of information and of action,* which may collect a speedy and perfect knowledge of all federal affairs, and by quick effectual operations take care of the whole. Can any thing be so absurd as to make the fate of Georgia depend on the exertions of New-Hampshire, when two or three months may elapse before an authentic information could be obtained; as many more be spent in deliberations; and the same time again taken up in the preparation for executing the resolves: The southern states may be conquered by a powerful enemy; before the northern troops had begun their march. The badness of the public roads, and the broken situation of the country divided by great rivers, bays, and many large creeks, are also great impediments of communication—an enemy may by establishing some posts, and by means of a fleet, extremely distress the country if not defended by a federal force. This very local situation necessarily lessens the reciprocal simpathy of different states. They cannot see those flames, that lay a town in ashes, and ruin in a few hours so many hundred families—they do not behold the fields deluged with blood, strewed with human limbs, with the dead and dying—they cannot hear the frantic shrieks of mothers, wives and daughters. Thus neither humanity nor self-interest are alarmed: the enemies' roaring artillery is heard only as the faint rumbling of a distant thunder storm, though it approaches fast, and will soon pour its deadly fury on the unfeeling and thoughtless. We read perhaps with indifferency, or with a transient emotion the sufferings of the back settlements from Indian barbarity; how different would the effect be, if the scenes were nearer! When there is a fire in the Northern Liberties, the people not only of Southwark, but in the city, are quite easy. *Thirdly,* though these reasons are quite sufficient, the present habits of the people require a strong federal government. Every person knows the exorbitant ideas of liberty so generally entertained, which render great numbers jealous of their rights, and fond of personal independency, to a degree absolutely incompatible with good government, the general welfare, and their own safety. The great attachment to property so common is visible, and in many respects pernicious to individuals and society. Carelessness about public affairs is another material characteristic, and palpable on numberless occasions. To cure a distemper, we must not contest it; every nation has its virtues and vices; a discreet apprehension of what is wrong, so far from affecting virtuous individuals, reflects the greater honor upon them. These three qualities in the present national character have originated from the peculiar circumstances of this country, as I have at large demonstrated and will be amended in the regular course of civilization and of an efficient government—at present this absolutely requires a strong federal power. The indolent and licentious man will say; *I shall pay my federal tax some time or other, when it suits me. The licentious miser says, my property is my right hand, I will not part with it.* The haughty independent spirit says—*I will grant the requisition of Congress; but they must come to me cup in hand, and wait my pleasure, they are but servants of the people.* The moderate and not ungenerous will naturally say—*I will do my part, if others will contribute; but why should the burden fall on a few, property is valuable, liberty is dear.* When marching orders come, one says, let who will be a butt for balls and bayonetts, for my part, I will stay at home, and *mind my business.* Another, I prefer a warm bed and hot supper, to sleeping on the ground with an empty stomach—A third is kept within the arms of a wife, who is more concerned for the safety than the honor of her dear—The generous and brave who cheerfully hazards his own life and property, and though with a tender pang leaves his family, is justly incensed by the selfishness of his fellow citizens; can he be very criminal if he forces the griping hand to contribute for the public safety, and drags the coward into the field, where he may at least do some good with the pickaxe.

Under these circumstances the union cannot possibly be safe without a strong federal government—*It must so far as the grand interest of the confederacy requires, have legislative, executive, and judiciary powers.* For the benefit of those readers who are less accustomed to political reasoning, I shall illustrate this matter by a plain simile. Suppose thirteen families are settled upon an island in this river, that is liable to be overflowed by the many accidental freshes dangerous to life and property. They must erect a strong bank, and keep it at all times in good repair. If the muskrats bore it through with many small holes, or if it is sunk in one or two places, a sudden storm may destroy the hay, grain, provisions, household goods; drown the cattle and the people themselves. Will they not then naturally appoint overseers, to inspect this bank, and with the most scrupulous attention keep it in order! They will fix a certain fund, to be collected by these men without any delay and opposition; and moreover impower them in case of any sudden danger to imploy all necessary hands; to press men and horses, take provisions and tools that are next at hand. The accounts may be settled when the danger is over. In proportion as all or some of these families are careless, stubborn, contentious, and selfish, those overseers must have greater powers. Suppose the case so bad, that one family keep loitering in their beds, while the water rises rapidly, another is groggy or foolish, and cannot see the danger; a third says, if I lose, my neighbour the rogue will lose more; a fourth will not expose its sons and fine horses to hardship and danger; a fifth is quarrelling and fighting when the furious waves threaten to swallow them up. But let the thirteen families be ever so good; future events are unknown—the overseers must have power adequate to any eventual situation. When those men are near relations of the families, and have themselves a great interest in the island, they may the more be trusted, and still more, if they are only for a time, and must be under other overseers in their turn. If we enlarge this idea, by supposing the island containing thirteen townships, and situated in the ocean, depending on the bank for its safety; the necessity of giving the overseers adequate powers, appears yet more striking. The inland people who seldom or never saw the sea, make hay and reap without any thought of the bank. While assistance is begged from house to house for twenty or thirty miles; or even while the generous hasten from shore to shore, the whole island may be buried in the briny waves; every wary mariner will shun the fatal strand with the reflexion—this land perished by the folly of its people.

XXV

My general sketch of additional federal powers has come very near to the plan of the Honorable Convention now published, and I am glad to have in one or two particulars rather gone beyond than below the mark. Unasked, unadvised, and unbiassed I have only sought truth on this important subject; and beg leave to observe that she is the same in American and European minds, invariable from the North to the South Pole; that this blessing, like the Great Giver of it, is found by all that earnestly seek it.

It is evident, that all the necessary powers of this federal government are fully consistent with every species of right and liberty of the people. *First,* This constitution has very few alluring objects of avarice and ambition: no standing armies, ecclesiastical establishments, pensions, and titles of nobility; and but a few offices in the revenue, foreign, and civil departments, that will be objects for men of easy fortunes either in profit or dignity. While land is so plenty, and consequently every kind of industry profitable, the lower offices will not be much affected by the middle classes as means of subsistence, nor as distinctions while a republican spirit is kept alive. This influence then is trifling to that in the best limited monarchies, where so great a part of the gentry and nobility depend more or less on the crown for support, honor, power; and the difficulty of subsistence with prejudices of ambition render the petty offices valuable to great numbers. As a further security, the 6th section of the 1st article, enacts, that no senator or representative shall, during the time for which he was elected, be appointed to any civil office under the authority of the United States, which shall have been created, or the emolument whereof shall have been encreased during such time; and no person holding any office under the United States, shall be a member of either house during his continuance in office."

Secondly. The conduct of members in both houses will be publicly known, because by 5th section of 1st article, "each house shall keep a journal of its proceedings, and from time to time publish the same—and the yeas and nays of the members of either house on any question shall, at the desire of one-fifth of those present, be entered on the journal." Any unpatriotic member may therefore be excluded at the new election. The representatives are chosen every second year, and the senators for six years; but with the proviso, that one third of them goes out at the end of two years, and another after four, so that only two thirds of them coexist for four and one third for six years. Art. 1 Sect. 3. This excellent regulation sufficiently prevents all combination; men that come together with different habits, principles and interests, could not in a short time form a dangerous collusion. What scheme of iniquity could ripen in two years? or by what supernatural means could the whole body of representatives, and the new third part of the senate, be corrupted? A quicker rotation would be prejudicial, because men of the best theoretic knowledge want practice; and among the great numbers who in their turn become members of Congress, many, however sensible in the common affairs of life, must be indifferent politicians, even when the public education is brought to great perfection. No solid system can be concerted in a continual change of legislators; neither plans or modes of execution can be fixed. Besides a member who but comes and goes, is less responsible for bad public measures, and consequently less animated by a sense of duty and honor. It is therefore necessary, that no part of the legislature should be changed too often, and that one part should remain for a longer time, in order to form and preserve the stamina of administration. A person who wants only a common dwelling house, does not change the master workmen every week. The high office of president is held only during the term of four years. His electors must not be representatives, senators, or persons holding an office of trust or profit under the United States. The person having the greatest number of votes, becomes president, if such number is a majority of the whole number of electors; if more than one have such majority, and an equal number of votes; the house of representatives immediately chooses by ballot one of them; if no person has a majority, then from the five highest on the list, the said house chooses in like manner the president. Art. 2. Sect. 1. This prudently guards against any aristocratic collusion between the executive power and the senate, as some members of this body may otherways take an undue advantage from their superiority of talents and fortunes, and from a longer continuance in power. *Thirdly*, though it is nearly impossible, that under these circumstances a majority of the congress with the president should conspire to subvert the constitution; yet supposing the worst—their design must be watched and opposed by the minority, who would give the nation an early alarm—they have not money to carry it on, because by the 9th sect. 1st art. "no money shall be drawn from the treasury, but in consequence of appropriations made by law; and a regular statement and account of the receipts and expenditures of all public money shall be published from time to time." They could not raise an army without a pretence of war, nor impose on the nation by a false alarm; and though they have a right "to call forth the militia to execute the laws of the union, and to suppress insurrections, sect. 8. art. 1; it is evident, that a people of tolerable virtue would never become tools for enslaving themselves: would any man be ordered to kill himself by his own sword? who but an idiot or a most dastardly wretch would not plunge it in the heart of the tyrant. For the raising and supporting armies no appropriation of money is allowed for more than two years by the 8th sect. 1st art. This term must be prolonged when necessary; but while an enemy is in the country, the army cannot be employed against its liberties; and after the war it is disbanded, or must be for the want of pay. The happy situation of America will generally guard her against long and severe wars—but should any such happen; even the power of a veteran army could not subdue a patriotic militia ten times its number, and rendered perfectly military in the course of such war. Besides, regular troops, who are natives of a country, allied by friendship and blood to the other citizens, bred in the principles of republican liberty, and who have for years defended this country with their blood against a powerful invader, cannot be so generally corrupted, as to turn their arms against those with whom they have so long shared danger and glory; to enslave and murder their friends, and relations, brothers, sons and fathers—in all probability a great part of this army would take part with the nation.

The constitution incorporates all the states as members of one body with a federal and generous spirit. Representatives and direct taxes are apportioned among them, according to their respective numbers, with proper allowance for the inferior value of *persons not free.* Art. 1. sect. 2. By this the people are wisely regarded more than property; because a multitude of virtuous, brave, industrious people is the real strength, glory, wealth, and prosperity of a country; especially in America, where no necessity renders great numbers indigent, consequently dependent, poor in spirit, and in many respects less valuable as men and citizens. By the 3d sect. 1st art. a generous indulgence is shown to the smaller states, who delegate two senators equally with the greater. In cases when the house of representatives chooses the president, the votes are also taken by states. Art. 2. sect. 1. All duties, imposts, and excises are uniform through the United States; likewise the rule of naturalization, and the laws on bankruptcies. No preference is given by any regulation of commerce or revenue to the ports of one state over those of another. Art. 1. sect. 9. The citizens of each state shall be entitled to all privileges and immunities of citizens in the several states. Art. 4. sect. 2. &c. It would be very unjust and impolitic to grant all the states an equal right in the house of representatives. Voting by states, though according to the established proportion, would only keep up a local antifederal spirit; it is therefore laid aside, even in the senate, notwithstanding the indulgence mentioned—The

United States in Congress assembled, should consider themselves as provinces of one empire: every member of either house is a federal citizen, sent there to think and act for the prosperity and glory of the UNION, and should never desire any thing for his own state, but an equitable share in the general happiness, which must be the result of *united wisdom and federal virtue.*

XXVIII

It is the singular happiness of America, to establish her federal empire at this enlightened era, when the principles of political union are in general pretty well understood; and when superstition, a passion for war, or other dangerous prejudices have no baneful influence. A sad experience of the evils that arise from an immoderate pursuit of wealth, and an overdriven love of liberty, is also very beneficial to a young nation, as it will impress the great maxims of moderation and integrity, without which neither individuals or civil societies can be happy. By the grace of Providence peace and tranquility favors a mature deliberation on the grand affairs of a national system. A solid confederation will secure the states against any external force, and prevent any dangerous internal tumults; but they may fear every calamity from the *evil genius of party,* that is the peculiar fiend of republics, and has ruined so many flourishing states—Let us then see, through what avenues this daemon may approach, and may they be shut up forever. No great or permanent national object can so differently affect individuals, as to create a general party through the states; but men may differ in sentiment on some capital matters to such a degree as to form opposite parties, which will afterwards, as usual, be variously blended with personal interest, pride, influence of leaders, mutual sympathy, antipathies, religious prejudices, &c. Extensive foreign connexions would among other great evils occasion this; because such complex systems are beyond the comprehension of great numbers, and cannot be regulated by fixed rules, but often require that reasoning of probability, in which men seldom agree. When foreign powers meddle in national affairs, foment animosities, and introduce a fatal corruption, great disasters are certain consequences—some of the greatest citizens will be their avowed partizans; and foreign gold will purchase yeas and nays in the most important debates. America, if wise, will enjoy her happy situation, and neither covet a greater share of the western continent, was it ten times more fertile, nor cast a wishful eye on the mines of Mexico; nor force over the friendly barrier of the Atlantic into the political labyrinths of Europe, in which she would lose her money, and many of her best sons. As to commerce, she will form a proper estimate of its advantages; not seek with danger and toil in remote climes what can be had at home; and value human blood more than liquors and toys.

The constitution itself often becomes an object of contention, even when it has no material faults, merely from a too refined political taste, irritated by pride, personal pique, and the other usual sauce of party. No human production was ever perfect; individuals should not presume to pick out little blemishes in systems composed by some of the best and wisest citizens. In a grand building a small omission in minute parts, is nothing—yet little minds can often espy this, but are not capable of admiring the great design, the beauty and strength of proportion, the skill in attaining advantages almost incompatible. The memorable expression of Solon, that his laws were the best his country would admit, should be well considered by all political critics. It is better to put up with some real imperfections, than to be always reforming—Hudibras justly ridicules those who seemed to think, that religion was only made to be mended—A political satirist relates how a nurse, in order to reduce the overgrown foot of a child, first squeezed, and then trimmed it, till it became necessary to cut it off. It is wisdom to be satisfied with that degree of perfection allotted our present state. The 5th article reserves a very proper mode for amending the federal constitution; it is certainly reasonable to give it a fair tryal by some years experience; and it must be madness *to pull down a house at the approach of winter because there may hereafter be a leak in the roof.*

It would be presumption not only in me, but I scruple not to say, in most native Americans, to define how far the federal union may in all cases be agreeable to the interest of the respective states; because they have as a nation just entered into the political world; and the very circumstance of being a young country not half improved is a source of many unknown complicated events. Should upon a fair trial any permanent inequality appear in favor of some states, it will no doubt be remedied—In the mean time all well-disposed Americans will pay a grateful regard to the faithful endeavors of the honorable Convention; the modesty and sensibility expressed in their address to Congress—"In all our deliberations on this subject we kept steadily in our view, &c. the greatest interest of every true American, the consolidation of our union, in which is involved our prosperity, &c. perhaps our national existence. This important consideration, seriously and deeply impressed on our minds, led each state in the convention to be less rigid on points of inferior magnitude—And thus the constitution which we now present, is the result of a spirit of amity, and of that mutual deference and concession, which the peculiarity of our situation then rendered indispensable." In a discussion of respective rights, the main question is, *to what states is the union most necessary?* Local situation, natural strength, and the temptation of advantage to foreign or internal enemies, must determine this. The small states want protection, those on the frontiers especially. The most powerful could not resist a formidable power. The southern states are more wealthy than strong; their situation and wealth would naturally invite a foreign attack. The union of Great-Britain was much opposed by those who extolled the superior wealth of England; but men of sense set a proper value on the military spirit of Scotland, and observed that *gold must be defended by steel.* If some states derive any superior advantage from the Inland carrying trade, it is a mark of their inferiority in a landed interest, and should not be a cause of envy; besides their maritime strength would upon occasion defend the other parts of the union. Thus the interest of property, which is a secondary object, may on the whole be not very unequally shared among the states.

Though the many small causes of parties cannot endanger the union, they will no doubt disturb its happiness, and should be carefully suppressed. It is an absurd maxim with some, that parties are happy symptoms of a public spirit, and support the balance of power. These men think that a person *must be mortally sick, or have a slight disorder.* A lethargy is indeed worse than a fever; but many constitutions are free from both. As to the balance, sober men will hold it better than those who are drunk. It is very pernicious merely for a temporary advantage to sour the public mind, and weaken all the social virtues, which are the bonds of civil union. I know, that furious flames are stopped by kindling a fire in a contrary direction; but I would not except in case of necessity, throw out a single spark. It is even dangerous to foment antipathy against foreign nations, because it contracts the heart, and raises an evil spirit, that often recoil upon those ungenerous silly politicians. How common is it to hear a rude person first vent his spleen in the most absurd and mean expressions against some European nation, and then with the same virulence curse his own government. Unhappily too many Americans know but little of Europe, and look upon it as a land of slaves—whereas though some parts of it are oppressed, others have as much liberty as they can bear, and much more real freedom, than America in her present anarchy. The many needy adventurers, bad characters, and low bred wretches, that flock hither from European countries, cannot but give unfavorable ideas; but it is wrong to judge from these; and happier would America be without this scum of the earth.

The United States are as yet not the most homogenial body politic—the federal union will gradually incorporate and animate it with one spirit; at the same time any ill humors and heterogeneous particles must be corrected. A diversity of manners and customs is found in all countries, and causes an agreeable variety; but any peculiarities that are objects of contempt, and aversion, should be prevented. An equal improvement of human nature through all the states is an important object; a superiority in virtue, learning, and manners would not only give some political ascendency, but inspire an antifederal disregard of their inferiors.

The rational opinion, that sincere worshippers in whatever religion are pleasing to Almighty God, is now pretty generally established in all civilized nations. It is of the highest consequence, because the belief that eternal happiness depends on a particular creed or mode of worship, will prompt even good men to establish such at all adventures. We must not however imagine that this species of bigotry has alone produced the many religious wars and tumults; for there are antipathies arising merely from the peculiar genius of a religion, capable of doing much hurt. Any thing that appears to another sect very absurd, mean, unsocial, &c. has an ill effect. A bad influence on manners and government is a serious affair. If it cannot be helped, *divide et impera* is a good maxim with religious as other parties—where any sect has a decided superiority, or a rapid increase, others may be encouraged. Indifferency is not the proper remedy against superstition; for a very defective religion is better than none. Let then the several professions respect the advantages of each other, and with candid benevolence criticise mutual infirmities—Let the bright luminary of reason gradually rise, and shed its majestic radiance over this western world; it will manifest to all the same great God, and the same road to happiness here and hereafter.

"Fabius"
[John Dickinson]

The Letters: I–III

John Dickinson was a delegate from Delaware to the Federal Convention. The "Penman of the Revolution," Dickinson had written the important *Letters from a Farmer in Pennsylvania to the Inhabitants of the British Colonies* (1768) and a good portion of the "Declaration of the Causes of Taking up Arms" (1775); yet, believing the document premature, he refused to sign the Declaration of Independence. Nevertheless he served loyally in the American Revolution. These Letters of Fabius originally appeared separately in newspapers in Delaware in 1788; they were collected and published in pamphlet form in 1797.

I

The Constitution proposed by the Federal Convention now engages the fixed attention of America.

Every person appears to be affected. Those who wish the adoption of the plan, consider its rejection as the source of endless contests, confusions, and misfortunes; and they also consider a resolution to alter, without previously adopting it, as a rejection.

Those who oppose the plan, are influenced by different views. Some of them are friends, others of them are enemies, to The United States. The latter are of two classes; either men without principles or fortunes, who think they may have a chance to mend their circumstances, with impunity, under a weak government, or in public convulsions, but cannot make them worse even by the last—or men who have been always averse to the revolution; and though at first confounded by that event, yet, their hopes reviving with the declension of our affairs, have since persuaded themselves, that at length the people, tired out with their continued distresses, will return to their former connection with Great Britain. To argue with these opposers, would be vain—The other opposers of the plan deserve the highest respect.

What concerns all, should be considered by all; and individuals may injure a whole society, by not declaring their sentiments. It is therefore not only their right, but their duty, to declare them. Weak advocates of a good cause or artful advocates of a bad one, may endeavour to stop such communications, or to discredit them by clamour and calumny. This, however, is not the age for such tricks of controversy. Men have suffered so severely by being deceived upon subjects of the highest import, those of religion and freedom, that *truth* becomes infinitely valuable to them, not as a matter of curious speculation, but of beneficial practice—A spirit of inquiry is excited, information diffused, judgment strengthened.

Before this tribunal of *the people,* let every one freely speak, what he really thinks, but with so sincere a reverence for the cause he ventures to discuss, as to use the utmost caution, lest he should lead any into errors, upon a point of such sacred concern as the public happiness.

It is not the design of this address, to describe the present derangement of our affairs, the mischiefs that must ensue from its continuance, the horrors, of a total dissolution of the union, or of the division of it into partial confederacies. Nor is it intended to describe the evils that will result from pursuing the plan of another Federal Convention; as if a better temper of conciliation, or a more satisfactory harmony of decisions, could be expected from men, after their minds are agitated with disgusts and disappointments, than before they were thus disturbed; though from an uncontradicted assertion it appears, that without such provocations, the difficulty of reconciling the interests of the several states was so near to *insuperable,* in the late convention, that after many weeks spent in the most faithful labours to promote concord, the members were upon the very point of dispersing in the utmost disorder, jealousy and resentment, and leaving the states exposed to all the tempests of passions, that have been so fatal to confederacies of republics.

All these things, with observations on particular articles of the constitution, have been laid before the public, and the writer of this address means not to repeat what has been already said. What he wishes, is to simplify the subject, so as to facilitate the inquiries of his fellow citizens.

Many are the objections made to the system proposed. They should be distinguished. Some may be called local, because they spring from the supposed interests of individual states. Thus, for instance, some inhabitants of large states may desire the system to be so altered, that they may possess more authority in the decisions of the government; or some inhabitants of commercial states may desire it to be so altered, that the advantages of trade may center almost wholly among themselves; and this predilection they may think compatible with the common welfare. Their judgment being thus warp'd, at the beginning of their deliberations, objections are accumulated as very important, that, without this prepossession, would never have obtained their approbation. Certain it is, that strong understandings may be so influenced by this insulated patriotism, as to doubt—whether general benefits can be communicated by a general government.

Probably nothing would operate so much for the correction of these errors, as the perusal of the accounts transmitted to us by the ancients, of the calamities occasioned in Greece by a conduct founded on similar mistakes. They are expressly ascribed to this cause—that each city meditated a part on its own profit and ends—insomuch that those *who seemed to contend for union,* could never relinquish their own interests and advancement, while they deliberated for the public.

Heaven grant! that our countrymen may pause in time—duly estimate the present moment—and solemnly reflect—whether their measures may not tend to draw down the same distractions upon us, that desolated Greece.

They may now tolerably judge from the proceedings of the Federal Convention and of other conventions, what are the sentiments of America upon her present and future prospects. Let the voice of her distress be venerated— and adhering to the generous Virginian declaration, let them resolve to "*cling to Union as the political Rock of our Salvation.*"

II

But besides the objections originating from the before mentioned cause, that have been called local, there are other objections that are supposed to arise from maxims of liberty and policy.—

Hence it is inferred, that the proposed system has such inherent vices, as must necessarily produce a bad administration, and at length the oppression of a monarchy and aristocracy in the federal officers.

The writer of this address being convinced by as exact an investigation as he could make, that such mistakes may lead to the perdition of his country, esteems it his indispensable duty, strenuously to contend, that—*the power of the people* pervading the proposed system, together with the *strong confederation of the states,* forms an adequate security against every danger that has been apprehended.

If this single assertion can be supported by facts and arguments, there will be reason to hope, that anxieties will be removed from the minds of some citizens, who are truly devoted to the interests of America, and who have been thrown into perplexities, by the mazes of multiplied and intricate disquisitions.

The objectors agree, that the confederation of the states will be strong, according to the system proposed, and so strong, that many of them loudly complain of that strength. On this part of the assertion, there is no dispute: But some of the objections that have been published, strike at another part of the principle assumed, and deny, that the system is sufficiently founded on the power of the people.

The course of regular inquiry demands, that these objections should be considered in the first place. If they are removed, then all the rest of the objections, concerning unnecessary taxations, standing armies, the abolishment of trial by jury, the liberty of the press, the freedom of commerce, the judicial, executive, and legislative authorities of the several states, and the rights of citizens, and the other abuses of federal government, must, of consequence, be rejected, if the principle contains the salutary, purifying, and preserving qualities attributed to it. The question then will be—not what may be done, when the government shall be turned into a tyranny; but how the government can be so turned?

Thus unembarrassed by subordinate discussions, we may come fairly to the contemplation of that superior point, and be better enabled to discover, whether our attention to it will afford any lights, whereby we may be conducted to peace, liberty, and safety.

The objections, denying that the system proposed is sufficiently founded on the power of the people, state, that the number of the federal trustees or officers, is too small, and that they are to hold their offices too long.

One would really have supposed, that smallness of number could not be termed a cause of danger, as influence must increase with enlargement. If this is a fault, it will soon be corrected, as an addition will be often made to the number of the senators, and a much greater and more frequently, to that of the representatives; and in all probability much sooner, than we shall be able and willing to bear the expence of the addition.

As to the senate, it never can be, and it never ought to be large, if it is to possess the powers which almost all the objectors seem inclined to allot to it, as will be evident to every intelligent person, who considers those powers.

Though small, let it be remembered, that it is to be created by the sovereignties of the several states; that is, by the persons, whom the people of each state shall judge to be most worthy, and who, surely, will be religiously attentive to making a selection, in which the interest and honour of their state will be so deeply concerned. It should be remembered too, that this is the same manner, in which the members of Congress are now appointed; and that herein, the sovereignties of the states are so intimately involved, that however a renunciation of part of these powers may be desired by some of the states, it *never* will be obtained from the rest of them. Peaceable, fraternal, and benevolent as these are, they think, the concessions they have made, ought to satisfy all.

That the senate may always be kept full, without the interference of Congress, it is provided in the system, that if vacancies happen by resignation or otherwise, during the recess of the legislature of the state, the executive thereof may make temporary appointments, until the next meeting of the legislature, which shall then fill up such vacancies.

As to the house of representatives, it is to consist of a number of persons, not exceeding one for every thirty thousand: But each state shall have at least one representative. The electors will reside, widely dispersed, over an extensive country. Cabal and corruption will be as impracticable, as, on such occasions, human institutions, can render them. The will of freemen, thus circumstanced, will give the fiat. The purity of election thus obtained, will amply compensate for the supposed defect of representation; and the members, thus chosen, will be most apt to harmonize in their proceedings, with the general interests, feelings, and sentiments of the people.

Allowing such an increase of population as, from experience and a variety of causes, may be expected, the representatives, in a short period, will amount to several hundreds, and most probably long before any change of manners for the worse, that might tempt or encourage our ruler to maladministration, will take place on this continent.

That this house may always be kept full, without the interference of Congress, it is provided in the system, that when vacancies happen in any state, the executive authority thereof shall issue writs of election to fill such vacancies.

But, it seems, the number of the federal officers is not only too small: They are to hold their offices too long.

This objection surely applies not to the house of representatives, who are to be chosen every two years, especially if the extent of empire, and the vast variety and importance of their deliberations, be considered. In that view, they and the senate will actually be not only legislative but also diplomatic bodies, perpetually engaged in the arduous talk of reconciling, in their determinations, the interests of several sovereign states, not to insist on the necessity of a competent knowledge of foreign affairs, relative to the states.

They who desire the representatives to be chosen every year, should exceed Newton in calculations, if they attempt to evince, that the public business would, in that case, be better transacted, than when they are chosen every two years. The idea, however, should be excused for the zeal that prompted it.

Is monarchy or aristocracy to be produced, without the consent of the people, by a house of representatives, thus constituted?

It has been unanimously agreed by the friends of liberty, that *frequent elections of the representatives of the people, are the sovereign remedy of all grievances in a free government.*—Let us pass on to the senate.

At the end of two years after the first election, one third is to be elected for six years; and at the end of four years, another third. Thus one third will constantly have but four years, and another but two years to continue in office. The whole number at first will amount to twenty-six, will be regularly renovated by the biennial election of one third, and will be overlooked, and overawed by the house of representatives, nearly three times more numerous at the beginning, rapidly and vastly augmenting, and more enabled to overlook and overawe them, by holding their offices for two years, as thereby they will acquire better information, respecting national affairs. These representatives will also command the public purse, as all bills for raising revenue, must originate in their house.

As in the Roman armies, when the Principes and Hastati had failed, there were still the Triarii, who generally put things to rights, so we shall be supplied with another resource.

We are to have a president, to superintend, and if he thinks the public weal requires it, to controul any act of the representatives and senate.

This president is to be chosen, not by the people at large, because it may not be possible, that all the freemen of the empire should always have the necessary information, for directing their choice of such an officer; nor by Congress, lest it should disturb the national councils; nor *by any one standing body whatever,* for fear of undue influence.

He is to be chosen in the following manner. Each state shall appoint, as the legislature thereof may direct, a number of electors, equal to the whole number of senators and representatives, to which the state shall be entitled in Congress: but no senator or representative, or person holding an office of trust or profit under the United States, shall be appointed an elector. As these electors are to be appointed, as the legislature of each state may direct, the fairest, freest opening is given, for each state to chuse such electors for this purpose, as shall be most signally qualified to fulfil the trust.

To guard against undue influence these electors, thus chosen, are to meet in their respective states, and vote by ballot; and still further to guard against it, Congress may determine the time of chusing the electors, and the days on which they shall give their votes—*which day shall be the same throughout the United States.* All the votes from the several states are to be transmitted to Congress, and therein counted. The president is to hold his office for four years.

When these electors meet in their respective states, utterly vain will be the unreasonable suggestions derived for partiality. The electors may throw away their votes, mark, with public disappointment, some person improperly favored by them, or justly revering the duties of their office, dedicate their votes to the best interests of their country.

This president will be no dictator. Two thirds of the representatives and the senate may pass any law, notwithstanding his dissent; and he is removable and punishable for misbehaviour.

Can this limited, fluctuating senate, placed amidst such powers, if it should become willing, ever become able, to make America pass under its yoke? The senators will generally be inhabitants of places very distant one from another. They can scarcely be acquainted till they meet. Few of them can ever act together for any length of time, unless their good conduct recommends them to a re-election; and then there will be frequent changes in a body dependant upon the acts of other bodies, the legislatures of the several states, that are altering every year. Machiavel and Cæsar Borgia together could not form a conspiracy in such a senate, destructive to any but themselves and their accomplices.

It is essential to every good government, that there should be some council, permanent enough to get a due knowledge of affairs internal and external; so constituted, that by some deaths or removals, the current of information should not be impeded or disturbed; and so regulated, as to be responsible to, and controulable by the people. Where can the authority for combining these advantages, be more safely, beneficially, or satisfactorily lodged, than in the senate, to be formed according to the plan proposed? Shall parts of the trust be committed to the president, with counsellors who shall subscribe their advices? If assaults upon liberty are to be guarded against, and surely they ought to be with sleepless vigilance, why should we depend more on the commander in chief of the army and navy of The United States, and of the militia of the several states, and on his counsellors, whom he may secretly influence, than of the senate to be appointed by the persons exercising the sovereign authority of the several states? In truth, the objections against the powers of the senate originated from a desire to have them, or at least some of them, vested in a body, in which the several states should be represented, in proportion to the number of inhabitants, as in the house of representatives. This method is *unattainable,* and the wish for it should be dismissed from every mind, that desires the existence of a confederation.

What assurance can be given, or what probability be assigned, that a board of counsellors would continue honest, longer than the senate? Or, that they would possess more useful information, respecting all the states, than the senators of all the states? It appears needless to pursue this argument any further.

How varied, balanced, concordant, and benign, is the system proposed to us? To secure the freedom, and promote the happiness of these and future states, by giving *the will of the people* a decisive influence over the whole, and over all the parts, with what a comprehensive arrangement does it embrace different modes of representation, from an election by a county to an election by an empire? What are the complicated ballot, and all the refined devices of Venice for maintaining her aristocracy, when compared with this plain-dealing work for diffusing the blessings of equal liberty and common prosperity over myriads of the human race?

All the foundations before mentioned, of the federal government, are by the proposed system to be established, in the most clear, strong, positive, unequivocal expressions, of which our language is capable. Magna charta, or any other law, never contained clauses more decisive and emphatic. While the people of these states have sense, they will understand them; and while they have spirit, they will make them to be observed.

III

The writer of this address hopes, that he will now be thought so disengaged from the objections against the principle assumed, that he may be excused for recurring to his assertion, that—the power of the people pervading the proposed system, together with the strong confederation of the states, will form an adequate security against every danger that has been apprehended.

It is a mournful, but may be a useful truth, that the liberty of single republics has generally been destroyed by some of the citizens, and of confederated republics, by some of the associated states.

It is more pleasing, and may be more profitable to reflect, that, their tranquility and prosperity have commonly been promoted, in proportion to the strength of their government for protecting the worthy against the licentious.[1]

As in forming a political society, each individual contributes some of his rights, in order that he may, from *a common stock* of rights, derive greater benefits, than he could from merely *his own;* so, in forming a confederation, each political society should contribute such a share of their rights, as will, from *a common stock* of these rights, produce the largest quantity of benefits for them.

But, what is that share? and, how to be managed? Momentous questions! Here, flattery is treason; and error, destruction.

Are they unanswerable? No. Our most gracious *Creator* does not condemn us to sigh for unattainable blessedness: But one thing he demands— that we should seek for happiness in his way, and not in our own.

Humility and benevolence must take place of pride and overweening selfishness. Reason, rising above these mists, will then discover to us, that we cannot be true to ourselves, without being true to others—that to love our neighbours as ourselves, is to love ourselves in the best manner—that to give, is to gain—and, that we never consult our own happiness more effectually, than when we most endeavour to correspond with *the divine designs,* by communicating happiness, as much as we can, to our fellow-creatures. *Inestimable truth!* sufficient, if they do not barely ask what it is, to melt tyrants into men, and to soothe the inflamed minds of a multitude into mildness—*Inestimable truth!* which our Maker in his providence, enables us, not only to talk and write about, but to adopt in practice of vast extent, and of instructive example.

1. For a discussion of this common theme of the American Founding period, see Gordon S. Wood, *Creation of the American Republic: 1776–1787* (Chapel Hill: University of North Carolina Press, 1969), 471–518.

Let us now enquire, if there be not some *principle,* simple as the laws of nature in other instances, from which, as from a *source,* the many benefits of society are deduced.

We may with reverence say, that our *Creator* designed men for society, because otherwise they cannot be happy. They cannot be happy without freedom; nor free without security; that is, without the absence of fear; nor thus secure, without society. The conclusion is strictly syllogistic—that men cannot be free without society. Of course, they cannot be equally free without society, *which freedom produces the greatest happiness.*

As these premises are invincible, we have advanced a considerable way in our enquiry upon *this deeply interesting subject.* If we can determine, what share of his rights, every individual must contribute to *the common stock* of rights in forming a society, for obtaining equal freedom, we determine at the same time, what share of their rights each political society must contribute to *the common stock* or rights in forming a confederation, which is only a larger society, for obtaining equal freedom: For, if the deposite be not proportioned to the magnitude of the association in the latter case, it will generate the same mischief among the component parts of it, from their inequality, that would result from a defective contribution to association in the former case, among the component parts of it, from their inequality.

Each individual then must contribute such a share of his rights, as is necessary for attaining that *security* that is essential to freedom; and he is bound to make this contribution by the law of his nature, which prompts him to a participated happiness; that is, by the command of his creator; therefore, he must submit his will, *in what concerns all,* to the will of all, that is of the whole society. What does he lose by this submission; The power of doing injuries to others—and the dread of suffering injuries from them. What does he gain by it? The aid of those associated with him, for his relief from the incommodities of mental or bodily weakness—the pleasure for which his heart is formed—of doing good—*protection* against injuries—a capacity of enjoying his undelegated rights to the best advantage—a repeal of his fears—and tranquility of mind—or, in other words, that perfect liberty better described in the Holy Scriptures, than any where else, in these expressions—"When every man shall sit under his vine, and under his fig-tree, and *none shall make him afraid.*"

The like submission, with a correspondent expansion and accommodation, must be made between states, for obtaining the like benefits in a confederation. *Men* are the materials of both. As the largest number is but a junction of *units*—a confederation is but an assemblage of individuals. The auspicious influence of the law of his nature, upon which the happiness of *man* depends in society, must attend him in confederation, or he becomes unhappy; for confederation should promote the happiness of individuals, or it does not *answer the intended purpose.* Herein there is a progression, not a contradiction. As *man,* he becomes a citizen; as a citizen, he becomes a federalist. The generation of one, is not the destruction of the other. He carries into society his naked rights: These thereby improved, he carries still forward into confederation. If that sacred law before mentioned, is not here observed, the confederation would not be real, but pretended. He would confide, and be deceived.

The dilemma is inevitable. There must either be one will, or several wills. If but one will, all the people are concerned: if several wills, few comparatively are concerned. Surprizing! that this doctrine should be contended for by those, who declare, that the constitution is not founded on a bottom broad enough; and, though *the whole people* of the United States are to be *trebly* represented in it in *three different modes* of representation, and their servants will have the most advantageous situations and opportunities of acquiring all requisite information for the welfare of the whole union, yet insist for a privilege of opposing, obstructing, and confounding all their measures taken with common consent for the general weal, by the delays, negligences, rivalries, or other selfish views of parts of the union.

Thus, while one state should be relied upon by the union for giving aid, upon a recommendation of Congress, to another in distress, the latter might be ruined; and the state relied upon, might suppose, it would gain by such an event.

When any persons speak of a consideration, do they, or do they not acknowledge, that the whole is interested in the safety of every part—in the agreement of parts—in the relation of parts to one another—to the whole—or, to other societies? If they do—then, the authority of the whole, must be co-extensive with its interests—and if it is, the will of the whole must and ought in such cases to govern; or else the whole would have interests without an authority to manage them—a position which prejudice itself cannot digest.

If they do not acknowledge, that the whole is thus interested, the conversation should cease. Such persons mean not a confederation, but something else.

As to the idea, that this superintending sovereign will must of consequence destroy the subordinate sovereignties of the several states, it is begging a concession of the question, by inferring, that a manifest and great usefulness must necessarily end in abuse; and not only so, but it requires an extinction of the principle of all society: for the subordinate sovereignties, or, in other words, the undelegated rights of the several states, in a confederation, stand upon the very same foundation with the undelegated rights of individuals in a society, the federal sovereign will being composed of the subordinate sovereign wills of the several confederated states. As some persons seem to think, a bill of rights is the best security of rights, the sovereignties of the several states have this best security by the proposed constitution, and more than this best security, for they are not barely declared to be rights, but are taken into it as component parts for their perpetual preservation—by themselves. In short, the government of each state is, and is to be, sovereign and supreme in all matters that relate to each state only. It is to be subordinate barely in those matters that relate to the whole; and it will be their *own faults* if the several states suffer the federal sovereignty to interfere in things of their respective jurisdictions. An instance of such interference with regard to any single state, will be a dangerous precedent as to all, and therefore will be guarded against by all, as the trustees or servants of the several states will not dare, if they retain their senses, so to violate the independent sovereignty of their respective states, *that justly darling object* of American affections, to which they are responsible, besides being endeared by all the charities of life.

The common sense of mankind agrees to the devolutions of individual wills in society; and if it has not been as universally assented to in confederation, the reasons are evident, and worthy of being retained in remembrance by Americans. They were want of opportunities, or the loss of them, through defects of knowledge and virtue. The principle, however, has been sufficiently vindicated in imperfect combinations, as their prosperity has generally been commensurate to its operation.

How beautifully and forcibly does the inspired Apostle Paul, argue upon a sublimer subject, with a train of reasoning strictly applicable to the present? His words are—"If the foot shall say, because I am not the hand, I am not of the body; is it therefore not of the body? and if the ear shall say, because I am not the eye, I am not of the body; is it therefore not of the body?" As plainly inferring, as could be done in that allegorical manner, the strongest censure of such partial discontents and dissentions, especially, as his meaning is enforced by his description of the benefits of union in these expressions—"But, now they are many members, yet but one body: and the eye *cannot* say to the hand, I have no need of thee."

When the commons of Rome upon a rupture with the Senate, seceded in arms at the Mons sacer, Menemius Agrippa used the like allusion to the human body, in his famous apologue of a quarrel among some of the members. The unpolished but honest-hearted Romans of that day, understood him, and were appeased.

Another comparison has been made by the learned, between a natural and a political body; and no wonder indeed, when the title of the latter was borrowed from the resemblance. It has therefore been justly observed, that if a mortification takes place in one or some of the limbs, and the rest of the body is sound, remedies may be applied, and not only the contagion prevented from spreading, but the diseased part or parts saved by the connection with the body, and restored to former usefulness. When general putrefaction prevails, death is to be expected. History sacred and profane tells us, that, *corruption of manners sinks nations into slavery.*

James Wilson

Speech

Pennsylvania Convention, 24 November 1787

James Wilson (1742–98), born in Scotland and an emigre to Pennsylvania in 1766, was one of the great American statesmen. In his lifetime, Wilson was a lawyer, an Associate Justice of the U.S. Supreme Court (appointed by Washington in 1789), a delegate to the Continental Congress, a signer of the Declaration of Independence, and one of the foremost individuals involved in drafting the Constitution. It was his influence and brilliance that would help win the Constitution's ratification in the divisive ratifying convention of Pennsylvania. For an insightful treatment of Wilson's political thought, see Ralph A. Rossum, "James Wilson and the Pyramid of Government," in Ralph A. Rossum and Gary L. McDowell, eds., *The American Founding: Politics, Statesmanship and the Constitution* (Port Washington, N.Y.: Kennikat Press, 1981).

This version of the 24 November speech is that of Thomas Lloyd. The errata by Lloyd have been included here in the text; Lloyd's notes are enclosed in { } throughout the text. Lloyd, secretary of the convention, charged that the original version, published as "The Substance of a Speech Delivered . . . Nov. 24th. [Reported by Alexander James Dallas]," was a misrepresentation of what Wilson had actually said. Nonetheless, the Dallas version was published in pamphlet form (Philadelphia: T. Bradford, 1787).

The system proposed, by the late Convention, for the government of the United States is now before you. Of that Convention I had the honor to be a member. As I am the only member of that body, who have the honor to be also a member of this, it may be expected that I should prepare the way for the deliberations of this assembly by unfolding the difficulties which the late Convention were obliged to encounter, by pointing out the end which they proposed to accomplish, and by tracing the general principles which they have adopted for the accomplishment of that end.

To form a good system of government for a single city or state, however limited as to territory or inconsiderable as to numbers, has been thought to require the strongest efforts of human genius. With what conscious diffidence, then, must the members of the Convention have revolved in their minds the immense undertaking, which was before them. Their views could not be confined to a small or a single community, but were expanded to a great number of states; several of which contain an extent of territory, and resources of population, equal to those of some of the most respectable kingdoms on the other side of the Atlantic. Nor were even these the only objects to be comprehended within their deliberations. Numerous states yet unformed, myriads of the human race, who will inhabit regions hitherto uncultivated, were to be affected by the result of their proceedings. It was necessary, therefore, to form their calculations on a scale commensurate to a large portion of the globe.

For my own part, I have been often lost in astonishment at the vastness of the prospect before us. To open the navigation of a single river was lately thought in Europe, an enterprise adequate to imperial glory. But could the commercial scenes of the Scheldt be compared with those, that, under a good government, will be exhibited on the Hudson, the Delaware, the Potomac, and the numerous other rivers, that water and are intended to enrich the dominions of the United States?

The difficulty of the business was equal to its magnitude. No small share of wisdom and address is requisite to combine and reconcile the jarring interests, that prevail, or seem to prevail, in a single community. The United States contain already thirteen governments mutually independent. Those governments present to the Atlantic a front of fifteen hundred miles in extent. Their soil, their climates, their productions, their dimensions, their numbers are different. In many instances a difference and even an opposition subsists among their interests. And a difference and even an opposition is imagined to subsist in many more. An apparent interest produces the same attachment as a real one; and is often pursued with no less perseverance and vigor. When all these circumstances are seen and attentively considered, will any member of this honorable body be surprised, that such a diversity of things produced a proportioned diversity of sentiment? Will he be surprised that such a diversity of sentiment rendered a spirit of mutual forbearance and conciliation indispensably necessary to the success of the great work, and will he be surprised that mutual concessions and sacrifices were the consequences of mutual forbearance and conciliation? When the springs of opposition were so numerous and strong, and poured forth their waters in courses so varying, need we be surprised that the stream formed by their conjunction was impelled in a direction somewhat different from that, which each of them would have taken separately?

I have reason to think that a difficulty arose in the minds of some members of Convention from another consideration—their ideas of the temper and disposition of the people for whom the Constitution is proposed. The citizens of the United States, however different in some other respects, are well-known to agree in one strongly marked feature of their character—a warm and keen sense of freedom and independence. This sense has been heightened by the glorious result of their late struggle against all the efforts of one of the most powerful nations of Europe. It was apprehended, I believe, by some, that a people so highly spirited, would ill brook the restraints of an efficient government. I confess that this consideration did not influence my conduct. I knew my constituents to be high-spirited, but I knew them also to possess sound sense. I knew that, in the event, they would be best pleased with that system of government, which would best promote their freedom and happiness. I have often revolved this subject in my mind. I have supposed one of my constituents to ask me, why I gave such a vote on a particular question? I have always thought it would be a satisfactory answer to say, "because I judged, upon the best consideration I could give, that such a vote was right." I have thought that it would be but a very poor compliment to my constituents to say—"that, in my opinion, such a vote would have been proper, but that I supposed a contrary one would be more agreeable to those who sent me to the Convention." I could not, even in idea, expose myself to such a retort, as, upon the last answer, might have been justly made to me. "Pray, sir, what reasons have you for supposing that a right vote would displease your constituents? Is this the proper return for the high confidence they have placed in you?" If they have given cause for such a surmise, it was by choosing a representative, who could entertain such an opinion of them. I was under no apprehension that the good people of this state would behold with displeasure the brightness of the rays of delegated power, when it only proved the superior splendor of the luminary, of which those rays were only the reflection.

A very important difficulty arose from comparing the extent of the country to be governed with the kind of government which it would be proper to establish in it. It has been an opinion, countenanced by high authority, "that the natural property of small states is to be governed as a republic; of middling ones, to be subject to a monarch; and of large empires, to be swayed by a despotic prince; and that the consequence is, that, in order to preserve the principles of the established government, the state must be supported in the extent it has acquired; and that the spirit of the state will alter in proportion as it extends or contracts its limits. {Montesquieu, b. 8. c. 20.} This opinion seems to be supported, rather than contradicted, by the history of the governments in the Old World. Here then the difficulty appeared in full view. On one hand, the United States contain an immense extent of territory, and, according to the foregoing opinion, a despotic government is best adapted to that extent. On the other hand, it was well-known, that, however the citizens of the United States might, with pleasure, submit to the legitimate restraints of a republican constitution, they would reject, with indignation, the fetters of despotism. What then was to be done? The idea of a confederate republic presented itself. This kind of constitution has been thought to have "all the internal advantages of a republican, together with the external force of a monarchical government." {Mont, b. 9. c. 1. 2. Paley 199. 202.} Its description is, "a convention, by which several states agree to become members of a larger one, which they intend to establish. It is a kind of assemblage of societies, that constitute a *new one*, capable of increasing by means of further association." {Montesquieu, b. 9. c. 1.} The *expanding* quality of such a government is peculiarly fitted for the United States, the greatest part of whose territory is yet uncultivated.

But while this form of government enabled us to surmount the difficulty last mentioned, it conducted us to another, of which I am now to take notice. It left us almost without precedent or guide; and consequently, without the benefit of that instruction, which, in many cases, may be derived from the

74

constitution, and history and experience of other nations. Several associations have frequently been called by the name of confederate states, which have not, in propriety of language, deserved it. The Swiss cantons are connected only by alliances. The United Netherlands are indeed an assemblage of societies; but this assemblage constitutes *no new one;* and, therefore, it does not correspond with the full definition of a confederate republic. The Germanic body is composed of such disproportioned and discordant materials, and its structure is so intricate and complex, that little useful knowledge can be drawn from it. Ancient history discloses, and barely discloses to our view, some confederate republics—the Achaean League, the Lycian Confederacy, and the Amphyctyonic Council. But the facts recorded concerning their constitutions are so few and general, and their histories are so unmarked and defective, that no satisfactory information can be collected from them concerning many particular circumstances, from an accurate discernment and comparison, of which alone legitimate and practical inferences can be made from one constitution to another. Besides, the situation and dimensions of those confederacies, and the state of society, manners, and habits in them, were so different from those of the United States, that the most correct descriptions could have supplied but a very small fund of applicable remark. Thus, in forming this system, we were deprived of many advantages, which the history and experience of other ages and other countries would, in other cases, have afforded us.

Permit me to add, in this place, that the science even of government itself seems yet to be almost in its state of infancy. Governments, in general, have been the result of force, of fraud, and of accident. After a period of six thousand years has elapsed since the Creation, the United States exhibit to the world, the first instance, as far as we can learn, of a nation, unattacked by external force, unconvulsed by domestic insurrections, assembling voluntarily, deliberating fully, and deciding calmly, concerning that system of government, under which they would wish that they and their posterity should live.[1] The ancients, so enlightened on other subjects, were very uninformed with regard to this. They seem scarcely to have had any idea of any other

---

1. *Cf. The Federalist,* Nos. 1 and 9.

kinds of governments than the three simple forms designed by the epithets, monarchical, aristocratical, and democratical. I know that much and pleasing ingenuity has been exerted, in modern times, in drawing entertaining parallels between some of the ancient constitutions and some of the mixed governments that have since existed in Europe. But I much suspect that, on strict examination, the instances of resemblance will be found to be few and weak; to be suggested by the improvements, which, in subsequent ages, have been made in government, and not to be drawn immediately from the ancient constitutions themselves, as they were intended and understood by those who framed them. To illustrate this, a similar observation may be made on another subject. Admiring critics have fancied that they have discovered in their favorite, Homer, the seeds of all the improvements in philosophy and in the sciences made since his time. What induces me to be of this opinion is that Tacitus—the profound politician Tacitus—who lived towards the latter end of those ages, which are now denominated ancient, who undoubtedly had studied the constitutions of all the states and kingdoms known before and in his time; and who certainly was qualified in an uncommon degree for understanding the full force and operation of each of them, considers, after all he had known and read, a mixed government, composed of the three simple forms, as a thing rather to be wished than expected. And he thinks, that if such a government could even be instituted, its duration could not be long. One thing is very certain, that the doctrine of representation in government was altogether unknown to the ancients. Now the knowledge and practice of this doctrine is, in my opinion, essential to every system that can possess the qualities of freedom, wisdom and energy.

It is worthy of remark, and the remark may, perhaps, excite some surprise, that representation of the people is not, even at this day, the sole principle of any government in Europe. Great Britain boasts, and she may well boast, of the improvement she has made in politics by the admission of representation. For the improvement is important as far as it goes, but it by no means goes far enough. Is the executive power of Great Britain founded on representation? This is not pretended. Before the Revolution [of 1688] many of the kings claimed to reign by divine right, and others by hereditary right; and even at the Revolution nothing further was effected or attempted than the recognition of certain parts of an original contract {Blackstone, 233} supposed, at some former remote period, to have been made between the king and the people. A contract seems to exclude, rather than to imply, delegated power. The judges of Great Britain are appointed by the Crown. The judicial authority, therefore, does not depend upon representation, even in its most remote degree. Does representation prevail in the legislative department of the British government? Even here it does not predominate; though it may serve as a check. The legislature consists of three branches, the King, the Lords, and the Commons. Of these only the latter are supported by the constitution to represent the authority of the people. This short analysis clearly shows to what a narrow corner of the British constitution the principle of representation is confined. I believe it does not extend further, if so far, in any other government in Europe. For the American states were reserved the glory and the happiness of diffusing this vital principle throughout the constituent parts of government. Representation is the chain of communication between the people and those to whom they have committed the exercise of the powers of government. This chain may consist of one or more links; but in all cases it should be sufficiently strong and discernible.[2]

To be left without guide or precedent was not the only difficulty, in which the Convention were involved, by proposing to their constituents a plan of a confederate republic. They found themselves embarrassed with another of peculiar delicacy and importance; I mean that of drawing a proper line between the national government and the government of the several states. It was easy to discover a proper and satisfactory principle on the subject. Whatever object of government is confined in its operation and effects within the bounds of a particular state should be considered as belonging to the government of that state; whatever object of government extends in its operation or effects beyond the bounds of a particular state should be considered as belonging to the government of the United States. But though this principle be sound and satisfactory, its application to particular cases would be accompanied with much difficulty; because in its application, room must be allowed for great discretionary latitude of construction of

2. See Rossum, "James Wilson and the Pyramid of Government."

the principle. In order to lessen or remove the difficulty arising from discretionary construction on this subject, an enumeration of particular instances, in which the application of the principle ought to take place, has been attempted with much industry and care. It is only in mathematical science that a line can be described with mathematical precision. But I flatter myself that upon the strictest investigation, the enumeration will be found to be safe and unexceptionable; and accurate too in as great a degree as accuracy can be expected in a subject of this nature. Particulars under this head will be more properly explained, when we descend to the minute view of the enumeration, which is made in the proposed Constitution.

After all, it will be necessary, that, on a subject so peculiarly delicate as this, much prudence, much candor, much moderation, and much liberality should be exercised and displayed both by the federal government and by the governments of the several states. It is to be hoped, that those virtues in government will be exercised and displayed, when we consider, that the powers of the federal government and those of the state governments are drawn from sources equally pure. If a difference can be discovered between them, it is in favor of the federal government, because that government is founded on a representation of the *whole* Union; whereas the government of any particular state is founded only on the representation of a part, inconsiderable when compared with the whole. Is it not more reasonable to suppose, that the counsels of the whole will embrace the interest of every part, than that the counsels of any part will embrace the interests of the whole?

I intend not, sir, by this description of the difficulties with which the Convention were surrounded to magnify their skill or their merit in surmounting them, or to insinuate that any predicament in which the Convention stood should prevent the closest and most cautious scrutiny into the performance, which they have exhibited to their constituents and to the world. My intention is of far other and higher aim—to evince by the conflicts and difficulties which must arise from the many and powerful causes which I have enumerated, that it is hopeless and impracticable to form a constitution, which, in every part, will be acceptable to every citizen, or even to every government in the United States; and that all which can be expected is to form such a constitution, as upon the whole, is the best that can possibly be obtained. Man and perfection!—a state and perfection!—an assemblage of states and perfection!—can we reasonably expect, however ardently we may wish, to behold the glorious union?

I can well recollect, though I believe I cannot convey to others the impression, which, on many occasions, was made by the difficulties which surrounded and pressed the Convention. The great undertaking, at some times, seemed to be at a stand; at other times, its motion seemed to be retrograde. At the conclusion, however, of our work, many of the members expressed their astonishment at the success with which it terminated.

Having enumerated some of the difficulties, which the Convention were obliged to encounter in the course of their proceedings, I shall next point out the end, which they proposed to accomplish. Our wants, our talents, our affections, our passions, all tell us that we were made for a state of society. But a state of society could not be supported long or happily without some civil restraint. It is true, that in a state of nature, any one individual may act uncontrolled by others; but it is equally true, that in such a state, every other individual may act uncontrolled by him. Amidst this universal independence, the dissensions and animosities between interfering members of the society would be numerous and ungovernable. The consequence would be, that each member, in such a natural state, would enjoy less liberty, and suffer more interruption, than he would in a regulated society. Hence the universal introduction of governments of some kind or other into the social state. The liberty of every member is increased by this introduction; for each gains more by the limitation of the freedom of every other member, than he loses by the limitation of his own. The result is, that civil government is necessary to the perfection and happiness of man. In forming this government, and carrying it into execution, it is *essential* that the *interest* and *authority* of the whole community should be binding in every part of it.

The foregoing principles and conclusions are generally admitted to be just and sound with regard to the nature and formation of single governments, and the duty of submission to them. In some cases they will apply, with much propriety and force, to states already formed. The advantages and necessity of civil government among individuals in society are not greater or stronger than, in some situations and circumstances, are the advantages and necessity of a federal government among states. A natural and a very important question now presents itself—is such the situation—are such the circumstances of the United States? A proper answer to this question will unfold some very interesting truths.

The United States may adopt any one of four different systems. They may become consolidated into one government, in which the separate existence of the states shall be entirely absorbed. They may reject any plan of union or association and act as separate and unconnected states. They may form two or more confederacies. They may unite in one federal republic. Which of these systems ought to have been formed by the Convention? To support, with vigor, a single government over the whole extent of the United States would demand a system of the most unqualified and the most unremitted despotism. Such a number of separate states, contiguous in situation, unconnected and disunited in government, would be, at one time, the prey of foreign force, foreign influence, and foreign intrigue; at another, the victim of mutual rage, rancor, and revenge. Neither of these systems found advocates in the late Convention. I presume they will not find advocates in this. Would it be proper to divide the United States into two or more confederacies? It will not be unadvisable to take a more minute survey of this subject. Some aspects, under which it may be viewed, are far from being, at first sight, uninviting. Two or more confederacies would be each more compact and more manageable than a single one extending over the same territory. By dividing the United States into two or more confederacies, the great collision of interests, apparently or really different and contrary, in the *whole extent* of their dominion, would be broken, and, in a great measure, disappear in the several parts. But these advantages which are discovered from certain points of view, are greatly overbalanced by inconveniences that will appear on a more accurate examination. Animosities, and perhaps wars, would arise from assigning the extent, the limits, and the rights of the different confederacies. The expenses of governing would be multiplied by the number of federal governments. The danger resulting from foreign influence and mutual dissensions would not, perhaps, be less great and alarming in the instance of different confederacies, than in the instance of different though more numerous unassociated states. These observations, and many others that might be made on the subject, will be sufficient to evince, that a division of the United States into a number of separate confederacies would probably be an unsatisfactory and an unsuccessful experiment. The remaining system which the American states may adopt is a union of them under one confederate republic. It will not be necessary to employ much time or many arguments to show, that this is the most eligible system that can be proposed. By adopting this system, the vigor and decision of a wide-spreading monarchy may be joined to the freedom and beneficence of a contracted republic. The extent of territory, the diversity of climate and soil, the number, and greatness, and connection of lakes and rivers, with which the United States are intersected and almost surrounded, all indicate an enlarged government to be fit and advantageous for them. The principles and dispositions of their citizens indicate that in this government, liberty shall reign triumphant. Such indeed have been the general opinions and wishes entertained since the era of independence. If those opinions and wishes are as well-founded as they have been general, the late Convention were justified in proposing to their constituents, *one* confederate republic as the best system of a national government for the United States.

In forming this system, it was proper to give minute attention to the interest of all the parts; but there was a duty of still higher import—to feel and to show a predominating regard to the superior interests of the whole. If this great principle had not prevailed, the plan before us would never have made its appearance. The same principle that was so necessary in forming it is equally necessary in our deliberations, whether we should reject or ratify it.

I make these observations with a design to prove and illustrate this great and important truth—that in our decisions on the work of the late Convention, we should not limit our views and regards to the State of Pennsylvania. The aim of the Convention was to form a system of good and efficient government on the more extensive scale of the United States. In this, and in every other instance, the work should be judged with the same spirit with which it was performed. A principle of duty as well as candor demands this.

We have remarked, that civil government is necessary to the perfection of society. We now remark that civil liberty is necessary to the perfection of civil government. Civil liberty is natural liberty itself, divested only of that part, which, placed in the government, produces more good and happiness to the community than if it had remained in the individual. Hence it follows, that civil liberty, while it resigns a part of natural liberty, retains the free and generous exercise of all the human faculties, so far as it is compatible with the public welfare.

In considering and developing the nature and end of the system before us, it is necessary to mention another kind of liberty, which has not yet, as far as I know, received a name. I shall distinguish it by the appellation of "*federal liberty*." When a single government is instituted, the individuals, of which it is composed, surrender to it a part of their natural independence, which they before enjoyed as men. When a confederate republic is instituted, the communities, of which it is composed, surrender to it a part of their political independence, which they before enjoyed as states. The principles, which directed, in the former case, what part of the natural liberty of the man ought to be given up and what part ought to be retained, will give similar directions in the latter case. The states should resign, to the national government, that part, and that part only, of their political liberty, which placed in that government will produce more good to the whole than if it had remained in the several states. While they resign this part of their political liberty, they retain the free and generous exercise of all their other faculties as states, so far as it is compatible with the welfare of the general and superintending confederacy.

Since *states* as well as *citizens* are represented in the Constitution before us, and form the objects on which that Constitution is proposed to operate, it was necessary to notice and define *federal* as well as *civil* liberty.

These general reflections have been made in order to introduce, with more propriety and advantage, a practical illustration of the end proposed to be accomplished by the late Convention.

It has been too well-known—it has been too severely felt—that the present Confederation is inadequate to the government and to the exigencies of the United States. The great struggle for liberty in this country, should it be unsuccessful, will probably be the last one which she will have for her existence and prosperity, in any part of the globe. And it must be confessed, that this struggle has, in some of the stages of its progress, been attended with symptoms, that foreboded no fortunate issue. To the iron hand of tyranny, which was lifted up against her, she manifested, indeed, an intrepid superiority. She broke in pieces the fetters, which were forged for her, and showed that she was unassailable by force. But she was environed with dangers of another kind, and springing from a very different source. While she kept her eye steadily fixed on the efforts of oppression, licentiousness was secretly undermining the rock on which she stood.

Need I call to your remembrance the *contrasted* scenes of which we have been witnesses? On the glorious conclusion of our conflict with Britain, what high expectations were formed concerning us by others! What high expectations did we form concerning ourselves! Have those expectations been realized? No. What has been the cause? Did our citizens lose their perseverance and magnanimity? Did they become insensible of resentment and indignation at any high-handed attempt that might have been made to injure or enslave them? No. What then has been the cause? The truth is, we dreaded danger only on one side. This we manfully repelled. But on another side, danger not less formidable, but more insidious, stole in upon us; and our unsuspicious tempers were not sufficiently attentive either to its approach or to its operations. Those, whom foreign strength could not overpower, have well-nigh become the victims of internal anarchy.

If we become a little more particular, we shall find that the foregoing representation is by no means exaggerated. When we had baffled all the menaces of foreign power, we neglected to establish among ourselves a government, that would insure domestic vigor and stability. What was the consequence? The commencement of peace was the commencement of every disgrace and distress, that could befall a people in a peaceful state. Devoid of national power, we could not prohibit the extravagance of our importations, nor could we derive a revenue from their excess. Devoid of national importance, we could not procure, for our exports, a tolerable sale at foreign markets. Devoid of national credit, we saw our public securities melt in the hands of the holders, like snow before the sun. Devoid of national dignity, we could not, in some instances, perform our treaties, on our parts; and, in other instances, we could neither obtain nor compel the performance of them on the part of others. Devoid of national energy, we could not carry into execution our own resolutions, decisions, or laws.

Shall I become more particular still? The tedious detail would disgust me. Nor is it now necessary. The years of languor are passed. We have felt the dishonor with which we have been covered. We have seen the destruction with which we have been threatened. We have penetrated to the causes of both, and when we have once discovered them, we have begun to search for the means of removing them. For the confirmation of these remarks, I need not appeal to an enumeration of facts. The proceedings of Congress, and of the several states, are replete with them. They all point out the weakness and insufficiency as the cause, and an *efficient* general government as the only cure of our political distempers.

Under these impressions, and with these views, was the late Convention appointed; and under these impressions, and with these views, the late Convention met.

We now see the great end which they propose to accomplish. It was to frame, for the consideration of their constituents, one federal and national constitution—a constitution, that would produce the advantages of good, and prevent the inconveniences of bad government—a constitution whose beneficence and energy would pervade the whole Union; and bind and embrace the interests of every part—a constitution that would insure peace, freedom, and happiness, to the states and people of America.

We are now naturally led to examine the means by which they proposed to accomplish this end. This opens more particularly to our view the important discussion before us. But previously to our entering upon it, it will not be improper to state some general and leading principles of government, which will receive particular applications in the course of our investigations.

There necessarily exists in every government a power from which there is no appeal; and which, for that reason, may be termed supreme, absolute, and uncontrollable. Where does this power reside? To this question, writers on different governments will give different answers. Sir William Blackstone will tell you, that in Britain the power is lodged in the British Parliament, that the Parliament may alter the form of the government; and that its power is absolute without control. The idea of a constitution, limiting and superintending the operations of legislative authority, seems not to have been accurately understood in Britain. There are, at least, no traces of practice conformable to such a principle. The British constitution is just what the British Parliament pleases. When the Parliament transferred legislative authority to Henry VIII, the act transferring could not in the strict acceptation of the term be called unconstitutional.

To control the power and conduct of the legislature by an overruling constitution was an improvement in the science and practice of government reserved to the American states.

Perhaps some politician, who has not considered, with sufficient accuracy, our political systems, would answer, that in our governments, the supreme power was vested in the constitutions. This opinion approaches a step nearer to the truth; but does not reach it. The truth is, that, in our governments, the supreme, absolute, and uncontrollable power *remains* in the people. As our constitutions are superior to our legislatures; so the people are superior to our constitutions. Indeed the superiority, in this last instance, is much greater; for the people possess, over our constitutions, control in *act,* as well as in right.

The consequence is, that the people may change the constitutions whenever and however they please. This is a right, of which no positive institution can ever deprive them.

These important truths, sir, are far from being merely speculative. We, at this moment, speak and deliberate under their immediate and benign influence. To the operation of these truths, we are to ascribe the scene, hitherto unparalleled, which America now exhibits to the world—a gentle, a peaceful, a voluntary, and a deliberate transition from one constitution of government to another. In other parts of the world, the idea of revolutions in government is, by a mournful and an indissoluble association, connected with the idea of wars and all the calamities attendant on wars. But happy experience teaches us to view such revolutions in a very different light—to consider them only as progressive steps in improving the knowledge of government, and increasing the happiness of society and mankind.

Oft have I viewed, with silent pleasure and admiration, the force and prevalence of this principle through the United States, that the supreme power resides in the people; and that they never part with it. It may be called the *panacea* in politics. There can be no disorder in the community but may here receive a radical cure. If the error be in the legislature, it may be corrected by the constitution. If in the constitution, it may be corrected by the people. There is a remedy, therefore, for every distemper in government; if the people are not wanting to themselves. For a people wanting to themselves, there is no remedy. From their power, as we have seen, there is no appeal. To their error, there is no superior principle of correction.

There are three simple species of government—monarchy, where the supreme power is in a single person; aristocracy, where the supreme power is in a select assembly, the members of which either fill up, by election, the vacancies in their own body, or succeed to their places in it by inheritance, property, or in respect of some *personal* right or qualification; a republic or democracy, where the people at large *retain* the supreme power, and act either collectively or by representation.

Each of these species of government has its advantages and disadvantages.

The advantages of a monarchy are strength, dispatch, secrecy, unity of counsel. Its disadvantages are tyranny, expense, ignorance of the situation and wants of the people, insecurity, unnecessary wars, evils attending elections or successions.

The advantages of aristocracy are wisdom, arising from experience and education. Its disadvantages are dissensions among themselves, oppression to the lower orders.

The advantages of democracy are liberty, equal, cautious, and salutary laws, public spirit, frugality, peace, opportunities of exciting and producing abilities of the best citizens. Its disadvantages are dissensions, the delay and disclosure of public counsels, the imbecility of public measures retarded by the necessity of a numerous consent.

A government may be composed of two or more of the simple forms above mentioned. Such is the British government. It would be an improper government for the United States; because it is inadequate to such an extent of territory; and because it is suited to an establishment of different orders of men. A more minute comparison between some parts of the British constitution and some parts of the plan before us may perhaps find a proper place in a subsequent period of our business.

What is the nature and kind of that government which has been proposed for the United States by the late Convention? In its principle, it is purely democratical. But that principle is applied in different forms, in order to obtain the advantages and exclude the inconveniences of the simple modes of government.

If we take an extended and accurate view of it, we shall find the streams of power running in different directions, in different dimensions, and at different heights watering, adorning, and fertilizing the fields and meadows thro which their courses are led; but if we trace them, we shall discover, that they all originally flow from one abundant fountain.

In THIS CONSTITUTION, *all authority is derived from the* PEOPLE.

Fit occasions will hereafter offer for particular remarks on the different parts of the plan. I have now to ask pardon of the house for detaining them so long.

"A Freeman"
[Tench Coxe]

Essays: I–III

Pennsylvania Gazette, Philadelphia, 23 and 30 January and
6 February 1788

Tench Coxe (1755–1824) was a leading defender of the proposed Constitution and is best remembered for his work in the area of political economy.
After ratification of the Constitution, he served as Assistant Secretary of
the Treasury from 1789 to 1792.

I

To the MINORITY of the CONVENTION of *Pennsylvania.*[1]

Gentlemen, The great question which at this time engages the attention of
the United States calls for the fairest and most dispassionate discussion. Mistakes in taking up the subject must lead to erroneous conclusions, and men
of pure intentions, both among yourselves and the people at large, should
misconceptions have arisen, may continue averse to the system, after it has
received the *fiat* of all the conventions. Well intended attempts to throw
light upon the interesting subject cannot, therefore, be unpleasing to you.
Without further introduction, then, I will proceed to a point of considerable
importance in itself and in its consequences, on which I conceive your opinions have been erroneously formed, and on which I earnestly hope we shall
finally concur.

---

1. The *Address and Reasons of Dissent of the Minority of the Convention of Pennsylvania to
Their Constituents* was published in the *Pennsylvania Packet* and the *Daily Advertiser* on 18
December 1787 because the minority could not use the official journal of the convention for
disseminating its views. According to Storing, Samuel Bryan, identified as Centinel, probably
wrote this. See Storing, 3:11; Allen, 53–70.

The consolidation of the United States into one government by the operation of the proposed constitution (in contradistinction from a confederacy) appears to you to be the consequence of the system, and the intention of its framers.[2] This is the point of difference which I mean to treat of, and for the present I shall confine my observations to it alone.

Were the parts of the fœderal government which you have particularized as much of the nature of consolidation as you seem to suppose, real nature and design, and the state sovereignties, would indeed be finally annihilated. The appearances which have misled you I shall remark on in the course of these papers, and I shall endeavour to exhibit clear and permanent marks and lines of *separate sovereignty*, which must ever distinguish and circumscribe each of the several states, and *prevent their annihilation* by the fœderal government, or any of its operations.

When the people of America dissolved their connexion with the crown of Britain, they found themselves separated from all the world, but a few powerless colonies, the principal of which indeed they expected to induce into their measures. The crown having been merely a centre of *union,* the act of independence dissolved the political ties that had formerly existed among the states, and it was attended with no absolute confederacy; but many circumstances conspired to render some new form of connexion desirable and necessary. We wished not to continue distinct bodies of people, but to form a respectable nation. The remains of our ancient governments kept us in the form of thirteen political bodies, and from a variety of just and prudent considerations, we determined to enter into an indissoluble and perpetual *union.* Though a confederacy of sovereign states was the mode of connexion which was wisely desired and actually adopted, yet in that feeble and inadequate bond of union to which we assented, articles strongly partaking of the nature of consolidation are observable.

2. The fear of consolidation was a major concern of most Anti-Federalists. While Publius in *The Federalist* could argue that the Constitution represented a "judicious modification of the federal principle," to the Anti-Federalists the modification had been anything but judicious. For the differences in the meanings of "federalism" and "confederalism" during the period, see Martin Diamond, "What the Framers Meant by Federalism," in Robert A. Goldwin, ed., *A Nation of States* (2d ed.; Chicago: Rand-McNally, 1974). For the best expression of the Anti-Federalist fears, see the essays of Brutus, Storing, 2:9; Allen, 269–74, 201–23, 102–11. See also the *Letters from the Federal Farmer to the Republican,* Storing, 2:8; Allen, 75–93, 177–201, 261–69.

We see, for example, that the free inhabitants of each state were rendered, to all intents and purposes, *free citizens of all the rest*. Persons fleeing from justice in one state were to be *delivered up* by any other in which they might take *refuge,* contrary to the laws prevailing among *distinct* sovereignties, whereby the jurisdiction of one state pervaded the territories of all the rest, to the effectual length of trial, condemnation and punishment. The right to judge of *the sums that should be expended for the use of the nation* lies, even under the old confederation, *solely* with Congress, and after the demand is fixed by them, and formally made, the states are *bound,* as far as they can be bound by any compact, to pay their respective quotas into the fœderal treasury, by which the power of the purse is fully given to them; nor can the states *constitutionally* refuse to comply. It is very certain that there is not in the present fœderal government vigor enough to carry *this actually delegated* power into execution; yet, if Congress had possessed energy sufficient to have done it, there is no doubt but they would have been justifiable in the measure, though the season of invasion was unfavorable for internal contests.

We shall also find, that *the right to raise armies and build navies* is also vested in Congress by the present confederation, and they are to be the sole judges of the occasion, and the force required. The state, therefore, that refuses to fulfil the requisitions of Congress on either of these articles, acts *unconstitutionally.* It appears, then, that it was thought necessary at the time of forming the old fœderal constitution, that Congress should have what is termed "*the powers of the purse and the sword.*" That constitution contained a delegation of them, because the framers of it saw that those powers were necessary to *the perpetuity and efficiency* of the union, and to obtain the desirable ends of it. It is certainly very true, that the means provided to enable Congress to apply those powers, which the constitution vested in them, were so liable to opposition, interruption and delay, that the clauses containing them became a mere dead letter. This however was not expected or desired by any of the states at the time, and their subsequent defaults are *infringements* of the letter and spirit of the confederation. On these circumstances I entreat your most dispassionate and candid consideration. I beg leave to remark, however, that as in the present constitution they are only *appearances* of consolidation, irrefragably contradicted by other facts and circumstances, so also are the facts and observations in your address *merely appearances* of a consolidation, which I hope to demonstrate does not exist. The matter will be better understood by proceeding to those points which shew, that, as under the old so under the new fœderal constitution, the thirteen United States were *not intended* to be, and really *are not consolidated,* in such manner as to *absorb or destroy* the sovereignties of the several states. In order to [have] a perfect understanding of each other, it may be proper to observe here, that by your term *consolidation* I understand you mean *the final annihilation of separate state government or sovereignty, by the nature and operations of the proposed constitution.* Among the proofs you adduce of such consolidation being the *intention* of the late convention, is the expression of—"We the People."—Tho' this is a mere form of words, it will be well to see what expressions are to be found in the constitution in opposition to this, and indicative of the intentions of the convention, before we consider those things, which, as I conceive, secure the states from a possibility of losing their respective sovereignties.

First, then, tho' the convention propose that it should be the act of the people, yet it is in their capacities as citizens of *the several members of our confederacy*—for they are expresly declared to be "the people of *the United States*"—to which idea the expression is *strictly* confined, and the *general* term of *America,* which is constantly used in speaking of us *as a nation,* is carefully omitted: a pointed view was evidently had to our *existing union.* But we must see at once, that the reason of *"the People"* being mentioned was, that alterations of several constitutions were to be effected, which the convention well knew could be done by no authority but that of *"the people,"* either determining themselves *in their several states,* or delegating adequate powers to their *state conventions.* Had the fœderal convention meant to exclude the idea of *"union,"* that is, of *several and separate* sovereignties joining in a confederacy, they would have said, we *the people of America;* for union necessarily involves the idea of component states, which complete consolidations exclude. But the severalty of the states is frequently recognized in the most distinct manner in the course of the constitution. The representatives are to be inhabitants of *the state* they represent—each *state* is to have a representative—the militia officers are to be appointed by the *several states*—and many other instances will be found in reading the constitution.

These, however, are all mere expressions, and I should not have introduced them, but to overbalance the words you have mentioned by a superior weight of the same kind. Let us, then, proceed to evidences against consolidation, of more force than the mere form of words.

It will be found, on a careful examination, that many things, which are indispensibly necessary to the existence and good order of society, cannot be performed by the fœderal government, but will require *the agency and powers* of the state legislatures or sovereignties, with their various appurtenances and appendages.

1st. Congress, under all the powers of the proposed constitution, can neither train the militia, nor appoint the officers thereof.

2dly. They cannot fix the qualifications of electors of representatives, or of the electors of the electors of the President or Vice-President.

3dly. In case of a vacancy in the senate or the house of representatives, they cannot issue a writ for a new election, nor take any of the measures necessary to obtain one.

4thly. They cannot appoint a judge, constitute a court, or in any other way interfere in determining offences against the criminal law of the states, nor can they in any way interfere in the determinations of civil causes between citizens of the same state, which will be innumerable and highly important.

5thly. They cannot elect a President, a Vice-President, a Senator, or a fœderal representative, without all of which their own government must remain *suspended,* and universal *Anarchy must ensue.*

6thly. They cannot determine the place of chusing senators, because that would be derogatory to *the sovereignty* of the state legislatures, who are to elect them.

7thly. They cannot enact laws for the inspection of the produce of the country, a matter of the utmost importance to the commerce of the *several* states, and the honor of *the whole.*

8thly. They cannot appoint or commission *any state officer,* legislative, executive or judicial.

9thly. They cannot interfere with the opening of rivers and canals; the making or regulation of roads, except post roads; building bridges; erecting ferries; establishment of state seminaries of learning; libraries; literary, religious, trading or manufacturing societies; erecting or regulating the police of cities, towns or boroughs; creating new state offices; building light houses, public wharves, county gaols, markets, or other public buildings; making sale of state lands, and other state property; receiving or appropriating the incomes of state buildings and property; executing the state laws; altering the criminal law; nor can they do any other matter or thing appertaining to the internal affairs of any state, whether legislative, executive or judicial, civil or ecclesiastical.

10thly. They cannot interfere with, alter or amend the constitution of any state, which, it is admitted, now is, and, from time to time, will be more or less necessary in most of them.

The proper investigation of this subject will require more of your time than I can take the liberty of engaging at present. I shall therefore leave what I have now written to your honest and cool reflection.

II

To the Minority of the Convention of *Pennsylvania.*

Gentlemen, The principal object of my last paper was to point out a variety of instances, in which *the agency and power of the state governments* are absolutely *necessary* to *the existence* of civil society, and to *the execution* of the fœderal constitution itself. I therein shewed that certain important matters, which must be done from time to time, cannot be attempted or performed by the general government. Here, then, we find, not only that the state powers will not be annihilated, but that they are so requisite to our system, *that they cannot be dispensed with.*

Having seen what Congress *cannot do,* let us now proceed to examine what the state governments *must or may do.*

First, then, each state can appoint every officer of its own militia, and can train the same, by which it will be sure of a powerful military support attached to, and even part of itself, wherein no citizen of any other state can be a private centinel, much less have influence or command.

2dly. Every regulation relating to religion, or the property of religious bodies, must be made by the state governments, since no powers affecting those points are contained in the constitution.

3dly. The state legislatures and constitutions must determine the qualifications of the electors for both branches of the fœderal government; and here let us remember to adhere firmly within our respective commonwealths to *genuine republican principles.* Wisdom, on this point which lies entirely in our hands, will pervade the whole system, and will *be a never failing antidote* to aristocracy, oligarchy and monarchy.

4thly. Regulating the law of descents, and forbidding the entail of landed estates, are exclusively in the power of the state legislatures. A perfect equality, at least among the males, and possibly among the females, should be established, not only in the strict line of descent, but in the most remote collateral branches. If a man *omits* to make a will, the public should distribute his property *equally* among those who have *equal* pretensions, and who are able to render *equal* services to the community. By these means, poverty and extreme riches would be avoided, and a republican spirit would be given to our laws, not only without a violation of private rights, but consistently with the principles of justice and sound policy. This power with that mentioned under the last head, if exercised with wisdom and virtue, will preserve the freedom of the states beyond any other means.

5thly. The elections of the President, Vice President, Senators and Representatives, are exclusively in the hands of the states, even as to filling vacancies. The smallest interference of Congress is not permitted, either in prescribing the qualifications of electors, or in determining what persons may or may not be elected.

The clause which enables the fœderal legislature to make regulations on this head, permits them only to say at what time in the two years the house of representatives shall be chosen, at what time in the six years the Senate shall be chosen, and at what time in the four years the President shall be elected; but these elections, by other provisions in the constitution, *must take place every two, four and six years,* as is declared in the several cases respectively.

6thly. The states elect, appoint and commission all their own officers, without any possible interference of the fœderal government.

7thly. The states can alter and amend their several constitutions, provided they do not make them aristocratical, oligarchic or monarchical—for the fœderal constitution restrains them from any alterations that are not *really republican.* That is, the sovereignty of the people is never to be infringed or destroyed.

8thly. The states have the power to erect corporations for literary, religious, commercial, or other purposes, which the fœderal government cannot prevent.

9thly. Every state can always give its dissent to fœderal bills, as each has *a vote* in the Senate secured by the constitution. Hence it appears, that the state governments are not only intended to remain in force within their respective jurisdictions, but they are always to be known to, and have their voices, *as states,* in the fœderal councils.

10thly. The states not only elect all their own officers, but they have *a check,* by their delegates to the Senate, on the appointment of *all fœderal officers.*

11thly. The states are to hold *separate territorial rights,* and the domestic jurisdiction thereof, exclusively of any interference of the fœderal government.

12thly. The states will regulate and administer the criminal law, *exclusively of Congress,* so far as it regards *mala in se,* or real crimes; such as murder, robbery, &c. They will also have a certain and large part of the jurisdiction, with respect to *mala prohibita,* or matters which are *forbidden* from political considerations, though not in themselves immoral; such as unlicenced public houses, nuisances, and many other things of the like nature.

13thly. The states are to determine all the innumerable disputes about property lying within their respective territories between their own citizens, such as titles and boundaries of lands, debts by assumption, note, bond, or account, mercantile contracts, &c. *none of which can ever be cognizable by any department of the fœderal government.*

14thly. The several states can create corporations civil and religious; prohibit or impose duties on the importation of slaves into their own ports; establish seminaries of learning; erect boroughs, cities and counties; promote and establish manufactures; open roads; clear rivers; cut canals; regulate descents and marriages; licence taverns; alter the criminal law; constitute new courts and offices; establish ferries; erect public buildings; sell, lease and appropriate the proceeds and rents of *their lands,* and of every other species of *state property;* establish poor houses, hospitals, and houses of employment; regulate the police; and many other things of the utmost importance to the happiness of their respective citizens. In short, besides the particulars enumerated, every thing of a domestic nature must or can be done by them.

In addition to this enumeration of the powers and duties of the state governments, we shall find many other instances under the constitution, which require or imply the existence or continuance of the sovereignty and severalty of the states.—The following are some of them:—

All process against criminals and many other law proceedings will be brought by and run in the name of *that commonwealth,* in which the offence or event has taken place.

The senate will be representatives of the several *state sovereignties.*

Every state must send *its own* citizens to the senate and to the house of representatives. No man can go thither, but from the state of which he is a complete *citizen,* and to which, if they choose, he shall be *sworn to be faithful.*

No state shall on any pretence be without *an equal voice* in the senate.

Any state may repel invasions or *commence a war* under emergent circumstances, without waiting for the consent of Congress.

The electors of the President and Vice-President must not nominate more than one person *of the state to which they belong:* so *careful* is the fœderal constitution *to preserve the rights of the states.*

In case of an equality of votes in the election of the President or Vice-President, a casting voice is given to *the states* from a due attention to their *sovereignty* in appointing the ostensible head of the fœderal government.

The President of the United States may require written communications from *the governors of the states.*

Provision is made for adjusting differences between *two states*—or *one state* and the citizens of *another. New states* may be admitted into *the union.* As all *the territory* of each state is *already* in the *union,* it is clear that any district will stand on different ground *when erected into a state,* from what it did when it composed a number of counties, or a part of an already existing member of the confederacy.

Two states may not become *one* without the consent of Congress, which proves clearly that the convention held *the severalty* of the states *necessary.* This is directly opposed to your idea, *that consolidation was intended. Each state* and the fœderal justiciary are to give faith and credit to the records and proceedings of *every other state.*

The states have, in the fœderal constitution, a guarantee of *a separate republican form of government.*

Two thirds of *the states* in the proposed confederacy can call a convention.

Three fourths of those *states* can alter the constitution.

From this examination of the proposed constitution for the United States, I trust it will appear, that though there are some parts of it, which, taken separately, look a little like consolidation, yet there are very many others of a nature, which proves, that no such thing was intended, and that it cannot ever take place.

It is but since the middle of the present century, that the principles and practice of free governments have been well understood, political science having been much slower in its progress than any other branch. Perhaps this has been caused by the greater degree of passion, to which, from its nature, this department of knowledge is subjected. The principles on which free sovereignties ought to confederate is quite a new question, and a new case. It is difficult to take it up at once in the proper way. One circumstance has exceedingly obscured the subject, and hid the truth from the eyes of many of us. Most of the states being in the possession of free governments, have looked for the same forms in *a confederating instrument,* which they have justly esteemed in their several *social compacts.* Recommending this distinction as necessary to be taken home to your minds when you examine the great subject before you, I shall cease to trespass on your time.

III

To the Minority of the Convention of *Pennsylvania.*

Gentlemen, In my former letters I endeavoured to point out certain provisions of the new Constitution, and several circumstances that must result from the proposed frame of government and the state constitutions, which might demonstrate, that there is no ground to apprehend a consolidation of the states, that shall join in the depending confederacy, into one government.

An observation of the honorable Mr. Wilson's has been adduced, among other arguments, to prove, that despotism would follow such a general government. I believe with him and with you that such would be the consequence of *a single national constitution, in which all the objects of society and government were so compleatly provided for, as to place the several states in the union on the footing of counties of the empire.*—But permit me to ask you, gentlemen, will such be the condition of the states? Where is the county that can independently train its own militia, appoint its civil and militia officers, establish *a peculiar system* of penal laws, issue criminal process *in its own name,* erect corporations, *impose direct taxes,* excises and duties, hold lands in its own right, *commence war* on any emergency, *regulate descents,* prescribe *the qualifications* of electors, alter its constitution or *the principles* of its government, divide itself into separate and *independent parts,* join itself to another state, issue writs for elections, and regulate the same, enact inspection laws, *erect courts,* appoint judges, *commission* all its officers, create new offices, sell and give away its lands, *erect fortifications,* and, in short where is the county in the union, or in the world, that can exercise in any instance *independent legislative, executive or judicial powers?*

Those three gentlemen[3] who with-held their names from the act of the fœderal convention could not have apprehended the annihilation of the state governments, while that house was sitting, or they would, under the influence of such a fear, certainly have pressed for a bill of rights.[4] It appears they did not think one so necessary, as to concert a single motion to obtain it: A conclusive proof, in my mind, that they saw no symptoms of a design to consolidate in the framers of the plan, and that they had no apprehensions of the kind themselves.

3. George Mason, Edmund Randolph, and Elbridge Gerry.

4. See Robert Rutland, *The Birth of the Bill of Rights* (Boston: Northeastern University Press, 1991); and Herbert J. Storing, "The Constitution and the Bill of Rights," in M. Judd Harmon, ed., *The Constitution of the United States* (Port Washington, N.Y.: Kennikat Press, 1978).

The construction of the senate affords an absolute certainty, that the states will not lose their present share of separate powers. No state is to lose its voice therein without *its own consent.* Governor Randolph justly observes, that the force of the constitution of any state can only be lessened *by the absolute grant of its own citizens.* Whatever therefore is now possessed will remain, unless transferred by new grants. The state legislatures too being the immediate representatives and guardians of their *respective* constituents, and being the powerful creators of the senators, it cannot be apprehended, either that they will give away their own powers, or that they will chuse men who are unfriendly to them; nor is it at all probable that a senator would hazard the displeasure of the people, or the vengeance of so potent a body as a state legislature, by sacrificing their interests or powers. Rather may it be expected, that his interest and connexions in the state will too partially attach him to it, to the injury of national objects; or that he may neglect general concerns, from a desire to please a legislature or a people, who will be to him *the source of honors, emolument and power.*

So *independent* will the state governments remain, that their laws may, and in some instances will, be *severer* than those of the union. Treason against the United States, for instance, cannot be attended with confiscation and corruption of blood; but by the existing laws of all the states, *the unoffending families* of attainted persons, stripped of all hereditary rights, and condemned to the bitter portion of extreme poverty, are left without their friend and parent, to meet the trials of the world alone: an awful monument of *the sovereign and avenging power* of their native state. Let the Representative or Senator who may meditate the annihilation of the government of his state duly consider this, before it be too late.

You apprehend the power of Congress to lay direct taxes will tend to produce consolidation. But the several states possess that power also, and by an *early,* wise and faithful exercise of it, can always supercede the use of it by Congress. For example; if ten thousand pounds were apportioned to Pennsylvania, to make up the interest on our foreign debts by the end of 1788, a tax for which would be laid in July, our legislature might proceed in the most easy and expeditious way to raise the money, against the time when the fœderal government must necessarily proceed, and by paying our quota into the fœderal treasury would fulfil the requisitions of the law. A fœderal government, that shall possess the least degree of policy or virtue, would never attempt to interfere with such honest, wise and effectual arrangements of any state. It cannot be reasonably feared that a fœderal legislature, chosen by *the equal voices* of all our citizens, *the poor, as well as the rich,* will ever wrest from the hands of the people and states, who respectively appoint them, powers so wisely placed and so honestly applied.

The check of the Senate on the appointment of officers will exceedingly favor the preservation of the state governments. Let us suppose an expedition on foot, which requires a number of general officers, whom a President might be inclined to appoint from the state to which he belongs, or for which several persons are nominated, that are too partially attached to the fœderal government, or desirous of lessening the powers of the separate states. *The Senate can reject them all,* and independently give their reasons to the people and the legislatures. That they will often do so, we cannot doubt, when we remember *where their private interests, affections and connexions lie,* to whom they will owe *their seats*—to whom they must look for *future favors* of the same kind.

The lordship of the soil is one of the most valuable and powerful appendages of sovereignty—This remains *in full perfection* with every state. From them must grants flow, to them must be paid *the annual acknowledgment,* whether it be a mere compliance with form in the rendering of a pepper corn, or *a solid revenue* in the payment of a quit-rent. To them also, as original and rightful proprietaries and *lords of the soil,* will the estates of extinct families revert.

Independent revenues and resources are indubitable proofs of *sovereignty.* The states will possess many of those which now exist, and which may hereafter be created. Taxes on state offices, fees for grants of lands, and various licences, tolls on rivers, canals, and roads not being post-roads, rents of public buildings, escheats, the mighty fund of quit-rents, and sales of lands; these and many others are (exclusively of Congress) within the power of the several states, besides their having access, in common with the fœderal government, to every source of revenue, but the duties on foreign merchandize and ships.

IMPEACHMENTS within the several states will afford them opportunities of exerting the most dignified and aweful powers of sovereignty. The people of every state, by their constitutional representatives, may impeach the public officer, however great or daring, that shall presume to violate their exclusive rights, or offend against the peace and dignity of their commonwealth, and may punish him, on conviction, by fine, imprisonment or death, without any possible interference of Congress.

But, Gentlemen, the subject is inexhaustible. Every section in the fœderal constitution, as we peruse it, affords new ideas opposed to consolidation: Every moment's reflexion, on the operation and tendency of the proposed government, adds to their number. I will not therefore trespass longer on your time. I will rest the matter on your own good sense and candor, confidently trusting that the removal of your apprehensions on this important point will render the new Constitution more agreeable to you. Thinking, as you did, consolidation was intended and would take place, and that it must produce a despotism, you would have been criminal in assenting to the plan proposed; but I will hope that the consideration of this point which we have taken together, will remove your fears, and open the door to comfortable hopes, rather than to apprehensions, from the great measure now waiting the Fiat of the people of the United States.

James Wilson

Speech

State House, 6 October 1787, *Pennsylvania Packet,* 10 October 1787

————•————

In this speech, one of the earliest defenses of the proposed Constitution,
Wilson canvasses the major Anti-Federal objections. For responses to the
speech, see *A Democratic Federalist,* Storing, 3:5; and *Letter by an Officer
of the Late Continental Army,* Storing, 3:8.

————•————

Mr. Chairman and Fellow Citizens, Having received the honour of an appointment to represent you in the late convention, it is, perhaps, my duty
to comply with the request of many gentlemen, whose characters and judg-
ments I sincerely respect, and who have urged that this would be a proper
occasion to lay before you any information, which will serve to elucidate
and explain the principles and arrangements of the constitution that has
been submitted to the consideration of the United States. I confess that I
am unprepared for so extensive and so important a disquisition: but the
insidious attempts, which are clandestinely and industriously made to per-
vert and destroy the new plan, induce me the more readily to engage in
its defence: and the impressions of four months constant attendance to the
subject, have not been so easily effaced, as to leave me without an answer
to the objections which have been raised.

It will be proper, however, before I enter into the refutation of the charges
that are alleged, to mark the leading discrimination between the state constitutions, and the constitution of the United States. When the people established the powers of legislation under their separate governments, they
invested their representatives with every right and authority which they did
not in explicit terms reserve: and therefore upon every question, respecting
the jurisdiction of the house of assembly, if the frame of government is silent,
the jurisdiction is efficient and complete. But in delegating fœderal powers,

another criterion was necessarily introduced: and the congressional authority is to be collected, not from tacit implication, but from the positive grant, expressed in the instrument of union. Hence, it is evident, that in the former case, everything which is not reserved, is given: but in the latter, the reverse of the proposition prevails, and every thing which is not given, is reserved. This distinction being recognized, will furnish an answer to those who think the omission of a bill of rights, a defect in the proposed constitution: for it would have been superfluous and absurd, to have stipulated with a fœderal body of our own creation, that we should enjoy those privileges, of which we are not divested either by the intention or the act that has brought that body into existence. For instance, the liberty of the press, which has been a copious subject of declamation and opposition: what controul can proceed from the fœderal government, to shackle or destroy that sacred palladium of national freedom? If, indeed, a power similar to that which has been granted for the regulation of commerce, had been granted to regulate literary publications, it would have been as necessary to stipulate that the liberty of the press should be preserved inviolate, as that the impost should be general in its operation. With respect, likewise, to the particular district of ten miles, which is to be the seat of government, it will undoubtedly be proper to observe this salutary precaution, as there the legislative power will be vested in the president, senate, and house of representatives of the United States. But this could not be an object with the convention: for it must naturally depend upon a future compact; to which the citizens immediately interested, will, and ought to be parties: and there is no reason to suspect, that so popular a privilege will in that case be neglected. In truth, then, the proposed system possesses no influence whatever upon the press; and it would have been merely nugatory, to have introduced a formal declaration upon the subject; nay, that very declaration might have been construed to imply that some degree of power was given, since we undertook to define its extent.

Another objection that has been fabricated against the new constitution, is expressed in this disingenuous form—"the trial by jury is abolished in civil cases." I must be excused, my fellow citizens, if, upon this point, I take advantage of my professional experience, to detect the futility of the assertion. Let it be remembered, then, that the business of the fœderal constitution was not local, but general—not limited to the views and establishments of a single state, but co-extensive with the continent, and comprehending the views and establishments of thirteen independent sovereignties. When, therefore, this subject was in discussion, we were involved in difficulties, which pressed on all sides, and no precedent could be discovered to direct our course. The cases open to a jury, differed in the different states; it was therefore impracticable, on that ground, to have made a general rule. The want of uniformity would have rendered any reference to the practice of the states idle and useless: and it could not, with any propriety, be said, that "the trial by jury shall be as heretofore:" since there has never existed any fœderal system of jurisprudence, to which the declaration could relate. Besides, it is not in all cases that the trial by jury is adopted in civil questions: for causes depending in courts of admiralty, such as relate to maritime captures, and such as are agitated in the courts of equity, do not require the intervention of that tribunal. How, then, was the line of discrimination to be drawn? The convention found the task too difficult for them: and they left the business as it stands—in the fullest confidence, that no danger could possibly ensue, since the proceedings of the supreme court are to be regulated by the congress, which is a faithful representation of the people: and the oppression of government is effectually barred, by declaring that in all criminal cases, the trial by jury shall be preserved.

This constitution, it has been further urged, is of a pernicious tendency, because it tolerates a standing army in the time of peace. This has always been a popular topic of declamation: and yet I do not know a nation in the world, which has not found it necessary and useful to maintain the appearance of strength in a season of the most profound tranquility. Nor is it a novelty with us; for under the present articles of confederation, congress certainly possesses this reprobated power: and the exercise of it is proved at this moment by the cantonments along the banks of the Ohio. But what would be our national situation, were it otherwise? Every principle of policy must be subverted, and the government must declare war before they are prepared to carry it on. Whatever may be the provocation, however important the object in view, and however necessary dispatch and secrecy may be, still the declaration must precede the preparation, and the enemy will be informed of your intention, not only before you are equipped for an attack, but even before you are fortified for a defence. The consequence is too obvious to require any further delineation; and no man, who regards the dignity and safety of his country, can deny the necessity of a military force, under the controul, and with the restrictions which the new constitution provides.

Perhaps there never was a charge made with less reason, than that which predicts the institution of a baneful aristocracy in the fœderal senate. This body branches into two characters, the one legislative, and the other executive. In its legislative character, it can effect no purpose without the co-operation of the house of representatives: and in its executive character, it can accomplish no object, without the concurrence of the president. Thus fettered, I do not know any act which the senate can of itself perform: and such dependence necessarily precludes every idea of influence and superiority. But I will confess, that in the organization of this body, a compromise between contending interests is discernible: and when we reflect how various are the laws, commerce, habits, population, and extent of the confederated states, this evidence of mutual concession and accommodation ought rather to command a generous applause, than to excite jealousy and reproach. For my part, my admiration can only be equalled by my astonishment, in beholding so perfect a system formed from such heterogenous materials.

The next accusation I shall consider, is that which represents the fœderal constitution as not only calculated, but designedly framed, to reduce the state governments to mere corporations, and eventually to annihilate them. Those who have employed the term corporation, upon this occasion, are not perhaps aware of its extent. In common parlance, indeed, it is generally applied to petty associations for the ease and conveniency of a few individuals; but in its enlarged sense, it will comprehend the government of Pennsylvania, the existing union of the states, and even this projected system is nothing more than a formal act of incorporation. But upon what pretence can it be alleged that it was designed to annihilate the state governments? For, I will undertake to prove that upon their existence depends the existence of the fœderal plan. For this purpose, permit me to call your attention to the manner in which the president, senate, and house of representatives, are proposed to be appointed. The president is to be chosen by electors, nominated in such manner as the legislature of each state may direct; so that if there is no legislature, there can be no senate. The house of representatives is to be composed of members chosen every second year by the people of the several states, and the electors in each state shall have the qualifications requisite to electors of the most numerous branch of the state legislature—unless, therefore, there is a state legislature, that qualification cannot be ascertained, and the popular branch of the fœderal constitution must likewise be extinct. From this view, then, it is evidently absurd to suppose, that the annihilation of the separate governments will result from their union; or, that, having that intention, the authors of the new system would have bound their connection with such indissoluble ties. Let me here advert to an arrangement highly advantageous; for you will perceive, without prejudice to the powers of the legislature in the election of senators, the people at large will acquire an additional privilege in returning members to the house of representatives—whereas, by the present confederation, it is the legislature alone that appoints the delegates to congress.

The power of direct taxation has likewise been treated as an improper delegation to the fœderal government; but when we consider it as the duty of that body to provide for the national safety, to support the dignity of the union, and to discharge the debts contracted upon the collective faith of the states, for their common benefit, it must be acknowledged that those, upon whom such important obligations are imposed, ought, in justice and in policy, to possess every means requisite for a faithful performance of their trust. But why should we be alarmed with visionary evils? I will venture to predict, that the great revenue of the United States must, and always will, be raised by impost; for, being at once less obnoxious, and more productive, the interest of the government will be best promoted by the accommodation of the people. Still, however, the object of direct taxation should be within reach in all cases of emergency; and there is no more reason to apprehend oppression in the mode of collecting a revenue from this resource, than in the form of impost, which, by universal assent, is left to the authority of the fœderal government. In either case, the force of civil constitutions will be adequate to the purpose; and the dread of military violence, which has been assiduously disseminated, must eventually prove the mere effusion of a wild imagination, or a factious spirit. But the salutary consequences that must flow from thus enabling the government to relieve and support the credit of the union, will afford another answer to the objections upon this ground. The state of Pennsylvania, particularly, which has encumbered itself with the assumption of a great proportion of the public debt, will derive considerable relief and advantage; for, as it was the imbecility of the present confederation, which gave rise to the funding law, that law must naturally expire, when a complete and energetic fœderal system shall be substituted— the state will then be discharged from an extraordinary burden, and the national creditor will find it to be to his interest to return to his original security.

After all, my fellow-citizens, it is neither extraordinary nor unexpected, that the constitution offered to your consideration, should meet with opposition. It is the nature of man to pursue his own interest, in preference to the public good; and I do not mean to make any personal reflection, when I add, that it is the interest of a very numerous, powerful, and respectable body, to counteract and destroy the excellent work produced by the late convention. All the officers of government, and all the appointments for the administration of justice and the collection of the public revenue, which are transferred from the individual to the aggregate sovereignty of the states, will necessarily turn the stream of influence and emolument into a new channel. Every person, therefore, who either enjoys, or expects to enjoy a place of profit under the present establishment, will object to the proposed innovation? not, in truth, because it is injurious to the liberties of his country, but because it effects his schemes of wealth and consequence. I will confess, indeed, that I am not a blind admirer of this plan of government, and that there are some parts of it, which, if my wish had prevailed, would certainly have been altered. But, when I reflect how widely men differ in their opinions, and that every man (and the observation applies likewise to every state) has an equal pretension to assert his own, I am satisfied that any thing nearer to perfection could not have been accomplished. If there are errors, it should be remembered, that the seeds of reformation are sown in the work itself, and the concurrence of two thirds of the congress may at any time introduce alterations and amendments. Regarding it, then, in every point of view, with a candid and disinterested mind, I am bold to assert, that it is the BEST FORM OF GOVERNMENT WHICH HAS EVER BEEN OFFERED TO THE WORLD.

"Philo-Publius"
[William Duer]

Essays

I: *Daily Advertiser*, New York, 30 October 1787; II: New York *Packet*, 16 November 1787; III and IV: *Daily Advertiser*, New York, 29 November and 1 December 1787

William Duer was originally to be one of the authors of *The Federalist*. According to James Madison, "William Duer was also included in the original plan; and wrote two or more papers, which though intelligent and sprightly, were not continued, nor did they make a part of the printed collection." Thus, Duer's choice of the pseudonym Philo-Publius. See the introduction to Jacob E. Cooke's edition of *The Federalist* (Middletown, Conn.: Wesleyan University Press, 1961).

I

In the first number of the Federalist, which appeared in the INDEPEN-DENT JOURNAL of Saturday, the interest of certain Officers, under the State establishments, to oppose an increase of Federal authority, is mentioned as a principal source of the opposition to be expected to the New Constitution.[1] The same idea has appeared in other publications, but has not hitherto been sufficiently explained. To ascertain its justness and extent, would, no doubt, be satisfactory to the public; and might serve to obviate misapprehensions.

A very natural enquiry presents itself on the subject:—How happens it,

---

1. As Publius puts it in *The Federalist*, No. 1: "Among the most formidable of the obstacles which the new Constitution will have to encounter, may readily be distinguished the obvious interest of a certain class of men in every state to resist all changes which may hazard a diminution of power, emolument, and consequence of the offices they hold under the state establishments."

that the interest of the Officers of a State should be different from that of its Citizens? I shall attempt an answer to this question.

The powers requisite to constitute Sovereignty, must be delegated by every people for their own protection and security. The people of each State have already delegated these powers; which are now lodged; partly in the PARTICULAR Government, and partly in the GENERAL Government. It is not necessary that they should grant greater or new ones. The only question with them is, in what manner the powers already granted shall be distributed; into what receptacles; and in what proportions. If they are represented in both, it will be immaterial to them, so far as concerns their individual authority, independence, or liberty, whether the principal share be deposited in the whole body, or in the distinct members. The repartition, or division, is a mere question of expediency; for, by whatever scale it be made, their personal rights will remain the same. If it be their interest to be united, it will be their interest to bestow as large a portion upon the Union, as may be required to render it solid and effectual; and if experience has shewn, that the portion heretofore conferred is inadequate to the object, it will be their interest to take away a part of that which has been left in the State reservoirs, to add it to the common stock.

But such a transfer of power, from the individual members to the Union, however it may promote the advantage of the citizens at large, may subtract not a little from the importance, and, what is with most men less easily submitted to, from the emolument of those, who hold a certain description of offices under the State establishments. These have one interest as Citizens, and another as OFFICERS. In the latter capacity, they are interested in the POWER and PROFIT of their offices, and will naturally be unwilling to put either in jeopardy. That men love power is no new discovery; that they are commonly attached to good salaries does not need elaborate proof; that they should be afraid of what threatens them with a loss of either, is but a plain inference from plain facts. A diminution of State authority is, of course, a diminution of the POWER of those who are invested with the administration of that authority; and, in all probability, will in many instances produce an eventual decrease of salary. In some cases it may annihilate the offices themselves. But, while these persons may have to repine at the loss of official importance or pecuniary emolument, the private citizen may feel himself exalted to a more elevated rank. He may pride himself in the character of a citizen of America, as more dignified than that of a citizen of any single State. He may greet himself with the appellation of an American as more honorable than that of a New-Yorker, a Pennsylvanian, or a Virginian.

From the preceding remarks, the distinction alluded to, between the private citizen and the citizen in office, will, I presume, be sufficiently apparent. But it will be proper to observe, that its influence does not reach near so far as might at first sight be imagined. The offices that would be affected by the proposed change, though of considerable importance, are not numerous. Most of the departments of the State Governments will remain, untouched, to flow in their accustomed channels. This observation was necessary, to prevent invidious suspicions from lighting where they would not be applicable.

II

The government of Athens was a democracy. The people, as is usual in all democratical governments, were constantly alarmed at the spectre of ARISTOCRACY; and it was common in that republic as it is in the republics of America to pay court to them by encouraging their jealousies, and gratifying their prejudices. Pericles, to ingratiate himself with the citizens of Athens, whose favour was necessary to his ambition, was a principal agent in mutilating the privileges and the power of the court of AREOPAGUS; an institution acknowledged by all historians to have been a main pillar of the State. The pretence was that it promoted the POWER of the ARISTOCRACY.

The same man undermined the constitution of his country TO ACQUIRE popularity—squandered the treasures of his country to PURCHASE popularity—and to avoid being accountable to his country precipitated it into a war which ended in its destruction. Pericles was, nevertheless, a man endowed with many amiable and shining qualities, and, except in a few instances, was always the favorite of the people.

III

PUBLIUS has shewn us in a clear light the utility, it might be said, the necessity of Union to the formation and support of a navy.[2] There is one point of view however on which he has left the subject untouched—the tendency of this circumstance to the preservation of liberty.

Will force be necessary to repell foreign attacks, or to guard the national rights against the ambition of particular members? A navy will be a much safer as well as a more effectual engine for either purpose. If we have a respectable fleet there will be the less call on any account for an army. This idea is too plain to need enlargement. Thus the salutary guardianship of the Union appears on all sides to be the palladium of American liberty.[3]

IV

UPON what basis does our Independence rest, so far as respects the recognition of Foreign Powers? Upon the basis of the UNION.—In what capacity did France first acknowledge our Independence? In the capacity of UNITED STATES. In what capacity did Britain accede to it, and relinquish her pretensions? In the capacity of UNITED STATES.—In what character have we formed Treaties with other Nations? In the character of UNITED STATES.—Are we, in short, known in any other Independent character to any Nation on the face of the Globe?

I admit, that in theory, our Independence may survive the Union; but can the Anti-federalists guarantee the efficacy of this theory upon the Councils of Europe? Can they ensure us against a fate, similar to that which lately befel the distracted and devoted Kingdom of Poland?

2. *The Federalist*, No. 11.
3. See *The Federalist*, Nos. 10, 14, and 51.

"State Soldier"

Essays: I, II, V

Virginia Independent Chronicle, Richmond, 16 January, 6 February, and 2 April 1788

———•———

The author of these essays may have been George Nicholas (1754?–99). Nicholas was a Charlottesville lawyer-planter, a former officer in the Continental army, and a supporter of the proposed Constitution in the Virginia State Convention. According to the editors of *Documentary History,* authorship may be attributable to Nicholas based on the fact that parts of a manuscript in his handwriting are similar to sections of the fourth letter in this series of essays. See *DH,* 8:303.

Changes to the first essay in this series have been made on the basis of a list of corresponding errata published in conjunction with the second essay.

———•———

I

An ADDRESS *to the* GOOD PEOPLE *of* VIRGINIA, *on the* NEW FŒDERAL CONSTITUTION, *by an old State Soldier, in answer to an Officer in the late American army.*[1]

A fellow-citizen whose life has once been devoted to your service, and knows no other interest now than what is common to you all, solicits your attention for a new few moments on the new plan of government submitted to your consideration.

Well aware of the feebleness of a Soldier's voice after his service shall be no longer requisite, and sensible of the superiority of those who have already appeared on this subject, he does not flatter himself that what he has now

1. According to Storing, William Findley was An Officer of the late Continental Army. This letter first appeared in the Philadelphia *Independent Gazetteer* on 6 November 1787, and was widely reprinted. See Storing, 3:8.

to say will have much weight—Yet it may serve to contradict some general opinions which may have grown out of circumstances too dangerous to our reputations, to remain unanswered.

Conscious of the rectitude of his own intentions however, and trusting that "in searching after error truth will appear," he flatters himself he should be excused, were he to leave the merits of this cause to that more able ADVOCATE, the CONSTITUTION itself, and confine himself wholly to those general, plain, and honest truths which flow from the feelings of the warmest heart.

FREEDOM has its charms, and authority its use—but there are certain points beyond which neither can be stretched without falling into licentiousness, or sinking under oppression.

Here then let us pause!—and before we approach these dreadful extremes, view well the ground on which we now stand, as well as that to which we are about to step. Let it be remembered that after a long and bloody conflict, we have been left in possession of that great blessing for which we so long contended—and which was only obtained, and could not be perfectly founded at a time when there was only a chance for succeeding in the claim. The one being separate and distinct from the other at all times, a happy REVOLUTION therefore, has necessarily left incomplete the labors of the war for the more judicious and permanent establishment of the calms of peace. It was not expected, or even wished, that a SYSTEM, which was the mere OFF-SPRING of NECESSITY, should govern and controul us when our object was changed, and another time than confusion should offer itself to our service for making choice of a better. But on the contrary the same mutual agreement which promised us success in our undertaking during the war, led us to hope for a happy settlement of those rights at the approach of peace—which alone can be done now by that policy which holds out at equal balance, strength and energy in the one hand, and justice, peace, and lenity in the other. Too much 'tis true may be surrendered up—but 'tis as certain too much may be retained, since there is no way more likely to lose ones liberty in the end than being too niggardly of it in the beginning. For he who grasps at more than he can possibly hold, will retain less than he could have handled with ease had he been moderate at first. *Omnes deteriores sumus licentia.* But how much is necessary to be given up is the difficulty to be ascertained. We all know however the more desperate any disease has become, so much more violent must be the remedy—that if there be now a danger in making the attempt, it is owing more to the putting off to this late period that which at some time or another is unavoidable, than to any thing in the design itself. Having neglected this business until necessity pressed us forward to it, we see an anxiety and hurry now in some which is extremely alarming to others—when in fact had it been attempted at the close of the war, it might have seemed nothing more perhaps than a necessary guard to that tender infant, INDEPENDENCE, to whom we had just given birth.

Long had the friends to the late REVOLUTION observed how incomplete the business was when we contented ourselves under that form of government, after the return of peace, which was only designed to bind us together the more effectually to carry on the war—and which could not be expected to operate effectually in many cases, the exspence of which no one at that time could foresee. At this late period then an attempt has been made to complete the designs of a war that ended many years before. And the first object which presented itself to our view in the business was the necessity of strengthening the UNION—the only probable way to do which, was the creating an authority whereby our credit could be supported—and in doing this (although it seems a single alteration in our old plan) the introduction of several other things was unavoidable. The credit of the UNION, like that of an individual, was only to be kept up by a prospect of being at some time or another able to pay the debts it had necessarily contracted—and that prospect could no way begin but by the establishment of some fund whereon the CONTINENT could draw with certainty. But the right of taxation (the only certain way of creating that fund) was too great a surrender to be made without [being] accompanied with some other alterations in the old plan. Among these the Senate, and the mode of proportioning the taxes with the representatives, seem to be the most material—the one acting as a curb, the other as a guide in the business. Though in fact the credit of the UNION depended on several other things besides the payment of its debts—Its internal defence, its compliance with its treaties, and the litigation of its own disputes, must be considered as inseparable from its national dignity. Therefore the additional authorities of the President, and the institution of the supreme court, were nothing more than necessary appendages to that AUTHORITY which every one seems to grant was necessary to be given up to strengthen our UNION and support our credit and dignity as a people—and when rightly considered can amount to nothing more than one alteration, so generally wished for, divided into several parts. One thing however appears to be entirely forgot: No one seems to remember that we had any fœderal constitution before this. Or if they do they have entirely forgotten what it was—it must be remembered however, that there was no other complaint made about that, but a want of energy and power. The removing this grand objection then, which seems to be the only material alteration made by this new Constitution, has not, as was expected, perfected the UNION; but it has served only to make way for the discovery of smaller imperfections which were not before seen. The want of a bill of rights, a charter for the press, and a thousand other things which are now discovered, have been heretofore unnoticed although they existed then in as great a degree as they now do. Whenever any alterations have been made in any of these lesser faults, they have universally been for the better. For instance the appropriation of monies under pretence of providing for our national defence, which then was without hesitation, is now restricted to two years: For although Congress could not absolutely keep a large standing force in time of profound peace, yet they had it in their power to provide for an army when there was not an absolute war: For the declaration being at their sole will, and they not accountable for the necessity, left the appropriation which was given them for supporting the one, entirely at their discretion in time of the other. That when this article shall be viewed independent of the grand object, and considered as one of the smaller faults, separate and distinct from the right of taxation, it must be confessed that part of our SYSTEM has been altered for the better. And thus too respecting a bill of rights, and the liberty of the press, it may also be said, the objection has been diminished by the new plan: For what security had we on this head before but that which was in our state constitutions? And of what is the republican form of government which Congress is now to guarantee to each state to consist?[2] Certainly of any thing each state shall think proper that does not take from Congress what this constitution absolutely claims. Even the very one we now have, or such parts of it as do not extend that far, may be that form of government which this new plan obliges Congress to guarantee. That so far from these objections being increased, they are diminished by the new plan; as there will not only be the same state security for these rights then, but also a continental conformation of them—there being nothing in the new system that excludes that part of the old. That it is not, because those smaller faults have not been before seen, they necessarily originate in, or are magnified by the new constitution: but the truth is, they have always been overlooked in beholding that grand blemish which marked the features of the old plan. The representation which was much more unequal and far more objectionable, then went unnoticed—as no one would observe the disproportion of the fingers while the whole carcase was disjointing for the want of sinews. The general cry and only wish then was, for more authority in our government. It was not expected the amendments would extend much further—yet they have: Many inferior objections which existed in the old plan, are in the new altered for the better. That when we came to enquire into the merits of this matter fairly, and set apart in the first place those things which are absolutely necessary to compose that alteration in our fœderal plan which we all so ardently wished for, and then in the next place give the proper credits to this new constitution for the amendments made in the more inferior faults of the old, we shall find there are but few things left worthy of grounding an opposition on. 'Tis much to be lamented however that we cannot avoid extremes on either side: For as all extremes are subject to a union in the end, it will be well if our violent opposition at this time, does not return to the most opposite submission at another. Indeed the comparrison of this opposition among ourselves to that of the

2. See William W. Wiecek, *The Guarantee Clause of the U.S. Constitution* (Ithaca, N.Y.: Cornell University Press, 1972).

late one towards our original situation, serves only to prove the likeness there is between the beginning and ending of our liberty—for there are no two things more strikingly alike than the first respirations of life and the last melancholy gasps of existence. But when confined to the likeness of situation itself, the same comparison is entirely unjust: For formerly we were governed by those who had no interest in our prosperity: But now it is our FRIENDS, our COUNTRYMEN, and our BRETHREN, on whom we are called to rely, whose very existence is so inseparable from our welfare as to render it impossible for them to injure us without giving a fatal stab to themselves and the happiness of their posterity. But to those who cannot distinguish between a cause and a people, a sentiment and an individual, the analogy may appear just, in its intended meaning—yet self-evident as the contrary is, it would illy become those whose reputations are immediately concerned to stifle an honest resentment on this occasion. When we behold the character of individuals held up to view as an argument in favor of any cause, we are sufficiently disgusted with the ignorance of the author; but when we see the credit of that ignorance (accompanied by illiberality) given to us who would willingly merit a better appellation than the secret movers of personal jealousy and detraction among citizens, we are doubly mortified—considering an endeavor to keep alive those distinctions now which owed their existence to the heat of war, as illiberal as a suspicion over our best friends would be unjust. The one serving only to keep up a perpetual war among ourselves; and the other to make distrust a justification for dishonesty—neither of which is a trait in the character of a real soldier it is presumed: For besides the dishonor, he who really knows what war is, would scarcely wish to keep it up when he could have peace. But it is a trite remark that he who is most violent in time of the one, has generally been the most mild during the other. It is not at all surprising however that you should be brought to believe your liberties are now in danger, when you are thus shewn how that bravery you have once felt in your favor, is likely to take residence in the breasts of those thus capable of any thing. By thus assuming our names and holding to view their own genuine characters, designing men do us more real injury, and their own cause more essential service, than those who insinuate that we shall be preferred from our former services to share the spoils when our country shall fall a prey to aristocratical invasion. These last only add insult to misfortune: For there is but little in our influence to rouse your jealousy, and much less in our situations to excite your envy, unless the nobleness of your gratitude should make you wish to share in our poverty and fears.—These being all we have obtained, there is but little prospect of our becoming your tyrants, since misery and wretchedness are seldom called in to share the dignities of oppression. In short, as there is nothing in this constitution itself that particularly bargains for a surrender of your liberties, it must be your own faults if you become enslaved. Men in power may usurp authorities under any constitution—and those they govern may oppose their tyranny: For although it be wrong to refuse the legal currency of one's country, yet there can be no harm in rejecting base coin, since there is no state in the world which compels a man to take that which is under its own standard.

It cannot be denied however but this constitution has its faults—yet when the whole of those objections shall be collected together and compared to the excellence of the main object, we cannot but conclude that the opposition will be like quarrelling about the division of straws, and neglecting the management of the grain. The period is not far distant however when it must be determined whether it be best to adopt it as it now stands, or run the risk of losing it by attempting amendments. This last consideration, deeply impressed on the minds of those who are interested in the welfare of America, cannot fail to call forth your attention, when a fitter season shall demand it, and another paper give it circulation.

II

To the good PEOPLE *of* VIRGINIA, *on the new*
FŒDERAL CONSTITUTION, *by an old*
STATE SOLDIER, *in answer to the proposition for
amendments.*

Under a persuasion of the utility of the UNION themselves, some persons till lately have been weak enough to suppose that no one would contend for the separation of the States. But all things have their duration—Politics as well as dress are often under the controul of fashion; and there are stated periods when the plainness and honesty of the old, must give way to the artifice and foppery of the new.

Impressed with the necessity in time of danger, each state was taught to believe, that it was by being "united they were to stand—and when divided to fall." And unaware of such open confessions as has lately been made of the contrary, I had intended to confine myself at present entirely to the subject of altering the new fœderal constitution—but finding the one so inseparably linked with the designs of the other, a few observations will necessarily occur in the course of this paper, as well to shew the necessity of continuing the UNION, as to strengthen the objections I had to offer against an attempt to alter the new plan of government.

It would be difficult, if not impossible however, to point out the difference between a public attempt to amend this new system, and a secret design to destroy it—yet it may not be hard to shew the evil tendency of either.

That no other method for bringing about so useful a business as the separation of the states could be devised but the framing a new constitution for the more effectually binding them together, and then destroying it, seems at least strange. GOVERNMENT being the foundation of all human happiness, untinctured with fickleness, should be the solid work of WISDOM and mature DELIBERATION—Children indeed may make impressions on the sands and rub them out when they become tired of looking at them; but states when they do childish things make impressions which their maturer days cannot efface.

For the noble purposes of combining us together and making us respectable as a nation abroad, and rich as individuals at home, a system of government is now offered to our service—which, though fraught with some lesser evils, has every important recommendation—but to correct the one we are now invited to risk the other—for as the principle objection to this constitution is the undue influence which some of the states will have over the others from their superiority in number, it is too obvious what must be the remedy applied in the first instance. For it being too well known to admit of a dispute that the same majority which the northern states now hold, will at another time be as great, it becomes as obvious that no alteration in that system at this time can correct this inconvenience but a dissolution of the UNION—yet a remedy may be found indeed in that very constitution itself as it now stands.

Through the feebleness of the UNION and popular turn of our system, the different interests of the states have heretofore been rendered somewhat discordant—Congress being entirely dependent on, and ever amenable to the state legislatures, that same fear of offending which has often operated on the state representative (in favor of a few to the prejudice of the many) extends itself to the continental delegate—which, when aided by the consideration of the dependence which most preferments have on the individual states, together with the insignificance of the present UNION, render the interest of a part more the object of fœderal consideration than the welfare of the whole—whence arises that contention of interests in which some states may have suffered; and is at this time so much dreaded.

Powerful however as that objection may appear against the existence of a general UNION, it has little to do with that question now: for to argue from what experience we have already had, would be nothing against the necessity of a UNION. Having never yet felt the effects of a perfect one, all that can be drawn from the experience of the old, will only prove the necessity of a new.

The present fœderal constitution, though under the name of a UNION, wanted every proper, strong, and well-tried string at its formation (if I may so express myself) to produce a perfect unison—the want of authority and independence rendered it too feeble an instrument to produce the wished for effects. When on the contrary had the general government of the continent been set at a proper distance above those of the states, the objections now started might never been known perhaps. The representative instead of contending for the particular interest of his own state, would then have had something of higher dignity in view—Congress being considered the only head of the continent, to ornament which so as to make a figure among the other nations of the world, would [have] been his only object—since from that source alone would spring the only political reputation worth adding to his name. And all preferments of the highest honor and emolument coming from the continent at large, it would thence have been immediately his interest to consult the dignity of the whole, and not the contracted, and too often illiberal interest of a part.

Whence we may consider the want of a perfect UNION the very cause of those evils which are so much dreaded, and now urged against a confederation of the states—For as men of contracted habits and moderate circumstances see no way of mending their fortunes but a selfish and narrow œconomy in their own system, so states will look no further than their own immediate interests, till a friendly intercourse with others has taught the benefit of making trivial sacrifices for double gain.

The use of trade has taught the benefit of loan—and favors with obligations by frequent and mutual intercourse become reciprocal interest at last. By a strict confederacy, under which the fruits of commerce would find a regular and general circulation, it would soon become the interest of each state to contribute to the profits of the whole—And acting under one uniform system, nothing but superior industry could give an advantage to any particular part: for it then being out of the power of each state to intrigue for its traders, party skill would necessarily give way to political wisdom—and thus the states, habituated by confederation to alternate sacrifices and advantages, growing into one grand EMPIRE, would gradually lose sight of every local and pernicious interest as the whole advanced into national perfection. And as the government became more and more fixed and freed from those local prejudices and interests, any necessary alterations might more easily be made.

But since those evils can no way be remedied at this time but by a separation of the states, I trust you will treat the attempt with that detestation which a design to ruin you forever would deserve.

For my part it is far from me to suspect any man of private designs in his public acts—But I fear every one will not be so liberal. The great opening which this doctrine leaves for suspicion to enter in, will not be long unoccupied I suspect. The many accomplishments which are necessary to entitle men to the presidency and other high offices under a government so extensive as this is likely [to] be; and on the contrary the few ingredients necessary to constitute that fitness where a state or two shall compose a UNION, render this darling scheme of disuniting the states too suspicious to go unnoticed by all. A general reputation throughout the continent,[3] both military and political, will be necessary in the one, and a few marches and retreats about Williamsburg at the beginning of the war, the taking a tory or two by surprise at their own houses by night, together with a popular eloquence, will be sufficient recommendations, both military and civil, in the other.

Though for my own part I should rather suppose that this strange, wild, and dangerous scheme has arisen from a mistaken zeal in some, and been kept up from a reverence for the opinions of particular men by others. For let a man whose wisdom, experience, or patriotism has been thought uncommon, advocate an opinion, however fallacious it may be, he will always find converts. And this I take to be the case in the present instance.

Some celebrated statesman perhaps has taken up an opinion that we cannot exist but by separate governments—and a number of others, who under an admiration of the man have adopted his opinions by way of recommending themselves, as if they thought it sufficient for that purpose if their wisdom could come up to a level with his folly.

Long, too long indeed my countrymen, have we been liable to be lulled into a fatal stupor by the musical eloquence of a single man!—Whence our government, free as it appears to be, has ever had the worst of tyranny lurking in it.

At all times liable to be governed by the breath of a single man, under a constitution subject to be swept away by his eloquence, no one can foretell at what instant we may fall a prey to his ambition. These being the only dangers you have to dread from designing men, you have it now in your powers to be relieved from every fear of the sort in future.

Under the general government of a UNION, whose members will be farther removed from those fears which spring from popular sources, another kind of eloquence than inflammatory declamation will be necessary for persuasion. And from an assembly composed of men (many of whom of equal abilities, or at least of too great an equality of pride and ambition

3. See James Ceaser, *Presidential Selection: Theory and Development* (Princeton, N.J.: Princeton University Press, 1979).

to suffer an individual of their own number to dictate to the rest) would flow laws founded on the combined abilities of all North America, and supersede those which were but the labours of some popular individual in each state.

Commerce then, freed from the oppressive hand of state jealousy and local interest, traversing the whole continent and seeking your commodities, would stamp a higher value on all your property. While policy and justice, unawed by popular resentment, extending their united hands, the one receiving from the delinquent states that portion of supplies which they have so long withheld, and the other placing it where it most righteously belongs—together with the assistance of a general impost, would soon relieve you from your debts both foreign and domestic, public and private. For as our present private embarrassments are in a great measure owing to the daily public demands which come against us, the[y] being relieved from the latter by any means whatever, will surely render us the more able to get rid of the former.

But while we impute to the taxes we pay towards supporting an ill-managed government our inability to discharge our private debts, let us recollect to what cause we owe that mismanagement itself;—and in doing this we shall probably find how inconsistent we are in opposing a government in every degree calculated to correct the evils of which we complain.

To look up for favors to others, without being willing to do a kindness in return, would be equally pitiful and unjust; and to expect to enjoy the benefits of a society to whose interests we are not always willing to adhere, would be unreasonable and absurd. Yet there are those who do not scruple to claim the most unbounded liberty, while they condemn the mismanagement of a government, the pressures of which are entirely owing to its being already too feeble and too popular to subsist but by relaxing first into the very lowest stages of existence, and then struggling and straining into vigor. Whence, though they are blinded to the cause, proceeds all the miseries they feel.—For that government which is distressed itself, by relenting in its demands at one time, must be the more rigid and severe at another.

To the different postponements of our taxes therefore, which have only been to please for the instant and not to give any lasting and permanent relief, we may justly [attribute] the most of our present distresses since the removing those necessary payments from time to time the further from us, only served to accumulate the load which at some time or another through necessity was doomed to fall on us with a threefold wretchedness—for the arrow that goes upwards is not rendered the less dangerous by being removed the further from us; but on the contrary the higher it ascends with so much the more force and weight it will return on our heads.

To an endeavor then to heal the wounds which that kind of policy has already made, which if too long irritated might become incurable at last, as well as to the causes before mentioned, the matter now under consideration owes its existence. But unfortunately that constitution, like all other human things, has its faults; and those faults are such as cannot be removed at this time without destroying it entirely—and what is worse, as I have before advanced, disuniting the whole of the states. And this last I trust, if sufficiently proved, will render the idea of amendments at this time as shocking in the eyes of the undesigning as the intent is treacherous in the minds and hearts of all others.

Let us for a moment however remove from our view the powerful tendency which the amendments themselves proposed by such men will have that way, and view them earnestly endeavoring to have those objectionable parts eradicated without a design of endangering the UNION. To that end it will only be necessary to consider the effects which the favorable reception that constitution may meet with from a part, will have on the UNION when met by such obstructions as amendments from the rest.

For it will not only be confessed, but it has already been urged as an objection to this new system of government, that it will be the interest of a majority of the states to oppress the rest—and it being the interest of that same majority to accede to any measure so highly favorable to that end as the new constitution will be, renders it at least probable that it will be adopted by a large majority of the states—which done, the proposing an amendment will be nothing less than a request to those states to undo and reconsider what they have already finally determined on;—and obstinately to persist in such amendments when that shall be the case, will be nothing less than in other words to withdraw ourselves from a connexion with them.

Though when we consider how numerous the objections as well as those who start them are, and how natural it is for all men to be attached to their own opinions, it will not be necessary to admit that nine states shall have adopted it to render an attempt to amend it the same with a design to destroy the UNION.

The many local interests which will rise up in opposition to each other throughout the continent, not being naturally reconcileable, if set in motion at a time when there is no legal restraint to their operations, will necessarily form the states into parties which no future exertions can reunite.—When on the contrary if under the interference of a government whose existence will depend on the welfare of the whole, those necessary amendments may be made by sacrificing a small share of the interest of different parts, without endangering that last and deepest interest of the whole—the existence of the UNION.

In securing to the states their different rights the larger received a considerable advantage over the smaller in the number of representatives they found themselves entitled to in Congress—and those smaller states could no way be prevailed on to join in a government which would only [have] been formed for the advantage of others and the destruction of themselves, had they not also been secured. To that end an equal representation has been allowed them in one of the branches of the legislature;—to deprive them of which, would be to take from them not only their only inducement to engage in the business as well as their only safety when united; but also the only possible means of bringing them up to a level with those parts with which their respectability was to join in making up the dignity of the whole.

Yet such is the anxiety of some to bring about a separation of the states that while they feign the most pious wish to perfect this new work, they plot its destruction by proposing amendments, the success of which they know must inevitably carry along with them the consequences they wish. For when any of the states shall be deprived of the only inducement they can have to unite themselves with, and what is worse, the only thing that can secure them from being swallowed up by the more important interests of the rest, how long must it be expected they will continue in that situation?—And to force others to withdraw from the UNION will no way differ from doing it ourselves, except that those who contrive this artful expedient to separate the states, will secretly effect the blackest design while they publicly wear the fairest face the most sincere love of their country could put on.

Nor would there be wanting pretences still more plausible than the representation in the senate to effect the dissolution of the UNION by pretending amendments. Objections which are called general, and really appear so at first, would be started and urged with a degree of plausibility that might impose on some of the best friends to the UNION.

It is well known that several of the states on the continent have never made any formal declaration of their rights. Well aware of the impossibility of enumerating all those blessings to which by nature they were entitled, and highly sensible of the danger there was intrusting to their recollection of them (knowing that when once they attempted to set to them legal bounds, what ever should by chance be left out, was of course given up) some of the states more prudently thought fit to enumerate on the other hand what should be the powers of their government, when of course what ever was omited on that side, remained as their natural and inviolable rights on the other. And but few states in the world have deemed it safe to do otherwise.

England itself until the reign of King John remained in this situation, when that foundation of the present British constitution, the Magna Charta of the land, made its appearance, under whose benign influence the plant of liberty was expected to grow and flourish. But unfortunately that bright luminary in the British constitution dawned but with a glimmering ray on this quarter of the world from its first settlement. America, though secured under the constitution of England, from time to time felt itself oppressed by its laws—till at length it was found, but little also than mercy, instead of our own rights, was left us in that government to depend on for safety— "when enquiring into the first principles of society, we became convinced that power, when its object was not the good of those who were subject to it, was nothing more than the right of the strongest, and might be repressed by the exertion of a similar right." And growing more and more restless the attempt soon followed the discovery.

The whole of the states at once becoming united, in what was considered the common cause of all, a general agitation took place, which increased as it extended itself across the continent "like the rolling waves of an extensive sea." When all the world, though interested in the event, stood motionless at first with astonishment at the attempt. Yet relying on the justness of their cause, while destitute of every resource, the thirteen states of America thus united and impressed with a true sense of the origin of power, most piously resolved to maintain those natural rights, the relinquishment of which to aggrandise any power on earth, would only be an insult on that divine authority from whence they sprung.

And to forge indiscriminately now those states into a declaration of their rights, who may think it still unsafe to rely on a bare recital of them, particularly in a general government which at its commencement must involve its authors in too great a variety of difficulties and cares, to be sufficiently mindful of every natural right necessary to be secured to each particular state, would be as unjust and inconsistent with our former pretentions, as its natural consequence—the separation of the states—would be contrary to that policy which gave us success.

But why need I labour thus to prove what is in itself so definitely clear?—The constitution itself admits of no amendments till put in force. To adopt it or reject it is all we have to do—The one I confess is the most ardent wish of my heart—though the other were to entitle me to the credit of prophesy; from whose foresight I should only most earnestly recommend to you to consider well before the approaching election whether a total dissolution of the UNION is desirable; for that I apprehend to be the only amendment which can be made in the new plan of government by our state convention.

V

To the GOOD PEOPLE *of* Virginia, *on the new* FŒDERAL CONSTITUTION, *by an old* STATE SOLDIER, *in answer to the objections.*

It is now my intention to examine into that class of objections in which it is said our interests are concerned; and in doing that I shall have answered such of the objections to the new constitution as appear worthy of notice.

If a general union be necessary for the preservation of the continent at large, whatever tends to that object most, comes nearest the interest of every particular part. Whence it follows that the interest of any individual state cannot be endangered by that policy which promotes the general welfare of the whole; but on the contrary must be strengthened with that of the rest, or else it never can be the interest of the union which is promoted.

It would only seem necessary therefore to prove that this constitution will promote the interest of the whole continent to shew its salutary effects on every particular state—yet, before I claim the advantage which so just a position in itself would give, I shall (in disseminating the seeds of refutation in other points) endeavor to supplant all doubts on that head, by means also, more local and particular. And in order the more clearly to do that, I shall endeavor to examine into the objections themselves;—the first of which, is that, which relates to the expensiveness of the plan;—and the next, a dread of the superiority of the northern states over the southern in Congress:—which together, acting in such diametrical contradiction to each other, render it necessary, to consider the two as nearly together as possible, thereby to prove the futility of both. The last of which however, so far as it respects the present instant, may perhaps hold good—and has indeed been admitted in a former paper,[4] and ought now to serve as a hint to shew the impropriety of attempting to amend the constitution at a time, when those states, whose influence we dread, will have it in their power to shape it as they please. But when considered as an objection to a government which is to last for many ages over a country like this, must appear not only trifling, but even applicable to the very reverse of things. For let us but consider this objection as connected with our geographical knowledge of America, and we shall find its weight preponderating in favor of the southern scale in the end.

The northern states, in comparison, contracted in their limits and already replete with inhabitants, even at this time feel the extent of their future influence in the union—whilst those to the south, though rich and extensive, yet thinly inhabited, look forward to a future population which presages a superiority unknown at present.

4. See State Soldier, *Friends,* 119–28.

But considering this constitution even as unconnected with future events, how contradictory is this objection in itself!—"This government is to promote the interest of the northern states," and at the same time hold out the destruction of the rest on whose approbation, as well as their own, its adoption and continuance depend. Whence alone we might infer that no such material objection could exist in reality should the constitution take place;—for as nothing less than the approbation of a large majority of the states can procure the adoption of this government, and nothing else than its being the interest of that majority could obtain such an approbation, so even the adoption of it, in itself, will imply its being the interest of more than seven of the northern states, since we know it will require more than the consent of that number to set it in motion. And thus too from the same mode of reasoning it may be reduced to a certainty that no such influence could be exerted even should it be found to exist;—for as the same causes which establishes must remain to support it, nothing need be apprehended from an influence, the very exercise of which would be a means of destroying the advantage itself, as nothing could induce so considerable a part of the continent to continue a connection which was to prove the destruction of themselves.

But let us now examine how this objection will square with that of the expensiveness of the plan. Between which, while we admit the propriety of the one, we shall destroy the force of the other. For if nothing but a separation of the states can cure the baneful influence of one part of the continent over the other, while that influence arises from a superiority of a number in that particular part, so nothing but a confederation of the whole can lessen the expence of the weakest part; and this I will prove from the two objections themselves, together with a short contrast on that head between a general confederation and two or more separate ones.

The advantages to be derived from one general government, are, that the necessary disbursements of state will be drawn from the whole continent and proportioned to the strength of each state—whereas under separate confederacies, though the expenditures of each would be nearly as great as the whole when united into one, they would be drawn from the few states within the separate union to which they belonged without regard to any inequality between them and the other states on the continent; which would make the expences of government, even were they no greater to the whole under one form than another, heavier to some, and lighter to others, than under one general head. And the difference, according to one of the foregoing objections itself, would unavoidably operate against the southern states;— for as it is on account of the disproportion of strength which the southern states hold to the northern that this constitution is in one instance objected to, so it will necessarily follow that the states which form southern confederacies will have most to pay, as those confederacies will be weakest when formed; and being weakest, and yet having the same to pay for their own support, will leave those states which form them with more to contribute than others forming stronger unions; as the fewer there are to make up the same sum at any time, so much the more must be contributed by each.

And thus this objection to the expensiveness of the plan, and that to the superior influence of the northern states, at present, operate in pointed contradiction to each other, and when taken together only serve to prove the advantages of this constitution to the southern states in particular.

But having already denied that the present superiority of the northern states will remain a lasting objection to a general Union, I shall endeavor to prove the particular advantages which some of the southern states will receive from this plan, on the score of œconomy, from another consideration.

From the establishment of the present confederation until this day the whole of the continental expences have been defrayed by little more than seven states, of which Virginia is one. I say by seven states because four only having complied fully with the requisitions of Congress, seven others having furnished about half their quotas, and the rest nothing at all, leaves still upwards of five proportions unpaid. So that we who have heretofore been making up the deficiencies of others, have little reason to complain of the expensiveness of a plan, the very first object of which was to force an equal compliance from all the states, as well to discharge our foreign as domestic debts; the first of which if left to be collected by coercion and distraint might fall equally severe on the punctual and delinquent.

Thus even in every local point of view this constitution is calculated to promote the interest of those very states which it has been supposed it would injure; and when examined into as distributing individual benefit by rendering general good, will be found equally interesting and desirable. And that being the general position laid down in the begining of this paper, I shall now advance to support it, and at once attack the main body of the enemy in their last retreat and strong hold,—which is, in the objection that makes the northern states the monopolisers of the carrying business.

Were I an East-Indian, a Turk, or an *Englishman,* I should in all probability find the same fault with this constitution; but as a Virginian and *a friend to my country,* I cannot object to the loss of an advantage which we never possessed, merely because it may be taken out of the hands of foreigners and put into those of our friends and neighbours; to enrich whom would be to strengthen ourselves.

Though even were there sacrifices to be made on that head by one state to another, the advantages arising from them would, on another principle, be felt in common by them all. For from the efforts necessary to give motion to a confederated republic, the different states, like the several parts of a complicated machine, must necessarily play into each other. Their sacrifices and advantages must be mutual and just;—for as there are certain proportions in mechanics necessary to form the powers of operation, so is there an equilibrium in government between the interests of its several parts necessary to give it force. That whilst a general operation remains, there must be felt a mutual assistance throughout the parts. And thus all those different advantages would revolve to each in turn, which under separate confederacies would centre where they first inclined.

But then, the carrying business is not one of the cases in which concessions are necessary to be made from one state to another;—for even were it to be entirely yielded into the hands of the northern states, there could be no great loss to the southern in consequence of the surrender, as would be proved by the very act of giving it up: for nothing but its being more the interest of the southern states to cultivate the commodities intended for exportation, than to carry them to market, could make them yield that business to the northern states, when they possessed every natural advantage in as great a degree as themselves for carrying it on. Blessed with a soil productive of every ingredient necessary for ship building; and environed, as well as interspersed with as advantageous bays and rivers as nature can bestow, Virginia might vie with any quarter of the globe in the profits of a maritime exertion—a competition in which, would not only redound to the dignity and safety, but also the interests of all America, as it would be the means of rearing a navy on the continent, as well as fixing all the profits arising *from* that business among ourselves, which now centre in foreign bottoms. And such a competition would naturally arise from what is now supposed will be the consequence of throwing such a business into the hands of the northern states. For as the only mischief that could arise from such a monopoly would be their having it in their power to raise the freightage, so the very evil itself would tend to produce the happiest of all effects. The different states compelled by their opposite interests, on such an occasion, would naturally struggle against each other, whereby they would render the most important of all public services to the continent at large, while they would be establishing a proper balance between the landed and mercantile interests of the different states.

In fine, there is no one instance in which the interest of an individual state can be injured by the promotion of that of the whole; but on the contrary must be particularly advanced. And the interests of every country being so inseparable from the dignity, the honor, and the credit of it, consequently renders that government most its immediate advantage which is best calculated to promote all those. Whence it only remains to enquire now how far the plan under consideration advances that way, to determine its real effects on the interests of the states.

Under a general and efficient government the powers of the different states, drawn to a single focus, would no longer be left to scatter their feeble rays in vain across the continent, but penetrating to the very bottom of the state authorities would bring forth that which would restore life to the decaying plant of PUBLIC FAITH; and with that would spring both private confidence and individual wealth:—for as it is by the extent of credit alone that the true value of property can be ascertained, so is it by honesty only that real wealth can exist. And to know that this government will promote honesty, it only remains to be told, that under it, no interference with private contracts in future can take place, as the states are "prohibited from passing any law impairing the obligation of contracts;" nor can the value of any debt be lessened, as at present by an emission of any kind of money of less value than that in which it was contracted, since the states are "prohibited making any thing but gold and silver coin a tender in payment of debts;" neither can our credit as a nation *hereafter* be injured in the eyes of the world by the interference of the individual states in any foreign treaty, as the sole right of declaring war or making peace, "unless when actually invaded," will be in the continental head.

And thus the day begins to dawn in America when all those pernicious authorities, now exercised in the different states, shall be lost in the general lustre of the whole government, whence PUBLIC JUSTICE in its usual splendor, firmly fixed, shall mark the NEW FEDERAL CONSTITU-TION as the rising SUN of the western world.

George Washington

Extract of Letter to Charles Carter

14 December 1787

———

Throughout the debate over the proposed Constitution, George Washington did not make public statements endorsing the document. In private correspondence, however, Washington added his own voice to the Federalist cause. The extract of the letter reprinted here is one such example. Written to Charles Carter (1733–96), a planter in Stafford County, Virginia, the letter discusses farming matters at some length and concludes with a brief opinion on the proposed Constitution.

The letter was first published on 27 December in the *Virginia Herald* under the heading, "Extract of a letter of a late date from a member of the Fœderal Convention, to his friend in this town." The letter was printed again on 3 January in the *Pennsylvania Mercury* and two days earlier in the *Maryland Journal* under the heading "*from the illustrious President of the late Federal Convention.*" By 27 March, Washington's letter was reprinted in the January issue of *American Museum* and in forty-nine newspapers.

Washington did not object to having his opinion on the Constitution made public but told Carter in a letter of 12 January that had he known, he would have used "less exceptional language." In the end, although both Carter and Washington were upset about the letter's publication, James Madison, who had wanted Washington to make his views known on the document, told Washington in a letter of 20 February that the letter's publication "may have been of service."

———

I thank you for your kind Congratulation on my safe Return from the Convention, and am pleased that the Proceedings of it have met your Approbation.—My *decided* Opinion of the Matter is, that there is *no Alternative* between the *Adoption* of it and *Anarchy.* If one State (however important it may conceive itself to be) or a Minority of them, should suppose that they can dictate a Constitution to the Union (unless they have the Power of applying the *ultima Ratio* to good Effect) they will find themselves deceived. All the Opposition to it that I have yet seen, is, I must confess, addressed more to the Passions than to the Reason; and *clear I am,* if another Federal Convention is attempted, that the Sentiments of the Members will be *more* discordant or *less* accommodating than the last. In fine, that they will agree upon no general Plan. General Government is now *suspended by a Thread,* I might go further, and say it is *really at an End,* and what will be the Consequence of a fruitless Attempt to amend the one which is offered, before it is tried, or of the Delay from the Attempt, does not in my Judgment need the *Gift of Prophesy to predict.*

"I am not a blind Admirer (for I saw the Imperfections) of the Constitution I aided in the Birth of, before it was handed to the Public; but I am fully persuaded it is the *best that can be obtained at this Time,* that it is free from many of the Imperfections with which it is charged, and that *it* or *Disunion* is before us to choose from. If the first is our Election, when the Defects of it are experienced, a constitutional Door is opened for Amendments, and may be adopted in a peaceable Manner, without Tumult or Disorder.

"A Citizen of New York"
[John Jay]

Address

New York, printed by Samuel and John Loudon, 1788

———•———

John Jay, appointed first Chief Justice of the Supreme Court under the new Constitution, had long been actively involved in public affairs by the time of the struggle over the Constitution. His expertise in foreign affairs was called upon when he collaborated with Alexander Hamilton and James Madison in writing *The Federalist;* due to illness, however, he contributed only five essays. He also served as a member of the New York ratifying convention.

———•———

Friends and Fellow Citizens: There are times and seasons, when *general evils* spread general alarm and uneasiness, and yet arise from causes too complicated, and too little understood by many, to produce an unanimity of opinions respecting their remedies. Hence it is, that on such occasions, the conflict of arguments too often excites a conflict of passions, and introduces a degree of discord and animosity, which, by agitating the public mind dispose it to precipitation and extravagance. They who on the ocean have been unexpectedly enveloped with tempests, or suddenly entangled among rocks and shoals, know the value of that serene, self-possession and presence of mind, to which in such cases they owed their preservation; nor will the heroes who have given us victory and peace, hesitate to acknowledge that we are as much indebted for those blessings to the calm prevision, and cool intrepidity which planned and conducted our military measures, as to the glowing animation with which they were executed.

While reason retains her rule, while men are as ready to receive as to give advice, and as willing to be convinced themselves, as to convince others, there are few political evils from which a free and enlightened people cannot deliver themselves. It is unquestionably true, that the great body of the people love their country, and wish it prosperity; and this observation is particularly applicable to the people of a *free* country, for they have more and stronger reasons for loving it than others. It is not therefore to vicious motives that the unhappy divisions which sometimes prevail among them are to be imputed; the people at large always mean well, and although they may on certain occasions be misled by the counsels, or injured by the efforts of the few who expect more advantage from the wreck, than from the preservation of national prosperity, yet the motives of these few, are by no means to be confounded with those of the community in general.

That such seeds of discord and danger have been disseminated and begin to take root in America, as unless eradicated will soon poison our gardens and our fields, is a truth much to be lamented; and the more so, as their growth rapidly increases, while we are wasting the season in honestly but imprudently disputing, not whether they shall be pulled up, but by whom, in what manner, and with what instruments, the work shall be done.

When the king of Great Britain, misguided by men who did not merit his confidence, asserted the unjust claim of binding us in all cases whatsoever, and prepared to obtain our submission by force, the object which engrossed our attention, however important, was nevertheless plain and simple, "What shall we do?" was the question—the people answered, let us unite our counsels and our arms. They sent Delegates to Congress, and soldiers to the field. Confiding in the probity and wisdom of Congress, they received their recommendations as if they had been laws; and that ready acquiesence in their advice enabled those patriots to save their country. Then there was little leisure or disposition for controversy respecting the expediency of measures—hostile fleets soon filled our ports, and hostile armies spread desolation on our shores. Union was then considered as the most essential of human means and we almost worshipped it with as much fervor, as pagans in distress formerly implored the protection of their tutelar deities. That union was the child of wisdom—heaven blessed it, and it wrought out our political salvation.

That glorious war was succeeded by an advantageous peace. When danger disappeared, ease, tranquility, and a sense of security loosened the bands of union; and Congress and soldiers and good faith depreciated with their apparent importance. Recommendations lost their influence, and requisitions were rendered nugatory, not by their want of propriety, but by their want of power. The spirit of private gain expelled the spirit of public good, and men became more intent on the means of enriching and aggrandizing themselves, than of enriching and aggrandizing their country. Hence the war-worn veteran, whose reward for toils and wounds existed in written promises, found Congress without the means, and too many of the States without the disposition, to do him justice. Hard necessity compelled him, and others under similar circumstances, to sell their honest claims on the public for a little bread; and thus unmerited misfortunes and patriotic distresses became articles of speculation and commerce.

These and many other evils, too well known to require enumeration, imperceptibly stole in upon us, and acquired an unhappy influence on our public affairs. But such evils, like the worst of weeds, will naturally spring up in so rich a soil; and a good Government is as necessary to subdue the one, as an attentive gardner or husbandman is to destroy the other—Even the garden of Paradise required to be dressed, and while men continue to be constantly impelled to error and to wrong by innumerable circumstances and temptations, so long will society experience the unceasing necessity of government.[1]

It is a pity that the expectations which actuated the authors of the existing confederation, neither have nor can be realized:—accustomed to see and admire the glorious spirit which moved all ranks of people in the most gloomy moments of the war, observing their steadfast attachment to Union, and the wisdom they so often manifested both in choosing and confiding in their rulers, those gentlemen were led to flatter themselves that the people of America only required to know what ought to be done, to do it. This amiable mistake induced them to institute a national government in such a manner, as though very fit to give advice, was yet destitute of power, and so constructed as to be very unfit to be trusted with it. They seem not to

---

1. "If men were angels," Publius argues in *The Federalist,* No. 51, "no government would be necessary."

have been sensible that mere advice is a sad substitute for laws; nor to have recollected that the advice even of the allwise and best of Beings, has been always disregarded by a great majority of all the men that ever lived.

Experience is a severe preceptor, but it teaches useful truths, and however harsh, is always honest—Be calm and dispassionate, and listen to what it tells us.

Prior to the revolution we had little occasion to inquire or know much about national affairs, for although they existed and were managed, yet they were managed *for* us, but not *by* us. Intent on our domestic concerns, our internal legislative business, our agriculture, and our buying and selling, we were seldom anxious about what passed or was doing in foreign Courts. As we had nothing to do with that department of policy, so the affairs of it were not detailed to us, and we took as little pains to inform ourselves, as others did to inform us of them. War, and peace, alliances, and treaties, and commerce, and navigation, were conducted and regulated without our advice or controul. While we had liberty and justice, and in security enjoyed the fruits of our "vine and fig tree," we were in general too content and too much occupied, to be at the trouble of investigating the various political combinations in this department, or to examine and perceive how exceedingly important they often were to the advancement and protection of our prosperity. This habit and turn of thinking affords one reason why so much more care was taken, and so much more wisdom displayed, in forming our State Governments, than in forming our Federal or national one.

By the Confederation as it now stands, the direction of general and national affairs is committed to a single body of men, viz. the Congress. They may make war, but are not empowered to raise men or money to carry it on. They may make peace, but without power to see the terms of it observed—They may form alliances, but without ability to comply with the stipulations on their part—They may enter into treaties of commerce, but without power to enforce them at home or abroad—They may borrow money, but without having the means of repayment—They may partly regulate commerce, but without authority to execute their ordinances— They may appoint ministers and other officers of trust, but without power to try or punish them for misdemeanors—They may resolve, but cannot execute either with dispatch or with secrecy—In short, they may consult, and deliberate, and recommend, and make requisitions, and they who please, may regard them.

From this new and wonderful system of Government, it has come to pass, that almost every national object of every kind, is at this day unprovided for; and other nations taking the advantage of its imbecility, are daily multiplying commercial restraints upon us. Our fur trade is gone to Canada, and British garrisons keep the keys of it. Our shipyards have almost ceased to disturb the repose of the neighborhood by the noise of the axe and hammer; and while foreign flags fly triumphantly above our highest houses, the American Stars seldom do more than shed a few feeble rays about the humble masts of river sloops and coasting schooners. The greater part of our hardy seamen, are plowing the ocean in foreign pay; and not a few of our ingenious shipwrights are now building vessels on alien shores. Although our increasing agriculture and industry extend and multiply our productions, yet they constantly diminish in value; and although we permit all nations to fill our country with their merchandises, yet their best markets are shut against us. Is there an English, or a French, or a Spanish island or port in the West-Indies, to which an American vessel can carry a cargo of flour for sale? Not one. The Algerines exclude us from the Mediterranean, and adjacent countries; and we are neither able to purchase, nor to command the free use of those seas. Can our little towns or larger cities consume the immense productions of our fertile country? or will they without trade be able to pay a good price for the proportion which they do consume? The last season gave a very unequivocal answer to these questions—What numbers of fine cattle have returned from this city to the country for want of buyers? What great quantities of salted and other provisions still lie useless in the stores? To how much below the former price, is our corn, and wheat and flour and lumber rapidly falling? Our debts remain undiminished, and the interest on them accumulating—our credit abroad is nearly extinguished, and at home unrestored—they who had money have sent it beyond the reach of our laws, and scarcely any man can borrow of his neighbor. Nay, does not experience also tell us, that it is as difficult to pay as to borrow? That even our houses and lands cannot command money—that law suits and usurious contracts abound—that our farms sell on executions for less than half their value, and that distress in various forms, and in various ways, is approaching fast to the doors of our best citizens.

These things have been gradually coming upon us ever since the peace— they have been perceived and proclaimed, but the universal rage and pursuit of private gain conspired with other causes, to prevent any proper efforts being made to meliorate our condition by due attention to our national affairs, until the late Convention was convened for that purpose. From the result of their deliberations, the States expected to derive much good, and should they be disappointed, it will probably be not less their misfortune than their fault. That Convention was in general composed of excellent and tried men—men who had become conspicuous for their wisdom and public services, and whose names and characters will be venerated by posterity. Generous and candid minds cannot perceive without pain, the illiberal manner in which some have taken the liberty to treat them; nor forbear to impute it to impure and improper motives, zeal for public good, like zeal for religion, may sometimes carry men beyond the bounds of reason, but it is not conceivable, that on this occasion, it should find means so to inebriate any *candid* American, as to make him forget what he owed to truth and to decency, or induce him either to believe or to say, that the almost unanimous advice of the Convention, proceeded from a wicked combination and conspiracy against the liberties of their country. This is not the temper with which we should receive and consider their recommendations, nor the treatment that would be worthy either of us or them. Let us continue careful therefore that facts do not warrant historians to tell future generations, that envy, malice and uncharitableness pursued our patriotic benefactors to their graves, and that not even pre-eminence in virtue, nor lives devoted to the public, could shield them from obloquy and detraction. On the contrary, let our bosoms always retain a sufficient degree of honest indignation to disappoint and discourage those who expect our thanks or applause for calumniating our most faithful and meritorious friends.

The Convention concurred in opinion with the people, that a national government, *competent to every national object,* was indispensibly necessary; and it was as plain to them, as it now is to all America, that the present confederation does not provide for such a government. These points being agreed, they proceeded to consider how and in what manner such a government could be formed, as on the one hand, should be sufficiently energetic to raise us from our prostrate and distressed situation, and on the other be perfectly consistent with the liberties of the people of every State. Like men to whom the experience of other ages and countries had taught wisdom, they not only determined that it should be erected by, and depend on the people; but remembering the many instances in which governments vested solely in one man, or one body of men, had degenerated into tyrannies, they judged it most prudent that the three great branches of power should be committed to different hands, and therefore that the executive should be separated from the legislative, and the judicial from both. Thus far the propriety of their work is easily seen and understood, and therefore is thus far *almost* universally approved—for no one man or thing under the sun ever yet pleased every body.

The next question was, what particular powers should be given to these three branches? Here the different views and interests of the different states, as well as the different abstract opinions of their members on such points, interposed many difficulties. Here the business became complicated, and presented a wide field for investigation; too wide for every eye to take a quick and comprehensive view of it.

It is said that "in a multitude of counsellors there is safety," because in the first place, there is greater security for probity; and in the next, if every member cast in only his mite of information and argument, their joint stock of both will thereby become greater than the stock possessed by any one single man out of doors. Gentlemen out of doors therefore should not be hasty in condemning a system, which probably rests on more good reasons than they are aware of, especially when formed under such advantages, and recommended by so many men of distinguished worth and abilities.

The difficulties before mentioned occupied the Convention a long time and it was not without mutual concessions that they were at last surmounted. These concessions serve to explain to us the reason why some parts of the system please in some states, which displease in others; and why many of the objections which have been made to it, are so contradictory and inconsistent with one another. It does great credit to the temper and talents of the Convention, that they were able so to reconcile the different views and interests of the different States, and the clashing opinions of their members as to unite with such singular and almost perfect unanimity in any plan whatever, on a subject so intricate and perplexed. It shews that it must have been thoroughly discussed and understood; and probably if the community at large had the same lights and reasons before them, they would, if equally candid and uninfluenced, be equally unanimous.

It would be arduous, and indeed impossible, to comprise within the limits of this address, a full discussion of every part of the plan. Such a task would require a volume, and few men have leisure or inclination to read volumes on any subject. The objections made to it are almost without number, and many of them without reason—some of them are real and honest, and others merely ostensible. There are friends to Union and a national Government who have serious doubts, who wish to be informed, and to be convinced; and there are others who, neither wishing for union, nor any national Government at all, will oppose and object to any plan that can be contrived.

We are told, among other strange things, that the liberty of the press is left insecure by the proposed Constitution, and yet that Constitution says neither more nor less about it, than the Constitution of the State of New York does. We are told that it deprives us of trial by jury, whereas the fact is, that it expressly secures it in certain cases, and takes it away in none—it is absurd to construe the silence of this, or of our own constitution, relative to a great number of our rights, into a total extinction of them—silence and blank paper neither grant nor take away anything. Complaints are also made that the proposed constitution is not accompanied by a bill of rights; and yet they who would make these complaints, know and are content that no bill of rights accompanied the Constitution of this State. In days and countries, where Monarchs and their subjects were frequently disputing about prerogative and privileges, the latter often found it necessary, as it were to run out the line between them, and oblige the former to admit by solemn acts, called bills of rights, that certain enumerated rights belonged to the people, and were not comprehended in the royal prerogative. But thank God we have no such disputes—we have no Monarchs to contend with, or demand admission from—the proposed Government is to be the government of the people—all its officers are to be their officers, and to exercise no rights but such as the people commit to them. The Constitution only serves to point out that part of the people's business, which they think proper by it to refer to the management of the persons therein designated—those persons are to receive that business to manage, not for themselves and as their own, but as agents and overseers for the people to whom they are constantly responsible, and by whom only they are to be appointed.

But the design of this address is not to investigate the merits of the plan, nor of the objections to it. They who seriously contemplate the present state of our affairs will be convinced that other considerations of at least equal importance demand their attention. Let it be admitted that this plan, like everything else devised by man, has its imperfections: That it does not please every body is certain and there is little reason to expect one that will. It is a question of great moment to you, whether the probability of your being able seasonably to obtain a better, is such as to render it prudent and advisable to reject this, and run the risque. Candidly to consider this question is the design of this address.

As the importance of this question must be obvious to every man, whatever his private opinions respecting it may be, it becomes us all to treat it in that calm and temperate manner, which a subject so deeply interesting to the future welfare of our country and prosperity requires. Let us therefore as much as possible repress and compose that irritation in our minds, which too warm disputes about it may have excited. Let us endeavour to forget that this or that man, is on this or that side; and that we ourselves, perhaps without sufficient reflection, have classed ourselves with one or the other party. Let us remember that this is not a matter to be regarded as a matter that only touches our local parties, but as one so great, so general, and so extensive in its future consequences to America, that for our deciding upon it according to the best of our unbiassed judgment, we must be highly responsible both here and hereafter.

The question now before us now naturally leads to *three* enquiries:

1. Whether it is probable that a better plan can be obtained?

2. Whether, if attainable, it is likely to be in season?

3. What would be our situation, if after rejecting this, all our efforts to obtain a better should prove fruitless?

The men, who formed this plan are Americans, who had long deserved and enjoyed our confidence, and who are as much interested in having a good government as any of us are, or can be. They were appointed to that business at a time when the States had become very sensible of the derangement of our national affairs, and of the impossibility of retrieving them under the existing Confederation. Although well persuaded that nothing but a good national government could oppose and divert the tide of evils that was flowing in upon us, yet those gentlemen met in Convention with minds perfectly unprejudiced in favour of any particular plan. The minds of their Constituents were at that time equally unbiased, cool and dispassionate. All agreed in the necessity of doing something, but no one ventured to say decidedly what precisely ought to be done—opinions were then fluctuating and unfixed, and whatever might have been the wishes of a few individuals, yet while the Convention deliberated, the people remained in silent suspence. Neither wedded to favourite systems of their own, nor influenced by popular ones abroad, the members were more desirous to receive light from, than to impress their private sentiments on, one another. These circumstances naturally opened the door to that spirit of candour, of calm enquiry, of mutual accommodation, and mutual respect, which entered into the Convention with them, and regulated their debates and proceedings.

The impossibility of agreeing upon any plan that would exactly quadrate with the local policy and objects of every State, soon became evident; and they wisely thought it better mutually to concede, and accommodate, and in that way to fashion their system as much as possible by the circumstances and wishes of different States, than by pertinaciously adhering, each to his own ideas, oblige the Convention to rise without doing anything. They were sensible that obstacles arising from local circumstances, would not cease while those circumstances continued to exist; and so far as those circumstances depended on differences of climate, productions, and commerce, that no change was to be expected. They were likewise sensible that on a subject so comprehensive, and involving such a variety of points and questions, the most able, the most candid, and the most honest men will differ in opinion. The same proposition seldom strikes many minds exactly in the same point of light; different habits of thinking, different degrees and modes of education, different prejudices and opinions early formed and long entertained, conspire with a multitude of other circumstances, to produce among men a diversity and contrariety of opinions on questions of difficulty. Liberality therefore as well as prudence, induced them to treat each other's opinions with tenderness, to argue without asperity, and to endeavor to convince the judgment without hurting the feelings of each other. Although many weeks were passed in these discussions, some points remained, on which a unison of opinions could not be effected. Here again that same happy disposition to unite and conciliate, induced them to meet each other; and enabled them, by mutual concessions, finally to complete and agree to the plan they have recommended, and that too with a degree of unanimity which, considering the variety of discordant views and ideas, they had to reconcile, is really astonishing.

They tell us very honestly that this plan is the result of accommodation—they do not hold it up as the best of all possible ones, but only as the best which they could unite in, and agree to. If such men, appointed and meeting under such auspicious circumstances, and so sincerely disposed to conciliation, could go no further in their endeavors to please every State, and every body, what reason have we at present to expect any system that would give more general satisfaction?

Suppose this plan to be rejected, what measures would you propose for obtaining a better? Some will answer, let us appoint another Convention, and as everything has been said and written that can well be said and written on the subject, they will be better informed than the former one was, and consequently be better able to make and agree upon a more eligible one.

This reasoning is fair, and as far as it goes has weight; but it nevertheless takes one thing for granted, which appears very doubtful; for although the new Convention might have more information, and perhaps equal abilities, yet it does not from thence follow that they would be equally *disposed to agree*. The contrary of this position is the most probable. You must have observed that the same temper and equanimity which prevailed among the people on the former occasion, no longer exists. We have unhappily become divided into parties; and this important subject has been handled with such indiscreet and offensive acrimony, and with so many little unhandsome artifices and misrepresentations, that pernicious heats and animosities have been kindled, and spread their flames far and wide among us. When therefore it becomes a question who shall be deputed to the new Convention; we cannot flatter ourselves that the talents and integrity of the candidates will determine who shall be elected. Federal electors will vote for Fœderal deputies, and anti-Fœderal electors for anti-Fœderal ones. Nor will either party prefer the most moderate of their adherents, for as the most staunch and active partizans will be the most popular, so the men most willing and able to carry points, to oppose, and divide, and embarrass their opponents, will be chosen. A Convention formed at such a season, and of such men, would be but too exact an epitome of the great body that named them. The same party views, the same propensity to opposition, the same distrusts and jealousies, and the same unaccommodating spirit which prevail without, would be concentred and ferment with still greater violence within. Each deputy would recollect *who* sent him, and *why* he was sent; and be too apt to consider himself bound in honor, to contend and act vigorously under the standard of his party, and not hazard their displeasure by prefering compromise to victory. As vice does not sow the seeds of virtue, so neither does passion cultivate the fruits of reason. Suspicions and resentments create no disposition to conciliate, nor do they infuse a desire of making partial and personal objects bend to general union and the common good. The utmost efforts of that excellent disposition were necessary to enable the late Convention to perform their task; and although contrary causes sometimes operate similar effects, yet to expect that discord and animosity should produce the fruits of confidence and agreement, is to expect "grapes from thorns, and figs from thistles."

The States of Georgia, Delaware, Jersey, and Connecticut, have adopted the present plan with unexampled unanimity; they are content with it as it is, and consequently their deputies, being apprized of the sentiments of their Constituents, will be little inclined to make alterations, and cannot be otherwise than averse to changes which they have no reason to think would be agreeable to their people—some other States, tho' less unanimous, have nevertheless adopted it by very respectable majorities; and for reasons so evidently cogent, that even the minority in one of them, have nobly

pledged themselves for its promotion and support. From these circumstances, the new Convention would derive and experience difficulties unknown to the former. Nor are these the only additional difficulties they
would have to encounter. Few are ignorant that there has lately sprung up
a sect of politicians who teach and profess to believe that the extent of our
nation is too great for the superintendance of one national Government,
and on that principle argue that it ought to be divided into two or three.
This doctrine, however mischievous in its tendency and consequences, has
its advocates; and, should any of them be sent to the Convention, it will
naturally be their policy rather to cherish than to prevent divisions; for well
knowing that the institution of any national Government, would blast their
favourite system, no measures that lead to it can meet with their aid or approbation.

Nor can we be certain whether or not any and what foreign influence
would, on such an occasion, be indirectly exerted, nor for what purposes—
delicacy forbids an ample discussion of this question. Thus much may be
said, without error or offence, viz. That such foreign nations as desire the
prosperity of America, and would rejoice to see her become great and powerful, under the auspices of a Government wisely calculated to extend her
commerce, to encourage her navigation and marine, and to direct the whole
weight of her power and resources as her interest and honour may require,
will doubtless be friendly to the Union of the States, and to the establishment
of a Government able to perpetuate, protect and dignify it. Such other foreign nations, if any such there be, who, jealous of our growing importance,
and fearful that our commerce and navigation should impair their own—
who behold our rapid population with regret, and apprehend that the enterprising spirit of our people, when seconded by power and probability
of success, may be directed to objects not consistent with their policy or
interests, cannot fail to wish that we may continue a weak and a divided
people.

These considerations merit much attention, and candid men will judge
how far they render it probable that a new Convention would be able either
to agree in a better plan, or with tolerable unanimity, in any plan at all.
Any plan forcibly carried by a slender majority, must expect numerous

opponents among the people, who, especially in their present temper, would be more inclined to reject than adopt any system so made and carried. We should in such case again see the press teeming with publications for and against it; for as the minority would take pains to justify their dissent, so would the majority be industrious to display the wisdom of their proceedings. Hence new divisions, new parties, and new distractions would ensue, and no one can foresee or conjecture when or how they would terminate.

Let those who are sanguine in their expectations of a better plan from a new Convention, also reflect on the delays and risque to which it would expose us. Let them consider whether we ought, by continuing much longer in our present humiliated condition, to give other nations further time to perfect their restrictive systems of commerce, to reconcile their own people to them, and to fence and guard and strengthen them by all those regulations and contrivances in which a jealous policy is ever fruitful. Let them consider whether we ought to give further opportunities to discord to alienate the hearts of our citizens from one another, and thereby encourage new Cromwells to bold exploits. Are we certain that our foreign creditors will continue patient, and ready to proportion their forbearance to our delays? Are we sure that our distresses, dissentions and weakness will neither invite hostility nor insult? If they should, how ill prepared shall we be for defence! without Union, without Government, without money, and without credit!

It seems necessary to remind you, that some time must yet elapse, before all the States will have decided on the present plan. If they reject it, some time must also pass before the measure of a new Convention, can be brought about and generally agreed to. A further space of time will then be requisite to elect their deputies, and send them on to Convention. What time they may expend when met, cannot be divined, and it is equally uncertain how much time the several States may take to deliberate and decide on any plan they may recommend—if adopted, still a further space of time will be necessary to organize and set it in motion:—In the mean time our affairs are daily going on from bad to worse, and it is not rash to say that our distresses are accumulating like compound interest.

But if for the reasons already mentioned, and others that we cannot now perceive, the new Convention, instead of producing a better plan, should give us only a history of their disputes, or should offer us one still less pleasing than the present, where should we be then? The old Confederation has done its best, and cannot help us; and is now so relaxed and feeble, that in all probability it would not survive so violent a shock. Then "to your tents Oh Israel!" would be the word. Then every band of union would be severed. Then every State would be a little nation, jealous of its neighbors, and anxious to strengthen itself by foreign alliances, against its former friends. Then farewell to fraternal affection, unsuspecting intercourse; and mutual participation in commerce, navigation and citizenship. Then would arise mutual restrictions and fears, mutual garrisons,—and standing armies, and all those dreadful evils which for so many ages plagued England, Scotland, Wales, and Ireland, while they continued disunited, and were played off against each other.

Consider my fellow citizens what you are about, before it is too late—consider what in such an event would be your particular case. You know the geography of your State, and the consequences of your local position. Jersey and Connecticut, to whom your impost laws have been unkind—Jersey and Connecticut, who have adopted the present plan, and expect much good from it—will impute its miscarriage and all the consequent evils to you. They now consider your opposition as dictated more by your fondness for your impost, than for those rights to which they have never been behind you in attachment. They cannot, they will not love you—they border upon you, and are your neighbors; but you will soon cease to regard their neighborhood as a blessing. You have but one port and outlet to your commerce, and how you are to keep that outlet free and uninterrupted, merits consideration.—What advantage Vermont in combination with others, might take of you, may easily be conjectured; nor will you be at a loss to perceive how much reason the people of Long Island, whom you cannot protect, have to deprecate being constantly exposed to the depredations of every invader.

These are short hints—they ought not to be more developed—you can easily in your own mind dilate and trace them through all their relative circumstances and connections.—Pause then for a moment, and reflect whether the matters you are disputing about, are of sufficient moment to justify your running such extravagant risques. Reflect that the present plan comes recommended to you by men and fellow citizens who have given you the highest proofs that men can give, of their justice, their love for liberty and their country, of their prudence, of their application, and of their talents. They tell you it is the best that they could form; and that in their opinion, it is necessary to redeem you from those calamities which already begin to be heavy upon us all. You find that not only those men, but others of similar characters, and of whom you have also had very ample experience, advise you to adopt it. You find that whole States concur in the sentiment, and among them are your next neighbors; both whom have shed much blood in the cause of liberty, and have manifested as strong and constant a predilection for a free Republican Government as any State in the Union, and perhaps in the world. They perceive not those latent mischiefs in it, with which some double-sighted politicians endeavor to alarm you. You cannot but be sensible that this plan or constitution will always be in the hands and power of the people, and that if on experiment, it should be found defective or incompetent, they may either remedy its defects, or substitute another in its room. The objectionable parts of it are certainly very questionable, for otherwise there would not be such a contrariety of opinions about them. Experience will better determine such questions than theoretical arguments, and so far as the danger of abuses is urged against the institution of a Government, remember that a power to do good, always involves a power to do harm. We must in the business of Government as well as in all other business, have some degree of confidence, as well as a great degree of caution. Who on a sick bed would refuse medicines from a physician, merely because it is as much in his power to administer deadly poisons, as salutary remedies.

You cannot be certain, that by rejecting the proposed plan you would not place yourself in a very awkward situation. Suppose nine States should nevertheless adopt it, would you not in that case be obliged either to separate from the Union, or rescind your dissent? The first would not be eligible, nor could the latter be pleasant—A mere hint is sufficient on this topic—You cannot but be aware of the consequences.

Consider then, how weighty and how many considerations advise and persuade the people of America to remain in the safe and easy path of Union: to continue to move and act as they hitherto have done, as a *band of brothers;* to have confidence in themselves and in one another; and since all cannot see with the same eyes, at least to give the proposed Constitution a fair trial, and to mend it as time, occasion and experience may dictate. It would little become us to verify the predictions of those who ventured to prophecy, that *peace:* instead of blessing us with happiness and tranquility, would serve only as the signal for factions, discords and civil contentions to rage in our land, and overwhelm it with misery and distress.

Let us also be mindful that the cause of freedom greatly depends on the use we make of the singular opportunities we enjoy of governing ourselves wisely; for if the event should prove, that the people of this country either cannot or will not govern themselves, who will hereafter be advocates for systems, which however charming in theory and prospect, are not reducible to practice. If the people of our nation, instead of consenting to be governed by laws of their own making, and rulers of their own choosing, should let licentiousness, disorder, and confusion reign over them, the minds of men every where, will insensibly become alienated from republican forms, and prepared to prefer and acquiesce in Governments, which, though less friendly to liberty, afford more peace and security.

Receive this Address with the same candor with which it is written; and may the spirit of wisdom and patriotism direct and distinguish your councils and your conduct.

Benjamin Franklin

Speech

The Federal Convention, 17 September 1787

———•———

Like Washington's, the views of Benjamin Franklin on the proposed Constitution carried great weight in the minds of his countrymen. In the final session of the Constitutional Convention on 17 September, Franklin gave James Wilson a speech to read which contained the elder statesman's reasons for assenting to the proposed document. Two days later the *Pennsylvania Gazette* reported that the speech was "extremely sensible" and that Franklin's support of the Constitution would recommend it to his fellow Pennsylvanians. At the request of Nathaniel Gorham, a delegate to the Convention from Massachusetts, Franklin provided him a version of the speech; Gorham's hope was that its publication in Massachusetts would influence those in his state who were still opposed to the document's ratification. Gorham deleted some portions of the speech and it appeared in the *Boston Gazette* on 3 December; this is also the version which appears here. By 21 December, the speech was reprinted twenty-six times.

———•———

I confess that I do not entirely approve of this Constitution at present, but Sir, I am not sure I shall never approve it: For having lived long, I have experienced many Instances of being oblig'd, by better Information or fuller Consideration, to change Opinions even on important Subjects, which I once thought right, but found to be otherwise. It is therefore that the older I grow the more apt I am to doubt my own Judgment and to pay more Respect to the Judgment of others. Most Men indeed as well as most Sects in Religion, think themselves in Possession of all Truth, and that wherever others differ from them it is so far Error. [Sir Richard] Steele, a Protestant, in a Dedication tells the Pope, that the only Difference between our two Churches in their Opinions of the Certainty of their Doctrine, is, the Romish Church is infallible, and the Church of England is never in the Wrong. But tho' many private Persons think almost as highly of their own Infallibility, as that of their Sect, few express it so naturally as a certain French lady, who in a little Dispute with her Sister, said, I don't know how it happens, Sister, but I meet with no body but myself that's *always* in the right.

In these Sentiments, Sir, I agree to this Constitution, with all its Faults, if they are such: because I think a General Government necessary for us, and there is no *Form* of Government but what may be a Blessing to the People if well administred; and I believe farther that this is likely to be well administred for a Course of Years, and can only end in Despotism as other Forms have done before it, when the People shall become so corrupted as to need Despotic Government, being incapable of any other. I doubt too whether any other Convention we can obtain, may be able to make a better Constitution: For when you assemble a Number of Men to have the Advantage of their joint Wisdom, you inevitably assemble with those Men all their Prejudices, their Passions, their Errors of Opinion, their local Interests, and their selfish Views. From such an Assembly can a perfect Production be expected? It therefore astonishes me, Sir, to find this System approaching so near to Perfection as it does; and I think it will astonish our Enemies, who are waiting with Confidence to hear that our Councils are confounded, like those of the Builders of Babel, and that our States are on the Point of Separation, only to meet hereafter for the Purpose of cutting one another's Throats. Thus I consent, Sir, to this Constitution because I expect no better, and because I am not sure that it is not the best. Much of the Strength and Efficiency of any Government, in procuring & securing Happiness to the People depends on Opinion, on the general Opinion of the Goodness of that Government as well as of the Wisdom & Integrity of its Governors. I hope therefore that for our own Sakes, as a Part of the People, and for the Sake of our Posterity, we shall act heartily & unanimously in recommending this Constitution, wherever our Influence may extend, and turn our future Thoughts and Endeavours to the Means of having it well administred.—

On the whole, Sir, I cannot help expressing a Wish, that every Member of the Convention, who may still have Objections to it, would with me on this Occasion doubt a little of his own Infallibility, and to make *manifest* our *Unanimity,* put his Name to this Instrument.—

Energetic but Limited Government

THE DEBATE between the Federalists and Anti-Federalists over the nature of the Union led naturally to the issue of governmental power and responsibility. The question was not only about the power of the central government *vis à vis* the states but also and more fundamentally about the power of the national representatives *vis à vis* the people. Federalists and Anti-Federalists generally agreed that in a free government a due dependence of the representatives on the people was required, otherwise there was no security for the people's rights and liberties. Anti-Federalists claimed that the proposed scheme of government, with a small number of representatives governing in a large territory, did not provide for the necessary degree of responsibility and that the liberty of the people was in danger. Federalists countered this charge, arguing that in the new order interest, reputation, and duty would bind the representatives to the Constitution and public opinion.

While the Federalists presented the case that the elective principle, separation of powers, bicameralism, and numerous governmental checks would work to prevent the representatives from overstepping their constitutional bounds, they did not develop a clear, united understanding about the nature of public opinion or how governmental dependence on it was to be fostered and maintained. Some Federalists echoed Anti-Federalists, arguing for a close, direct dependence of the representatives on the will of their constituents, such that the representatives would act as mirrors reflecting the people's interests and views. Unlike the Anti-Federalists, however, such Federalist writers as "Socius," "America," and Roger Sherman claimed that the proposed constitutional system was sufficient to maintain a close connection between the government and the people. The interests of the representatives and the interests of the people will be the same, they asserted.

Other proponents of the Constitution, such as Fisher Ames, James Wilson, and John Dickinson, set forth a subtler theory of representation in which the governing officials were responsible to the general opinion or sense of the public but not dependent on fleeting impulses or narrow, supposed interests. While most of the leading Federalists shared in this view, their position was not without some ambiguity. United in the general claim that the authoritative force in the American republic is the reason or sense of the people, they left unresolved the issue of what precisely constituted the public sense and how it was to be achieved by the people and depended on by the representatives. Fisher Ames, for example, understood the proposed system, with its large territory and insulation from the rule of faction, to encourage a certain degree of independence in the representatives during the ordinary business of public policy-making. The power of the representatives is the power of the people, Ames said; the watchfulness of the people's representatives is the guard of the people themselves. In the delegation of power to *trustees,* Ames argued, the true sovereignty of the people and the real protection of liberty become manifest. John Dickinson also believed that the will of the people must be a reasonable and not a distracted will, and that it was "the sense of the people" that the representatives were to express. However Dickinson further declared that the people's will is the "superior will" and that to preserve liberty the people must "trust to their own spirit" and practice the "living principle of watchfulness and controul" over their representatives.

Only a few years later, in the early 1790s, there would occur a split within the Federalist camp partly because this matter of what constituted the public sense, and a due dependence of the representatives on it, was never settled. In 1792, some of the Federalists formed the first American political party— the Republican Party—to oppose the Federalist administration of government. These former Federalists, led by James Madison and Thomas Jefferson, were joined by many who had been Anti-Federalists in the 1780s. One of their major criticisms of the Federalist administration was that the government was not sufficiently responsible to public opinion, and that it was in fact charting an antirepublican course largely independent of the people themselves.

The disagreement in respect to the theory of representation between the Federalists and Anti-Federalists, as well as among the Federalists themselves, points to the fundamental democratic challenge of the Founding generation: how to retain the spirit and principles of popular government without falling prey to its defects. The leading Federalist argument demonstrated that if representation was merely a vehicle for the expression of the narrow, unmodified interests and views of the populace, then the defects of democracy are not cured. What was necessary, powerful Federalist voices contended, was the establishment of a constitutional system that effectively placed limitations on the power of governmental officials so that they could not tyrannize over the people and that also controlled the collective power of the people so that they could not tyrannize over themselves. The solution they offered is summed up in the term "constitutionalism." American constitutionalism meant that the people are sovereign and the supreme law of the land is of their own making. Further it involved the republican idea that the people never act directly but only through the refining filter of representation. The representatives are dependent on the people's authority, but they are responsible first and foremost to the Constitution because it embodies the most fundamental, sovereign power of the people and is the source of all legitimate governmental activity. Accordingly, the Constitution is a higher law than legislative law, and government is limited in its powers to those delegated to it by the people and enumerated in the Constitution.

In the debate between Federalists and Anti-Federalists over the need for a bill of rights, Anti-Federalists generally believed that the absence of a written declaration was a major defect of the proposed Constitution. Without a bill of rights, they claimed, the government may become one of unlimited powers and trample on the rights and liberties of the people. Most Federalists argued that a written declaration of rights was unnecessary in theory and ineffectual in practice. In practical terms, Federalists claimed that the people's rights and liberties are protected by the numerous constitutional safeguards that provide for mutual checks among the departments of government. Further, they insisted, the real security for the people's rights is achieved by connecting the interests of the rulers with the interests of the people so that the rulers will have no motive to invade the rights of the people; or they argued that the true security for rights and the preservation of liberty can only be achieved by the ongoing perseverance of a freedom-loving people of sound sense and honest hearts. In theoretical terms, many Federalists claimed that the very idea of a constitution of enumerated and limited powers removes the need for a bill of rights. Elaborating on the notion of constitutionalism, they maintained that because the people delegate power to the government, and not vice versa, all powers that are not delegated are necessarily reserved to them as men or as citizens. The enumeration of the rights of the people carries with it the potential for abuse, for in the future it may be presumed that only those rights listed belong to the people. And it would be sheer folly, they said, to attempt to enumerate all the rights of mankind.

Some Federalists, James Wilson for example, demonstrated more fully the theoretical underpinnings of this argument. Wilson argued that all government derives its authority from the people, and government is obliged to act *for* the people; it must, however, act for the people only on the basis of the authority granted it *by* the people. Those who would have government do more than this misunderstand "the principle on which this system was constructed"—that is, the supreme and absolute authority of the people. The "inherent and unalienable right of the people" to establish government and organize its just powers, Wilson showed, is derived from the truths of the Declaration of Independence. In regard to the Declaration's teaching, he proclaimed: "This is the broad basis on which our independence was placed; on the same certain and solid foundation this system is erected." Precisely because the Constitution is erected on the foundation that all men are created equal and their rights are inalienable, there is no need for a bill of rights; because this is the only legitimate basis for government, there is no wisdom in risking a contrary understanding.

Despite the forceful reasoning of Wilson and others, the issue of where sovereignty ultimately resides in the American republic was neither unanimously agreed to nor practically solved by the Founding generation. "Alfredus," for example, asserted that the state constitution of New Hampshire is a compact between individuals; the federal Constitution, however, "is not a compact between individuals, but between several sovereign and independent political societies already formed and organized." Although he quotes Wilson at length and claims only to add to his reasoning, one must question whether this is a mere addition or rather a radical alteration of Wilson's view. According to Wilson, not only do the American people possess supreme power, they have not and ought not "to part with it to any government whatsoever." They may delegate certain powers in such proportions to the various governments as they think appropriate, but it is they, and only they, who are and always remain supremely and absolutely sovereign.

To complicate matters further, Tench Coxe blithely stated that "the contracting parties in the federal compact are *the people of the several states* and *the federal state governments.*" Thus we see that during the Founding era there is not only a divergence of opinion on the issue of sovereignty but a lack of clarity in the meaning of the term itself. Indeed the word "sovereignty" was often used in two different senses—one referring only to the federal nature of the polity and the constitutional division of power between the national and state governments, and the other referring to who or what possesses the fundamental and absolutely final authority in the regime.

In respect to the degree of power in the federal head, Federalists contended that in order to regulate trade, restore public and private credit, give respectability to the states both at home and abroad, safeguard property, and enlarge commerce, a federal government of limited powers but sufficient energy was absolutely necessary. Furthermore many of them forcefully attacked Anti-Federalist reasoning at its core, arguing that only a government of substantial energy can protect liberty. If the people are to retain their liberty, they must be protected against the influence of licentious passion within themselves. Thus drawing the distinction between liberty and license, Dickinson identified the issue of the character of the "predominant authority" in the polity as critical. His discussion of this issue sets forth the substantive republican grounds for the new Constitution and the corollary purpose for the principle of representation. He taught that nothing short of the formation of a people of sound, republican character will answer the cause of liberty in America. The predominance of "the true spirit of republicanism" requires that "life and vigor [be] communicated through the whole, by the popular representation of each part, and the close combination of all."

"*Socius*"

Essay

Carlisle Gazette, 14 November 1787

Some THOUGHTS on the FEARS which many appear to entertain about the FEDERAL CONSTITUTION.

As the Federal Government, now under consideration, is a subject of the highest importance to our happiness, as a nation, it is certainly of great consequence, that we lay down right principles, upon which we may form the judgment of it. While the fears of the people are alarmed, on the one side or the other, they are not capable of such a cool examination, and deliberate choice, as the weight of the case requires; and it is certain that this has been the effect of such writings as have appeared upon this grand question. If the grounds of fear are real, they indeed ought to affect us; but it becomes us to submit them to a serious and impartial inquiry, before we suffer them to blind judgment or precipitate our conclusions.

The very idea of government supposes power to be committed to our rulers; and power is always capable of being abused. Various arrangements have been invented to restrain this abuse of power; but it does not appear, that any possible arrangements thereof can merely of themselves, secure the rights and liberties of the people, in all cases, from oppression. Some are without doubt, better calculated for this purpose, than others; but when the people have chosen the best devisable form, there are other sources from which they must also derive their safety, and on which they must depend.

The form of government proposed appears to be organized with great wisdom to guard against this abuse, as the very powers will be a watch upon one another, and act as centinels in giving the alarm, should any one attempt any unreasonable encroachments on our liberties. They are all of the people, and have the same rights and privileges, in all respects, to defend. They are chosen at such times as is sufficient to secure their responsibility, and in such a manner as must ever prevent their permanency. The objects of power have all a federal nature, [or are absolutely] necessary to the hon[or and safety] of the nation. But toget[her with all] this, our political liberty requires the aid of other motives and principles, which if we duly consider, with the operation and force they are allowed to have, under this constitution, it would tend greatly to allay any unreasonable fears which have been raised about it.

One great security we have of men in power, is interest, when their places are so often changeable, as is ordained in this constitution. There is no great danger of men abusing the power committed to them, to destroy those rights and liberties, in which they themselves are as much interested, as any other of the people; while they know, at the same time, that they must shortly return to that condition, which will render these privileges so precious and estimable. If they were indeed a permanent body independent [of] the people, and holding their places for themselves and their heirs, the motives to self-aggrandisement would prevail over all others, and our liberties were gone. But so far is this constitution from favouring such a permanency, that it cannot take place without the utter destruction of this plan of government. They will always be chosen by the people; and by the assemblies, which excludes every idea of permanency, though the Centinel[1] has affected to argue it out according to his method of reason.

Now, apply this to some of the objections, which have been made to this plan of government. The countenancing [of] a standing army—if in the present depraved state of human nature, any military force should be necessary to support the honour, and promote the safety of the nation, and protect our trade by land or sea; surely there can be no reasonable objection against it. But to imagine that the Congress, our own representatives, whose power depends entirely on the people, and whose interests, liberties and safety are at stake, in common with every person in the union, that these should wilfully impose an unnecessary burden, or subject us to unnecessary danger, is surely an unreasonable suspicion. To speak of thirty or fifty thousands of a standing army, or any thing like it, is only calculated to alarm the fears of the people, with an evil entirely imaginary.

1. For information on the Centinel essays, see *Friends,* 37 nn. 1, 2.

The same may be said of the power of direct taxation. As the grand revenue will arise from another source, this mode may never be applied to, but on such occasions, as may require great exertions; and if in such cases, the Congress should make use of this method, what reason have we to think, that it should be so dreadfully oppressive? Are not the estates of those in power, as liable as others! and if they are the great and the mighty (as one writer observes) will they not be peculiarly affected. However it is certain, that the command of a sufficient revenue should be in their hands, otherwise they can never support the dignity or safety of the United States.

Another grand security, and indeed the principal one, which the people have against the abuse of power, is the freedom of choice. This is the very essence of political liberty—while this remains it is impossible they can be enslaved, and if their rulers incroach upon their privileges it must be of their own fault, and not that of the government. Now this privilege cannot be taken away without destroying this constitution; under which no one, in the several branches of government, can hold a place, but by the fair choice of the people, immediately, or by electors chosen by them. They are still the sovereign masters, and may choose whom they will; all depends on their own virtue and the wisdom of their choice. While this freedom is allowed, and the power returns to us at proper intervals, not so near, as to keep us in a perpetual electionary ferment, nor so distant, as to prevent a proper responsibility in the rulers, there can be no danger from the government; we will be happy.

Indeed it is surmised, that the Congress may render this privilege difficult or impossible, by the power the constitution gives them over elections. But why should we fear such an injurious exercise of power as it is wantonly said this will be?—The assemblies have authority to fix the mode and places of elections in every country, yet we never have been afraid, that they would make a law, to oblige us to meet [in in]convenient places, or drag us from one country to another to give our votes, and why should we be so exceedingly jealous of our own representatives in this case? The reason of such a power appears as good in the one, as in the other. It is of consequence to our freedom that we have a fair and honest representation in Congress, and that no one be admitted as our representative who is not lawfully chos[en]. This will require a power of judging in all disputed elections, which often happen, and this implies a law, whereby the qualifications of members shall be ascertained, and as these qualifications include the regularity of the choice, as to time and mode and place, it is proper that these should be fixed by one general election-law. This will be necessary, not only to enable the respective houses to judge of the qualifications of their own members, but also for the greater case and regularity of proceeding, having all their members chosen in the same manner, and returnable at the same time. As such a law therefore will be necessary, it cannot be questioned but that the Congress is the proper authority to make it—and to assert, that, in making such a law, they would not have a regard to the ease and convenience of the people, is very unreasonable to say, that they will frame it so, as to put it out of our power to chuse, is absolutely extravagant.

The most of those fears, which have given strength to the objections against the government, have arisen from this excessive distrust in the representatives we are to chuse; surely we ought to put some confidence in them, to whom we commit so great a trust. To be so jealous, as to excite our watchfulness against their abusing their power, is useful and salutary; but to put no confidence at all in them; to believe that as soon as we chuse them, we set them at variance with our liberties, and make them enemies to all our dearest privileges; that they will surely abuse their power, to aggrandise themselves; this is a jealousy utterly unreasonable and absurd. It is an ungenerous reflection on them we chuse, and a vile reproach upon our own wisdom. It is a principle which would set aside all government intirely.—No man in common life, acts upon so absurd a principle as this, yet most of the fears about this constitution have had only this foundation—on this principle, the Centinel has raised the most alarming apprehensions, of aristocracy, a standing army, oppression of taxes, the annihilation of state assemblies, suppression of the press, and all his catalogue of evils—and upon this also the Old Whig[2] appears to have raised his wonderful superstructures

2. The essays of An Old Whig first appeared in the Philadelphia *Independent Gazetteer* between 6 October 1787 and 6 February 1788. They were fairly widely reprinted in Pennsylvania, New York, and Massachusetts. See Storing, 3:3; Allen, 27–30.

of possibles and probables, perhaps's, maybe's and awful predictions, which have so terrified him, as to conclude that "whether it is a good constitution or a bad one, it will remain forever unamended." These writers seem to take it for granted, and I fear too many follow them in it, that we are not, nor ought to be one people; that the interest of the several states must be different from that of the union; and there must be an eternal variance between the Congress and the state Assemblies. This appears visibly in their writings, as the ground of their charges against the constitution.—The absurdity of these principles is evident, the ruin that must attend the adoption of them and proceeding upon them, every one must see, and consequently how groundless those jealousies are, which have no other foundation.

With all the securities, then, which we have against the abuse of power, why should we fear [that] the constitution is free? in its nature and construction—the interest of the rulers and ours is the same—the power of displacing them is still in our own hands—and besides these, the equality among the citizens, the prohibition of hereditary property or honours—the freedom of the press—the jealousy and watchfulness of the Assemblies, whose power, after all that has been said, I cannot see to be abridged or destroyed with respect to any branch of internal policy, or in any cases but such as are federal, except the impost, and this is by all granted to Congress. With all these securities we surely cannot be in so great danger, as is apprehended by many. But after all, if it should prove dangerous and intollerable, it is capable of alteration, and it may reasonably be expected that when the people feel it so, they will alter it. The manner of process is not more difficult, in altering than making it—and the accomplishment of the one, is an evidence that the other, if found necessary, is neither impossible nor improbable.

"America"
[Noah Webster]

Essay

Daily Advertiser, New York, 31 December 1787

---·---

A lexicographer and the author of *An American Dictionary of the English Language* (1828), Noah Webster was a man of many interests. He was a publisher and editor of newspapers and magazines and an author of scholarly works in education, history, politics, medicine, and the natural sciences.

---·---

To the DISSENTING MEMBERS of the late CONVENTION OF PENNSYLVANIA.

Gentlemen, Your long and elaborate publication,[1] assigning the reasons for your refusing to subscribe the ratification of the NEW FEDERAL CONSTITUTION, has made its appearance in the public papers, and, I flatter myself, will be read throughout the United States. It will feed the flame of opposition among the weak, the wicked, the designing, and the factious; but it will make many new converts to the proposed Government, and furnish the old friends of it with new weapons of defence. The very attempt to excite uneasiness and disturbance in a State, about a measure legally and constitutionally adopted, after a long and ample discussion in a Convention of the people's Delegates, marks a disposition, beyond all conception, obstinate, base, and politically wicked. But *obstinacy* is the leading trait in your public characters, and, as it serves to give *consistency* to your actions, even in error, it cannot fail to procure you that share of respect which is paid to the *firmness* of Satan and his fellow apostates, who, after their expulsion

---

1. See *Friends,* 88 n. 1.

from Heaven, had too much pride to *repent* and *ask for a re-admission*. My address to you will not be so lengthy as your publication; your arguments are *few*, altho' your harangue is *long* and *insidious*.

You begin with telling the world, that *no defect was discovered in the present Confederation, till after the war.* Why did you not publish the truth? You know, Gentlemen, that during six years of the war, we had *no Confederation at all.* You know that the war commenced in April, 1775, and that we had *no Confederation* till March, 1781. You know (for some of you are men of abilities and reading) or ought to know, a principle of *fear,* in time of war, operates more powerfully in binding together the States which have a common interest, than all the parchment compacts on earth. Could we, then, discover the defects of our present Confederation, with *two years'* experience only, and an enemy in our country? You know we could not.

I will not undertake to detect the falshood of every assertion, or the fallacy of all your reasoning on each article. In the most of them the public will anticipate any thing I could say, and confute your arguments as fast as they read them. But I must tell you, Gentlemen, that your reasoning against the *New Constitution* resembles that of Mr. Hume on miracles. You begin with some *gratis dicta,* which are denied; you assume *premises* which are *totally false,* and then reason on them with great address. Your whole reasoning, and that of all the opposers of the Federal Government, is built on this *false principle,* that the *Federal Legislature* will be a body *distinct from* and *independent* of the people. Unless your opposition is grounded on *that principle,* it stands on *nothing;* and on any *other* supposition, your arguments are but *declamatory nonsense.*

But the principle is false. The Congress, under the proposed Constitution, will have the *same interest* as the people—they are a *part* of the people—their interest is *inseparable* from that of the people; and this union of interest will eternally remain, while the right of election shall continue in the people. Over this right Congress will have no control: the time and manner of exercising that right are very wisely vested in Congress, otherwise a delinquent State might embarrass the measures of the Union. The safety of the public requires that the Federal body should prevent any particular delinquency; but the *right of election* is above their control: it *must* remain in the people, and be exercised once in two, four or six years. A body thus organized, with thirteen Legislatures watching their measures, and several millions of jealous eyes inspecting their conduct, would not be apt to betray their constituents. Yet this is not the best ground of safety. The first and almost only principle that governs men, is *interest. Love of our country* is a powerful auxiliary motive to patriotic actions; but rarely or never operates against *interest.* The only requisite to secure liberty, is to connect the *interest* of the *Governors* with that of the *governed.* Blend these interests—make them inseparable—and both are safe from voluntary invasion. How shall this union be formed? This question is answered. The union is formed by the equal principles on which the people of these States hold their property and their rights. But how shall this union of interests be perpetuated? The answer is easy—bar all perpetuities of estates—prevent any exclusive rights— preserve all preferment dependent on the choice of the people—suffer no power to exist independent of the people or their Representatives. While there exists no power in a State, which is independent on the will of the electors, the rights of the people are secure. The only barrier against tyranny, that is necessary in any State, is *the election of Legislators* by the yeomanry of that State. Preserve *that,* and every privilege is safe. The Legislators thus chosen to represent the people, should have all the power that the people would have, were they assembled in one body to deliberate upon public measures. The distinction between the powers of the *people* and of their *Representatives* in the Legislature, is as absurd in *theory,* as it proves pernicious in *practice.* A distinction, which has already countenanced and supported *one rebellion* in America; has prevented many *good* measures; has produced many *bad;* has created animosities in many States, and embarrassments in all. It has taught the people a lesson, which, if they continue to practise, will bring laws into contempt, and frequently mark our country with blood.

You object, Gentlemen, to the powers vested in Congress. Permit me, to ask you, where will you limit their powers? What bounds will you pre- scribe? You will reply, *we will reserve certain rights, which we deem invaluable, and restrain our rulers from abridging them.* But, Gentlemen, let me ask you, how will you define these rights? would you say, *the liberty of the Press shall not be restrained?* Well, what is this liberty of the Press? Is it an unlimited licence to publish *any thing and every thing* with impunity? If so, the Author, and Printer of any treatise, however obscene and blasphemous, will be screened from punishment. You know, Gentlemen, that there are books extant, so shockingly and infamously obscene and so daringly blasphemous, that no society on earth, would be vindicable in suffering the publishers to pass unpunished. You certainly know that such cases *have* happened, and *may* happen again—nay, you know that they are *probable*. Would not that indefinite expression, *the liberty of the Press,* extend to the justification of every *possible publication?* Yes, Gentlemen, you know, that under such a general licence, a man who should publish a treatise to *prove his maker a knave,* must be screened from legal punishment. I shudder at the thought!—But the truth must not be concealed. The Constitutions of several States *guarantee that very licence.*

But if you attempt to define the *liberty of the Press,* and ascertain what cases shall fall within that privilege, during the course of centuries, where will you *begin?* Or rather, where will you *end?* Here, Gentlemen, you will be puzzled. Some publications certainly *may* be a breach of civil law: You will not have the effrontery to deny a truth so obvious and intuitively evident. Admit that principle; and unless you can define precisely the cases, which are, and are not a breach of law, you have no right to say, the liberty of the Press shall not be restrained; for such a license would warrant *any breach of law.* Rather than hazard such an abuse of privilege, is it not better to leave the right altogether with your rulers and your posterity? No attempts have ever been made by a Legislative body in America, to abridge that privilege; and in this free enlightened country, no attempts could succeed, unless the public should be convinced that an abuse of it would warrant the restriction. Should this ever be the case, you have no right to say, that a future Legislature, or that posterity shall not abridge the privilege, or punish its abuses. The very attempt to establish a permanent, unalterable Constitution, is an act of consummate arrogance. It is a presumption that we have all possible wisdom—that we can foresee all possible circumstances—and judge for future generations, better than they can for themselves.

But you will say, that trial by jury, is an unalienable right, that ought not to be trusted with our rulers. Why not? If it is such a darling privilege, will not Congress be as fond of it, as their constituents? An elevation into that Council, does not render a man insensible to his privileges, nor place him beyond the necessity of securing them. A member of Congress is liable to all the operations of law, except during his attendance on public business; and should he consent to a law, annihilating any right whatever, he deprives himself, his family and estate, of the benefit resulting from that right, as well as his constituents. This circumstance alone, is a sufficient security.

But, why this outcry about juries? If the people esteem them so highly, why do they ever neglect them, and suffer the trial by them to go into disuse? In some States, *Courts of Admiralty* have no juries—nor Courts of Chancery at all. In the City-Courts of some States, juries are rarely or never called, altho' the parties may demand them; and one State, at least, has lately passed an act, empowering the parties to submit both *law* and *fact* to the Court. It is found, that the judgment of a Court, gives as much satisfaction, as the verdict of a jury, as the Court are as good judges of fact, as juries, and much better judges of law. I have no desire to abolish trials by jury, although the original design and excellence of them, is in many cases superseded.— While the people remain attached to this mode of deciding causes, I am confident, that no Congress can wrest the privilege from them.

But, Gentlemen, our legal proceedings want a reform. Involved in all the mazes of perplexity, which the chicanery of lawyers could invent, in the course of 500 years, our road to justice and redress is tedious, fatiguing and expensive. Our Judicial proceedings are capable of being simplified, and improved in almost every particular. For God's sake, Gentlemen, do not shut the door against improvement. If the people of America, should ever spurn the shackles of opinion, and venture to leave the road, which is so overgrown with briers and thorns, as to strip a man's cloaths from his back as he passes, I am certain they can devise a more easy, safe, and expeditious mode of administering the laws, than that which harrasses every poor mortal, that is wretched enough to want *legal* justice. In Pennsylvania, where very respectable merchants, have repeatedly told me, they had rather lose a debt of fifty pounds, than attempt to recover it by a legal process, one would think that men, who value liberty and property, would not restrain any Government from suggesting a remedy for such disorders.

Another right, which you would place beyond the reach of Congress, is the writ of *habeas corpus*. Will you say that this right may not be suspended in *any* case? You dare not. If it may be suspended in any case, and the Congress are to judge of the necessity, what security have you in a declaration in its favor? You had much better say nothing upon the subject.

But you are frightened at a standing army. I beg you, Gentlemen, to define a *standing army*. If you would refuse to give Congress power to raise troops, to guard our frontiers, and garrison forts, or in short, to enlist men for any purpose, then we understand you—you tie the hands of your rulers so that they cannot defend you against any invasion. This is protection indeed! But if Congress can raise a body of troops for a year, they can raise them for a *hundred years,* and your declaration against *standing armies* can have no other effect, than to prevent Congress from denominating their troops, a *standing army.* You would only introduce into this country, the English farce of mechanically passing an annual bill for the support of troops which are never disbanded.

You object to the indefinite power of taxation in Congress. You must then limit the exercise of that power by the sums of money to be raised; or leaving the sums indefinite, must prescribe the *particular mode* in which, and the *articles* on which the money is to be raised. But the sums cannot be ascertained, because the necessities of the States cannot be foreseen nor defined. It is beyond even *your* wisdom and profound knowledge, Gentlemen, to ascertain the public exigencies, and reduce them to the provisions of a Constitution. And if you would prescribe the mode of raising money, you will meet with equal difficulty. The different States have different modes of taxation, and I question much whether even *your* skill, Gentlemen, could invent a uniform system that should sit easy upon every State. It must therefore be left to experiment, with a power that can correct the errors of a system, and suit it to the habits of the people. And if no uniform mode will answer this purpose, it will be in the power of Congress to lay taxes in each State, according to its particular practice. But you know, Gentlemen, that an efficient Federal Government will render taxes unnecessary—*that it will ease the people of their burdens,* and *remove their complaints,* and therefore when you raise a clamor about the right of taxation, you must be guilty of the *basest design*—your hearts must be as *malignant* as your actions have been *insidious*. You know that requisitions on the States are ineffectual— That they cannot be rendered effectual, but by a compulsory power in Congress—You know that without an efficient power to raise money, Government cannot secure person, property or justice—Nay, you know further, that such power is as safely lodged in your *Representatives* in Congress, as it is in your *Representatives* in your distinct Legislatures.

You would likewise restrain Congress from requiring *excessive bail,* or imposing *excessive fines* and *unusual punishment.* But unless you can, in every possible instance, previously define the words *excessive* and *unusual*—if you leave the discretion of Congress to define them on occasion, any restriction of their power by a general indefinite expression, is a nullity—mere *formal nonsense.* What consummate arrogance must you possess, to presume you can *now* make *better* provision for the Government of these States, during the course of ages and centuries, than the future Legislatures can, on the spur of the occasion! Yet your whole reasoning on the subject implies this arrogance, and a presumption that you have a right to legislate for posterity!

But to complete the list of unalienable rights, you would insert a clause in your declaration, *that every body shall, in good weather, hunt on his own land, and catch fish in rivers that are public property.* Here, Gentlemen, you must have exerted the whole force of your genius! Not even the *all-important* subject of *legislating for a world* can restrain my laughter at this clause! As a supplement to that article of your bill of rights, I would suggest the following restriction:—"That Congress shall never restrain any inhabitant of America from eating and drinking, *at seasonable times,* or prevent his lying on his *left side,* in a long winter's night, or even on his back, when he is fatigued by lying on his *right*."—This article is of just as much consequence as the 8th clause of your proposed bill of rights.

But to be more serious, Gentlemen, you must have had in idea the forest-laws in Europe, when you inserted that article; for no circumstance that ever took place in America, could have suggested the thought of a declaration in favor of hunting and fishing. Will you forever persist in error? Do you not reflect that the state of property in America, is directly the reverse of what it is in Europe? Do you not consider, that the forest-laws in Europe originated in *feudal tyranny,* of which not a trace is to be found in America? Do you not know that in this country almost every farmer is Lord of his own soil? That instead of suffering under the oppression of a Monarch and Nobles, a class of haughty masters, totally independent of the people, almost every man in America is a *Lord himself*—enjoying his property in fee? Where then the necessity of laws to secure hunting and fishing? You may just as well ask for a clause, giving licence for every man to till *his own land,* or milk *his own cows.* The Barons in Europe procured forest-laws to secure the right of hunting on *their own land,* from the intrusion of those who had no property in lands. But the distribution of land in America, not only supersedes the necessity of any laws upon this subject, but renders them absolutely trifling. The same laws which secure the property in land, secure to the owner the right of using it as he pleases.

But you are frightened at the prospect of a *consolidation of the States.* I differ from you very widely. I am afraid, after all our attempts to unite the States, that contending interests, and the pride of State-Sovereignties, will either prevent our union, or render our Federal Government weak, slow and inefficient. The danger is all on this side. If any thing under Heaven now endangers our liberties and independence, it is that single circumstance.

You harp upon that clause of the New Constitution, which declares, that the laws of the United States, &c. shall be the supreme law of the land; when you know that the powers of the Congress are defined, to extend only to those matters which are in their nature and effects, *general.* You know, the Congress cannot meddle with the internal police of any State, or abridge its Sovereignty. And you know, at the same time, that in all general concerns, the laws of Congress must be *supreme,* or they must be *nothing.*

But the public will ask, who are these men that so violently oppose the New Constitution? I will tell them. You are the heads of that party, Gentlemen, which, on the celebration of a very glorious event in Philadelphia, at the close of the war, collected in a mob, and broke the windows of the Quakers, and committed the most detestable outrages, because their religion would not suffer them to illuminate their windows, and join in the rejoicings. You are the men, Gentlemen, that wrested the Charter from the Bank, without the least justifiable pretence; sporting with a grant which *you* had made, and which had never been forfeited. You are the men, that, without a show of right, took away the Charter of the University, and vested it in the hands of your own tools. Yes, Gentlemen, you are the men, who prescribed a test law and oath of abjuration in Pennsylvania, which excluded more than half the Citizens of the State from all Civil Offices. A law, which, had it not been altered by the efforts of more reasonable men, would have established you, and your adherents, as an Aristocratic junto, in all the offices and emoluments of the State. Could your base designs have been accomplished, *you* would have rioted in all the benefits of Government, and Pennsylvania would now, have been subject to as tyrannical an Aristocracy, as ever cursed Society. Such has been the uniformly infamous conduct of the men, who now oppose the best Constitution of Government, ever devised by human wisdom.

But the most bare-faced act of tyranny and wickedness, which has distinguished your political characters, remains to be mentioned. You are the men, Gentlemen, who have abandoned your parts of duty, and betrayed the constitutional rights of the State of Pennsylvania, by *seceding from the Legislature,* with the design of defeating the measures of a constitutional quorum of the House. Yes, Gentlemen, and to add to the infamy of your conduct, you have the audacity to *avow the intention.* Will you then attempt to palliate the crime, by saying it was *necessary?* Good Heavens! *necessary* that a State should be *ruled by a minority!* *necessary* that the sense of a legislature should be defeated by a junto, which had labored incessantly, for four years, to establish an *Aristocracy* in the State! The same principle which will vindicate you, will justify any *one* man in defeating the sense of the *whole* State. If a minority may prevent a law, one man may do it; but is this liberty? Is this your concern for the rights of the State? Dare you talk of rights, which you have so flagrantly invaded? Will the world expect *you* to be the guardians of privileges? No, Gentlemen, they will sooner expect lessons of morality from the wheel-barrowed criminals, that clank their chains along your streets.

Do you know, Gentlemen, that you are treading in the steps of the Governors before the revolution? Do you know that from the first settlement of Pennsylvania, there was a contest between the people and the deputies of the proprietaries? And that when a Governor could not bring the Assembly to resign their rights, he would *prevail on certain members to leave the House,* and prevent their measures. Yes, Gentlemen, you are but following the precedents of your tyrannical Governors. You have begun, and pursued, with unwearied perseverance, the same plan of Despotism which wrought the late revolution; and, with a calm, hypocritical phiz, pretend to be *anxious for the liberties of the people.*

These facts stare you in the face! They are *felt* in Pennsylvania—and *known* to the world! There is not a spot in the United States, where the solemnity of contracts and grants, has been so sacrilegiously violated—and the rights of men so wantonly and perseveringly abused, as by you and your junto in Pennsylvania—except only, in the little detestable corner of the Continent, called *Rhode-Island.* Thanks be to the Sovereign Ruler of events, you are checked in your career of tyranny—your power is dwindling into impotence—and your abuse of the respectable Convention, and of the friends of our Federal Union, will shroud you in oblivion, or accelerate your progress to merited contempt.

"A Countryman"
[Roger Sherman]

The Letters: II

New Haven Gazette, 22 November 1787

A delegate to both Continental Congresses and member of the committee that drafted the Declaration of Independence, Sherman was influential at the Constitutional Convention, wrote essays in favor of the Constitution, and supported the Constitution during ratification in Connecticut. Afterward he served in the House of Representatives (1789–91) and the Senate (1791–93).

To the PEOPLE *of* Connecticut.

It is fortunate that you have been but little distressed with that torrent of impertinence and folly, with which the newspaper politicians have overwhelmed many parts of our country.

It is enough that you should have heard, that one party has seriously urged, that we should adopt the *New Constitution* because it has been approved by *Washington* and *Franklin:* and the other, with all the solemnity of apostolic address to *Men, Brethren, Fathers, Friends and Countrymen,* have urged that we should reject, as dangerous, every clause thereof, because that *Washington* is more used to command as a soldier, than to reason as a politician—*Franklin* is *old*—others are *young*—and *Wilson* is *haughty.* You are too well informed to decide by the opinion of others, and too independent to need a caution against undue influence.

Of a very different nature, tho' only one degree better than the other reasoning, is all that sublimity of *nonsense* and *alarm,* that has been thundered against it in every shape of *metaphoric terror,* on the subject of a *bill of rights,* the *liberty of the press, rights of conscience, rights of taxation and election, trials in the vicinity, freedom of speech, trial by jury,* and a *standing army.* These last are undoubtedly important points, much too important to depend on mere paper protection. For, guard such privileges by the strongest expressions, still if you leave the legislative and executive power in the hands of those who are or may be disposed to deprive you of them—you are but slaves. Make an absolute monarch—give him the supreme authority, and guard as much as you will by bills of right, your liberty of the press, and trial by jury;—he will find means either to take them from you, or to render them useless.

The only real security that you can have for all your important rights must be in the nature of your government. If you suffer any man to govern you who is not strongly interested in supporting your privileges, you will certainly lose them. If you are about to trust your liberties with people whom it is necessary to bind by stipulation, that they shall not keep a standing army, your stipulation is not worth even the trouble of writing. No bill of rights ever yet bound the supreme power longer than the *honey moon* of a new married couple, unless the *rulers were interested* in preserving the rights; and in that case they have always been ready enough to declare the rights, and to preserve them when they were declared.—The famous English *Magna Charta* is but an act of parliament, which every subsequent parliament has had just as much constitutional power to repeal and annul, as the parliament which made it had to pass it at first. But the security of the nation has always been, that their government was so formed, that at least *one branch* of their legislature must be strongly interested to preserve the rights of the nation.

You have a bill of rights in Connecticut (i.e.) your legislature many years since enacted that the subjects of this state should enjoy certain privileges. Every assembly since that time, could, by the same authority, enact that the subjects should enjoy none of those privileges; and the only reason that it has not long since been so enacted, is that your legislature were as strongly interested in preserving those rights as any of the subjects; and this is your only security that it shall not be so enacted at the next session of assembly: and it is security enough.

Your General Assembly under your present constitution are supreme. They may keep troops on foot in the most profound peace, if they think proper. They have heretofore abridged the trial by jury in some causes, and they can again in all. They can restrain the press, and may lay the most burdensome taxes if they please, and who can forbid? But still the people are perfectly safe that not one of these events shall take place so long as the members of the General assembly are as much interested, and interested in the same manner as the other subjects.

On examining the new proposed constitution, there can not be a question, but that there is authority enough lodged in the proposed federal Congress, if abused, to do the greatest injury. And it is perfectly idle to object to it, that there is no bill of rights, or to propose to add to it a provision that a trial by jury shall in no case be omitted, or to patch it up by adding a stipulation in favor of the press, or to guard it by removing the paltry objection to the right of Congress to regulate the time and manner of elections.

If you can not prove by the best of all evidence, viz. by the *interest of the rulers,* that this authority will not be abused, or at least that those powers are not more likely to be abused by the Congress, than by those who now have the same powers, you must by no means adopt the constitution:—No, not with all the bills of rights and all the stipulations in favour of the people that can be made.

But if the members of Congress are to be interested just as you and I are, and just as the members of our present legislatures are interested, we shall be just as safe, with even supreme power, (if that were granted) in Congress, as in the General Assembly. If the members of Congress can take no improper step which will not affect them as much as it does us, we need not apprehend that they will usurp authorities not given them to injure that society of which they are a part.

The sole question, (so far as any apprehension of tyranny and oppression is concerned) ought to be, how are Congress formed? how far are the members interested to preserve your rights? how far have you a controul over them?—Decide this, and then all the questions about their power may be dismissed for the amusement of those politicians whose business it is to catch flies, or may occasionally furnish subjects for *George Bryan's*[1] POMPOSITY, or the declamations of *Cato*[2]—*An Old Whig*[3]—*Son of Liberty*[4]—*Brutus*[5]—*Brutus junior*[6]—*An Officer of the Continental Army,*[7]—the more contemptible *Timoleon*[8]—and the residue of that rabble of writers.

1. For information on George Bryan, see *Friends,* 37 n. 2.

2. Cato was a pseudonym especially popular with the Anti-Federalists. See Storing, 2:6, 5:7, and 5:10; Essays V, VI, and VII by Cato are in Allen, 159–69.

3. For biographical information on An Old Whig, see *Friends,* 167 n. 2.

4. A Son of Liberty's list of objections first appeared in the *New York Journal* on 8 November 1787. See Storing, 6:2.

5. Among the most important of Anti-Federalist writings, the essays of Brutus were published in the *New York Journal* between October 1787 and April 1788. The essays of Brutus generally are attributed to Robert Yates; however, Storing questions this attribution. See Storing, 2:9; Essays I, III, IV, V, XI, XII, and XV are in Allen, 102–17, 201–23, and 269–74.

6. This essay was published in the *New York Journal* on 8 November 1787. See Storing, 6:3.

7. For information see *Friends,* 113 n. 1.

8. The letter of Timoleon was published in an "extraordinary" issue of the *New York Journal* on 1 November 1787. It was subsequently reprinted and distributed in the Hudson River Valley and Connecticut. See *DH,* 13:534–38.

"A Citizen of Philadelphia"
[Peletiah Webster]

"The Weakness of Brutus Exposed"

Philadelphia, 1787

———•———

Peletiah Webster, a Philadelphia merchant, was a staunch patriot throughout the American Revolution. This item was a pamphlet printed in Philadelphia and advertised in the *Pennsylvania Packet* and other newspapers.
The first twenty pages were reprinted in the New York *Daily Advertiser.*
See *DH*, 14:63–74.

———•———

The long piece signed BRUTUS,[1] (which was first published in a New-York
paper, and was afterwards copied into the Pennsylvania Packet of the 26th
instant) is wrote in a very good stile; the language is easy, and the address
is polite and insinuating: but the sentiments, I conceive, are not only un-
sound, but wild and chimerical; the dreary fears and apprehensions, altogether groundless; and the whole tendency of the piece, in this important
crisis of our politics, very hurtful. I have therefore thought it my duty to
make some animadversions on it; which I here offer, with all due deference,
to the Author and to the Public.

His first question is, *Whether a confederated government is best for the
United States?*

I answer, If Brutus, or any body else, cannot find any benefit resulting
from the union of the Thirteen States; if they can do *without* as well as *with*
the respectability, the protection, and the security, which the States might
derive from that union, I have nothing further to say: but if that union is
to be supported in any such manner as to afford respectability, protection,

1. For information on Brutus, see *Friends,* 182 n. 5. Webster is addressing Essay I by Brutus,
which is reprinted in Storing, 2:9; and Allen, 102–11.

or security to the States, I say it must be done by an adequate government, and cannot be otherwise done.

This government must have a supreme power, *superior to and able to controul* each and all of its parts. 'Tis essential to all governments, that such a power be somewhere existing in it; and if *the place* where the proposed Constitution has fixed it, does not suit Brutus and his friends, I will give him leave to stow it away in any *other place that is better:* but I will not consent to have it *annihilated;* neither will I agree to have it *cramped and pinched* for room, so as to lessen its energy; for that will *destroy* both its nature and use.

The supreme power of government ought to be *full, definite, established,* and *acknowledged.* Powers of government too limited, or uncertain and disputed, have ever proved, like *Pandora's* box, a most fruitful source of quarrels, animosities, wars, devastation, and ruin, in all shapes and degrees, in all communities, states, and kingdoms on earth.

Nothing tends more to the honour, establishment, and peace of society, than public decisions, grounded on principles of right, natural fitness, and prudence; but when the powers of government are *too limited,* such decisions can't be made and enforced; so the mischief goes without a remedy: dreadful examples of which we have felt, in instances more than enough, for seven years past.

Further, where the powers of government are not *definite* but *disputed,* the administration dare not make decisions on the footing of impartial justice and right; but must temporise with the parties, lest they lose friends or make enemies: and of course the *righteous* go off injured and disgusted, and the *wicked* go grumbling too; for 'tis rare that any sacrifices of a court can satisfy a prevailing party in the state.

'Tis necessary in States, as well as in private families, that controversies should have a just, *speedy,* and effectual decision, that right may be done before the contention has *time* to grow up into habits of malignity, resentment, ill nature, and ill offices. If a controversy happens between two states, must it continue undecided, and daily increase, and be more and more aggravated, by the repeated insults and injuries of the contending parties, 'till they are ripe for the decision of the sword? or must the weaker states suffer, without remedy, the groundless demands and oppressions of their stronger neighbours, because they have no avenger, or umpire of their disputes?

Or shall we institute a supreme power with full and effectual authority to controul the animosities, and decide the disputes of these strong contending bodies? In the one proposed to us, we have perhaps every chance of a *righteous judgment,* that we have any reason to hope for; but I am clearly of opinion, that even a *wrongful decision,* would, in most cases, be preferable to the continuance of such destructive controversies.

I suppose that neither Brutus nor any of his friends would wish to see our government *embroiled abroad;* and therefore will admit it necessary to institute some federal authority, sufficient to punish *any individual or State,* who shall violate our treaties with foreign nations, insult their dignity, or abuse their citizens, and compel due reparation in all such cases.

I further apprehend, that Brutus is willing to have the *general* interest and *welfare* of the States well provided for and supported, and therefore will consent that there shall exist in the states, an authority to *do* all this *effectually;* but he seems grieved that Congress should be the *judges of this general welfare* of the states. If he will be kind enough to point out any other more suitable and proper judges, I will consent to have them admitted.

Indeed I begin to have hopes of Brutus, and think he may come right at last; for I observe (after all his fear and tremblings about the new government) the constitution he *defines and adopts,* is the very same as that which the federal convention have proposed to us, *viz.* "that the Thirteen States should continue thirteen confederated republics under the *direction and controul* of a supreme federal head, for certain defined national purposes, only." Where we may observe,

1. That the new Constitution leaves all the Thirteen States, complete republics, as it found them, but all confederated under the direction and controul of a federal head, for certain defined national purposes only, *i.e.* it leaves all the dignities, authorities, and internal police of each State in free, full, and perfect condition; unless when national purposes make the controul of them by the federal head, or authority, necessary to the general benefit.

2. These powers of controul by the federal head or authority, are *defined* in the new constitution, as minutely as may be, in their principle; and any detail of them which may become necessary, is committed to the wisdom of Congress.

3. It extends the controuling power of the federal head to no one case, to which the jurisdiction or power of definitive decision of any one state, can be competent. And,

4. In every such case, the controuling power of the federal head, is absolutely necessary to the support, dignity, and benefit of the national government, and the safety of individuals; neither of which can, by any possibility, be secured without it.

All this falls in pretty well with Brutus's sentiments; for he does not think that the new Constitution in *its present state* so very bad, but fears that it will not preserve its purity of institution; but if adopted, will immediately verge to, and terminate in *a consolidation,* i.e. a destruction of the state governments. For argument, he suggests the avidity of power natural to rulers; and the eager grasp with which they hold it when obtained; and their strong propensity to abuse their power, and encroach on the liberties of the people.

He dwells on the vast powers vested in Congress by the new Constitution, *i.e.* of levying taxes, raising armies, appointing federal courts, *&c.;* takes it for granted, that all these powers will be abused, and carried to an oppressive excess; and then harrangues on the dreadful case we shall be in, when our *wealth* is all devoured by taxes, our *liberty* destroyed by the power of the army, and our *civil rights* all sacrificed by the unbounded power of the federal courts, *&c.*

And when he has run himself out of breath with this dreary declamation, he comes to the conclusion he set out with, *viz.* That the Thirteen States are too big for a republican government, which requires *small territory,* and can't be supported in *more extensive nations;* that in large states liberty will soon be swallowed up, and lost in the magnitude of power requisite in the government, *&c.*

If any conclusion at all can be drawn from this baseless assemblage of gloomy thoughts, I think it must be *against any union at all;* against *any kind of federal government.* For nothing can be plainer than this, *viz.* that *the union can't by any possibility be supported with success, without adequate and effectual powers of government?*

We must have *money* to support the union, and therefore the power of raising it must be lodged somewhere; we must have *a military force,* and of consequence the power of raising and directing it must exist; civil and criminal causes of national concern will arise, therefore there must be somewhere a power of appointing *courts* to hear and determine them.

These powers must be vested in Congress; for nobody pretends to wish to have them vested in any other body of men.

The Thirteen States have a territory very extensive, and inhabitants very numerous, and every day rapidly increasing; therefore the powers of government necessary to support their union must be great in proportion. If the ship is large, the mast must be proportionably great, or it will be impossible to make her sail well. The federal powers must extend to every part of the federal territory, *i.e.* to the utmost limits of the Thirteen States, and to every part of them; and must carry with them, sufficient authority to secure the execution of them; and these powers must be vested in Congress, and the execution of them must be under their direction and controul.

These powers are *vast,* I know, and the trust is of the most *weighty kind* that can be committed to human direction; and the execution and administration of it will require the greatest *wisdom, knowledge, firmness,* and *integrity* in that august body; and I hope they will have all the *abilities and virtues* necessary to their important station, and will *perform their duty well;* but if they fail, the fault is in them, not in the constitution. The best constitution possible, even a divine one, badly administered, will make a bad government.

The members of Congress will be the best we can get; they will all of them derive their appointment from the States, and if the States are not wise enough to send *good and suitable* men, great *blame,* great *sin* will lie at their door. But I suppose nobody would wish to mend this fault by taking away the election of the people, and directing the appointment of Congress to be made in any other way.

When we have gotten the best that can be obtained, we ought to be quiet and cease complaining. 'Tis not in the power of human wisdom to do more; 'tis the fate of human nature to *be imperfect and to err;* and no doubt but Congress, with all their *dignity of station and character,* with all their *opportunities* to gain *wisdom and information,* with all their *inducements to virtue and integrity,* will err, and abuse or misapply their powers in more or less instances. I have no expectation that they will make *a court of angels,* or be any thing more than *men:* 'tis probable many of them will be *insufficient* men, and some of them may be *bad men.*

The greatest wisdom, care, and caution, has been used in the *mode* of their appointment; in the *restraints and checks* under which they must act; in the numerous *discussions and deliberations* which all their acts must pass through, before they can receive the stamp of authority; in the terrors of *punishment* if they misbehave. I say, in all *these ways* the greatest care has been used to procure and form a good Congress.

The *dignity and importance* of their station and character will afford all the inducements to virtue and effort, which can influence a mind *capable* of their force.

Their own *personal reputation,* with the eyes of all the world on them,—the *approbation of their fellow citizens,* which every man in public station naturally wishes to enjoy,—and the *dread of censure and shame,* all contribute very forceable and strong inducements to noble, upright and worthy behavior.

The *particular interest* which every member of Congress has in every public order and resolution, is *another strong motive* to right action. For every act to which any member gives his sanction, if it be raising an *army,* levying a *tax,* instituting a *court,* or any other act to bind the *States,*—such act will equally bind *himself, his nearest connections, and his posterity.*

Another mighty influence to the noblest principle of action will be *the fear of God before their eyes;* for while they sit in the place of God, to give law, justice, and right to the States, they must be *monsters indeed* if they do not regard *his law,* and imitate *his character.*

If all this will not produce a Congress fit to be trusted, and worthy of the public confidence, I think we may give the matter up as impracticable.

But still we must make ourselves as easy as we can, under a *mischief* which admits *no remedy,* and bear with patience an *evil* which can't be *cured:* for a government we must have; there is no safety without it; though we know it will be imperfect, we still must prefer it to anarchy or no government at all. 'Tis the height of folly and madness to reject a necessary convenience, because it is not a perfect good.

Upon this statement of facts and principles (for the truth and reality of which, I appeal to every candid man,) I beg leave to remark,

1. That the federal Convention, in the constitution proposed to us, have exerted their utmost to produce *a Congress worthy of the public confidence,* who shall have *abilities* adequate to their important duty, and shall act under every possible inducement to execute it *faithfully.*

2. That this affords every chance which the nature of the thing will admit, of a wise and upright administration.

3. Yet all this notwithstanding, 'tis very possible that Congress *may err, may abuse, or misapply* their powers, which no precaution of human wisdom can prevent.

4. 'Tis *vain,* 'tis *childish,* 'tis *contentious* to object to a constitution thus framed and guarded, on pretence that the commonwealth may suffer by a bad administration of it; or to *withhold* the *necessary powers* of government, from the supreme rulers of it, least they should *abuse* or *misapply* those powers. This is an objection which will operate with equal force against every institution that can be made in this world, whether of policy, religion, commerce, or any other humane concern, which can require regulations: for 'tis not possible to form any institution however necessary, wise, and good, whose uses may not be lessened or destroyed by bad management.

If Brutus, or any body else, can point out any *checks, cautions,* or *regulations,* which have been hitherto omitted, which will make Congress more *wise,* more *capable,* more *diligent,* or more *faithful,* I am willing to attend to them. But to set Congress at the head of the government, and object to their being vested with full and sufficient power to manage all the great departments of it, appears to me *absurd,* quite *wild,* and *chimerical:* it would produce a plan which would destroy itself as it went along, would be a sort of counter position of contrary parts, and render it impossible for rulers to render those services, and secure those benefits to the States, which are the only great ends of their appointment.

The constitution under Brutus's corrections, would stand thus, *viz.* Congress would have power to *raise money,* but must not direct the *quantity,* or *mode of levying* it; they might raise *armies,* but must not judge of the *number* of soldiers necessary, or direct their destination; they ought to provide for the *general welfare,* but must not be judges of what that welfare *consists in,* or in *what manner* 'tis to be provided for; they might controul the several States, for *defined national purposes,* but must not be judges of *what purposes* would come within that *definition,* &c.

Any body with half an eye, may see what sort of administration the constitution, thus corrected, would produce, *e.g.* it would require much greater trouble to leave the work *undone,* than would be necessary to get it *well done,* under a constitution of sufficient powers. If any one wishes to view more minutely this blessed operation, he may see a lively sample of it, in the last seven years practice of our federal government.

5. Brutus all along founds his objections, and fears on *extreme cases* of abuse or misapplication of supreme powers, which may *possibly* happen, under the administration of a wild, weak, or wicked Congress; but 'tis easy to observe that all institutions are liable to *extremes,* but ought not *to be judged by them;* they do not often appear, and perhaps never may; but if they should happen in the cases supposed, (which God forbid,) there is *a remedy pointed out, in the Constitution itself.*

'Tis not supposeable that such abuses could arise to any ruinous height, before they would affect the States so much, that at least *two-thirds* of them would unite in pursuing a remedy, in the mode prescribed by the Constitution, which will always be liable to amendment, whenever any mischiefs or abuses appear in the government, which the Constitution in its present state, can't reach and correct.

6. Brutus thinks we can never be too much afraid of the *encroaching avidity of rulers;* but 'tis pretty plain, that however great the natural *lust of power in rulers* may be, the *jealousy of the people in giving it,* is about equal; these two opposite passions, will always operate in opposite directions to each

other, and like *action and reaction* in natural bodies, will ever tend to a good ballance.

At any rate, the Congress can never *get* more power than the people will *give,* nor *hold* it any longer than they will *permit;* for should they assume tyrannical powers, and make incroachments on liberty without the consent of the people, they would soon attone for their temerity, with shame and disgrace, and probably with their heads.

But 'tis here to be noted, that all the danger does not arise from the extreme of power *in the rulers;* for when the ballance verges to the contrary extreme, and the power of the rulers becomes too much *limited and cramped,* all the nerves of government are weakened, and the administration must unavoidably sicken, and lose that energy which is absolutely necessary for the support of the State, and the security of the people. For 'tis a truth worthy of great attention, that laws are not made so much for the *righteous* as for the *wicked;* who never fail to shelter themselves from punishment, whenever they can, under the *defects of the law, and the weakness of government.*

I now come to consider the grand proposition which Brutus sets out with, concludes with, and interlards all along, and which seems to be the great gift of his performance, viz. *That a confederation of the Thirteen States into one great republic is not best for them:* and goes on to prove by a variety of arguments, that *a republican form of government is not compatible, and cannot be convenient to so extensive a territory as the said States possess.* He begins by taking one assumption for granted (for I can't see that his arguments prove it at all) *viz.* That the Constitution proposed will melt down and destroy the *jurisdiction* of the particular States, and *consolidate* them all into one great republic.

I can't see the least reason for this sentiment; nor the least tendency in the new Constitution to produce this effect. For the Constitution does not suffer the federal powers to controul in the least, or so much as to interfere in the internal policy, jurisdiction, or municipal rights of any particular State; except where great and manifest *national purposes and interests* make that controul necessary. It appears very evident to me, that *the Constitution gives an establishment, support, and protection* to the *internal* and *separate police* of each State, under the superintendency of the federal powers, which it could not possibly enjoy in an independent state. Under the confederation each State derives strength, firmness, and permanency from its compact with the other States. Like a stave in a cask well bound with hoops, it stands *firmer,* is not so easily *shaken, bent,* or *broken,* as it would be were it set up by itself alone, without any connexion with its neighbours.

There can be no doubt that each State will receive from the union great *support and protection* against the *invasions and inroads* of foreign enemies, as well as against *riots and insurrections* of their own citizens; and of consequence, the course of their internal administration will be secured by this means against any *interruption or embarrassment* from either of these causes.

They will also derive their share of benefit from the respectability of the union abroad, from the treaties and alliances which may be made with foreign nations, *&c.*

Another benefit they will receive from the controul of the supreme power of the union is this, *viz.* they will be restrained from making *angry, oppressive, and destructive laws,* from declaring *ruinous wars* with their neighbours, from fomenting *quarrels and controversies,* &c. all which ever *weaken* a state, tend to its fatal *disorder,* and often end in its dissolution. *Righteousness exalts* and strengthens *a nation; but sin is a reproach* and weakening of *any people.*

They will indeed have the privilege of oppressing *their own citizens* by bad laws or bad administration; but the moment the mischief extends beyond their own State, and begins to affect the citizens of other States strangers, or the national welfare,—the salutary controul of the supreme power will check the evil, and restore *strength and security,* as well as *honesty and right,* to the offending state.

It appears then very plain, that the natural effect and tendency of the supreme powers of the union is to give *strength, establishment, and permanency* to the internal police and jurisdiction of each of the particular States; not to *melt down and destroy,* but to *support and confirm* them all.

By what sort of assurance, then, can *Brutus* tell us that the new Constitution, *if executed, must certainly and infallibly terminate in a consolidation of the whole, into one great republic, subverting all the State authorities.* His only argument is, that the federal powers *may be corrupted, abused,* and *mis-applied,* 'till this effect shall be produced. 'Tis true, that the constitution, like every other on earth, committed to human management, *may be corrupted by a bad administration,* and be made to operate to the *destruction* of the very capital benefits and uses, which were the great end of its institution. The same argument will prove with equal cogency, that the constitution of each particular State, may be corrupted in practice, become tyranical and inimical to liberty. In short the argument proves *too much,* and therefore proves *nothing:* 'tis empty, childish, and futile, and a serious proposal of it, is, I conceive, an affront to the human understanding.

But after all, supposing this event should take place, and by some strange fatality, the several States should be melted down, and merged in the great commonwealth, in the form of counties, or districts; I don't see why *a commonwealth mode of government, would not be as suitable and convenient for the great State, as any other form whatever;* I cannot see any sufficient ground or reason, for the position pretty often and boldly advanced, *that a republican form of government can never be suitable for any nation of extensive territory, and numerous population:* for if Congress can be chosen by the several States, though under the form and name of *counties, or election districts,* and be in every respect, instituted as directed by the new constitution, I don't see but we shall have as suitable a *national council,* as wise a *legislative,* and as strong and safe an *executive power,* as can be obtained under any form of government whatever; let our territory be ever so extensive or populous.

The most despotic monarch that can exist, must have his councils, and officers of state; and I can't see any one circumstance of their being appointed under a monarchy, that can afford any chance of their being any wiser or better, than ours may be. 'Tis true indeed, the despot may, if he pleases, act without any advice at all; but when he does so, I conceive it will be very rare that the nation will receive greater advantages from his unadvised edicts, than may be drawed from the deliberate acts and orders of our supreme powers. All that can be said in favour of *those,* is, that they will have less chance of delay, and more of secrecy, than *these;* but I think it probable, that the latter will be grounded on better information, and greater wisdom; will carry more weight, and be better supported.

The Romans rose, from small beginnings, to a very great extent of territory, population, and wisdom; I don't think their constitution of government, was near so good as the one proposed to us, yet we find their power, strength, and establishment, were raised to their utmost height, under *a republican form of government*. Their State received very little acquisition of territory, strength, or wealth, after their government became imperial; but soon began to weaken and decay.

The *Carthagenians* acquired an amazing degree of strength, wealth, and extent of dominion, under *a republican form of government*. Neither *they* or *the Romans,* owed their dissolation to any causes arising from *that kind of government:* 'twas the *party rage,* animosity, and violence of their citizens, which destroyed them both; it weakened them, 'till *the one* fell under the power of their enemy, and was thereby reduced to ruin; *the other* changed their form of government, to a monarchy, which proved in the end, equally fatal to them.

The same causes, if they can't be restrained, will weaken or destroy any nation on earth, let their form of government be what it will; witness the *division and dissolution* of the Roman empire; the late *dismemberment* of *Poland;* the intestine divisions, rage, and wars of *Italy,* of *France,* of *Spain,* and of *England.*

No form of government can preserve a nation which can't controul the party rage of its own citizens; when any one citizen can rise *above the controul* of the laws, *ruin* draws near. 'Tis not possible for any nation on earth, to hold their strength and establishment, when the dignity of their government is lost, and this dignity will forever depend on the *wisdom* and *firmness* of the officers of government, aided and supported by the *virtue* and *patriotism* of their citizens.

On the whole, I don't see but that any form of government may be safe and practicable, where the controuling authority of the supreme powers, is strong enough to effect the ends of its appointment, and at the same time, sufficiently *checked* to keep it within due bounds, and limit it to the objects of its duty; and I think it appears, that the constitution proposed to us, has all these qualities in as great perfection, as any form we can devise.

But after all, the *grand secret of forming a good government,* is, *to put good men into the administration:* for *wild, vicious, or idle men,* will ever make a bad government, let its principles be ever so good; but *grave, wise, and faithful men,* acting under a good constitution, will afford the best chance of security, peace, and prosperity, to the citizens, which can be derived from civil police, under the present disorders, and uncertainty of all earthly things.

Fisher Ames

Speech

Massachusetts Convention, 15 January 1788

A brilliant lawyer and writer, Fisher Ames was a leading Federalist and would become one of the most important interpreters of the Constitution. During Washington's administration (1789–97), he was a member of the lower house of the U.S. Congress. His distinguished public life earned him widespread fame.

I do not regret, Mr. President, that we are not unanimous upon this question. I do not consider the diversity of sentiment which prevails, as an impediment in our way to the discovery of truth. In order that we may think alike upon this subject at last, we shall be compelled to discuss it by ascending to the principles upon which the doctrine of representation is grounded.

Without premeditation, in a situation so novel, and awed by the respect which I feel for this venerable assembly, I distrust extremely my own feelings, as well as my competency to prosecute this inquiry. With the hope of an indulgent hearing, I will attempt to proceed. I am sensible, sir, that the doctrine of frequent elections has been sanctified by antiquity; and it is still more endeared to us by our recent experience, and uniform habits of thinking. Gentlemen have expressed their zealous partiality for it. They consider this as a leading question in the debate, and that the merits of many other parts of the constitution are involved in the decision. I confess, sir, and I declare, that my zeal for frequent elections is not inferior to their own. I consider it as one of the first securities for popular liberty, in which its very essence may be supposed to reside. But how shall we make the best use of this pledge and instrument of our safety?

A right principle, carried to an extreme, becomes useless. It is apparent that a declaration for a very short term, as for a single day, would defeat the design of representation. The election in that case would not seem to the people to be of any importance, and the person elected would think as lightly of his appointment. The other extreme is equally to be avoided. An election for a very long term of years, or for life, would remove the member too far from the control of the people, would be dangerous to liberty, and, in fact, repugnant to the purposes of the delegation. The truth, as usual, is placed somewhere between the extremes, and, I believe, is included in the proposition: the terms of election must be so long that the representative may understand the interests of the people, and yet so limited, that his fidelity may be secured by a dependence upon their approbation.

Before I proceed to the application of this rule, I cannot forbear to premise some remarks upon two opinions which have been suggested.

Much has been said about the people's divesting themselves of power, when they delegate it to representatives; and that all representation is to their disadvantage, because it is but an image, a copy, fainter and more imperfect than the original, the people, in whom the light of power is primary and unborrowed, which is only reflected by their delegates. I cannot agree to either of these opinions. The representation of the people is something more than the people. I know, sir, but one purpose which the people can effect without delegation, and that is, to destroy a government. That they cannot erect a government, is evinced by our being thus assembled on their behalf. The people must govern by a majority, with whom all power resides. But how is the sense of this majority to be obtained? It has been said that a pure democracy is the best government for a small people who assemble in person. It is of small consequence to discuss it, as it would be inapplicable to the great country we inhabit. It may be of some use in this argument, however, to consider that it would be very burdensome, subject to faction and violence; decisions would often be made by surprise, in the precipitancy of passion, by men who either understand nothing, or care nothing about the subject; or by interested men, or those who vote for their own indemnity. It would be a government not by laws, but by men.

Such were the paltry democracies of Greece and Asia Minor, so much extolled, and so often proposed as a model for our imitation. I desire to be thankful, (said Mr. Ames) that our people are not under any temptation to adopt the advice. I think it will not be denied that the people are gainers by the election of representatives. They may destroy, but they cannot exercise, the powers of government in person; but by their servants *they* govern; they do not renounce their power; they do not sacrifice their rights; they become the true sovereigns of the country when they delegate that power, which they cannot use themselves, to their trustees.

I know, sir, that the people talk about the liberty of nature, and assert that we divest ourselves of a portion of it when we enter into society. This is declamation against matter of fact. We cannot live without society; and as to liberty, how can I be said to enjoy that which another may take from me when he pleases? The liberty of one depends not so much on the removal of all restraint from him, as on the due restraint upon the liberty of others. Without such restraint, there can be no liberty. Liberty is so far from being endangered or destroyed by this, that it is extended and secured. For I said that we do not enjoy that which another may take from us. But civil liberty cannot be taken from us, when any one may please to invade it; for we have the strength of the society on our side.

I hope, sir, that these reflections will have some tendency to remove the ill impressions which are made by proposing to divest the people of their power.

That they may never be divested of it, I repeat, that I am in favor of frequent elections. They who commend annual elections are desired to consider, that the question is, whether biennial elections are a defect in the Constitution; for it does not follow, because annual elections are safe, that biennial are dangerous; for both may be good. Nor is there any foundation for the fears of those, who say that if we, who have been accustomed to choose for one year only, now extend it to two, the next stride will be to five or seven years, and the next for term of life; for this article, with all its supposed defects, is in favor of liberty. Being inserted in the Constitution, it is not subject to be repealed by law. We are sure that it is the worst of the case. It is a fence against ambitious encroachments, too high and too strong to be passed; in this respect, we have greatly the advantage of the people of England, and of all the world. The law which limits their Parliaments is liable to be repealed.

I will not defend this article by saying, that it was a matter of compromise in the federal Convention; it has my entire approbation as it stands. I think that we ought to prefer, in this article, biennial elections to annual; and my reasons for this opinion are drawn from these sources:

From the extent of the country to be governed;
The objects of their legislation;
And the more perfect security of our liberty.

It seems obvious that men who are to collect in Congress from this great territory, perhaps from the Bay of Fundy, or from the banks of the Ohio, and the shore of Lake Superior, ought to have a longer term in office than the delegates of a single state, in their own legislature. It is not by riding post to and from Congress, that a man can acquire a just knowledge of the true interests of the Union. This term of election is inapplicable to the state of a country as large as Germany, or as the Roman empire in the zenith of its power.

If we consider the objects of their delegation, little doubt will remain. It is admitted that annual elections may be highly fit for the state legislature. Every citizen grows up with a knowledge of the local circumstances of the state. But the business of the federal government will be very different. The objects of their power are few and national. At least two years in office will be necessary to enable a man to judge of the trade and interests of the state which he never saw. The time, I hope, will come, when this excellent country will furnish food, and freedom (which is better than food, which is the food of the soul) for fifty millions of happy people. Will any man say, that the national business can be understood in one year?

Biennial elections appear to me, sir, an essential security to liberty. These are my reasons:

Faction and enthusiasm are the instruments by which popular governments are destroyed. We need not talk of the power of an aristocracy. The people, when they lose their liberties, are cheated out of them. They nourish factions in their bosoms, which will subsist so long as abusing their honest credulity shall be the means of acquiring power. A democracy is a volcano, which conceals the fiery materials of its own destruction. These will produce an eruption, and carry desolation in their way. The people always mean right, and, if time is allowed for reflection and information, they will do right. I would not have the first wish, the momentary impulse of the public mind, become law; for it is not always the sense of the people, with whom I admit that all power resides. On great questions, we first hear the loud clamors of passion, artifice, and faction. I consider biennial elections as a security that the sober, second thought of the people shall be law. There is a calm review of public transactions, which is made by the citizens, who have families and children, the pledges of their fidelity. To provide for popular liberty, we must take care that measures shall not be adopted without due deliberation. The member chosen for two years will feel some independence in his seat. The factions of the day will expire before the end of his term.

The people will be proportionably attentive to the merits of a candidate. Two years will afford opportunity to the member to deserve well of them, and they will require evidence that he has done it.

But, sir, the representatives are the grand inquisition of the Union. They are, by impeachment, to bring great offenders to justice. One year will not suffice to detect guilt, and to pursue it to conviction; therefore, they will escape, and the balance of the two branches will be destroyed, and the people oppressed with impunity. The senators will represent the sovereignty of the States. The representatives are to represent the people. The offices ought to bear some proportion in point of importance. This will be impossible if they are chosen for one year only.

Will the people then blind the eyes of their own watchmen? Will they bind the hands which are to hold the sword for the defence? Will they impair their own power by an unreasonable jealousy of themselves?

For these reasons, I am clearly of opinion that the article is entitled to our approbation as it stands; and as it has been demanded, why annual elections were not preferred to biennial, permit me to retort the question, and to inquire, in my turn, what reason can be given, why, if annual elections are good, biennial elections are not better?

The inquiry in the latter part of Mr. Ames's speech being directed to the Hon. Mr. Adams, that gentleman said, he only *made the* inquiry for information, and that he had heard sufficient to satisfy himself of its propriety.

James Wilson

Speech

Pennsylvania Convention, 4 December 1787, afternoon

This version of Wilson's speech is that of Thomas Lloyd. Lloyd's notes have been included here and are indicated by { }.

Before I proceed to consider those qualities in the Constitution before us, which I think will insure it our approbation, permit me to make some remarks, and they shall be very concise, upon the objections that were offered this forenoon, by the member from Fayette (John Smilie).[1] I do it, at this time, because I think it will be better to give a satisfactory answer to the whole of the objections, before I proceed to the other part of my subject. I find that the doctrine of a single legislature is not to be contended for in this Constitution. I shall therefore say nothing on that point. I shall consider that part of the system, when we come to view its excellencies. Neither shall I take particular notice of his observation on the qualified negative of the President, for he finds no fault with it; he mentions, however, that he thinks it a vain and useless power, because it can never be executed. The reason he assigns for this is, that the king of Great Britain, who has an absolute negative over the laws proposed by Parliament, has never exercised it, at least, not for many years. It is true, and the reason why he did not exercise it was, that during all that time, the king possessed a negative before the bill had passed through the two houses, a much stronger power than a negative after debate. I believe, since the Revolution, at the time of William III, it was never known that a bill disagreeable to the Crown passed both houses. At one time in the reign of Queen Anne, when there appeared some danger of this being effected, it is well-known that she created twelve peers, and by that means effectually defeated it. Again, there was some risk of late

---

1. For John Smilie's remarks, see *DH*, 2:465–67.

years in the present reign, with regard to Mr. [Charles James] Fox's East India bill, as it is usually called, that passed through the House of Commons, but the king had interest enough in the House of Peers, to have it thrown out; thus it never came up for the royal assent. But that is no reason why this negative should not be exercised here, and exercised with great advantage. Similar powers are known in more than one of the states. The governors of Massachusetts and New York have a power similar to this; and it has been exercised frequently to good effect.

I believe the governor of New York, under this power, has been known to send back five or six bills in a week; and I well recollect that at the time the funding system was adopted by our legislature, the people in that state considered the negative of the governor as a great security, that their legislature would not be able to encumber them by a similar measure. Since that time an alteration has been supposed in the governor's conduct, but there has been no alteration in his power.

The honorable gentleman from Westmoreland (William Findley),[2] by his highly refined critical abilities, discovers an inconsistency in this part of the Constitution, and that which declares in [Article I,] section first: "All legislative powers, herein granted, shall be vested in a congress of the United States, which shall consist of a senate and a house of representatives," and yet here, says he, is a power of legislation given to the President of the United States, because every bill, before it becomes a law, shall be presented to him. Thus he is said to possess legislative powers. Sir, the Convention observed on this occasion strict propriety of language; "if he approve the bill when it is sent, he shall sign it, but if not he shall return it"; but no bill passes in consequence of having his assent—therefore he possesses no legislative authority.

The effect of his power upon this subject is merely this, if he disapproves a bill, two-thirds of the legislature become necessary to pass it into a law, instead of a bare majority. And when two-thirds are in favor of the bill, it becomes a law, not by his, but by authority of the two houses of the leg-

2. See *DH,* 2:461.

islature. We are told, in the next place, by the honorable gentleman from Fayette (John Smilie)[3] that in the different orders of mankind, there is that of a natural aristocracy. On some occasions, there is a kind of magical expression, used to conjure up ideas, that may create uneasiness and apprehension. I hope the meaning of the words is understood by the gentleman who used them. I have asked repeatedly of gentlemen to explain, but have not been able to obtain the explanation of what they meant by a consolidated government. They keep round and round about the thing, but never define. I ask now what is meant by a natural aristocracy? I am not at a loss for the etymological definition of the term, for, when we trace it to the language from which it is derived, an aristocracy means nothing more or less than a government of the best men in the community, or those who are recommended by the words of the constitution of Pennsylvania, where it is directed, that the representatives should consist of those most noted for wisdom and virtue. Is there any danger in such representation? I shall never find fault, that such characters are employed. Happy for us, when such characters can be obtained. If this is meant by a natural aristocracy, and I know no other, can it be objectionable, that men should be employed that are most noted for their virtue and talents? And are attempts made to mark out these as the most improper persons for the public confidence?

I had the honor of giving a definition, and I believe it was a just one, of what is called an aristocratic government. It is a government where the supreme power is not retained by the people, but resides in a select body of men, who either fill up the vacancies that happen, by their own choice and election, or succeed on the principle of descent, or by virtue of territorial possessions, or some other qualifications that are not the result of personal properties. When I speak of personal properties, I mean the qualities of the head and the disposition of the heart.

We are told that the Representatives will not be known to the people, nor the people to the Representatives, because they will be taken from large districts where they cannot be particularly acquainted. There has been some

3. For John Smilie's remarks, see *DH,* 2:465–66.

experience in several of the states, upon this subject, and I believe the experience of all who have had experience demonstrates that the larger the district of election, the better the representation. It is only in remote corners of a government, that little demagogues arise. Nothing but real weight of character can give a man real influence over a large district. This is remarkably shown in the Commonwealth of Massachusetts. The members of the House of Representatives are chosen in very small districts, and such has been the influence of party cabal and little intrigue in them, that a great majority seem inclined to show very little disapprobation of the conduct of the insurgents in that state.

The governor is chosen by the people at large, and that state is much larger than any district need be under the proposed Constitution. In their choice of their governor, they have had warm disputes; but however warm the disputes, their choice only vibrated between the most eminent characters. Four of their candidates are well-known: Mr. [John] Hancock, Mr. [James] Bowdoin, General [Benjamin] Lincoln, and Mr. [Nathaniel] Gorham, the late President of Congress.

I apprehend it is of more consequence to be able to know the true interest of the people, than their faces, and of more consequence still, to have virtue enough to pursue the means of carrying that knowledge usefully into effect. And surely when it has been thought hitherto, that a representation in Congress of from five to two members was sufficient to represent the interest of this state, is it not more than sufficient to have ten members in that body and those in a greater comparative proportion than heretofore? The citizens of Pennsylvania will be represented by eight, and the state by two. This, certainly, though not gaining enough, is gaining a good deal; the members will be more distributed through the state, being the immediate choice of the people, who hitherto have not been represented in that body. It is said that the House of Representatives will be subject to corruption, and the Senate possess the means of corrupting, by the share they have in the appointment to office. This was not spoken in the soft language of attachment to government. It is perhaps impossible, with all the caution of legislators and statesmen, to exclude corruption and undue influence entirely from government. All that can be done, upon this subject, is done in the Constitution before you. Yet it behooves us to call out, and add, every guard and preventative in our power. I think, sir, something very important on this subject is done in the present system. For it has been provided, effectually, that the man that has been bribed by an office shall have it no longer in his power to earn his wages. The moment he is engaged to serve the Senate, in consequence of their gift, he no longer has it in his power to sit in the House of Representatives. For "no representative shall, during the term for which he was elected, be appointed to any civil office, under the authority of the United States, which shall have been created, or the emoluments whereof shall have been encreased during such time." And the following annihilates corruption of that kind: "And no person holding any office under the United States, shall be a member of either house, during his continuance in office." So that the mere acceptance of an office as a bribe effectually destroys the end for which it was offered. Was this attended to when it was mentioned that the members of the one house could be bribed by the other? "But the members of the Senate may enrich themselves" was an observation made as an objection to this system. As the mode of doing this has not been pointed out, I apprehend the objection is not much relied upon. The Senate are incapable of receiving any money, except what is paid them out of the public treasury. They cannot vote to themselves a single penny, unless the proposition originates from the other house. This objection therefore is visionary, like the following one, "that pictured group, that numerous host, and prodigious swarm of officers, which are to be appointed under the general government." The gentlemen tell you that there must be judges of the supreme, and judges of the inferior courts, with all their appendages; there will be tax gatherers swarming throughout the land. Oh! say they, if we could enumerate the offices, and the numerous officers that must be employed every day, in collecting and receiving, and comptrolling the monies of the United States, the number would be almost beyond imagination. I have been told, but I do not vouch for the fact, that there are in one shape or another, more than a thousand persons in this very state, who get their living in assessing and collecting our revenues from the other citizens. Sir, when this business of revenue is conducted on a general plan, we may be able to do the business of the thirteen states, with an equal, nay, with a less number—instead of thirteen comptrollers general, one comptroller will be sufficient. I apprehend that the number of officers under this system will be greatly reduced from the number now employed. For as Congress can now do nothing effectually, the states are obliged to do everything. And in this very point, I apprehend, that we shall be great gainers.

Sir, I confess I wish the powers of the Senate were not as they are. I think it would have been better if those powers had been distributed in other parts of the system. I mentioned some circumstances in the forenoon, that I had observed on this subject.[4] I may mention now, we may think ourselves very well off, sir, that things are as well as they are, and that that body is even so much restricted. But surely objections of this kind come with a bad grace from the advocates, or those who prefer the present Confederation, and who wish only to increase the powers of the present Congress. A single body not constituted with checks, like the proposed one, who possess not only the power of making treaties, but executive powers, would be a perfect despotism; but, further, these powers are, in the present Confederation, possessed without control.

As I mentioned before, so I will beg leave to repeat, that this Senate can do nothing without the concurrence of some other branch of the government. With regard to their concern in the appointment to offices, the President must nominate before they can be chosen; the President must acquiesce in that appointment. With regard to their power in forming treaties, they can make none, they are only auxiliaries to the President. They must try all impeachments; but they have no power to try any until presented by the House of Representatives; and when I consider this subject, though I wish the regulations better, I think no danger to the liberties of this country can arise even from that part of the system. But these objections, I say, come with a bad grace from those who prefer the present Confederation, who think it only necessary to add more powers to a body organized in that form. I confess, likewise, that by combining those powers, of trying impeach-

4. James Wilson's morning speech is included in this volume. See *Friends*, 231–49.

ments, and making treaties, in the same body, it will not be so easy as I think it ought to be, to call the Senators to an account for any improper conduct in that business.

Those who proposed this system were not inattentive to do all they could. I admit the force of the observation made by the gentleman from Fayette (John Smilie)[5] that when two-thirds of the Senate concur in forming a bad treaty, it will be hard to procure a vote of two-thirds against them, if they should be impeached. I think such a thing is not to be expected; and so far they are without that *immediate* degree of responsibility, which I think requisite, to make this part of the work perfect. But this will not be *always* the case. When a member of Senate shall behave criminally, the criminality will not expire with his office. The Senators may be called to account after they shall have been changed, and the body to which they belonged shall have been altered. There is a rotation; and every second year one-third of the whole number go out. Every fourth year two-thirds of them are changed. In six years the whole body is supplied by a new one. Considering it in this view, responsibility is not entirely lost. There is another view in which it ought to be considered, which will show that we have a greater degree of security. Though they may not be convicted on impeachment before the Senate, they may be tried by their country; and if their criminality is established, the law will punish. A grand jury may present, a petit jury may convict, and the judges will pronounce the punishment. This is all that can be done under the present Confederation, for under it there is no power of impeachment; even here then we gain something. Those parts that are exceptionable in this Constitution are improvements on that concerning which so much pains are taken to persuade us, that it is preferable to the other.

The last observation respects the judges. It is said that if they dare to decide against the law, one house will impeach them, and the other will convict them. I hope gentlemen will show how this can happen, for bare supposition ought not to be admitted as proof. The judges are to be impeached because they decide an act null and void that was made in defiance

5. For John Smilie's remarks, see *DH,* 2:460–61.

of the Constitution! What House of Representatives would dare to impeach, or Senate to commit judges for the performance of their duty? These observations are of a similar kind to those with regard to the liberty of the press.

I will now proceed to take some notice of those qualities in this Constitution, that I think entitle it to our respect and favor. I have not yet done, sir, with the great principle on which it stands; I mean the practical recognition of this doctrine, that in the United States the people retain the supreme power.

In giving a definition of the simple kinds of government known throughout the world, I had occasion to describe what I meant by a democracy; and I think I termed it, that government in which the people retain the supreme power, and exercise it either collectively or by representation—this Constitution declares this principle in its terms and in its consequences, which is evident from the manner in which it is announced: "WE, THE PEOPLE OF THE UNITED STATES." After all the examination, which I am able to give the subject, I view this as the only sufficient and the most honorable basis, both for the people and government, on which our Constitution can possibly rest. What are all the contrivances of states, of kingdoms, and empires? What are they all intended for? They are all intended for man, and our natural character and natural rights are certainly to take place, in preference to all artificial refinements that human wisdom can devise.

I am astonished to hear the ill-founded doctrine, that states alone ought to be represented in the federal government; these must possess sovereign authority forsooth, and the people be forgot. No, let us *reascend* to first principles. That expression is not strong enough to do my ideas justice. Let us RETAIN first principles. The people of the United States are now in the possession and exercise of their original rights, and while this doctrine is known, and operates, we shall have a cure for every disease.

I shall mention another good quality, belonging to this system. In it the legislative, executive, and judicial powers are kept nearly independent and distinct. I express myself in this guarded manner, because I am aware of some powers that are blended in the Senate. They are but few; and they are not dangerous. It is an exception, yet that exception consists of but few instances, and none of them dangerous. I believe [that] in no constitution for any country on earth is this great principle so strictly adhered to, or marked with so much precision and accuracy, as in this. It is much more accurate, than that which the honorable gentleman [John Smilie] so highly extols, I mean the constitution of England. There, sir, one branch of the legislature can appoint the members of another. The king has the power of introducing members into the House of Lords. I have already mentioned that in order to obtain a vote, twelve peers were poured into that house at one time; the operation is the same, as might be under this Constitution, if the President had a right to appoint the members of the Senate. This power of the king's extends into the other branch, where, though he cannot immediately introduce a member, yet he can do it remotely by virtue of his prerogative, as he may create boroughs with power to send members to the House of Commons. The House of Lords form a much stronger exception to this principle than the Senate in this system; for the House of Lords possess judicial powers, not only that of trying impeachments, but that of trying their own members, and civil causes when brought before them, from the courts of chancery, and the other courts in England.

If we therefore consider this Constitution, with regard to this special object, though it is not so perfect as I would wish, yet it is more perfect than any other government that I know.

I proceed to another property which I think will recommend it to those who consider the effects of beneficence and wisdom. I mean the *division of this legislative authority* into two branches. I had an opportunity of dilating somewhat on this subject before. And as it is not likely to afford a subject of debate, I shall take no further notice of it, than barely to mention it. The next good quality, that I remark is, that the *executive authority is one;* by this means we obtain very important advantages. We may discover from history, from reasoning, and from experience, the security which this furnishes. The executive power is better to be trusted when it has no *screen.* Sir, we have a responsibility in the person of our President; he cannot act improperly, and hide either his negligence, or inattention; he cannot roll upon any other person the weight of his criminality. No appointment can take place without his nomination; and he is responsible for every nomination he makes. We secure *vigor;* we well know what numerous executives are. We know there is neither vigor, decision, nor responsibility in them. Add to all this, that officer is placed high, and is possessed of power, far from being contemptible, yet not a *single privilege* is annexed to his character; far from being *above the laws,* he is *amenable* to them in his *private character* as a *citizen,* and in his public character by impeachment.

Sir, it has often been a matter of surprise, and frequently complained of even in Pennsylvania, that the independence of the judges is not properly secured. The servile dependence of the judges, in some of the states that have neglected to make proper provision on this subject, endangers the liberty and property of the citizen; and I apprehend that whenever it has happened that the appointment has been for a less period than during good behavior, this object has not been sufficiently secured—for if every five or seven years, the judges are obliged to make court for a reappointment to office, they cannot be styled independent. This is not the case with regard to those appointed under the general government. For the judges here shall hold their offices during good behavior. I hope no further objections will be taken, against this part of the Constitution, the consequence of which will be, that private property (so far as it comes before their courts) and personal liberty, so far as it is not forfeited by crimes, will be guarded with firmness and watchfulness.

It may appear too professional to descend into observations of this kind, but I believe, that public happiness, personal liberty, and private property depend essentially upon the able and upright determinations of independent judges.

Permit me to make one more remark on the subject of the judicial department. Its objects are intended *beyond* the bounds or power of every particular state, and therefore must be proper objects of the general government. I do not recollect any instance where a case can come before the judiciary of the United States, that could possibly be determined by a particular state, except one, which is, where citizens of the same state claim lands under the grant of different states, and in that instance, the power of the two states necessarily comes in competition; wherefore there would be great impropriety in having it determined by either.

Sir, I think there is another subject with regard to which this Constitution deserves approbation. I mean the *accuracy* with which the *line is drawn* between the powers of the *general government,* and that of the *particular state governments.* We have heard some general observations on this subject, from the gentlemen who conduct the opposition. They have asserted that these powers are unlimited and undefined. These words are as easily pronounced as limited and defined. They have already been answered by my honorable colleague (Thomas M'Kean)[6] therefore, I shall not enter into an explanation; but it is not pretended, that the line is drawn with mathematical precision; the inaccuracy of language must, to a certain degree, prevent the accomplishment of such a desire. Whoever views the matter in a true light will see that the powers are as minutely enumerated and defined as was possible, and will also discover that the general clause [Article I, section 8], against which so much exception is taken, is nothing more than what was necessary to render effectual the particular powers that are granted.

But let us suppose (and the supposition is very easy in the minds of the gentlemen on the other side) that there is some difficulty in ascertaining where the true line lies. Are we therefore thrown into despair? Are disputes between the general government and the state governments to be necessarily the consequence of inaccuracy? I hope, sir, they will not be the enemies of each other, or resemble comets in conflicting orbits mutually operating destruction. But that their motion will be better represented by that of the planetary system, where each part moves harmoniously within its proper sphere, and no injury arises by interference or opposition. Every part, I trust, will be considered as a part of the United States. Can any cause of distrust arise here? Is there any increase of risk, or rather are not the enumerated powers as well defined here, as in the present Articles of Confederation?

Permit me to proceed to what I deem another excellency of this system— all authority of every kind *is derived by* REPRESENTATION *from the* PEOPLE, *and the* DEMOCRATIC *principle is carried into every part of the government.* I had an opportunity when I spoke first of going fully into an elucidation of this subject. I mean not now to repeat what I then said.

6. For Thomas McKean's remarks, see *DH,* 2:411–21.

I proceed to another quality that I think estimable in this system—*it secures in the strongest manner the right of suffrage.* Montesquieu, book 2d, ch. 2d, speaking of laws relative to democracy, says, "when the body of the people is possessed of the SUPREME POWER, this is called a *democracy.* When the SUPREME POWER is lodged in the hands of a part of the people, it is then an *aristocracy.*

"In a democracy the people are in some respects the sovereign, and in others the subject.

"There can be no exercise of sovereignty but by their suffrages, which are their own will; now, the sovereign's will is the sovereign himself. The laws, therefore, which establish the right of suffrage are fundamental to this government. And indeed it is as important to regulate, in a republic, in what manner, by whom, to whom, and concerning what, suffrages are to be given, as it is in a monarchy, to know who is the prince, and after what manner he ought to govern."

In this system it is declared, that the electors in each state shall have the qualification requisite for electors of the most numerous branch of the state legislature. This being made the criterion of the right of suffrage, it is consequently secured, because the same Constitution *guarantees* to every state in the Union a *republican* form of government. The right of suffrage is fundamental to republics.

Sir, there is another principle that I beg leave to mention. *Representation and direct taxation,* under this Constitution, are to be according to numbers. As this is a subject which I believe has not been gone into in this house, it will be worthwhile to show the sentiments of some respectable writers thereon. Montesquieu, in considering the requisites in a confederate republic, book 9th, ch. 3d, speaking of Holland observes, "it is difficult for the united states to be all of equal power and extent. The Lycian republic {Strabo, lib. 14} was an association of twenty-three towns; the large ones had three votes in the common council, the middling ones two, and the small towns one. The Dutch republic consists of seven provinces, of different extent of territory, which have each one voice."

The cities of Lycia {Strabo, lib. 14} *contributed to the expenses of the state, according to the proportion of suffrages.* The provinces of the United Netherlands cannot follow this proportion; they must be directed by that of their power.

In Lycia {Strabo, lib. 14} the judges and town magistrates were elected by the common council, *and according to the proportion already mentioned.* In the republic of Holland, they are not chosen by the common council, but each town names its magistrates. Were I to give a model of an excellent confederate republic, I should pitch upon that of Lycia.

I have endeavored, in all the books that I could have access to, to acquire some information relative to the Lycian republic, but its history is not to be found; the few facts that relate to it are mentioned only by Strabo; and however excellent the model it might present, we were reduced to the necessity of working without it. Give me leave to quote the sentiments of another author, whose peculiar situation and extensive worth throws a luster on all he says, I mean Mr. Neckar,[7] whose ideas are very exalted both in theory and practical knowledge on this subject. He approaches the nearest to the truth in his calculations from experience, and it is very remarkable that he makes use of that expression. His words are, {Neckar on Finance, Vol. 1. p. 308} "population can therefore be only looked on as an exact measure of comparison, when the provinces have resources nearly equal; but even this imperfect rule of proportion ought not to be neglected; and of all the objects which may be subjected to a determined and positive calculation, that of the taxes, to the population, approaches nearest to the truth."

Another good quality in this Constitution is, that the members of the *legislature cannot hold offices under the authority of this government.* The operation of this I apprehend would be found to be very extensive, and very salutary in this country, to prevent those intrigues, those factions, that corruption, that would otherwise rise here, and have risen so plentiful in every other country. The reason why it is necessary in England to continue such influence is that the Crown, in order to secure its own influence against two other branches of the legislature, must continue to bestow places, but those *places* produce the opposition which frequently runs so strong in the British Parliament.

---

7. Jacques Necker, *De L'Administration des Finances de la France* (n.p., 1785). See *DH,* 2:47.

Members who do not enjoy offices combine against those who do enjoy them. It is not from principle, that they thwart the ministry in all its operations. No, their language is, let us turn them out and succeed to their places. The great source of corruption in that country is that persons may hold offices under the Crown, and seats in the legislature at the same time.

I shall conclude at present, and I have endeavored to be as concise as possible, with mentioning, that in my humble opinion, the powers of the general government are necessary, and well defined—that the restraints imposed on it, and those imposed on the state governments, are rational and salutary, and that it is entitled to the approbation of those for whom it was intended.

I recollect, on a former day, the honorable gentleman from Westmoreland (William Findley)[8] and the honorable gentleman from Cumberland (Robert Whitehill)[9] took exceptions against the first clause of the 9th section, Article I, arguing very unfairly, that because Congress might impose a tax or duty of ten dollars on the importation of slaves, within any of the United States, Congress might therefore permit slaves to be imported within this state, contrary to its laws. I confess I little thought that this part of the system would be excepted to.

I am sorry that it could be extended no further; but so far as it operates, it presents us with the pleasing prospect, that the rights of mankind will be acknowledged and established throughout the Union.

If there was no other lovely feature in the Constitution, but this one, it would diffuse a beauty over its whole countenance. Yet the lapse of a few years and Congress will have power to exterminate slavery from within our borders.

How would such a delightful prospect expand the breast of a benevolent and philanthropic European? Would he cavil at an expression? Catch at a phrase? No, sir, that is only reserved for the gentleman [William Findley] on the other side of your chair to do. What would be the exultation of that great man, whose name I have just now mentioned, we may learn from the

8. For William Findley's remarks, see *DH*, 2:462.
9. For Robert Whitehill's remarks, see *DH*, 2:464.

following sentiments on this subject. They cannot be expressed so well as in his own words. {Neckar on Finance, Vol. i, page 329}

"The colonies of France contain as we have seen, near five hundred thousand slaves, and it is from the number of these wretches, that the inhabitants set a value on their plantations. What a fatal prospect and how profound a subject for reflection! Alas! How inconsequent we are, both in our morality, and our principles. We preach up humanity, and yet go every year to bind in chains twenty thousand natives of Africa! We call the Moors barbarians and ruffians, because they attack the liberty of Europeans, at the risk of their own; yet these Europeans go, without danger, and as mere speculators, to purchase slaves, by gratifying the cupidity of their masters; and excite all those bloody scenes which are the usual preliminaries of this traffic! In short, we pride ourselves on the superiority of man, and it is with reason that we discover this superiority, in the wonderful and mysterious unfolding of the intellectual faculties; and yet a trifling difference in the hair of the head, or in the color of the epidermis, is sufficient to change our respect into contempt, and to engage us to place beings like ourselves, in the rank of those animals devoid of reason, whom we subject to the yoke; that we may make use of their strength, and of their instinct, at command.

"I am sensible, and I grieve at it, that these reflections which others have made much better than me, are unfortunately of very little use! The necessity of supporting sovereign power has its peculiar laws, and the wealth of nations is one of the foundations of this power. Thus the sovereign who should be the most thoroughly convinced of what is due to humanity, would not singly renounce the service of slaves in his colonies; time alone could furnish a population of free people to replace them, and the great difference that would exist in the price of labor, would give so great an advantage to the nation that should adhere to the old custom, that the others would soon be discouraged in wishing to be more virtuous. And yet, would it be a chimerical project to propose a general compact, by which all the European nations should unanimously agree to abandon the traffic of African slaves! They would in that case, find themselves exactly in the same proportion relative to each other as at present; for it is only on comparative riches that the calculations of power are founded.

"We cannot as yet indulge such hopes; statesmen in general, think that every common idea must be a low one; and since the morals of private people stand in need of being curbed, and maintained by the laws, we ought not to wonder, if those of sovereigns conform to their independence.

"The time may nevertheless arrive, when, fatigued of that ambition which agitates them, and of the continual rotation of the same anxieties, and the same plans, they may turn their views to the great principles of humanity; and if the present generation is to be witness of this happy revolution, they may at least be allowed to be unanimous in offering up their vows for the perfection of the social virtues, and for the progress of public beneficial institutions." These are the enlarged sentiments of that great man.

Permit me to make a single observation in this place on the restraints placed on the state governments. If only the following lines were inserted in this Constitution, I think it would be worth our adoption: "No state shall hereafter *emit bills of credit;* make any thing, but gold and silver coin, a *tender* in payment of debts; pass any bills of attainder; ex post facto law; *or law impairing the obligation of contracts.*" Fatal experience has taught us, dearly taught us, the value of these restraints. What is the consequence even at this moment? It is true we have no tender law in Pennsylvania; but the moment you are conveyed across the Delaware you find it haunts your journey and follows close upon your heels. The paper passes commonly at twenty-five or thirty percent discount. How insecure is property!

These are a few of those properties in this system, that I think recommend it to our serious attention, and will entitle it to receive the adoption of the United States. Others might be enumerated, and others still will probably be disclosed by experience.

"Fabius"
[John Dickinson]

The Letters: IV–VI

IV

Another question remains. How are the contributed rights to be managed? The resolution has been in great measure anticipated, by what has been said concerning the system proposed. Some few reflections may perhaps finish it.

If it be considered separately, a *constitution* is the *organization* of the contributed rights in society. *Government* is the *exercise* of them. It is intended for the benefit of the governed; of course can have no just powers but what conduce to that end: and the awfulness of the trust is demonstrated in this— that it is founded on the nature of man, that is, on the will of his *Maker*, and is therefore sacred. It is then an offence against Heaven, to violate that trust.

If the organization of a constitution be defective, it may be amended.

A good constitution promotes, but not always produces a good administration.

The government must never be lodged in a single body. From such an one, with an unlucky composition of its parts, rash, partial, illegal, and when intoxicated with success, even cruel, insolent and contemptible edits, may at times be expected. By these, if other mischiefs do not follow, the national dignity may be impaired.

Several inconveniences might attend a division of the government into two bodies, that probably would be avoided in another arrangement.

The judgment of the most enlightened among mankind, confirmed by multiplied experiments, points out the propriety of government being committed to such a number of great departments, as can be introduced without confusion, distinct in office, and yet connected in operation. It seems to be agreed, that three or four of these departments are a competent number.

Such a repartition appears well calculated to express the sense of the people, and to encrease the safety and repose of the governed, which with the advancement of their happiness in other respects, are the objects of government; as thereby there will be more obstructions interposed; against errors, feuds, and frauds, in the administration, and the extraordinary interference of the people need be less frequent. Thus, wars, tumults, and uneasinesses, are avoided. The departments so constituted, may therefore be said to be balanced.

But, notwithstanding, it must be granted, that a bad administration may take place.—What is then to be done? The answer is instantly found—Let the Fasces be lowered before—the supreme sovereignty of the people. *It is their duty to watch, and their right to take care, that the constitution be preserved;* or in the Roman phrase on perilous occasions—*to provide, that the republic receive no damage.*

Political bodies are properly said to be balanced, with respect to this *primary origination* and *ultimate destination,* not to any intrinsic or constitutional properties. It is the *power* from which they *proceed,* and which they *serve,* that *truly and of right balances* them.

But, as a good constitution [does] not always produces a good administration, a defective one [does] not always excludes it. Thus in governments very different from those of United America, general manners and customs, improvement in knowledge, and the education and disposition of princes, not unfrequently soften the features, and qualify the defects. Jewels of value are substituted, in the place of the rare and genuine orient of highest price and brightest lustre: and though the sovereigns cannot even in their ministers, be brought to account by the governed, yet there are instances of their conduct indicating a veneration for the rights of the people, and an internal conviction of the guilt that attends their violation. Some of them appear to be fathers of their countries. Revered princes! Friends of mankind! May peace be in their lives—and in their deaths—Hope.

By this superior will of the people, is meant a reasonable, not a distracted will. When frenzy seizes the mass, it would be equal madness to think of their happiness, that is, of their freedom. They will infallibly have a Philip or a Cæsar, to bleed them into soberness of mind. At present we are cool; and let us attend to our business.

Our government under the proposed confederation, will be guarded by a repetition of the strongest cautions against excesses. In the senate the sovereignties of the several states will be equally represented; in the house of representatives, the people of the whole union will be equally represented; and, in the president, and the federal independent judges, so much concerned in the execution of the laws, and in the determination of their constitutionality, the sovereignties of the several states and the people of the whole union, may be considered as conjointly represented.

Where was there ever and where is there now upon the face of the earth, a government so diversified and attempered? If a work formed with so much deliberation, so respectful and affectionate an attention to the interests, feelings, and sentiments of all United America, will not satisfy, what would satisfy all United America?

It seems highly probable, that those who would reject this labour of public love, would also have rejected the Heaven-taught institution of *trial by jury*, had they been consulted upon its establishment. Would they not have cried out, that there never was framed so detestable, so paltry, and so tyrannical a device for extinguishing freedom, and throwing unbounded domination into the hands of the king and barons, under a contemptible pretence of preserving it? "What! Can freedom be preserved by imprisoning its guardians? Can freedom be preserved, by keeping twelve men closely confined without meat, drink, fire, or candle, until they unanimously agree, and this to be innumerably repeated? Can freedom be preserved, by thus delivering up a number of freemen to a monarch and an aristocracy, fortified by dependant and obedient judges and officers, to be shut up, until under duress they speak as they are ordered? Why cannot the twelve jurors separate, after hearing the evidence, return to their respective homes, and there take time, and think of the matter at their ease? Is there not a variety of ways, in which causes have been, and can be tried, without this *tremendous, unprecedented inquisition*? Why then is it insisted on; but because the fabricators of it know that it will, and intend that it shall reduce the people to slavery? Away with it—Freemen will never be enthralled by so insolent, so execrable, so pitiful a contrivance."

Happily for us our ancestors thought otherwise. They were not so over-nice and curious, as to refuse blessings, because, they might possibly be abused.

They perceived, that the uses included were great and manifest. Perhaps they did not foresee, that from this acorn, as it were, of their planting, would be produced a perpetual vegetation of political energies, that "would secure the just liberties of the nation for a long succession of ages, and elevate it to the distinguished rank it has for several centuries held." As to abuses, they trusted to their own spirit for preventing or correcting them: And worthy is it of deep consideration by every friend of freedom, that abuses that seem to be but "trifles," may be attended by fatal consequences. What can be "trifling," that diminishes or detracts from the only defence, that ever was found against "open attacks and secret machinations?" This establishment originates from a knowledge of human nature. With a superior force, wisdom, and benevolence united, it rives the difficulties concerning administration of justice, that have distressed, or destroyed the rest of mankind. It reconciles contradictions—vastness of power, with safety of private station. It is ever new, and always the same.

Trial by jury and the dependence of taxation upon representation, those corner stones of liberty, were not obtained by a bill of rights, or any other records, and have not been and cannot be preserved by them. They and all other rights must be preserved, by *soundness of sense and honesty of heart.* Compared with these, what are a bill of rights, or any characters drawn upon paper or parchment, those frail remembrances? Do we want to be reminded, that the sun enlightens, warms, invigorates, and cheers? or how horrid it would be, to have his blessed beams intercepted, by our being thrust into mines or dungeons? Liberty is the sun of society. Rights are the beams.

"It is the duty which every man owes to his country, his friends, his posterity, and himself, to maintain to the utmost of his power this valuable palladium in all its rights; to restore it to its ancient dignity, if at all impaired by the different value of property, or otherwise deviated from its first institution; to amend it, wherever it is defective; and above all to guard with the most jealous circumspection against the new and arbitrary methods of trial, which, under a variety of plausible pretences, may in time imperceptibly undermine this best preservative of liberty." Trial by Jury is our birthright; and tempted to his own ruin, by some seducing spirit, must be the man, who in opposition to the genius of United America, shall dare to attempt its subversion.

In the proposed confederation, it is preserved inviolable in criminal cases, and cannot be altered in other respects, but when United America demands it.

There seems to be a disposition in men to find fault, no difficult matter, rather than to act as they ought. The works of creation itself have been objected to: and one learned prince declared, that if he had been consulted, they would have been improved. With what book has so much fault been found, as with the Bible? Perhaps, principally, because it so clearly and strongly enjoins men *to do right*. How many, how plausible objections have been made against it, with how much ardor, with how much pains? Yet, the book has done more good than all the books in the world; would do much more, if duly regarded; and might lead the objectors against it to happiness, if they would value it as they should.

When objections are made to a system of high import, should they not be weighed against the benefits? Are these great, positive, immediate? Is there a chance of endangering them by rejection or delay? *May they not be attained without admitting the objections at present,* supposing the objections to be well founded? If the objections are well founded, may they not be hereafter admitted, without danger, disgust, or inconvenience? Is the system so formed, that they may be thus admitted? May they not be of less efficiency, than they are thought to be by their authors? are they not designed to hinder evils, which are generally deemed to be sufficiently provided against? May not the admission of them prevent benefits, that might otherwise be obtained? In political affairs, is it not more safe and advantageous, for all to agree in measures that may not be best, than to quarrel among themselves, what are best?

When questions of this kind with regard to the plan proposed, are calmly considered, it seems reasonable to hope, that every faithful citizen of United America, will make up his mind, with much satisfaction to himself, and advantage to his country.

V

It has been considered, what are the rights to be contributed, and how they are to be managed; and it has been said, that republican tranquility and prosperity have commonly been promoted, in proportion to the strength of government for protecting the worthy against the licentious.

The protection herein mentioned, refers to cases between citizens and citizens, or states and states: But there is also a protection to be afforded to all the citizens, or states, against foreigners. It has been asserted, that this protection never can be afforded, but under an appropriation, collection, and application, of the general force, by the will of the whole combination. This protection is in a degree dependent on the former, as it may be weakened by internal discords and especially where the worst party prevails. Hence it is evident, that such establishments as tend most to protect the worthy against the licentious, tends most to protect all against foreigners. This position is found to be verified by indisputable facts, from which it appears, that when nations have been, as it were, condemned for their crimes, unless they first became suicides, foreigners have acted as executioners.

This is not all. As government is intended for the happiness of the people, the protection of the worthy against those of contrary characters, is calculated to promote the end of legitimate government, that is the general welfare; for *the government will partake of the qualities of those whose authority is prevalent.* If it be asked, who are the worthy, we may be informed by a heathen poet—

"Vir bonus est quis?
"Qui consulta patrum, qui leges juraque servat."*

The best foundations of this protection, that can be laid by man, are a constitution and government secured, as well as can be, from the undue influence of passions either in the people or their servants.[1] Then in a contest

---

*He who reverses the constitution, liberties and laws of his country.—

1. In *The Federalist,* No. 49, Publius argues that "it is the reason alone, of the public, that ought to controul and regulate the government. The passions ought to be controuled and regulated by the government."

between citizens and citizens, or states and states, the standard of laws may be displayed, explained and strengthened by the well-remembered sentiments and examples of our fore-fathers, which will give it a sanctity far superior to that of their eagles so venerated by the former masters of the world. This circumstance will carry powerful aids to the true friends of their country, and unless counteracted by the follies of Pharsalia, or the accidents of Philippi, may secure the blessings of freedom to succeeding ages.

It has been contended that the plan proposed to us, adequately secures us against the influence of passions in the federal servants. Whether it as adequately secures us against the influence of passions in the people, or in particular states, time will determine, and *may the determination be propituous.*

Let us now consider the tragical play of the passions in similar cases; or, in other words, the consequences of their irregularities. Duly governed, they produce happiness.

Here the reader, is respectfully requested, to assist the intentions of the writer, by keeping in mind, the ideas of a single republic with one democratic branch in its government, and of a confederation of republics with one or several democratic branches in the government of the confederation, or in the government of its parts, so that as he proceeds, a comparison may easily run along, between any of these and the proposed plan.

History is entertaining and instructive; but if admired chiefly for amusement, it may yield little profit. If read for improvement, it is apprehended, a slight attention only will be paid to the vast variety of particular incidents, unless they be such as may meliorate the heart. A knowledge of the distinguishing features of nations, the principles of their governments, the advantages and disadvantages of their situations, the methods employed to avail themselves of the first, and to alleviate the last, their manners, customs, and institutions, the sources of events, their progresses, and determining causes, may be eminently useful, tho' obscurity may rest upon a multitude of attending circumstances. Thus one nation may become prudent and happy, not only by the wisdom and success, but even by the errors and misfortunes of another.[2]

2. See Douglass Adair, *Fame and the Founding Fathers.*

In Carthage and Rome, there was a very numerous senate, strengthened by prodigious attachments, and in a great degree independent of the people. In Athens, there was a senate strongly supported by the powerful court of Areopagus. In each of these republics, their affairs at length became convulsed, and their liberty was subverted. What cause produced these effects? Encroachments of the senate upon the authority of the people? No! but directly the reverse, according to the unanimous voice of historians; that is, encroachments of the people upon the authority of the senate. The people of these republics absolutely *laboured* for their own destruction; and never thought themselves so free, as when they were promoting their own subjugation. Though even after these encroachments had been made, and ruin was spreading around, yet the remnants of senatorial authority delayed the final catastrophe.

In more modern times, the Florentines exhibited a memorable example. They were divided into violent parties; and the prevailing one vested exorbitant powers in the house of Medici, then possessed, as it was judged, of more money than any crowned head in Europe. Though that house engaged and persevered in the attempt, yet the people were never despoiled of their liberty, until they were overwhelmed by the armies of foreign princes, to whose enterprizes their situation exposed them.

Republics of later date and various form have appeared. Their institutions consist of old errors tissued with hasty inventions, somewhat excusable, as the wills of the Romans, made with arms in their hands. Some of them were condensed, by dangers. They are still compressed by them into a sort of union. Their well-known transactions witness, that their connection is not enough compact and arranged. They have all suffered, or are suffering through that defect. Their existence seems to depend more upon others, than upon themselves. There might be an impropriety in saying more, considering the peculiarity of their circumstances at this time.

The wretched mistake of the great men who were leaders in the long parliament of England, in attempting, by not filling up vacancies, to extend their power over a brave and sensible people, accustomed to *popular representation,* and their downfal, when their victories and puissance by sea and land had thrown all Europe into astonishment and awe, shew, how difficult it is for rulers to usurp over a people who are not wanting to themselves.

Let the fortunes of confederated republics be now considered.

"The Amphictionic council," or "general court of Greece," claims the first regard. Its authority was very great: But, the parts were not sufficiently combined, to guard against the ambitious, avaricious, and selfish projects of some of them; or, if they had the power, they dared not to employ it, as the turbulent states were very sturdy, and made a sort of partial confederacies.

"The Achæan league" seems to be the next in dignity. It was at first, small, consisting of few states: afterwards, very extensive, constituting of many. In their diet or Congress, they enacted laws, disposed of vacant employments, declared war, made peace, entered into alliances, compelled every state of the union to obey its ordinances, and managed other affairs. Not only their laws, but their magistrates, council, judges, money, weights and measures, were the same. So uniform were they, that all seemed to be but one state. Their chief officer called Strategos, was chosen in the Congress by a majority of votes. He presided in the Congress, commanded the forces, and was vested with great powers, especially in time of war: but was liable to be called to an account by the Congress, and punished, if convicted of misbehaviour.

The states have been oppressed by the kings of Macedon, and insulted by tyrants. "From their incorporation," says Polybius, "may be dated the birth of that greatness, that by a constant augmentation, at length arrived to a marvellous height of prosperity. The same of their wise laws and mild government reached the Greek colonies in Italy, where the Grotoniates, the Sybarites, and the Cauloniates, agreed to adopt them, and to govern their states conformably."

Did the delegates to the Amphictionic council, or to the Congress of the Achæan league destroy the liberty of their country, by establishing a monarchy or an aristocracy among themselves? Quite the contrary. *While the several states continued faithful to the union, they prospered.* Their affairs were shattered by dissensions, emulations, and civil wars, artfully and diligently fomented by princes who thought it their interest; and in the case of the Achæan league, partly, by the folly and wickedness of Greeks not of the league, particularly the Ætolians, who repined at the glories, that constantly attended the banner of freedom, supported by virtue and conducted by prudence. Thus weakened, they all sunk together, the envied and the envying, under the domination, first of Macedon, and then of Rome.

Let any man of common sense peruse the gloomy but instructive pages of their mournful story, and he will be convinced, that if any nation could successfuly have resisted those conquerors of the world, the illustrious deed had been achieved by Greece; that cradle of republics, if the several states had been cemented by some such league as the Achæan, and had honestly fulfilled its obligations.

It is not pretended, that the Achæan league was perfect, or that they were not monarchical and aristocratical factions among the people of it. Every concession of that sort, that can be asked, shall be made. It had many defects; every one of which, however, has been avoided in the plan proposed to us.

With all its defects, with all its disorders, yet such was the life and vigor communicated through the whole, by the popular representation of each part, and the close combination of all, that the true spirit of republicanism *predominated,* and thereby advanced the happiness and glory of the people to so pre-eminent a state that *our* ideas upon the pleasing theme cannot be too elevated. Here is the proof of this assertion. When the Romans had laid Carthage in ashes; had reduced the kingdom of Macedon to a province; had conquered Antiochus the great, and got the better of all their enemies in the East; these Romans, masters of so much of the then known world, determined to humble the Achæan league, because as history expressly informs us, "their great power began to raise no small jealousy at Rome."— Polybius.

What a vast weight of argument do these facts and circumstances add to the maintenance of the principle contended for by the writer of this address?

VI

Some of our fellow-citizens have ventured to predict the future state of United America, if the system proposed to us, shall be adopted.

Though every branch of the constitution and government is to be popular, and guarded by the strongest provisions, that until this day have occurred to mankind, yet the system will end, they say, in the oppressions of a monarchy or aristocracy by the federal servants or some of them.

Such a conclusion seems not in any manner suited to the premises. It startles, yet, not so much from its novelty, as from the respectability of the characters by which it is drawn.

We must not be too much influenced by our esteem for those characters: But, should recollect, that when the fancy is warmed, and the judgment inclined, by the proximity or pressure of particular objects, very extraordinary declarations are not unfrequently made. Such are the frailties of our nature, that genius and integrity sometimes afford no protection against them.

Probably, there never was, and never will be, such an instance of dreadful denunciation, concerning the fate of a country, as was published while the union was in agitation between England and Scotland. The English were for a joint legislature, many of the Scots for separate legislatures, and urged, that they should be in a manner swallowed up and lost in the other, as then they would not possess one eleventh part in it.

Upon that occasion lord Belhaven, one of the most distinguished orators of the age, made in the Scottish parliament a famous speech, of which the following extract is part:

"My lord Chancellor,

"When I consider this affair of an union between the two nations, as it is expressed in the several articles thereof, and now the subject of our deliberation at this time, I find my mind crowded with a variety of very melancholy thoughts, and I think it my duty to disburthen myself of some of them, by laying them before and exposing them to the serious consideration of this honourable house.

"I think, *I see a free and independent kingdom* delivering up that, which all world hath been fighting for since the days of Nimrod; yea, that, for which most of all the empires, kingdoms, states, principalities, and dukedoms of Europe, are at this very time engaged in the most bloody and cruel wars that ever were; to wit, *a power to manage their own affairs by themselves, without the assistance and council of any other.*

"I think I see *a National Church,* founded upon a rock, secured by a claim of right, hedged and fenced about by the strictest and pointedest legal sanctions that sovereignty could contrive, voluntarily descending into a plain upon an equal level with Jews, Paptists, Socinians, Armenians, and Anabaptists, and other Sectaries, &c.

"I think I see *the noble and honorable peerage of Scotland,* whose valiant predecessors led against their enemies upon their own proper charges and expences, now divested of their followers and vassalages, and put upon such an equal foot with their vassals, that I think, I see a petty English *excise-man* receive more homage and respect, than what was paid formerly to their quondam Mackallamors.

"I think, I see *the present peers of Scotland,* whose noble ancestors, conquered provinces, over-run countries, reduced and subjected towns and fortified places, exacted tribute through the greatest part of England, now walking in the *court of requests,* like so many English Attornies, laying aside their walking swords when in company with the English Peers, lest their self-defence should be found murder.

"I think, I see *the honorable Estate of Barons,* the bold assertors of the nations rights and liberties in the worst of times, now setting *a watch upon their lips* and *a guard upon their tongues,* lest they be found guilty of *scandalum magnatum.*

"I think I see *the royal State of Boroughs,* walking their *desolate streets,* hanging down their heads *under disappointments;* worm'd out of *all the branches of their old trade,* uncertain *what hand to turn to,* necessitated to become apprentices to their unkind neighbors, and yet after all finding their *trade so fortified by companies* and secured by prescriptions, that they despair of any success therein.

"I think, I see *our learned Judges* laying aside their practiques and decisions, studying the common law of England, gravelled with certioraries, *nisi priuses,* writs of error, *ejectiones firmæ,* injunctions, demurrers, &c. and frighted with *appeals* and *avocations,* because of *the new regulations,* and *rectifications* they meet with.

"I think, I see *the valiant and gallant soldiery,* either sent to learn the plantation trade abroad, or at home petitioning for *a small subsistence,* as the reward of their honourable exploits, while their old corps are broken, the common soldiers left to beg, and the youngest English corps kept standing.

"I think, I see the *honest industrious tradesman* loaded with *new taxes and impositions,* disappointed of the equivalents, drinking water in place of ale, eating his saltless pottage, petitioning for *encouragement to his manufactories,* and answered by counter petitions.

"In short, I think I see the *laborious ploughman,* with his corn spoiling upon his hands *for want of sale,* cursing the day of his birth; dreading the expence of his burial, and uncertain whether to marry or do worse.

"I think I see the incurable difficulties of *landing men,* fettered under the golden chain of equivalents, their pretty daughters petitioning for want of husbands, and their sons for want of employments.

"I think I see *our mariners delivering up their ships* to their Dutch partners, and what through *presses and necessity* earning their bread as underlings in the English navy. But above all, my lord, I think, I see *our ancient mother Caledonia,* like Cæsar, sitting in the midst of our senate, ruefully looking round about her, covering herself with her royal garment, attending the fatal blows and breathing out her last with a ————*Et tu quoque mi fili.*

"Are not these, my lord, very afflicting thoughts? And yet they are the least part suggested to me by these dishonorable articles. Should not the considerations of these things vivify these dry bones of ours? Should not the memory of our noble predecessors' valor and constancy rouse up our drooping spirits? Are our noble predecessors' souls got so far into the English cabbage-stalks and cauliflowers, that we should shew the least inclination that way? Are our eyes so blinded? Are our ears so deafened? Are our hearts so hardened? Are our tongues so faultered? Are our hands so fettered? that in this our day, I say, my lord, that in this our day, we should not mind the things that concern the very being and well being of our ancient kingdom, before the day be hid from our eyes.

"When I consider this treaty as it hath been explained, and spoke to, before us these three weeks by past; I see the *English* constitution remaining firm, the same *two houses* of Parliament, the same *taxes,* the same *customs,* the same *excises,* the same *trading companies,* the same municipal laws and courts of judicature; *and all ours either subject to regulations or annihilations,* only we are to have *the honor* to pay *their old debts,* and to have some few persons present for witnesses, to the validity of the deed, when they are pleased to contract more."

Let any candid American deliberately compare that transaction with the present, and laying his hand upon his heart, solemnly answer this question to himself—Whether, he does not verily believe the eloquent Peer before mentioned, had ten-fold more cause to apprehend evils from such an unequal match between the two kingdoms, that any citizen of these states has to apprehend them from the system proposed? Indeed not only that Peer, but other persons of distinction, and large numbers of the people of Scotland were filled with the utmost aversion to the union; and if the greatest diligence and prudence had not been employed by its friends in removing misapprehensions and refuting misrepresentations, and by the then subsisting government for preserving the public peace, there would certainly have been a rebellion.

Yet, *what were the consequences* to Scotland of that *dreaded* union with England? The cultivation of her virtues and the correction of her errors—The emancipation of one class of her citizens from the yoke of her superiors—A relief of other classes from the injuries and insults of the great—Improvements in agriculture, science, arts, trade, and manufactures—The profits of industry and ingenuity enjoyed under the protection of laws—peace and security at home, and encrease of respectability abroad. Her Church is still eminent—Her laws and courts of judicature are safe—Her boroughs grown into cities—Her mariners and soldiery possessing a larger subsistence than she could have afforded them, and her tradesmen, ploughmen, landed men, and her people of every rank, in a more flourishing condition, not only than they ever were, but in a more flourishing condition, than the clearest understanding could, at the time, have thought it possible for them to attain in so short a period, or even in many ages. England participated in the blessings. The stock of their union or ingraftment, as perhaps it may be called, being strong and capable of drawing better nutriment and in greater abundance, than they could ever have done apart,

"Ere long, to Heaven the soaring branches shoot,
And wonder at their height, and more than native fruit."

James Wilson

Speech

Pennsylvania Convention, 4 December 1787, morning

This version of Wilson's speech is that of Thomas Lloyd. Lloyd's errata have been included here and are indicated by { }.

I shall take this opportunity, of giving an answer to the objections already urged against the Constitution; I shall then point out some of those qualities, that entitle it to the attention and approbation of this Convention; and after having done this, I shall take a fit opportunity of stating the consequences, which I apprehend will result from rejecting it and those which will probably result from its adoption. I have given the utmost attention to the debates and the objections, that from time to time have been made by the three gentlemen who speak in opposition. I have reduced them to some order, perhaps not better than that in which they were introduced. I will state them; they will be in the recollection of the house, and I will endeavor to give an answer to them—in that answer, I will interweave some remarks, that may tend to elucidate the subject.

A good deal has already been said concerning a bill of rights; I have stated, according to the best of my recollection, all that passed in Convention relating to that business. Since that time, I have spoken with a gentleman who has not only his memory but full notes that he had taken in that body; and he assures me, that upon this subject, no direct motion was ever made at all; and certainly, before we heard this so violently supported out of doors, some pains ought to have been taken to have tried its fate within; but the truth is, a bill of rights would, as I have mentioned already, have been not only unnecessary but improper. In some governments it may come within the gentleman's [John Smilie][1] idea, when he says it can do no harm; but

1. For John Smilie's remarks, see *DH*, 2:440–41.

even in these governments, you find bills of rights do not uniformly obtain; and do those states complain who have them not? Is it a maxim in forming governments, that not only all the powers which are given, but also that all those which are reserved, should be enumerated? I apprehend, that the powers given and reserved form the whole rights of the people as men and as citizens. I consider that there are very few who understand the *whole* of these rights. All the political writers, from Grotius and Puffendorf down to Vattel, have treated on this subject; but in no one of those books, nor in the aggregate of them all, can you find a complete enumeration of rights, appertaining to the people as men and as citizens.

There are two kinds of government; that where general power is intended to be given to the legislature and that where the powers are particularly enumerated. In the last case, the implied result is, that nothing more is intended to be given, than what is so enumerated, unless it results from the nature of the government itself. On the other hand, when general legislative powers are given, then the people part with their authority, and on the gentleman's principle of government, retain nothing. But in a government like the proposed one, there can be no necessity for a bill of rights. For, on my principle, the people never part with their power. Enumerate all the rights of men! I am sure, sir, that no gentleman in the late Convention would have attempted such a thing. I believe the honorable speakers in opposition on this floor were members of the Assembly which appointed delegates to that Convention; if it had been thought proper to have sent them into that body, how luminous would the *dark conclave* have been! So the gentleman [William Findley][2] has been pleased to denominate that body. Aristocrats as they were, they pretended not to define the rights of those who sent them there. We are asked repeatedly, what *harm* could the addition of a bill of rights do? If it can do no *good,* I think that a sufficient reason to refuse having any thing to do with it. But to whom are we to report this bill of rights, if we should adopt it? Have we authority from those who sent us here to make one?

It is true we may propose, as well as any other private persons; but how shall we know the sentiments of the citizens of this state and of the other

2. For William Findley's remarks, see *DH,* 2:439–40.

states? Are we certain that any one of them will agree with our definitions and enumerations?

In the second place, we are told, that there is no check upon the government but the people; it is fortunate, sir, if their superintending authority is allowed as a check. But I apprehend that in the very construction of this government, there are numerous checks. Besides those expressly enumerated, the two branches of the legislature are mutual checks upon each other. But this subject will be more properly discussed, when we come to consider the form of government itself; and then I mean to show the reason, why the right of *habeas corpus* was secured by a particular declaration in its favor.

In the third place we are told, that there is no security for the rights of conscience. I ask the honorable gentleman [John Smilie], what part of this system puts it in the power of Congress to attack those rights? When there is no power to attack, it is idle to prepare the means of defense.

After having mentioned, in a cursory manner, the foregoing objections, we now arrive at the leading ones against the proposed system.

The very manner of introducing this Constitution, by the recognition of the authority of the people, is said to change the principle of the present Confederation, and to introduce a *consolidating* and absorbing government!

In this confederated republic, the sovereignty of the states, it is said, is not preserved. We are told, that there cannot be two sovereign powers, and that a subordinate sovereignty is no sovereignty.

It will be worthwhile, Mr. President, to consider this objection at large. When I had the honor of speaking formerly on this subject,[3] I stated, in as concise a manner as possible, the leading ideas that occurred to me, to ascertain where the supreme and sovereign power resides. It has not been, nor, I presume, will it be denied, that somewhere there is, and of necessity must be, a supreme, absolute and uncontrollable authority. This, I believe, may justly be termed the sovereign power; for from that gentleman's (William Findley's)[4] account of the matter, it cannot be sovereign unless it is

---

3. James Wilson's 24 November 1787 speech is included in this volume. See *DH*, 2:350–63; *Friends*, 71–87.

4. For William Findley's remarks, see *DH*, 2:445–46.

supreme; for, says he, a subordinate sovereignty is no sovereignty at all. I had the honor of observing, that if the question was asked, where the supreme power resided, different answers would be given by different writers. I mentioned, that Blackstone will tell you, that in Britain, it is lodged in the British Parliament; and I believe there is no writer on this subject on the other side of the Atlantic but supposes it to be vested in that body. I stated further, that if the question was asked, some politician, who had not considered the subject with sufficient accuracy, where the supreme power resided in our governments, he would answer, that it was vested in the state constitutions. This opinion approaches near the truth, but does not reach it; for the truth is, that the supreme, absolute, and uncontrollable authority *remains* with the people. I mentioned also, that the practical recognition of this truth was reserved for the honor of this country. I recollect no constitution founded on this principle. But we have witnessed the improvement, and enjoy the happiness, of seeing it carried into practice. The great and penetrating mind of Locke seems to be the only one that pointed towards even the theory of this great truth.

When I made the observation, that some politicians would say the supreme power was lodged in our state constitutions, I did not suspect that the honorable gentleman from Westmoreland (William Findley) was included in that description; but I find myself disappointed; for I imagined his opposition would arise from another consideration. His position is, that the supreme power resides in the states, as governments; and mine is, that it *resides* in the PEOPLE, as the fountain of government; that the people have not—that the people mean not—and that the people ought not to part with it to any government whatsoever. In their hands it remains secure. They can delegate it in such proportions, to such bodies, on such terms, and under such limitations as they think proper. I agree with the members in opposition, that there cannot be two sovereign powers on the same subject.

I consider the people of the United States, as forming one great community; and I consider the people of the different states, as forming communities again on a lesser scale. From this great division of the people into distinct communities, it will be found necessary, that different proportions of legislative powers should be given to the governments, according to the nature, number, and magnitude of their objects.

Unless the people are considered in these two views, we shall never be able to understand the principle on which this system was constructed. I view the states as made *for* the People, as well as *by* them, and not the People as made for the states; the People, therefore, have a right, whilst enjoying the undeniable powers of society, to form either a general government, or state governments, in what manner they please; or to accommodate them to one another; and by this means preserve them all; this, I say, is the inherent and unalienable right of the people; and as an illustration of it, I beg to read a few words from the Declaration of Independence, made by the representatives of the United States and recognized by the whole Union.

"We hold these truths to be self-evident, that all men are created equal; that they are endowed by their Creator with certain unalienable rights; that among these are life, liberty, and the pursuit of happiness. That to secure these rights, *governments* are instituted among men, *deriving their just powers from the consent of the governed;* that whenever any form of government becomes destructive of these ends, it is the RIGHT of the People, to alter or to abolish it, and institute new governments, laying its foundation on such principles, and organizing its powers in such forms, as to them shall seem most likely to effect their safety and happiness."

This is the broad basis on which our independence was placed; on the same certain and solid foundation this system is erected.

State sovereignty, as it is called, is far from being able to support its weight. Nothing less than the authority of the people could either support it or give it efficacy. I cannot pass over this subject, without noticing the different conduct pursued by the late Federal Convention and that observed by the convention which framed the constitution of Pennsylvania; on that occasion you find an attempt made to deprive the people of this right, so lately and so expressly asserted in the Declaration of Independence. We are told in the preamble to the declaration of rights, and frame of government, that *we* "do, by virtue of the authority vested in *us* [by our constituents], ordain, declare and establish, the following declaration of rights, and frame of government, to be the constitution of this commonwealth, and to remain in force therein UNALTERED, except in such articles as shall hereafter, on experience, be found to require improvement, and which shall, by the same authority of the people, [be] fairly delegated *as this frame of government directs.*" An honorable gentleman (Stephen Chambers) was well warranted in saying, that all that could be done, was done, to cut off the people from the right of amending; for if it {*cannot*} be amended by any other mode than that which it directs; then any number more than one-third may control any number less than two-thirds.

But I return to my general reasoning. My position is, sir, that in this country the supreme, absolute, and uncontrollable power resides in the people at large; that they have vested certain proportions of this power in the state governments; but that the fee simple continues, resides, and remains with the body of the people. Under the practical influence of this great truth, we are now sitting and deliberating, and under its operation, we can sit as calmly, and deliberate as coolly, in order to change a constitution, as a legislature can sit and deliberate under the power of a constitution, in order to alter or amend a law. It is true the exercise of this power will not probably be so frequent, nor resorted to on so many occasions in one case as in the other; but the recognition of the principle cannot fail to establish it more firmly; {*but*} because this recognition is made in the proposed Constitution, an exception is taken to the whole of it; for, we are told, it is a violation of the present Confederation—a CONFEDERATION of SOVEREIGN STATES. I shall not enter into an investigation of the present Confederation, but shall just remark, that its principle is not the principle of free governments. The PEOPLE of the United States are not as such represented in the present Congress; and considered even as the component parts of the several states, they are not represented in proportion to their numbers and importance.

In this place I cannot help remarking on the general inconsistency which appears between one part of the gentleman's [John Smilie] objections and another. Upon the principle we have now mentioned, the honorable gentleman contended, that the powers ought to flow from the states; and that all the late Convention had to do was to give additional powers to Congress. What is the present form of Congress? A single body, with some legislative, but little executive and no effective judicial power. What are these additional powers that are to be given? In some cases legislative are wanting, in others judicial, and in others executive; these, it is said, ought to be allotted to the general government; but the impropriety of delegating such extensive trust to one body of men is evident; yet in the same day, and perhaps in the same hour, we are told, by honorable gentlemen, that these three branches of government are not kept sufficiently distinct in this Constitution; we are told also that the Senate, possessing some executive power, as well as legislative, is such a monster that it will swallow up and absorb every other body in the general government after having destroyed those of the particular states.

Is this reasoning with consistency? Is the Senate under the proposed Constitution so tremendous a body, when checked in their legislative capacity by the House of Representatives, and in their executive authority by the President of the United States? Can this body be so tremendous as the present Congress, a single body of men possessed of legislative, executive, and judicial powers? To what purpose was Montesquieu read to show that this was a complete tyranny? The application would have been more properly made by the advocates of the proposed Constitution, against the patrons of the present Confederation.

It is mentioned that this federal government will annihilate and absorb all the state governments. I wish to save as much as possible the time of the house, I shall not, therefore, recapitulate what I had the honor of saying last week[5] on this subject; I hope it was then shown, that instead of being abolished (as insinuated) from the very nature of things, and from the organization of the system itself, the state governments must exist, or the general government must fall amidst their ruins; indeed so far as to the forms, it is admitted they may remain; but the gentlemen seem to think their power will be gone.

I shall have occasion to take notice of this power hereafter, and, I believe, if it was necessary, it could be shown that the state governments, as states, will enjoy as much power, and more dignity, happiness, and security than

5. For James Wilson's 28 November 1787 speech, see *DH,* 2:403–6.

they have hitherto done. I admit, sir, that some of the powers will be taken from them, by the system before you; but it is, I believe, allowed on all hands, at least it is not among us a disputed point, that the late Convention was appointed with a particular view to give more power to the government of the Union. It is also acknowledged, that the intention was to obtain the advantage of an efficient government over the United States; now, if power is to be given to that government, I apprehend it must be taken from some place. If the state governments are to retain all the powers they held before, then, of consequence, every new power that is given to Congress must be taken from the people at large. Is this the gentleman's intention? I believe a strict examination of this subject will justify me in asserting, that the states, as governments, have assumed too much power to themselves, while they left little to the people. Let not this be called cajoling the people—the elegant expression used by the honorable gentleman from Westmoreland (William Findley); it is hard to avoid censure on one side or the other. At some time it has been said, that I have not been at the pains to conceal my contempt of the people; but when it suits a purpose better, it is asserted that I cajole them. I do neither one nor the other. The voice of approbation, sir, when I think that approbation well earned, I confess is grateful to my ears; but I would disdain it, if it is to be purchased by a sacrifice of my duty or the dictates of my conscience. No, sir, I go practically into this system, I have gone into it practically when the doors were shut; when it could not be alleged that I cajoled the people, and I now endeavor to show that the true and only safe principle for a free people is a practical recognition of their original and supreme authority.

I say, sir, that it was the design of this system to take some power from the state government and to place it in the general government. It was also the design, that the people should be admitted to the exercise of some powers, which they did not exercise under the present Confederation. It was thought proper, that the citizens, as well as the states should be represented; how far the representation in the Senate is a representation of states, we shall see by and by, when we come to consider that branch of the federal government.

This system, it is said, "unhinges and eradicates the state governments, and was systematically intended so to do"; to establish the *intention,* an argument is drawn from Article Ist, section 4th on the subject of elections. I have already had occasion to remark upon this, and shall therefore pass on to the next objection.

That the last clause of the 8th section of the Ist Article gives the power of self-preservation to the general government, *independent* of the states. For in case of their *abolition,* it will be alleged in behalf of the general government, that self-preservation is the first law, and necessary to the exercise of *all other* powers.

Now let us see what this objection amounts to. Who are to have this self-preserving power? The Congress. Who are Congress? It is a body that will consist of a Senate and a House of Representatives. Who compose this Senate? Those who are *elected* by the *legislatures* of the different states. Who are the electors of the House of Representatives? Those who are *qualified* to *vote* for the most numerous branch of the *legislature* in the separate states. Suppose the state legislatures annihilated, where is the criterion to ascertain the qualification of electors? And unless this be ascertained, they cannot be admitted to vote; if a state legislature is not elected, there can be no Senate, because the Senators are to be chosen by the *legislatures only.*

This is a plain and simple deduction from the Constitution, and yet the objection is stated as conclusive upon an argument expressly drawn from the last clause of this section.

It is repeated, with confidence, "that this is not a *federal* government, but a complete one, with legislative, executive and judicial powers. It is a *consolidating* government." I have already mentioned the misuse of the term; I wish the gentleman [William Findley] would indulge us with his definition of the word. If, when he says it is a consolidation, he means so far as relates to the general objects of the Union—so far it was intended to be a consolidation, and on such a consolidation, perhaps our very existence, as a nation, depends. If, on the other hand (as something which has been said seems to indicate) he (William Findley) means that it will absorb the governments of the individual states, so far is this position from being admitted, that it is unanswerably controverted. The existence of the state government is one of the most prominent features of this system. With regard to those purposes which are allowed to be for the general welfare of the Union, I think it no objection to this plan, that we are told it is a complete government. I think it no objection, that it is alleged the government will possess legislative, executive, and judicial powers. Should it have only legislative authority! We have had examples enough of such a government to deter us from continuing it. Shall Congress any longer continue to make requisitions from the several states, to be treated sometimes with silent and sometimes with declared contempt? For what purpose give the power to make laws, unless they are to be executed? And if they are to be executed, the executive and judicial powers will necessarily be engaged in the business.

Do we wish a return of those insurrections and tumults to which a sister state was lately exposed or a government of such insufficiency as the present is found to be? Let me, sir, mention one circumstance in the recollection of every honorable gentleman who hears me. To the determination of Congress are submitted all disputes between states concerning boundary, jurisdiction, or right of soil. In consequence of this power, after much altercation, expense of time, and considerable expense of money, this state was successful enough to obtain a decree in her favor, in a difference then subsisting between her and Connecticut; but what was the consequence? The Congress had no power to carry the decree into execution. Hence the distraction and animosity, which have ever since prevailed, and still continue in that part of the country. Ought the government then to remain any longer incomplete? I hope not; no person can be so insensible to the lessons of experience as to desire it.

It is brought as an objection "that there will be a rivalship between the state governments and the general government; on each side endeavors will be made to increase power."

Let us examine a little into this subject. The gentlemen tell you, sir, that they expect the states will not possess any power. But I think there is reason to draw a different conclusion. Under this system their respectability and power will increase with that of the general government. I believe their happiness and security will increase in a still greater proportion; let us attend a moment to the situation of this country; it is a maxim of every government, and it ought to be a maxim with us, that the increase of numbers increases the dignity, the security, and the respectability of all governments; it is the first command given by the Deity to man, increase and multiply; this applies with peculiar force to this country, the smaller part of whose territory is yet inhabited. We are representatives, sir, not merely of the present age, but of future times; not merely of the territory along the seacoast, but of regions immensely extended westward. We should fill, as fast as possible, this extensive country, with men who shall live happy, free, and secure. To accomplish this great end ought to be the leading view of all our patriots and statesmen. But how is it to be accomplished, but by establishing peace and harmony among ourselves, and dignity and respectability among foreign nations. By these means, we may draw numbers from the other side of the Atlantic, in addition to the natural sources of population. Can either of these objects be attained without a protecting head? When we examine history, we shall find an important fact, and almost the only fact, which will apply to all confederacies. They have all fallen to pieces, and have not absorbed the subordinate government{*s*}.

In order to keep republics together they must have a strong binding force, which must be either external or internal. The situation of this country shows, that no foreign force can press us together, the bonds of our Union ought therefore to be indissolubly strong.

The powers of the states, I apprehend, will increase with the population and the happiness of their inhabitants. Unless we can establish a character abroad, we shall be unhappy from foreign restraints or internal violence. These reasons, I think, prove sufficiently the necessity of having a federal head. Under it the advantages enjoyed by the whole Union would be participated [in] by every state. I wish honorable gentlemen would think not only of themselves, not only of the present age, but of others and of future times.

It has been said, "that the state governments will not be able to make head against the general government," but it might be said with more propriety, that the general government will not be able to maintain the powers given it against the encroachments and combined attacks of the state governments. They possess some particular advantages, from which the general government is restrained. By this system, there is a provision made in the Constitution that no Senator or Representative shall be appointed to any civil office under the authority of the United States, which shall have been created, or the emoluments whereof shall have been increased during the time for which he was elected; and no person holding any office under the United States can be a member of either house; but there is no similar security against state influence, as a Representative may enjoy places and even sinecures under the state governments. On which side is the door most open to corruption? If a person in the legislature is to be influenced by an office, the general government can give him none unless he vacate his seat. When the influence of office comes from the state government, he can retain his seat and salary too. But, it is added, under this head "that state governments will lose the attachment of the people, by losing the power of conferring advantages, and that the people will not be at the expense of keeping them up." Perhaps the state governments have already become so expensive as to alarm the gentlemen on that head. I am told that the civil list of this state amounted to £40,000 in one year. Under the proposed government, I think it would be possible to obtain in Pennsylvania every advantage we now possess, with a civil list that shall not exceed one-third of that sum.

How differently the same thing is talked of, if it be a favorite or otherwise! When advantages to an officer are to be derived from the general government, we hear them mentioned by the name of *bribery*, but when we are told of the states' governments losing the power of conferring advantages, by the disposal of offices, it is said they will lose the *attachment* of the people. What is in one instance corruption and bribery, is in another the power of conferring advantages.

We are informed "that the state elections will be ill-attended, and that the state governments will become mere boards of electors." Those who have a due regard for their country will discharge their duty and attend; but those who are brought only from interest or persuasion had better stay away; the public will not suffer any disadvantage from their absence. But the honest citizens, who know the value of the privilege, will undoubtedly attend to secure the man of his choice. The power and business of the state legislatures relates to the great objects of life, liberty, and property; the same are also objects of the general government.

Certainly the citizens of America will be as tenacious in the one instance as in the other. They will be interested, and I hope will exert themselves to secure their rights not only from being injured by the state governments, but also from being injured by the general government.

"The power over election, and of judging of elections, gives absolute sovereignty"; this power is given to every state legislature, yet I see no necessity, that the power of absolute sovereignty should accompany it. My general position is, that the absolute sovereignty never goes from the people.

We are told, "that it will be in the power of the Senate to prevent any addition of Representatives to the lower house."

I believe their power will be pretty well balanced, and though the Senate should have a desire to do this, yet the attempt will answer no purpose; for the House of Representatives will not let them have a farthing of public money, till they agree to it. And the latter influence will be as strong as the other.

"Annual assemblies are necessary" it is said—and I answer in many instances they are very proper. In Rhode Island and Connecticut they are elected for six months. In larger states, that period would be found very inconvenient, but in a government as large as that of the United States, I presume that annual elections would be more disproportionate, than elections for six months would be in some of our largest states.

"The British Parliament took to themselves the prolongation of their sitting to seven years. But even in the British Parliament the appropriations are annual."

But, sir, how is the argument to apply here? How are the Congress to assume such a power? They cannot assume it under the Constitution, for that expressly provides "the members of the house of representatives shall be chosen every two years, by the people of the several states, and the senators for six years." So if they take it at all, they must take it by usurpation and force.

"Appropriations may be made for two years, though in the British Parliament they are made but for one"; for some purposes, such appropriations may be made annually, but for every purpose they are not; even for a standing army, they may be made for seven, ten, or fourteen years—the civil list is established, during the life of a prince. Another objection is "that the members of the Senate may enrich themselves—they may hold their office as long as they live, and there is not power to prevent them; the Senate will swallow up everything." I am not a blind admirer of this system. Some of the powers of the Senators are not with me the favorite parts of it, but as they stand connected with other parts, there is still security against the efforts of that body. It was with great difficulty that security was obtained, and I may risk the conjecture, that if it is not now accepted, it never will be obtained again from the same states. Though the Senate was not a favorite of mine, as to some of its powers, yet it was a favorite with a majority in the Union, and we must submit to that majority, or we must break up the Union. It is but fair to repeat those reasons, that weighed with the Convention. Perhaps, I shall not be able to do them justice, but yet I will attempt to show, why additional powers were given to the Senate, rather than to the House of Representatives. These additional powers, I believe, are, that of trying impeachments, that of concurring with the President in making treaties, and that of concurring in the appointment of officers. These are the powers that are stated as improper. It is fortunate, that in the exercise of every one of them, the Senate stands controlled. If it is that monster which it [is] said to be, it can only show its teeth; it is unable to bite or devour. With regard to impeachments, the Senate can try none but such as will be brought before them by the House of Representatives.

The Senate can make no treaties; they can approve of none unless the President of the United States lay it before them. With regard to the appointment of officers, the President must nominate before they can vote. So that if the powers of either branch are perverted, it must be with the approbation of some one of the other branches of government. Thus checked on each side, they can do no one act of themselves.

"The powers of Congress extend to taxation—to direct taxation—to internal taxation—to poll taxes—to excises—to other state and internal purposes." Those who possess the power to tax, possess all other sovereign power. That their powers are thus extensive is admitted; and would any thing short of this have been sufficient? Is it the wish of these gentlemen? If it is, let us hear their sentiments—that the general government should subsist on the bounty of the states. Shall it have the power to contract, and no power to fulfill the contract? Shall it have the power to borrow money, and no power to pay the principal or interest? Must we go on, in the track that we have hitherto pursued and must we again compel those in Europe, who lent us money in our distress, to advance the money to pay themselves interest on the certificates of the debts due to them?

This was actually the case in Holland, the last year. Like those who have shot one arrow, and cannot regain it, they have been obliged to shoot another in the same direction, in order to recover the first. It was absolutely necessary, sir, that this government should possess these rights, and why should it not, as well as the state governments? Will this government be fonder of the exercise of this authority, than those of the states are? Will the states, who are equally represented in one branch of the legislature, be more opposed to the payment of what shall be required by the future, than what has been required by the present Congress? Will the people, who must indisputably pay the whole, have more objections to the payment of this tax, because it is laid by persons of their own immediate appointment, even if those taxes were to continue as oppressive as they now are? But under the general power of this system, that cannot be the case in Pennsylvania. Throughout the Union, direct taxation will be lessened, at least in proportion to the increase of the other objects of revenue. In this Constitution, a power is given to Congress to collect imposts, which is not given by the present Articles of Confederation. A very considerable part of the revenue of the United States will arise from that source; it is the easiest, most just, and most productive mode of raising revenue; and it is a safe one, because it is voluntary. No man is obliged to consume more than he pleases, and each buys in proportion only to his consumption. The price of the commodity is blended with the tax, and the person is often not sensible of the payment. But would it have been proper to have rested the matter there? Suppose this fund should not prove sufficient, ought the public debts to remain unpaid or the exigencies of government be left unprovided for? Should our tranquility be exposed to the assaults of foreign enemies, or violence among ourselves, because the objects of commerce may not furnish a sufficient revenue to secure them all? Certainly Congress should possess the power of raising revenue from their constituents, for the purpose mentioned in the eighth section of the first Article, that is "to pay the debts and provide for the common defence and general welfare of the United States." It has been common, with the gentlemen on this subject, to present us with frightful pictures. We are told of the hosts of tax gatherers that will swarm through the land; and whenever taxes are mentioned, military force seems to be an attending idea. I think I may venture to predict, that the taxes of the general government (if any shall be laid) will be more equitable, and much less expensive, than those imposed by the state government.

I shall not go into an investigation of this subject; but it must be confessed, that scarcely any mode of laying and collecting taxes can be more burdensome than the present.

Another objection is, "that Congress may borrow money, keep up standing armies, and command the militia." The present Congress possesses the power of borrowing money and of keeping up standing armies. Whether it will be proper at all times to keep up a body of troops will be a question to be determined by Congress; but I hope the necessity will not subsist at all times; but if it should subsist, where is the gentleman that will say that they ought not to possess the necessary power of keeping them up?

It is urged, as a general objection to this system, that "the powers of Congress are unlimited and undefined, and that they will be the judges, in all cases, of what is necessary and proper for them to do." To bring this subject to your view, I need do no more than point to the words in the Constitution, beginning at the 8th section, Article 1st. "The Congress," it says, "shall have power, etc." I need not read over the words, but I leave it to every gentleman to say whether the powers are not as accurately and minutely defined, as can be well done on the same subject, in the same language. The old constitution is as strongly marked on this subject; and even the concluding clause, with which so much fault has been found, gives no more, or other powers; nor does it in any degree go beyond the particular enumeration; for when it is said, that Congress shall have power to make all laws which shall be necessary and proper, those words are limited, and defined by the following, "for carrying into execution the foregoing powers." It is saying no more than that the powers we have already particularly given shall be effectually carried into execution.

I shall not detain the house, at this time, with any further observations on the liberty of the press, until it is shown that Congress have any power whatsoever to interfere with it, by licensing it, or declaring what shall be a libel.

I proceed to another objection, which was not so fully stated as I believe it will be hereafter; I mean the objection against the judicial department. The gentleman from Westmoreland [William Findley] only mentioned it to illustrate his objection to the legislative department. He said "that the judicial powers were coextensive with the legislative powers, and extend even to capital cases." I believe they ought to be coextensive, otherwise laws would be framed, that could not be executed. Certainly, therefore, the executive and judicial departments ought to have power commensurate to the extent of the laws; for, as I have already asked, are we to give power to *make* laws, and no power to *carry them into effect?*

I am happy to mention the punishment annexed to one crime. You will find the current running strong in favor of humanity. For this is the first instance in which it has not been left to the legislature, to extend the crime and punishment of treason so far as they thought proper. This punishment and the description of this crime are the great sources of danger and persecution, on the part of government against the citizen. Crimes against the state! and against the officers of the state!; history informs us, that more wrong may be done on this subject than on any other whatsoever. But under this Constitution, there can be no treason against the United States, except such as is defined in this Constitution. The manner of trial is clearly pointed out; the positive testimony of two witnesses to the same overt act or a confession in open court is required to convict any person of treason. And after all, the consequences of the crime shall extend no further than the life of the criminal; for no attainder of treason shall work corruption of blood, or forfeiture, except during the life of the person attainted.

I come now to consider the last set of objections that are offered against this Constitution. It is urged, that this is not such a system as was within the powers of the Convention; they assumed the *power of proposing.* I believe they might have made proposals without going beyond their powers. I never heard before, that to make a proposal was an exercise of power. But if it is an exercise of power, they certainly did assume it; yet they did not act as that body who framed the present constitution of Pennsylvania acted; they did not by an ordinance attempt to rivet the constitution on the people, before they could vote for members of Assembly under it. Yet such was the effect of the ordinance that attended the constitution of this commonwealth. I think the late Convention have done nothing beyond their powers. The fact is, they have exercised no power at all. And in point of validity, this Constitution, proposed by them for the government of the United States, claims no more than a production of the same nature would claim, flowing from a private pen. It is laid before the citizens of the United States, unfettered by restraint; it is laid before them to be judged by the natural, civil, and political rights of men. By their FIAT, it will become of value and authority; without it, it will never receive the character of authenticity and power. The business, we are told, which was entrusted to the late Convention was merely to amend the present Articles of Confederation. This observation has been frequently made, and has often brought to my mind a story that is related of Mr. [Alexander] Pope, who, it is well known, was not a little deformed. It was customary with him to use this phrase, "God mend me," when any little accident happened. One evening a linkboy was lighting him along, and coming to a gutter, the boy jumped nimbly over it. Mr. Pope called to him to turn, adding, "God mend me." The arch rogue turned to light him—looked at him, and repeated "God mend you! He would sooner make half a dozen new ones." This would apply to the present Confederation; for it would be easier to make another than to mend this. The gentlemen urge, that this is such a government as was not expected by the people, the legislatures, nor by the honorable gentlemen who mentioned it. Perhaps it was not such as was expected, *but it may be* BETTER; and is that a reason why it should not be adopted? It is not worse, I trust, than the former. So that the argument of its being a system not expected is an argument more strong in its favor than against it. The letter which accompanies this Constitution, must strike every person with the utmost force. "The friends of our country have long seen and desired the power of war, peace, and treaties, that of levying money and regulating commerce, and the corresponding executive and judicial authorities, should be fully and effectually vested in the general government of the union; but the impropriety of delegating such extensive trust to one body of men, is evident. *Hence results the necessity of a different organization.*[6] I therefore do not think that it can be urged as an objection against this system, that it was not expected by the people. We are told, to add greater force to these objections, that they are not on local, but on general principles, and that they are uniform throughout the United States. I confess I am not altogether of that opinion; I think some of the objections are inconsistent with others, arising from a different quarter, and I think some are inconsistent, even with those derived from the same source. But, on this occasion, let us take the fact for granted, that they are all on general principles, and uniform throughout the United States. Then we can judge of their full amount; and what are they, BUT TRIFLES LIGHT AS AIR? We see the whole force of them; for according to the sentiments of opposition, they can nowhere be stronger, or more fully stated than here. The conclusion, from all these objections, is reduced to a point, and the plan is declared to be inimical to our liberties. I have said nothing, and mean to say nothing, concerning the dispositions or characters of those that framed the work now before you. I agree that it ought to be judged by its own intrinsic qualities. If it has not merit, weight of character ought not to carry it into effect. On the other hand, if it has merit, and is calculated to secure the blessings of liberty, and to promote the general welfare, then such objections as have hitherto been made ought not to influence us to reject it.

I am now led to consider those qualities that this system of government possesses, which will entitle it to the attention of the United States. But as I have somewhat fatigued myself, as well as the patience of the honorable members of this house, I shall defer what I have to add on this subject until the afternoon.

6. *The President of the Convention to the President of Congress,* 17 September 1787. *DH,* 1:305–6.

"*Alfredus*"
[Samuel Tenny]

Essay: I

Freeman's Oracle, Exeter, 18 January 1788

Samuel Tenny was a New Hampshire surgeon fairly active in public affairs.

I

Messeurs PRINTERS, In your Oracle of the 11th current I observed an address to the Farmers of the State, by one who pretends to belong to that respectable class of citizens.[1] Whether he does or not is of no consequence. In this address he labors hard to tincture the public mind with jealouses and prejudicies against the new Constitution. Having possessed himself of that wretched hobby-horse, a Bill of Rights, which has been best ridden by every antifederal scribbler thro' the United States, till he is jaded into a perfect hack equally unfit for service and shew, he has mounted him, armed *cap-a-pre* with Federal courts, trial by Jury, liberty of the Press. Standing armies, etc. and etc. Thus accoutred and mounted and perfectly resembling Don Quixote and the Renaissance in their memorable attack as the Wind-Mill, he Sallies out against the new Constitution, calling on his brethren to witness his amazing prowess and address in the dangerous conflict. But the patrons of this admirable system, of federal government, need be under no apprehensions for its fate in this expedition. Whatever may be the valor of the Rider, the steed has no mettle and will certainly fail him in the terrible onset. For a proof of this I shall insert in this address the Speech of Mr. [James] Wilson in the Pennsylvania Convention on the subject of a Bill of

---

1. Alfredus refers to the first essay in a series by A Farmer, which was printed in the New Hampshire *Freeman's Oracle* and the *New Hampshire Advertiser* between January and June 1788. Storing identifies Colonel Thomas Cogswell, Chief Justice of the New Hampshire Court of Common Pleas, as A Farmer. See Storing, 4:17.

Rights, by which it will appear that it is not only *unnecessary* in the new Constitution, but would be *impractical* and *dangerous*. The substance of this speech is as follows.

"Mr. President,"

"We are repeatedly called upon to give some reason why a bill of rights has not been annexed to the proposed plan. I not only think that enquiry is at this time unnecessary and out of order, but I expect, at least, that those who desire us to shew why it was omitted will furnish some arguments to shew that it ought to have been inserted; for the proof of the affirmative naturally falls upon them. But the truth is, Sir, that this circumstance, which has since occasioned so much clamour and debate, never struck the mind of any member in the late convention until, I believe, within three days of the dissolution of that body, and even then, of so little account was the idea, that it passed off in a short conversation, without introducing a formal debate, or assuming the shape of a motion. For, Sir, the attempt to have thrown into the national scale an instrument in order to evince that any power not mentioned in the constitution was reserved, would have been formed at as an insult to the common understanding of mankind. In civil governments it is certain, that bills of rights are unnecessary and useless, nor can I conceive whence the contrary notion has arisen. Virginia has no bill of rights, and will it be said that her constitution was the less free? Has South Carolina no security for her liberties?—That state has no bill of rights. Are the citizens of Delaware more secured in their freedom, or more enlightened in the subjects of government than the citizens of Maryland? New-Jersey has no bill of rights; New-York has none; and Rhode Island has none. Thus, Sir, it appears from the sample of other states, as well as from principle, that a bill of rights is neither essential nor a necessary instrument in forming a system of government, since liberty may exist and be as well secured without it. But it was not only unnecessary, but on this occasion, it was found impracticable; for who will be bold enough to undertake to enumerate all the rights of the people? And when the attempt to enumerate them is made, it will be remembered that if the enumeration is not complete, every thing not expressly mentioned will be presumed to be purposely omitted. So it must be with a bill of rights, and an omission in stating the powers granted to the government, is not so dangerous as an omission in recapitulating the rights reserved by the people. We have already seen the reign of magna charta, and tracing the subject still further, we find the petition of rights claiming the liberties of the people, according to the laws and statutes of the realm, of which the great charter was, the most material; so that here again recourse is had to the old source from which their liberties are derived, the grant of the king. It was not until the revolution that the subject was placed upon a different footing, and even then the people did not claim their liberties as an inherent right, but as the result of an original contract between them and the sovereign. Thus, Mr. President, an attention to the situation of England will shew that the conduct of that country in respect to bills of rights, cannot furnish an example to the inhabitants of the United States, who by the revolution have regained all their natural rights, and possess their liberty neither by grant nor contract. In short, Sir, I have said that a bill of rights would have been improperly annexed to the federal plan, and for this plain reason, that it would imply that whatever is not expressed was given, which is not the principle of the proposed constitution."[2]

To these reasonings of Mr. Wilson it may be added that the Constitution for the United States and a constitution for an individual State are essentially different. When we framed our State Constitution we were in a state of Nature, possessing individually all the rights, privileges and immunities that belong to men before they enter into political society. The question was which of those we should retain. The Bill of Rights prefixed to our constitution innumerated and defined them. The rest were given up. But to whom were they resigned? Not to a sovereign power independent of our controul, but to each other. It was a social compact between individuals possessed of equal power and authority in which every thing that was not expressly reserved and guaranteed to individuals was resigned to the direction of the majority. The Constitution now before the public is not a compact between individuals, but between several sovereign and independent political societies already formed and organized. These societies have general

2. For the newspaper version of James Wilson's speech, see the *Pennsylvania Herald and General Advertiser*, vol. 5, no. 97, 12 December 1787, 386.

and particular interests and concerns. Those which respect the whole are submitted to the direction of the federal government; while those which respect individual states only are left, as they ought to be, in the hands of the state assemblies. To prevent any interference between the federal and state governments, the objects of the former are pointed out in the preamble to the Constitution, viz. *"To form a more perfect union—establish justice—insure domestic tranquility—provide for the common defence—promote the general welfare—and secure the blessings of liberty to ourselves and posterity."* These objects are all national and important. The powers vested in the supreme authority for the accomplishment of these purposes are accurately defined in the 8th section of the first article, and limited in the section following. It must therefore be taken for granted that every thing not expressly given up is retained by the states. If this is not enough to secure the liberties of the subject, *The United States guarantee to each separate state a republican form of government.* Of these, the Bill of Rights, where they have any prefixed, is an essential part; of consequence the Bill of Rights is as effectually secured by the Constitution proposed as if it had been expressly mentioned.—What can the most suspicious patriot want further? The Farmer himself acknowledges that he is silenced by Mr. Wilson's arguments in favour of the omission—tho' he pretends not to be convinced. Perhaps a man of more candor than he appears to be would have been perfectly satisfied. The clause in the constitution which he recites to prove the necessity of a Bill of Rights is very little to his purpose, even in appearance, and in reality still less.—By this Constitution the Congress of the United States will be invested with several powers, which now belong only to individual states. For the exercise of these powers laws must necessarily be enacted. They must also be the supreme law of the land, otherwise they would be useless and insignificant. Now it is evident that, although these laws may apparently clash with the Constitutions of the several states as they at present stand, yet they will be perfectly consistent with the exercise of all the powers the states still retain; because they will be founded on those rights which they have voluntarily divested themselves of and placed in the hands of the United States.

The Bill of Rights being the Burden of the Farmer's song; and in having been clearly shewn that those of the several states are confirmed and guaranteed to them by the new Constitution, I might here terminate my strictures on the publication. But there are several other things calculated to mislead the class of men to whom they are addressed and therefore deserve a few remarks by way of reply. Among these his hints concerning the *Federal Courts* first present themselves. Of these courts, especially after Congress have mounted their hobby horse of a federal jurisdiction over a certain district of country, he has the most fearful apprehensions, except this horse is well *guarded* and *fettered.* But whence can these apprehensions arise in this gentleman's mind? Certainly no good member of society can have any grounds to fear passing through, or residing within the jurisdiction of those rulers whom he has had a hand in appointing, and who are accountable to him for the use they make of their delegated authority. Good laws and magistrates are a terror to evil doers, but those who do well may ever expect from them both protection and praise. An honest man therefore can never be in danger from legal authority, whether established by a single state or thirteen combined.

The Farmer thinks a Trial by Jury is indispensably necessary to the security of the liberties of the people. A person who had never read the new constitution would suppose that the institution was to be entirely abolished in the federal courts. But how would he be surprized to find that that "Trial of all crimes except in cases of impeachment, shall be by jury?" Life and Liberty are therefore as well secured by the federal Constitution as by those of the several states: for in cases of impeachment juries have never been employed. But who has informed this writer that any causes shall be tried in the federal courts without jury? The constitution does not prescribe it, but leaves it to the direction of Congress.

But after all, what are the advantages of this boasted *trial by Jury,* and on which side do they lie? Not certainly on the side of *justice:* for one unprincipled juror secured in the interest of the opposite party will frequently divert her from her course. And I believe every gentleman much acquainted in our judicial courts will agree in sentiment with me that in four cases out of five, where injustice is done, it is by the ignorance of knavery of the jury, in opposition to the opinion of the judges. The fact is that under the present regulation, which most unreasonably (at least in civil cases) requires an unanimity in the verdict, juries favor the guilty much more than the innocent party. It is therefore no wonder that certain characters, in this as well as in other States, shudder on the idea of courts in which justice will more generally take place. Let those who for sake of the wages, love and practice the *works of righteousness* clamour at such an establishment: Honest men will justify and supplant it. Laws were made and judicatories established for the punishment of the former, and the security of the latter. Upon their faithful execution greatly depends the happiness of society: and however the vicious and disorderly may fare, the virtuous and honest can never suffer by them except when they permit *violence, injustice* and *fraud* to escape with impunity.

The next engine, the Farmer brings into play to alarm the fears of the people is that tedious Bug-bear, *a standing army in time of peace.* This he and some others would represent as a monster ever possessed both of the will and power to swallow up the liberties of the country at a meal. But let us for a moment inquire into the idea of a standing army, and ask what it is? Certainly not an army voted, raised and supported by the people. Such an army *stands* no longer than the people direct. The same voice that gave it being last year may now annihilate it.—How then can it be called a *standing army?* In fact, a free government knows no such thing, nor can it: and the writer who endeavors to excite jealousies against the new Constitution in the minds of the good citizens of the United States, by representing that it licences standing armies in times of peace, is either grossly ignorant or scandalously dishonest. A standing army is that which the supreme executive magistrate can raise by his own authority and support by permanent revenues placed beyond the controul of his subjects. It is against standing armies thus circumstanced that so much reasoning and declamation have been levelled, and not against such bodies of men as may be necessary for the protection of a state, and under the direction of its legislature. Such an army, it must be confessed, is a most dangerous instrument in the hands of arbitrary power, and too much cannot be said against it: But when I hear a man of the least knowledge in such matters expressing his apprehensions of danger to the liberties of America from that quarter, under the new constitution without a Bill of Rights, I cannot help considering him as an unhappy HYPOCHONDRIAC, whose fears must be calmed by medicine rather than by argumentation.

To trace this writer, Messeurs Printers, thro' all his ramblings from the point, and to make a reply to every scandalous innuendo, foolish proposition, impertinent observation, and groundless assertion, would equally fatigue the patience and insults the understandings of your readers. I shall therefore conclude with this remark on his observation in the last sentence of his address elegantly introduced by the *fox* and the *hen-roost*, that however cautious we ought to be in our choice of public officers, when we have got the most patriotic, virtuous and colightened characters we can find, they ought never to be degraded by mean jealousies and groundless distrusts, but to be honored with our full confidence; because by such jealousies and distrusts we should in some measure authorize them to betray their trust: as many a husband has procured a growth of horns on his front by unjustly calling in question the fidelity of his Wife.

"An American Citizen"
[Tench Coxe]

"Thoughts on the Subject of Amendments": II–III

Pennsylvania Gazette, Philadelphia, 10 December and 24 December 1788

II

To moderate the ardor and diminish the fears of the friends of *amendment,* we took a cursory view, in the last paper, of the ground upon which liberty is fixed in this enlightened time, and particularly in the United States. It clearly appeared, that the dangers to property, peace, liberty and life, so far as they have heretofore proceeded from the abuse of ecclesiastical power, are now done away by the total suppression of that species of authority. It was also evident, that instead of *general feeling* and *opinion,* on which the liberties of the ancient republics precariously rested, the progress of political knowledge had given us the more certain basis of *the acknowledged rights* of man, and *the established principles* of freedom. Being possessed of constitutions formed out of these *rights and principles,* it was argued, that no sudden inroads upon the liberties of the people could be made, no insidious encroachments could be effected. Wherefore, it was further observed, the business of amendment, equally important to *liberty and government,* need not be precipitated, from any dangerous circumstances that attend our present situation.

The amendments that have been hitherto suggested may not improperly be divided into two kinds—1st. Those which are supposed immediately to regard the liberties of the people; and 2dly. Those which would effect a diminution of the powers of the federal legislature.

In considering those amendments which immediately relate to the rights of individuals, we must call to mind that the United States have successfully concluded an important contest, the grounds of which principally were, their assertion of their general and common rights, in the utmost extent to which the theory of a free government could carry them. We must remember also, that our federal and state governments are and will be, so far as a very large majority goes, in the hands of those men who originated that contest, or maintained it to an happy issue. If we give ourselves a moment's time for reflection, we shall be satisfied that the leaders of the general and state councils from 1775 to 1778, both civil and military characters, who are now entering upon the duties of the new government, will not betray that liberty they then asserted, nor be silent spectators of its destruction by the plans of their fellow-citizens. When the body of the new Congress shall be assembled—when the state legislatures shall see in the Senate the representatives of their various interests, *created by a deliberate exercise of their own powers*—when the people at large shall behold in the House of Representatives *the men of their freest choice,* and in their Chief Magistrate, *the creature of their breath* and *the venerated object of their warmest affections*—they will not unreasonably and ungenerously suppose that such a body, formed at a juncture so important and [by] means so just, will be inattentive to any consideration, which may affect the happiness of a country on whose fortunes hang all their joys and sorrows. Shall we not then *calmly* wait the short period of their meeting? Shall we formally elect them for the most important duties, and immediately withdraw from them the confidence their station demands? 'Till their conduct gives us some shadow of cause to censure them, let us rationally expect that they will examine, with becoming anxiety and care, what further checks in favor of liberty can be introduced, what further explanations of the constitution time and reflection prove to be necessary. Should they discover that the preservation of freedom, or *even the restoration of general harmony,* renders it necessary that a declaration of the rights of conscience, the freedom of the press, and other articles, should be expressed as fully in the constitution of the union as they are in those of the states, we should be wanting to ourselves, and cruelly unjust to them, to suppose they will neglect to propose them.

If we consider the manner in which a general convention must be created, *by the election of the state legislatures*—if we remember at the same time, that one branch of the new Congress are to be chosen by those bodies, and the other by the people at large—if we bear in mind also, that *the rights of the states,* as well as those of *the people,* are involved in the proposed amendments—we shall see that a General Convention would not be as competent to decide on alterations, as the new Congress, from the nature of its two branches, will be to propose them for the determination of the legislatures or people of the states. Considering the mixed nature of the new constitution, made up as it is of the rights of the people and the rights of the states, a mixed body only, created *by both the parties concerned,* can safely and equitably amend it. The contracting parties in the federal compact are *the people of the several states* and *the federal state governments.* Amendments originated by the representatives of either, alone, cannot be just, and may be dangerous to the other.

Considering, then, that the present situation of the United States is peculiarly free from those rocks on which the liberties of the people have formerly been lost,—that we may place our affairs, both in the state and general governments, under the guidance of our most enlightened citizens,—that there *is* every reason to believe the interest, the wisdom and the virtue of those, whom the people and the legislatures shall elect, will ensure a due attention to the peace and safety of our country,—that precipitation, warmth, and unreasonable prejudices may possibly mar the constitution, but cannot amend it—we must deem it at once our interest and duty, calmly to wait the first operations of the federal legislature. Impatience under assumed powers has been the just characteristic of Americans. Let not our enemies, in this our political infancy, be able to charge us with the same temper towards the just authority, *which we ourselves have deliberately created.*

III

In examining those amendments which relate to the powers vested in Congress by the new constitution, we find the principle ground of objection to be, the effect which the general government will have upon the governments of the states. And here it may be well for us briefly to notice the principle causes of opposition throughout the United States, which unhappily can be too easily ascertained. Considerations with regard to personal rights no doubt have affected many worthy men, but we trust we have already shewn, that every amendment really affecting liberty may be expected of the new Congress. The event must very soon prove the prediction to be true or false, and in the mean time it must be evident that there is no danger from an unorganized government, from a constitution yet on paper.

The first great cause of objection which presents itself is, that the federal constitution will prevent those legal invasions of *the rights of property,* which have shewn themselves in *paper emissions, lawful tenders, installment laws, and valuation laws.* To all arguments drawn from *such* considerations, it would be an insult to the integrity of an honest opponent to the constitution to offer an answer. He will reject them of his own accord. Only to remind him of the facts will be sufficient. He will find, on examination, that a majority of the state legislatures had committed trespasses of this kind, prior to the meeting of the late general convention, and that attempts were making in some one of the remaining states at every session.

The second objection to the constitution of the United States which occurs, and which is of too general influence, is, that it aims to restore *energy,* and to give *effect* to government. The delay of justice, and in the collection of taxes and debts, in the interior parts of some, and every part of other states, is too convenient, too agreeable to many. To all arguments drawn from *such* considerations, also, it would be an insult to the integrity of an honest opponent of the constitution to offer an answer. Measures, which will remedy these two evils, must be acceptable to good men of both parties, and are indispensably necessary to the prosperity and honor of the United States.

The third objection to the powers of the federal government, which create a strong and warm body of opponents, is the influence, 'tis said, it will have on the powers of the state governments.

The constitutions of a majority of the states establish, in many important particulars, an equality among their respective counties, tho' they differ in their number of freemen in the proportion of ten to one, and in their contributions to government much more. This is surely a violation of justice and the equal rights of man. Such constitutions are not *the codes of liberty,* nor can a just and safe administration take place under them.

Several of the state constitutions impose religious tests. One of them disfranchises the whole body of the clergy of all denominations—another disfranchises all christian sects but one. Would not the friends of religious men, and the meritorious advocates of religious liberty, be well employed in obtaining amendments of these articles.

If the state constitutions thus violate the rights of man, both *temporal* and *spiritual,* the administration under them must always be precarious, and has been already extremely unjust. Foreigners, and the merchants and tradesmen of New Hampshire, Massachusetts, Connecticut, Pennsylvania and Maryland (where special payments can be compelled) have placed large properties in goods in the hands of the merchants, traders, planters and farmers in Georgia, the Carolinas, Virginia, New Jersey and Rhode Island. The *legal* impediments, which the several legislatures of the latter states have thrown in the way, or which they have purposely omitted to remove, though within their powers, have long detained, and yet continue to keep the rightful property of the former out of their hands. The consequence to the unhappy creditor, who is within the reach of a just and efficient government, is a loss of those profits, which would maintain his family and educate his children, injurious sales of his landed property to make his payments, too often forced by legal executions, or even a distressful bankruptcy. The public debts and the public revenues might be enlarged on; but the picture of our country, as it stood at the time of the establishment of the federal constitution, arising principally from the defects and faults in the state constitutions, or the mal-administration of them, would be too painful. Let our own reflexion and these facts, which are *as true* as they are *deplorable,* suffice. Let us, however, deduce from these observations the conclusion to which they were meant to lead, that *a diminution of the powers of the state governments, and a transfer of a due portion of them to a national body, was necessary to the salvation of our country.*

In the formation of this national body a careful examination was previously made. It was seen, that the United States were made up of *the people at large,* and of *thirteen local governments,* and that both must be completely represented in the general government. Hence an entire body was assigned to the people, called *the House of Representatives,* without whose consent *nothing* can be done, and whose election is always to be made in a manner as consistent with equality and liberty, as that of any body upon earth. Hence, also, an entire representative body was assigned to the state legislatures, called *the Senate,* in which the thirteen governments are completely represented, and their equal rights are duly maintained. To preserve unimpaired the independency of *the freemen* of the United States, no inequality was permitted to be introduced, to the prejudice of any man, in the election of the federal representatives; so also, to preserve inviolate the independency of *the states,* no inequality was allowed, to the injury of any one of them, in the election of their representatives, *the Federal Senators.* How just and safe to both is this arrangement.

We are now electing *the men of our choice* to represent us in the two houses of the general government. Let us, 'till the short period of their meeting, give them a generous credit for the amendments they will propose, affecting the rights of conscience, the liberty of the press, and other topics, concerning which our apprehensions have been some times honestly, and at other times dishonestly, excited. Let us remember, what we will all admit, that they love virtue and freedom no less than ourselves.

"A Citizen of New Haven"
[Roger Sherman]

The Letters: I–II

New Haven Gazette, 18 and 25 December 1788

I

*Observations on the Alterations Proposed as Amendments to
the new Federal Constitution.*

Six of the states have adopted the new constitution without proposing any alteration, and the most of those proposed by the conventions of other states may be provided for by congress in a code of laws without altering the constitution. If congress may be safely trusted with the affairs of the Union, and have sufficient powers for that purpose, and possess no powers but such as respect the common interest of the states (as I have endeavored to show in a former piece),[1] then all the matters that can be regulated by law may safely be left to their discretion, and those will include all that I have noticed except the following, which I think on due consideration will appear to be improper or unnecessary.

I. It is proposed that the consent of two-thirds or three-fourths of the members present in this branch of the congress shall be required for passing certain acts.

On which I would observe, that this would give a minority in congress power to controul the majority, joined with the concurrent voice of the president, for if the president dissents, no act can pass without the consent of two-thirds of the members in each branch of congress; and would not that be contrary to the general principles of republican government?

1. According to the editor of the *New Haven Gazette,* the piece referred to was actually letter II, published after this one. See the *New Haven Gazette,* vol. 3, no. 50, 18 December 1788.

2. That impeachments ought not to be tried by the senate, or not by the senate alone.

But what good reason can be assigned why the senate is not the most proper tribunal for that purpose? The members are to be chosen by the legislatures of the several states, who will doubtless appoint persons of wisdom and probity, and from their office can have no interested motives to partiality. The house of peers in Great Britain try impeachments and are also a branch of the legislature.

3. It is said that the president ought not to have power to grant pardons in cases of high treason, but the congress.

It does not appear that any great mischief can arise from the exercise of this power by the president (though perhaps it might as well have been lodged in congress). The president cannot pardon in case of impeachment, so that such offenders may be excluded from office notwithstanding his pardon.

4. It is proposed that members of congress be rendered ineligible to any other office during the time for which they are elected members of that body.

This is an objection that will admit of something plausible to be said on both sides, and it was settled in convention on full discussion and deliberation. There are some offices which a member of congress may be best qualified to fill, from his knowledge of public affairs acquired by being a member, such as minister to foreign courts, &c., and on accepting any other office his seat in congress will be vacated, and no member is eligible to any office that shall have been instituted or the emoluments increased while he was a member.

5. It is proposed to make the president and senators ineligible after certain periods.

But this would abridge the privilege of the people, and remove one great motive to fidelity in office, and render persons incapable of serving in offices, on account of their experience, which would best qualify them for usefulness in office—but if their services are not acceptable they may be left out at any new election.

6. It is proposed that no commercial treaty should be made without the consent of two-thirds of the senators, nor any cession of territory, right of

navigation or fishery, without the consent of three-fourths of the members present in each branch of congress.

It is provided by the constitution that no commercial treaty shall be made by the president without the consent of two-thirds of the senators present, and as each state has an equal representation and suffrage in the senate, the rights of the state will be as well secured under the new constitution as under the old; and it is not probable that they would ever make a cession of territory or any important national right without the consent of congress. The king of Great Britain has by the constitution a power to make treaties, yet in matters of great importance he consults the parliament.

7. There is one amendment proposed by the convention of South Carolina respecting religious tests, by inserting the word *other,* between the words *no* and *religious* in that article, which is an ingenious thought, and had that word been inserted, it would probably have prevented any objection on that head. But it may be considered as a clerical omission and be inserted without calling a convention; as it now stands the effect will be the same.

On the whole it is hoped that all the states will consent to make a fair trial of the constitution before they attempt to alter it; experience will best show whether it is deficient or not, on trial it may appear that the alterations that have been proposed are not necessary, or that others not yet thought of may be necessary; everything that tends to disunion ought to be avoided. Instability in government and laws tends to weaken a state and render the rights of the people precarious.

If another convention should be called to revise the constitution, 'tis not likely they would be more unanimous than the former; they might judge differently in some things, but is it certain that they would judge better? When experience has convinced the states and people in general that alterations are necessary, they may be easily made, but attempting it at present may be detrimental if not fatal to the union of the states.

The judiciary department is perhaps the most difficult to be precisely limited by the constitution, but congress have full power to regulate it by law, and it may be found necessary to vary the regulations at different times as circumstances may differ.

Congress may make requisitions for supplies previous to direct taxation, if it should be thought to be expedient, but if requisitions be made and some states comply and others not, the noncomplying states must be considered and treated as delinquents, which will tend to excite disaffection and disunion among the states, besides occasioning delay; but if congress lay the taxes in the first instance these evils will be prevented, and they will doubtless accommodate the taxes to the customs and convenience of the several states.

Some suppose that the representation will be too small, but I think it is in the power of congress to make it too large, but I believe that it may be safely trusted with them. Great Britain contains about three times the number of the inhabitants in the United States, and according to Burgh's account in his political disquisitions, the members of parliament in that kingdom do not exceed 131, and if 69 more be added from the principal cities and towns the number would be 200; and strike off those who are elected by the small boroughs, which are called the rotten part of the constitution by their best patriots and politicians, that nation would be more equally and better represented than at present; and if that would be a sufficient number for their national legislature, one-third of that number will be more than sufficient for our federal legislature who will have few general matters to transact. But these and other objections have been considered in a former paper, before referred to. I shall therefore conclude this with my best wishes for the continuance of the peace, liberty and union of these states.

II

Observations on the New Federal Constitution.

In order to form a good Constitution of Government, the legislature should be properly organized, and be vested with plenary powers for all the purposes for which the government was instituted, to be exercised for the public good as occasion may require.

The greatest security that a people can have for the enjoyment of their rights and liberties, is that no laws can be made to bind them nor any taxes imposed upon them without their consent by representatives of their own chusing, who will participate with them in the public burthens and benefits; this was the great point contended for in our controversy with Great Britain, and this will be fully secured to us by the new constitution. The rights of the people will be secured by a representation in proportion to their numbers in one branch of the legislature, and the rights of the particular states by their equal representation in the other branch.

The President and Vice-President as well as the members of Congress will be eligible for fixed periods, and may be re-elected as often as the electors shall think fit, which will be a great security for their fidelity in office, and give greater stability and energy to government than an exclusion by rotation, and will be an operative and effectual security against arbitrary government, either monarchial or aristocratic.

The immediate security of the civil and domestic rights of the people will be in the government of the particular states. And as the different states have different local interests and customs which can be best regulated by their own laws, it should not be expedient to admit the federal government to interfere with them, any farther than may be necessary for the good of the whole. The great end of the federal government is to protect the several states in the enjoyment of those rights, against foreign invasion, and to preserve peace and a beneficial intercourse among themselves; and to regulate and protect our commerce with foreign nations.

These were not sufficiently provided for by the former articles of confederation, which was the occasion of calling the late Convention to make amendments. This they have done by forming a new constitution containing the powers vested in the federal government, under the former, with such additional powers as they deemed necessary to attain the ends the states had in view, in their appointment. And to carry those powers into effect, they thought it necessary to make some alterations in the organization of the government: this they supposed to be warranted by their commission.

The powers vested in the federal government are clearly defined, so that each state still retain its sovereignty in what concerns its own internal government, and a right to exercise every power of a sovereign state not particularly delegated to the government of the United States. The new powers vested in the United States, are, to regulate commerce; provide for a uniform practice respecting naturalization, bankruptcies, and organizing, arming and training the militia; and for the punishment of certain crimes against the United States; and for promoting the progress of science in the mode therein pointed out. There are some other matters which Congress has power under the present confederation to require to be done by the particular states, which they will be authorized to carry into effect themselves under the new constitution; these powers appear to be necessary for the common benefit of the states, and could not be effectually provided for by the particular states.

The objects of expenditure will be the same under the new constitution, as under the old; nor need the administration of government be more expensive; the number of members of Congress will be the same, nor will it be necessary to increase the number of officers in the executive department or their salaries; the supreme executive will be in a single person, who must have an honourable support; which perhaps will not exceed the present allowance to the President of Congress, and the expence of supporting a committee of the states in the recess of Congress.

It is not probable that Congress will have occasion to sit longer than two or three months in a year, after the first session, which may perhaps be something longer. Nor will it be necessary for the Senate to sit longer than the other branch. The appointment of officers may be made during the session of Congress, and trials on impeachment will not often occur, and will require but little time to attend to them. The security against keeping up armies in time of peace will be greater under the new constitution than under the present, because it can't be done without the concurrence of two branches of the legislature, nor can any appropriation of money for that purpose be in force more than two years; whereas there is no restriction under the present confederation.

The liberty of the press can be in no danger, because that is not put under the direction of the new government.

If the federal government keeps within its proper jurisdiction, it will be the interest of the state legislatures to support it, and they will be a powerful and effectual check to its interfering with their jurisdiction. But the objects of federal government will be so obvious that there will be no great danger of any interference.

The principal sources of revenue will be imposts on goods imported, and sale of the western lands, which will probably be sufficient to pay the debts and expences of the United States while peace continues; but if there should be occasion to resort to direct taxation, each state's quota will be ascertained according to a rule which has been approved by the legislatures of eleven of the states, and should any state neglect to furnish its quota, Congress may raise it in the same manner that the state ought to have done; and what remedy more easy and equitable could be devised, to obtain the supplies from a delinquent state?

Some object, that the representation will be too small; but the states have not thought fit to keep half the number of representatives in Congress that they are entitled to under the present confederation; and of what advantage can it be to have a large assembly to transact the few general matters that will come under the direction of Congress.—The regulating of time, place and manner of elections seems to be as well secured as possible; the legislature of each state may do it, and if they neglect to do it in the best manner, it may be done by Congress;—and what motive can either have to injure the people in the exercise of that right? the qualifications of the electors are to remain as fixed by the constitutions and laws of the several states.

It is by some objected, that the executive is blended with the legislature, and that those powers ought to be entirely distinct and unconnected, but is not this a gross error in politics? The united wisdom and various interests of a nation should be combined in framing the laws. But the execution of them should not be in the whole legislature; that would be too troublesome and expensive; but it will not thence follow that the executive should have no voice or influence in legislation. The executive in Great Britain is one branch of the legislature, and has a negative on all laws; perhaps that is an extreme not to be imitated by a republic, but the partial negative vested in the President by the new Constitution on the acts of Congress and the subsequent revision, may be very useful to prevent laws being passed without mature deliberation.

The Vice-President while he acts as President of the Senate will have nothing to do in the executive department; his being elected by all the states will incline him to regard the interests of the whole, and when the members of the senate are equally divided on any question, who so proper to give a casting vote as one who represents all the states?

The power of the President to grant pardons extends only to offences committed against the United States, which can't be productive of much mischief, especially as those on Impeachment are excepted, which will exclude offenders from office.

It was thought necessary in order to carry into effect the laws of the Union, to promote justice, and preserve harmony among the states, to extend the judicial powers of the United States to the enumerated cases, under such regulations and with such exceptions as shall be provided by law, which will doubtless reduce them to cases of such magnitude and importance as cannot safely be trusted to the final decision of the courts of particular states; and the constitution does not make it necessary that any inferior tribunals should be instituted, but it may be done if found necessary; 'tis probable that the courts of particular states will be authorized by the laws of the union, as has been heretofore done in cases of piracy, &c., and the Supreme Court may have a circuit to make trials as convenient, and as little expensive as possible to the parties; nor is there anything in the constitution to deprive them of trial by jury in cases where that mode of trial has been heretofore used. All cases in the courts of common law between citizens of the same state, except those claiming lands under grants of different states, must be finally decided by courts of the state to which they belong, so that it is not probable that more than one citizen to a thousand will ever have a cause that can come before a federal court.

Every department and officer of the federal government will be subject to the regulation and control of the laws, and the people will have all possible securities against oppression. Upon the whole, the constitution appears to be well framed to secure the rights and liberties of the people and for preserving the governments of the individual states, and if well administered, to restore and secure public and private credit, and to give respectability to the states both abroad and at home. Perhaps a more perfect one could not be formed on mere speculation; and if upon experience it shall be found deficient, it provides an easy and peaceable mode to make amendments. Is it not much better to adopt it than to continue in present circumstances? Its being agreed to by all the states present in Convention, is a circumstance in its favour, so far as any respect is due to their opinions.

Hugh Williamson

"Remarks on the New Plan of Government"

Daily Advertiser, New York, 25–27 February 1788

Hugh Williamson was a member of the Continental Congress and North Carolina delegate to the Federal Convention; he served in the House of Representatives from 1789 to 1793. This speech was printed in three installments over 25, 26, and 27 February 1788. During 1788 a version of the "Remarks" was also published in the *State Gazette of North Carolina,* New Bern, as well as in Pennsylvania, South Carolina, and Massachusetts.

The following Remarks on the New Plan of Government are handed us as the substance of Doctor WILLIAMSON's *Address to the Freemen of Edenton and the County of Chowan, in North-Carolina, when assembled to instruct their Representatives.*

Though I am conscious that a subject of the greatest magnitude must suffer in the hands of such an advocate, I cannot refuse, at the request of my fellow-citizens, to make some observations on the new Plan of Government.

It seems to be generally admitted, that the system of Government which has been proposed by the late Convention, is well calculated to relieve us from many of the grievances under which we have been laboring. If I might express my particular sentiments on this subject, I should describe it as more free and more perfect than any form of government that ever has been adopted by any nation; but I would not say it has no faults. Imperfection is inseparable from every human device. Several objections were made to this system by two or three very respectable characters in the Convention, which have been the subject of much conversation;[1] and other objections,

---

1. This is apparently a reference to Elbridge Gerry, George Mason, and Edmund Randolph. See Storing, 2:1, 2:2, and 2:5. The objections of Mason and Gerry are also in Allen, 11–13 and 20–22, respectively.

by citizens of this State, have lately reached our ears. It is proper that you should consider of these objections. They are of two kinds; they respect the things that are in the system, and the things that are not in it. We are told that there should have been a section for securing a Trial by Jury in Civil cases, and the Liberty of the Press: that there should also have been a Declaration of Rights. In the new system it is provided, that "*The Trial of all crimes,* except in cases of Impeachment," *shall be by Jury,* but this provision could not possibly be extended to all *Civil* cases. For it is well known that the Trial by Jury is not general and uniform throughout the United States, either in cases of Admiralty or of Chancery; hence it became necessary to submit the question to the General Legislature, who might accommodate their laws on this occasion to the desires and habits of the nation. Surely there is no prohibition in a case that is untouched.

We have been told that the Liberty of the Press is not secured by the New Constitution. Be pleased to examine the plan, and you will find that the Liberty of the Press and the laws of Mahomet are equally affected by it. The New Government is to have the power of protecting literary property; the very power which you have by a special act delegated to the present Congress. There was a time in England, when neither book, pamphlet, nor paper could be published without a licence from Government. That restraint was finally removed in the year 1694 and by such removal, their press became perfectly free, for it is not under the restraint of any licence. Certainly the new Government can have no power to impose restraints. The citizens of the United States have no more occasion for a second Declaration of Rights, than they have for a section in favor of the press. Their rights, in the several States, have long since been explained and secured by particular declarations, which make a part of their several Constitutions. It is granted, and perfectly understood, that under the Government of the Assemblies of the States, and under the Government of the Congress, every right is reserved to the individual, which he has not expressly delegated to this, or that Legislature. The other objections that have been made to the new plan of Government, are: That it absorbs the powers of the several States: That the national Judiciary is too extensive: That a standing army is permitted: That Congress is allowed to regulate trade: That the several States are prevented from taxing exports, for their own benefit.

When Gentlemen are pleased to complain, that little power is left in the hands of the separate States; they should be advised to cast an eye upon the large code of laws, which have passed in this State since the peace. Let them consider how few of those laws have been framed, for the general benefit of the Nation. Nine out of ten of them, are domestic; calculated for the sole use of this State, or of particular citizens. There must still be use for such laws, though you should enable the Congress to collect a revenue for National purposes, and the collection of that revenue includes the chief of the new powers, which are now to be committed to the Congress.

Hitherto you have delegated certain powers to the Congress, and other powers to the Assemblies of the States. The portion that you have delegated to Congress is found to have been useless, because it is too small, and the powers that are committed to the assemblies of the several States, are also found to be absolutely ineffectual for national purposes, because they can never be so managed as to operate in concert. Of what use is that small portion of reserved power? It neither makes you respectable nor powerful. The consequence of such reservation is national contempt abroad, and a state of dangerous weakness at home. What avails the claim of power, which appears to be nothing better than the empty whistling of a name? The Congress will be chosen by yourselves, as your Members of Assembly are. They will be creatures of your hands, and subject to your advice. Protected and cherished by the small addition of power which you shall put into their hands, you may become a great and respectable nation.

It is complained that the powers of the national Judiciary are too extensive.[2] This objection appears to have the greatest weight in the eyes of gentlemen who have not carefully compared the powers which are to be delegated with those that had been formerly delegated to Congress. The powers that are now to be committed to the national Legislature, as they are detailed

2. See especially the criticisms by Brutus, Storing, 2:9, 130–96, and the Federal Farmer, Storing, 2:8, 183–95. For more on Brutus, see *Friends*, 182 n. 5. The exact identity of Federal Farmer, one of the ablest of the Anti-Federalists and quite popular, is unsettled. While Richard Henry Lee is generally thought to be the author, Storing is unconvinced. See the introduction to Storing, 2:8. Essays I, III, IV, V, XI, XII, and XV of Brutus are in Allen, 102–17, 201–23, and 269–74. Letters I, II, III, VII, VIII, IX, XII, and XVII of Federal Farmer are in Allen, 75–93, 177–201, and 261–69.

in the 8th section of the first article, have already been chiefly delegated
to the Congress under one form or another, except those which are contained in the first paragraph of that section. And the objects that are now
to be submitted to the Supreme Judiciary, or to the Inferior Courts, are those
which naturally arise from the constitutional laws of Congress. If there is
a single new case that can be exceptionable, it is that between a foreigner
and a citizen, or that between the citizens of different States. These cases
may come up by appeal. It is provided in this system that there shall be
no fraudulent tender in the payments of debts. Foreigners, with whom we
have treaties, will trust our citizens on the faith of this engagement. And
the citizens of different States will do the same. If the Congress had a negative
on the laws of the several States, they would certainly prevent all such laws
as might endanger the honor or peace of the nation, by making a tender
of base money; but they have no such power, and it is at least possible that
some State may be found in this Union, disposed to break the Constitution,
and abolish private debts by such tenders. In these cases the Courts of the
offending States would probably decide according to its own laws. The foreigner would complain; and the nation might be involved in war for the
support of such dishonest measures. Is it not better to have a Court of Appeals in which the Judges can only be determined by the laws of the nation?
This Court is equally to be desired by the citizens of different States. But
we are told that justice will be delayed, and the poor will be drawn away
by the rich to a distant Court. The authors of this remark have not fully
considered the question, else they must have recollected that the poor of
this country have little to do with foreigners, or with the citizens of distant
States. They do not consider that there may be an Inferior Court in every
State; nor have they recollected that the appeals being *with such exceptions,*
and *under such regulations* as Congress shall make, will never be permitted
for trifling sums, or under trivial pretences, unless we can suppose that the
national Legislature shall be composed of knaves and fools. The line that
separates the powers of the national Legislature from those of the several
States is clearly drawn. The several States reserve every power that can be
exercised for the particular use and comfort of the State. They do not yield
a single power which is not purely of a national concern; nor do they yield

a single power which is not absolutely necessary to the safety and prosperity of the nation, nor one that could be employed to any effect in the hands of particular States. The powers of Judiciary naturally arise from those of the Legislature. Questions that are of a national concern, and those cases which are determinable by the general laws of the nation, are to be referred to the national Judiciary, but they have not any thing to do with a single case either civil or criminal, which respects the private and particular concerns of a State or its citizens.

The possibility of keeping regular troops in the public service has been urged as another objection against the new Constitution. It is very remarkable that the same objection has not been made against the original Confederation, in which the same grievance obtained without the same guards. It is now provided, that no appropriation of money for the use of the army shall be for a longer time than two years. Provision is also made for having a powerful militia, in which case there never can be occasion for many regular troops. It has been objected in some of the Southern States, that the Congress, by a majority of votes, is to have the power to regulate trade. It is universally admitted that Congress ought to have this power, else our commerce, which is nearly ruined, can never be restored; but some gentlemen think that the concurrence of two thirds of the votes in Congress should have been required. By the sundry regulations of commerce, it will be in the power of Government not only to collect a vast revenue for the general benefit of the nation, but to secure the carrying trade in the hands of citizens in preference to strangers. It has been alledged that there are few ships belonging to the Southern States, and that the price of freight must rise in consequence of our excluding many foreign vessels: but when we have not vessels of our own, it is certainly proper that we should hire those of citizens in preference to strangers; for our revenue is promoted and the nation is strengthened by the profits that remain in the hands of citizens; we are injured by throwing it into the hands of strangers; and though the price of freight should rise for two or three years, this advantage is fully due to our brethren in the Eastern and middle States, who, with great and exemplary candor, have given us equal advantages in return. A small encrease in the price of freight would operate greatly in favor of the Southern States: it would promote the spirit of ship building; it would promote a nursery for native seamen, and would afford support to the poor who live near the sea coast; it would encrease the value of their lands, and at the same time it would reduce their taxes. It has finally been objected that the several States are not permitted to tax their exports for the benefit of their particular Treasuries. This strange objection has been occasionally repeated by citizens of this State. They must have transplanted it from another State, for it could not have been the growth of North-Carolina. Such have been the objections against the new Constitution.

Whilst the honest patriot, who guards with a jealous eye the liberties of his country, and apprehends danger under every form: the placeman in every State, who fears lest his office should pass into other hands; the idle, the factious, and the dishonest, who live by plunder or speculation on the miseries of their country; while these, assisted by a numerous body of secret enemies, who never have been reconciled to our Independence, are seeking for objections to this Constitution; it is a remarkable circumstance, and a very high encomium on the plan, that nothing more plausible has been offered against it; for it is an easy matter to find faults.

Let us turn our eyes to a more fruitful subject; let us consider the present condition of the United States, and the particular benefits that North Carolina must reap by the proposed form of Government. Without money, no Government can be supported; and Congress can raise no money under the present Constitution: They have not the power to make commercial treaties, because they cannot preserve them when made. Hence it is, that we are the prey of every nation: We are indulged in such foreign commerce, as must be hurtful to us: We are prohibited from that which might be profitable, and we are accordingly told, that on the last two years, the Thirteen States have hardly paid into the Treasury, as much as should have been paid by a single State. Intestine commotions in some of the States: Paper Money in others, a want of inclination in some, and a general suspicion throughout the Union, that the burthen is unequally laid; added to the general loss of trade have produced a general bankruptcy, and loss of honor. We have borrowed money of Spain—she demands the principal, but we cannot pay the interest. It is a circumstance perfectly humiliating, that we should remain under obligations to that nation: We are Considerably indebted to France but she is too generous to insist upon what she knows we cannot pay, either the principal or interest. In the hour of our distress, we borrowed money in Holland; not from the Government, but from private citizens. Those who are called the Patriots were our friends, and they are oppressed in their turn by hosts of enemies: They will soon have need of money: At this hour we are not able to pay the interests of their loan. What is to be done? Will you borrow money again from other citizens of that oppressed Republic, to pay the interest of what you borrowed from their brethren? This would be a painful expedient, but our want of Government may render it necessary. You have two or three Ministers abroad; they must soon return home, for they cannot be supported. You have four or five hundred troops scattered along the Ohio to protect the frontier inhabitants, and give some value to your lands; those troops are ill paid, and in a fair way for being disbanded. There is hardly a circumstance remaining; hardly one external mark by which you can deserve to be called a nation. You are not in a condition to resist the most contemptible enemy. What is there to prevent an Algerine Pirate from landing on your coast, and carrying your citizens into slavery? You have not a single sloop of war. Does one of the States attempt to raise a little money by imposts or other commercial regulations.—A neighboring State immediately alters her laws and defeats the revenue, by throwing the trade into a different channel. Instead of supporting or assisting, we are uniformly taking the advantage of one another. Such an assemblage of people are not a nation. Like a dark cloud, without cohesion or firmness, we are ready to be torn asunder and scattered abroad by every breeze of external violence, or internal commotion.

Is there a man in this State who believes it possible for us to continue under such a Government?—Let us suppose but for a minute, that such a measure should be attempted.—Let us suppose that the several States shall be required and obliged to pay their several quotas according to the original plan. You know that North-Carolina, on the last four years, has not paid one dollar into the Treasury for eight dollars that she ought to have paid.

We must encrease our taxes exceedingly, and those taxes must be of the most grievous kind; they must be taxes on lands and heads; taxes that cannot fail to grind the face of the poor; for it is clear that we can raise little by imports and exports. Some foreign goods are imported by water from the Northern States, such goods pay a duty for the benefit of those States, which is seldom drawn back; this operates as a tax upon our citizens. On this side, Virginia promotes her revenue to the amount of 25,000 dollars every year, by a tax on our tobacco that she exports: South-Carolina on the other side, may avail herself of similar opportunities. Two thirds of the foreign goods that are consumed in this State are imported by land from Virginia or South-Carolina; such goods pay a certain impost for the benefit of the importing States, but our Treasury is not profited by this commerce. By such means our citizens are taxed more than one hundred thousand dollars every year, but the State does not receive credit for a shilling of that money. Like a patient that is bleeding at both arms, North-Carolina must soon expire under such wasteful operations. Unless I am greatly mistaken, we have seen enough of the State of the Union, and of North-Carolina in particular, to be assured that another form of Government is become necessary. Is the form now proposed well calculated to give relief? To this, we must answer in the affirmative. All foreign goods that shall be imported into these States, are to pay a duty for the use of the nation. All the States will be on a footing, whether they have bad ports or good ones. No duties will be laid on exports; hence the planter will receive the true value of his produce, wherever it may be shipped. If excises are laid on wine, spirits, or other luxuries, they must be uniform throughout the States. By a careful management of imposts and excises, the national expences may be discharged without any other species of tax; but if a poll-tax, or land-tax shall ever become necessary, the weight must press equally on every part of the Union. For in all cases, such taxes must be according to the number of inhabitants. Is it not a pleasing consideration that North-Carolina, under all her natural disadvantages, must have the same facility of paying her share of the public debt as the most favored, or the most fortunate State? She gains no advantage by this plan, but she recovers from her misfortunes. She stands on the same footing with her sister States, and they are too generous to desire that she should stand on lower ground. When you consider those parts of the new System which are of the greatest import—those which respect the general question of liberty and safety, you will recollect that the States in Convention were unanimous; and you must remember that some of the members of that body have risqued their lives in defence of liberty; but the system does not require the help of such arguments; it will bear the most scrupulous examination.

When you refer the proposed system to the particular circumstances of North-Carolina, and consider how she is to be affected by this plan; you must find the utmost reason to rejoice in the prospect of better times—this is a sentiment that I have ventured with the greater confidence, because it is the general opinion of my late Honorable Colleagues, and I have the utmost reliance in their superior abilities. But if our constituents shall discover faults where we could not see any, or if they shall suppose that a plan is formed for abridging their liberties when we imagined that we had been securing both liberty and property on a more stable foundation; if they perceive that they are to suffer a loss where we thought they must rise from a misfortune; they will at least do us the justice to charge those errors to the head, and not to the heart.

The proposed system is now in your hands, and with it the fate of your country. We have a common interest, for we are embarked in the same vessel. At present she is in a sea of troubles, without sails, oars, or pilot; ready to be dashed into pieces by every flaw of wind. You may secure a port, unless you think it better to remain at sea. If there is any man among you that wishes for troubled times and fluctuating measures, that he may live by speculations, and thrive by the calamities of the State; this Government is not for him.

If there is any man who envies the prosperity of a native citizen, who wishes that we should remain without native merchants or seamen, without shipping, without manufactures, without commerce; poor and contemptible, the tributaries of a foreign country; this Government is not for him.

And if there is any man who has never been reconciled to our Independence, who wishes to see us degraded and insulted abroad, oppressed by anarchy at home, and torn into pieces by factions; incapable of resistance and ready to become a prey to the first invader; this Government is not for him.

But it is a Government, unless I am greatly mistaken, that gives the fairest promise of being firm and honorable; safe from Foreign Invasion or Domestic Sedition. A Government by which our commerce must be protected and enlarged; the value of our produce and of our lands must be encreased; the labourer and the mechanic must be encouraged and supported. It is a form of Government that is perfectly fitted for protecting Liberty and Property, and for cherishing the good Citizen and the Honest Man.

"A Freeman"

Essay to the People of Connecticut

Connecticut Courant, Hartford, 31 December 1787

This is a day, by way of eminence, for political deliberation, and we are amused with reasons against and reasons for the new Constitution from one part of the continent to the other. Held up to our view as something magnificent are the *reasons of the Honorable Mr.* [Elbridge] *Gerry* for not subscribing to the Constitution. From Virginia, we have the *objections of the Honorable George Mason,* pompously set forth. In New York, a factious genius pours a flood of eloquence against the Constitution. And our printers possess so much candor as to keep their presses open to all parties. Amid all these publications, a Freeman of Connecticut ventures to make his remarks and professes to do it in the spirit of candor.

In the course of some late publications, several things have been discussed relating to the new Constitution that might have a tendency to prevent prejudices and clear off objections, to give the landholders and farmers an opportunity to judge for themselves as to the defects or excellencies of it. And, as the season for the sitting of the state Convention approaches, so I would call your attention still further to the interesting subject.

Our country now seems to hang in anxious suspense, not knowing whether she is to have a good and efficient government or none at all, or a despotic one imposed upon her by some daring adventurer. She has fought, her enemies must do her the justice to own, gallantly with one of the most powerful kingdoms on the globe; a kingdom which had spread the glory of its arms and the terror of its name over every quarter of the world. She has bled, we are all mournful witnesses, at a thousand veins through a bloody and long war. She has nobly conquered, to the astonishment of the nations of Europe. On account of her splendid victories and passion for freedom approaching to enthusiasm, her fame has diffused itself far and wide. Her generals, her soldiers, her perseverance and patience under every difficulty, her statesmen and her resources are the admiration of distant nations, and probably will be of applauding posterity, if she improve aright the present eligible situation for adopting a good federal system of policy. The grand question is—shall she be happy in a good or wretched in a bad form of government? Shall all her blood and treasures expended in the late war be lost? Shall the advantages which she now possesses, prodigal-like be squandered away? When peace was established and the horrors of war terminated, the most of us mistakenly concluded that all was done for us, and that we had nothing left but to reach out the eager hand and take hold of happiness. Independence we fondly believed would cost us little or nothing—good government, national faith, national honor, and national dignity would take place of course, without any exertions of our own. But an arduous task was still to be performed. We had an empire to build. The American Revolution is a distinguished era in the history of mankind. And the present is to us a period as important, as delicate and as critical, and perhaps more so, than any that has yet been. To fight battles and vanquish enemies is far less difficult than to curb selfish passions, to liberalize the narrow-minded, to eradicate old prejudices (as the most stupid and silly and ungenerous prejudices have subsisted in the several states against each other), to give up local attachments, and to cement together as *one great people,* pursuing one general interest. An opportunity now presents of realizing the richest blessings. The new Constitution holds out to us national dignity, respectability, and an energetic form of government. I wish to see candidly discussed the most material objections against it as they may appear in the public papers, be proposed by gentlemen of sense and merit, or be started by the common people and be enlarged upon with malignant pleasure by popular drudges, who clamor plausibly about the rights of the people, but whose intentions invariably are to promote and secure their own lucrative posts or honorable employments.

In this publication, I shall consider that objection to the Constitution upon which much is confidently advanced by many, *that if we adopt the Constitution our liberties are gone forever, that moment the nation receives this form of government, that moment we become a nation of slaves.* It is incumbent upon those who make this objection to point out the dangerous clause. They should be challenged to show where we may find it. Designing and factious men throw out this objection; and many honest, well-meaning farmers and landholders are frightened with it. They hear others, of whose wisdom, knowledge in politics, and character, they have an exalted opinion, speak of the Constitution as a dangerous one, an insidious one, which is to betray the liberties of the people, while it professes to defend and guard them. They consequently fear the worst of evils lie hidden under a fair guise. For themselves, they see no danger, and never would dream of any, were it not from the base surmises of the designing. With their own eyes they can see no evils, but the more shrewd have eyes to see. Such, and such characters, important men—men in high posts—men of reputed principles and integrity—object against the Constitution as designed to annihilate the state sovereignties, undermine our rights, and to end either in a corrupt aristocracy or absolute monarchy. Thus stands the objection. Let the well-meaning who fear no loss of lucrative posts view the *mighty scarecrow.* O ye my countrymen, be not deceived with fair words and plausible speeches. You have eyes; use them for yourselves—employ your own good sense—read and examine the Constitution—trust not to others to do it for you—narrowly inspect every part of it. Then, you will be convinced that the objection is wholly groundless, having no existence but in imagination. Believe for once that many who pretend to be so tender for your rights, and are so deeply concerned for your liberties, and on all occasions boast of their love and veneration for liberty, only mean to dupe you. I am credibly informed that in a certain town, when the inhabitants were convened in pursuance of the order of the General Court to choose delegates to sit in Convention to determine whether this state will assent to and ratify a Constitution which has for its object the establishment of the dignity, freedom, and happiness of our country, a great man made a great speech, in length two hours, in breadth one hair, and closed with this striking observation: *My fellow citizens, this is the day in which you are to vote whether you will be freemen or slaves; if we reject the Constitution, we shall be free; if we adopt it, we shall be slaves.* The candor and justice of this representation, I presume, will be discerned by every man of common sense. Such an observation not obliquely, but directly insinuates that the Constitution will infallibly make us a nation of slaves. There certainly is nothing in it that looks this way.

On the contrary it seems to guard you on every side from despotism and shows an uncommon solicitude to prevent any infringement upon the liberties of the people; gives all the liberty which a judicious people could desire. Liberty, a word that has charms sufficient to captivate a generous mind, is revered in the Constitution; and is totally different from licentiousness. Many have no other idea of liberty, but for everyone to do as he pleases—to be as honest as he pleases—to be as knavish as he pleases—to revere the laws and authority of the state as much as he pleases—and to traduce and revile the rulers as much as he pleases. Such a liberty, which to our shame has for several years been our idol, ought to be done away and never more stop the progress of justice or with its foul streams pollute this beautiful country. Every government which is worth having and supporting must have a competent degree of power in it to answer the great ends of its creation—the happiness of the people, the protection of their persons, and security of their property. A government without such a power is only a burden. That government, provided for us by the concentered wisdom of the states, secures all our liberties that ought to be secured.

"A Landholder"
[Oliver Ellsworth]

The Letters: I–V, VIII

Connecticut Courant, Hartford, 5, 12, 19, 26 November, 3 and
24 December 1787

———•———

Delegate to the Continental Congress and Judge of the Connecticut Supreme Court, Ellsworth was a member of the Constitutional Convention
of 1787. After ratification he served as U.S. Senator from Connecticut
(1789–96) and Chief Justice of the Supreme Court (1796–1800).

———•———

I

To the Holders and Tillers of Land.

The writer of the following passed the first part of his life in mercantile
employments and, by industry and economy, acquired a sufficient sum on
retiring from trade to purchase and stock a decent plantation on which he
now lives in the state of a farmer. By his present employment he is interested
in the prosperity of agriculture and those who derive a support from cultivating the earth. An acquaintance with business has freed him from many
prejudices and jealousies which he sees in his neighbors, who have not intermingled with mankind nor learned by experience the method of man-
aging an extensive circulating property. Conscious of an honest intention,
he wishes to address his brethren on some political subjects which now engage the public attention and will in the sequel greatly influence the value
of landed property. The new Constitution for the United States is now before the public; the people are to determine, and the people at large generally
determine right when they have had means of information.

It proves the honesty and patriotism of the gentlemen who composed
the General Convention that they chose to submit their system to the people
rather than the legislatures, whose decisions are often influenced by men
in the higher departments of government, who have provided well for them-

selves and dread any change lest they should be injured by its operation. I would not wish to exclude from a state convention those gentlemen who compose the higher branches of the assemblies in the several states, but choose to see them stand on an even floor with their brethren, where the artifice of a small number cannot negative a vast majority of the people.

This danger was foreseen by the Federal Convention, and they have wisely avoided it by appealing directly to the people. The landholders and farmers are more than any other men concerned in the present decision; whether the proposed alteration is best they are to determine, but that an alteration is necessary, an individual may assert. It may be assumed as a fixed truth that the prosperity and riches of the farmer must depend on the prosperity and good national regulation of trade. Artful men may insinuate the contrary, tell you let trade take care of itself, and excite your jealousy against the merchant because his business leads him to wear a gayer coat than your economy directs. But let your own experience refute such insinuations. Your property and riches depend on a ready demand and generous price for the produce you can annually spare. When and where do you find this? Is it not where trade flourishes and when the merchant can freely export the produce of the country to such parts of the world as will bring the richest return? When the merchant doth not purchase, your produce is low, finds a dull market—in vexation you call the trader a jockey and curse the men whom you ought to pity. A desire of gain is common to mankind and the general motive to business and industry. You cannot expect many purchasers when trade is restricted, and your merchants are shut out from nine-tenths of the ports in the world. While they depend on the mercy of foreign nations, you are the first persons who will be humbled. Confined to a few foreign ports, they must sell low, or not at all; and can you expect they will greedily buy in at a high price, the very articles which they must sell under every restriction?

Every foreign prohibition on American trade is aimed in the most deadly manner against the holders and tillers of the land, and they are the men made poor. Your only remedy is such a national government as will make the country respectable, such a supreme government as can boldly meet the supremacy of proud and self-interested nations. The regulation of trade ever was and ever must be a national matter. A single state in the American Union cannot direct, much less control it. This must be a work of the whole, and requires all the wisdom and force of the continent, and until it is effected our commerce may be insulted by every overgrown merchant in Europe. Think not the evil will rest on your merchants alone; it may distress them, but it will destroy those who cultivate the earth. Their produce will bear a low price and require bad pay, the laborer will not find employment, the value of lands will fall, and the landholder become poor.

While our shipping rots at home by being prohibited from ports abroad, foreigners will bring you such articles and at such price as they please. Even the necessary article of salt has the present year been chiefly imported in foreign bottoms, and you already feel the consequence; your flaxseed in barter has not returned you more than two-thirds of the usual quantity. From this beginning learn what is to come.

Blame not our merchants; the fault is not in them but in the public. A federal government of energy is the only means which will deliver us, and now or never is your opportunity to establish it on such a basis as will preserve your liberty and riches. Think not that time without your own exertions will remedy the disorder. Other nations will be pleased with your poverty; they know the advantage of commanding trade and carrying in their own bottoms. By these means they can govern prices and breed up a hardy race of seamen to man their ships of war when they wish again to conquer you by arms. It is strange the holders and tillers of the land have had patience so long. They are men of resolution as well as patience, and will I presume be no longer deluded by British emissaries, and those men who think their own offices will be hazarded by any change in the constitution. Having opportunity, they will coolly demand a government which can protect what they have bravely defended in war.

II

To the Holders and Tillers of Land.

Gentlemen, You were told in the late war that peace and independence would reward your toil, and that riches would accompany the establishment of your liberties, by opening a wider market and consequently raising the price of such commodities as America produces for exportation.

Such a conclusion appeared just and natural. We had been restrained by the British to trade only with themselves, who often reexported to other nations, at a high advance, the raw materials they had procured from us. This advance we designed to realize, but our expectation has been disappointed.

The produce of the country is in general down to the old price, and bids fair to fall much lower. It is time for those who till the earth in the sweat of their brow to inquire the cause, and we shall find it neither in the merchant or farmer, but in a bad system of policy and government, or rather in having no system at all. When we call ourselves an independent nation, it is false: we are neither a nation, nor are we independent. Like thirteen contentious neighbors, we devour and take every advantage of each other, and are without that system of policy which gives safety and strength, and constitutes a national structure. Once we were dependent only on Great Britain; now we are dependent on every petty state in the world and on every customhouse officer of foreign ports. If the injured apply for redress to the assemblies of the several states, it is in vain, for they are not, and cannot be known abroad. If they apply to Congress, it is also vain, for however wise and good that body may be, they have not power to vindicate either themselves or their subjects.

Do not, my countrymen, fall into a passion on hearing these truths, nor think your treatment unexampled. From the beginning it hath been the case that people without policy will find enough to take advantage of their weakness, and you are not the first who have been devoured by their wiser neighbors. But perhaps it is not too late for a remedy; we ought at least to make a trial, and if we still die shall have this consolation in our last hours, that we tried to live.

I can foresee that several classes of men will try to alarm your fears, and however selfish their motives, we may expect that *liberty, the encroachments of* power, *and the inestimable privileges of dear posterity* will with them be fruitful topics of argument. As Holy Scripture is used in the exorcisms of Romish priests to expel imaginary demons; so the most sacred words will be conjured together to oppose evils which have no existence in the new Constitution, and which no man dare attempt to carry into execution among a people of so free a spirit as the Americans. The first to oppose a federal government will be the old friends of Great Britain, who in their hearts cursed the prosperity of your arms and have ever since delighted in the perplexity of your councils. Many of these men are still among us, and for several years their hopes of a reunion with Britain have been high; they rightly judge that nothing will so soon effect their wishes as the deranged state we are now in, if it should continue. They see that the merchant is weary of a government which cannot protect his property, and that the farmer, finding no benefit from the revolution, begins to dread much evil; and they hope the people will soon supplicate the protection of their old masters. We may therefore expect that all the policy of these men will center in defeating those measures which will protect the people and give system and force to American councils.

I was lately in a circle where the new Constitution was discussed. All but one man approved; he was full of trembling for the liberties of poor America. It was strange! It was wondrous strange to see his concern after several of his arguments had been refuted by an ingenious farmer in the company. But says he, it is against the treaty of peace. We received independence from Great Britain on condition of our keeping the old constitution. Here the man come out! We had beat the British with a bad frame of government, and with a good one he feared we should eat them up.

Debtors in desperate circumstances, who have not resolution to be either honest or industrious, will be the next men to take the alarm. They have long been upheld by the property of their creditors and the mercy of the public, and daily destroy a thousand honest men who are unsuspicious. *Paper money* and *tender acts* is the only atmosphere in which they can breathe and live. This is now so generally known that by being a friend to such measures a man effectually advertises himself a bankrupt. The opposition of these we expect, but for the sake of all honest and industrious debtors, we most earnestly wish the proposed Constitution may pass, for whatever gives a new spring to business will extricate them from their difficulties.

There is another kind of people will be found in the opposition. Men of much self-importance and supposed skill in politics, who are not of sufficient consequence to obtain public employment, but can spread jealousies in the little districts of country where they are placed; these are always jealous of men in place and of public measures, and aim at making themselves consequential by distrusting every one in the higher offices of society.

It is a strange madness of some persons immediately to distrust those who are raised by the free suffrages of the people to sustain powers which are absolutely necessary for public safety. Why were they elevated but for a general reputation of wisdom and integrity; and why should they be distrusted, until by ignorance or some base action they have forfeited a right to our confidence?

To fear a general government on energetic principles lest it should create tyrants, when without such a government all have an opportunity to become tyrants and avoid punishment, is fearing the possibility of one act of oppression more than the real exercise of a thousand. But in the present case, men who have lucrative and influential state offices, if they act from principles of self-interest, will be tempted to oppose an alteration which would doubtless be beneficial to the people. To sink from a controlment of finance, or any other great department of the state, thro want of ability or opportunity to act a part in the federal system must be a terrifying consideration. Believe not those who insinuate that this is a scheme of great men to grasp more power. The temptation is on the other side. Those in great offices never wish to hazard their places by such a change. This is the scheme of the people, and those high and worthy characters who, in obedience to the public voice, offer the proposed amendment of our federal constitution thus esteemed it, or they would not have determined state conventions as the tribunal of ultimate decision. This is the last opportunity you may have to adopt a government which gives all protection to personal liberty and, at the same time, promises fair to afford you all the advantages of a sovereign empire. While you deliberate with coolness, be not duped by the artful surmises of such as from their own interest or prejudice are blind to the public good.

III

To the Holders and Tillers of Land.

GENTLEMEN, When we rushed to arms for preventing British usurpation, liberty was the argument of every tongue.

This word would open all the resources of the country and draw out a brigade of militia rapidly as the most decisive orders of a despotic government. Liberty is a word which, according as it is used, comprehends the most good and the most evil of any in the world. Justly understood it is sacred next to those which we appropriate in divine adoration; but in the mouths of some it means any thing, which will enervate a necessary government, excite a jealousy of the rulers who are our own choice, and keep society in confusion for want of a power sufficiently concentered to promote its good. It is not strange that the licentious should tell us a government of energy is inconsistent with liberty, for being inconsistent with their wishes and their vices, they would have us think it contrary to human happiness. In the state this country was left by the war, with want of experience in sovereignty, and the feelings which the people then had; nothing but the scene we had passed thro' could give a general conviction that an internal government of strength is the only means of repressing external violence, and preserving the national rights of the people against the injustice of their own brethren. Even the common duties of humanity will gradually go out of use, when the constitution and laws of a country, do not insure justice from the public and between individuals. American experience, in our present deranged state, hath again proved these great truths, which have been verified in every age since men were made and became sufficiently numerous to form into public bodies. A government capable of controling the whole, and bringing its force to a point is one of the prerequisites for national liberty. We combine in society, with an expectation, to have our persons and properties defended against unreasonable exactions either at home or abroad. If the public are unable to protect us against the unjust impositions of foreigners, in this case we do not enjoy our natural rights, and a weakness in government is the cause. If we mean to have our natural rights and properties protected, we must first create a power which is able to do it, and in our case there is no want of resources, but only of a civil constitution which may draw them out and point their force.

The present question is shall we have such a constitution or not? We allow it to be a creation of power; but power when necessary for our good is as much to be desired as the food we eat or the air we breathe. Some men are mightily afraid of giving power lest it should be improved for oppression;

this is doubtless possible, but where is the probability. The same objection may be made against the constitution of every state in the union, and against every possible mode of government; because a power of doing good always implies a power to do evil if the person or party be disposed.

The right of the legislature to ordain laws binding on the people, gives them a power to make bad laws.

The right of the judge to inflict punishments, gives him both power and opportunity to oppress the innocent; yet none but crazy men will from thence determine that it is best to have neither a legislature nor judges.

If a power to promote the best interest of the people, necessarily implies a power to do evil, we must never expect such a constitution in theory as will not be open in some respects to the objections of carping and jealous men. The new Constitution is perhaps more cautiously guarded than any other in the world, and at the same time creates a power which will be able to protect the subject; yet doubtless objections may be raised, and so they may against the constitution of each state in the union. In Connecticut the laws are the constitution by which the people are governed, and it is generally allowed to be the most free and popular in the thirteen states. As this is the state in which I live and write, I will instance several things which with a proper colouring and a spice of jealousy appear most dangerous to the natural rights of the people, yet they never have been dangerous in practice, and are absolutely necessary at some times to prevent much greater evil.

The right of taxation or of assessing and collecting money out of the people, is one of those powers which may prove dangerous in the exercise, and which by the new constitution is vested solely in representatives chosen for that purpose. But by the laws of Connecticut, this power called so dangerous may be exercised by the selectmen of each town, and this not only without their consent but against their express will, where they have considered the matter, and judge it improper. This power they may exercise when and so often as they judge necessary! Three justices of the quorum, may tax a whole county in such sums as they think meet, against the express will of all the inhabitants. Here we see the dangerous power of taxation vested in the justices of the quorum and even in Select men, men whom we should suppose as likely to err and tyrannize as the representatives of three millions of people, in solemn deliberation, and amenable to the vengeance of their constituents, for every act of injustice. The same town officers have equal authority where personal liberty is concerned, in a matter more sacred than all the property in the world, the disposal of your children. When they judge fit, with the advice of one justice of the peace, they may tear them from the parents embrace, and place them under the absolute control of such masters as they please; and if the parents reluctance excites their resentment, they may place him and his property under overseers. Fifty other instances fearfull as these might be collected from the laws of the state, but I will not repeat them least my readers should be alarmed where there is no danger. These regulations are doubtless best, we have seen much good and no evil come from them. I adduced these instances to shew, that the most free constitution when made the subject of criticism may be exhibited in frightful colours, and such attempts we must expect against that now proposed. If my countrymen, you wait for a constitution which absolutely bars a power of doing evil, you must wait long, and when obtained it will have no power of doing good. I allow you are oppressed, but not from the quarter that jealous and wrong-headed men would insinuate. You are oppressed by the men, who to serve their own purposes would prefer the shadow of government to the reality. You are oppressed for want of a power which can protect commerce, encourage business, and create a ready demand for the productions of your farms. You are become poor, oppression continued will make wise men mad. The landholders and farmers have long borne this oppression, we have been patient and groaned in secret, but can promise for ourselves no longer; unless relieved madness, may excite us to actions we now dread.

IV

To the Landholders and Farmers.

Remarks on the objections made by the Honorable ELBRIDGE GERRY to the new Constitution.[1]

1. Gerry, a wealthy Massachusetts merchant with vast public securities, was a member of the Philadelphia Convention. Charles Beard argued that the Founding Fathers supported the

To censure a man for an opinion in which he declares himself honest, and in a matter of which all men have a right to judge, is highly injurious; at the same time, when the opinions even of honorable men are submitted to the people, a tribunal before which the meanest citizen hath a right to speak, they must abide the consequence of public stricture. We are ignorant whether the honorable gentleman possesses state dignities or emoluments which will be endangered by the new system, or hath motives of personality to prejudice his mind and throw him into the opposition; or, if it be so, do not wish to evade the objections by such a charge. As a member of the General Convention, and deputy from a great state, this honorable person hath a right to speak and be heard. It gives us pleasure to know the extent of what may be objected or even surmised, by one whose situation was the best to espy danger, and mark the defective parts of the Constitution, if any such there be. Mr. Gerry, tho in the character of an objector, tells us "he was fully convinced that to preserve the Union, an efficient government was indispensably necessary, and that it would be difficult to make proper amendments to the old Articles of Confederation," therefore, by his own concession, there was an indispensable necessity of a system in many particulars entirely new. He tells us further "that if the people reject this altogether, anarchy may ensue," and what situation can be pictured more awful than a total dissolution of all government. Many defects in the Constitution had better be risked than to fall back into that state of rude violence in which every man's hand is against his neighbor, and there is no judge to decide between them or power of justice to control. But we hope to show that there are no such alarming defects in the proposed structure of government, and that, while a public force is created, the liberties of the people have every possible guard.

Constitution because they stood to gain economically under the new regime. However, Gerry, who stood to profit substantially under the new system, refused to sign the Constitution and steadfastly opposed its ratification. As Forrest McDonald has wryly remarked, "except in opposing the Constitution, Gerry fits Professor Beard's description of suffering personalty interests in every way and on a large scale." Forrest McDonald, *We the People: The Economic Origins of the Constitution* (Chicago: University of Chicago Press, 1958), 44. See Storing, 2:1. Gerry's objections are also in Allen, 20–22.

Several of the honorable gentleman's objections are expressed in such vague and indecisive terms that they rather deserve the name of insinuations, and we know not against what particular parts of the system they are pointed. Others are explicit and, if real, deserve serious attention. His first objection is "that there is no adequate provision for a representation of the people." This must have respect either to the number of Representatives or to the manner in which they are chosen. The proper number to constitute a safe representation is a matter of judgment in which honest and wise men often disagree. Were it possible for all the people to convene and give their personal assent, some would think this the best mode of making laws; but, in the present instance, it is impracticable. In towns and smaller districts where all the people may meet conveniently and without expense this is doubtless preferable. The state representation is composed of one or two from every town and district, which composes an assembly not so large as to be unwieldy in acting, nor so expensive as to burden the people. But if so numerous a representation were made from every part of the United States, with our present population, the new Congress would consist of three thousand men; with the population of Great Britain, to which we may arrive in half a century, of ten thousand; and with the population of France, which we shall probably equal in a century and half, of thirty thousand.

Such a body of men might be an army to defend the country in case of foreign invasion, but not a legislature, and the expense to support them would equal the whole national revenue. By the proposed Constitution the new Congress will consist of nearly one hundred men. When our population is equal to Great Britain of three hundred men, and when equal to France of nine hundred. Plenty of lawgivers! Why any gentleman should wish for more is not conceivable.

Considering the immense territory of America, the objection with many will be on the other side; that, when the whole is populated, it will constitute a legislature unmanageable by its numbers. [The] Convention, foreseeing this danger, have so worded the article that if the people should at any future time judge necessary, they may diminish the representation.

As the state legislatures have to regulate the internal policy of every town and neighborhood, it is convenient enough to have one or two men, particularly acquainted with every small district of country, its interests, parties, and passions. But the federal legislature can take cognizance only of national questions and interests, which in their very nature are general, and for this purpose five or ten honest and wise men chosen from each state, men who have had previous experience in state legislation, will be more competent than an hundred. From an acquaintance with their own state legislatures, they will always know the sense of the people at large, and the expense of supporting such a number will be as much as we ought to incur.

If the honorable gentleman, in saying "there is no adequate provision for a representation of the people," refers to the manner of choosing them, a reply to this is naturally blended with his second objection, "that they have no security for the right of election." It is impossible to conceive what greater security can be given, by any form of words, than we here find.

The federal Representatives are to be chosen by the votes of the people. Every freeman is an elector. The same qualifications which enable you to vote for state representatives give you a federal voice. It is a right you cannot lose, unless you first annihilate the state legislature and declare yourselves incapable of electing, which is a degree of infatuation improbable as a second deluge to drown the world.

Your own assemblies are to regulate the formalities of this choice, and unless they betray you, you cannot be betrayed. But perhaps it may be said, Congress have a power to control this formality as to the time and places of electing; and we allow they have. But this objection, which at first looks frightful, was designed as a guard to the privileges of the electors. Even state assemblies may have their fits of madness and passion. This, tho not probable, is still possible.

We have a recent instance in the State of Rhode Island, where a desperate junto are governing contrary to the sense of a great majority of the people. It may be the case in any other state, and should it ever happen that the ignorance or rashness of the state assemblies in a fit of jealousy should deny you this sacred right, the deliberate justice of the continent is enabled to interpose and restore you a federal voice. This right is therefore more inviolably guarded than it can be by the government of your state, for it is guaranteed by the whole empire. Tho out of the order in which the honorable gentleman proposes his doubts, I wish here to notice some questions which he makes. The proposed plan among others, he tells us, involves these questions: "Whether the several state governments shall be so altered as in effect to be dissolved? Whether in lieu of the state governments the national Constitution now proposed shall be substituted?" I wish for sagacity to see on what these questions are founded. No alteration in the state governments is even proposed, but they are to remain identically the same that they now are. Some powers are to be given into the hands of your federal Representatives, but these powers are all in their nature general, such as must be exercised by the whole or not at all, and such as are absolutely necessary; or your commerce, the price of your commodities, your riches, and your safety will be the sport of every foreign adventurer. Why are we told of the dissolution of our state governments, when by this plan they are indissolubly linked? They must stand or fall, live or die together. The national legislature consists of two houses, a Senate and House of Representatives. The Senate is to be chosen by the assemblies of the particular states; so that if the assemblies are dissolved, the Senate dissolves with them. The national Representatives are to be chosen by the same electors, and under the same qualifications, as choose the state representatives; so that if the state representation be dissolved, the national representation is gone of course.

State representation and government is the very basis of the congressional power proposed. This is the most valuable link in the chain of connection and affords double security for the rights of the people. Your liberties are pledged to you by your own state and by the power of the whole empire. You have a voice in the government of your own state and in the government of the whole. Were not the gentleman on whom the remarks are made very honorable, and by the eminence of office raised above a suspicion of cunning, we should think he had, in this instance, insinuated merely to alarm the fears of the people. His other objections will be mentioned in some future number of the LANDHOLDER.

V

To the Landholders and Farmers.

Continuation of remarks on the Honorable ELBRIDGE GERRY's objections to the new Constitution.

It is unhappy both for Mr. Gerry and the public that he was not more explicit in publishing his doubts. Certainly this must have been from inattention, and not thro any want of ability; as all his honorable friends allow him to be a politician even of metaphysical nicety.

In a question of such magnitude, every candid man will consent to discuss objections which are stated with perspicuity; but to follow the honorable writer into the field of conjecture and combat phantoms, uncertain whether or not they are the same which terrified him, is a task too laborious for patience itself. Such must be the writer's situation in replying to the next objection, *"That some of the powers of the legislature are ambiguous, and others indefinite and dangerous."* There are many powers given to the legislature. If any of them are dangerous, the people have a right to know which they are, and how they will operate, that we may guard against the evil. The charge of being ambiguous and indefinite may be brought against every human composition, and necessarily arises from the imperfection of language. Perhaps no two men will express the same sentiment in the same manner, and by the same words; neither do they connect precisely the same ideas with the same words. From hence arises an ambiguity in all languages, with which the most perspicuous and precise writers are in a degree chargeable. Some persons never attain to the happy art of perspicuous expression, and it is equally true that some persons, thro a mental defect of their own, will judge the most correct and certain language of others to be indefinite and ambiguous. As Mr. Gerry is the first and only man who has charged the new Constitution with ambiguousness, is there not room to suspect that his understanding is different from other men's, and whether it be better or worse, the Landholder presumes not to decide.

It is an excellency of this Constitution that it is expressed with brevity and in the plain common language of mankind.

Had it swelled into the magnitude of a volume, there would have been more room to entrap the unwary, and the people who are to be its judges would have had neither patience nor opportunity to understand it. Had it been expressed in the scientific language of law, or those terms of art which we often find in political compositions, to the honorable gentleman it might have appeared more definite and less ambiguous, but to the great body of the people altogether obscure, and to accept it they must leap in the dark.

The people, to whom in this case the great appeal is made, best understand those compositions which are concise and in their own language. Had the powers given to the legislature been loaded with provisos and such qualifications as a lawyer who is so cunning as even to suspect himself would probably have intermingled, there would have been much more danger of a deception in the case. It would not be difficult to show that every power given to the legislature is necessary for national defense and justice, and to protect the rights of the people who create this authority for their own advantage; but to consider each one particularly would exceed the limits of my design.

I shall therefore select two powers given them, which have been more abused to oppress and enslave mankind than all the others with which this or any legislature on earth is clothed: the right of taxation, or of collecting money from the people, and of raising and supporting armies.

These are the powers which enable tyrants to scourge their subjects; and they are also the very powers by which good rulers protect the people against the violence of wicked and overgrown citizens, and invasion by the rest of mankind. Judge candidly what a wretched figure the American empire will exhibit in the eye of other nations, without a power to array and support a military force for its own protection. Half a dozen regiments from Canada or New Spain might lay whole provinces under contribution, while we were disputing who has power to pay and raise an army. This power is also necessary to restrain the violence of seditious citizens. A concurrence of circumstances frequently enables a few disaffected persons to make great revolutions unless government is vested with the most extensive powers of self-defense. Had [Daniel] Shays, the malcontent of Massachusetts, been a man of genius, fortune, and address, he might have conquered that state and, by the aid of a little sedition in the other states and an army proud by victory, become the monarch and tyrant of America. Fortunately he was checked, but should jealousy prevent vesting these powers in the hands of men chosen by yourselves and who are under every constitutional restraint, accident or design will in all probability raise up some future Shays to be the tyrant of your children.

A people cannot long retain their freedom whose government is incapable of protecting them.

The power of collecting money from the people is not to be rejected because it has sometimes been oppressive.

Public credit is as necessary for the prosperity of a nation as private credit is for the support and wealth of a family.

We are this day many millions poorer than we should have been had a well-arranged government taken place at the conclusion of the war. All have shared in this loss, but none in so great proportion as the landholders and farmers.

The public must be served in various departments.

Who will serve them without a meet recompense? Who will go to war and pay the charges of his own warfare? What man will any longer take empty promises of reward from those who have no constitutional power to reward or means of fulfilling them? Promises have done their utmost, more than they ever did in any other age or country. The delusive bubble has broke, and in breaking it has beggared thousands and left you an unprotected people, numerous without force and full of resources but unable to command one of them. For these purposes there must be a general treasury with a power to replenish it as often as necessity requires. And where can this power be more safely vested than in the common legislature, men chosen by yourselves from every part of the Union, and who have the confidence of their several states, men who must share in the burdens they impose on others, men who by a seat in Congress are incapable of holding any office under the states, which might prove a temptation to spoil the people for increasing their own income?

We find another objection to be "that the executive is blended with and will have an undue influence over the legislative." On examination you will find this objection unfounded. The supreme executive is vested in a President of the United States. Every bill that hath passed the Senate and Representatives must be presented to the President, and if he approve, it becomes law. If he disapproves, but makes no return within ten days, it still becomes law. If he returns the bill with his objections, the Senate and Representatives consider it a second time, and if two-thirds of them adhere to the first resolution, it becomes law notwithstanding the President's dissent. We allow the President hath an influence, tho strictly speaking he hath not a legislative voice, and think such an influence must be salutary. In the President, all the executive departments meet, and he will be a channel of communication between those who make and those who execute the laws. Many things look fair in theory which in practice are impossible. If lawmakers in every instance, before their final decree, had the opinion of those who are to execute them, it would prevent a thousand absurd ordinances, which are solemnly made, only to be repealed and lessen the dignity of legislation in the eyes of mankind.

The Vice President is not an executive officer while the President is in discharge of his duty; and when he is called to preside, his legislative voice ceases. In no other instance is there even the shadow of blending or influence between the two departments. We are further told "that the judicial department, or those courts of law to be instituted by Congress, will be oppressive."

We allow it to be possible, but from whence arises the probability of this event? State judges may be corrupt, and juries may be prejudiced and ignorant, but these instances are not common; and why shall we suppose they will be more frequent under a national appointment and influence, when the eyes of a whole empire are watching for their detection?

Their courts are not to intermeddle with your internal policy and will have cognizance only of those subjects which are placed under the control of a national legislature. It is as necessary there should be courts of law and executive officers, to carry into effect the laws of the nation, as that there be courts and officers to execute the laws made by your state assemblies. There are many reasons why their decisions ought not to be left to courts instituted by particular states.

A perfect uniformity must be observed thro the whole Union, or jealousy and unrighteousness will take place; and for a uniformity, one judiciary must pervade the whole. The inhabitants of one state will not have confidence in judges appointed by the legislature of another state, in which they have no voice. Judges who owe their appointment and support to one state will be unduly influenced and not reverence the laws of the Union. It will at any time be in the power of the smallest state, by interdicting their own judiciary, to defeat the measures, defraud the revenue, and annul the most sacred laws of the whole empire. A legislative power without a judicial and executive under their own control is in the nature of things a nullity. Congress under the old Confederation had power to ordain and resolve, but having no judicial or executive of their own, their most solemn resolves were totally disregarded. The little State of Rhode Island was purposely left by Heaven to its present madness for a general conviction in the other states that such a system as is now proposed is our only preservation from ruin. What respect can anyone think would be paid to national laws, by judicial and executive officers who are amenable only to the present Assembly of Rhode Island? The rebellion of Shays and the present measures of Rhode Island ought to convince us that a national legislature, judiciary, and executive must be united or the whole is but a name; and that we must have these or soon be hewers of wood and drawers of water for all other people.

In all these matters and powers given to Congress, their ordinances must be the supreme law of the land or they are nothing. They must have authority to enact any laws for executing their own powers, or those powers will be evaded by the artful and unjust, and the dishonest trader will defraud the public of its revenue.

As we have every reason to think this system was honestly planned, we ought to hope it may be honestly and justly executed. I am sensible that speculation is always liable to error. If there be any capital defects in this Constitution, it is most probable that experience alone will discover them. Provision is made for an alteration if on trial it be found necessary.

When your children see the candor and greatness of mind with which you lay the foundation, they will be inspired with equity to furnish and adorn the superstructure.

VIII

To the Hon. ELBRIDGE GERRY, Esquire.

Sir, When a man in public life first deviates from the line of truth and rectitude, an uncommon degree of art and attention becomes necessary to secure him from detection. Duplicity of conduct in him requires more than double caution; a caution which his former habits of simplicity have never furnished him the means of calculating; and his first leap into the region of treachery and falshood is often as fatal to himself as it was designed to be to his country. Whether you and Mr. Mason may be ranked in this class of transgressors I pretend not to determine. Certain it is, that both your management and his for a short time before and after the rising of the fœderal convention impress us with a favorable opinion, that you are great novices in the arts of dissimulation. A small degree of forethought would have taught you both a much more successful method of directing the rage of resentment which you caught at the close of the business at Philadelphia, than the one you took. You ought to have considered that you resided in regions very distant from each other, where different parts were to be acted, and then made your *cast* accordingly. Mr. Mason was certainly wrong in telling the world that he acted a double part—he ought not to have published two setts of *reasons for his dissent to the constitution. His New-England reasons* would have come better from you. He ought to have contented himself with haranguing in the southern states, *that it was too popular, and was calculated too much for the advantage of the eastern states.* At the same time you might have come on, and in the Coffee-House at New-York you might have found an excellent sett of objections ready made to your hand; a sett that with very little alteration would have exactly suited the latitude of New-England, the whole of which district ought most clearly to have been submitted to your protection and patronage. A Lamb, a Willet, a Smith, a Clinton, a Yates,[2] or any other gentleman whose salary is paid by the state impost, as they had six months the start of you in considering the subject, would have furnished you with a good discourse upon the "*liberty of the press,*" the "*bill of rights,*" the "*blending of the executive and legislative,*" "*internal taxation,*" or any other topic which you did not happen to think of while in convention.

It is evident that this mode of proceeding would have been well calculated for the security of Mr. Mason; he there might have vented his antient enmity against the independence of America, and his sore mortification for the loss

2. John Lamb, Marinus Willetts, Melancton Smith, George Clinton, and Robert Yates were prominent New York Anti-Federalists. See Storing, 6 and passim. In Allen, see Robert Yates and John Lansing's "Reasons of Dissent," 14–16, and Melancton Smith's speech to the New York ratifying convention on 20 June 1788, 171–77.

of his favorite motion respecting the navigation-act; and all under the mask of sentiments, which with a proper caution in expressing them, might have gained many adherents in his own state. But, although Mr. Mason's conduct might have been easily guarded in this particular, your character would not have been entirely safe even with the precaution above mentioned. Your policy, Sir, ought to have led you one step farther back. You have been so precipitate and unwary in your proceedings, that it will be impossible to set you right, even in idea, without recurring to previous transactions and recalling to your view the whole history of your conduct in the convention as well as the subsequent display of patriotism contained in your publication. I undertake this business, not that I think it possible to help you out of your present embarrassments; but, as those transactions have evidently slipt your memory, the recollection of the blunder into which your inexperience has betrayed you, may be of eminent service in forming future schemes of popularity, should the public ever give you another opportunity to traduce and deceive them.

You will doubtless recollect the following state of facts; if you do not, every member of the Convention will attest them—that almost the whole time during the setting of the Convention, and until the Constitution had received its present form, no man was more plausible and conciliating upon every subject than Mr. Gerry—he was willing to sacrifice every private feeling and opinion—to concede every state interest that should be in the least incompatible with the most substantial and permanent system of general government—that mutual concession and unanimity were the whole burden of his song; and although he originated no ideas himself, yet there was nothing in the system as it now stands to which he had the least objection—indeed Mr. Gerry's conduct was agreeably surprising to all his acquaintance, and very unlike that turbulent obstinacy of spirit which they had formerly affixed to his character. Thus stood Mr. Gerry; till, towards the close of the business, he introduced a motion respecting the redemption of the old Continental Money—that it should be placed upon a footing with other liquidated securities of the United States. As Mr. Gerry was supposed to be possessed of large quantities of this species of paper, his motion appeared to be founded in such barefaced selfishness and injustice, that it at once accounted for all his former plausibility and concession, while the rejection of it by the Convention inspired its author with the utmost rage and intemperate opposition to the whole system he had formerly praised. His resentment could no more than embarrass and delay the completion of the business for a few days; when he refused signing the Constitution and was called upon for his reasons. These reasons were committed to writing by one of his colleagues and likewise by the Secretary, as Mr. Gerry delivered them. These reasons were totally different from those which he has published, neither was a single objection which is contained in his letter to the legislature of Massachusetts ever offered by him in convention.

Now, Mr. Gerry, as this is generally known to be the state of facts, and as neither the reasons which you publish nor those retained on the Secretary's files can be supposed to have the least affinity to truth, or to contain the real motives which induced you to withhold your name from the constitution, it appears to me that your plan was not judiciously contrived. When we act without principle, we ought to be prepared against embarrassments. You might have expected some difficulties in realizing your continental money; indeed the chance was rather against your motion even in the most artful shape in which it could have been proposed. An experienced hand would therefore have laid the whole plan beforehand, and have guarded against a disappointment. You should have begun the business with doubts, and expressed your sentiments with great ambiguity upon every subject as it passed. This method would have secured you many advantages. Your doubts and ambiguities, if artfully managed, might have passed, like those of the Delphic Oracle, for wisdom and deliberation; and at the close of the business you might have acted either for or against the constitution, according to the success of your motion, without appearing dishonest or inconsistent with yourself. One farther precaution would have brought you off clear. Instead of waiting till the Convention rose, before you consulted your friends at New-York, you ought to have applied to them at an earlier period, to know what objections you should make. They could have instructed you as well in August as October. With these advantages you might have past for a complete politician, and your duplicity might never have been detected.

The enemies of America have always been extremely unfortunate in concerting their measures. They have generally betrayed great ignorance of the true spirit and feeling of the country, and they have failed to act in concert with each other. This is uniformly conspicuous, from the first Bute Parliament in London to the last Shays Parliament at Pelham. The conduct of the enemies of the new constitution compares with that of the other enemies above mentioned only in two particulars, its *object* and its *tendency.* Its object was self interest built on the ruins of the country, and its tendency is the disgrace of its authors and the final prosperity of the same country they meant to depress. Whether the constitution will be adopted at the first trial in the conventions of nine states is at present doubtful. It is certain however, that its enemies have great difficulties to encounter arising from their disunion; in the different states where the opposition rages the most, their principles are totally opposite to each other and their objections discordant and irreconcilable; so that no regular system can be formed among you, and you will betray each other's motives.

In Massachusetts the opposition began with you, and from motives most pitifully selfish and despicable; you addressed yourself to the feelings of the Shays faction, and that faction will be your only support. In New-York the opposition is not to this constitution in particular, but to the federal impost; it is confined wholly to salary men and their connections, men whose salary is paid by the state impost. This class of citizens are endeavouring to convince the ignorant part of the community that an annual income of fifty thousand pounds, extorted from the citizens of Massachusetts, Connecticut and New-Jersey, is a great blessing to the state of New-York. And although the regulation of trade and other advantages of a federal government would secure more than five times that sum to the people of that state; yet, as this would not come through the same hands, these men find fault with the constitution. In Pennsylvania the old quarrel respecting their state constitution has thrown the state into parties for a number of years. One of these parties happened to declare for the new federal constitution, and this was a sufficient motive for the other to oppose it: the dispute there is not upon the merits of the subject, but it is their old warfare carried on with different weapons, and it was an even chance that the parties had taken different sides from what they have taken, for there is no doubt but either party would sacrifice the whole country to the destruction of their enemies. In Virginia the opposition wholly originated in two principles; the madness of Mason, and the enmity of the Lee faction to General Washington. Had the General not attended the convention nor given his sentiments respecting the constitution, the Lee party would undoubtedly have supported it, and Col. Mason would have vented his rage to his own negroes and to the wind. In Connecticut, our wrongheads are few in number and feeble in their influence. The opposition here is not one half so great to the federal government, as it was three years ago to the federal impost; and the faction, such as it is, is from the same blindfold party.

I thought it my duty to give you these articles of information, for the reasons above mentioned. Wishing you more caution and better success in your future manœuvers, I have the honour to be, Sir, with great respect your very humble servant.

Popular Government and Civic Virtue

DESPITE NUMEROUS Anti-Federalist accusations that the Federalists were advancing aristocratic government in America, virtually all Federalists defended the cause of popular government. The Federalist case for popular government rested on both the natural right of the people to institute government and the concomitant duty to establish and preserve good government. Even "Caesar," who with "blunt and ungracious reasoning" fully admitted that he considered the "unthinking masses" ill qualified to evaluate the Constitution, and that he was "not much attached to the *majesty of the multitude*," nonetheless recognized the inherent right of the people to receive or reject the Constitution. He simply exhorted them to look to the opinions of their more learned superiors in deciding the case. In contrast to the deferential role "Caesar" advised the people to take, Noah Webster argued that "it is not only the *right,* but the indispensable *duty* of every citizen to examine the principles" of the proposed government.

Though strongly committed to popular government, the Federalists were not inattentive to the problems and excesses of democracy. Unwilling to defend "popular government with a vengeance" or "licentious democracy," they sought a way to retain the principles and spirit of democratic government and at the same time avoid the defects toward which it tended. In response to the Anti-Federalist view that a large territory is unfit for popular government and that only in small territories are the republican virtues of public spiritedness and moderation possible, Federalists charged that the small republic thesis was flawed. The problem of small republics, they said, is that they are prone to turbulence, licentiousness, and faction. To counteract these diseases, Federalists asserted the need for a large republic.

How did the Federalists understand the purpose of republican government? How did they think such a government was to be preserved and perpetuated? Was there a Federalist vision of republicanism that was more than a defense against Anti-Federalist criticisms? The following selections demonstrate that many of the Federalists did not simply react to their opponents' charges, but presented philosophically thoughtful, albeit sometimes competing, views about the nature of republican government. The "State Soldier" ridicules the "chimerical and speculative enjoyments" that amused the political imaginations of his opponents and declares that "the only desirable purpose of any government is, the security of men's persons and property." According to Noah Webster, a general distribution of property is "the very *soul of a republic.*" Indeed, Montesquieu was wrong; it is not virtue that provides the sturdiest support of free government but property and dominion.

In contrast, Nicholas Collin warns against an "overdriven spirit of commerce," for the desire to accumulate wealth and dominion, left unchecked by moral and religious principles, fosters base passions. Put simply "there can be no liberty without virtue." In his view, the moral and intellectual qualities that ennoble men and make them capable of self-government are the very soul of the republic. A people of good manners, morals, and learning make the political union stronger, animating it "by the same generous spirit." In turn, a noble republican civilization gradually enhances "the dispositions necessary for civil government." John Dickinson agreed. He believed that while government ought to safeguard the liberty and property of the people, the perpetuation of the people's virtue and the advancement of their happiness is the final purpose of government. Dickinson's understanding of the rights of man places the individual "in a close connection with all his duties." The right of the people to establish a constitution and institute government is inextricably bound to the purpose of a constitution and government: to advance the general welfare and happiness of the people in the way ordained by the Creator and the law of nature.

The competing views on the nature of republican government represent two different poles of political science in the eighteenth century. According to the narrower vision, not only is free government limited in its powers, but it is also limited in its purpose. The aim of republican government is the security of the individual and his property, or in other words the prevention of injustice; republican government neither attempts to form nor depends upon a virtuous citizenry. Proponents of the broader vision agreed that republican government must be limited in its powers, for only a government of constitutionally limited authority is consistent with the rights of man. They did not, however, believe that the recognition of man's natural rights reduced the ends of politics. Rather than lowering the ends of political association, the discovery and recognition of the rights of man offered the just basis on which to construct the political community and to accomplish the highest of political tasks. There can be no self-government without liberty, they believed, but further there can be no genuine liberty and self-government without virtue.

Despite the lack of unanimity about the purpose of republican government, most Federalists understood that the regime they were about to establish would affect the manners and souls of the citizens. They also generally agreed that the perpetuation of republicanism depends ultimately on the character of the citizens. The need for ethical and religious instruction in the polity was widely felt and frequently spoken of, though as a whole the Federalists did not draw a detailed roadmap for the journey of moral education in the United States. Instead, they tended to speak to their fellow citizens in generalities, almost in matter-of-fact tones, about the need for and the benefits that would derive from religion, education, good statesmanship, and law.

Having said this, it is important to point out that there were indeed some Federalists who confronted certain moral and religious matters explicitly. It is not sufficient to assume a common consensus on the "universally established principles of humanity and common equity," Collin said. These principles must be applied in practice. Thus he, Tench Coxe, "Crito," and others raised their voices in condemnation of the cruel, inhuman practice of slavery in America. Presaging the poignant appeal of Abraham Lincoln during the Civil War era, "Crito" reminds his fellow citizens of the principles to which the American union is dedicated. "It was repeatedly declared," he says, " . . . that *all men* are created equal; That they are endowed by their Creator with certain *unalienable rights*. That among these are *life, liberty,* and the *pursuit of happiness*." Pointing out the striking contradiction between the sacred principles and the profane practices of America, "Crito" continues:

> The Africans, and the blacks in servitude among us, were really as much included in these assertions as ourselves; and their right, *unalienable right* to liberty, and to procure and possess property, is as much asserted as ours, if they be *men*. And if we have not allowed them to enjoy these unalienable rights, but violently deprive them of liberty and property, and are still taking, as far as in our power, all liberty, and property from the nations in Africa, we are guilty of a ridiculous wicked contradiction and inconsistence: and practically authorize any nation or people, who have power to do it, to make us their slaves.

It would seem that David Ramsay of South Carolina could not hear the pleas of "Crito," or the "bitter sighs, groans, and tears" of the distressed men and women held in bondage. Congress is prohibited from outlawing the slave trade for twenty-one years, Ramsay points out. It does not follow that they must or will forbid it after 1808; indeed, "it is probable that they will not." Ramsay's prediction is premised on his calculation of the economic self-interest of both the South and the North, implying that the desire for wealth will decide the question of the future of the slave trade in the United States. "One of the People Called Quakers" saw things very differently. The Virginia delegates to the Constitutional Convention, he says, were obdurately opposed to slavery and agreed to the limited importation of slaves only because it was the best compromise they could then attain. "The new federal government," he concludes, " . . . would eagerly embrace the opportunity not only of putting an end to the importation of slaves, but of abolishing slavery forever."

In matters of religious conviction, the Federalists concurred that liberty requires the unrestrained exercise of the conscience and prohibits religious tests for office. This did not mean to "Elihu" that the impious and the immoral were not fools nor to Oliver Ellsworth that the law must be indifferent to gross impieties and immoralities. Indeed in matters of morality the law serves not only to punish indiscretions but also to induce good habits and educate to virtue. For the vast majority of the Founders, liberty was compatible with morality; it was not compatible with, or even secure in, a polity that failed or refused to make moral distinctions. The concern for the relationship between liberty and morality was also applied to economic matters. Some of the Federalists viewed the life of commerce and manufacturing as incompatible with an independent, simple-mannered, virtuous republican citizenry. More often than not, however, Federalists concluded that there is no incongruity between scientific progress and commercial prosperity on the one hand, and the preservation of a virtuous citizenry on the other. In fact according to Collin, Dickinson, Ellsworth, and Wilson, the moderate and just pursuit of wealth is perfectly compatible with, and may even provide a mutual support for, the ethical life.

Many leading Federalists contended that adherence to the just principles of republican government requires both a dependence on the character of the citizenry and guidance from intelligent and virtuous leaders. The call for a republican spirit throughout the government and across the land is echoed by a host of voices in choral array. Dickinson tells of how this may be achieved, teaching that a popular government in a large territory acting according to the principles of representation and federalism can be characterized by an "animated moderation." Similarly Wilson calls for the union of public-spiritedness and moderation. In his Fourth of July oration of 1788 he exhorts the American people to the cause of their celebrated independence and union, demonstrating at once the profoundly popular character of the American polity and the crucial task that must be performed by statesmen-educators if republican government is to endure. One can almost hear the sonorous echoes of the Federalists sounding across the many July Fourths that separate us in time but connect us in spirit, calling out their hope for a "constellation of noble minds" to continue the trial of self-government and thus shedding "a bright day over America till time is no more."

"One of Four Thousand"

Essay

Independent Gazetteer, Philadelphia, 15 October 1787

To the FREEMEN OF PENNSYLVANIA.

A publication has lately appeared in several of our papers, said to be signed by *sixteen* members of the late Assembly of Pennsylvania, which challenges a few remarks.[1]

The first remark that occurs is, that the paper was neither written by any *one* of them, nor signed by *all* of them. They are too illiterate to compose such an address, and it can be proved that several of the persons whose names are subscribed to it left the city on Saturday, before there was time to collect the materials of the address, or to receive it from the *person* who is well known to have written it.

A second remark that occurs in this place is, that there was a fixed resolution of the anti-federal junto to oppose the federal government, *long before* it made its appearance. In the month of July last, at a meeting of this junto, it was agreed, "that if the new constitution of Congress interfered in the least with the constitution of Pennsylvania, it ought to be opposed and rejected, and that even the name of a WASHINGTON should not carry it down." Happily it requires a reduction of the enormous expenses, and some other alterations of our constitution. Hence the reason of their opposition. Had it been much more perfect, or had it, like the Jewish theocracy, been framed by the hand of the SUPREME BEING himself, it would have been equally unpopular among them, since it interferes with their expensive hobby-horse, the Constitution of Pennsylvania.

The address, and all the opposition to the new government, originate from the officers of government, who are afraid of losing their salaries or

---

1. The unknown author of this essay is responding to An Address of the Minority of the Pennsylvania House of Representatives. For the address see *DH,* 2:112–17.

places. This will not surprise those of us who remember the opposition which our Independence received from a few officers of government in the years 1775 and 1776. Recollect the FRIENDLY ADDRESSES and the CATOS, which appeared in those years in all our newspapers. Remember too, that these publications came from men of as great understandings, and of more extensive influence, than Randolph, Mason or Gerry. Which of them is fit to be named with Hutchinson, Bernard, Tryon or Kemp?

The Address begins with two palpable falsehoods. "We lamented (it says) at the time, that a majority of our legislature appointed men to represent this state, who were all citizens of Philadelphia, and none of them calculated to represent the landed interest of Pennsylvania."

It is a well known fact, that a seat in the Convention was offered to William Findley, and that he objected to it, because no wages were to be connected with it. It became, therefore, a matter of economy, as well as convenience, to fill up the delegation with members from Philadelphia. If this was a crime, the sixteen concurred in it, for they *all* voted for five of the delegation, and for three other men who were at that time citizens of Philadelphia, viz. Thomas McKean, Charles Pettit, and John Boyard, Esquires.

The story of the delegates from Pennsylvania having no interest in the landed property of the state is equally groundless with the foregoing. They are all land holders, and one of them alone owns a greater landed estate than the whole sixteen absconders; and has for many years past punctually and justly paid more taxes on it, than are paid by the whole antifederal junto—and, unfortunately, for the support of the men who compose this junto.

The address confesses that the sixteen absconded, to prevent the majority of the House from calling a convention, to consider the new form of government. Is this right, Freemen of Pennsylvania?—Is it agreeable to democratic principles, that the *Minority* should govern the *Majority?*—Is not this aristocracy in good earnest?—Is it not tyranny, that a *few* should govern the *many?*—By absconding, and thereby obstructing the public business, they dissolved the constitution. They annihilated the first principles of government, and threw the commonwealth into a *state of nature*. Under these circumstances, the citizens of Philadelphia appealed to the *first* of nature's laws, viz. self-preservation. They seized two of the sixteen absconders, and compelled them to form a House by their attendance. In this they acted wisely and justly—as much so as the man who seizes a highwayman, who is about to rob him. If they were wrong in this action, then the men who drove Galloway, Skinner, Delancey, and other miscreants, from our states, by force, in the year 1776, were wrong likewise. What justified all the outrages that were committed against the tories in the beginning of the war? Nothing but the dissolution of our governments.—What was the foundation of the dissolution of these governments? Nothing but a resolution of Congress.—What determined us to establish new governments on the ruins of the old? Nothing but a recommendation of Congress.—Why, then, do these men fly in the faces of the Convention and Congress?—It was from similar bodies of men, similarly constituted, that their present form of government derived its independence. It cannot exist without a Congress—it is meet, therefore, that it should harmonize with it.

The objections to the federal government are weak, false, and absurd. The neglect of the Convention to mention the *Liberty of the Press* arose from a respect to the state constitutions, in each of which this palladium of liberty is secured, and which is guaranteed to them as an essential part of their republican forms of government. But supposing this had not been done, the *Liberty of the Press* would have been an inherent and political right, as long as nothing was said *against* it. The Convention have said nothing to secure the privilege of eating and drinking, and yet no man supposes that right of nature to be endangered by their silence about it.

Considering the variety of interests to be consulted, and the diversity of human opinions upon all subjects, and especially the subject of government, it is a matter of astonishment, that the government formed by the Convention has so few faults. With these faults, it is a phenomenon of human wisdom and virtue, such as the world never saw before. It unites in its different parts all the advantages, without any of the disadvantages of the three well known forms of government, and yet it preserves the attributes of a republic. And lastly, if it should be found to be faulty in any particular, it provides an easy and constitutional method of curing its faults.

I anticipate the praise with which this government will be viewed by the friends of liberty and mankind in Europe. The philosophers will no longer consider a republic as an impracticable form of government, and pious men of all denominations will thank God for having provided in our federal constitution, an Ark for the preservation of the remains of the justice and liberties of the world.

Freemen of Pennsylvania, consider the character and services of the men who made this government. Behold the venerable FRANKLIN, in the 70th year of his age, cooped up in the cabin of a small vessel, and exposing himself to the dangers of a passage on the ocean, crowded with British cruisers, in a winter month, in order to solicit from the court of France that aid, which finally enabled America to close the war with so much success and glory—and then say, is it possible that this man would set his hand to a constitution that would endanger your liberties? From this aged servant of the public, turn your eyes to the illustrious American hero, whose name has ennobled human nature—I mean our beloved WASHINGTON. Behold him, in the year 1775, taking leave of his happy family and peaceful retreat, and flying to the relief of a distant, and at that time an unknown part of the American continent. See him uniting and cementing an army, composed of the citizens of thirteen states, into a band of brothers. Follow him into the field of battle, and behold him the *first* in danger, and the *last* out of it. Follow him into his winter quarters, and see him sharing in the hunger, cold and fatigues of every soldier in his army. Behold his fortitude in adversity, his moderation in victory, and his tenderness and respect upon all occasions for the civil power of his country. But above all, turn your eyes to that illustrious scene he exhibited at Annapolis in 1782, when he resigned his commission, and laid his sword at the feet of Congress, and afterwards resumed the toils of an American farmer on the banks of the Potomac. Survey, my countrymen, these illustrious exploits of patriotism and virtue, and then say, is it possible that the deliverer of our country would have recommended an unsafe form of government for that liberty, for which he had for eight long years contended with such unexampled firmness, constancy and magnanimity?

Pardon me, if I here ask—Where were the sixteen absconders and their advisers, while these illustrious framers of our federal constitution were exposing their lives and exerting their talents for your safety and happiness? Some of them took sanctuary in offices, under the constitution of Pennsylvania, from the dangers of the year 1776, and the rest of them were either inactive, or known only on the muster-rolls of the militia during the war.

Look around you, my fellow citizens, and behold the confusion and distresses which prevail in every part of our country.[2] Behold, from the weakness of the government of Massachusetts, the leaders of rebellion making laws to exempt *themselves* from punishment. See, in Rhode Island, the bonds of society and the obligations of morality dissolved by paper money and tender laws. See the flames of courthouses in Virginia, kindled by debtors to stop the course of justice. Hear the complaints of our farmers, whose unequal and oppressive taxes in every part of the country amount to nearly the rent of their farms. Hear too the complaints of every class of public creditors. Look at the records of bankruptcies that fill every newspaper. Look at the melancholy countenances of our mechanics, who now wander up and down the streets of our cities without employment. See our ships rotting in our harbors, or excluded from nearly all the ports in the world. Listen to the insults that are offered to the American name and character in every court of Europe. See order and honor everywhere prostrate in the dust, and religion, with all her attending train of virtues, about to quit our continent forever. View these things, my fellow citizens, and then say that we do not require a new, a protecting, and efficient federal government, if you can. The picture I have given you of the situation of our country is not an exaggerated one. I challenge the boldest enemy of the federal constitution to disprove any one part of it.

It is not to be wondered at, that *some* of the rulers and officers of the government of Pennsylvania are opposed to the new constitution of the United States. It will lessen their power, number and influence—for it will necessarily reduce the expenses of our government from nearly 50,000 l. to

2. Consider the following catalogue of political evils in light of the arguments by Publius in *The Federalist,* No. 10.

10,000 l., or, at most, 15,000 l. a year. I am very happy in being able to except many worthy officers of our government from concurring in this opposition. Their names, their conduct, and their characters, are well-known to their Fellow Citizens, and I hope they will all be rewarded by a continuance and accumulation of public favor and confidence.

The design of this address is not to inflame the passions of my fellow citizens; I know the feelings of the people of Pennsylvania are sufficiently keen. It becomes me not, therefore (to use the words of the address of the sixteen absconders), to add to them, by dwelling longer "upon the distresses and dangers of our country. I have laid a real state of facts before you; it becomes you, therefore, to judge for yourselves."

The absconders have endeavored to sanctify their false and seditious publication by a solemn address to the Supreme Being. I shall conclude the truths I have written, by adopting some of their own words, with a short addition to them.

"May HE, who alone has dominion over the passions and understandings of men, preserve you from the influence of rulers, who have upon many occasions *held fellowship with iniquity, and established mischief by law.*"

The author of this Address is one of the FOUR THOUSAND Citizens of Philadelphia and its neighborhood, who subscribed the petition to the late Assembly, immediately to call a Convention, in order to adopt the proposed FEDERAL CONSTITUTION.

"Caesar"

The Letters: II

Daily Advertiser, New York, 17 October 1787

---·---

In his editorial notes to *Essays on the Constitution of the United States,* Paul L. Ford identifies Alexander Hamilton as the author of the Caesar letters. But as Jacob E. Cooke has shown, Ford's reasons are "not altogether convincing." Cooke has cast enough doubt on Hamilton's authorship to attribute the letters simply to the effort of an anonymous Caesar. See Cooke, "Alexander Hamilton's Authorship of the Caesar Letters," *William and Mary Quarterly* 17 (1960): 78.

---·---

II

> "The great source of all the evils which afflict Republics, is, that the people are too apt to make choice of rulers, who are either Politicians without being Patriots, or Patriots without being Politicians."

MR. CHILDS: When I took notice of Cato's[1] prefatory address to the Citizens of the State of New York, in your paper of the first instant, I had no serious intention of becoming a controversial defendant of the new constitution. Indeed, if the system required defence, I was neither so weak nor so vain as to suppose myself competent to the task. To obviate difficulties which may arise, when such weighty affairs as the principles of legislation are under discussion, I am sensible requires talents far beyond my limited abilities.

---

1. The letters of Cato began appearing in the *New York Journal* on 27 September 1787. Paul L. Ford attributed authorship to George Clinton, but in the wake of additional research by Jacob Cooke and Linda Grant DePauw, it appears, as Storing has remarked, that the attribution is "almost entirely groundless." See especially the appendix to DePauw, *The Eleventh Pillar* (Ithaca: American Historical Association, Cornell University Press, 1966). Cato's letters are in Storing, 2:6.

When I offered a few remarks on Cato's introduction, I was strongly impressed with the idea that even the most substantial criticisms, promulgated by the most influential *avowed Citizens,* could have no good tendency at *this time.* I viewed the public mind as wound up to a great pitch of dissatisfaction, by the inadequacy of the powers of the present Congress to the general good and conversation of the union. I believed then, as I do now, that the people were determined and prepared for a *change.* I conceived, therefore, that the wish of every good man would be, that *this change might be peaceably effected.* With this view I opposed myself to Cato. I asserted, in my last, *that the door of recommendation was shut, and cannot be opened by the same men—that the Convention was dissolved.* If I am wrong, it will be of great importance to Cato's future remarks that he make it appear. If he will declare from sufficient authority, that the members of the late Convention have only adjourned to give time to hear the sentiments of every political disputant, that after the numerous presses of America have groaned with the heavy productions of speculative politicians, they will *again meet,* weigh their respective merits, and accommodate accordingly—I say, if Cato can do this, I make no hesitation in acknowledging the utility of his plan. In the mean time, I positively deny having any, the most distant desire of shutting the door of free discussion, on any subject which may benefit the people; but I maintain (until Cato's better information refutes me) that the door, as far as relates to *this subject,* is already shut, not by me, but by the highest possible authority which the case admits, even by those great Patriots who were delegated by the people of the United States to *open such a door,* as might enable them to escape from impending calamities and political shipwreck. This distinction is clear, I conceive, and ought to have some weight even with Cato, as well as those for whom he writes. I am not one of those who gain an influence by cajoling the unthinking mass (tho' I pity their delusions), and ringing in their ears the gracious sound of their *absolute Sovereignty.* I despise the trick of such dirty policy. I know there are Citizens, who, to gain their own private ends, enflame the minds of the well-meaning, tho' less intelligent parts of the community, by sating their vanity with that cordial and unfailing specific, that *all power is seated in the people.* For my part, I am not much attached to the *majesty of the multitude,* and therefore waive all pretensions (founded on such conduct), to their countenance. I consider them in general as very ill qualified to judge for themselves what government will best suit their peculiar situations; nor is this to be wondered at. The science of government is not easily understood. Cato will admit, I presume, that men of good education and deep reflection, only, are judges of the *form* of a government; whether it is constituted on such principles as will restrain arbitrary power, on the one hand, and equal to the exclusion of corruption and the destruction of licentiousness on the other; whether the New Constitution, if adopted, will prove adequate to such desirable ends, time, the mother of events, will show. For my own part, I sincerely esteem it a system, which, without the finger of *God,* never could have been suggested and agreed upon by such a diversity of interests. I will not presume to say that a more perfect system might not have been fabricated; but who expects perfection at once? And it may be asked, *who are judges of it?* Few, I believe, who have leisure to study the nature of Government scientifically, but will frequently disagree about the quantum of power to be delegated to Rulers, and the different modifications of it. Ingenious men will give every plausible, and, it may be, pretty substantial reasons, for the adoption of two plans of Government, which shall be fundamentally different in their construction, and not less so in their operation; yet both, if honestly administered, might operate with safety and advantage. When a new form of government is fabricated, it lies with the people at large to receive or reject it—that is, their *inherent right.* Now, I would ask (without intending to triumph over the weaknesses or follies of any men), how are the people to profit by this inherent right? By what conduct do they discover that they are sensible of their own interests in this situation? Is it by the exercise of a well-disciplined reason, and a correspondent education? I believe not. How then? As I humbly conceive, by a tractable and docile disposition, and by honest men endeavoring to keep their minds easy, while others, of the same disposition, with the advantages of genius and learning, are constructing the bark that may, by the blessing of Heaven, carry them to the port of rest and happiness, if they will embark without diffidence and proceed without mutiny. I know this is blunt and ungracious reasoning; it is the best, however, which I am prepared to offer on this momentous business; and, since my own heart does not reproach me, I shall not be very solicitous about its reception. If truth, then, is permitted to speak, the mass of the people of America (any more than the mass of other countries) cannot judge with any degree of precision concerning the fitness of this New Constitution to the peculiar situation of America; they have, however, done wisely in delegating the power of framing a government to those every way worthy and well-qualified; and, if this Government is snatched, untasted, from them, it may not be amiss to inquire into the causes which will probably occasion their disappointment. Out of several, which present to my mind, I shall venture to select *one,* baneful enough, in my opinion, to work this dreadful evil. There are always men in society of some talents, but more ambition, in quest of *that* which it would be impossible for them to obtain in any other way than by working on the passions and prejudices of the less discerning classes of citizens and yeomanry. It is the plan of men of this stamp to frighten the people with ideal bugbears, in order to mould them to their own purposes. The unceasing cry of these designing croakers is, My friends, your liberty is invaded! Have you thrown off the yoke of one tyrant to invest yourselves with that of another? Have you fought, bled and conquered for *such a change*? If you have—go—retire into silent obscurity, and kiss the rod that scourges you.

To be serious: These state empirics leave no species of deceit untried to convince the unthinking people that they have power to do—what? Why truly to do much mischief, and to occasion anarchy and wild uproar. And for what reason do these political jugglers incite the peaceably disposed to such extravagant commotions? Because until the people really discover that they have *power,* by some outrageous act, they never can become of any importance. The misguided people never reflect during this frenzy, that the moment they become riotous, they renounce, from that moment, their independence, and commence vassals to their ambitious leaders, who instantly, and with a high hand, rob them of their consequence, and apply it to their own present or future aggrandisement; nor will these tyrants over the people stick at sacrificing *their* good, if an advantageous compromise can be effected for *themselves.*

Before I conclude, I cannot refrain from observing that Cato states very disingenuously the manner in which the Federal System came abroad. He tells us, Congress were sensible that the late Convention exercised a power which no authority could delegate to them. The Convention, says Cato, have taken upon them to make a perfectly new system, which by its operations will absorb the sovereignties of the individual States; this new government founded on *usurpation,* (Cato, this expression is very indecent— but I will rouse no passions against you) this consolidated system Congress did not approve and *therefore* have been *silent* on its character. That Congress was silent on its character is true, but could Cato find no other reason for their silence than that of disapprobation? I believe Congress were by no means dissatisfied with the freedom the Convention took with the Articles of Confederation; I believe further that with very few exceptions, that honorable body approves of the New Constitution; and that they did not accompany it to the States with a recommendatory capitation or circular letter, proceeded from a delicate attention to the members of the late Convention, to a few of their own body, and to the people of America at large. That the Convention went so earnestly into the business committed to their care ought, instead of being matter of chagrin, to occasion the liveliest expressions of approbation and gratitude—as matters stand just now. I think it may be fairly said, that no *generous plan of government* for the *United States* has ever been constructed, (the plan only excepted which is under consideration) so that it seems quite unnecessary in Cato to disturb the peace of society by a bombast appeal to their feelings, on the *generous plan of power delivered down by their renowned forefathers.* I venerate the memory of the slaughtered patriots of America, and rejoice as much as Cato that they did not bleed in vain, but I would have America profit by their death in a different manner from him. I believe they sought to obtain liberty for no particular State, but for the whole Union, indissolubly connected under one controlling and supreme head.

Cato complains of my anticipating parts of his subject which he intended for future periods. I shall break in no more upon his *arrangements.* All he can say against the New Constitution has been already disseminated in a neighboring State by the glorious defenders of *Shayism.* I shall therefore leave Cato to the wicked influences of his own heart, in the fullest persuasion that all good citizens will combine their influence to establish the fair fabric of American liberty beyond the reach of suspicion, violence, anarchy, and tyranny. When this glorious work is accomplished, what may America not hope to arrive at? I will venture to prophesy that the day on which the Union under the new government shall be ratified by the American States, that *that day* will begin an era which will be recorded and observed by future ages as a day which the Americans had marked by their wisdom in circumscribing the *power* and ascertaining the *decline* of the ancient nations in Christendom.

"Atticus"

Essays: I–IV

Independent Chronicle and the Universal Advertiser, Boston, 9 August, 18 October, 22 November, and 27 December 1787

I

For the Independent Chronicle.

Mess'rs. PRINTERS. If you think the following worth the public notice, please to insert it in your paper.

> *L'Homme est un animal guide par la coutume—*
> *Ses changemens subits la font un Protée.*
> —K. of PRUSSIA.

IT will often be the lot of him, who is a calm, and Philosophical Spectator of the movements of human beings, to remark the sudden changes of their sentiments, and passions. The first observations will create great surprize; but the vehemence of wonder will abate, when a variety of experiments shall have proved the truth of my motto, *viz.* That man is a being governed by *custom,* whose frequent changes make *her* a true Proteus.

Did the capricious power of *fashion* only extend to regulating the attire of ladies and petit-maitres, the Philosopher would have no cause to complain. But it requires a good degree of patience, calmly to behold her interfering in the province of wisdom, subverting the sciences and perplexing the most important concerns of human kind.

What but fashion teaches the smart and popular divine to talk, in these days, of the absolute necessity of human actions; and that God has *acted out* his wisdom and goodness, that is, done his utmost in the formation of the universe. But a few years ago, the Deity was thought unsearchable, and man a free agent.

Newtonianism was not long since the fashionable Philosophy; but now is scarcely to be admitted by the beaux-esprits. No, without some tincture of Cartesian, or Hutchinsonian principles, by tasty Philosophers, a man is thought a novice.

Ideas enjoyed a former brilliant day under the patronage of *the* illustrious Locke. But common sense (the only metaphysics worth a farthing) afterwards seemed to be regaining her authority, supported by Beattie and Reid. But her reign was short; for men will not long be contented with such a homespun mistress as common sense. Ideas have revived their reign, in all their tinsel and splendor.

In physic, not long since, the hot regimen was all in all for the small-pox, and other eruptive disorders. To this succeeded the Suttonian system, and fevers were to be cooled by frost. A simple process indeed! Of late some Physicians have practised inoculation, on the temperate regimen, with great success. And perhaps, after all, this is the very dictate of nature.

Republicanism, a few years ago, was all the vogue of politicians. "A government of laws and not of men." But now the aristocratics and monarchy-men on the one hand, and the insurgent party on the other, are with different views contending for a "government of men, and not of laws." The weakness of republics is become the everlasting theme of speculative politicians. While a man of less enthusiasm, on remarking the extravagancies of parties, is ready to say,

> For forms of government let fools contest,
> Whate'er is best administ'red is best.
> —POPE.[1]

But even this is not strictly true. A government may be deficient in its form: and afford no principles on which the executive power shall proceed. We may therefore define a good government thus. It *is that which contains a good system of laws, with provision suitable and sufficient, for the putting them into execution.* By whatever name such a government be called, it is a good one. The goodness of forms of government is, however, almost wholly *relative.* Some agree with one nation, with respect to their temper

---

1. See *The Federalist,* No. 68. Publius there insists that one must not acquiesce in the "political heresy" of Pope, but he goes on to argue that "the true test of a good government is its aptitude and tendency to produce a good administration."

and circumstances, some with another. Habit and actual experience alone, can absolutely determine that which is fit for any individual State.

Liberty, when considered as a power, *is the unrestrained power of acting reasonably: As a privilege, it is the security which a man feels in acting rightly and enjoying the fruit of his own labor.* When either of these are wanting, the people are not free, although their government may be called a *democracy.* When these exist, the people are free, although the government may be stiled an *absolute monarchy.* For an absolute, and arbitrary government, are very different things.[2]

If a government shall contain a good system of laws, then it is a good one, if these laws can be executed, and guarded from abuse. The form of government is then such as it ought to be; and the evils of such a government are either only accidental, or such as no *form* can remedy. If false opinions prevail among the people, let common-sense have fair play; and matters will come right again. If the *temper* and principles of the nation be wholly corrupt, their ruin is certain in the nature of things. They must of necessity be slaves.[3] In vain did Brutus think to make the Romans free by killing Caesar. The spirit of Romans had so totally forsaken them, that any man, who could assemble an army of desperadoes, might be a Caesar if he pleased. In all these things the form of the government was not at fault.

Such as above defined is the system of government we enjoy. The laws are indisputably good. The provision for executing them amply sufficient. We have evidently seen the force of our government, in the surprising rapidity and success, with which the active powers of the State, demolished a rebellion, which, from late facts, appears to have comprehended, in one form or another, a full third part of the people in the State. If any say it is weak, because certain persons under sentence of death, are not executed; let them ask themselves, Whether the Executive are *not able* to do it? That the government is *afraid,* or *unable,* to execute the laws, can only enter the

2. Consider, for example, the plan of government Alexander Hamilton introduced in the Federal Convention. Farrand, *Records,* 1:282–93.

3. The problems posed to republican government by the moral degeneracy of the people was a common political theme during the Founding period. For an interesting discussion of the problem (and one which many of that generation were familiar with), see Adam Ferguson, *An Essay on the History of Civil Society* (Edinburgh, 1776).

head of some distracted party-man. They, who could bring a man to the gallows, and keep him there, till within two minutes of the time of execution, doubtless could have suggested their authority two minutes longer.

You will then say, There is a faulty remissness in the Executive.—So there might be if the government were absolutely despotic. But perhaps we are too positive, when we affirm this absolutely—we may not see all that they do—we have not seen the full result of their administration—when we have, we may be better judges. To publish inflammatory libels in news-papers; or revile, and oppose, the present government, is doing, ourselves what we before censured in others. It is insurrection and rebellion. If the present Executive, acquired, hold, and exercise their *powers* constitutionally, they cannot lawfully be reviled or opposed. *The spirit of all parties is the same, and it ought to be received as a political maxim, that no violent party-man can be a good citizen.*[4]

As for the perfection of monarchies, in force, in wisdom, in dispatch of operations, in security of private property, it is merely ideal, the *fashionable cant* of the day, which experience abundantly refutes. No government, in these respects, can claim a preference to our own if we consider its form. Did not the government of France under the administration of the despotic Louis XIV, with an army of 80,000 men, dally with a body of insurgents, for several years; and finally treat with the leaders, give them full indemnity, and admission to places in the government? Who claimed to be more despotic, yet who governed with less force, than the three last Kings of France, of the family of Valois? Who claimed to be more despotic in England, and who governed with less force, than the family of the Stuarts? Did not the whole army of James II. desert him, tho' raised in his name, supported by his bread, and paid by his order? Even the all powerful Sultan of Turkey, whose subjects scarcely dare whisper of politics, often sees his favourite minister torne in pieces by the populace; and his hands and feet respectfully laid before the door of his palace. While HE trembles from within; and dares not assist his dearest friend.

The folly of Ishbosheth King of Israel; the uxoriousness of Ahab; the inconsistency of James II. of England, Lewis XIV. and XV. of France, governed

---

4. See Publius's famous discussion of this problem in *The Federalist*, Nos. 10, 49, and 51.

by women; the madness of Caligula the Roman Emperor, who made his horse a Consul; the South Sea bubble of England when the king was the head of the company; the madness of France in pursuing the schemes of *LAW,* the Scotch financier, (the very paper money whim of our own country) sufficiently shew, that wisdom is not intailed on monarchies.

What nation ever made more glorious marches, and more quick and vigourous expeditions, than the Greeks? 'Twas the custom of the Romans, according to Virgil, to meet their enemies before they thought of it. Lincoln's expedition of last winter, proves what republics can do—when the administration is *equal* to the form.

Property is so insecure in France that the cultivation of lands is greatly neglected. The great men trample on the peasants. The merchant in England is secure, but the tenant often sees his fields destroyed without remedy, if the Squire be fond of hunting. For Spain, Germany, and the dominions of the Pope, no advocate will appear.

Let the people of this Commonwealth, give up their idle whim of *tender-acts,* and *legal alteration of bargains;*[5] let us lay aside all violence of party spirit, and esteem the laws which we ourselves have adopted; then our government will appear wise, good, and sufficiently forceable. If we will destroy ourselves, not all the *despotism* on earth, could save us.

II

For the Independent Chronicle.

Letter II. *From a gentleman in the Country to his friend in town.*

> "Thus jarring interests, of themselves create,
> Th' according music of a well mix'd State."
> —POPE.

---

5. One of the major problems of the period, exemplified in the minds of many by Daniel Shays's uprising, was what Publius calls the "rage for paper money" (*The Federalist,* No. 10) and the ability of the legislatures to nullify contracts and absolve debtors from their obligations under them.

YES, as I observed sometime ago, no violent party man can ever be a good citizen. He seeks to destroy all interests but his own; and to ride triumphant over the prostrate necks of his opposers. Such is his delirium and fury, that he pays no regard to the wisest laws, or the most unquestionable rights of mankind. Yet, by the wisdom of Patriots, occasional good may be drawn from the storm of party-rage. The wrath of parties, when not suffered to reach the extreme to which it tends, shall work the good of the State. When the troops which were ordered to Concord, the last September, to support the Court of Common Pleas, were countermanded, it was not difficult for a person of but moderate skill in political movements, to foresee, that thenceforth there would be two parties, or factions, in the State. That one of these, that of the populace, would tend to general levelism, and democratic turbulence. That the other, that of the rich, and of men of austere political principles, would tend to an alteration of the constitution of our State, and the subjection of the people to a rigid aristocracy.

The first of these factions arises from the impatience and *uneasiness,* which they who compose it feel, under their *embarrassed circumstances,* which they commonly attribute to rich men, and officers of the State. From this uneasiness arises their licentious humour and their envy of the rich, and powerful—The latter of these factions arises from the *love of property and the desire of preserving it.* The reason why these appeared distinct, at the time above mentioned, was this; that then the populace tho't they might, without fear of punishment, shake off subjection to those laws, which obliged them to fulfil their obligations to men of property. And perhaps some even wished to seize on that wealth which was not their own. While the men of wealth judged from the countermanding of the troops, that the laws were not sufficient to defend them in the possession of that property which they had acquired. Thus both parties, with mortal animosity against each other, agreed in reprobating the then present system of government.[6]

6. A fear held by many was of what they termed the "leveling spirit," a rampant egalitarianism. In the Federal Convention James Madison spoke of the political problem presented by "those who . . . labour under all the hardships of life & secretly sigh for a more equal distribution of its blessings" (Farrand, *Records,* 1:422). In *The Federalist,* No. 10 he would argue that "the most common and durable source of factions has been the various and unequal dis-

Here it will be instructive to inspect the basis on which each party is formed. That of the first is composed, (unless we have been deceived in our attentive observations) of men of some, but small property, much embarrassed, and devoured by the interest of their debts. That of the latter, of men of large estates, especially those which consist in money. And to these parties are joined many, not immediately interested; but as their relations in life, their dependence, their mode of education, or caprice may lead them. They, we think, properly speaking, are the factions of the m[e]n of *large estates,* and the men of *small estates;* but for convenience, we shall call them by names, invented long ago, the democratic and aristocratic factions. And they will exist, as long as uneasiness at embarrassments will dare to express itself on the one hand; or the love of property have scope to exert itself on the other—nor can they be stilled so long as laws, and not men, claim dominion. They will not be silent, till despotism render all subjects of government as silent as the grave.

The tears of a patriot are worthily shed for dying laws. Nothing represents mankind to a true philosopher in so pityable a situation, as their rising in wrath, against those laws, which defend to them their lives, their liberty, their religion, their possessions, and all that is dear to the human heart.

Yet for a professed politician, to turn pale at the rise of parties, while the laws are preserved, is as much out of character, as for a veteran soldier to tremble at the discharge of cannon. Parties are the materials of which the most perfect societies are formed. As in the making of PUNCH the ingredients are perfect contradictions; and each in excessive quantities,

---

tribution of property. Those who hold, and those who are without property, have ever formed distinct interests in society. . . . The regulation of these various and interfering interests forms the principal task of modern Legislation, and involves the spirit of party and faction in the necessary and ordinary operations of Government."

To Madison's way of thinking, the Constitution would provide such regulation by its embrace of an "extended republic" with a "great variety of interests, parties and sects." Such a multiplicity of interests would weaken the division between rich and poor. As Martin Diamond has shown, the science of politics presented in *The Federalist,* with its "novel contribution" that republican liberty is safer in a large than in a small republic, substituted conflict over *kinds* of property for conflicts over *amounts* of property. See Martin Diamond, *The Founding of the Democratic Republic* (Itasca, Ill.: F. E. Peacock, 1981).

would disturb, if not destroy, the human frame, but the composition is generally thought excellent. The most opposite interests rightly blended, make the harmony of the State.[7]

Parties give life to the moving powers of the State, and when properly checked and balanced, are productive of much good. The dishonest, and ambitious, excite the rage of parties, to promote their own designs; but the patriot directs their force, like that of fire, to the profit of the State, and not to its destruction. Fire in its own nature tends to dissipate the most solid bodies. But the skilful artist suffers it not to proceed so far. When the iron becomes pliable by means of heat, he shapes it according to his wisdom; and then leaves it to cool. Thus a patriot deals with parties.

Parties always keep alive, an attention to public measures. While men are immersed in their own concerns, public officers may act as they please. The materials of which the Commonwealth is composed, become like the waters of a stagnant pool. They must be ruffled by the hurricane of parties, before they will become wholesome.

Parties produce great attendance and carefulness respecting elections. Among the various evils, arising from the disturbances of the last year, this hopeful symptom appear'd. The people were never so attentive to elections before. And, if the effect was not in every case, what a judicious person would wish for; it ought to be ascribed to the agitation of their minds at the time of election. This great attention to elections, if continued, will one day produce excellent effects.

Parties keep any one interest from swallowing up the rest. The idea of an opposite party influence, renders every part of the community anxious to secure itself. And a warm emulation is excited. Each wishes to recommend itself by illustrious deeds, which shall increase the numbers of its advocates. Each interest equips itself with all kinds of powers, for reducing the exorbitance of other parties, and strengthening itself. The chieftains, seek to excel in all the arts of policy. Each separate interest marks out, and publicly exposes the errors and illegal proceedings of the rest. The history of England, will convince any impartial observer, that, since the rise of the memorable fac-

7. *Cf. The Federalist,* No. 51.

tions of the whigs and tories, the government of that country has been much more mild and favourable to the interests of the whole community, than before.

But here lies the danger of parties. Two factions of nearly equal strength, violently played off against each other by ill designing or mistaken men, would either mutually destroy each other, and suffer a third power to prevail, or the contest would terminate in the utter extinction of one, and the insolent triumph of the other. Either event would introduce a most insupportable tyranny. Hence the necessity of a third power sufficient to check the exorbitances of each. Of aristocracy and democracy our State has enough. The partizans are animated sufficiently against each other. Have we a third power sufficient to restrain them? This is the question. But it must be answered at some future day, if you have the candor to read the speculations of *ATTICUS*.

III

Observations

On the letter of the Hon. E. G. *Esq;*[8] *published in the* Independent Chronicle, *Nov.* 8, 1787, *and other pieces lately published in opposition to the* Federal Constitution: *In* LETTER III.

From a Gentleman in the country, to his friend in town.

> *"Who shall decide when Doctors disagree,—*
> And soundest Casuists doubt."
> —POPE

I Must postpone my designed answer to the question, with which I concluded my last letter, (whether there be any power, or principle, in our Commonwealth, sufficient to keep within proper bounds, the contests of the

---

8. Elbridge Gerry. His objections to the Constitution are in Storing, 2:1; Allen, 20–22.

great and *little* men amongst us?) and must now attend to your favour of November 14th.

You have read the letter of the Hon. E[lbridge] G[erry] and it seems to have given you some disturbance. The letter I have several times perused, with great attention; yet find not, that it contains any thing which ought greatly to offend us. It seems to be an excuse for *his* d[issent] from the *federal system.* Ought we to resent his apology with anger? We too, must think for ourselves. The only question here, seems to be, Whether, after the business of the delegation was finished, a delegate, any more than any private gentleman, could *with propriety,* write to the Legislature, either for or against the adopted system? Especially as a *State Convention,* and not the *Legislature,* were to decide the important question.

His observation, "that the greatest men may err," is of real importance, and leads to this conclusion, that the Hon. E[lbridge] G[erry] *may err.* If the authority of a Washington, a Franklin, or a Rufus King, supported by the authority of all the *States* in Convention, be no *good* argument in favour of their system; then, by parity of reason, the authority of the Hon. E[lbridge] G[erry] or a Randolph, or a Mason, can be *no better* argument against it. Between these great Casuists, the people, in Convention assembled, must judge; and to this decision, we hope, they will bring *cool heads* and *pure hearts.*

The federal system determines, that every branch of its Legislature shall be *elective;* the qualifications of electors are ascertained; and caution is taken that elections be not held at an inconvenient place. *The time,* whether in July, May or August, or other month of the year; *the manner,* whether by ballot or otherwise, is to be regulated by state, or federal laws. Here I can see no great "insecurity of the right of elections." Nor do I fear, that the federal government will not be as likely as the State Legislatures, to fix on some method, by which the sense of the people shall be fairly taken. As to the representation, it seems to be as large, as the state of our country will well admit of; and as well defined, as numbers can make it. If those observations be just, is "the representation inadequate," or "elections insecure?"

Yet the Hon. E[lbridge] G[erry] has reasons on which his objections are founded, to be divulged when he shall return to Massachusetts. If reasons he hath, by all means let us hear them; and let us confront them by better reasons, if we can.

The Hon. E[lbridge] G[erry] and others, complain, that the system has not the security of *a bill of rights.* That series of propositions commonly called *a bill of rights,* is taken out of lawbooks, and is only an extract of the rights of persons.—Now let us suppose, that it stands in a law-book, which is appealed to, as an authority, in all the Courts of judicature, or is tacked (without pains or penalty annexed to the violation of it) as a preface to the Constitution. In which case is it likely to afford the greatest security to the rights of persons? Let the unbiased judge. On this point we may appeal to fact. There is a Commonwealth, with which we are not wholly uncon-nected, which hath a bill of rights prefixed to its Constitution. Yet ask those of either of the great parties, into which that State hath lately been divided, if this bill of rights hath not been frequently violated? If you confide in the zealots of each party, will you not be ready to conceive, that the actual Leg-islators have had as poor an opinion of the bill of rights, as Cromwell had of Magna Charta? If you speak to the moderate men in that same State, they will perhaps shrug their shoulders, and shake their heads, and give you *no answer.*

When the powers to be exercised, under a certain system, are in them-selves consistent with the people's liberties, are legally defined, guarded and ascertained, and ample provision made for bringing to condign punishment all such as shall overstep the limitations of law,—it is hard to conceive of a greater security for the rights of the people.

It hath been said, that the Constitution proposed, "has few federal fea-tures, but is rather a system of national government." Perhaps the features of a confederacy, and of a national government, are happily blended; as a child may have a resemblance of both its parents. If so, may not the event be happy for us? For is it not for want of national government, that com-merce, husbandry, mechanics, the arts and manufactures, are now languish-ing and seem ready to die? was it not for want of *this,* that the States of Greece, were enslaved by a petty monarchy, that Switzerland is destitute of national importance, and Holland torn with all the distresses of a civil war? Must not the States of America, without this, serve with the fruits of their hardy industry, their enemies in Britain. *Dean Tucker* (whose political prophecies have mostly been verified) hath predicted concerning America, "that they will be a contemptible people to the end of time." Without national government, must it not be so in fact? for a confederacy, without energy sufficient to bring the confederates to joint-action, is a mere *nullity.* Let us not quarrel about words and sounds, *national* or *federal;* it is a good system if its tendency be to make us a happy people.

It is said that it "dissolves the state governments, because it makes the federal laws supreme in each State." *What bond of union could there be without this?* It ought to be allowed, however, that the powers given to Congress in this system, are the utmost extent of the federal legislation. If these relate to matters of merely national concern, they do not interfere, any more than they ought, with the legislative powers of particular States.

It is suggested that this system may be "amended" before its adoption. On this two questions arise; when are the people groaning under present burthens, to be eased of the expences of conventions and assemblies, for settling government? and will there probably be fewer dissentients from the amendments, than from the system as it now stands?

Should it be received as it now stands, it is suggested "that our liberties *may* be lost." The caution expressed in the word *may,* is commendable, because many persons whose abilities the modesty of the Hon. E[lbridge] G[erry] would not suffer him to undervalue, think quite otherwise. Too, too long it hath been the humour of our countrymen, to be so fearful of giving their rulers power to do hurt, that they never have given them power to do good. *This is the very reason why the public authority, hath been so much despised by the people; and why the people have so little attachment to their civil institutions.*

When such a great affair is depending, parties, disputes, and objections, are to be expected. It is best I believe that they should, in a certain degree, take place. I hope they will not proceed to violent extremes. The State of Massachusetts is not bound to imitate Pennsylvania: Let not our good citizens mistake *passion* for *council;* but let them choose men of clear heads, and honest minds, for their State Convention. When the "greatest of men" differ, the assembled people must decide. And let them, after the affair is impartially examined, and thoroughly sifted, receive, amend, or utterly reject the Federal Constitution. Let not the leading characters among us, in the mean time, forget that excellent advice of the Hon. E[lbridge] G[erry] worthy to be written for their use in letters of gold, that they *preserve moderation.*

Further communications and correspondence on those interesting subjects, will be agreeable to your friend *ATTICUS.*

IV

LETTER IV,
From a gentleman in the country, to his friend in town.

"But Heaven hath a hand in these events,
To whose high will we bound our calm contents."[9]
—SHAKESPEARE.

EVERY State, of any considerable magnitude, contains three classes of men. Those who have small estates in land, and little money: those who have large estates in one, or both of these: and those who depend for their support, upon salaries, or wages given for personal service. The influence of the first mentioned class, tends to a mere democracy; that of the second evidently to aristocracy; and, of the last, a monarch is the natural defender, and patron. This latter class will always find, that great men will oppress them; men of small estates will pay them ill; but a monarch will defend them; for they are in turn the instruments of his power.—To make the citizens peaceable, the government of every country, of an considerable extent, should be mixed, and should consist of the combined influence of all these three classes of men.

It is certain that in a country like ours, mere democracy can never be the prevailing government. That class of people who favour it, have no regular system of action. Their force is exerted only by starts, and on sudden

9. *Richard II* 5.2.

occasions. Their domestic concerns soon call them back to their ordinary employments.—They cannot become soldiers themselves, unless they leave their families to perish, and they have not money to hire others to fight for them. They cannot bring the rich down to their class, nor prevent the dependant sort from feeling the influence of money. They pay the learned professions ill, and particularly are apt to leave the clergy unsupported. So that the influence of learning and of religious instruction, is against them.—This class is very apt to lose its patrons. If they become eminent, they acquire riches, or power, and their ideas change.—If they are unfortunate, they sink into the dependant part of the community.—Were the people actually brought to an equality, you could not keep them so. An entire massacre of all the great men (were it possible) once in seven years, would not effect the purpose. So that in so large a territory as that of Massachusetts, whose inhabitants are so variously employed, and of such an active, ambitious and enterprising spirit, a pure democracy can never prevail.

There are also very great obstacles to the establishment of an aristocracy. We have no intailed estates, no hereditary offices.—Our aristocracies are all, such as nature, personal merit, present office, and not *standing laws* have made. Offices and estates are continually changing from man to man. If the father of a family shall amass a large estate, it is soon divided thro' a numerous family, or dissipated by some pamper'd heir. There are only two supposeable cases, in which it is possible for an aristocracy to prevail. Either the people must sink into a state of stupidity and total inattention to public affairs, which I conceive party-spirit must forbid; or they must by insurrections give occasion to the rich and politic to raise an army, and maintain it. Otherwise an aristocracy cannot be established. If the laws under our present Constitution, were allowed to have their full effect, it would forever be impossible.

Considering then, the natural obstacles there are to the prevalence of either party: Is not the force of the executive and judicial departments, sufficient to hold the balance between them? Were our state not influenced by the policy of other states, I am certain it would be. Any number of spirited citizens, with law, money, discipline, and experience on their side, would be equal to three times their number without them. That Governour will scarcely be found, who will not dread, more than death, the infamy of having the state subverted when he is at the head. Nor will his dependence on the people for his office utterly enervate the power of that motive for defending the state. Thro' inexperience of a new government, some of the dependant part of the community lost their places in a late grand contest; but they will soon learn to range themselves under the banners of the executive power. You will find most of the learned professions disposed to give strength to the monarchical principle. And by a most natural connection, the kingdom and the priesthood always go together.

Did we consider these principles of reasoning only, we should be ready to pronounce, that our constitution was a most happy one, and calculated for a long duration. But we are in a kind of ambiguous connection with twelve other republics; whose separate interests will often lead them to measures injurious to us. If we enact laws, seemingly wise and wholesome, to prevent unnecessary importations; to oblige our rivals in trade to deal with us on equal footing; to relieve the public wants and establish the state's credit, by duties and excises; the neighbouring states are sure to counteract us, and take advantage of our laws for their own emolument.—Then an artificial scarcity of money is created; lands depreciate, every kind of business is stagnated, and taxes which compared with estates are not heavy, yet are too severely felt in the collection. All public and private credit is lost. The people at large not seeing whence their evils arise, charge them on the government and laws. They clamor for tender-acts, paper-money, and all the engines of fraud. Harpy speculators join the din of complaint. The democratic party are aroused to arms, and proceed to open rebellion. But here they find themselves weak, being destitute of discipline, and resources for war. They are defeated. But on the field of election they have better success; turn out their former representatives, and executive officers, and choose new ones; and perhaps seem appeased for a while. They find out the weak side of government, and will keep it always in view at their annual elections, and prevent it from ever rising to strength and respectability.

Nor do I conceive that it is possible, without a government over the whole thirteen States, invested with the powers to transact all concerns, which are properly national, with Judicial Courts and all the apparatus of civil power, ever to remedy the contentions in particular States, between the great men and the adverse party. But we must be tossing from one wretched measure, and expedient to another; continually quarrelling, and making laws which discourage arts and industry, and discountenance honesty itself; till we, being sick of our boasted equal liberty, shall gladly embrace the offer of some hero, of plausible character, to give us a good government, and establish it by the sword.

The Americans are of quick understanding, lively and enterprising: They possess great means of information: They will not therefore be long in finding out that government which shall be a balance to their passions: Under that, and that only, will they rest: From this, I am almost confident that the government, proposed by the Federal Convention, will take place: They who think that it will bear to be much relaxed, or amended, may be honest; but they are short-sighted men. *Powers must be adequate to their end.*[10] And let any man judge from facts that have already appeared, whether any linsey-woolsey, half formed expedients, will deliver us from the wretched perplexity of our affairs. If this does not take place, I am about as certain as I can be of any thing, short of fact and demonstration, that in less than ten years, perhaps in less than five, a bold push will be made to establish a monarchy. And it may succeed to the loss of thousands of lives, and of the liberties of the people. I rather think that a government; either the federal or one very like it, will take place: Or that the states will divide, and the northern establish a mixed government; and the southern a monarchy, *or else go to perdition.*

You seem to be anxious, my friend, lest we should lose all government: Never fear it, we shall have an efficient government, and that very soon: The great first cause has constructed the universe, better than you imagine. He has inserted in it principles which will give *us* government; and the rage

10. See *The Federalist,* No. 31. Publius elaborates this point by arguing that a "government ought to contain within itself every power requisite to the full accomplishment of the objects committed to its care, and to the complete execution of the trusts for which it is responsible, free from every other control but a regard to the public good and to the sense of the people."

See also the opinion of Chief Justice John Marshall in *McCulloch v. Maryland,* 4 Wheat. 416 (1819), and his public defense of that opinion in Gerald Gunther, ed., *John Marshall's Defense of McCulloch v. Maryland* (Stanford: Stanford University Press, 1969).

of parties, will only quicken their operation: My fears are, lest we reject the milder government, and be obliged to receive the more severe. The principles, which of late have appeared, are productive of the most efficient governments. The hand of the Supreme is in all these things, and we can do nothing against his established laws.

Your love to your country, my friend, must needs be tender, since every trifle alarms you: A *Mason*,[11] angry at being left almost alone in a favourite opinion; and pleading in one breath for a bill of rights, and in the next for expost-facto laws, (which are destructive of all right) alarms you. A plausible and artful *Brutus*[12] alarms you: But pay a little attention to his argument, and you will see it flatly contradicts itself. In one part of his argument, the Federal government is so *enormously powerful,* that it swallows up all before it, the State governments with all their appurtenances! In the other part it is *so weak,* that it cannot command the obedience of the people: But if it proves any thing, it proves, that we ought to establish a royal government: For I presume this will not be denied, that these States, as governments, utterly unconnected with each other, cannot subsist. We shall become the prey of every invader. From this proceeds Brutus, and says, We cannot subsist as a national republican government; because the people, in different States, differ in climate, manners, interest, &c.—But for a much stronger reason, we cannot subsist, as confederated sovereign States, differing as we do, in climate, manners, interest, &c.—Therefore we cannot subsist as republican governments at all. And I have known several persons, who oppose the federal Constitution, do it in order to compel us at least to submit to a monarchy. I wish that they and all other politicians were more honest. Of this, however, I am secure, that we shall soon have an effective government. The rich, the wise, the brave, the industrious, and enterprising, I am sure, will not be content to lie at the mercy of the idle, and licentious; and be the prey of harpy speculators. But as to the precise method of bringing it to pass, I cheerfully submit to the power that rules the Glove.—Adieu, remember your friend, *ATTICUS.*

11. See Storing, 2:2; Allen, 11–13.
12. See Storing, 2:9; Allen, 102–13, 201–3, 269–74.

"Cato"

Essay

Country Journal and *Advertiser,* Poughkeepsie,
12 December 1787

IN my address to you in the spring of 1766, on the subject of our political concerns, I promised at a future period to continue my observations; but was happy to find, that the general voice of the nation superseded the necessity of them. The radical defects in the constitution of the confederate government, was too obvious to escape the notice of a sensible, enlightened people—they saw with concern the danger their former caution & jealousy had involved them in; and very wisely called a general Convention of the States to devise a plan to check the mischief of anarchy in its bud—happily for this country many of the wisest men and most distinguished characters, independent in their principles and circumstances, and disconnected with party influence, were appointed to the important trust; and their unanimity in the business affords a pleasing presage of the happiness that will result from their deliberation.

It is but a groveling business, and commonly ruinous policy, to repair by peace-meal a shattered defective fabric—it is better to raise the disjointed building to its formation, and begin a new. The confederation was fraught with so many defects, and these so interwoven with its substantial parts, that to have attempted to revise it would have been doing business by the halves, and therefore the Convention with a boldness and decision becoming freemen, wisely carried the remedy to the root of the evil; and have offered a form of government to your consideration on an entire new system—much depends on your present deliberations.—It is easy to foresee that the present crisis will form a principal epoch in the politics of America, from whence we may date our national consequence and dignity, or anarchy,

Cato was a pseudonym especially popular with the Anti-Federalists. See Storing, 2:6, 5:7, and 5:10; Allen, 159–69.

discord and ruin; the arguments made use of by a certain class of political scribblers, I conceive calculated (instead of throwing light on the subject) to deceive the ignorant but perhaps honest part of the community; and to misguide the thoughtless and unweary—in our present enquiry it is of no consequence who are the authors of these inflamatory productions, whether they are the result of the vanity of a northern champion to become the head of a party; the expiring groans of a principal magistrate of a state; or the last effort of the *patriotic bower* of a Treasury to gain popularity; or all together, I trust will bare equal rights on the minds of the public. It is natural enough to suppose that, when any general plan is proposed, that thwarts the private interests or views of a party, that, such party will draw the most unpleasing picture of the plan, and blacken it with all the false colouring that a gloomy imagination can invent: thus are we told by these evil prospects, that the system is impracticable; smallness of territory being essential to a republican government—in support of this doctrine, Montesquieu (who was born and educated under a monarchical government and knew nothing of any other but in theory) is quoted as an uncontrovertable authority, and after all, I presume they have mistaken the meaning of this author,[1] for if I comprehend him right he is speaking of a pure democracy, such as Athens where the people all met in council; to be sure in such a government, extensive territory would be inconvenient, but a remedy to this evil has long since been found out: when the territory of any state became too large for the general assembling of the people, it was thought best to transact the business of the Commonwealth by representation: and thus large states may be governed as well by delegates from twenty districts, as small ones are from two or three; but this is what we are told by the politicians of the day constitutes a *dangerous aristocracy*, for say they in their learned definition, it is *a government of the few;* on this shameful quibble they attempt to ketch the attention of the rabble and frighten them into the measure of rejecting the proposed government—if I understand any

1. For an elaboration of this argument that the Anti-Federalists failed to grasp the full implications of Montesquieu's argument in behalf of small republics, see *The Federalist,* Nos. 9 and 10. For a study of Montesquieu's political philosophy, see Thomas Pangle, *Montesquieu's Philosophy of Liberalism* (Chicago: University of Chicago Press, 1973).

thing of the meaning of the term, aristocracy signifies a government by a body of Nobles, who derive their power either from hereditary succession or from self appointment; and are no way dependent on the people for their rank in the state. By the plan offered to us, both the legislative and executive, derive their appointments either directly from the people, or from the representatives chosen directly from the people: how this can be called aristocracy exceeds the limits of my comprehension; it is true that we are told that the better sort of people will be appointed to govern; I pray God the prediction may not be a false one. But should that be the case, say these political empirics, we shall not have an equal representation. Why? Because every class of people will not be represented. God knows that fools and knaves have voice enough in government already; it is to be hoped these wise prophesiers of evil would not wish to give them a constitutional privilege to send members in proportion to their numbers. If they mean by classes the different professions in the state, their plan is totally new, and it is to be feared the system once adopted, there would be no end to their democratical purity; to take in every profession from the Clergy to the Chimneysweep, will besides composing a motley assemblage of heterogeneous particles, enlarge the representation so that it will become burthensome to the Community; had the representation in Massachusetts been no larger than that in the proposed government of the Union, Shays would never have had a follower:—I think my judgment will not be impeached when I say that if our representation in this state was less, we should be better represented, and the public saved a very great expence—to judge of the future by the past, it is easy to perceive, that small states are as subject to aristocratic oppressions, as large ones; witness the small territory of Venice, at present the purest aristocracy in the world: Geneva, the circumference of which may be traversed in an hour's march is now oppressed by a dangerous aristocracy; while the democratic branch of the legislature in England retains its primitive purity. Who was it that enslaved the extensive empire of Rome, but an abandoned democracy? Who defended the republic at the battle of Pharsallia, but the better sort of people? Caesar can be considered in no other light than a more fortunate Cattiline, and the latter in no other than that of an ambitious demagogue attempting to ruin the Commonwealth, at the head of licentious democracy. In the present crisis of our public affairs I confess with the frankness of a free man and the concern of a patriot, that I apprehend more danger from a licentious democracy, than from aristocratic oppression.

I clearly perceive there will be no mid-way in the present business; we must either adopt the advice of these pretended democratical puritans, and then carry their doctrines to the point they evidently lead, viz. To divide the present union into at least five hundred independent sovereign states, build a council-house in the centre of each, and by a general law declare all the servants and apprentices free, and then let the multitude meet and govern themselves—or on the other hand, fall to the plain road of common sense, and govern the union by representatives in one collective council; as pointed-out in the system offered to your consideration: In the first you will possess popular liberty with a vengeance, and like a neighbour* state, no man's property will be secure, but each one defrauding his neighbor under the sanction of law,—thus subverting every principle of morality and religion.—In the second you will enjoy the blessing of a well balanced government, capable of inspiring credit and respectability abroad, and virtue, confidence, good order and harmony at home.—Should the Author have leisure to attend to it, the dangerous consequences that will inevitably flow from dividing the union, will be the subject of another paper.

*Rhode-Island

"A Democratic Federalist"

Essay

Independent Gazetteer, Philadelphia, 26 November 1787

Although the evidence is not conclusive, the editors of *The Documentary History of the Ratification of the Constitution* suggest that "it is possible that Tench Coxe wrote 'A Democratic Federalist.' On the address page of a letter he wrote on 26 November, Coxe states: 'The enclosed paper is also mine. I wish you would have it republished in New York, but do not mention the writer, as my attempt to *conciliate* our Constitutionals (the design of the paper) may be deemed uniting with them. You know I am of no party.' " *DH,* 2:298 n. 1.

The examination of the principle of liberty and civil polity is one of the most delightful exercises of the rational faculties of man. Hence the pleasure we feel in a candid, unimpassioned investigation of the grounds and probable consequences of the new frame of government submitted to the people by the Federal Convention. The various doubts, which the subject has created, will lead us to consider it the more by awakening our minds to that attention with which every freeman should examine the intended constitutions of his country.

Several zealous defenders of liberty in America, and some of them of the *first* reputation, have differed from the bulk of the nation in their speculative opinions on the best constitution for a legislative body. In Pennsylvania this question has formed *the line of division* between two parties, in each of which are to be found men of sound judgment and very general knowledge. As this diversity of opinion has not arisen from any peculiarity in our situation or circumstances, it must have been produced by the imperfections of our political researches and by the fallibility of the human mind, ever liable to unfavorable influence even from laudable and necessary passions. The sincere and zealous friend of liberty is naturally in love with a refined democracy, beautiful and perfect as a theory, and adapted to the government of the purest beings; and he views with jealousy, apprehension and dislike not only *real* deviations from democratic principles, but *the appearance* of aristocracy. Hence the idea of an *upper* house (a term erroneously adopted from the British constitution) has been disagreeable and even alarming to many, who were equally friends to perfect and real liberty and to an effective government. Among the various regulations and arrangements of the new Federal Constitution the *peculiar* ground on which the Senate is placed is on this account the most striking and perhaps estimable. A careful comparison of our *second* branch, as proposed by the Convention, with the upper house in the British constitution, will show, I hope, that there is something like *a middle ground* on which the wise and good of both opinions may meet and unite.

The ancestors of the upper house in England originally derived all their power from the feudal system. Possessed by lawless force of extensive domains, which, after a certain period, became hereditary in their families, they established a permanent power through *the military service* of their tenants, for upon those terms were all the lands of the kingdom once held under them. When the address and spirit of the people, exerted upon every proper occasion, obtained for them the interesting privileges of holding in their families also the tenanted estates of the lords, and of alienating their tenancies to such as would perform the conditions on which they were held— when, by the extinction of the families of some of the barons, their tenants remained in possession of their lands—when by the increase of the property, the knowledge and the power of the tenants (or Commons of England) and from other favorable circumstances, the people of that country obtained a portion of that independence which Providence intended for them, such of their nobles as stood the shock, which fell from these circumstances on their order, were formed into a separate independent body. They claimed an absolute right to act in their proper persons, and not by representatives, in the formation of the laws. Being from their wealth, their hereditary power to legislate and judge, and their extraordinary learning in those times, perfectly independent of the rest of the nation, they have often been useful in checking the encroachments of the crown, and the precipitation and inadvertance of the people. In that country they have really held *the balance* between the king and the Commons. But though such a balance may be proper in a royal government, it does not appear necessary *merely in that view* in a genuine republic—which ought to be a government of laws. Yet there are striking and capital advantages resulting from a second, not an *upper* house, if they can be obtained without departing, in our practice, from the real principles of liberty. The arts and influence of popular and unworthy men; too hasty, careless, incautious and passionate proceedings; breaches of wholesome order and necessary form are evils we must wish to avoid, if to be effected without the hazard of greater. Let us examine how far the *peculiar* constitution of our federal Senate will give us the advantages of a second legislative branch without subjecting us to the dangers usually apprehended from such bodies, that the sincere friends of freedom and mankind in America, if there is no longer reason for their differing upon a point of speculation may harmonize and unite.

The federal Senate, from the nature of our governments, will not be hereditary, nor will they possess, like the British barons, a power originally usurped by lawless violence and supported by military tenants. They will not necessarily have even an influential property, for they will have a greater number of fellow citizens, as rich as themselves; and no qualification of wealth exists in the Constitution at present, nor can it be introduced without the consent of *three-fourths of the people of the Union.* It cannot be apprehended, that the people at large of these free commonwealths will consent to disqualify themselves for the senatorial office, which God and the Constitution have intended they should fill. The members of the Senate should certainly be men of very general information, but through the goodness of Providence, numbers will be found in every state, equally well qualified in that respect to execute a trust for which two persons only will be necessary. Instead of their possessing all the knowledge of the state, an equal proportion will be found in some of the members of the House of Representatives, and even a greater share of it will often adorn persons in private walks of life. They will have no distinctions of rank, for the persons over whom a Senator might be weak enough to affect a superiority will be really equal to him and may in a short time change situations with him. The Senator will again become a private citizen and the citizen may become a Senator—nay more—a president of the Senate or President of the Union. The upper house in England have an interest different and separate from the people and, whether in the execution of their office or not, are a distinct body of men, a superior order. Many little circumstances tend to favor and promote this unjust and preposterous distinction. If an ambassador is sent to their court by France or Spain, he is a nobleman of his own country, and a nobleman must be sent from England in return, which operates as a deprivation of the rights of every well-qualified commoner in the kingdom. This is a hardship, which *cannot* arise from our second branch, but exists in Britain not only in the case particularized, but in regard to many other employments of honor and profit. But a greater and more essential distinction between the upper house in England and our federal Senate yet remains. The members of the former claim and possess all their powers and honors in their *own* right, their own *hereditary* right, while the new Constitution renders our Senate merely a *representative* body without one distinction in favor of the birth, rank, wealth or power of the Senators or their fathers. There has arisen out of the particular nature of our affairs, a *peculiar* happiness in the formation of this body. The federal Senate are *the representatives of the sovereignties of their respective states.* A second branch, *thus constituted,* is a novelty in the history of the world. Instead of an hereditary upper house, the American Confederacy has created a body, the temporary representatives of their component sovereignties, dignified only by their being the immediate delegates and guardians of sovereign states selected from the body of the people for that purpose, and for no reasons, but their possessing the qualifications necessary for their station. We find then in this body, none of the evils of aristocracy apprehended by those who have drawn their reasonings from an erroneous comparison with the upper house of Britain, and all the benefits of a second branch, without hazarding the rights of the people in the smallest particular. As our federal Representatives and state legislatures will be composed of men, who, the moment before their election, were a part of the people and who on the expiration of their time, will return to the same private situations, so the members of our federal Senate will be elected from out of the body of the people, without one quali-

fication being made necessary, but mere citizenship, and at the expiration
of their term will again be placed in private life. The Senate, therefore, will
be as much a democratic body as the House of Representatives, with this
advantage, that they will be elected by the state legislatures to whom, on
account of their superior wisdom and virtue, the people at large will have
previously committed the care of their affairs.

The plan of federal government proposed by the Convention has another
merit of essential consequence to our national liberties. Under the old Confederation, the people at large had no voice in the election of their rulers.
The collected wisdom of the state legislatures will hereafter be exercised in
the choice of the Senate, but our federal Representatives will be chosen *by
the votes of the people themselves.* The Electors of the President and Vice President of the Union may also, by laws of the separate states, be put on the
same footing.

The separation of the judicial power from the legislative and executive
has been justly deemed one of the most inestimable improvements in modern polity; yet no country has ever completely accomplished it in their actual
practice. The British peers are criminal judges in cases of impeachment, and
are a court of appeal in civil cases. The power of impeachment, vested in
our federal Representatives, and the right to hear those cases, which is vested
in the Senate, can produce no punishment in person or property, *even on
conviction.* Their whole judicial power lies within a narrow compass. They
can take no cognizance of a private citizen and can only declare any dangerous public officer no longer worthy to serve his country. To punish him
for his crimes, in body or estate, is not within their constitutional powers.
They must consign him to a jury and a court, with whom the deprivation
of his office is to be no proof of guilt.

The size of the Senate has been considered by some, as an objection to
that body. Should this appear of any importance it is fortunate that there
are reasons to expect an addition to their number. The legislature of Virginia
have taken measures preparatory to the erection of their western counties
into a separate state, from which another good consequence will follow, that
the free persons, which will remain within the Dominion of Virginia, will
perhaps be nearly or quite as well represented in the Senate as Pennsylvania

or Massachusetts. Should Vermont, at some future time, be also introduced into the Union, a further addition to the number of our Senators will take place. If therefore there is any importance in the objection to the size of our federal Senate, or if any such objection prevails in the minds of the people, it is in a way of being removed.

The executive powers of the Union are separated in a higher degree from the legislative than in any government now existing in the world. As a check upon the President, the Senate may disapprove of the officers he appoints, but no person holding *any office* under the United States can be a member of the federal legislature. How differently are things circumstanced in the two houses in Britain where an officer of any kind, naval, military, civil or ecclesiastical, may hold a seat in either house.

This is a most enlightened time, but more especially so in regard to matters of government. The divine right of kings, the force of ecclesiastical obligations in civil affairs, and many other gross errors, under which our forefathers have lain in darker ages of the world, are now done away. The natural, indefeasible and unalienable rights of mankind form the more eligible ground on which we now stand.

The United States are in this respect *"the favored of Heaven."* The Magna Charta, Bill of Rights, and common law of England furnished in 1776 a great part of the materials out of which were formed our several state constitutions.[1] *All these* were more or less recognized in the old Articles of Confederation.

On this solid basis is reared the fabric of our new federal government. These taken together form THE GREAT WHOLE OF THE AMERICAN CONSTITUTIONS, the fairest fabric of liberty that ever blessed mankind, immovably founded on a solid rock, whose mighty base is laid at the center of the earth.

1. See Willi Paul Adams, *The First American Constitutions: Republican Ideology and the Making of the State Constitutions in the Revolutionary Era* (Chapel Hill: University of North Carolina Press, 1980).

"*Convention*"

Essay

Massachusetts Centinel, Boston, 13 October 1787

Mr. Russell,
"It is impossible but that offenses will come."

The above sentence of holy writ occurred to me on reading some paragraphs in the *Massachusetts Gazette* of Tuesday last.[1] The late Continental Convention could not entertain the idea of suiting the AMERICAN CONSTITUTION to the whims, caprices, prejudices, and self-interest of every individual in the United States.—Such an anticipation would have been as absurd as the conduct of the old man in the fable, who set out to carry his ass to market.

This paragraphist observes, "That a Confederation for purposes merely national, would undoubtedly be exceedingly beneficial to these States."—What his ideas of a nation are, is difficult to ascertain. If the nation is composed of individual States, it evidently follows that a confederation must fall short of answering any national purpose, except it has influence on the concerns of particular States—and here the Confederation under which we at present are languishing, fainting, and expiring, discovers its total inefficiency—The new Constitution is happily calculated not only to restore us to animation and vigour, but to diffuse a national spirit, and inspire every man with sentiments of dignity, when he reflects that he is not merely the individual of a State, but a CITIZEN of AMERICA. This leads to his second paragraph, respecting, "the mode of publick business, being conformable to the habits of the people"—Is this antifederalist to be informed at this time of day, that the "habits" of the citizens of America are very dissimilar?—And that this is owing in a great measure to the disuniting and discordant principles of the separate Constitutions of the States, and the

---

1. The anonymous essay is in Storing, 4:1.

355

want of a federal Government?—It is in vain to expect a national trait in our characters, or a similitude of habits, but as the effect of a national efficient government—Virtue or good habits are the result of good laws—and from the excellent American Constitution those habits will be induced, that shall lead to those exertions, manufactures and enterprises, which will give a scope to the American genius, and "find employment for their activity."

His third paragraph contains the basest anti-federal insinuations and suspicions—Although the Representative body is by the new Constitution to be much larger than at present, he represents it as a "small number;"[2] and the period for which they are chosen every one knows is short enough to acquire that legislative knowledge which the great concerns of such an extensive government must require—Fatal experience has evinced the absurdity of a rapid rotation of publick officers; and a more frequent recurrence to elections would deprive us of the whole advantage of a national government: But the Congress of the United States "is to be invested with almost every branch of Legislative authority"—Well, in the name of reason, why should they not?—Does this paragraphist mean to treat the publick as children or as fools? Are we to exist as a nation without laws, and without legislators?—And another dreadful circumstance with him is, the Congress will not set in ALL the States at one and the same time!—How long are we to be troubled by such ridiculous cavillings of moonshine politicians?

Fourthly—Congress by the new Constitution are to regulate commerce, external and internal—"a consummation devoutly to be wished"—"But they are "NOT" to keep up standing armies within the States at all times," although this paragraphist wickedly and falsely asserts it—Look at the Constitution, see if the supreme power has there delegated to it greater authority in this respect than what the very nature of things requires? How the States lose the right of compelling the obedience of their own subjects, I cannot devise—it is true we resign those rights that are incompatible with our NATIONAL INTEREST, and no others.

2. A common Anti-Federal argument was that the new Constitution was insufficiently representative. As Richard Henry Lee saw it, even the most democratic institution, the House of Representatives, was "a mere shread or rag of representation."

Fifthly—This paragraphist asserts that no State will be able to pay its debts but by a dry tax—Where he acquired this knowledge I cannot determine—the Constitution says no such thing—It is true that the right (not an exclusive one by the bye) of levying Impost and Excise is to be vested in the Congress, and if the domestick debts of the States are put upon a continental establishment, as justice, policy, and the facilitating publick business evidently point out, this bugbear of a dry tax vanishes—What the paragraphist means by the States not having a right to certify their own debts, he must write more paragraphs to explain.

His Sixth paragraph is equally enigmatical respecting lands—That the Continental Government will operate unequally for a time may be true—but this is an evil merely temporary, and better to be indured than no government—this State will have an equal chance, and time and experience will doubtless effect an equality—That the State of Vermont will be excluded from the union is a meer assertion, or rather vile incendiary insinuation—one of the group that certain restless spirits are anxious to disseminate for the sole purpose of [advising] the people, and keeping themselves in power.

His Seventh paragraph is full of that mean suspicion which has too long prevailed, and been one chief mean of bringing the whole continent into its present deplorable circumstances. That "we are every day coalescing under a wise and moderate, but firm government," all our senses contradict:—But that the good people through the States are earnestly desiring such a government, is undoubtedly a fact—The people appear to be united in sentiment, that the American Constitution will give them such a government—why then, in the name of honesty, should they be plagued with the groundless surmises and falsehoods of those who fear for themselves, but for the publick have no bowels of compassion? Why should any man be so vain, so self-sufficient, as to palm his individual judgment upon the people, as superiour to that of the concentered wisdom of America, in its late glorious CONVENTION?

"State Soldier"

Essays: III–IV

Virginia Independent Chronicle, Richmond, 12 and 19 March 1788

III

To the GOOD PEOPLE *of* Virginia, *on the new*
FŒDERAL CONSTITUTION, *by an old*
STATE SOLDIER, *respecting the influence of great
names.*

When I first entered the list among the patriotic advocates for the new constitution, which I look up to now as the salvation of America, I had nothing
else in view than just to expose the folly of those who made use of the names
and characters of private men to support the insignificance of their own
arguments.

But alarmed at the thoughts of a dissolution of the UNION, which I
consider the greatest curse that could befall America, I determined to suspend my answer to those authors, to which my first address was only an
introduction, until I cautioned you against laying the foundation of your
own destruction by electing men for the approaching convention, who, under a pretence of amending and perfecting this new work, mean to dissolve
the confederation.

And having in the fullest manner, I trust, proved to you in my last the
impossibility of amending this new plan of government, at this time, without disuniting the states, I shall now return to my first design.

The adversaries to the constitution have not only held up the *chief heroes*
of their party as the infallible guides on this occasion, but have spoken of
some of its friends with such asperity and* disingenuousness as would induce those who were unacquainted with the dispute, to suppose, that it was

---

The Am. Off. The Centinel, etc. of Gen. Washington, Franklin, and Wilson.

nothing more than a private *quarrel* among some leading individuals, under whose standards all the rest of America had servilely enlisted as their vassals.

If in answering those *ingenuous, polite,* and *liberal* authors, I should bring to view some truths which have not yet appeared, by using their own method of arguing as the only means to refute their folly, I trust I shall be excused, as they have not only taught the useful lesson, but absolutely driven those who attempt to answer them into the necessity.

But notwithstanding all that has been said about the liberty of the press being destroyed by the new constitution, I scarcely expect to find a sufficient remnant of that great blessing even in our present system to bring this paper to your view.

For to those very causes which some attribute the destruction of the liberty of the press, I look up for its becoming more unbounded—since clear it is, there are great restraints of that sort already, nor can any thing else be expected in a government as popular as this is.

The liberty of the press is not always one of the most lovely traits of the freest governments:—for as the most popular kinds have generally been thought the most free, it follows that the most free will not be the most favorable to that spirit which is necessary to constitute the liberty of the press.

It is in popular governments that men obtain that very superiority over others, by consent, which is held in other governments by hereditary right; with this only difference, that as the one is always the attainment of superior abilities, and the other too often the right of fools, the just sense we have of the one's being capable of doing us more real good or harm than the other, renders the influence of merit much greater than that of birth.

Whence it follows that men in popular repute over-awe the actions of others much more than those who are only the favorites of fortune. For in kingly governments where men are statesmen by birth, and perhaps only revered for their empty titles, dignity remains protected no longer than it is unattacked—which in general is not long—for superior merit ever anxious to float uppermost in the stream of life, those who possess it necessarily strive to sink others who have only risen above them by the partial hand of fortune. When instantly, that same superiority of talents which adheres to the side of government in the one instance, shifts its influence to the side of liberty in the other.

And thus the press becomes influenced, not by the absolute interference of any government, but by the mere complexion of it—and is nothing more at last than an adherence to the popular side.

In those governments whose heads are the free choice of the people, it is ever to be found on the side of the state, as the same voice which promotes will protect its favorite; and where the success of an author depends on the breath of those who have thus promoted the man at whose character he aims, it would be deemed madness to make the attempt, and nothing less than treason to aid him in it.

When on the other hand, in those governments whose heads are the establishment of birth, and the detestation of the majority, the assistance of the press is to be found on the side of the people. And this it is that is called the liberty of the press.

In England where government has always had some of the ablest men for its opponents, with the popular voice of the people on their side, the liberty of the press is such that even the dignity of the crown does not protect men from ridicule and abuse.

But in America where the dignity of an individual depends on the voice of the people at large, the very reverse has already been seen.

In the course of the late war many attempts were made by General Lee to publish different pieces in abuse of General Washington, only one of which ever made its appearance, and for publishing that, the printer was severely handled, not by government, but by the populace. Which we cannot now but consider as improper:—for sacred as the character of any individual may be, yet the voice of another should be fairly heard—since ridicule, when unconnected with truth, not only ceases to be severe, but degenerating into scurrility, renders the author, and not the person pointed at, the object of contempt.

Under this consideration no good man could object to seeing his character fully stated to the world—and much less would HE whose merits like the purest gold could only become the brighter by being the more frequently handled;—and whose character when held up to public view would only serve to dazzle the eye of envy itself.

That however justly General Lee might have merited our hatred on that occasion, we cannot but lament the consequences of such a disposition. For as no one can judge of the merits of another before he hears them fairly investigated, it would be wrong to shut our eyes against an attack on any one until we were convinced thereby of his purity. The impropriety of which however will be still more clearly seen in a much more recent affair—The recital of which will bring me to the principal object of this paper, from which I have already too long digressed.

As late as in the contest now subsisting about the constitution under consideration, a printer in this state for some time refused to publish a piece because it contained some reflections on one Richard Henry Lee—when, had he measured the dignity of that name by the merits of the letter to which we have lately seen it annexed, he would have had no such scruples perhaps.[1]

But it is not at all surprising that folly should come off with impunity where even vice itself meets with protection.

Fortunately however for this country, we are now likely to profit from both. This gentleman at length, led by his vanity to give us a true attested copy of the powers of his genius, has relieved us from any fear we might have had of being deluded by his abilities; and being long convinced how far we might rely on his integrity, we feel ourselves more and more at ease under any political opinions he may advance. From the commencement of his political career until the publication of his letter, we have been in doubt about the one; but from the *stamp-act* until the present day, we have been clear in the other.

But whatever could have induced the opponents to the constitution, and Mr. Lee above all, to hint at the designs of its friends, I cannot conceive. Did they expect that the mere name of Lee or Mason would be sufficient protection to such barefaced impudence and folly? Did they expect that no enquiry would be made, and no return given to such uncharitable methods?—Or did they expect their characters, abilities, or designs would bear a stricter scrutiny than those aimed at on the other side?—Nothing but the vain manner in which one of those gentlemen ushered his pamphlet forth, could make us suspect either of them of such ill-grounded hopes.

1. See Storing, 5:6; Allen, 22–27.

It is not at all surprising however that Mr. Lee should be opposed to a government, which will probably begin with a man at its head, to procure whose disgrace he has once before convinced us he would cheerfully have sacrificed all America. This is a circumstance too fresh in the minds of all to be forgotten, though it might not have been mentioned at this time, had not this gentleman's own imprudence forced it from me.

Had those two *great statesmen* but sent forth their objections to the new constitution through the verbal medium of their friends; or, had they, like another author of the same stamp, but sent them forth in the more *important* form of *parables* for others to comment* upon, they would have had much more weight, I suspect, than even the objections of a Lycurgus or a Solon, supported by the printed arguments of a Lee or a Mason.

But how far the dignity of names may go towards making up for a deficiency of argument, I am incapable of ascertaining—Or how far the name of Lee may be considered as such, I only shall appeal to his own pamphlet to determine—where, whenever it shall be seen deprived of every other ornament but the genius of the man, the mighty name of—Lee—in weight, as well as size, will only be found to be the *picture* of *greatness* in *miniature* at best.

Mr. Lee begins his objections to the constitution by observing that "to say (as many do) that a bad government must be established for fear of anarchy, is really saying that we must kill ourselves for fear of dying."—From which, as simplicity of thought generally denotes a goodness of heart, I should suppose this gentleman to be one of the best creatures in nature, and if considered as similar only to what he meant should follow after, was as just as it is inelegant and inapplicable if intended to answer any other end.

For how does he prove this to be a bad government?—Is it by comparing it with the perfection of his own scheme, for I observe he has been graciously pleased to offer us his amendments to the constitution?

The present Governor, who gave out his objections to the constitution, and then left them like a parcel of poor little helpless orphans to be supported by a contribution of arguments from his friends.[2]

2. Letter of Edmund Randolph, Storing, 2:5.

It is a pity this gentleman had not given a sample of what he could do before the appointment to the grand convention was made, that he might have offered his *amendments* in a more seasonable place. For had he convinced the world that he was superior to either of the nine, who were in the course of the business appointed by this state, I have no doubt but he would have been in that honorable Assembly, where he might have shewn that superiority, of which he thinks himself possessed over the thirty nine who signed the constitution, without exposing his name at this time to the ridicule of the world.

In respect to the tyranny those gentlemen paint in such horrid colours, it appears to me, but little need be said; for it is not only true, that those who are the loudest about liberty, have always been the greatest tyrants themselves when they have had it in their power; but it is also clear that while in the very act of the one, they are even then exercising the very worst kind of the other. For it being a fixed point that human nature cannot exist without the assistance of government, and there being no power to which mankind are incident, more terrible than fear, it follows, that to keep men under a perpetual alarm about what they cannot, agreeable to their own natures, get rid of, is to worry them out with one oppression and thereby fit them for every other. And this too being generally done by the most insignificant members of the community, renders the tyranny of popular alarm much worse than the fixed oppressions of the most formidable government—and in *the present* instance far more degrading, as it would be much more honorable to be devoured alive by a LION, than frightened to death by a *monkey*.

But I should not deal thus in trifles were it not for two reasons: The first is, having set out solely with a view of exposing in this paper the meanness and folly of being led away by the mere sound of names, I could not pass by this self-sufficient politician in silence—and the other is, that were we determined to pay no attention to trifles, Mr. Lee's whole letter would go unnoticed—which would be rather mortifying, after the hints he dropped to get it printed;—notwithstanding which, however, it had nearly died in manuscript. For unfortunately that gentleman's correspondent was either too good a judge of literary performances to suppose, as he did, that the mere name of Richard Henry Lee would stamp it with the title of perfection;

or else, he had not clearly determined, at that time, on taking his side of the question, as he has since *prudently* taken *both:*—and that being the case, I shall say nothing to caution you against relying on his opposition to the constitution; as there are few I presume willing to rely much on the command of a general who will not openly head his own army for fear of offending the enemy.

As for Mr. Mason, poor old man, he appears to have worn his judgment entirely thread-bare and ragged in the service of his country.[3] But however faint his present endeavors may be to render public good, his past services can never be forgot while his *great zeal* in the Indiana cause remains so lasting a monument of his *righteous* endeavors, and *happy effects* of his land-office scheme have shewn themselves so clearly—*at least in favor of his own fortune.*

To a man thus *zealous,* the want of authority to pass ex post facto laws may be a great objection to the new constitution indeed, as they might be rendered highly useful to, and a great improvement on, the *art of speculation.* But in all other cases they have ever been considered a great curse, since they can only be productive of a halter to the innocent and ignorant.

Whatever this gentleman might have intended when he said that this government would "vibrate for some time between aristocracy and monarchy," and then that "it will settle at last between the one and the other," I will not undertake to say, as I would not presume to dive into the meanings of so profound a man. But if its *vibrating between* the two—and then *settling between* the two, proves any thing, it must be that it will not end in either—*and this is what we wish.*

But what do you suppose are the real motives of such gentlemen for advocating the cause of liberty so strenuously at this time?—Is it that Mr. Mason, who is a man of immense fortune, and Mr. Lee, who possesses as much pride and ambition as he does fortune, are really anxious to see all men raised up to an equality with themselves?—Or is it not rather from a fear that they themselves shall be reduced below the level of some others?

Two things appear to me to operate most powerfully against the adoption of this constitution. The one is dignity—the other debt. And to both of

---

3. See Mason's "Objections," Storing, 2:7; Allen, 11–13.

those causes I attribute the opposition of a *man* whose designs and ingenuity are much more to be dreaded than any I have yet mentioned. The constant propensity he has ever shewn to soar upwards on the breath of popular applause, justifies my surmising the one; and his uniform opposition to the payment of certain debts, in which the majority of this country are little interested, and the establishment of this government will certainly bring about, warrants me in asserting the other.

For he who was willing but a few years ago to vest Congress with the power of raising taxes by the absolute assistance of* armies, could have little objection to a plan at this time, which only proposes to raise them by moderate means, was there not something of secret consequence involved in it.

But as this gentleman has been too wise to trust his objections to the new constitution to the eyes of the public, I shall not mention his name; though I should have little scruple in exposing to view the name of a man, who after all his patriotic canting and whining has been among the first to speculate on the unfortunate credit of his country, and that too when he enjoyed one of the first posts in government. And should a proper opening ever offer, I shall let loose such a train of hyprocricy and deceit upon you, as will astonish you to behold.

But admitting all the enemies to the constitution to be equally honest in their opposition, that in itself is the strongest proof of the necessity there is of adopting it before we attempt to amend it. For if their different designs cannot be offered as an excuse for their differing so widely as they do about the faults of the constitution, nothing I am sure but an acknowledgement that some of them are wrong can account for it; and since we know not on which to rely, nothing but experience can teach us which is right.

Thus having remarked on the designs of some of the principal enemies to the constitution with that freedom which becomes the spirit of an independent man, to which none of those gentlemen themselves can with propriety object, since they are all such *great friends to the Liberty of the press,* I shall return again to the more pleasing subject of the constitution, and

---

* See *Journals of Assembly of Virginia 1784,* resolution proposing to give Congress a right to compel the states to comply with their requisitions by force of arms—Who by?—

endeavor in my next to answer, in as plain a manner as I can, such objections to it as I think worthy of notice.

IV

To the GOOD PEOPLE of Virginia, on the new FŒDERAL CONSTITUTION, by an old STATE SOLDIER, in answer to the objections.

I have now shewn you the *effects which an attempt to amend the new constitution, at this time, would have on the* Union; and also the meanness there is *in being influenced by the mere sound of names* on this important occasion.

And in doing this, I have been unavoidably led to answer some of the individual objections to the constitution themselves—among these are *the want of a bill of rights, the equality in the senate, and the liberty of the press*—all of which I shall avoid recapitulating at this time, with an intention of confining myself wholly to those objections which I have not heretofore entered fully into.

All the objections to the constitution appear to be contained under two heads—the one respects our liberties, the other our interests. To those which respect our liberties, only, I mean to reply in this paper; and in order the more effectually to do that, I shall head this first class of objections under that assertion, which holds forth, that *by the adoption of this constitution we shall be deprived of our liberties.*

And considering that as the *ne plus ultra* of antifœderal workmanship, I shall, after viewing it in the light of a slender fabrick built in air, and filled with imaginary bugbears, first examine into its foundation as a general assertion; and then prove its feebleness by trying the arguments on which it depends for support.

The only desirable purpose of any government, is, the security of men's persons and property; and that which advances farthest that way, is not only the most perfect, but the most free.

Chimerical and speculative enjoyments may amuse the imagination; but justice and safety alone can ensure real happiness—and liberty without happiness is but emptiness and sound.

The more independent a government is therefore of the people, under proper restraints, the more likely it is to produce that justice; and the more substantial and efficient under such restraints, the better calculated to protect both the persons and property of mankind. And the efficiency and energy, of this government being acknowledged in this *general objection* itself, the only necessary enquiry will be, whether the restraints are sufficient to prevent its becoming too formidable in the end.

In respect to restraints on government, there are but three things necessary to be guarded against, the first is a power to deprive men of their personal rights or property by direct laws; the second, is, a power to depress those natural rights into a meanness of person by preventing men from acquiring property from loading them unequally with the public burthens of the state; and the third is, a power to destroy the equality of right by a partial administration of justice. That government which is guarded against those powers, may be said to have all the restraints necessary to constitute a rational happiness under any society.

Let us examine then how far the proposed constitution may be valued on that head.

Under this government neither the Congress nor state legislature could, by direct laws, deprive us of any property we might hold under the general law of the land, or punish us for any offence committed previous to the passage of such laws, since they are prohibited from passing ex post facto laws. Nor could they injure the value of any species of property by partial taxes, since from the proportion laid down in that government, to affect the value of slaves, for instance, in this state, they must ruin all the free persons in several others. Nor could they injure the property of an individual in any state, since the same proportion must be observed throughout a part as well as the whole.

Neither could they in the third instance destroy the equality of right, or injure the value of property in a particular state, or belonging to any individual by a partial administration of justice, since the same doors of one general tribunal would be opened to all—which would on the contrary enhance the value of all property on the continent by giving confidence to foreign creditors, and an equal security to citizens of every state.

Under such restraints and useful regulations, it cannot be denied but that the authorities contained in a firm and efficient government are necessary to procure safety, and give to that machine a proper motion; unless there be those so chimerical and speculative as to expect government, like a wind-mill, to go on by airy efforts only.

But in order the more clearly to view that *great objection* still on general principles, as I first proposed to examine it, let us next try it by the simple test of facts.

That there will go no more power out of the peoples' hands by the adoption of this constitution than what is already given up, is obvious, because the state legislature and Congress together have in their hands, at this time, every authority which is proposed to be given to the new head, and that too without any restraints on those of the state. The right of passing ex post facto laws, the power of administering partial taxation, and a right to procrastinate justice, or interfere, in their legislative capacity, in private affairs, make up the only compound necessary to give a dismal *hue* to the finest features of any government. Yet such are the powers already given into the hands of government as to justify and produce all those acts.

The only difference therefore between our present situation and under the new government will be, that the most of the powers already given up will be in the hands of Congress instead of the legislature of the state; which change will only be felt by the leading men in each state, and not by the people. Whence we shall experience all the security which an efficient government can afford, without being subject to its oppressions. For in the proposed plan will be exercised all the useful authorities which already belong to the state, with all the salutary and safe restraints inseparable from the new system.

Thus having shewn on general principles the fallacy of that doctrine which holds out that we shall be deprived of our liberties by the adoption of this constitution, I shall now examine how this general assertion stands supported by the individual objections themselves.

The first I shall touch upon, is, that to the *authorities of the supreme court.*

There were three things in the first place which made it necessary to establish this court—the first is, the disputes that might arise between the different states, which could not otherwise [have] been determined but by a recourse to arms—the second is, in disputes between foreigners and citizens, without which general and impartial mode of trial under a fœderal government, an end would soon be put to foreign credit, and of course to that extensive commerce which alone can ensure a lasting value to our property—and the third is, in disputes between citizens of different states, which alone could prevent that jealousy that must have been excited by trials in the state where only one of the parties resided; and which would have been destructive of that confidence and harmony which will ever be requisite to preserve that union and agreement, without which, this new government itself would cease to exist. And the two last are the only cases in which the people can be much affected; and that in most instances only by appeal.

The next objection I shall take notice of, is, that against standing armies.

There are but two ways in which armies are ever employed, the one is defending, the other abusing, mens' rights; and in order to do the one, they must first begin with a pretence of intending the other. Nor can they long go undiscovered in acting thus, as the difference between the two is very easily observed; and as it will only become necessary to make the discovery to put an end to its progress, so in order to become a lasting evil, they must have some other foundation to depend on, than the will of those they are to injure. Either the separate interests or popular influence of those who employ them, have ever been the causes of their being used for a bad purpose. Hence it follows that a body of men so numerous as to make a division of power but a small object to any; and who only enjoy that power under the will of those they would endeavor to enslave, would neither wish to succeed in such a design, even were it practicable, nor expect to find it practicable should they make the attempt. As long therefore as the representatives of a people are elected by them, and under the necessity of returning among them at stated periods, when they will be liable to their resentments, there is but little danger of their committing an open outrage on their liberties. It cannot be then for the abuse of our rights that Congress are to have a power of raising armies, as it is clearly on the will of the people the right of creating them depends—and therefore for our protection alone can be employed.

The right of laying direct taxes is also objected to, though this is among the powers already given up by the people, and necessary for the existence of every government. Whether it extends itself over the whole continent or only a single state therefore, the effects will be the same to the people; and all the difference there will be, is, that less will be collected by the states individually, and more by the continent than now is.—But this, like all the other powers to be exercised by a representative who holds his authority under the will of those he is to govern; cannot be exercised but for their immediate benefit.

But then "the laws made under this constitution are to be the supreme laws of the land." Under this clause it is said every authority is included.

It is with this objection however as with that about taxation; it would [have] availed but little to have attempted altering our system, and at the same time withhold from the new plan every thing that was useful. The great object which we had in view when we first called for the assistance of a convention, was, the strengthening the hands of the UNION; and if there are to be left in the hands of the different states sufficient powers to supersede those of Congress, little after all has been effected. At least a contention for supremacy between the different states and Congress would have been the consequence, had not some such distinguishing mark been set up to decide the superiority; the consequence of which would have been, that each in vieing with the other would be provoked to make daily experiments of its power, while the people would be left between the two rival authorities as the subject of their *anatomy.*

But this objection is a contradiction in itself; and if of any weight, only serves to operate against every other objection that has been made to the constitution; for if there be an objection to any other part of the constitution, it must be because there is an authority some where else besides in that general clause, which is a contradiction, because, an absolute and unbounded authority admits of no rivalship—And on the other hand, by viewing it in the light of a general authority given to Congress without controul, we render null and void all the other authorities, of which, in the same breath are so loudly complained; and in doing that, we destroy at a single blow every other objection, since there can be no objection to any part, where there is to be no power.

But to view it in a still more serious light, the saying that the laws made under that constitution shall be the supreme laws of the land, never could [have] been intended to bear that construction which has been put on it by some, because, if it had been intended or wished that Congress should have possessed such an unbounded power as is said, it would have been needless to run the risk of losing that *desirable* point, by adding to it, things which were to be of no use. And as it is not, that the laws made under that particular clause of the constitution, but the laws made under the whole system, of which that is but a small part, shall be the supreme laws of the land, so any law made in contradiction to any other clause, will be as void of effect as another made in direct compliance with that will be binding.

That this part of the constitution is neither so contradictory in itself as it appears when made an objection, nor are the other parts so useless and insignificant as they are made by giving that particular clause absolute power—but each in their several places form the different useful authorities and checks which are necessary to give both stability to our laws and safety to the people.

These, together with the other three assertions which I have endeavored to refute in some previous papers, form the most important supports of that grand objection to the constitution which respects our liberties; though there are many others which might have come under the same head; for it is a rule with artists, that in rearing the superstructure of all fabrics, to have as good a foundation and as firm supporters as possible; but when they cannot support the edifice by strength of braces, they naturally have recourse to [a] number of posts; and when they far exceed the number, which if found, would answer, it does not require much reasoning to prove that they themselves have but little confidence in any.

That from what has been said already on either side, it may I think be concluded that our liberties so far from being diminished, will be increased by the adoption of the new constitution, as it will be a means of depriving the states of the right of exercising the most unbounded acts of injustice, under which, both the persons and property of men are insecure; and under such insecurity, every earthly consideration is lessened in its value. Whence, as there is no species of liberty but what is connected either with the person or property of mankind, so there is no species of it also but what is increased by adding confidence and safety to the one, and permanence and value to the other. And that government therefore which is best calculated to ensure both, is most consistent with every rational idea of liberty and happiness.

"A Citizen of America"
[Noah Webster]

"An Examination into the Leading Principles of the Federal Constitution"

Philadelphia, 17 October 1787

Of all the memorable æras that have marked the progress of men from the savage state to the refinements of luxury, that which has combined them into society, under a wise system of government, and given form to a nation, has ever been recorded and celebrated as the most important. Legislators have ever been deemed the greatest benefactors of mankind—respected when living, and often deified after their death. Hence the fame of Fohi and Confucius—of Moses, Solon and Lycurgus—of Romulus and Numa—of Alfred, Peter the Great, and Mango Capac; whose names will be celebrated through all ages, for framing and improving constitutions of government, which introduced order into society and secured the benefits of law to millions of the human race.

This western world now beholds an æra important beyond conception, and which posterity will number with the age of Czar of Muscovy, and with the promulgation of the Jewish laws at Mount Sinai. The names of those men who have digested a system of constitutions for the American empire, will be enrolled with those of Zamolxis and Odin, and celebrated by posterity with the honors which less enlightened nations have paid to the fabled demi-gods of antiquity.

But the origin of the AMERICAN REPUBLIC is distinguished by peculiar circumstances. Other nations have been driven together by fear and necessity—the governments have generally been the result of a single man's observations; or the offspring of particular interests. In the formation of our constitution, the wisdom of all ages is collected—the legislators of antiquity are consulted—as well as the opinions and interests of the millions who are concerned. In short, it is *an empire of reason.*

In the formation of such a government, it is not only the *right,* but the indispensable *duty* of every citizen to examine the principles of it, to compare them with the principles of other governments, with a constant eye to our particular situation and circumstances, and thus endeavor to foresee the future operations of our own system, and its effects upon human happiness.[1]

Convinced of this truth, I have no apology to offer for the following remarks, but an earnest desire to be useful to my country.

In attending to the proposed Federal Constitution, the first thing that presents itself to our consideration, is the division of the legislative into two branches. This article has so many advocates in America, that it needs not any vindication.*—But it has its opposers, among whom are some respectable characters, especially in Pennsylvania; for which reason, I will state some of the arguments and facts which incline me to favor the proposed division.

On the first view of men in society, we should suppose that no man would be bound by a law to which he had not given his consent. Such would be our first idea of political obligation. But experience, from time immemorial, has proved it to be impossible to unite the opinions of all the members of a community, in every case; and hence the doctrine, that the opinions of a *majority* must give law to the *whole State:* a doctrine as universally received, as any intuitive truth.

Another idea that naturally presents itself to our minds, on a slight consideration of the subject, is, that in a perfect government, all the members of a society should be present, and each give his suffrage in acts of legislation, by which he is to be bound. This is impracticable in large states; and even were it not, it is very questionable whether it would be the *best* mode of legislation. It was however practised in the free states of antiquity; and was the cause of innumerable evils. To avoid these evils, the moderns have invented the doctrine of *representation,* which seems to be the perfection of human government.

Another idea, which is very natural, is, that to complete the mode of legislation, all the representatives should be collected into *one body,* for the

---

1. See *The Federalist,* No. 1, for a similar sentiment.

*A division of the legislature has been adopted in the new constitution of every state except Pennsylvania and Georgia.

purpose of debating questions and enacting laws. Speculation would suggest the idea; and the desire of improving upon the systems of government in the old world, would operate powerfully in its favor.

But men are ever running into extremes. The passions, after a violent constraint, are apt to run into licentiousness; and even the reason of men, who have experienced evils from the *defects* of a government, will sometimes coolly condemn the *whole system.*

Every person, moderately acquainted with human nature, knows that public bodies, as well as individuals, are liable to the influence of sudden and violent passions, under the operation of which, the voice of reason is silenced. Instances of such influence are not so frequent, as in individuals; but its effects are extensive in proportion to the numbers that compose the public body. This fact suggests the expediency of dividing the powers of legislation between the two bodies of men, whose debates shall be separate and not dependent on each other: that, if at any time, one part should appear to be under any undue influence, either from passion, obstinacy, jealousy of particular men, attachment to a popular speaker, or other extraordinary causes, there might be a power in the legislature sufficient to check every pernicious measure. Even in a small republic, composed of men, equal in property and abilities, and all meeting for the purpose of making laws, like the old Romans in the field of Mars, a division of the body into two independent branches, would be a necessary step to prevent the disorders, which arise from the pride, irritability and stubborness of mankind. This will ever be the case, while men possess passions, easily inflamed, which may bias their reason and lead them to erroneous conclusions.

Another consideration has weight: A single body of men may be led astray by one person of abilities and address, who, on the first starting [of] a proposition, may throw a plausible appearance on one side of the question, and give a lead to the whole debate. To prevent any ill consequence from such a circumstance, a separate discussion, before a different body of men, and taken up on new grounds, is a very eligible expedient.

Besides, the design of a senate is not merely to check the legislative assembly, but to collect wisdom and experience. In most of our constitutions, and particularly in the proposed federal system, greater age and longer residence are required to qualify for the senate, than for the house of representatives. This is a wise provision. The house of representatives may be composed of new and unexperienced members—strangers to the forms of proceeding, and the science of legislation. But either positive institutions, or customs, which may supply their place, fill the senate with men venerable for age and respectability, experienced in the ways of men, and in the art of governing, and who are not liable to the bias of passions that govern the young. If the senate of Rhode Island is an exception to this observation, it is a proof that the mass of the people are corrupted, and that the senate should be elected less frequently than the other house: Had the old senate in Rhode Island held their seats for three years; had they not been chosen, amidst a popular rage for paper money, the honor of that state would probably have been saved. The old senate would have stopped the measure for a year or two, till the people could have had time to deliberate upon its consequences. I consider it as a capital excellence of the proposed constitution, that the senate can be wholly renewed but once in six years.

Experience is the best instructor—it is better than a thousand theories. The history of every government on earth affords proof of the utility of different branches in a legislature. But I appeal only to our own experience in America. To what cause can we ascribe the absurd measures of Congress, in times past, and the speedy recision of whole measures, but to the want of some check? I feel the most profound deference for that honorable body, and perfect respect for their opinions; but some of their steps betray a great want of consideration—a defect, which perhaps nothing can remedy, but a division of their deliberations. I will instance only their *resolution* to build a *Federal Town.* When we were involved in a debt, of which we could hardly pay the interest, and when Congress could not command a shilling, the very proposition was extremely absurd. Congress themselves became ashamed of the resolution, and rescinded it with as much silence as possible. Many other acts of that body are equally reprehensible—but respect forbids me to mention them.

Several states, since the war, have experienced the necessity of a division of the legislature. Maryland was saved from a most pernicious measure, by her senate. A rage for paper money, bordering on madness, prevailed in their house of delegates—an emission of £.500,000 was proposed; a sum equal to the circulating medium of the State. Had the sum been emitted, every shilling of specie would have been driven from circulation, and most of it from the state. Such a loss would not have been repaired in seven years—not to mention the whole catalogue of frauds which would have followed the measure. The senate, like honest, judicious men, and the protectors of the interests of the state, firmly resisted the rage, and gave the people time to cool and to think. Their resistance was effectual—the people acquiesced, and the honor and interest of the state were secured.

The house of representatives in Connecticut, soon after the war, had taken offence at a certain act of Congress. The upper house, who understood the necessity and expediency of the measure, better than the people, refused to concur in a remonstrance to Congress. Several other circumstances gave umbrage to the lower house; and to weaken or destroy the influence of the senate, the representatives, among other violent proceedings, resolved, not merely to remove the seat of government, but to make every county town in the state the seat of government, by rotation. This foolish resolution would have disgraced school-boys—the senate saved the honor of the state, by rejecting it with disdain—and within two months, every representative was ashamed of the conduct of the house. All public bodies have these fits of passion, when their conduct seems to be perfectly boyish; and in these paroxisms, a check is highly necessary.

Pennsylvania exhibits many instances of this hasty conduct. At one session of the legislature, an armed force is ordered, by a precipitate resolution, to expel the settlers at Wioming from their possessions—at a succeeding session, the same people are confirmed in their possessions. At one session, a charter is wrested from a corporation—at another, restored. The whole state is split into parties—everything is decided by party—any proposition from one side of the house, is sure to be damned by the other—and when one party perceives the other has the advantage, they play truant—and an officer or a mob hunt the absconding members in all the streets and alleys in town. Such farces have been repeated in Philadelphia—and *there alone.* Had the legislature been framed with some check upon rash proceedings, the honor of the state would have been saved—the party spirit would have died with the measures proposed in the legislature. But now, any measure may be carried by party in the house; it then becomes a law, and sows the seeds of dissension throughout the state.*

A thousand examples similar to the foregoing may be produced, both in ancient and modern history. Many plausible things may be said in favor of pure democracy—many in favor of uniting the representatives of the people in one single house—but uniform experience proves both to be inconsistent with the peace of society, and the rights of freemen.

The state of Georgia has already discovered such inconveniences in its constitution, that a proposition has been made for altering it; and there is a prospect that a revisal will take place.

People who have heard and read of the European governments, founded on the different ranks of *monarch, nobility and people,* seem to view the *senate* in America, where there is no difference of ranks and titles, as a useless branch—or as a servile imitation of foreign constitutions of government, without the same reasons. This is a capital mistake. Our senates, it is true, are not composed of a different order of men; but the same reasons, the same necessity for distinct branches of the legislature exists in all governments. But in most of our American constitutions, we have all the advantages of checks and balance, without the danger which may arise from a superior and independent order of men.

It is worth our while to institute a brief comparison between our American forms of government, and the two *best constitutions* that ever existed in Europe, the *Roman* and the *British.*

---

*I cannot help remarking the singular jealousy of the constitution of Pennsylvania, which requires that a bill shall be published for the consideration of the people, before it is enacted into a law, except in extraordinary cases. This annihilates the legislature, and reduces it to an advisory body. It almost wholly supersedes the uses of *representation,* the most excellent improvement in modern governments. Besides the absurdity of constituting a legislature, without supreme power, such a system will keep the state perpetually embroiled. It carries the spirit of discussion into all quarters, without the means of reconciling the opinions of men, who are not assembled to hear each others' arguments. They debate with themselves—form their own opinions, without the reasons which influence others, and without the means of information. Thus the warmth of different opinions, which, in other states, dies in the legislature, is diffused through the state of Pennsylvania, and becomes personal and permanent. The seeds of dissension are sown in the constitution, and no state, except Rhode Island, is so distracted by factions.

In England, the king or supreme executive officer, is hereditary. In America, the president of the United States, is elective. That this is an advantage will hardly be disputed.

In ancient Rome, the king was elective, and so were the consuls, who were the executive officers in the republic. But they were elected by the body of the people, in their public assemblies; and this circumstance paved the way for such excessive bribery and corruption as are wholly unknown in modern times. The president of the United States is also elective; but by a few men—chosen by the several legislatures—under their inspection— separated at a vast distance—and holding no office under the United States. Such a mode of election almost precludes the possibility of corruption. Besides, no state however large, has the power of chusing a president in that state; for each elector must choose at least one man, who is not an inhabitant of that State to which he belongs.

The crown of England is hereditary—the consuls of Rome were chosen annually—both these extremes are guarded against in our proposed constitution. The president is not dismissed from his office, as soon as he is acquainted with business—he continues four years, and is re-eligible, if the people approve his conduct. Nor can he canvass for his office, by reason of the distance of the electors; and the pride and jealousy of the states will prevent his continuing too long in office.

The age requisite to qualify for this office is thirty-five years.* The age requisite for admittance to the Roman consulship was forty-three years. For this difference, good reasons may be assigned—the improvements in science, and particularly in government, render it practicable for a man to qualify himself for an important office, much earlier in life, than he could among the Romans; especially in the early part of their commonwealth, when the office was instituted. Besides it is very questionable whether any inconvenience would have attended admission to the consulship at an earlier age.

---

*In the decline of the republic, bribery or military force obtained this office for persons who had not attained this age—Augustus was chosen at the age of twenty; or rather obtained it with his sword.

The powers vested in the president resemble the powers of the supreme magistrates in Rome. They are not so extensive as those of the British king; but in one instance, the president, with concurrence of the senate, has powers exceeding those of the Roman consuls; I mean in the appointment of judges and other subordinate executive officers. The prætors or judges in Rome were chosen annually by the people. This was a defect in the Roman government. One half the evils in a state arise from a lax execution of the laws; and it is impossible that an executive officer can act with vigor and impartiality, when his office depends on the popular voice. An annual popular election of executive officers is the sure source of a negligent, partial and corrupt administration. The independence of the judges in England has produced a course of the most just, impartial and energetic judicial decisions, for many centuries, that can be exhibited in any nation on earth. In this point therefore I conceive the plan proposed in America to be an improvement on the Roman constitution. In all free governments, that is, in all countries, where *laws govern,* and not *men,* the supreme magistrate should have it in his power to execute any law, however unpopular, without hazarding his person or office. The laws are the sole *guardians* of right, and when the magistrate dares not act, every person is insecure.

Let us now attend to the constitution and the powers of the senate.

The house of lords in England is wholly independent of the people. The lords spiritual hold their seats by office; and the people at large have no voice in disposing of the ecclesiastical dignities. The temporal lords hold their seats by hereditary right or by grant from the king: And it is a branch of the king's prerogative to make what peers he pleases.

The senate in Rome was elective; but a senator held his seat for life.*

---

*I say the senate was *elective*—but this must be understood with some exceptions; or rather qualifications. The constitution of the Roman senate has been a subject of enquiry, with the first men in modern ages. Lord Chesterfield requested the opinion of the learned Vertot, upon the manner of chusing senators in Rome; and it was a subject of discussion between Lord Harvey and Dr. Middleton. The most probable account of the manner of forming the senate, and filling up vacancies, which I have collected from the best writers on this subject, is here abridged for the consideration of the reader.

Romulus chose one hundred persons, from the principal families in Rome, to form a council or senate; and reserved to himself the right of nominating their successors; that is of filling vacancies. "Mais comme Romulus avoit lui même choisi les premiers senateurs il se reserva

The proposed senate in America is constituted on principles more favorable to liberty: The members are elective, and by the separate legislatures: They hold their seats for six years—they are thus rendered sufficiently dependent on their constituents; and yet are not dismissed from their office as soon as they become acquainted with the forms of proceeding.

It may be objected by the larger states, that the representation is not equal; the smallest states having the privilege of sending the same number of senators as the largest. To obviate this objection, I would suggest but two or three ideas.

I. If each state had a representation and a right in deciding questions, proportional to its property, three states would almost command the whole. Such a constitution would gradually annihilate the small states; and finally melt down the whole United States into one undivided sovereignty. The free states of Spain and the heptarchy in England, afford striking examples of this.

---

le droit de nommer a son gré, leurs successeurs."—Mably, sur les Romains. Other well informed historians intimate that Romulus retained the right of nominating the president only. After the union of the Sabines with the Romans, Romulus added another hundred members to the senate, but by *consent of the people.* Tarquin, the *ancient,* added another hundred; but historians are silent as to the manner.

On the destruction of Alba by Hostilius, some of the principal Alban families were added to the senate, *by consent of the senate and people.*

After the demolition of the monarchy, Appius Claudius was admitted into the senate by *order of the people.*

Cicero testifies that, from the extinction of the monarchy, all the members of the senate were admitted by *command of the people.*

It is observable that the first creation of the senators was the act of the monarch; and the first patrician families claimed the sole right of admission into the senate. "Les familles qui descendoient des deux cent senateurs que Romulus avoit créés,—se crurent seules en droit d'entrer dans le senat."—Mably.

This right however was not granted in its utmost extent; for many of the senators in the Roman commonwealth, were taken from plebian families. For sixty years before the institution of the *censorship,* which was A. U. C. 311, we are not informed how vacancies in the senate were supplied. The most probable method was this; to enrol, in the list of senators, the different magistrates; viz., the consuls, prætors, the two quæstors of patrician families, the five tribunes (afterwards ten) and the two ædiles of plebian families: The office of quæstor gave an immediate admission into the senate. The tribunes were admitted two years after their creation. This enrollment seems to have been a matter of course; and likewise their confirmation by the people in their comitia or assemblies.

Should it be said that such an event is desirable, I answer; the states are all entitled to their respective sovereignties, and while they claim independence in international jurisdiction, the federal constitution ought to guarantee their sovereignty.

2. Another consideration has weight—There is, in all nations, a tendency toward an accumulation of power in some point. It is the business of the legislator to establish some barriers to check the tendency. In small societies, a man worth £.100,000 has but one vote, when his neighbors, who are worth but fifty pounds, have each one vote likewise. To make property the sole basis of authority, would expose many of the best citizens to violence and oppression. To make the number of inhabitants in a state, the rule of apportioning power, is more equitable; and were the United States one indivisible interest, would be a perfect rule for representation. But the detached situation of the states has created some separate interests—some local institutions, which they will not resign nor throw into the hands of other states. For these peculiar interests, the states have an *equal* attachment—for the preservation and enjoyment of these, an *equal* sovereignty is necessary;

On extraordinary occasions, when the vacancies of the senate were numerous, the consuls used to nominate some of the most respectable of the equestrian order to be chosen by the people.

On the institution of the censorship, the censors were invested with full powers to inspect the manners of the citizens,—enrol them in their proper ranks according to their property,—make out lists of the senators and leave out the names of such as had rendered themselves unworthy of their dignity by any scandalous vices. This power they several times exercised; but the disgraced senators had an appeal to the people.

After the senate had lost half its members in the war with Hannibal, the dictator, M. Fabius Buteo, filled up the number with the magistrates, with those who had been honored with a civic crown, or others who were respectable for age and character. One hundred and seventy new members were added at once, with *the approbation of the people.* The vacancies occasioned by Sylla's proscriptions amounted to three hundred, which were supplied by persons nominated by Sylla and *chosen by the people.*

Before the time of the Gracchi, the number of senators did not exceed three hundred. But in Sylla's time, so far as we can collect from direct testimonies, it amounted to about five hundred. The age necessary to qualify for a seat in the senate is not exactly ascertained; but several circumstances prove it to have been about thirty years.

See Vertot, Mably, and Middleton on this subject.

In the last ages of Roman splendor, the property requisite to qualify a person for a senator, was settled by Augustus at eight hundred sestertia—more than six thousand pounds sterling.

and the sovereignty of each state would not be secure, had each state, in both branches of the legislature an authority in passing laws, proportioned to its inhabitants.

3. But the senate should be considered as representing the confederacy in a body. It is a false principle in the vulgar idea of representation, that a man delegated by a particular district in a state, is the representative of that district only; whereas in truth a member of the legislature from any town or county, is the representative of the whole state. In passing laws, he is to view the whole collective interest of the state, and act from that view; not from a partial regard to the interest of the town or county where he is chosen.

The same principle extends to the Congress of the United States. A delegate is bound to represent the true local interest of his constituents—to state in its true light to the whole body—but when each provincial interest is thus stated, every member should act for the *aggregate interest* of the whole confederacy. The design of representation is to bring the collective interest into view—a delegate is not the legislator of a single state—he is as much the legislator of the whole confederacy as of the particular state where he is chosen; and if he gives his vote for a law which he believes to be beneficial to his own state only, and pernicious to the rest, he betrays his trust and violates his oath. It is indeed difficult for a man to divest himself of local attachments and act from an impartial regard to the general good; but he who cannot for the most part do this, is not a good legislator.

These considerations suggest the propriety of continuing the senators in office, for a longer period, than the representatives. They gradually lose their partiality, generalize their views, and consider themselves as acting for the whole confederacy. Hence in the senate we may expect union and firmness—here we may find the *general good* the object of legislation, and a check upon the more partial and interested acts of the other branch.

These considerations obviate the complaint, that the representation in the senate is not equal; for the senators represent the whole confederacy; and all that is wanted of the members is information of the true situation and interest of each state. As they act under the direction of the several legislatures, two men may as fully and completely represent a state, as twenty;

and when the true interest of each state is known, if the senators perform the part of good legislators, and act impartially for the whole collective body of the United States, it is totally immaterial where they are chosen.*

The house of representatives is the more immediate voice of the separate states—here the states are represented in proportion to their number of inhabitants—here the separate interests will operate with their full force, and the violence of parties and the jealousies produced by interfering interests, can be restrained and quieted only by a body of men, less local and dependent.

It may be objected that no separate interests should exist in a state; and a division of the legislature has a tendency to create them. But this objection is founded on mere jealousy, or a very imperfect comparison of the Roman and British governments, with the proposed federal constitution.

The house of peers in England is a body originally and totally independent of the people—the senate in Rome was mostly composed of patrician or noble families, and after the first election of a senator, he was no longer dependent on the people—he held his seat for life. But the senate of the

---

*It is a capital defect of most of the state-constitutions, that the senators, like the representatives, are chosen in particular districts. They are thus inspired with local views, and however wrong it may be to entertain them, yet such is the constitution of human nature, that men are almost involuntarily attached to the interest of the district which has reposed confidence in their abilities and integrity. Some partiality therefore for constituents is always expectable. To destroy it as much as possible, a political constitution should remove the grounds of local attachment. Connecticut and Maryland have wisely destroyed this attachment in their senates, by ordaining that the members shall be chosen in the *state at large*. The senators hold their seats by the suffrages of the state, *not of a district;* hence they have no particular number of men to fear or to oblige.—They represent *the state;* hence that union and firmness which the senates of those states have manifested on the most trying occasions, and by which they have prevented the most rash and iniquitous measures.

It may be objected, that when the election of senators is vested in the people, they must choose men in their own neighborhood, or else those with whom they are unacquainted. With respect to representatives, this objection does not lie; for they are chosen in small districts; and as to senators, there is, in every state, a small number of men, whose reputation for abilities, integrity and good conduct will lead the people to a very just choice. Old experienced statesmen should compose the senate; and people are generally, in this free country, acquainted with their characters. Were it possible, as it is in small states, it would be an improvement in the doctrine of representation, to give every freeman the right of voting for every member of the legislature, and the privilege of choosing the men in any part of the state. This would totally exclude bribery and undue influence; for no man can bribe a state; and it would almost annihilate partial views in legislation. But in large states it may be impracticable.

United States can have no separate interests from the body of the people; for they live among them—they are chosen by them—they *must* be dismissed from their place once in six years and *may* at any time be impeached for mal-practices——their property is situated among the people, and with their persons, subject to the same laws. No title can be granted, but the temporary titles of office, bestowed by the voluntary election of the people; and no pre-eminence can be acquired but by the same means.

The separation of the legislature divides the power—checks—restrains—amends the proceedings—at the same time, it creates no division of interest, that can tempt either branch to encroach upon the other, or upon the people. In turbulent times, such restraint is our greatest safety—in calm times, and in measures obviously calculated for the general good, both branches must always be unanimous.

A man must be thirty years of age before he can be admitted into the senate—which was likewise a requisite in the Roman government. What property was requisite for a senator in the early ages of Rome, I cannot inform myself; but Augustus fixed it at six hundred sestertia—between six and seven thousand pounds sterling. In the federal constitution, money is not made a requisite—the places of senators are wisely left open to all persons of suitable age and merit, and who have been citizens of the United States for nine years; a term in which foreigners may acquire the feelings and acquaint themselves with the interests, of the native Americans.

The house of representatives is formed on very equitable principles; and is calculated to guard the privileges of the people. The English house of commons is chosen by a small part of the people of England, and continues for seven years. The Romans never discovered the secret of representation—the whole body of citizens assembled for the purposes of legislation—a circumstance that exposed their government to frequent convulsions, and to capricious measures. The federal house of representatives is chosen by the people qualified to vote for state representatives,* and continues two years.

*It is said by some, that no property should be required as a qualification for an elector. I shall not enter into a discussion of the subject; but remark that in most free governments, some property has been thought requisite, to prevent corruption and secure government from the influence of an unprincipled multitude.

Some may object to their continuance in power *two years*. But I cannot see any danger arising from this quarter. On the contrary, it creates less trouble for the representatives, who by such choice are taken from their professions and obliged to attend Congress, some of them at the distance of at least seven hundred miles. While men are chosen by the people, and responsible to them, there is but little danger from ambition or corruption.

If it should be said that Congress may in time become triennial, and even septennial, like the English parliaments, I answer, this is not in their power. The English parliament had power to prolong the period of their existence—but Congress will be restrained by the different legislatures, without whose constitutional concurrence, no alteration can be made in the proposed system.

In ancient Rome none but the free citizens had the right of a suffrage in the *comitia* or legislative assemblies. But in Sylla's time the Italian cities demanded the rights of the Roman citizens; alledging that they furnished two-thirds of the armies, in all their wars, and yet were despised as foreigners. Vell Paterc. lib. 2. cap. 15. This produced the *Marsic* or *social* war, which lasted two years, and caried off 300,000 men. Ibm. It was conducted and concluded by Pompey, father of Pompey the Great, with his lieutenants Sylla and Marius. But most of the cities eventually obtained *the freedom of Rome;* and were of course entitled to the rights of suffrage in the comitia. "Paulatim deinde recipiendo in civitatem, qui arma aut non ceperant aut deposuerant maturiùs, vires refectæ sunt." Vell. Paterc. 2. 16.

But Rome had cause to deplore this event, for however reasonable it might appear to admit the allies to a participation of the rights of citizens, yet the concession destroyed all freedom of election. It enabled an ambitious demagogue to engage and bring into the assemblies, whole towns of people, slaves and foreigners;—and everything was decided by faction and violence. This Montesquieu numbers among the causes of the decline of the Roman greatness. De la grandeur des Romains, c. 9.

Representation would have, in some measure, prevented the consequences; but the admission of every man to a suffrage will ever open the door to corruption. In such a state as Connecticut, where there is no conflux of foreigners, no introduction of seamen, servants, &c., and scarcely an hundred persons in the state who are not natives, and very few whose education and connexions do not attach them to the government; at the same time few men have property to furnish the means of corruption, very little danger could spring from admitting every man of age and discretion to the privilege of voting for rulers. But in the large towns of America there is more danger. A master of a vessel may put votes in the hands of his crew, for the purpose of carrying an election for a party. Such things have actually taken place in America. Besides, the middle states are receiving emigrations of poor people, who are not at once judges of the characters of men, and who cannot be safely trusted with the choice of legislators.

"A Citizen of America"

The fourth section, article I, of the new constitution declares that "The times, places, and manner of holding elections for senators and representatives, shall be prescribed in "each state by the legislature thereof; *but the Congress may at any time by law make or alter such regulations, except as to the places of chusing senators.*" Here let us pause——What did the convention mean by giving Congress power to *make regulations,* prescribed by the legislatures? Is this expression accurate or intelligible? But the word *alter* is very intelligible, and the clause puts the election of representatives *wholly,* and the senators *almost wholly,* in the power of Congress.

The views of the convention I believe to be perfectly upright—They might mean to place the election of representatives and senators beyond the reach of faction—They doubtless had good reasons, in *their* minds, for the clause—But I see no occasion for any power in Congress to interfere with the choice of their own body—They will have power to suppress insurrections, as they ought to have; but the clause in *Italics* gives *needless* and *dangerous* powers—I hope the states will reject it with decency, and adopt the whole system, without altering another syllable.

The method of passing laws in Congress is much preferable to that of ancient Rome or modern Britain. Not to mention other defects in Rome, it lay in the power of a single tribune to obstruct the passing of a law. As the tribunes were popular magistrates, the right was often exercised in favor of liberty; but it was also abused, and the best regulations were prevented, to gratify the spleen, the ambition, or the resentment of an individual.

The king of Great-Britain has the same power, but seldom exercises it. It is however a dangerous power—it is absurd and hazardous to lodge in *one man* the right of controlling the will of a state.

Every bill that passes a majority of both houses of Congress, must be sent to the president for his approbation; but it must be returned in ten days, whether approved by him or not; and the concurrence of two thirds of both houses passes the bill into a law, notwithstanding any objections of the president. The constitution therefore gives the supreme executive a check but no negative, upon the sense of Congress.

The powers lodged in Congress are extensive; but it is presumed that they are not too extensive. The first object of the constitution is to *unite* the states into one *compact society,* for the purpose of government. If such *union* must exist, or the states be exposed to foreign invasions, internal discord, reciprocal encroachments upon each others property—to weakness and infamy, which no person will dispute; what powers must be collected and lodged in the supreme head or legislature of these states. The answer is easy: This legislature must have exclusive jurisdiction in all matters in which the states have a mutual interest. There are some regulations in which all the states are equally concerned—there are others, which in their operation, are limited to one state. The first belongs to Congress—the last to the respective legislatures. No one state has a right to supreme control, in any affair in which the other states have an interest, nor should Congress interfere in any affair which respects one state only. This is the general line of division, which the convention have endeavored to draw, between the powers of Congress and the rights of the individual states. The only question therefore is, whether the new constitution delegates to Congress any powers which do not respect the general interest and welfare of the United States. If these powers intrench upon the present sovereignty of any *state,* without having for an object the *collective interest* of the whole, the powers are too extensive. But if they do not extend to all concerns, in which the states have a mutual interest, they are too limited. If in any instance, the powers necessary for protecting the *general* interest, interfere with the constitutional rights of an *individual* state, such state has assumed powers that are inconsistent with the safety of the United States, and which ought instantly to be resigned. Considering the states as individuals, on equal terms, entering into a social compact, no state has a right to any power which may prejudice its neighbors. If therefore the federal constitution has collected into the federal legislature no more power than is necessary for the *common defence and interest,* it should be recognized by the states, however particular clauses may supersede the exercise of certain powers by the individual states.

This question is of vast magnitude. The states have very high ideas of their separate sovereignty; altho' it is certain, that while each exists in its full latitude, we can have no *Federal sovereignty.* However flattered each state may be by its independent sovereignty, we can have no union, no respectability, no national character, and what is more, no national justice, till the states resign to one *supreme head* the exclusive power of *legislating, judging*

388

and executing, in all matters of a general nature. Every thing of a private or provincial nature, must still rest on the ground of the respective state-constitutions.[2]

After examining the limits of the proposed congressional powers, I confess I do not think them too extensive—I firmly believe that the life, liberty and property of every man, and the peace and independence of each state, will be more fully secured under such a constitution of federal government, than they will under a constitution with more limited powers; and infinitely more safe than under our boasted distinct sovereignties. It appears to me that Congress will have no more power than will be necessary for our union and general welfare; and such power they must have or we are in a wretched state. On the adoption of this constitution, I should value real estate twenty per cent. higher than I do at this moment.

I will not examine into the extent of the powers proposed to be lodged in the supreme federal head; the subject would be extensive and require more time than I could bestow upon it. But I will take up some objections, that have been made to particular points of the new constitution.

Most of the objections I have yet heard to the constitution, consist in mere insinuations unsupported by reasoning or fact. They are thrown out to instil groundless jealousies into the minds of the people, and probably with a view to prevent all government; for there are, in every society, some turbulent geniuses whose importance depends solely on faction. To seek the insidious and detestable nature of these insinuations, it is necessary to mention, and to remark on a few particulars.

I. The first objection against the constitution is, that the legislature will be more expensive than our present confederation. This is so far from being true, that the money we actually lose by our present weakness, disunion and *want of government* would support the civil government of every state in the confederacy. Our public poverty does not proceed from the expensiveness of Congress, nor of the civil list; but from want of power to command our own advantages. We pay more money to foreign nations, in the course of business, and merely for *want of government,* than would, under an efficient government, pay the annual interest of our domestic debt. Every

2. See Madison to Washington, 16 April 1787.

man in business knows this to be *truth;* and the objection can be designed only to delude the ignorant.

2. Another objection to the constitution, is the division of the legislature into two branches. Luckily this objection has no advocates but in Pennsylvania; and even here their number is dwindling. The factions that reign in this state, the internal discord and passions that disturb the government and the peace of the inhabitants, have detected the errors of the constitution, and will some time or other produce a reformation. The division of the legislature has been the subject of discussion in the beginning of this essay; and will be deemed, by nineteen-twentieths of the Americans, one of the principal excellencies of the constitution.

3. A third insinuation, is that the proposed federal government will annihilate the several legislatures. This is extremely disingenuous. Every person, capable of reading, must discover, that the convention have labored to draw the line between the federal and provincial powers—to define the powers of Congress, and limit them to those general concerns which *must* come under federal jurisdiction, and which *cannot* be managed in the separate legislatures—that in all internal regulations, whether of civil or criminal nature, the states retain their sovereignty, and have it guaranteed to them by this very constitution. Such a groundless insinuation, or rather mere surmise, must proceed from dark designs or extreme ignorance, and deserves the severest reprobation.

4. It is alledged that the liberty of the press is not guaranteed by the new constitution. But this objection is wholly unfounded. The liberty of the press does not come within the jurisdiction of federal government. It is firmly established in all the states either by law, or positive declarations in *bills of right;* and not being mentioned in the federal constitution, is not—and cannot be abridged by Congress. It stands on the basis of the respective state-constitutions. Should any state resign to Congress the exclusive jurisdiction of a certain district, which should include any town where presses are already established, it is in the power of the state to reserve the liberty of the press, or any other fundamental privilege, and make it an immutable condition of the grant, that such rights shall never be violated. All objections therefore on this score are *"baseless visions."*

5. It is insinuated that the constitution gives Congress the power of levying internal taxes at pleasure. This insinuation seems founded on the eighth section of the first article, which declares, that "Congress shall have power to lay and collect taxes, duties, imposts and excises, to pay the debts and provide for the common defence and general welfare of the United States."

That Congress should have power to collect duties, imposts and excises, in order to render them uniform throughout the United States will hardly be controverted. The whole objection is to the right of levying internal taxes.

But it will be conceded that the supreme head of the states must have power, competent to the purposes of our union, or it will be, as it now is, a *useless body*, a mere expense, without any advantage. To pay our public debt, to support foreign ministers and our own civil government, money must be raised; and if the duties and imposts are not adequate to these purposes, where shall the money be obtained? It will be answered, let Congress apportion the sum to be raised, and leave the legislatures to collect the money. Well this is all that is intended by the clause under consideration; with the addition of a federal power that shall be sufficient to oblige a delinquent state to comply with the requisition. Such power must exist somewhere, or the debts of the United States can never be paid. For want of such power, our credit is lost and our national faith is a bye-word.

For want of such power, one state now complies fully with a requisition, another partially, and a third absolutely refuses or neglects to grant a shilling. Thus the honest and punctual are doubly loaded—and the knave triumphs in his negligence. In short, no honest man will dread a power that shall enforce an equitable system of taxation. The dishonest are ever apprehensive of a power that shall oblige them to do what honest men are ready to do voluntarily.

Permit me to ask those who object to this power of taxation, how shall money be raised to discharge our honest debts which are universally acknowledged to be just? Have we not already experienced the inefficacy of a system without power? Has it not been proved to demonstration, that a voluntary compliance with the demands of the union can never be expected? To what expedient shall we have recourse? What is the resort of all governments in cases of delinquency? Do not the states vest in the legislature, or even in the governor and council, a power to enforce laws, even with the militia of the states? And how rarely does there exist the necessity of exerting such a power? Why should such a power be more dangerous in Congress than in a legislature? Why should more confidence be reposed in a member of one legislature than of another? Why should we choose the best men in the state to represent us in Congress, and the moment they are elected arm ourselves against them as against tyrants and robbers? Do we not, in this conduct, act the part of a man, who, as soon as he has married a woman of unsuspected chastity, locks her up in a dungeon? Is there any spell or charm, that instantly changes a delegate to Congress from an honest man into a knave—a tyrant? I confess freely that I am willing to trust Congress with any powers that I should dare lodge in a state-legislature. I believe life, liberty, and property is as safe in the hands of a federal legislature, organized in the manner proposed by the convention, as in the hands of any legislature, that has ever been or ever will be chosen in any particular state.

But the idea that Congress can levy taxes *at pleasure* is false, and the suggestion wholly unsupported. The preamble to the constitution is declaratory of the purposes of our union, and the assumption of any powers not necessary to *establish justice, insure domestic tranquility, provide for the common defence, promote the general welfare, and to secure the blessings of liberty to ourselves and our posterity,* will be unconstitutional, and endanger the existence of Congress. Besides, in the very clause which gives the power of levying duties and taxes, the purposes to which the money shall be appropriated are specified, viz. *to pay the debts and provide for the common defence and general welfare of the United States.** For these purposes money must be collected, and the

* The clause may at first appear ambiguous. It may be uncertain whether we should read and understand it thus—"The Congress shall have power to lay and collect taxes, duties, imposts and excises *in order to pay the debts,*" &c. or whether the meaning is—"The Congress shall have power to lay and collect taxes, duties, imposts and excises, and *shall have power to pay the debts,*" &c. On considering the construction of the clause, and comparing it with the preamble, the last sense seems to be improbable and absurd. But it is not very material; for no powers are vested in Congress but what are included under the general expressions, of *providing for the common defence and general welfare of the United States.* Any powers not promotive of these purposes, will be unconstitutional;—consequently any appropriations of money to any other purpose will expose the Congress to the resentment of the states, and the members to impeachment and loss of their seats.

power of collection must be lodged, sooner or later, in a federal head; or the common defence and general welfare must be neglected.

The states in their separate capacity, cannot provide for the *common* defence; nay in case of a civil war, a state cannot secure its own existence. The only question therefore is, whether it is necessary to unite, and provide for our *common defence and general welfare.* For this question being once decided in the affirmative, leaves no room to controvert the propriety of constituting a power over the whole United States, adequate to these general purposes.

The states, by granting such power, do not throw it out of their own hands—they only throw, each its proportion, into a common stock—they merely combine the powers of the several states into one point, where they *must* be collected, before they *can* be exerted. But the powers are still in their own hands; and cannot be alienated, till they create a body independent of themselves, with a force at their command, superior to the whole yeomanry of the country.

6. It is said there is no provision made in the new constitution against a standing army in time of peace. Why do not people object that no provision is made against the introduction of a body of Turkish Janizaries; or against making the Alcoran the rule of faith and practice, instead of the Bible? The answer to such objections is simply this—*no such provision is necessary.* The people in this country cannot forget their apprehensions from a British standing army, quartered in America; and they turn their fears and jealousies against themselves. Why do not the people of most of the states apprehend danger from standing armies from their own legislatures? Pennsylvania and North Carolina, I believe, are the only states that have provided against this danger at all events. Other states have declared that "no standing armies shall be kept up without the consent of the legislature." But this leaves the power entirely in the hands of the legislature. Many of the states however have made *no provision* against this evil. What hazards these states suffer! Why does not a man pass a law in his family, that no armed soldier shall be quartered in his house by his consent? The reason is very plain: no man will suffer his liberty to be abridged, or endangered—his disposition and his power are uniformly opposed to any infringement of his rights. In the same manner, the principles and habits, as well as the power of the Americans

are directly opposed to standing armies; and there is as little necessity to guard against them by positive constitutions, as to prohibit the establishment of the Mahometan religion. But the constitution provides for our safety; and while it gives Congress power to raise armies, it declares that no appropriation of money to their support shall be for a longer term than two years.

Congress likewise are to have power to provide for organizing, arming and disciplining the militia, but have no other command of them, except when in actual service. Nor are they at liberty to call out the militia at pleasure—but only, to execute the laws of the union, suppress insurrections, and repel invasions. For these purposes, government must always be armed with a military force, if the occasion should require it; otherwise laws are nugatory, and life and property insecure.

7. Some persons have ventured to publish an intimation, that by the proposed constitution, the trial by jury is abolished in all *civil cases*. Others very modestly insinuate, that it is in *some cases* only. The fact is, that trial by jury is not affected in *any* case, by the constitution; except in cases of impeachment, which are to be tried by the senate. None but persons in office in or under Congress can be impeached; and even after a judgment upon an impeachment, the offender is liable to a prosecution, before a common jury, in a regular course of law. The insinuation therefore that trials by jury are to be abolished, is groundless, and beyond conception, wicked. It must be wicked, because the circulation of a barefaced falsehood, respecting a privilege, dear to freemen, can proceed only from a depraved heart and the worst intentions.

8. It is also intimated as a probable event, that the federal courts will absorb the judiciaries of the federal states. This is a mere suspicion, without the least foundation. The jurisdiction of the federal states is very accurately defined and easily understood. It extends to the cases mentioned in the constitution, and to the execution of the laws of Congress, respecting commerce, revenue, and other general concerns.

With respect to other civil and criminal actions, the powers and jurisdiction of the several judiciaries of each state, remain unimpaired. Nor is there anything novel in allowing appeals to the supreme court. Actions are mostly to be tried in the state where the crimes are committed—But appeals are allowed under our present confederation, and no person complains; nay, were there no appeal, every man would have reason to complain, especially when a final judgement, in an inferior court, should affect property to a large amount. But why is an objection raised against an appellate jurisdiction in the supreme court, respecting *fact* as well as *law*? Is it less safe to have the opinions of two juries than of one? I suspect many people will think this is no defect in the constitution. But perhaps it will destroy a material requisite of a good jury, viz. their vicinity to the cause of action. I have no doubt, that when causes were tried, in periods prior to the Christian æra, before twelve men, seated upon twelve stones, arranged in a circular form, under a huge oak, there was great propriety in submitting causes to men *in the vicinity.* The difficulty of collecting evidence, in those rude times, rendered it necessary that juries should judge mostly from their own knowledge of facts or from information obtained out of court. But in these polished ages, when juries depend almost wholly on the testimony of witnesses; and when a complication of interests, introduced by commerce and other causes, renders it almost impossible to collect men, in the vicinity of the parties, who are wholly disinterested, it is no disadvantage to have a cause tried by a jury of strangers. Indeed the latter is generally the most eligible.

But the truth is, the creation of all inferior courts is in the power of Congress; and the constitution provides that Congress may make such exceptions from the right of appeals as they shall judge proper. When these courts are erected, their jurisdictions will be ascertained, and in small actions, Congress will doubtless direct that a sentence in a subordinate court shall, to a certain amount, be definite and final. All objections therefore to the judicial powers of the federal courts appear to me as trifling as any of the preceding.

9. But, say the enemies of slavery, negroes may be imported for twenty-one years. This exception is addressed to the quakers; and a very pitiful exception it is.

The truth is, Congress cannot prohibit the importation of slaves during that period; but the laws against the importation into particular states, stand unrepealed. An immediate abolition of slavery would bring ruin upon the whites, and misery upon the blacks, in the southern states. The constitution has therefore wisely left each state to pursue its own measures, with respect to this article of legislation, during the period of twenty-one years.[3]

Such are the principal objections that have yet been made by the enemies of the new constitution. They are mostly frivolous, or founded on false constructions, and a misrepresentation of the true state of facts. They are evidently designed to raise groundless jealousies in the minds of well meaning people, who have little leisure and opportunity to examine into the principles of government. But a little time and reflection will enable most people to detect such mischievous intentions; and the spirit and firmness which have distinguished the conduct of the Americans, during the conflict for independence, will eventually triumph over the enemies of union, and bury them in disgrace or oblivion.

But I cannot quit this subject without attempting to correct some of the erroneous opinions respecting *freedom and tyranny,* and the principles by which they are supported. Many people seem to entertain an idea, that liberty consists in *a power to act without any control.* This is more liberty than even the savages enjoy. But in civil society, political liberty consists in *acting conformably to a sense of a majority of the society.* In a free government every man binds himself to obey the *public voice,* or the opinions of a majority; and the *whole society* engages to *protect each individual.* In such a government a man is *free* and safe. But reverse the case; suppose every man to act without control or fear of punishment—every man would be free, but no man would be sure of his freedom one moment. Each would have the power of taking his neighbor's life, liberty, or property; and no man would command more than his own strength to repel the invasion. The case is the same with states. If the states should not unite into one compact society, every state may trespass upon its neighbor, and the injured state has no means of redress but its own military force.

The present situation of our American states is very little better than a state of nature—Our boasted state sovereignties are so far from securing

3. See Storing, "Slavery and the Moral Foundations of the American Republic," in Robert Horowitz, ed., *The Moral Foundations of the American Republic* (Charlottesville: University Press of Virginia, 1977).

our liberty and property, that they, every moment, expose us to the loss of both. That state which commands the heaviest purse and longest sword, may at any moment, lay its weaker neighbor under tribute; and there is no superior power now existing, that can regularly oppose the invasion or redress the injury. From such liberty, O Lord, deliver us!

But what is tyranny? Or how can a free people be deprived of their liberties? Tyranny is the exercise of some power over a man, which is not warranted by law, or necessary for the public safety. A people can never be deprived of their liberties, while they retain in their own hands, a power sufficient to any other power in the state. This position leads me directly to enquire, in what consists the power of a nation or of an order of men?

In some nations, legislators have derived much of their power from the influence of religion, or from that implicit belief which an ignorant and superstitious people entertain of the gods, and their interposition in every transaction of life. The Roman senate sometimes availed themselves of this engine to carry their decrees and maintain their authority. This was particularly the case, under the aristocracy which succeeded the abolition of the monarchy. The augurs and priests were taken wholly from patrician families.* They constituted a distinct order of men—had power to negative any law of the people, by declaring that it was passed during the taking of the auspices.† This influence derived from the authority of opinion, was less perceptible, but as tyrannical as a military force. The same influence constitutes, at this day, a principal support of federal governments on the Eastern continent, and perhaps in South America. But in North America, by a singular concurrence of circumstances, the possibility of establishing this influence, as a pillar of government, is totally precluded.

Another source of power in government is a military force. But this, to be efficient, must be superior to any force that exists among the people, or which they can command: for otherwise this force would be annihilated,

---

*"Quod nemo plebeius auspicia haberet, ideoque decemviros connubium diremisse, ne incerta prole auspicia turbarentur." Tit. Liv. lib. 4. cap. 6.

†Auguriis certe sacerdotisque augurum tantus honos accessit, ut nihil belli domique postea, nisi auspicato, gereretur: concilia populi, exercitus vocati, summa rerum, ubi aves non admisissent, dirimerentur. Liv. lib. I. cap. 37.

on the first exercise of acts of oppression. Before a standing army can rule, the people must be disarmed; as they are in almost every kingdom in Europe. The supreme power in America cannot enforce unjust laws by the sword; because the whole body of the people are armed, and constitute a force superior to any band of regular troops that can be, on any pretence, raised in the United States. A military force, at the command of Congress, can execute no laws, but such as the people perceive to be just and constitutional; for they will possess the *power,* and jealousy will instantly inspire the *inclination,* to resist the execution of a law which appears to them unjust and oppressive. In spite of all the nominal powers, vested in Congress by the constitution, were the system once adopted in its fullest latitude, still the actual exercise of them would be frequently interrupted by popular jealousy. I am bold to say, that *ten* just and constitutional measures would be resisted, where *one* unjust or oppressive law would be enforced. The powers vested in Congress are little more than *nominal;* nay *real* power cannot be vested in them, nor in any body, but in the *people.* The source of power is in the *people* of this country, and cannot for ages, and probably never will, be removed.

In what then does *real* power consist? The answer is short and plain—in *property.* Could we want any proofs of this, which are not exhibited in this country, the uniform testimony of history will furnish us with multitudes. But I will go no farther for proof, than the two governments already mentioned, the Roman and the British.

Rome exhibited a demonstrative proof of the inseparable connexion between property and dominion. The first form of its government was an elective monarchy—its second, an aristocracy; but these forms could not be permanent, because they were not supported by property. The kings at first and afterwards the patricians had nominally most of the power; but the people, possessing most of the lands, never ceased to assert their privileges, till they established a commonwealth. And the kings and senate could not have held the reigns of government in their hands so long as they did, had they not artfully contrived to manage the established religion, and play off the superstitious credulity of the people against their own power. "Thus this weak constitution of government," says the ingenious Mr. Moyle, speaking of the aristocracy of Rome, "not founded on the true *center of dominion, land,* nor on any standing foundation of authority, nor rivetted in the esteem and affections of the people; and being attacked by strong passion, general interest and the joint forces of the people, mouldered away of course, and pined of a lingering consumption, till it was totally swallowed up by the prevailing faction, and the nobility were moulded into the mass of the people."* The people, notwithstanding the nominal authority of the patricians, proceeded regularly in enlarging their own powers. They first extorted from the senate, the right of electing *tribunes,* with a negative upon the proceedings of the senate.† They obtained the right of proposing and debating laws; which before had been vested in the senate; and finally advanced to the power of enacting laws, without the authority of the senate.‡ They regained the rights of election in their comitia, of which they had been deprived by Servius Tullius.§ They procured a permanent body of laws, collected from the Grecian institutions. They destroyed the influence of augurs, or diviners, by establishing the *tributa comitia,* in which they were not allowed to consult the gods. They increased their power by large accessions of conquered lands. They procured a repeal of the law which prohibited marriages between the patricians and plebians. ‖ The Licinian law limited all possessions to five hundred acres of land; which, had it been fully executed, would have secured the commonwealth.#

The Romans proceeded thus step by step to triumph over the aristocracy, and to crown their privileges, they procured the right of being elected to the highest offices of the state. By acquiring *the property* of the plebians, the nobility, several times, held most of the power of the state; but the people,

---

*Essay on the Roman government.[4]

4. Walter Moyle, *A Select Collection of Tracts . . . Containing, I. An Essay Upon the Roman Government . . .* (Glasgow, 1750).

†Livy, 2. 33.

‡Livy, 3. 54.

§Livy, 3. 33.

‖ Livy, 4. 6.

#Livy, 6. 35. 42. "Ne quis plus quingenta jugera agri possideret."

by reducing the interest of money, abolishing debts, or by forcing other advantages from the patricians, generally held the power of governing in their own hands.

In America, we begin our empire with more popular privileges than the Romans ever enjoyed. We have not to struggle against a monarch or an aristocracy—power is lodged in the mass of the people.

On reviewing the English history, we observe a progress similar to that in Rome—an incessant struggle for liberty from the date of Magna Charta, in John's reign, to the revolution. The struggle has been successful, by abridging the enormous power of the nobility. But we observe that the power of the people has increased in an exact proportion to their acquisitions of property. Wherever the right of primogeniture is established, property must accumulate and remain in families. Thus the landed property in England will never be sufficiently distributed, to give the powers of government wholly into the hands of the people. But to assist the struggle for liberty, commerce has interposed, and in conjunction with manufacturers, thrown a vast weight of property into the democratic scale. Wherever we cast our eyes, we see this truth, that *property* is the basis of *power;* and this, being established as a cardinal point, directs us to the means of preserving our freedom. Make laws, irrevocable laws in every state, destroying and barring entailments; leave real estates to revolve from hand to hand, as time and accident may direct; and no family influence can be acquired and established for a series of generations—no man can obtain dominion over a large territory—the laborious and saving, who are generally the best citizens, will possess each his share of property and power, and thus the balance of wealth and power will continue where it is, in the *body of the people.*

A general and tolerably equal distribution of landed property is the whole basis of national freedom: The system of the great Montesquieu will ever be erroneous, till the words *property or lands in fee simple* are substituted for *virtue,* throughout his *Spirit of Laws.*

Virtue, patriotism, or love of country, never was and never will be, till men's natures are changed, a fixed, permanent principle and support of government. But in an agricultural country, a general possession of land in fee simple, may be rendered perpetual, and the inequalities introduced by commerce, are too fluctuating to endanger government. An equality of property, with a necessity of alienation, constantly operating to destroy combinations of powerful families, is the very *soul of a republic*—While this continues, the people will inevitably possess both *power* and *freedom;* when this is lost, power departs, liberty expires, and a commonwealth will inevitably assume some other form.

The liberty of the press, trial by jury, the Habeas Corpus writ, even Magna Charta itself, although justly deemed the palladia of freedom, are all inferior considerations, when compared with a general distribution of real property among every class of people.* The power of entailing estates is more dangerous to liberty and republican government, than all the constitutions that

---

*Montesquieu supposed *virtue* to be the principle of a republic. He derived his notions of this form of government, from the astonishing firmness, courage and patriotism which distinguished the republics of Greece and Rome. But this *virtue* consisted in pride, contempt of strangers and a martial enthusiasm which sometimes displayed itself in defence of their country. These principles are never permanent—they decay with refinement, intercourse with other nations and increase of wealth. No wonder then that these republics declined, for they were not founded on fixed principles; and hence authors imagine that republics cannot be durable. None of the celebrated writers on government seems to have laid sufficient stress on a general possession of real property in fee-simple. Even the author of the *Political Sketches,* in the *Museum* for the month of September, seems to have passed it over in silence; although he combats Montesquieu's system, and to prove it false, enumerates some of the principles which distinguish our governments from others, and which he supposes constitutes the support of republics.

The English writers on law and government consider Magna Charta, trial by juries, the Habeas Corpus act, and the liberty of the press, as the bulwarks of freedom. All this is well. But in no government of consequence in Europe, is freedom established on its true and immoveable foundation. The property is too much accumulated, and the accumulations too well guarded, to admit the *true principle of republics.* But few centuries have elapsed, since the body of the people were vassals. To such men, the smallest extension of popular privileges, was deemed an invaluable blessing. Hence the encomiums upon trial by juries, and the articles just mentioned. But these people have never been able to mount to the source of *liberty, estates in fee,* or at least but partially; they are yet obliged to drink at the streams. Hence the English jealousy of certain rights, which are guaranteed by acts of parliament. But in America, and here alone, we have gone at once to the *fountain of liberty,* and raised the people to their true dignity. Let the lands be possessed by the people in fee-simple, let the fountain be kept pure, and the streams will be pure of course. Our jealousy of *trial by jury, the liberty of the press,* &c., is totally groundless. Such rights are inseparably connected with the *power* and *dignity* of the people, which rest on their *property.* They cannot be abridged. All *other* nations have wrested *property* and *freedom* from *barons* and *tyrants; we* begin our empire with full possession of property and all its attending rights.

can be written on paper, or even than a standing army. Let the people have property, and they *will* have power—a power that will for ever be exerted to prevent a restriction of the press, and abolition of trial by jury, or the abridgement of any other privilege. The liberties of America, therefore, and her forms of government, stand on the broadest basis. Removed from the fears of a foreign invasion and conquest, they are not exposed to the convulsions that shake other governments; and the principles of freedom are so general and energetic, as to exclude the possibility of a change in our republican constitutions.

But while *property* is considered as the *basis* of the freedom of the American yeomanry, there are other auxiliary supports; among which is the *information of the people.* In no country, is education so general—in no country, have the body of the people such a knowledge of the rights of men and the principles of government. This knowledge, joined with a keen sense of liberty and a watchful jealousy, will guard our constitutions, and awaken the people to an instantaneous resistance of encroachments.

But a principal bulwark of freedom is the *right of election.* An equal distribution of property is the *foundation* of a republic; but *popular elections* form the *great barrier,* which defends it from assault, and guards it from the slow and imperceptible approaches of corruption. Americans! never resign that right. It is not very material whether your representatives are elected for one year or two—but the *right* is the Magna Charta of your governments. For this reason, expunge that clause of the new constitution before mentioned, which gives Congress an influence in the election of their own body. The *time, place* and *manner* of chusing senators or representatives are of little or no consequence to Congress. The number of members and time of meeting in Congress are fixed; but the *choice* should rest with the several states. I repeat it—reject the clause with decency, but with unanimity and firmness.

Excepting that clause the constitution is good—it guarantees the *fundamental principles* of our several constitutions—it guards our rights—and while it vests extensive powers in Congress, it vests no more than are necessary for our union. Without powers lodged somewhere in a single body, fully competent to lay and collect equal taxes and duties—to adjust controversies between different states—to silence contending interests—to suppress insurrections—to regulate commerce—to treat with foreign nations, our confederation is a cobweb—liable to be blown asunder by every blast of faction that is raised in the remotest corner of the United States.

Every motive that can possibly influence men ever to unite under civil government, now urges the unanimous adoption of the new constitution. But in America we are urged to it by a singular necessity. By the local situation of the several states *a few* command *all* the advantages of commerce. Those states which have no advantages, made equal exertions for independence, loaded themselves with immense debts, and now are utterly unable to discharge them; while their richer neighbors are taxing them for their own benefit, merely because they *can*. I can prove to a demonstration that Connecticut, which has the heaviest internal or state debt, in proportion to its number of inhabitants, of any in the union, cannot discharge its debt, on any principles of taxation ever yet practised. Yet the state pays in duties, at least 100,000 dollars annually, on goods consumed by its own people, but imported by New York. This sum, could it be saved to the state by an equal system of revenue, would enable that state to gradually sink its debt.*

New Jersey and some other states are in the same situation, except that their debts are not so large, in proportion to their wealth and population.

The boundaries of the several states were not drawn with a view to independence; and while this country was subject to Great Britain, they produced no commercial or political inconveniences. But the revolution has placed things on a different footing. The advantages of some states, and the disadvantages of others are so great—and so materially affect the business and interest of each, that nothing but an equalizing system of revenue, that shall reduce the advantages to some equitable proportion, can prevent a civil war and save the national debt. Such a system of revenue is the *sine qua non* of public justice and tranquillity.

It is absurd for a man to oppose the adoption of the constitution, because *he* thinks some part of it defective or exceptionable. Let every man be at liberty to expunge what *he* judges to be exceptionable, and not a syllable of the constitution will survive the scrutiny. A painter, after executing a mas-

*The state debt of Connecticut is about 3,500,000 dollars, its proportion of the federal debt about the same sum. The annual interest of the whole 420,000 dollars.

terly piece, requested every spectator to draw a pencil mark over the part that did not please him; but to his surprise, he soon found the *whole piece* defaced. Let every man examine the most perfect building by his *own* taste, and like some microscopic critics, condemn the *whole* for small deviations from the rules of architecture, and not a part of the *best* constructed fabric would escape. But let *any* man take a *comprehensive view* of the whole, and he will be pleased with the general beauty and proportions, and admire the structure. The same remarks apply to the new constitution. I have no doubt that *every* member of the late convention has exceptions to *some part* of the system proposed. Their constituents have the same, and if *every* objection must be removed, before we have a national government, the Lord have mercy on us.

Perfection is not the lot of humanity. Instead of censuring the small faults of the constitution, I am astonished that so many clashing interests have been reconciled—and so many sacrifices made to the *general interest*! The mutual concessions made by the gentlemen of the convention, reflect the highest honor on their candor and liberality; at the same time, they prove that their minds were deeply impressed with a conviction, that such mutual sacrifices are *essential to our union*. They *must* be made sooner or later by every state; or jealousies, local interests and prejudices will unsheath the sword, and some Cæsar or Cromwell will avail himself of our divisions, and wade to a throne through streams of blood.

It is not our duty as freemen, to receive the opinions of any men however great and respectable, without an examination. But when we reflect that some of the greatest men in America, with the venerable FRANKLIN and the illustrious WASHINGTON at their head; *some* of them the *fathers* and *saviors* of their country, men who have labored at the helm during a long and violent tempest, and guided us to the haven of peace—and *all* of them distinguished for their abilities [and] their acquaintance with ancient and modern governments, as well as with the temper, the passions, the interests and the wishes of the Americans;—when we reflect on these circumstances, it is impossible to resist impressions of respect, and we are almost impelled to suspect our own judgements, when we call in question any part of the system, which they have recommended for adoption. Not having the same means of information, we are more liable to mistake the nature and tendency of particular articles of the constitution, or the reasons on which they were admitted. Great confidence therefore should be reposed in the abilities, the zeal and integrity of that respectable body. But after all, if the constitution should, in its future operation, be found defective or inconvenient, two-thirds of both houses of Congress or the application of two-thirds of the legislatures, may open the door for amendments. Such improvements may then be made, as experience shall dictate.

Let us then consider the *New Federal Constitution,* as it really is, an *improvement* on the *best* constitutions that the world ever saw. In the house of representatives, the people of America have an equal voice and suffrage. The choice of men is placed in the freemen or electors at large; and the frequency of elections, and the responsibility of the members, will render them sufficiently dependent on their constituents. The senate will be composed of older men; and while their regular dismission from office, once in six years, will preserve their dependence on their constituents, the duration of their existence will give firmness to their decisions, and temper the factions which must necessarily prevail in the other branch. The president of the United States is elective, and what is a capital improvement on the best governments, the mode of chusing him excludes the danger of faction and corruption. As the supreme executive, he is invested with power to enforce the laws of the union and give energy to the federal government.

The constitution defines the powers of Congress; and every power not expressly delegated to that body, remains in the several state-legislatures. The sovereignty and the republican form of government of each state is guaranteed by the constitution; and the bounds of jurisdiction between the federal and respective state governments, are marked with precision. In theory, it has all the energy and freedom of the British and Roman governments, without their defects. In short, the privileges of freemen are interwoven into the feelings and habits of the Americans; *liberty* stands on the immoveable basis of a general distribution of property and diffusion of knowledge; but the Americans must cease to contend, to fear, and to hate, before they can realize the benefits of independence and government, or enjoy the blessings, which heaven has lavished, in rich profusion, upon this western world.

"A Foreign Spectator"
[Nicholas Collin]

"An Essay on the Means of Promoting Federal Sentiments in the United States": I, IV, VI, VII, X, XV, XX, XXI, XXIII

Independent Gazetteer, Philadelphia, 6, 10, 16, 17, 24 August and 4, 12, 13, 17 September 1787

I

An ESSAY on the Means of Promoting Federal Sentiments in the United States, by a Foreign Spectator.

It is an old maxim, that no Republican Government can be lasting without the good will of its subjects. What majority of loyal citizens, or what degree of public virtue, are indispensable, depends indeed on many circumstances; but the greater they are, the more safe and happy is a state; and in many cases an apparently small defect in either may produce very critical dangers. Republican Liberty is inseparable from a certain want of energy in the Government: The indolent and selfish can often with impunity clog its most important operations: The disaffected may go deep into rebellion, before they can be legally impeached: Infernal traitors may sometimes assume the heavenly form of patriots, and while they point a dagger to the bosom of their country, are by insane multitudes idolized as its guardian angels.

The people of a Federal Republic stand in the double relation, as citizens of a particular state, and citizens of the United States: In the former they think and act for their respective Republics, in the latter for the whole Confederacy. As Federal subjects it is their duty to promote the general interest—to regard their own state only as a Member of the Union—and to allow it only a just proportion. Those rights of the Federal Republic, and of each particular state, which are defined by the articles of Confederation, must be faithfully supported. The Federal Allegiance is supreme, and obligates every person to be an enemy of his own state, if it should prove treacherous to the Union. In cases not clearly defined by the Constitution, or when the occasional surrender of a right is very beneficial to the Confederacy, for another state, a generous condescension, and a Federal affection are very salutary.

In Federal Monarchies or Aristocracies the people in general need not have any high Federal sentiments; it is enough, that they are attached to their own governments, and that these act their part in the Federal System. But in United Republics a general Federal spirit is necessary: because a want of it will naturally be visible in the several Legislatures, which bear the complexion of their constituents, and often are the mere interpreters of their wishes; and because Federal measures adopted by a wise and patriotic state government could not be inforced against the sense of its people. My design is to inquire, by what means this happy Federal spirit may be improved, and not to hazard any thoughts on the political arrangement of the Confederation, except what are inseparable from my subject.

Four grand operations appear to me necessary—to promote a general disposition for order and Government—to limit the political Union of the respective states—to prevent any partial affection between two or more—and to render the Confederacy an object of general attachment. These operations admirably support and facilitate each other, and being more or less performed by the same means, cannot be treated separately. The Ruler of the Universe has disposed the principles of our political felicity in this charming harmony; woe be to those discordant minds, that wish to frustrate his divine design.

Man is naturally an unruly animal, little capable of governing himself, and very averse to controul from others. Any person in the least acquainted with human life, knows how fatal unrestrained liberty is to the individual and society. It is absurd to expect, that a man, whose will was never curbed, can be a dutiful subject of any Government; but whoever has by a cultivated reason, and the salutary check of others, learnt to govern his passions, will easily submit to a legal civil authority. Several causes of long standing have very generally marked the American character with an overdriven sense of liberty. Parents are very indulgent to their children—very few families have private tutors—some country places have no public schools, many only at times, and often kept by indifferent masters. The facility of subsisting by very moderate industry makes every person independent. Superiority of birth, fortune, and office has hitherto been very trifling. Ecclesiastical authority has been little or nothing. The Negro slavery has no doubt often created habits of pride, dominion and severity. Taxes, and other burdens of civil Government have till the revolution been extremely easy. This high sense of liberty has indeed, even in ruder minds, produced a fierce independent spirit, without which the revolution could not have been effected, but it has also in too many created a licentiousness, at present very detrimental, and incompatible with good Government.

The jealous fondness of liberty so common among republicans, makes them very loth to grant the necessary powers of Government to their duly elected Representatives: the more ignorant and turbulent pretend, that the people have a right to disobey any disagreeable law—nay, to call their Legislators to an account—a doctrine subversive of all Government. In Federal Republics these ideas are still more prevalent; because, if it is dangerous, to give full power of attorney to a person of our own choice, it is much more so to delegate it to one chosen by him. In America, an excessive love of liberty and the novelty of a Federal constitution, combine to render great numbers averse from the so necessary and rational Government of a Supreme Congress; though it has proved so worthy of the public trust.

Knowledge, prudence, temperence, industry, honor, decency, justice, benevolence—all those qualities, which enable men to govern themselves, to regard the rights of others, to respect superior merit, to love order and tranquillity, are so many excellent dispositions for civil Government. They are necessary in Republics, where the energy of Government depends on a chearful obedience. As the people cannot be led as children, or drove as mules, the only method is, to make them rational beings. Men of reflection have the advantage, not only to see things in extensive combinations, and remote consequences, but to feel an important truth with more sensibility;

because in a chain of reasoning the result does not forcibly strike the mind, except it can rapidly run through the links—doubts or slow apprehension dull the feeling. This accounts for the great difficulty of persuading thought-less people in the greatest concerns, even when their understanding is at last convinced. Thus a man well acquainted with political principles, and the fate of Empires, will feelingly perceive the dreadful catastrophes, that must ensue from a weakness of Federal Union; but let an ignorant clown hear the clearest discourse on the subject—he will at the conclusion think; this may be; that looks very likely: however I'll think farther on it. Political knowledge cannot be too much encouraged. Pope's maxim is here appli-cable: a little learning is a dangerous thing—drink deep, or touch not the Castalian spring. America has many great politicians; but as a sensible gentleman very justly observed, the people in general have too much, and too little. The wretched dialogues on politics so frequent in the taverns and elsewhere, please the mirthy not less than the novel of Peregrine Pickle, while they enrage the splenetic, and grieve the serious patriot. These political tink-ers think themselves capable of governing a universal monarchy: speak with contempt of their Legislators, as *the servants of the public,* and declaim with more than royal pride, on *the Majesty of the people,* meaning in fact their own servants, and their own majesty.

By various excellent improvements in the public education, the institu-tion of political societies throughout the continent, much may be done. We must however not form a Utopian scheme of making every citizen an enlightened patriot. God has not granted such perfection to human nature in the present state; but ordered the wise and good to direct their weaker brethren, and to chastise refractory members of society. Far be it from me, to recommend passive obedience, or too mechanical habits of discipline: I would rather have the people turbulent than servile. But if men submit to the fidelity and better knowledge of others in their greatest concerns—if they trust their lives in the hands of a physician—if they commit themselves, their families, and properties to the care of an experienced mariner; it is unreasonable to deny their best fellow-citizens, whom they freely chose, those powers of Government absolutely necessary for the well-being of the community, and their own. The majority of a Legislature may indeed sometimes do wrong; but it is very improbable, that there should be less wisdom and integrity in the flower of a nation, chosen as such, than in tumultuary multitudes, or the discontented individuals scattered over the country, whose number and grievances often appear great only from the loudness and frequency of their complaints. The necessity of human affairs requires even obedience to laws evidently wrong; and nothing but measures atrociously and immediately pernicious can justify resistance, when the people have the right to remonstrate, and to change the Legislators in a short time. These principles are the plain dictates of sound common sense, and should be engraved on every American heart. Religion itself sanctifies them: it commands us to be subject for conscience sake, to regard the civil power as the minister of God for our good. Rom: 13, and not to use liberty as a cloak of maliciousness 1 Pet: 2. If the almighty has made civil Government an indispensable means for human felicity, and if the greatest miseries and most horrid crimes are the certain fruits of anarchy; loyalty to a legal Government is a sacred duty to him, and disobedience an atrocious sin. This doctrine should be held up in the pulpit, and be taught in the catechism of every denomination. Grown children will understand it equally well with the first principles of morality. I would even insert the words *to honor and obey the Congress,* &c. Sentiments of loyalty thus imbibed with the first ideas of religion, among the best and happiest sensations of a young heart; and afterwards confirmed by reason and experience, will be dear and sacred through life.

IV

Civil society becomes, in its natural progress, by degrees more happy. The faculties of human nature are unfolded and improved; consequently better enabled to pursue and attain the means of felicity, which lie in man himself and in external nature—the many wants of reciprocal assistance in these pursuits call forth the social affections—the very competition of interests, and clashing of passions, teach the necessity of good manners, and moral government. I say, *a natural progress*—because a civil society may set out in a wrong way; or in a prosperous career be retarded, misled, and entangled by the ignorance or ill designs of the guides, or the laziness, obstinacy, disorder of its members. The progress of civilization in the United States will, if properly conducted, gradually improve the dispositions necessary for civil government, and the federal in particular. The rapid encrease of population will soon multiply and draw closer the links of society. Idleness and a slovenly œconomy will then be corrected by a sense of real want, or at least the loss of great comforts. The labouring people must work more; yet will be much happier by a greater sobriety and frugality. Smaller portions of land must be improved with more assiduous, orderly, and ingenious industry. A competition in the several trades and manufactures will produce a greater emulation, in workmanship, and complaisance to customers. Commercial dealings will require more punctuality and exactness. In Europe the payment of a small sum to the very day is often indispensable; because a trader depending on several such, cannot, if disappointed, discharge his contracts, or carry on the branches of his business; and one disappointment creates many hundred, where national industry has formed extensive and intricate connexions—In America, the neglect of payment is not so pernicious; people expect to be disappointed by each other; they can easily find credit; and the great majority, depending on agriculture, or the most useful trades, cannot at the worst want necessaries. Hence, merchants, shopkeepers, tradesmen, and farmers are in accounts with each other for years: money-hunting is a common expression, and very proper, as many hunt for days, and cannot get a shilling.

The multiplicity of interests and connexions, that increases in every progressive society, and is in America quickened by a rapid population, will improve the general manners by a deeper and more frequent sense of the necessity, propriety, and advantage of an equitable, obliging, and decent conduct—men will from interest and examples learn to check rude and selfish passions; to yield, not only to the rights, but sometimes even the fancies of others; and will be easily reconciled to this self-denial, because they receive the same good treatment from others. The civil arts will in their progress visit the ruder parts of the country; procure ease and affluence, and thereby taste and means for education, reading, social pleasures, and for the genuine elegancies of human life, which improve the understanding, embellish the imagination, and refine the passions. The necessity of civil order encreases with the multiplicity and reciprocal connexion of civil affairs—The many objects of wealth and pleasure raise eager competitions, and excite the ill-disposed to acts of violence and fraud; they also produce inordinate gratifications in luxuries—Fortune and talents will claim an invidious distinction—moral prejudices and high principles of honor may sometimes raise warm contentions—Not only malice and selfishness of individuals, but in many cases their neglect, may destroy the property and lives of thousands—Local situation, wealth, &c. may expose a nation to foreign attacks—This and commercial affairs, may involve it in extensive connexions with other powers. All this will point out the necessity of legislation, police, public defence; of a general powerful government; which cannot be supported without a chearful obedience, personal services, and pecuniary contributions—Let us compare, in this respect, a peasant from a wilder part of the country with a citizen of Philadelphia. The first has every necessary of simple life within himself; he has no law-suits, fears no thieves and robbers; knows nothing of a foreign enemy—The latter finds a jail the most necessary building in the city; he must trust a great part of his property among strangers, for which a regular administration of justice is his only security—He sees the necessity of strict police, not only for conveniency, but health, life, and his dearest interests—a rude carter may drive over his children—unlucky boys may set his house on fire by their squibs—the stinking dock may cause a putrid fever, by which he may die or lose his wife. He knows, that in case of war, a frigate may burn the city, if the river is not fortified; and that the whole militia of Pennsylvania could not defend him without a federal power. The events of Massachusetts Bay confirm my assertions; the rebellion broke out in the remoter counties—Boston and other great-towns are loyal. In Europe riots are more frequent in great towns, where a numerous and indigent populace is more corrupt than the poorest country people. In America the cities have yet but a small mob; the great body of people live in the country; and numbers have, from ignorance, rude manners, and a weak sense of social dependence, dispositions very unfavorable to civil, and especially federal, government. The civil corruption, so visible in many ancient states, and aggravated by the pens of some great political writers, has made it a very common opinion—that high civilization brings on political diseases, and final dissolution. But we should consider, that a refined civilization is not principally an immense apparatus of wealth and luxury: such a corrupt national taste will indeed be fatal—that although every period of the political body, like that of the human frame, has its peculiar disorders; yet there is not such a corruption in human nature, that men by too near approach must infect each other—that the United States, whose constitution is young, and tainted with no mortal distemper, may hope by a genuine civilization *to live forever.* Human reason is a ray from the eternal MIND, and true goodness an image of his loveliest attribute. They can in conjunction plan the felicity of the greatest political systems; must they then be confined to narrow spheres? Must they be conquered by the night of ignorance and vice! No! the constellation of noble minds shall, we hope, shed a bright day over America till time is no more.

VI

It cannot be too well considered, that as Republicans govern themselves and each other, they must be good and wise; that in this confederacy, so free and extensive, benevolence and integrity are the very elements of political union. Manners ought then to be a capital object, in all the operations of government, and patriotic exertions of individuals. There is an immediate necessity for improveing the public education. The encreasing idleness, profligacy, thieving, and robbing, among the populace of great towns, call aloud for the erection of *free schools:* without them Philadelphia will soon have a numerous and desperate mob. Reflect on the consequence—The mad rabble of a crazy *Lord Gordon,* had nearly burnt *London*—The children, that lisp horrid imprecations, and strike the pavement with impotent rage, may, when 12 years old, murder your son—The many idle boys, who do nothing but beg, play, and fight,—will soon be the very men for a rebel Shays. In the country, every town should have one or more good schools. For want of clergymen, schoolmasters are in many parts the only moral teachers; I hope to God then none among them will hereafter be illiterate knavish vagabonds: can such instructors and patterns qualify a people for domestic, social, and civil duties? for the important functions of jurymen, magistrates, electors, legislators? In some places we see good plantations with convenient buildings, well kept taverns, and shops with many articles of luxury; but no house of public worship, and miserable schools. Silly people may admire such improvement; for my part I lament this unequal civilization, and find ample reason for it: The owner of this fine plantation got it by cheating illiterate wretches, who did not know what they signed; another lately belonged to a spendthrift, who, because he knew no higher enjoyment, drank grog, and followed horse racing—Several likely girls have been seduced, under promise of marriage, by fellows, who are too free and independent for the bonds of matrimony; and besides cannot support a family, because they hate work, and must ride an *English horse*—Gentlemen of superior fortune and character, who for many years have been in civil authority, are turned out, because *they are against paper money;* and ignorant, knavish demagogues chosen for legislators—A number of labourers play at quoits for the whole day at the taverns, running in debt for liquors, while their wives and children want bread—Numerous law-suits arise from drunken frais, malice, lying, fraud, extortion, inability and unwillingness of paying debts—executions are common, and often ruinous to whole families. It is a great maxim in government, to balance the human passions: objects of wealth and pleasure are dangerous without a proper check of moral and religious principles, and sense to see the consequences of ill conduct, though in many cases remote and intricate: and the desire of these objects is not to be estimated by their real value, but the circumstances of the people. One person gets drunk on rum, another on claret. A common farmer may long as much for his neighbour's meadow, as a wealthy proprietor for a fine country seat. A chintz gown is the wish of a country girl, as a diamond stomacher of a peeress; a young rake in bright buff on a fine horse is as dangerous to her, as an embroidered beau in a coach and six is to the other. The necessary moral and religious instruction in public schools need not be impeded by the difference of religious professions. Moral principles are universal—*Whatsoever ye would that men should do unto you, even so do unto them, love thy neighbour as thyself.* These principles of equity and benevolence, are engraven on all human hearts by the same Almighty hand; known in Japan and America, in Lapland

and Otabeite. The moral precepts of Christianity are the same plain dictates of natural conscience, refined and exalted by motives of religion. I have seen in Europe, a treatise on the whole system of natural religion and morality, comprised in a small duodecimo under the title of *Dialogues between an old man and a boy of eight years:* the author in a clear and affecting manner impresses the young mind with a sense of every moral duty; even humanity to the brute creation; and the political virtues of citizens, and nations: such a book is a treasure. In the Christian religion, the catechism of Dr. Watts would be the best system, for perspicuity, and universality. In schools, where the bible, and moral writings are used, the great defect is: not to explain, apply, and combine the several moral duties; which a judicious teacher may do to the satisfaction of elder children. Some virtues are peculiarly important in a certain state of national affairs, or the circumstances of a particular county, and even township. There is an intimate connexion between the moral virtues; they defend, support and adorn each other, so that one cannot be violated without hurting the other. Few men are so ill disposed as to have no good affections; most have some tender part in the heart, by which they can be led—if therefore all the consequences of virtue and vice were clearly and pathetically pointed out to a young person; he would behold so much dignity in one virtue, beauty in another, delight in the third; he would feel the meanness, anguish, horror of the several vices; he would find the impossibility of indulging one vicious inclination, without stabbing his favourite virtue, the mistress of his heart—he must, if not of the worst clay, become a tolerable character; and if naturally good, grow excellent. Men do more frequently rush into crimes and miseries from blindness, than the impulse of a wicked heart. Many, when they awake from intoxicating passions, or behold the sparks wantonly thrown, kindle a dreadful fire; stand aghast at their woeful gilt; and unable to pluck the daggers from their hearts, plunge with despair into a dark eternity.

That religion is a most valuable security to states, by its general influence on men of diverse characters and conditions, is an opinion held not only by all the good and wise in the world, but by every thinking man. *Montesquieu* values it more than all the fear of despotism, the honor of monarchies, and the political virtue of republics. There is a striking similarity

in the sentiments of truly great minds in every age and country: Cyrus the
Great never begun a battle, before he had sacrificed to *Jupiter the ruler and
preserver;** and the great Gustavus Adolphus King of Sweden used to say,
that the best Christian was the best soldier.** The fears of religion have a
salutary check on many: if not on every vicious disposition: on some—if
not constantly; at some periods; would it then be wise, to take off one strong
chain from ungovernable beasts, and to let others quite loose on society?
Mixed characters are highly improved by the blended effect of hopes and
fears, instruction, and a certain air of tender solemnity. Minds naturally
good must derive the greatest strength and noblest elevation from a firm
belief—that every deed, and every virtuous thought are known by a most
holy God, who values moral excellency above all that is great and beautiful,
as a mirror of his own perfection—that all the toils and sufferings in the
cause of virtue, are so many dear proofs of our fidelity to HIM; and so
many steps to immortal glory and perfect felicity; where the good of every
nation shall meet, and the remembrance of every noble deed will be a source
of rapture through all eternity. How will these sentiments warm and exalt
the human mind? Happy the nation, that has such heroes and statesmen!
A firm belief in the soul's immortality is a necessary support for the best
affections. You wish to mark every day of your life by some good action—
You can sacrifice ease, property, health, popular applause for your duty—
You can die in tortures for your country; but alas! every step in this bright
career hurries you to that dark goal, where the head, that plans the felicity
of an empire, and the heart that glowes with philanthropy, shall lose every
thought and feeling—where an Henry the Fourth, and a Ravailac, Washington and Arnold, shall mingle in the parent-dust—at such a thought
heaven soaring genius droops; virtue sighs with anguish; the noblest minds
wish to be a worm. The letter of the late King of Prussia to Marshal Keith,
on the death of Count Saxe, Marshal of France, breathes a spirit of melancholy horror through all the consolation of a false philosophy, and the
charms of poetry.† But, he was a great man? ask that question from the many

*Xenophon's life of Cyrus, page 367.
**Hart's history of Gustavus Adolphus.
†Oeuvres du philosophe de sans souci.

hundred thousands in the shades below; by whose blood every acre in Silesia was bought—God preserve America and the world from such great men.

VII

Unbelief of a future state is often the offspring of immorality, and never fails to encrease national iniquity. Providence has awfully warned mankind against it by the ruin of the greatest empire in the world. The corruption, that like a gangrene so rapidly dissolved the Roman Republic, grew from that Epicurean doctrine dressed up by Lucretius in all the beauties of poetry. The historians and moral poets of the age prove it sufficiently. Horace, who certainly was no bigot, laments the neglect of public worship, and the ruinous condition of the temples.* The severe, but judicious Juvenal exclaims—To what dire cause can we ascribe these crimes—but to that reigning atheism of the times—ghosts, Stygian lakes—*are now thought fables*—He then strongly paints the grief and indignation felt in the Elysian abodes by Curius, Camillus, the Fabii, and Scipios, and by all the brave Romans slain at Canna, at seeing a glorious Republic, reared by their virtues, blood and victories, ruined by this vile doctrine. The Roman constitution was originally interwoven with strong principles of religion; which continued in force during the prosperous times of the Republic. Polybious, an eminent politician, ascribes to these her superiority over other nations, and very justly censures those as wretched politicians, who at that time endeavoured to eradicate the fear of a future state out of the minds of a people. He draws a very striking contrast between the Roman integrity, and the corruption of Greece already prophane by this false philosophy—trust, he says, but a single talent to a Greek, who has been used to finger the public money; and though you have the security of ten counterparts, drawn up by as many public notaries, backed by as many feats, and the testimony of as many witnesses; yet with all these precautions you cannot possibly prevent him from proving a rogue; whilst the Romans, who by their various offices are intrusted with large sums of public money, pay so conscientious

*Lib. 3. Ode 6.

417

a regard to the religion of their office oath, that they were never known to violate their faith, though restrained only by that single tie.* Wealth and dominion fostered avarice, luxury, ambition—the execrable doctrine imported from Greece, grew rapidly in this soil, destroyed public virtue—and the republic. Cicero, and Sallust paint the corruption as dreadful; conspiracies and civil wars were inevitable consequences of it. Among the** banditti of Cataline were such as had committed sacrilege, murdered parents, and made a livelihood by false swearing. In the debates of the Senate on the best mode of punishing these rebels, Caesar openly asserted, that beyond the grave is neither pleasure nor pain, and that death could not be a severe punishment to them who only regarded it as the end of all troubles.†

The political corruption of the British Empire, which undoubtedly is dangerous even for a limited Republic, proceeds in a great measure from irreligion. Among the higher classes many are neither good Christians, nor sound Deists. The instruction of the lower classes has been extremely neglected, 'til the frequency and enormity of crimes has at last forced a thoughtless government into expedients which might easily have been adopted long ago. The immediate benefit from Sunday schools is a proof, how many lives would have been saved, *and* what losses and misfortunes avoided by that simple remedy. But alas! nations, like silly individuals, are often intent on show and pleasure, while a cancer gains on their vital parts. Irreligion is peculiarly baneful to Republics even in this respect, that it weakens or annihilates the sacredness of oaths, which are so frequent in the many public charges, and may, especially in juries and elections be considered as the bulwark of the constitution.‡ The excellent Lord Kames§ reproves the abuse and careless administration of oaths—a most salutary advice even to America—I hope, magistrates will not tender an oath in a hasty muttering manner equally prophane and disgraceful; and that other states will not learn from a neighbouring assembly to swear people for a pound of sugar, and a quart of rum.

*Montague on the rise and fall of the ancient Republics. Page 304 and 307.
** Sallust P. 25.
† Ibidem, Pag. 94.
‡ Montague, P. 307.
§ Sketches—man.

I speak here of religion only as a political blessing, given by the Universal Parent to all his children, that will accept of it. In this view we find often among dark superstitions some bright and fixed principles, that like polar stars lead mankind to virtue and happiness. Virgil's description of a future state is not indeed perfect; but it is far superior to the picture drawn by many Christians, who people heaven with such a multitude of knaves and fools, men of *faith without works,* saints without common honesty, and bigotted tyrants; and doom to eternal misery a Plato and Marcus Aurelius, nay millions of the human race, and, I shudder at the thought, numbers of innocent children, who did not know the right hand from the left. In Virgil's hell you find unkind brothers, unnatural sons and daughters, knaves, misers, adulterers, rebels and traitors. In his paradise there is not one bad character—but the good and wise, who have been the benefactors of mankind, inventors and promoters of useful arts, moral sublime poets, holy priests, and those who for their country have freely bled, and nobly died.*

Contempt for religion is by no means general in America; the great mass of people has rather a spirit of devotion; which however in some cases must be animated, and in others regulated. The want of regular worship in so great a part of the country is a severe evil: many learn absolutely nothing— others acquire absurd and dangerous ideas in religion—and many of good principles degenerate, because they are seldom or never animated by the persuasive address of good and sensible teachers. A sermon every Sunday is a powerful antidote against selfish and malicious passions,—it would often dispose people for good government better than the wisest laws, and by promoting all the civil virtues, enable them to pay taxes, and to fulfil all the duties of a good citizen. This want is often caused by neglect and a penurious disposition, which throws the whole burden of supporting public worship on a few generous persons—in that case it is a mark of ignorance and a depravity incompatible with public virtue; because people, who begrudge a few shillings for what they really believe will be of importance to their future happiness, and that of their children, cannot surely be liberal in the support of government. Another cause is the mixture of several religious professions, and will I doubt not be in part removed by the progress

Aneidos lib. 6 v. 608. &c. *ditto* 660, &c.

of liberal sentiments. The greater majority hold now the sound principle, that all faithful worshipers please the Supreme Being; why then should smaller differences prevent so great a national blessing as a general public worship; why do not the several denominations, who admit of regular teachers, join in supporting some kind of worship, as in some parts of Germany and Swisserland, where Protestants and Catholics worship under one roof. Ministers, who are real Christian philosophers, would easily please all rational hearers, because they teach only what is necessary, good, and sublime—no mithology, no metaphysic jargon, no dull mysteries, no useless controversies will disgrace their preaching. It must be a bad religion, that is not preferable to irreligion. Such, says an American author,* is my veneration for every religion, that reveals the attributes of the Deity, and a future state of rewards and punishments, that I had rather see the opinions of Confucius or Mahomed inculcated upon our youth, than see them grow up wholly devoid of a system of religious principles. A sentiment so just cannot be too much enforced. The main question in matters of religion is *useful truth:* and even errors that improve the heart without impairing, the judgement in other things, are valuable. Without this generous association of religious professions, some of the most cultivated parts of the country will suffer yet a long time from the want of public worship, and the influence of ignorant, gloomy enthusiasts; and the scattered settlement, will become very savage.

In this friendly concert the harsher notes of religious discord would be excluded; because a preacher could not without giving offence, insist on peculiarities, but must dwell on the essentials of religion. By this, only the most valuable parts of each religious system would be retained, and gradually formed into a system more refined and sublime. The limits of an essay will not permit me to pursue this important subject, but it demands a serious consideration. The clergy in America are sufficiently respected, but often badly supported; which is very detrimental to religion. A clergyman should not desire wealth; but he ought to live according to his station, and have means for private and public beneficence. If this is with-held, the clerical profession will frequently be taken up by persons of low education, who

---

Thoughts upon the mode of education proper in a Republic, Page 15.

have no prospect in life, and by ignorant, intemperate devotees, who may infect multitudes with a pernicious superstition. In this lies the danger of being *priest-ridden* in America. The clergy are not prompted either by sentiments or circumstances to ambitious designs. The examples of hierarchy in other countries need not raise any suspicion. They arose from an overdriven and mistaken devotion, not any original plans of the clergy; and have in general been less oppressive than aristocracies.* It is reasonable to suppose some good dispositions in a person who takes upon him a sacred function, and he must be very bad not to grow better in the exercise of it. Clergymen must be sensible of the importance of civil order to the interest of religion, and the good of mankind. So far as I know, those in America are general friends of true liberty, and supporters of a federal government.

X

In America, the sudden influx of money and foreign luxury, could not have produced the extravagance so much complained of without the aid of an overdriven principle of equality. I have often heard fellows complain, *how hard it is that a poor man cannot get his belly full of rum like other people.* However, this hardship is not deemed a disgrace; nor is a luxurious table as yet reckoned honorable in America. Besides the inferiority in costly fare can generally be concealed. But disadvantage in external appearance so visible to the public eye revolts against this levelling principle—as poverty, it is a serious evil where wealth is in high estimation—as want of gentility, it is peculiarly obnoxious to those that associate the ideas of wealth and refinement.

Inequality of property dictates a difference in living; if people do not comply with this from principle; pride, luxury, vanity will urge them to a thousand tricks of knavery and violence, and perhaps to mutiny and open rebellion—extreme liberty, untempered by religious and moral principles, is the source of agrarian laws, and all the foul monsters of anarchy. I despise aristocracies, and abhor the idea of making religion an engine of slavery— but I wish to make people sensible, that Almighty God has established an

---

* *Hume's history—Moore's travels in Italy.*

order in human affairs, on which political happiness absolutely depends. Great disparity of property is bad; but some must arise from the inequality of genius and industry, inheritance, and that chance, which in fact is the disposition of providence. Whatever is the quantity of national wealth, the great body of a people can never be rich; an easy, decent competency, is the utmost they can obtain, and should be the height of their wishes. The people of America cannot complain of poverty—the land is generally fertile, and amply sufficient—all useful trades are profitable—nay, every pair of industrious hands is a competent estate—the present difficulties may easily be removed by a proper federal government. America equally removed from the distress of poverty, and the danger of wealth, has obtained from all-bountiful heaven that happy lot, which Solomon in all his glory thought the most desirable[;]* why then that *love of money!* which has been *the root of so much* evil, and *pierced her through with so many sorrows.*** As to distinction; *integrity, goodness, manly sense, an independent spirit, invincible fortitude, patriotic virtue, are the genuine honors of a Republic;* honors open to all; honors, without which all the gems of India, and all the gold of Peru, are shining toys. The wealthy are only more respectable, if they excell in these qualities: if grateful to God and their country, they enjoy their wealth with dignity, humanity, generosity and public spirit. Whoever acts honorably in a lower station, is infinitely superior to one that disgraces the highest: There is no comparison between sound feet and a dropsical head. A labourer, who by honest industry supports his family, whose heart can feel, and hand can act for his country, is a far greater man than a volumptous, idle, selfish beau, though he was covered with rubies—the one is a *rough solid stone* in the ground work of the federal system; the other *a rotten piece* in the gilded dome. That labourer's wife, who continually studies the comfort of her husband, who toils for her numerous children, and often gives them the bread from her own mouth, is infinitely *more of a lady,* than those women of quality, who carry a dress twice the value of their husband's income; who gad about from place to place to show their finery, and prattle nonsense; who find no pleasure in the nursery; nay, ruin husband and children by a cruel dissipation.

*Prov. 30. 8 *give me neither poverty nor riches.*
**1 *Tim.* 6. 10.

These are the sentiments of the noblest men and women in every nation, and in every station of life; and they cannot be too much impressed on America. If wealth and show is the great object, people will all run mad after gugaws, scuffle and trample on each other, and raise a bloody fray. Neither laws nor habits can here authorise any man to say *keep your distance;* and your right to a more *glittering bauble* will be disputed by many—what then can be done, but to teach all poorer or richer, not to overvalue these trifles, and at any rate to acquire them honestly. In Europe, an established order of civil society prevents a general infection by luxury—the middle gentry does not emulate the first nobility; and is not rivalled by the yeomanry: such vanity would be ridiculous. In America the maid too often vies with her mistress, and a common laborer can with propriety dress like a governor.

The question is not, whether other countries do not surpass America in avarice, luxury, and vanity; it is a poor consolation to a sick man, that his neighbour is worse. The symptoms of corruption so feelingly described by many good and wise Americans are not trifling, and they are founded on open well-known facts. The civil war in Massachusetts, and the treason of Rhode-Island are alarming proofs. Early marriages are marks of national prosperity, and have been very general in America; they are not so now, especially in the great towns—because women *not worth a groat* speak with scorn of 200 *a year;* and because pretty beaus and smart bucks prefer *English buttons* and Madeira wine to *the best American girl.* The patriots of America will then be sensible, that *a putrid fever is not to be trifled with;* principiis obsta, fera medicina paratur.

A regular progress of national wealth under the direction of virtue and taste, will considerably promote national happiness. The unequal civilization of America has in a great measure occasioned that false taste so well criticized by judicious writers.* That dress, says one, which unites the articles of convenience, simplicity, and neatness in the greatest perfection, must be considered as the most elegant. But true taste goes farther—it has reference to age, to shape, to complexion, and to the season of the year. The same dress which adorns a miss of 15, will be frightful on a venerable lady of 70—

---

* *Webster[,] Pennsylvania Packet, 15th February,* 1787.

But the passive disposition of Americans in receiving every mode that is offered them, sometimes reduces all ages, shapes, and complexions to a level. Our distance also from our models of dress, &c—a thin garment which will scarcely form a visible shadow, and was designed for summer dress in Europe, may just be introduced into America when frost begins. Yet the garment must be worn; for before the arrival of a proper season there will perhaps be a new fashion.—He justly commends the simplicity and neatness of the Quaker ladies, who by neglect of superfluous finery, dress with two-thirds of the common expence; and after a handsome compliment to the native charms of his country women, entreats them not to be implicitly directed by the milliners and mantoa-makers on the other side of the Atlantic. "We behold," says Dr. Rush, "our ladies panting in a heat of ninety degrees, under a hat and cushion, which were calculated for the temperature of a British summer.*—It is high time to awake from this servility—to study our own character—to examine the age of our country—In particular, we must make ornamental accomplishments yield to principles and knowledge in the education of our women."

A good taste is not the spontaneous product of sense and delicacy; it implies an accuracy of judgment, a refinement of sentiment, a perception of order and propriety, not to be acquired without long observation on men and things. Hence the greatest genius has an imperfect taste in youth—and the taste of a young nation cannot be perfect, for want of regularity in many things. The states of Northern Europe have suffered much from an indiscreet adoption of French manners—It is no wonder that [in] America a young easy country girl should prejudice herself by an unreserved imitation of Europe, and especially of her grandam Great-Britain.

XV

I have now shewn, how federal sentiments must be acquired by education, manners, laws, morals, and religion; and proceed to consider how they may be promoted by civil institutions—my reader will please to remember, that

*Thoughts upon female education—United States. page 19. *a piece wrote with taste and judgment.*

the political arrangement of a federal system is my object only in this view. There can be no republican liberty, but where the great body of the people does by representatives exercise the sovereign power. A great number should therefore be qualified to rule in their turn—the far greater majority should have the knowledge and virtue of electors—the whole nation ought to have a warm zeal for liberty, integrity and courage to intimidate the boldest ambition; yet be generous enough to love and respect a good government, and to support it with their lives and fortunes. We may heartily despise those politicians, who pretend to establish a noble republican system only by a nice balance of civil powers. Can a Palladio erect a palace, that shall be the wonder of ages, with untempered mortar, soft bricks, and rotten timbers! Can a Vauban with such materials form national bulwarks, that shall mock the fury of batteries, and the disperate attack of the forlorn hope. Suppose the Turkish Sultan had a mind to transform his vast despotic empire into a federal republic, and had for this purpose all the best politicians in Europe and America, and the honorable Federal Convention; do you think, he could do it? No, a dreadful civil war would kindle from the Black Sea to Lybia, and the blood of a million would only cement the vast prison of slavery. In the republican edifice, the people are not inanimate materials, but *living stones.* They must not only be sound and proper, but also willing to lie, to stand, *to join* as the architect wishes, nay, to go into their proper places; because in a free country there is no machinery strong enough to hoist massy stones and heavy timbers against their will—no iron capable of trussing a roof, when the rafters will not join—no force to fix a kingpost against his inclination—to make the stately columns, that bear up the dome, stand in their places—The very stones of the foundation can, if they please, begin to fight, and like a fatal earthquake shake the whole fabric into a heap of rubbish. Reflect on this ye federal people! Spurn the *crooked stick;* let the unwieldly mass *stick in the mire;* despise every *showy but hollow hearted tree;* be like the *best freestone; firm, sound, invariable,* as your live oaks and evergreen cedars—consider also, that the stones, however solid, must be smoothed and joined by the *yielding well tempered mortar;* that discord is a bursting mine. Ye political architects! exert all your skill; poise your centers of gravity; calculate the weights and bearings; Consult the plans of Montesquieu, Harrington, Stuart, Hume, Smith,* and others—but consider that never did so much depend on the quality of the materials; ameliorate and innoble them therefore by all means; improve their solidity, firmness, cohesion; animate them with the generous spirit of true freedom: make them say—*here we are, place us where we suit best: that is the post of honor, whether in the lowest part of the foundation, or in the towering arch.* Then shall your masterly hands rear *a grand temple of federal liberty,* perennial as this western continent, and the sun that gildes it with his mild evening rays.

THE PRINCIPLES of SENTIMENTAL POLITICAL UNION.

Not only the necessaries and conveniencies of life, but the principal enjoyments of human nature, depend on society. The Great Creator has therefore given us strong social passions, and the best minds have the most of this moral magnetism: The little girl that weeps for her doll, will be an excellent wife and mother—A man of sensibility would in a wilderness place his affections on the most beautiful trees. A well-ordered political society is a theatre for the noblest exertions of human genius, the best feelings of the human heart. To be the guardian Angels of a nation, to chain the monsters that ravage it; to repel daring foes; to diffuse the heavenly light of virtue and knowledge; continually to open some rich source for the ease and comfort of mankind—must indeed be a glorious delightful employment. To form connexions with persons of enlightened and exalted minds; mutually to give and receive the glad applause, and respectful affection; to have the grateful esteem of the good and just; nay, to dispise the rage and falshood of the wicked; to pity and forgive well meaning enemies—all this is high enjoyment. While man is wrapt up in himself he is a mean little being; but when he steps out from his prison, he becomes great, and rises to an amazing glory. The generous patriot lives but for his country, and will gladly dye for it—his country's love of him is his very soul, entwined with every fibre of his heart; the dear thought of it is his last in this world, and remains with him through an happy eternity.

*On the wealth of nations.

426

Inferior men will be also much improved by a social union. There is a native dignity in the generous affections, that strikes even the selfish, and often makes them forget themselves. Society calls many of these into play. The common object is a center, that attracts numbers of dissimilar dispositions, and thus brings them near each other—it becomes a source of reciprocal good-will, because they expect to attain it by joint endeavors; in this pursuit they frequently must exchange mutual good offices, and upon trying occasions sacrifice ease, humour, interest; leading characters will by their talents and public virtue, animate and attach the less sanguine; in action and conversation will arise the sympathetic passions of hopes and fears, grief and joy, admiration of worthy members, dislike of the bad, with all the congenial sentiments on the common cause. Self love itself, if not too sordid, is gratified in a social union—Besides a share in the common object, a new and often superior interest is acquired: the pleasure of acting as a member; the honor, dignity, importance, and whatever advantage that attend it; a participation of the merit and glory of eminent fellow citizens, and of the whole society, *all* which in a great measure reflect on every member. If therefore the common object of attachment is interesting, and a sufficient majority has those moral principles, which are the stamina of all rational government; the political union has a natural tendency to grow stronger—because the selfish passions will necessarily be weakened, or take a better direction; and all the sentiments of integrity, honor, private attachment, and public spirit, will encrease; by the exercise of social duties, by civil habits, and the gradual incorporation of the body politic, which will be finally moulded into an excellent form, and animated by the same generous spirit. Let us then consider the principal bonds of a sentimental political union, and apply the theory to the United States.

XX

The grand federal interest, which is to preserve independency, safety and peace, requires, next to a solid military union, a concert in some other important affairs. The states must be *reciprocal guarantees of their several constitutions,* when they shall be properly settled; because an alteration in these may break or prejudice the union—As if any state should unanimously or by a great majority, set up monarchy, aristocracy, or democracy; or should annul the habeas corpus law, tryal by juries, and the like institutions, which are the pillars of republican liberty. If corruption becomes so rife in any state, that a party could establish itself in oppression; the federal power should redress the grievance, though it might not threaten the confederacy with danger—because such an evil may be worse than a rebellion, or a foreign invasion; and the states ought surely to guarantee each other that happiness, which is the end of all political union.

All external commerce must be under a federal regulation in all cases, when it involves foreign treaties and political connexions; affects the federal revenue; or creates a collision of interest between the states. It is evident that internal commerce will also, in many cases, become a federal object in a country that has 3000 miles extent of coast, and an inland navigation of the same length, with large bays, many great rivers, and numberless inlets. There cannot be any doubt, but a federal power will, whenever its interference is necessary, manage the national commerce to the best advantage. It will obtain from foreign powers, every advantage that the situation of the United States can procure—it will prevent disagreement and war with other nations—it will do justice to the respective states, and keep peace among them, when it would be disturbed by numberless collisions. But I am persuaded, that with every exertion of federal wisdom and integrity, no subject is more likely to become a bone of contention, than this, if the states do not display that reciprocal generosity, and confidence in the federal head, which I have so warmly recommended. First, commerce is in its nature very variable, and more so in America, where its regular course has been so disturbed, and where new channels of industry from manufactures not yet formed, and products of regions not yet explored, will arise and mingle in many intricate windings—in consequence of this, the respective commercial rights of the states cannot be fixed at present, but require successive alterations. Secondly, the people of America have an overdriven spirit of trade; and great numbers that formerly derived wealth and support from it, are by the present stagnation in great difficulties, or what to some appears very hard, cannot make money as they used to do. Thirdly, many have too sanguine and unreasonable expectations of commercial benefit from the exertions of an adequate federal power. I shall beg leave to observe, that in some respects that very decay of trade so much lamented, is a real advantage. Before the war, America was continually in debt to Great-Britain for articles of luxury. After the peace, all Europe poured in an immensity of goods upon her; the one was as foolish to give, as the other to receive an unbounded credit. Many of the European merchants expected to find Mexican wealth in the United States; and these chearfully went in debt for trinkets and finery in the high spirits and golden dreams that naturally followed a war closed with so much honor and success.*

"Triumphant over a great enemy, courted by the most powerful nations in the world, it was not in human nature, that America should immediately comprehend her new situation—really possessed of the means of future greatness, she anticipated the most distant benefits of the revolution, and considered them as already in her hands." Is it not very happy that these thoughtless adventures and imprudent credits from foreign countries have ceased! that some silver and gold is left! that the demands of foreign nations are not become so great as to make us insolvents, and bring on a war to compel payment! Necessity and good sense will, I hope, stop that torrent of iniquity, which a ridiculous fondness of glittering toys has poured over the land; which threatened to annihilate *the landmarks of common honesty, and to break down the barriers of national integrity, honor, liberty, and in-dependency.* Far be it from me to dissuade from those measures, which may alleviate the distresses of the commercial interest, and its dependencies; but when this is done, I sincerely wish to check, for the future, the overdriven spirit of commerce, so unsuitable to America, and in many respects per-nicious. "So uninformed," says the last mentioned author,** "or mistaken have many of us been, that commerce has been stated as the great object, and I fear it is yet believed to be the most important interest in New-England. But from the best calculations I have been able to make, I cannot raise the proportion of property, or the number of men employed in manu-factures, fisheries, navigation, and trade, to one-eighth of the property and

Principles of a commercial system for the United States, by Tench Coxe, merchant of Phila-delphia.
** *Tench Coxe.*

people occupied by agriculture, even in that commercial quarter of the union." This author very judiciously ranks agriculture, manufactures, internal trade, and foreign commerce in the first, second, &c. places, respectively. It is but just to pay this gentleman the compliment, that his ideas of national œconomy are not warped by professional habits, but just and liberal. His theory corresponds with the principles of an excellent modern author, who ought to be generally perused.* At present, necessary manufactures are a great object, and may by prudent spirited exertion soon flourish beyond expectation. These will improve agriculture and promote internal trade. With them jointly, America will be a great, powerful, and *in a just sense,* wealthy country, without any dependence on foreign nations. She will easily obtain the few valuable articles really wanted, without any solicitations or compliments. China, Indostan, and ancient Egypt, countries of high population and wealth, have had but little external commerce. The coal trade between New-Castle and London, employs more shipping than all the carrying trade of England.**

What would you think of a great Virginia proprietor turning shop-keeper! weighing a pound of sugar, drawing a quart of molasses twenty times a day; measuring inches of tobacco; disputing with sordid customers about weight and measure; cajoling and humoring huckster women, or ladies who in sentiment are not above such, for their custom; solicitous from morn till night how to make a penny. Can such a man have noble, generous, independent sentiments, suitable to his fortune? what will he be in two or three years? Is he, or will he be, qualified to command a brigade, to act as a governor, or member of Congress? America is a great heiress of an immense landed estate, with fruitful plains, charming meadows, green stately woods full of game, mountains of ore, glimmering lakes stored with fish, numberless limpid brooks that embellish and fertilise the land, fragrant orchards and blooming gardens. She can keep a plentiful table, dress in fine cloth, linen and silk of her own, build stone, brick and cedar-houses with her own

*Smith on the wealth of nations. See the second book, fifth chapter.
**Smith, in the book and chapter mentioned.

materials; she can make her own ploughs, boats and fishing tackle; she need not go abroad for *steel, guns and powder.* By swapping a little tobacco for paint and some little trifles, she can even ride round her estate in a coach and six. Her fine flour will furnish her tea-table, and purchase rum for her hunters and fishermen. This great lady need not, with Nicholas Frog, look for suckers in every puddle, or hunt in distant forests for drugs among serpents and tigers.* She need not, with Highland Peggy, knitt stockings till her hands are all in blisters;** nor with John Bull† hammar hardware, and comb wool till she becomes sore-eyed and phthisical—coax the fancy of customers with frying-pan and gridiron-buttons, and by forcing the scarlet on a haughty lord Strutt,‡ get a black eye and a broken pate.

It would require many papers to shew all the evils arising from an absurd spirit of trade. Let a few facts speak. How many robust fellows cry limes and clams about the street, who ought to work in iron forges! What number of huckster women sit with a few apples and gingerbread, who should be at the spinning-wheel! how many lads and grown men stand leaning over the rum-barrel! We have half as many sellers as buyers; how shall they live! will not shifting, turning, going in debt, gradually weaken the principles of honesty? can a continual minute attention to interest be consistent with generous and patriotic sentiments! when you continually handle brass, will not your hands smell of it? Among the country people a spirit of petty trading and sordid speculation is, in some places, too common—The most interesting conversation is *how poultry and butter* sell in the market— swapping horses is a favorite trade—vendues are entertainments, where they vie in buying on trust; this nuisance has occasioned a very common saying, that one vendue is the mother of many; consequently of law-suits, executions, and moral depravity, complaint of hard times, and murmurs against government. In every country excess of petty trading is marked with cunning

---

Allusion to the herring fishery, and spice trade of Holland.
**Scotch Highlands.*
†*England, where consumption, &c. have encreased with assiduous sedentary manufactures.*
‡*Swift's history of John Bull—Competition in manufactures and commerce, have created many wars.*

and sordid selfishness. The Chinese are very fraudulent: I have been informed that some of the crew in the late China ships, were imposed upon by pieces of wood in the shape and colour of gammons.

An extensive foreign commerce would involve America in troublesome political connexions, perhaps in wars, and undoubtedly create parties at home. A spirit of commerce is unfavourable to those high sentiments of honor and military virtue, which are the only real bulwarks of a nation. China, with a million or more of standing troops, was conquered by a small army of Tartars, who established their empire and yet have a prince of their blood on the throne. Montesquieu remarks, "that when Carthage made war with her opulence against the Roman poverty, her great disadvantage arose from what she esteemed her greatest strength and chief dependence. Gold and silver may easily be exhausted, but public virtue, constancy, firmness of mind, and fortitude are inexhaustible." The Carthaginians in their wars employed foreign mercenaries. A defeat or two at sea obstructed their commerce and stopped the spring, which supplied their exchequer. The loss of a battle in Africa reduced them to submit to any terms. Regulus in the first punic war cooped them up in their capital after one defeat by sea, and one by land. Their final ruin arose from a mean spirit of avarice, that denied the gallant Hannibal the necessary supplies of men and money.* Holland is in great part defended by foreign mercenaries. Great-Britain to her shame cannot do without them in time of war—It is a mark of dreadful corruption, when a nation will entrust such with her *safety, her honor, even that wealth she doats upon, because her own people can earn more at the loom.* What is the consequence. The pretender with 6000 half disciplined ragged High-landers took all Scotland, advanced into England, and struck a panic on London, which alone could furnish 100,000 fighting men. *America was lost because Great-Britain was intent on turning buttons, and making Manchester fluff.* O! horrid, base! America became independent, not by those wretches, whose political sentiments depended on hard money, salt, molasses; but by those who without shoes and stockings marched day and night in the snow; who naked and half starved, met every dreary form of death—by those who

Montague on the rise and fall of the ancient republics. page 339, ditto 219.

made a generous sacrafice of property, when the selfish would contribute nothing. I mean not to depreciate British valour, and I have told America harsh truth; I am neither Briton or American—what I say is evident. Had Great Britain been less commercial, and America more, this had yet been a province of the other. A rich fleet of merchantmen may be taken or destroyed only by an unlucky change of the wind: Great cities may be pillaged, or ruined by the fatal bombs:—But the land can neither sink or burn; and a brave people of a great landed interest is invincible. They cannot be starved into a compliance: If their forts are taken, every noble heart is an impregnable castle.

XXI

By the 9th article of confederation "the United States in Congress assembled, have the sole and exclusive right and power of regulating the alloy and value of coin struck by their own authority, or by that of the respective states." Consequently no state can have a right to enact tender-laws, emit any sort of paper currency, or adopt any plan of finance that may affect the union, without the consent of a federal head. Neither ought it to have any such right to the prejudice of its own people, or foreigners; because the states are guarantees to each other, and must, without any special treaty, guarantee to every foreign nation the *jus gentium,* mutual rights of nations, regarded as sacred in every civilized country, nay among savages. The United States are known as a nation only in their federal quality. If a nation is injured by any state it looks up to the union for satisfaction, and if refused, has a right to procure it by force. If a Spanish merchant f [or] e[xample] is defrauded by a trader of Rhode-Island, it is a private affair; but if he is injured by a tender law that pays him a dollar with a shilling, his government may demand satisfaction from Congress, and if refused, seize the property of a Philadelphian. What disgrace and danger may not then arise from such a weakness of federal power, that cannot restrain a wicked state government from robbing its own people, and the world at large! What antifederal impression must it not make on every mind! Money is a universal object, in which every person is concerned, some daily and hourly: it is a general standard by which all commodities are measured; to be harrassed, wronged, and trifled with, by a medium depending on every body's caprice, must create hatred and contempt of the sovereign power. But a coin of permanent universal value, struck by federal authority, would impress all the citizens of the United States with a constant sense of this power, and of its salutary protection. Federal emblems and mottos on the different species of coin, would also have a good effect. As these must significantly express the most interesting federal sentiments in few words, they are objects for a fine genius.

As there can be no liberty without virtue, there can be none without a very general share of learning. An overdriven spirit of wealth has, both in Great Britain and America, nearly established the false maxim, that national liberty is safest in the hands of the rich, because they have a greater share in the public interest. This can be admitted so far only as wealth is attended with superior virtue and wisdom. Avarice and luxury is as little satisfied with 10,000 l. a year, as 100 l. and a person may have his *pockets full of money with empty brains.* The public education throughout the states, is a great federal concern, as without it no state can be well governed, nor act its part in the confederation with dignity, honor and a federal spirit.

There is of late an honorable exertion for the interest of learning very general; but, as may naturally be expected, in many cases ill directed. A smattering of Greek is nothing in comparison to the essential parts of learning which we continually want in public and private life. The great science of politics is the capital learning of republics, and three years at least should be dedicated to it in every state college, by those that expect to be legislators. What can we expect from men who know nothing but the little affairs of their own townships, who not only have no reading, but want the knowledge and reflection acquired by travelling through different parts of the country, and conversation with men of science and political experience? Their affections are too often equally narrow with their ideas—The union is an object by far too grand for them. It is a most important consideration, that *ignorance creates suspicion*—it is a law of nature for our good. A man of common sense, who knows nothing about fine horses, will not give 200 l. for one, without solicitous consultation with men on whose knowledge and integrity he can depend—For the same reason an ignorant assemblyman will refuse the most necessary grant of a federal requisition; because he don't understand the fatal consequence of a refusal to the union, his own state, and finally to himself; but he knows that his neighbours must pay a share of it, and *feels* that some must come out of his own pocket. What is remarkable, this suspicion not seldom influences electors; they are afraid of choosing men *who know too much.* Hence an infatuated multitude place their confidence either in those who are *too stupid* to do either good or harm; or in quacks who promise to cure every political disorder with a *six pence nostrum.*

When the public education shall distinguish many by political abilities and a polite taste; and enable great numbers to esteem these qualities; the most eminent characters will be chosen for the legislature, civil administration, and military command—consequently the government will not only in reality be so much better, but acquire that love and respect from the people, so necessary for its efficacy. What can you expect when a legislator or a magistrate can, over his bowl of grog, talk of nothing but hogs, potatoes, and the necessity of lessening the taxes! What may you not expect when such men are enlightened patriots, gentlemen in ideas, sentiments, and behaviour; who at the same time as they mix in chearful society with their fellow citizens, by instruction and example, make them wiser and better, more patriotic and federal.

A gentleman under the signature of *Nestor,* some months ago, gave the public a hint for erecting a *Federal University.* How much this will promote learning in general, is evident from the situation of this young country, whose pecuniary and literary resources cannot yet be great enough for more than one *illustrious assembly of the muses.* It would be an excellent institution for promoting federal sentiments. In the happy spring of youth all our best affections bloom—the high sense of honor, the warmth of friendship, the glow of patriotic virtue then animate the enraptured soul—Sublime and elegant literature has then its highest relish, refines and exalts these noble passions. What glorious effects may not then a nation expect from a *concourse of her best sons at the temple of wisdom!* Society in the sweet enjoyment of literature, and the many social pleasures of an academic life, will create a mutual endearment, and form those charming friendships, that will continue to the grave. When after a finished education they depart to their different stations, and places of residence, they will be so many *capital links of the federal union, so many stately columns under the grand fabric, so many bright luminaries to shed a radiance through the whole federal system, and so many powerful centripetal forces to give it eternal stability.* Infinitely above the local prejudices of vulgar bosoms, they will think and feel as genuine sons of America. I scruple not to say, that though a State College is formed on the most liberal plan, its education cannot be so patriotic as that in a Federal University. Let us propose these questions to the respective students. Where did you spend the happiest part of your life? In, f [or] e[xample] Pennsylvania. Where did you acquire those sciences and liberal arts which you value more than Peruvian treasures? In Pennsylvania. Where did you know the best politicians, philosophers and poets? In Pennsylvania. Where are your most faithful and admired friends? In Pennsylvania. When the dearest objects of the human heart are thus confined within a narrow sphere, it must be uncommonly noble to embrace unknown persons and objects however near politically related. But all these questions are answered by the federal student—in America. His learning, his virtues, his graces, all the blessings of education were acquired in the *center of the confederacy.** The friends of his youth, *for whom he would die,* are Americans, some in Georgia, others in New-Hampshire, or in Kentucky—Military officers, clergymen, magistrates, members of legislatures, delegates in congress.

XXIII

This institution is separate from the university, and will be on the same footing as the philosophical societies: only more extensive, both in a federal view, and to render it more respectable by a combination of all the sons of Apollo. Distant members may correspond, and besides form the like societies on a smaller scale in their respective states. This federal academy of belles letters will not require any public expense, nor any other care from government than encouragement and protection. In proportion as elegant learning is

* *The university should be where Congress meets.*

436

cultivated, it will tincture manners, religion, laws, and government. The great admiration of the British constitution, which is not confined to Great-Britain, is in great part owing to the enthusiastic eulogiums on it blended with the finest English compositions. When the federal system shall be established, this federal academy of polite learning will be an ornamental and not feeble support to it. The large western territory is in several views a great federal object. A firm union will prevent those dissentions, which may otherwise arise between some states about lands so valuable—Extent of dominion is immaterial, when they are united provinces of one empire—What other advantage may be had from possession, is the same, when thrown into a common stock, and impartially administered. It is highly necessary to settle this territory *slowly and regularly;* otherwise this part of the union can neither be civilized, governed, nor secured. Among those who flock hither from the different states, some are bold and enterprizing; many of the most idle and licentious character; not a few fled from criminal and civil justice. The well disposed will generally degenerate in bad society, under want of education, public worship, and other means of civilization. A continual warfare with the Indians will render them fierce and warlike. Constant hunting naturally creates a ferocious temper: humanity is undoubtedly weakened by the constant destruction of animals, sight of blood and mortal agonies in various forms. In consequence of all this, the back inhabitants would for a while be like the wild herds of Tartars and Arabs; and with an encreasing population form many petty states unconnected with the union, and in perpetual war among themselves—if attacked by a federal force they would unite and erect a considerable empire. This is a serious consideration; in comparison to which it is but a small evil, that so many hands withdraw into the wilderness from the scenes of industry, to the great hurt of necessary manufactures, and agriculture itself. The vast frontiers of Persia, Turkey and Russia have always been infested with rebellions—The last Russian rebel Pugaschef was a mean wretch; yet he seduced a multitude of ignorant, savage people, gave the government great trouble; and caused the destruction of many thousands:* What may not America dread from such men as

---

* Cox's travels in Russia.

Sullivan—If the letter signed by that name, and addressed to the Spanish Governor of Florida, is genuine, what may not be feared from such a daring ambition, such ardour for war, such a military genius improved by liberal knowledge.

Though the federal power should not interfere in the internal management of the states; yet some extraordinary affairs demand an exception. At present the negro slavery is a federal object—It revolts against the plainest and universally established principles of humanity and common equity; it is in that respect a national disgrace; it is a standing proof and example of corruption. In a political view the effect is dangerous—A man who exercises absolute power over some hundred fellow creatures, although he should not abuse it, cannot easily have a heart-felt sensibility of the equal rights of mankind, the moderation of a republican, and a genuine love of liberty. It is impossible but the cruelty of some masters, and the obstinacy of some slaves should often create horrid excesses.* Who does not know many examples, that shock humanity! This national evil must indeed be abolished with prudence, and by degrees; but let it be done with all possible speed, and in the mean time be mitigated by the humanity and wisdom of federal government. Let no barbarian with impunity starve, mangle, and kill in lingering tortures a miserable defenceless fellow-creature! Let not a brute, who never felt parental, filial or conjugal affection, by a cruel separation inflict on husband and wife, parents and children, agonies worse than the most dreadful death—agonies from which the most affectionate bosoms often seek from the poison, the dagger, the friendly wave that relief which an impotent or inhuman government will not give. America! Africa is thy sister; thy children may one day become her slaves, if thou wilt not regard thy honor, the sacred rights of humanity, that liberty which is thy pride, and that GREAT GOD, who is the universal father of mercies, and a terrible avenger of his injured children.

In all national affairs, and especially in the modern state of political society, money is a great and necessary instrument. The federal government,

---

*See in the American Museum an account of a negro enclosed in an iron cage, and miserably devoured by birds of prey.

though frugal, has a considerable expence in time of peace: it must have certain and adequate resources for an eventual war; and for discharging the national debt. No person of any sense can believe that foreign powers will wait for ever. When they cannot even obtain interest for a generous loan, what must they think of national honor, integrity, gratitude! Will they think America worthy of their friendship, or even common civility! will they again spend their blood and treasure for her independency! In case of war with any formidable power, how will an army be raised and equipped! Will the troops again list for money, of which a month's pay will soon scarcely buy a morning dram? Will men of honor suffer hunger and cold, bleed and dye, for a country that will not do them common justice? While the states are disputing whether they shall grant the federal requisitions or not; an enemy may penetrate into the heart of a country, and cut off some members of the union. In the midst of a debate whether a few hundred pounds more or less shall be granted, an enemies' grenadiers may step in, and say *deliver* or *die:* raise immediately so many thousand pounds, or have your city pillaged and burnt! This is plain sense; those who will not comprehend it, are insane, and if nothing else will cure them, had better *be bled* by their own citizens, than massacreed by an enemy. Was I an American, my sword would not sleep in the scabbard, while sordid wretches ruined my country. Is it not horrible that at this very time the savages riot in blood and destruction, because the federal government cannot support a regiment of soldiers on the frontiers! The wail of the babe, who dies under the tomahawk on the mothers breast, the shrieks of the mother that fill the wilderness, and pierce the very rocks—the expiring groans of the father writhing in slow fires, do they not cry to heaven for vengeance over that cruel avarice, which is the cause of such woe.[1]

It is high time then to have done with those requisitions of Congress so neglected, and even treated with contempt.* This head of the Empire

---

1. This paragraph was reprinted in the *Freeman's Journal,* 26 September and the *Pennsylvania Packet,* 12 October.

Col. Hamilton's speech in the Assembly of New-York. 18th February, forcibly treats of this matter—but alas rocks will not as in ancient times move for the best music—the impost was strangled by a band of mutes.

has been forced to declare publicly in pathetic addresses to the States that the confederacy is in danger, and that it cannot answer for the cruel accidents that may befall the body politic.

The federal government must have a *fixed and ample revenue to be furnished by certain taxes in every state, and collected by officers of its own appointment, and under its own direction.* Without this we shall either have foreign soldiers or our own Shayses for collectors; or the brave and generous must join, and with the bayonet to every ignoble breast, say *deliver.*

"Crito"
[Stephen Hopkins]

Essay on the African Slave Trade: I

Providence Gazette and Country Journal, 6 October 1787

—————

This essay was written while the Federal Convention was still sitting, and thus is not strictly speaking either a Federalist or Anti-Federalist tract. It does, however, address many of the themes touched upon by other Federalist writers. Its date of publication and the importance of the topic recommend its inclusion in this collection.

Stephen Hopkins was a leading statesman from Rhode Island and a signer of the Declaration of Independence. Given his participation in that event, his views on slavery and the slave trade contribute a good deal to our understanding of these issues during the Founding period. See Herbert J. Storing, "Slavery and the Moral Foundations of the American Republic"; and Walter Berns, "The Constitution and the Migration of Slaves," *Yale Law Journal* 78 (1968): 198.

The second part of this essay followed on 13 October in the *Providence Gazette and Country Journal.* Like the first part, it deals with the inconsistency of practicing the slave trade whilst continuing to affirm the founding principles expounded in the Declaration of Independence. Yet the second installment of the Crito essays goes further in admonishing the American people for this great "national sin." In addition to warning America's citizens—and in a larger sense, all peoples everywhere engaged in the slave trade—of a divine retribution, it directly ties "repentance and reformation" to the future success of the great experiment in self-government then under consideration. Crito writes: "If we persist in thus transgressing the laws of Heaven, and obstinately refuse to do unto us, we cannot prosper."

Also, like the connection Crito draws between the British and slavery in the first part, he develops a connection between slavery and the Algerine problem in the second. The war with Algiers, not officially declared until the war with England ended in 1812, was the result of prolonged Algerine pirating of American ships and the enslavement of the captured seamen.

Crito draws the reader's attention to the inconsistency of American cries
for retribution against Algiers for their crimes while continuing the practice
of like crimes at home.

———•———

I

When the public, or any part of the community, are taking those measures
or going into that practice, which may issue in ruin, and most certainly
will, unless reformed; he who foresees the approaching evil cannot act a
benevolent or faithful part, unless he gives warning of the danger, and does
his utmost to reform and save his fellow-citizens, even though he should
hereby incur the displeasure and resentment of a number of individuals.
In this view, Crito asks the candid attention of the public to what he has
to say on the following interesting and important subject.

Some, perhaps, will not chuse to read any farther; but drop this paper
with a degree of uneasy disgust, when they are told the subject to which
their attention is asked is, The AFRICA SLAVE TRADE, which has been
practiced and in which numbers in these United States are now actually
engaged.

So much has been published within a few years past on this subject, describing the fertile country of Africa, and the ease and happiness which the
natives of that land enjoy, and might enjoy to a yet greater degree, were
it not for their own ignorance and folly, and the unhappy influence which
the Europeans and Americans have had among them, inducing them to
make war upon each other, and by various methods to captivate and kidnap
their brethren and neighbours, and sell them into the most abject and perpetual slavery—and at the same time giving a well-authenticated history
of this commerce in the human species, pointing out the injustice, inhu-
manity and barbarous cruelty of this trade, from beginning to end, until
the poor Africans, are fixed in a state of the most cruel bondage, in which,
without hope, they linger out a wretched life; and then leave their posterity,
if they are so unhappy as to have any, in the same miserable state: So much
has been lately published, I say, on these subjects, that it is needless particularly to discuss them here. It is sufficient to refer the inquisitive to the

following books, viz.—Several tracts collected and published by the late Anthony Benezet, of Philadelphia—*A Dialogue concerning the Slavery of the Africans,* lately reprinted at New York, by order of the society here, for promoting the admission of slaves, and protecting such of them as have been or may be liberated; and especially, *An Essay on the Slaves and Commerce of the Human Species, particularly the Africans,* by Thomas Clarkson, which was honoured with the first prize in the University of Cambridge, for the year 1785.

If the African slave trade, and the consequent slavery of the Negroes in the West-Indies, and in the United States of America, be an open and gross violation of the rights of mankind, a most unrighteous, inhuman and cruel practice, which has been the occasion of the death of millions, and of violently forcing millions of others from their dear native country, and their most tender and desirable connexions, and of bringing them to a land of slavery, where they have not a friend to pity and relieve them, but are doomed to cruel bondage, without hope of redress, till kind death shall release them, as is represented, and seems to be abundantly proved in the above mentioned publications, and many others, a conviction of which is fast spreading among all ranks of men in Europe and America; then the following terrible consequence, which may well make all shudder and tremble who realize it, *forces* itself upon us, viz. all who have had any hand in this iniquitous business, whether more directly or indirectly, have used their influence to promote it, or have consented to it, or ever connived at it, and have not opposed it, by all proper exertions of which they have been capable; All these are, in a greater or less degree, chargeable with the injuries and miseries which millions have suffered, and are suffering, in consequence of this trade; and are guilty of the blood of millions who have lost their lives by this traffic of the human species! Not only the merchants who have been engaged in this trade, and for the sake of gain have sacrificed the liberty and happiness, yea the lives of millions of their fellow men, and the captains and men who have been tempted by the love of money to engage in this cruel work, to buy and sell and butcher men; and the slave holders of every description, are guilty of shedding rivers of blood: But all the Legislatures who have authorized, encouraged, or even neglected to suppress it, to the utmost of their power; and all the individuals in private stations, who have any way aided in this business, consented to it, or have not opposed it to the utmost of their ability, have a share in this guilt. It is therefore become a *national sin,* and a sin of the first magnitude; a sin which righteous Heaven has never suffered to pass unpunished in this world. For the truth of this assertion we may appeal to history, both sacred and profane.

We will leave the inhabitants of Britain, and other European nations, who have been and still are concerned in the slave trade, to answer for themselves; and consider this subject as it more immediately concerns the United States of America.—Hundreds of thousands of slaves have been imported into these States, many thousands are now in slavery here, and many more thousands have been brought from Africa by the inhabitants of these States, and sold in the West-Indies, where slavery is attended with cruelty and horrors beyond description. And who can reckon upon the numbers who have lost their lives, and been really murdered, by this trade, or have a full conception of the suffering and distressed of body and mind, which have been the attendants and effects of it: All this blood which has been shed, constantly cries to Heaven; and all the bitter sighs, groans, and tears, of these injured, distressed, helpless poor, have entered into the ears of the Lord of hosts, and are calling and waiting for the day of vengeance.

The inhabitants of Rhode-Island, especially those of Newport, have had by far the greatest share in this traffic of all these United States. This trade in the human species has been the first wheel of commerce in Newport, on which every other movement in business has chiefly depended: That town has been built up and flourished, in times past, at the expence of the blood, the liberty and happiness, of the poor Africans; and the inhabitants have lived on this, and by it have gotten most of their wealth and riches.—If a bitter woe is pronounced on "him who buildeth his house by unrighteousness, and his chambers by wrong," (Jer.xxii.13) "to him who buildeth a town by blood, and establisheth a city by iniquity." (Heb.ii.12) "to the *bloody* city," (Ezek.xxiv.6) what a heavy, dreadful woe hangs over the heads of all those, whose hands are defiled by the blood of the Africans, especially the inhabitants of that State, and of that town, who have had a distinguished share in this unrighteous, bloody commerce!

444

All this, and more, follows as a necessary consequence, which, it is presumed, none will dispute, on supposition the before mentioned publications give in any measure a just representation of the slave trade, and the consequent slavery of the Africans; and unless thousands and millions of all ranks, and of the most disinterested, and many of them men of the best abilities and character for knowledge, uprightness, and benevolence, and who are under the greatest advantages to know the truth, and judge right of this matter, both in Europe and America; unless *all those* are grossly deluded.

But if all these may be fairly confuted, and the African slave trade, and the consequent treatment of those who are by means of this reduced to slavery, can be justified and shown to be confident with justice, humanity and universal benevolence, then the whole of this consequence will be obviated, and all the supposed guilt of injuring our fellow men in the highest degree, and of shedding rivers of innocent blood, will be wiped away as a mere phantom, and vanish as the baseless fabric of a night vision. It is earnestly to be desired therefore, if this be possible, that some able, disinterested advocate for the slave trade, if such an one can be found, would step forth, and do it. But if there be no such man, let the interested, and those who are in this traffic, and the slavery of the Africans, arise, and shew it to be just and benevolent if they can. We will promise you a candid and patient hearing; for we desire to justify you, if it were possible. If this can be done to the satisfaction of all, it would remove from our minds a sett of painful feelings, which cannot be easily described, and dissipate a gloom which now hangs heavy upon us, in the view of the exceeding depravity, uprighteousness and cruelty of men, who, for a little gain, will deluge millions in slavery, and blood, with an unfeeling heart, and their eyes fast shut against the floating light which condemns their horrid deeds; and in the painful prospect of the dreadful vengeance of Heaven, for such daring outrage against our fellow-men, our brethren!

But until this be done, this business must be unavoidably viewed in the most disagreeable, odious, horrible light, by us. And we must be suffered to consider, and lay before the public some of the great aggravations which attend the continuation of this practice by us in these American States.

When the inhabitants of these States found themselves necessarily involved in convention with Britain, in order to continue a free people, and had the distrusting prospect of a civil war, they, being assembled in Congress, in October 1774, did agree and resolve in the following words: "We will neither import nor purchase any slave imported, after the first day of December next: After which time we will wholly discontinue the slave trade; and will neither be concerned in it ourselves, nor will we hire our vessels, nor sell our commodities or manufactures, to those who are concerned in it." This reasonable, noble and important resolution, was approved by the people in general, and they adhered to it through the war; during which time there was much publicly said and done, which was, at least, an implicit and practical declaration of the unreasonableness and injustice of the slave trade, and of the slavery in general. It was repeatedly declared in Congress, as the language and sentiment of all these States, and by other public bodies of men, "that we hold these truths to be self-evident, that *all men* are created *equal;* That they are endowed by their Creator with certain *unalienable rights.* That among these are *life, liberty,* and the *pursuit of happiness:* "That all men are born, *equally free and independent,* and have certain natural, inherent, and *unalienable* rights, among which are the defending and enjoying *life* and *liberty,* acquiring, possessing and protecting *property,* and pursuing and obtaining happiness and safety. By the immutable laws of nature, all men are entitled to life and liberty." etc. etc.[1]

The Africans, and the blacks in servitude among us, were really as much included in these assertions as ourselves; and their right, *unalienable right* to liberty, and to procure and possess property, is as much asserted as ours, if they be *men.* And if we have not allowed them to enjoy these unalienable rights, but violently deprive them of liberty and property, and are still taking, as far as in our power, all liberty, and property from the nations in Africa, we are guilty of a ridiculous wicked contradiction and inconsistence: and

1. Compare Hopkins's view with that of Chief Justice Roger B. Taney in *Dred Scott v. Sanford,* 19 How. 393 (1857), and the responses of Abraham Lincoln to that decision. See Don E. Fehrenbacher, *Prelude to Greatness: Lincoln in the 1850's* (Stanford: Stanford University Press, 1962); and Harry V. Jaffa, *Crisis of the House Divided* (New York: Doubleday, 1959).

practically authorize any nation or people, who have power to do it, to make us their slaves.

The whole of our war with Britain was a contest for Liberty: By which we, when brought to the severest test, practically adhered to the above assertions, so far as they concerned ourselves, at least, and we declared, in words and actions, that we chose rather to die than to be slaves, or have our liberty and property taken from us. We viewed the British in an odious and contemptible light, purely because they were attempting, by violence, to deprive us, in some measure, of those our unalienable rights. But if at the same time, or since we have taken or withheld these same rights from the Africans, or any of our fellow men, we have justified the inhabitant of Britain in all they have done against us, and declared that all the blood which has been shed in consequence of our opposition to them, is chargeable on us. If we do not allow this, and abide by the above declarations, we charge ourselves with the guilt of all the blood which has been shed by means of the slave trade; and of an unprovoked and most injurious conduct in depriving innumerable Africans of their just, unalienable rights, in violently taking and withholding from them all liberty and property; holding them as our own property, and buying and selling them, as we do our horses, and cattle; reducing them to the most vile, humiliating, and painful situation.

This whole contest, it must be again observed, was suited to bring and keep in our view, and impress on our minds, a deep and lasting sense of the worth of liberty, and the unrighteousness of taking it from any man; and consequently of our unrighteousness and cruelty towards the Africans—If it were known, that the wise Governor of the world had determined to take some method to convince us of the injustice of the slave trade, and of the slavery of the Africans, had manifest his displeasure with us for it, and use means suited to reform us, could we conceive of any measures which might be better suited to answer this end, than those which have actually taken place in this war considered in all the circumstances of it; It would be thought impossible that every one who then was, or had been, active in reducing the Africans to the abject and suffering state in which they are in the West Indies, and even among us, should not reflect upon it with self-condemnation, regret and horror, had not experiment proved the contrary. And while we execrated the British for taking out men, and ordering them to be transported to the East Indies, and for crowding so many of our people into prisons, and prisonships, where they died by the thousands, without any relief or pity from them, was it possible for us not to reflect upon our treatment of the Africans, in transporting so many thousands of them from their native country, to a land of slavery, while multitudes, being crowded and shackled in our ships, have died on their passage, without one to help or pity them? Could any avoid seeing the righteous hand of GOD stretched out against us and retaliating our unrighteous, cruel treatment of them, in a way suited to strike conviction into our minds of our guilt, and of the righteous displeasure of Heaven with us for these horrid deeds which had been done by us? Surely we had good reason to espouse the language of the brethren of Joseph in a similar case: "We are verily guilty concerning our brethren, the Africans, in that we saw the anguish of their souls, under our cruel bards, and they besought us, and cried for pity; but we would not hear: Therefore is this distress come upon us."

Is it possible that the Americans should, after all this, and in the face of all this light and conviction, and after they had obtained liberty and independence for themselves, continue to hold hundreds of thousands of their fellow men in the most abject slavery? And not only so, but notwithstanding their resolutions and declarations, renew and carry on the slave trade; and from year to year convey thousands of their fellow-men from the native country, to a state of most severe and perpetual bondage: This would have been thought impossible was it not known to be true in fact. And who can describe the aggravated guilt which the Americans have brought upon themselves by this? If this was an Heaven daring crime, of the first magnitude, before the war with Britain, how much more criminal must we be now, when, instead of regarding the admonitions of Heaven, and the light and conviction set before us, and repenting and reforming, we persist in this evil practice: What name shall be given to their daring presumption and hardiness, who, from a thirst for gold, have renewed this trade in slaves, in the bodies and souls of men, and of those whom they employ in this unhuman horrid business!

> "Is there not some chosen curse,
> Some hidden thunder, in the stores of Heaven,
> Red with wrath, to blast these men."

who owe their riches to such aggravated, detestable crimes, now necessarily involved in carrying on this trade!

"Civis"
[David Ramsay]

"An Address to the Freemen of South Carolina on the Subject of the Federal Constitution"

Columbian Herald, Charleston, 4 February 1787

———•———

A member of the Continental Congress and the South Carolina ratifying convention, Ramsay was also a physician and a noted historian.

———•———

Friends, Countrymen, and Fellow Citizens, You have at this time a new federal constitution proposed for your consideration. The great importance of the subject demands your most serious attention. To assist you in forming a right judgment on this matter, it will be proper to consider,

1st. It is the manifest interest of these states to be united. Eternal wars among ourselves would most probably be the consequence of disunion. Our local weakness particularly proves it to be for the advantage of South-Carolina to strengthen the federal government; for we are inadequate to secure ourselves from more powerful neighbours.

2d. If the thirteen states are to be united in reality, as well as in name, the obvious principle of the union should be, that the Congress or general government, should have power to regulate all general concerns. In a state of nature, each man is free and may do what he pleases; but in society, every individual must sacrifice a part of his natural rights; the minority must yield to the majority, and the collective interest must controul particular interests. When thirteen persons constitute a family, each should forego every thing that is injurious to the other twelve. When several families constitute a parish, or county, each may adopt any regulations it pleases with regard to its domestic affairs, but must be abridged of that liberty in other cases, where the good of the whole is concerned.

When several parishes, counties or districts form a state, the separate interests of each must yield to the collective interest of the whole. When thirteen states combine in one government, the same principles must be observed. These relinquishments of natural rights, are not real sacrifices: each person, county or state, gains more than it loses, for it only gives up a right of injuring others, and obtains in return aid and strength to secure itself in the peaceable enjoyment of all remaining rights. If then we are to be an united people, and the obvious ground of union must be, that all continental concerns should be managed by Congress—let us by these principles examine the new constitution. Look over the 8th section, which enumerates the powers of Congress, and point out one that is not essential on the before recited principles of union. The first is a power to lay and collect taxes, duties, imposts and excises, to pay the debts, and provide for the common defence and general welfare of the United States.

When you authorised Congress to borrow money, and to contract debts for carrying on the late war, you could not intend to abridge them of the means of paying their engagements, made on your account. You may observe, that their future power is confined to provide for the *common defence* and *general welfare* of the United States. If they apply money to any other purposes, they exceed their powers. The people of the United States who pay, are to be judges how far their money is properly applied. It would be tedious to go over all the powers of Congress, but it would be easy to shew that they all may be referred to this single principle, "that the general concerns of the union ought to be managed by the general government." The opposers of the constitution, cannot shew a single power delegated to Congress, that could be spared consistently with the welfare of the whole, nor a single one taken from the states, but such as can be more advantageously lodged in the general government, than in that of the separate states.

For instance—the states cannot emit money; this is not intended to prevent the emission of paper money, but only of state paper money. Is not this an advantage? To have thirteen paper currencies in thirteen states is embarrassing to commerce, and eminently so to travellers. It is obviously our interest, either to have no paper, or such as will circulate from Georgia to New-Hampshire. Take another instance—the Congress are authorised to provide and maintain a navy—Our sea coast in its whole extent needs the protection thereof; but if this was to be done by the states, they who build ships, would be more secure than they who do not. Again, if the local legislatures might build ships of war at pleasure, the Eastern would have a manifest superiority over the Southern states. Observe how much better this business is referred to the regulations of Congress. A common navy, paid out of the common treasury, and to be disposed of by the united voice of a majority for the common defence of the weaker as well as of the stronger states, is promised, and will result from the federal constitution. Suffer not yourselves to be imposed on by declamation. Ask the man who objects to the powers of Congress two questions. Is it not necessary that the supposed dangerous power be lodged somewhere? and secondly, where can it be lodged consistently with the general good, so well as in the general government? Decide for yourselves on these obvious principles of union.

It has been objected, that the eastern states have an advantage in their representation in Congress. Let us examine this objection—the four eastern states send seventeen members to the house of representatives, but Georgia, South-Carolina, North-Carolina and Virginia, send twenty-three. The six northern states send twenty-seven, the six southern thirty. In both cases we have a superiority;—but, say the objectors, add Pennsylvania to the northern states, and there is a majority against us. It is obvious to reply, add Pennsylvania to the Southern states, and they have a majority. The objection amounts to no more than that seven are more than six. It must be known to many of you, that the Southern states, from their vast extent of uncultivated country, are daily receiving new settlers; but in New-England their country is so small, and their land so poor, that their inhabitants are constantly emigrating. As the rule of representation in Congress is to vary with the number of inhabitants, our influence in the general government will be constantly increasing. In fifty years, it is probable that the Southern states will have a great ascendency over the Eastern. It has been said that thirty-five men, not elected by yourselves, may make laws to bind you. This objection, if it has any force, tends to the destruction of your state government. By our constitution, sixty-nine make a quorum, of course, thirty-five members may make a law to bind all the people of South-Carolina.—Charleston, and any one of the neighbouring parishes send collectively thirty-six members; it is therefore possible, in the absence of all others, that three of the lower parishes might legislate for the whole country. Would this be a valid objection against your own constitution? It certainly would not—neither is it against the proposed federal plan. Learn from it this useful lesson—insist on the constant attendance of your members, both in the state assembly, and Continental Congress: your representation in the latter, is as numerous in a relative proportion with the other states as it ought to be. You have a thirteenth part in both houses; and you are not, on principles of equality, entitled to more.

It has been objected, that the president, and two-thirds of the senate, though not of your election, may make treaties binding on this state. Ask these objectors—do you wish to have any treaties? They will say yes.—Ask then who can be more properly trusted with the power of making them, than they to whom the convention have referred it? Can the state legislatures? They would consult their local interests—Can the Continental House of Representatives? When sixty-five men can keep a secret, they may. Observe the cautious guards which are placed around your interests. Neither the senate nor president can make treaties by their separate authority.— They must both concur.—This is more in your favor than the footing on which you now stand. The delegates in Congress of nine states, without your consent can not bind you;—by the new constitution there must be two thirds of the members present, and also the president, in whose election you have a vote. Two thirds are to the whole nearly as nine to thirteen. If you are not wanting to yourselves by neglecting to keep up the states compliment of senators, your situation with regard to preventing the controul of your local interests by the Northern states, will be better under the proposed constitution than now it is under the existing confederation.

It has been said, we will have a navigation act, and be restricted to American bottoms, and that high freight will be the consequence. We certainly ought to have a navigation act, and we assuredly ought to give a preference, though not a monopoly, to our own shipping.

If this state is invaded by a maritime force, to whom can we apply for immediate aid?—To Virginia and North-Carolina? Before they can march by land to our assistance, the country may be over run. The Eastern states, abounding in men and in ships, can sooner relieve us, than our next door neighbours. It is therefore not only our duty, but our interest, to encourage their shipping. They have sufficient resources on a few months notice, to furnish tonnage enough to carry off all your exports; and they can afford, and doubtless will undertake to be your carriers on as easy terms as you now pay for freight in foreign bottoms.

On this subject, let us consider what we have gained, & also what they have lost by the revolution. We have gained a free trade with all the world, and consequently a higher price for our commodities, it may be said, and so have they; but they who reply in this manner, ought to know, that there is an amazing difference in our favor: their country affords no valuable exports, and of course the privilege of a free trade is to them of little value, while our staple commodity commands a higher price than was usual before the war. We have also gained an exemption from quit rents, to which the eastern states were not subjected. Connecticut and Rhode-Island were nearly as free before the revolution as since. They had no royal governor or councils to control them, or to legislate for them. Massachusetts and New-Hampshire were much nearer independence in their late constitutions than we were. The eastern states, by the revolution, have been deprived of a market for their fish, of their carrying-trade, their ship building, and almost of every thing but their liberties.

As the war has turned out so much in our favor, and so much against them, ought we to begrudge them the carrying of our produce, especially when it is considered, that by encouraging their shipping, we increase the means of our own defence. Let us examine also the federal constitution, by the principle of reciprocal concession. We have laid a foundation for a navigation act.—This will be a general good; but particularly so to our northern brethren. On the other hand, they have agreed to change the federal rule of paying the continental debt, according to the value of land as laid down in the confederation, for a new principle of apportionment, to be founded on the numbers of inhabitants in the several states respectively. This is an immense concession in our favor. Their land is poor; our's rich; their numbers great; our's small; labour with them is done by white men, for whom they pay an equal share; while five of our negroes only count as equal to three of their whites. This will make a difference of many thousands of pounds in settling our continental accounts. It is farther objected, that they have stipulated for a right to prohibit the importation of negroes after 21 years. On this subject observe, as they are bound to protect us from domestic violence, they think we ought not to increase our exposure to that evil, by an unlimited importation of slaves. Though Congress may forbid the importation of negroes after 21 years, it does not follow that they will. On the other hand, it is probable that they will not.[1] The more rice we make, the more business will be for their shipping: their interest will therefore coincide with our's. Besides, we have other sources of supply—the importations of the ensuing 20 years, added to the natural increase of those we already have, and the influx from our northern neighbours, who are desirous of getting rid of their slaves, will afford a sufficient number for cultivating all the lands in this state.

Let us suppose the union to be dissolved by the rejection of the new constitution, what would be our case? The United States owe several millions of dollars to France, Spain, and Holland. If an efficient government is not adopted, which will provide for the payment of our debt, especially of that which is due to foreigners—who will be the losers? Most certainly the southern states. Our exports, as being the most valuable, would be the first objects of capture on the high seas; or descents would be made on our defenceless coasts, till the creditors of the United States had paid themselves at the expence of this weaker part of the union. Let us also compare the present confederation, with the proposed constitution. The former can neither protect us at home, nor gain us respect abroad: it cannot secure the payment of our debts, nor command the resources of our country, in case of danger. Without money, without a navy, or the means of even supporting an army of our own citizens in the field, we lie at the mercy of every invader; our sea port towns may be laid under contribution, and our country ravaged.

By the new constitution, you will be protected with the force of the union, against domestic violence and foreign invasion. You will have a navy to defend your coasts.—The respectable figure you will make among the nations, will so far command the attention of foreign powers, that it is probable you

1. See One of the People Called Quakers, *Friends,* 457.

will soon obtain such commercial treaties, as will open to your vessels the West-India islands, and give life to your expiring commerce.

In a country like ours, abounding with free men all of one rank, where property is equally diffused, where estates are held in fee simple, the press free, and the means of information common; tyranny cannot readily find admission under any form of government; but its admission is next to impossible, under one where the people are the source of all power, and elect either mediately by their representatives, or immediately by themselves the whole of their rulers.

Examine the new constitution with candor and liberality. Indulge no narrow prejudices to the disadvantage of your brethren of the other states; consider the people of all the thirteen states, as a band of brethren, speaking the same language, professing the same religion, inhabiting one undivided country, and designed by heaven to be one people. Consent that what regards all the states should be managed by that body which represents all of them; be on your guard against the misrepresentations of men who are involved in debt; such may wish to see the constitution rejected, because of the following clause "no state shall emit bills of credit, make any thing but gold and silver coin, a tender in payment of debts, pass any *expost facto* law, or law impairing the obligation of contracts." This will doubtless bear hard on debtors who wish to defraud their creditors, but it will be of real service to the honest part of the community. Examine well the characters & circumstances of men who are averse to the new constitution. Perhaps you will find that the above recited clause is the real ground of the opposition of some of them, though they may artfully cover it with a splendid profession of zeal for state privileges and general liberty.

On the whole, if the proposed constitution is not calculated to better your country, and to secure to you the blessings for which you have so successfully contended, reject it: but if it is an improvement on the present confederation, and contains within itself the principles of farther improvement suited to future circumstances, join the mighty current of federalism, and give it your hearty support. You were among the first states that formed an independent constitution; be not among the last in accepting and ratifying the proposed plan of federal government; it is your sheet anchor; and without it, independence may prove a curse.

"One of the People Called Quakers"

Essay

Virginia Independent Chronicle, Richmond, 12 March 1788

Mr. DAVIS, *"A Virginian"* [1] might have a right to expect, and would perhaps have received, the thanks of *"the people called Quakers in Virginia,"* for the *"hint"* he hath given them, if they thought it was wholly dictated by an unfeigned regard for their interests and happiness: but its seeming want of candor, the criterion, by which a plain simple people, lovers of truth, are led to judge, inclines them to think that it springs from some other motive.

He tells the Quakers, that they should *"disapprove of the new constitution"*—["] *because it admits of the importation of slaves to America for a limited time."* Hence it would seem, as if he inferred, and would have them to believe that the new constitution would introduce slaves into Virginia contrary to the inclination of the people: which the Quakers apprehend is not the case. Virginia indeed, may import slaves, but she may, as she now does, also prohibit, and which it is reasonable to expect she will continue to do; and therefore, the Quakers, or any other society opposed to the slave trade, have nothing to apprehend on that score; and more especially, when it is considered that the late convention, used every means in their power, to prevail upon the Carolina's and Georgia, the only states in the union, that at present import slaves, at once to put an end to this unjust traffic; but the representatives of these states being inflexible in their opposition thereto, occasioned the limited importation as the best compromise that could be made; hence it is but just to conclude, that the new fœderal government, if established, would eagerly embrace the opportunity not only of putting an end to the importation of slaves, but of abolishing slavery forever.

---

1. The author is responding to a letter from a "Virginian," published in the *Virginia Independent Chronicle,* 13 February 1788.

Though the Quakers, are fully sensible of the favors and protection that they have hitherto experienced under the present constitution, and government of Virginia, they see no great reason to apprehend that their principles would not be as safe under the new constitution, and better secured and protected, under a government of more weight, dignity, and stability.

This *"hint"* like most of the other hints and objections that have hitherto appeared, rather tend to fix, than to remove any favorable impressions that *"the people called Quakers in Virginia"* have received of the new constitution. A good cause, will always be supported by plain reasons, addressed to the most common understanding; while a bad one, stands in need of sophistry, subtilty, and even trifling *"hints,"* calculated to operate upon the passions and prejudices of man, in order to mislead and confound, where they cannot convince.

"An American Citizen"
[Tench Coxe]

"An Examination of the Constitution of the United States"

Independent Gazetteer, Philadelphia, 26–29 September 1788

Essays I, II, and III in this series appeared in the *Independent Gazetteer* on 26, 28, and 29 September. On or before 21 October, a reprint of the series was printed by Hall and Sellers of the *Pennsylvania Gazette,* Philadelphia, in which the fourth essay first appeared.

I

It is impossible for an honest and feeling mind, of any nation or country whatever, to be insensible to the present circumstances of America. Were I an East Indian, or a Turk, I should consider this singular situation of a part of my fellow creatures, as most curious and interesting. Intimately connected with the country, as a citizen of the Union, I confess it entirely engrosses my mind and feelings.

To take a proper view of the ground on which we stand, it may be necessary to recollect the manner in which the United States were originally settled and established. Want of charity in the religious systems of Europe and of justice in their political governments were the principal moving causes which drove the emigrants of various countries to the American continent. The Congregationalists, Quakers, Presbyterians and other British dissenters, the Catholics of England and Ireland, the Huguenots of France, the German Lutherans, Calvinists, and Moravians, with several other societies, established themselves in the different colonies, thereby laying the ground of that catholicism in ecclesiastical affairs, which has been observable since the late Revolution. Religious liberty naturally promotes corresponding dispositions in matters of government. The constitution of England, as it stood on paper, was one of the freest at that time existing in the world, and the American colonies considered themselves as entitled to the fullest enjoyment of it. Thus when the ill-judged discussions of latter times in England brought into question the rights of this country, as it stood connected with the British Crown, we were found more strongly impressed with their importance and accurately acquainted with their extent, than the wisest and most learned of our brethren beyond the Atlantic. When the greatest names in Parliament insisted on the power of that body over the commerce of the colonies, and even the right to bind us in all cases whatsoever, America, seeing that it was only another form of tyranny, insisted upon the immutable truth, that taxation and representation are inseparable, and while a desire of harmony and other considerations induced her into an acquiescence in the commercial regulations of Great Britain, it was done from the declared necessity of the case, and with a cautious, full and absolute saving of our voluntarily suspended rights. The Parliament was persevering, and America continued firm till hostilities and open war commenced, and finally the late Revolution closed the contest forever.

Tis evident from this short detail and the reflections which arise from it, that the quarrel between the United States and the Parliament of Great Britain did not arise so much from objections to the form of government, *though undoubtedly a better one by far is now within our reach,* as from a difference concerning certain important rights resulting from the essential principles of liberty, which the constitution preserved to all the subjects actually residing within the realm. It was not asserted by America that the people of *the island of Great Britain* were slaves, but that *we,* though possessed absolutely of the same rights, were not admitted to enjoy *an equal degree of freedom.*

When the Declaration of Independence completed the separation between the two countries, new governments were necessarily established.[1]

---

1. See Adams, *The First American Constitutions.*

Many circumstances led to the adoption of the republican form, among which was the predilection of the people. In devising the frames of government it may have been difficult to avoid extremes opposite to the vices of that we had just rejected; nevertheless many of the state constitutions we have chosen are truly excellent. Our misfortunes have been, *that in the first instance we adopted no national government at all,* but were kept together by common danger only, *and that in the confusions of a civil war we framed a federal constitution now universally admitted to be inadequate to the preservation of liberty, property, and the Union.* The question is not then how far our state constitutions are good or otherwise—the object of our wishes is *to amend and supply the evident and allowed errors and defects of the federal government.* Let us consider awhile, that which is now proposed to us. Let us compare it with the so much boasted British form of government, and see how much more it favors the people and how completely it secures their rights, remembering at the same time that we did not dissolve our connection with that country so much on account of its constitution as the perversion and maladministration of it.

In the first place let us look at the nature and powers of the head of that country, and those of the ostensible head of ours.

The British king is the great bishop or supreme head of an established church, with an immense patronage annexed. In this capacity he commands a number of votes in the House of Lords, by creating bishops, who, besides their great incomes, have votes in that assembly, and are judges in the last resort. They have also many honorable and lucrative places to bestow, and thus from their wealth, learning, dignities, powers and patronage give a great luster and an enormous influence to the Crown.

In America our President will not only be *without* these influencing advantages, *but they will be in the possession of the people at large, to strengthen their hands in the event of a contest with him.* All religious funds, honors and powers are in the gift of numberless, unconnected, disunited, and contending corporations, wherein the principle of perfect equality universally prevails. In short, danger from ecclesiastical tyranny, that longstanding and still remaining curse of the people—that sacrilegious engine of royal power in

461

some countries, can be feared by no man in the United States. In Britain their king is for life. In America our President will always be *one of the people* at the end of four years. In that country the king is hereditary and may be an idiot, a knave, or a tyrant by nature, or ignorant from neglect of his education, yet cannot be removed, for *"he can do no wrong."* In America, as the President is to be one of the people at the end of his short term, so will he and his fellow citizens remember, *that he was originally one of the people; and that he is created by their breath.* Further, he cannot be an idiot, probably not a knave or a tyrant, for those whom nature makes so, discover it before the age of thirty-five, until which period he cannot be elected. It appears we have not admitted that he can do no wrong, but have rather presupposed he may and will sometimes do wrong, by providing for *his impeachment, his trial, and his peaceable and complete removal.*

In England the king has a power to create members of the upper house, who are judges in the highest court, as well as legislators. Our President not only cannot make members of the upper house, but their creation, like his own, is by *the people* through their representatives, and a member of assembly may and will be as certainly dismissed at the end of his year for electing a weak or wicked Senator, as for any other blunder or misconduct.

The king of England has legislative power, while our President can only use it when the other servants of the people are divided. But in all great cases affecting the national interests or safety, his modified and restrained power must give way to the sense of two-thirds of the legislature. In fact it amounts to no more, than a serious duty imposed upon him to request both houses to reconsider any matter on which he entertains doubts or feels apprehensions; and here the people have a strong hold upon him *from his sole and personal responsibility.*

The president of the upper house (or the chancellor) in England is appointed by the king, while our Vice President, who is chosen *by the people* through the Electors and the Senate, *is not at all dependent on the President,* but may exercise equal powers on some occasions. In all royal governments an helpless infant or an inexperienced youth may wear the crown. *Our President must be matured by the experience of years,* and being born among us, his character at thirty-five must be fully understood. Wisdom, virtue, and active qualities of mind and body can alone make him the first servant of a free and enlightened people.

Our President will fall very far short indeed of any prince in his annual income,[2] which will not be hereditary, but *the absolute allowance of the people passing through the hands of their other servants from year to year as it becomes necessary*. There will be no burdens on the nation to provide for his heir or other branches of his family. Tis probable, from the state of property in America and other circumstances, that many citizens will *exceed* him in show and expense, those dazzling trappings of kingly rank and power. He will have no authority to make a treaty without *two-thirds of the Senate*, nor can he appoint ambassadors or other great officers *without their approbation*, which will remove the idea of *patronage and influence*, and of personal obligation and dependence. The appointment of even the inferior officers may be taken out of his hands by an act of Congress at any time; he can create no nobility or titles of honor, nor take away offices during good behavior. *His person is not so much protected as that of a member of the House of Representatives; for he may be proceeded against like any other man in the ordinary course of law.* He appoints *no officer of the separate states.* He will have no influence *from placemen in the legislature*, nor can he prorogue or dissolve it. He will have no power *over the treasures of the state;* and lastly, as he is *created* through the Electors by the people at large, *he must ever look up to the support of his creators.* From such a servant with powers so limited and transitory, there can be no danger, especially when we consider the solid foundations on which our national liberties are immovably fixed by the other provisions of this excellent Constitution. Whatever of dignity or au-

2. In the Federal Convention, Franklin spoke in favor of *not* paying the chief executive *at all*. To Franklin's way of thinking, payment would serve only to unite the passion of avarice with the passion of ambition in those who would seek the executive office: "Place before the eyes of such men a post of *honour* that shall at the same time be a place of *profit*, and they will move heaven and earth to obtain it." The "pleasure of doing good & serving their Country and the respect such conduct entitles them to," Franklin insisted, "are sufficient motives" to draw the most capable men into public affairs. The suggestion was not taken seriously. As Madison recorded in his notes, "No debate ensued." Farrand, *Records*, 1:81–85.

thority he possesses is *a delegated part of their majesty and their political omnipotence, transiently vested in him by the people themselves for their own happiness.*

II

We have seen that the late Honorable Convention, in designating the nature of the chief executive office of the United States, *have deprived it of all the dangerous appendages of royalty,* and provided for *the frequent expiration of its limited powers.* As our President bears *no resemblance to a king,* so we shall see the Senate have *no similitude to nobles.*

First then not being hereditary, their *collective* knowledge, wisdom and virtue are not precarious, *for by these qualities alone are they to obtain their offices;* and they will have none of the *peculiar* follies and vices of those men *who possess power merely because their fathers held it before them,* for they will be educated (under equal advantages and with equal prospects) among and on a footing with the other sons of a free people. If we recollect the characters, who have, at various periods, filled the seats of Congress, we shall find this expectation *perfectly reasonable.* Many *young* men of genius and *many characters of more matured abilities, without fortunes,* have been honored with that trust. *Wealth has had but few representatives there, and those have been generally possessed of respectable personal qualifications.* There have also been many instances of persons, not eminently endowed with mental qualities, who have been sent thither *from a reliance on their virtues, public and private.* As the Senators *are still to be elected by the legislatures of the states,* there can be no doubt of *equal safety and propriety* in their future appointment, especially as no further pecuniary qualification is required by the Constitution.

They can hold *no other office* civil or military under the United States, nor can they join *in making provisions for themselves,* either by creating new places or increasing the emoluments of old ones. As their sons are not to succeed them, they will not be induced to aim at an increase or perpetuity of their powers, at the expense of the liberties of the people of which those sons will be a part. They possess *a much smaller share of the judicial power* than the upper house in Britain, for they are not, as there, the highest court in civil affairs. Impeachments *alone* are the cases cognizable before them, and in what other place could matters of that nature be so properly and safely determined? The judges of the federal courts will owe their appointments to the President and Senate, therefore may not feel so perfectly free *from favor, affection and influence* as the upper house, who receive their power from the people, through their state representatives, and are immediately responsible to those assemblies, and finally to the nation at large. Thus we see when a daring or dangerous offender is brought to the bar of public justice, the people *who alone can impeach him by their immediate representatives* will cause him to be tried, *not by the judges appointed in the heat of the occasion,* but by two-thirds of *a select body, chosen a long time before, for various purposes by the collected wisdom of their state legislatures.* From a pretense or affection of extraordinary purity and excellence of character *their word of honor* is the sanction under which these high courts in other countries have given their sentence. But with us, like the other judges of the Union, like the rest of the people *of which they are never to forget they are a part,* it is required that they be on oath.

No ambitious, undeserving or unexperienced youth can acquire a seat in this house by means of the most enormous wealth or most powerful connections, *till thirty years have ripened his abilities and fully discovered his merits to his country*—a more rational ground of preference surely than mere property.

The Senate, though more independent of the people as to *the free exercise of their judgment and abilities* than the House of Representatives, by the longer term of their office, must be older and more experienced men, and the public treasures, *the sinews of the state,* cannot be called forth by their original motion. They may *restrain the profusion or errors* of the House of Representatives, *but they cannot take the necessary measures to raise a national revenue.*

The people, through the Electors, *prescribe* them such a President as shall be *best qualified to control them.*

They can only, by conviction on impeachment, *remove and incapacitate a dangerous officer,* but the punishment of him as a criminal *remains within the province of the courts of law to be conducted under all the ordinary forms and precautions,* which exceedingly diminishes the importance of their judicial powers. They are *detached,* as much as possible, from *local* prejudices in favor of their respective states by having *a separate and independent vote,* for the sensible and conscientious use of which, every member will find *his person, honor and character* seriously bound. He cannot shelter himself, *under a vote in behalf of his state,* among his immediate colleagues. As there are only *two,* he cannot be voluntarily or involuntarily governed *by the majority of the deputation.* He will be obliged, by wholesome provisions, *to attend his public duty,* and thus in great national questions *must give a vote* of the honesty of which he will find it necessary to convince his constituents.

The Senate *must always receive the exceptions of the President* against any of their legislative acts, which, without *serious deliberation and sufficient reasons,* they will seldom disregard. They will also feel a considerable check *from the constitutional powers of the state legislatures,* whose rights they will not be disposed to infringe, since they are the bodies *to which they owe their existence,* and are moreover to remain *the immediate guardians of the people.*

And lastly the Senate will feel *the mighty check of the House of Representatives*—a body *so pure in its election,* so intimately connected, by its interests and feelings, *with the people at large,* so guarded against *corruption and influence*—so much, from its nature, *above all apprehensions,* that it *must ever be able to maintain the high ground assigned to it by the Federal Constitution.*

III

In pursuing the consideration of the new Federal Constitution, it remains now to examine the nature and powers of the House of Representatives—*the immediate delegates of the people.*

Each member of this truly popular assembly will be chosen by about six thousand electors, *by the poor as well as the rich.* No decayed and venal borough will have an *unjust* share in their determinations. No old *Sarum* will send thither a Representative *by the voice of a single elector.* As we shall have no royal ministries to purchase votes, so we shall have no votes for sale. *For*

466

the suffrages of six thousand enlightened and independent freemen are above all price. When the increasing population of the country shall render the body too large at the rate of one member for every thirty thousand persons, they will be returned at the greater rate of one for every forty or fifty thousand, which will render the electors still more incorruptible. For this regulation is only designed to prevent a *smaller number* than thirty thousand from having a Representative. Thus we see a provision follows, that no state shall have less than one member; for if a new and greater number should hereafter be fixed on, which shall exceed the whole of the inhabitants of any state, such state, without this wholesome provision, would lose its voice in the House of Representatives, a circumstance which the Constitution renders *impossible.*

The people of England, whose House of Commons is filled with military and civil officers and pensioners, say their liberties would be perfectly secured by triennial parliaments. *With us no placemen can sit among the Representatives of the people, and two years are the constitutional term of their existence.* Here again, lest wealth, powerful connections, or even *the unwariness of the people* should place in this important trust an undeserving, unqualified or inexperienced youth, the wisdom of the Convention has proposed *an absolute incapacity till the age of twenty-five.* At twenty-one a young man is made the guardian of his *own* interests, *but he cannot for a few years more be entrusted with the affairs of the nation.* He must be an inhabitant of the state that elects him, that he may be intimately acquainted with their *particular circumstances.* The House of Representatives is not, *as the Senate,* to have a president chosen *for them* from *without* their body, *but are to elect their speaker from their own number.* They will also appoint *all their other officers.* In great state cases, they will be *the grand inquest of the nation,* for they possess *the sole and uncontrollable power of impeachment.* They are neither *to wait the call* nor *abide the prorogations and dissolutions of a perverse or ambitious prince,* for they are to meet at least once in every year, and sit on adjournments to be agreed on between themselves and the other servants of the people. Should they differ in opinion, the President, who is a temporary fellow servant and not their hereditary master, has *a mediatorial power* to adjust it for them, *but cannot prevent their constitutional meeting within the year.* They can compel the attendance of their members, that their public duty may not be *evaded* in times of difficulty or danger. The vote of each Representative can be always known, as well as the proceedings of the House, *that so the people may be acquainted with the conduct of those in whom they repose so important a trust.* As was observed of the Senators, they cannot make *new* offices *for themselves,* nor increase, *for their own benefit,* the emoluments of old ones, *by which the people will be exempted from needless additions to the public expenses on such sordid and mercenary principles.* They are not to be restrained from *the firm and plain language* which becomes the independent representatives of freemen, *for there is to be a perfect liberty of speech.* Without their consent *no monies can be obtained, no armies raised, no navies provided.* They *alone* can originate bills for drawing forth the revenues of the Union, and *they will have a negative upon every legislative act of the other house.* So far, in short, as the sphere of federal jurisdiction extends, they will be controllable *only by the people,* and in contentions with the other branch, so far as they shall be right, *they must ever finally prevail.*

Such, my countrymen, are some of *the cautionary provisions* of the frame of government your faithful Convention have submitted to your consideration—such *the foundations of peace, liberty and safety,* which have been laid by their unwearied labors. They have guarded you against *all servants* but those "whom choice and common good ordain," against *all masters* "save preserving Heaven."

IV

In considering the respective powers of the President, the Senate and the House of Representatives, under the fœderal constitution, we have seen a part of the wholesome precautions, which are contained in the new system. Let us examine what further securities for the safety and happiness of the people are contained in the general stipulations and provisions.

The United States guarantee to every state in the union a separate republican form of government. From thence it follows, that any man or body of men, however rich or powerful, who shall make an alteration in the form of government of any state, whereby the powers thereof shall be attempted to be taken out of the hands of the people at large, will stand guilty of high treason; or should a foreign power seduce or over-awe the people of any state, so as to cause them to vest in the families of any ambitious citizens or foreigners the powers of hereditary governors, whether as Kings or Nobles, that such investment of powers would be void in itself, and every person attempting to execute them would also be guilty of treason.

No religious test is ever to be required of any officer or servant of the United States. The people may employ any wise or good citizen in the execution of the various duties of the government. In Italy, Spain, and Portugal, no protestant can hold a public trust. In England every Presbyterian, and other person not of their established church, is incapable of holding an office. No such impious deprivation of the rights of men can take place under the new fœderal constitution. The convention has the honour of proposing the first public act, by which any nation has ever divested itself of a power, every exercise of which is a trespass on the Majesty of Heaven.

No qualification in monied or landed property is required by the proposed plan; nor does it admit any preference from the preposterous distinctions of birth and rank. The office of the President, a Senator, and a Representative, and every other place of power or profit, are therefore open to the whole body of the people. Any wise, informed and upright man, be his property what it may, can exercise the trusts and powers of the state, provided he possesses the moral, religious and political virtues which are necessary to secure the confidence of his fellow citizens.

The importation of slaves from any foreign country is, by a clear implication, held up to the world as equally inconsistent with the dispositions and the duties of the people of America. A solid foundation is laid for exploding the principles of negro slavery, in which many good men of all parties in Pennsylvania, and throughout the union, have already concurred.[3] The temporary reservation of any particular matter must ever be deemed an admission that it should be done away. This appears to have been well understood. In addition to the arguments drawn from liberty, justice and religion, opinions against this practice, founded in sound policy, have no

---

3. See Crito, *Friends,* 441–49; One of the People Called Quakers, *Friends,* 457–58; Cf. Civis, *Friends,* 450–56.

doubt been urged. Regard was necessarily paid to the peculiar situation of our southern fellow-citizens; but they, on the other hand, have not been insensible of the delicate situation of our national character on this subject.[4]

The people will remain, under the proposed constitution, the fountain of power and public honour. The President, the Senate, and the House of Representatives, will be the channels through which the stream will flow—but it will flow from the people, and from them only. Every office, religious, civil and military will be either their immediate gift, or it will come from them through the hands of their servants. And this, as observed before, will be guaranteed to them under the state constitution which they respectively approve; for they cannot be royal forms, cannot be aristocratical, but must be republican.

The people of those states which have faithfully discharged their duty to the union will be no longer subjected alone to the weight of the public debts. Proper arrangements will call forth the just proportion of their sister states, and our national character will again be as unstained as it was once exalted. Elevation to independence, with the loss of our good name, is only to be conspicuous in disgrace. The liberties of a people involved in debt are as uncertain as the liberty of an individual in the same situation. Their virtue is more precarious. The unfortunate citizen must yield to the operation of the laws, while a bankrupt nation too easy annihilates the sacred obligations of gratitude and honour, and becomes execrable and infamous. I cannot refrain from reminding my fellow-citizens of our near approach to that deplorable situation, which must be our miserable condition, if the defects of the old confederation remain without amendment. The proposed constitution will cure the evil, and restore us to our rank among mankind.

Laws, made after the commission of the fact, have been a dreadful engine in the hands of tyrannical governors. Some of the most virtuous and shining characters in the world have been put to death, by laws formed to render them punishable, for parts of their conduct which innocence permitted, and to which patriotism impelled them. These have been called ex post facto laws, and are exploded by the new system. If a time of public contention shall hereafter arrive, the firm and ardent friends to liberty may know the

4. See Storing, "Slavery and the Moral Foundations of the American Republic."

length to which they can push their noble opposition, on the foundation of the laws. Should their country's cause impel them further, they will be acquainted with the hazard, and using those arms which Providence has put into their hands, will make a solemn appeal to "the power above."

The destruction of the ancient republics was occasioned in every instance by their being ignorant of a great political position, which was left for America to discover and establish. Self-evident as the truth appears, we find no friend to liberty in ancient Greece or Rome asserting, that taxation and representation were inseparable. The Roman citizens, proud of their own liberty, imposed, in the freest times of the commonwealth, the most grievous burdens on their wretched provinces. At other times we find thousands of their citizens, though residing within the walls of Rome, deprived of legislative representatives. When America asserted the novel truth, Great Britain, though boasting herself as alone free among the modern nations, denied it by her legislature, and endeavoured to refute it by her arms—the reasoning of tyrants.[5] But the attempt was vain, for the voice of truth was heard above the thunders of the war, and reached the ears of all nations. Henceforth the people of the earth will consider this position as the only rock on which they can found the temple of liberty, that taxation and representation are inseparable. Our new constitution carries it into execution on the most enlarged and liberal scale, for a Representative will be chosen by six thousand of his fellow-citizens, a Senator by half a sovereign state, a President by a whole nation.

The old fœderal constitution contained many of the same things, which from error or disingenousness are urged against the new ones. Neither of them have a bill of rights, nor does either notice the liberty of the press, because they are already provided for by the state constitutions; and relating only to personal rights, they could not be mentioned in a contract among foreign states.

Both the old and new fœderal constitutions, and indeed the constitution of Pennsylvania, admit of courts in which no use is made of a jury. The board of property, the court of admiralty, and the high court of errors and

---

5. As Chief Justice John Marshall would have occasion to instruct in *McCulloch v. Maryland:* "The power to tax involves the power to destroy."

appeals, in the state of Pennsylvania, as also the court of appeals under the old confederation, exclude juries. Trial by jury will therefore be in the express words of the Pennsylvania constitution, "as heretofore,"—almost always used, though sometimes omitted. Trials for lands lying in any state between persons residing in such state, for bonds, notes, book debts, contracts, trespasses, assumptions, and all other matters between two or more citizens of any state, will be held in the state courts by juries, as now. In these cases the fœderal courts cannot interfere.* But when a dispute arises between the citizens of any state about lands lying out of the bounds thereof, or when a trial is to be had between the citizens of any state and those of another, or the government of another, the private citizen will not be obliged to go into a court constituted by the state, with which, or with the citizens of which, his dispute is. He can appeal to a disinterested fœderal court. This is surely a great advantage, and promises a fair trial, and an impartial judgment. The trial by jury is not excluded in these fœderal courts. In all criminal cases, where the property, liberty or life of the citizen is at stake, he has the benefit of a jury. If convicted on impeachment, which is never done by a jury in any country, he cannot be fined, imprisoned or punished, but only may be disqualified from doing public mischief by losing his office, and his capacity to hold another. If the nature of his offence, besides its danger to his country, should be criminal in itself—should involve a charge of fraud, murder or treason—he may be tried for such crime, but cannot be convicted without a jury. In trials about property in the fœderal courts, which can only be as above stated, there is nothing in the new constitution to prevent a trial by jury. No doubt it will be the mode in every case, wherein it is practicable. This will be adjusted by law, and it could not be done otherwise. In short, the sphere of jurisdiction for the fœderal courts is limited, and that sphere only is subject to the regulations of our fœderal government. The known principles of justice, the attachment to trial by jury whenever it can be used, the instructions of the state legislatures, the instructions of the people at large, the operation of the fœderal regulations on the property of a president, a senator, a representative, a judge, as well as on that of a

---

*Trials between a state and its own Citizens, and between Citizens of the same state, involving questions concerning state laws that infringe this constitution, may be carried by appeal, it is presumed, into a fœderal court.

private citizen, will certainly render those regulations as favorable as possible to property; for life and liberty are put more than ever into the hands of the juries. Under the present constitution of all the states, a public officer may be condemned to imprisonment or death on impeachment, without a jury; but the new fœderal constitution protects the accused, till he shall be convicted, from the hands of power, by rendering a jury the indispensible judges of all crimes.

The influence which foreign powers may attempt to exercise in our affairs was foreseen, and a wholesome provision has been made against it; for no person holding an office under the United States is permitted to enjoy any foreign honours, powers or emoluments.

The apprehensions of the people have been excited, perhaps by persons with good intentions, about the powers of the new government to raise an army. Let us consider this point with moderation and candour. As enemies will sometimes insult us, invade our country and capture our property, it is clear a power in our government to oppose, restrain or destroy them, is necessary to our honor, safety and existence. The military should, however, be regarded with a watchful eye; for it is a profession that is liable to dangerous perversion. But the powers vested in the fœderal government do not go the length which has been said. A standing army is not granted or intended, for there can be no provision for its continuing three years, much less for its permanent establishment. Two years are the utmost time for which the money can be given. It will be under all the restrictions which wisdom and jealousy can suggest, and the original grant of the supplies must be made by the House of representatives, the immediate delegates of the people. The Senate and President, who also derive their power from the people, appoint the officers; and the heads of the departments, who must submit their accounts to the whole legislature, are to pay and provide them, as shall be directed by the laws that shall contain the conditions of the grant. The militia, who are in fact the effective part of the people at large, will render many troops quite unnecessary. They will form a powerful check upon the regular troops, and will generally be sufficient to over-awe them—for our detached situation will seldom give occasion to raise an army, though a few scattered companies may often be necessary. But whenever, even on the most obvious reasons, an army shall be raised, the several states will be called, by the nature of things, to attend to the condition of the militia. Republican jealousy, the guardian angel of these states, will watch the motions of our military citizens, even though they will be the soldiers of a free people. There is a wide difference however between the troops of such commonwealths as ours, founded on equal and unalterable principles, and those of a regal government, where ambition and oppression are the profession of the king. In the first case, a military officer is the occasional servant of the people, employed for their defence; in the second, he is the ever ready instrument to execute the schemes of conquest or oppression, with which the mind of his royal master may be disturbed.

Observations have been made on the power given to the fœderal Government in regard to the elections of Representatives and Senators. The regulations of these elections are, by the first part of the clause, to be prescribed by the state legislatures, who are certainly the proper bodies, if they will always execute the duty. But in case the union or the public safety should be endangered by an omission of this duty, as in the case of Rhode-Island, then the legislature of the United States can name for the people a convenient time, and do other matters necessary to insure the free exercise of their right of election. The exception, in regard to the places of chusing Senators, was made from due respect to the sovereignty of the state legislatures, who are to elect the senators, and whose place of meeting ought not to be prescribed to them by any authority, except, indeed, as we always must, by the authority of the people. This power given to the fœderal legislature is no more than what is possessed by the governments of all the states. The constitution of Pennsylvania permits two thirds of such cities and counties, as shall elect representatives, to exercise all the powers of the General Assembly, "as fully and amply as if the whole were present," should any part of the state neglect or refuse to perform their duty in this particular. In short, it is a power necessary to preserve the social compact of each state and the confederation of the United States.

Besides the securities for the liberties of the people arising out of the fœderal government, they are guarded by their state constitutions, and by the nature of things in the separate states.[6] The Governor or President in

6. Cf. The Federalist, No. 51.

each commonwealth, the Councils, Senates, Assemblies, Judges, Sheriffs, Grand and Pettit Juries, Officers of Militia, Clergy and Lay Officers of all churches, state and county Treasurer, Prothonotaries, Registers, Presidents and other officers of Universities, Colleges and Academies, Wardens of ports and cities, Burgesses of towns, Commissioners of counties, County Lieutenants, and many other officers of power and influence, will still be chosen within each state, without any possible interference of the fœderal Government. The separate states will also choose all the members of the legislative and executive branches of the United States. The people at large in each state will choose their fœderal representative, and, unless ordered otherwise by state legislatures, may choose the electors of the President and Vice-President of the Union. And lastly, the legislature of the state will have the election of the senate, as they have heretofore had of the Members of Congress. Let us then, with a candor worthy of the subject, ask ourselves, whether it can be feared, that a majority of the Representatives, each of whom will be chosen by six thousand enlightened freemen, can betray their country?—Whether a majority of the Senate, each of whom will be chosen by the legislature of a free, sovereign and independent state, without any stipulations in favour of wealth or the contemptible distinctions of birth or rank, and who will be closely observed by the state legislatures, can destroy our liberties, controuled as they are too by the house of representatives? or whether a temporary, limited, executive officer, watched by the fœderal Representatives, by the Senate, by the state legislatures, by his personal enemies among the people of his own state, by the jealousy of the people of rival states, and by the whole of the people of the Union, can ever endanger our Freedom.*

*There is one grand operation of the new fœderal constitution, favorable to general liberty, which I do not remember to have heard from any of its friends. It is well known, that in most of the states the members of their Houses of Representatives are chosen in equal numbers from each county, and in the eastern states, in equal numbers from each town, without any regard to the number of taxable inhabitants, or the number of souls. Hence it is very frequent for a county, with ten thousand souls, to send only the same number of members to the state house of representatives, as a county with two thousand souls, by which each person in the least populous county has five times as great a voice in electing representatives, as his fellow citizen of the most populous county. This is clearly a departure from the principles of equal liberty, and ought to be altered in the several states. I speak the more plainly because our state constitution is free from that fault in the formation of our house of Assembly. Now the new

Permit me, my fellow-citizens, to close these observations by remarking, that there is no spirit of arrogance in the new fœderal constitution. It addresses you with becoming modesty, admitting that it may contain errors. Let us give it a trial; and when experience has taught its mistakes, the people, whom it preserves absolutely all powerful, can reform and amend them. That I may be perfectly understood, I will acknowledge its acceptance by all the states, without delay, is the second wish of my heart. The first is, that our country may be virtuous and free.

---

constitution expressly declares, that the fœderal Representatives shall be in the proportion of one to every thirty thousand, which accords with reason and the true principles of liberty. This house, therefore, so far as national matters go, will remedy the evil spoken of in the several states, and is one more great step towards the perfection of equal liberty and genuine republicanism in America. It must strongly recommend the fœderal constitution to the serious reflecting patriot, even though he may formerly have had doubts, and it will suggest to the several states the propriety of reconsidering that point in their respective constitutions. Pennsylvania, though right in the principles on which her legislative elections are and will be held, is less safe from the existence of this fault in the adjoining sister states of Virginia, Maryland, Jersey, Delaware and New York, and in others more remote.

"Elihu"

Essay

American Mercury, Hartford, 18 February 1788

I was afraid, and durst not shew mine opinion. I said days should speak and multitude of years should teach wisdom. Great men are not always wise, neither doth age understand judgment. I will answer. I also will shew mine opinion. The Spirit within me constraineth me. I will speak that I may be refreshed. Let me not accept any man's person, neither let me give flattering titles unto man. etc. Job, chap. XXXII.

It was an objection against the Constitution, urged in the late Convention, that the being of a God was not explicitly acknowledged in it. It has been reported that an honorable gentleman, who gave his vote in favor of the Constitution, has since expressed his discontent by an expression no less remarkable than this, "that they (speaking of the framers of the Constitution) had not allowed God a seat there"!!

Another honorable gentleman who gave his vote in like manner, has published a *specimen of an introductory acknowledgment of a God* such as should have been *in his opinion* prefixed to the Constitution, viz.: *We the people of the United States, in a firm belief of the being and perfections of the one living and true God, the creator and supreme Governor of the world, in His universal providence and the authority of His laws: that He will require of all moral agents an account of their conduct, that all rightful powers among men are ordained of, and mediately derived from God, therefore in a dependence on His blessing and acknowledgment of His efficient protection in establishing our Independence, whereby it is become necessary to agree upon and settle a Constitution of federal government for ourselves*—This introduction is likewise to serve as a religious test, for he says "*instead of none, no other religious test should ever be required, etc.*"

In treating of a *being* who is above comprehension there may be a certain degree of propriety in using language that is so; if any reader's brain is too weak to obtain a distinct idea of a writer's meaning, I am sensible it may be retorted that a writer is not obliged to furnish his readers with comprehension. Neither is there any law to oblige him to write comprehensible matter, which is a great comfort to me; as I shall not stop to think, but proceed to give mine opinion! Should any body of men, whose characters were unknown to me, form a plan of government, and prologue it with a long pharisaical harangue about God and religion, I should suspect a design to cheat and circumvent us, and their cant, and semblance of superior sanctity would be the ground of my suspicion. If they have a plan founded on good sense, wisdom, and experience, what occasion have they to make use of God, His providence, or religion, like old cunning monks to gain our assent to what is in itself rational and just? "There must be (tis objected) some proof, some evidence that we the people acknowledge the being of a God." Is this a thing that wants proof? Is this a thing that wants constitutional establishment in the United States? It is almost the only thing that all universally are agreed in; everybody believes there is a God; not a man of common sense in the United States denies or disbelieves it. *The fool hath said in his heart there is no God,* but was there ever a wise man said such a thing? No, not in any age or in any country. Besides, if it was not so, if there were unbelievers, as it is a matter of faith, it might as well be admitted; for we are not to bind the consciences of men by laws or constitutions. The mind is free; it may be convinced by reasoning, but cannot be compelled by laws *or constitutions,* no, nor by fire, faggot, or the halter. Such an acknowledgment is moreover useless *as a religious test*—it is calculated to exclude from office *fools* only, who believe there is no God; and the people of America are now become so enlightened that no fool hereafter (it is hoped) will ever be promoted to any office or high station.

An honorable gentleman objects that God has no seat allowed him. Is this only to find fault with the Constitution because he had no hand in making it? Or is he serious? Would he have given God a seat there? For what purpose? To get a name for sanctity that he might have it in his power to impose on the people? The time has been when nations could be kept in awe with stories of gods sitting with legislators and dictating laws; with this lure, cunning politicians have established their own power on the credulity of the people, shackling their uninformed minds with incredible tales. But the light of philosophy has arisen in these latter days, miracles have ceased, oracles are silenced, monkish darkness is dissipated, and even witches at last hide their heads. Mankind are no longer to be deluded with fable. Making the glory of God subservient to the temporal interest of men is a wornout trick, and a pretense to superior sanctity and special grace will not much longer promote weakness over the head of wisdom.

A low mind may imagine that God, like a foolish old man, will think himself slighted and dishonored if he is not complimented with a seat or a prologue of recognition in the Constitution, but those great philosophers who formed the Constitution had a higher idea of the perfection of that INFINITE MIND which governs all worlds than to suppose they could add to his honor or glory, or that He would be pleased with such low familiarity or vulgar flattery.

The most shining part, the most brilliant circumstance in honor of the framers of the Constitution is their avoiding all appearance of craft, declining to dazzle even the superstitious by a hint about grace or ghostly knowledge. They come to us in the plain language of common sense and propose to our understanding a system of government as the invention of mere human wisdom; no deity comes down to dictate it, not even a God appears in a dream to propose any part of it.

A knowledge of human nature, the aid of philosophy, and the experience of ages are seen in the very face of it; whilst it stands forth like a magnificent STATUE of gold. Yet, there are not wanting FANATICS who would crown it with the periwig of an old monk and wrap it up in a black cloak— whilst *political quackery* is contending to secure it with fetters and decorate it with a leather apron!!

"A Landholder"
[Oliver Ellsworth]

The Letters: VII, XIII

Connecticut Courant, Hartford, 17 December 1787
and 24 March 1788

VII

To the Landholders and Farmers.

I have often admired the spirit of candour, liberality, and justice, with which the Convention began and completed the important object of their mission. "In all our deliberations on this subject," say they, "we kept steadily in our view, that which appears to us the greatest interest of every true American, the consolidation of our union, in which is involved our prosperity, felicity, safety, perhaps our national existence. This important consideration, seriously and deeply impressed on our minds, led each state in the Convention to be less rigid on points of inferior magnitude, than might otherwise have been expected; and thus the Constitution which we now present, is the result of a spirit of amity, and of that mutual deference and concession, which the peculiarity of our political situation rendered indispensible."

Let us, my fellow citizens, take up this constitution with the same spirit of candour and liberality; consider it in all its parts; consider the important advantages which may be derived from it, and the fatal consequences which will probably follow from rejecting it. If any objections are made against it, let us obtain full information on the subject, and then weigh these objections in the balance of cool impartial reason. Let us see, if they be not wholly groundless; But if upon the whole they appear to have some weight, let us consider well, whether they be so important, that we ought on account of them to reject the whole constitution. Perfection is not the lot of human institutions; that which has the most excellencies and fewest faults, is the best that we can expect.

Some very worthy persons, who have not had great advantages for information, have objected against that clause in the constitution, which provides, that *no religious Test shall ever be required as a qualification to any office or public trust under the United States.*[1] They have been afraid that this clause is unfavourable to religion. But, my countrymen, the sole purpose and effect of it is to exclude persecution, and to secure to you the important right of religious liberty. We are almost the only people in the world, who have a full enjoyment of this important right of human nature. In our country every man has a right to worship God in that way which is most agreeable to his own conscience. If he be a good and peaceable citizen, he is liable to no penalties or incapacities on account of his religious sentiments; or in other words, he is not subject to persecution.

But in other parts of the world, it has been, and still is, far different. Systems of religious error have been adopted, in times of ignorance. It has been the interest of tyrannical kings, popes, and prelates, to maintain these errors. When the clouds of ignorance began to vanish, and the people grew more enlightened, there was no other way to keep them in error, but to prohibit their altering their religious opinions by severe persecuting laws. In this way persecution became general throughout Europe. It was the universal opinion that one religion must be established by law; and that all, who differed in their religious opinions, must suffer the vengeance of persecution. In pursuance of this opinion, when popery was abolished in England, and the church of England was established in its stead, severe penalties were inflicted upon all who dissented from the established church. In the time of the civil wars, in the reign of Charles I. the presbyterians got the upper hand, and inflicted legal penalties upon all who differed from them in their sentiments respecting religious doctrines and discipline. When Charles II. was restored, the church of England was likewise restored, and the presbyterians and other dissenters were laid under legal penalties and incapacities. It was in this reign, that a religious test was established as a qualification for office; that is, a law was made requiring all officers civil and military (among other things)

---

1. See the letter of William Williams, "A Letter to The Landholder," in Paul Leicester Ford, *Essays on the Constitution of the United States* (New York: Historical Printing Club, 1892), 207–9.

to receive the Sacrament of the Lord's Supper, according to the usage of the church of England, written six months after their admission to office, under the penalty of 500 l. and disability to hold the office. And by another statute of the same reign, no person was capable of being elected to any office relating to the government of any city or corporation, unless, within a twelvemonth before, he had received the Sacrament according to the rites of the church of England. The pretence for making these severe laws, by which all but churchmen were made incapable of any office civil or military, was to exclude the papists; but the real design was to exclude the protestant dissenters. From this account of test-laws, there arises an unfavourable presumption against them. But if we consider the nature of them and the effects which they are calculated to produce, we shall find that they are useless, tyrannical, and peculiarly unfit for the people of this country.

A religious test is an act to be done, or profession to be made, relating to religion (such as partaking of the sacrament according to certain rites and forms, or declaring one's belief of certain doctrines,) for the purpose of determining, whether his religious opinions are such, that he is admissible to a public office. A test in favour of any one denomination of christians would be to the last degree absurd in the United States. If it were in favour of either congregationalists, presbyterians, episcopalions, baptists, or quakers; it would incapacitate more than three fourths of the American citizens for any public office; and thus degrade them from the rank of freemen. There needs no argument to prove that the majority of our citizens would never submit to this indignity.

If any test-act were to be made, perhaps the least exceptionable would be one, requiring all persons appointed to office, to declare, at the time of their admission, their belief in the being of a God, and in the divine authority of the scriptures. In favour of such a test, it may be said, that one who believes these great truths, will not be so likely to violate his obligations to his country, as one who disbelieves them; we may have greater confidence in his integrity. But I answer: His making a declaration of such belief is no security at all. For suppose him to be an unprincipled man, who believes neither the word nor the being of a God; and to be governed merely by selfish motives; how easy is it for him to dissemble? how easy is it for him to make a public declaration of his belief in the creed which the law prescribes; and excuse himself by calling it a mere formality? This is the case with the test-laws and creeds in England. The most abandoned characters partake of the sacrament, in order to qualify themselves for public employments. The clergy are obliged by law to administer the ordinance unto them; and thus prostitute the most sacred office of religion; for it is a civil right in the party to receive the sacrament. In that country, subscribing to the thirty-nine articles is a test for admission into holy orders. And it is a fact, that many of the clergy do this; when at the same time, they totally disbelieve several of the doctrines contained in them. In short, test-laws are utterly ineffectual; they are no security at all; because men of loose principles will, by an external compliance, evade them. If they exclude any persons, it will be honest men, men of principle, who will rather suffer an injury, than act contrary to the dictates of their consciences. If we mean to have those appointed to public offices, who are sincere friends to religion; we the people who appoint them, must take care to choose such characters; and not rely upon such cob-web barriers as test-laws are.

But to come to the true principle, by which this question ought to be determined: The business of civil government is to protect the citizen in his rights, to defend the community from hostile powers, and to promote the general welfare. Civil government has no business to meddle with the private opinions of the people. If I demean myself as a good citizen, I am accountable, not to man, but to God, for the religious opinions which I embrace, and the manner in which I worship the supreme being. If such had been the universal sentiments of mankind, and they had acted accordingly, persecution, the bane of truth and nurse of error, with her bloody axe and flaming hand, would never have turned so great a part of the world into a field of blood.

But while I assert the right of religious liberty; I would not deny that the civil power has a right, in some cases, to interfere in matters of religion. It has a right to prohibit and punish gross immoralities and impieties; because the open practice of these is of evil example and public detriment. For this reason, I heartily approve of our laws against drunkenness, profane swearing, blasphemy, and professed atheism. But in this state, we have never thought it expedient to adopt a test-law; and yet I sincerely believe we have as great a proportion of religion and morality, as they have in England, where every person who holds a public office, must be either a saint by law, or a hypocrite by practice. A test-law is the parent of hypocrisy, and the offspring of error and the spirit of persecution. Legislatures have no right to set up an inquisition, and examine into the private opinions of men. Test-laws are useless and ineffectual, unjust and tyrannical; therefore the Convention have done wisely in excluding this engine of persecution, and providing that no religious test shall ever be required.

XIII

The attempt to amend our federal Constitution, which for some time past hath engrossed the public regard, is doubtless become an old and unwelcome topic to many readers whose opinions are fixed, or who are not concerned for the event. There are other subjects which claim a share of attention, both from the public and from private citizens. It is good government which secures the fruits of industry and virtue; but the best system of government cannot produce general happiness unless the people are virtuous, industrious and œconomical.

The love of wealth is a passion common to men, and when justly regulated it is condusive to human happiness. Industry may be encouraged by good laws—wealth may be protected by civil regulations; but we are not to depend on these to create it for us, while we are indolent and luxurious. Industry is most favourable to the moral virtue of the world, it is therefore wisely ordered by the Author of Nature, that the blessings of this world should be acquired by our own application in some business useful to society; so that we have no reason to expect any climate or soil will be found, or any age take place, in which plenty and wealth will be spontaneously produced. The industry and labour of a people furnish a general rule to measure their wealth, and if we use the means we may promise ourselves the reward. The present state of America will limit the greatest part of its inhabitants to agriculture; for as the art of tilling the earth is easily acquired, the price of land low, and the produce immediately necessary for life, greater encouragement to this is offered here than in any country on earth.—But still suffer me to enquire whether we are not happily circumstanced and actually able to manage some principal Manufactories with success, and encrease our wealth by encreasing the labour of the people, and saving the surplus of our earnings, for a better purpose than to purchase the labour of European nations. It is a remark often made, and generally believed, that in a country so new as this, where the price of lands is low and the price of labour high, manufactories cannot be conducted with profit. This may be true of some manufactures, but of others it is grossly false. It is now in the power of New-England to make itself more formidable to Great-Britain, by rivaling some of her principal manufactures, than ever it was by separating from her government. Woolen cloaths the principal English manufacture, may more easily be rivaled than any other. Purchasing all the materials and labour at the common price of the country, cloths of three quarters width, may be fabricated for six shillings per yard, of fineness and beauty equal to English cloths of six quarters width, which sell at twenty shillings. The cost of our own manufacture is little more than half of the imported, and for service it is allowed to be much preferable. It is found that our wool is of equal quality with the English, and that what we once supposed the defect of our wool, is only a deficiency in cleansing, sorting and dressing it.

It gives me pleasure to hear that a number of gentlemen in Hartford and the neighbouring towns are forming a fund for the establishment of a great Woolen Manufactory—The plan will doubtless succeed, and be more profitable to the stockholders than money deposited in trade. As the manufacture of cloths is introduced, the raising of wool and flax the raw materials, will become an object of the farmers attention.

Sheep are the most profitable part of our stock, and the breed is much sooner multiplied than horses or cattle. Why do not our opulent farmers avail themselves of the profit? An experiment would soon convince them there is no better method of advancing property, and their country would thank them for the trial. Sheep are found to thrive and the wool to be of a good quality in every part of New-England, but as this animal delights in grazing, and is made healthy by coming often to the earth, our sea coasts with the adjacent country, where snow is of short continuance, are particularly favourable to their propagation. Our hilly coasts were designed by nature for this, and every part of the country that abounds in hills ought to make an experiment by which they will be enriched.

In Connecticut, the eastern and south-eastern counties, with the highlands on Connecticut river towards the sea, ought to produce more wool than would cloath the inhabitants of the state. At present the quantity falls short of what is needed for our own consumption; if a surplusage could be produced, it would find a ready market and the best pay.

The culture of flax, another principal material for manufacturing, affords great profit to the farmer. The seed of this crop when it succeeds well will pay the husbandman for his labour, and return a better ground rent than many other crops which are cultivated. The seed is one of our best articles for remittance and exportation abroad. Dressing and preparing the flax for use is done in the most leisure part of the year, when labour is cheap, and we had better work for six pence a day and become wealthy, than to be idle and poor.

It is not probable the market can be overstocked, or if it should chance for a single season to be the case, no article is more meliorated by time, or will better pay for keeping, by an increase of quality. A large flax crop is one most certain sign of a thrifty husbandman. The present method of agriculture in a course of different crops is well calculated to give the husbandman a sufficiency of flax ground, as it is well known that this vegetable will not thrive when sown successively in the same place.

The Nail Manufacture might be another source of wealth to the northern states. Why should we twice transport our own iron, and pay other nations for labour which our boys might perform as well. The art of nail making is easily acquired. Three thousand men and boys in Connecticut, might spend our long and idle winters in this business, without detriment to their agricultural service. Remittances have actually been made from some parts of the state in this article, the example is laudable and ought to be imitated. The sources of wealth are open to us, and there needs but industry to become as rich as we are free.

"Fabius"
[John Dickinson]

The Letters: VII–IX

VII

Thus happily mistaken was the ingenious, learned, and patriotic lord Belhaven, in his prediction concerning the fate of his country; and thus happily mistaken, it is hoped, some of our fellow-citizens will be, in their prediction concerning the fate of their country.

Had they taken large scope, and assumed in their proposition the vicissitude of human affairs, and the passions that so often confound them, their prediction might have been a tolerably good guess. Amidst the mutabilities of terrestrial things, the liberty of United America may be destroyed. As to that point, it is our duty, humbly, constantly, fervently, to implore the protection of our most gracious maker, "who doth not afflict willingly nor grieve the children of men," and incessantly to strive, as we are commanded, to recommend ourselves to that protection, by "doing his will," diligently exercising our reason in fulfilling the purposes for which that and our existence were given to us.

How the liberty of this country is to be destroyed, is another question. Here, the gentlemen assign a cause, in no manner proportioned, as it is apprehended, to the effect.

The uniform tenor of history is against them. That holds up the *licentiousness* of the people, and *turbulent temper* of some of the states, as *the only causes* to be dreaded, not the conspiracies of federal officers. Therefore, it is highly probable, that, if our liberty is ever subverted, it will be by one of the two causes first mentioned. Our tragedy will then have the same acts, with those of the nations that have gone before us; and we shall add one more example to the number already too great, of people that would not take warning, not, "know the things which belong to their peace." But, we ought not to pass such a sentence against our country, and the interests of freedom: Though, no sentence whatever can be equal to the atrocity of our guilt, if through enormity of obstinacy or baseness, we betray the cause of our posterity and of mankind, by providence committed to our parental and fraternal care. There is reason to believe, that the calamities of nations are the punishments of their sins.

As to the first mentioned cause, it seems unnecessary to say any more upon it.

As to the second, we find, that the misbehaviour of the constituent parts acting separately, or in partial confederacies, debilitated the Greeks under The Amphictionic Council, and under The Achæan League. As to the former, it was not entirely an assembly of strictly democratical republics. Besides, it wanted a sufficiently close connection of its parts. After these observations, we may call our attention from it.

'Tis true, The Achæan League was disturbed by the misconduct of some parts, but it is as true, that it surmounted these difficulties, and wonderfully prospered, until it was dissolved in the manner that has been described.

The glorious operations of its principles bear the clearest testimony to this distant age and people, that the wit of man never invented such an antidote against monarchical and aristocratical projects, as a strong combination of truly democratical republics. By strictly or truly democratical republics, the writer means republics in which all the principal officers, except the judicial, are from time to time chosen by the people.

The reason is plain. As liberty and equality, or as well termed by Polybius, *benignity,* were the foundations of their institutions, and the energy of the government pervaded all the parts in things relating to the whole, it counteracted for the common welfare, the designs hatched by selfishness in separate councils.

If folly or wickedness prevailed in any parts, friendly offices and salutary measures restored tranquility. Thus the public good was maintained. In its very formation, tyrannies and aristocracies submitted, by consent or compulsion. Thus, the Ceraunians, Trezenians, Epidaurians, Megalopolitans, Argives, Hermionians, and Phlyayzrians were received into the league. A happy exchange! For history informs us, that so true were they to their noble and benevolent principles, that, in their diet, "*no resolutions were taken, but what were equally advantageous to the whole confederacy, and the interest of each part so consulted, as to leave no room for complaints!"*

How degrading would be the thought to a citizen of United America, that the people of these states, with institutions beyond comparison preferable to those of The Achæan league, and so vast a superiority in other respects, should not have wisdom and virtue enough, to manage their affairs, with as much prudence and affection of one for another as these ancients did.

Would this be doing justice to our country? The composition of her temper is excellent, and seems to be acknowledged equal to that of any nation in the world. Her prudence will guard its warmth against two faults, to which it may be exposed—The one, an imitation of *foreign fashions,* which from small things may lead to great. May her citizens aspire at a national dignity in every part of conduct, private as well as public. This will be influenced by the former. May *simplicity* be the characteristic feature of their manners, which, inlaid with their other virtues and their forms of government, may then indeed be compared, in the Eastern stile, to "apples of gold in pictures of silver." Thus will they long, and may they, while their rivers run, escape the contagion of luxury—that motley issue of innocence debauched by folly, and the lineal predecessor of tyranny, prolific of guilt and wretchedness. The other fault, of which, as yet, there are no symptoms among us, is the *thirst of empire.* This is a vice, that ever has been, and from the nature of things, ever must be, fatal to republican forms of government. Our wants, are sources of happiness: our irregular desires, of misery. The abuse of prosperity, is rebellion against Heaven; and succeeds accordingly.

Do the propositions of gentlemen who object, offer to our view, any of *the great points* upon which, the fate, fame, or freedom of nations has turned, excepting what some of them have said about trial by jury; and which has been frequently and fully answered? Is there one of them calculated to regulate, and if needful, to *controul* those tempers and measures of constituent parts of an union, that have been so baneful to the weal of every confederacy that has existed? Do not some of them tend to enervate the authority evidently designed thus to regulate and controul? Do not others of them discover a bias in their advocates to particular connections, that if indulged to them, would enable persons of less understanding and virtue, to repeat the disorders, that have so often violated public peace and honor? Taking them altogether, would they afford as strong a security to our liberty, as the frequent election of the federal officers by the people, and the repartition of power among those officers, according to the proposed system?

It may be answered, that, they would be an additional security. In reply, let the writer be permitted at present to refer to what has been said.

The principal argument of gentlemen who object, involves a direct proof of the point contended for by the writer of this address, and as far as it may be supposed to be founded, a plain confirmation of Historic evidence.

They generally agree, that the great danger of a monarchy or aristocracy among us, will arise from the federal senate.

The members of this senate, are to be chosen by men exercising the sovereignty of their respective states. These men therefore must be monarchically or aristocratically disposed, before they will chuse federal senators thus disposed; and what merits particular attention, is, that these men must have obtained an overbearing influence in their respective states, before they could with such disposition arrive at the exercise of the sovereignty in them: or else, the like disposition must be prevalent among the people of such states.

Taking the case either way, is not this a disorder in parts of the union, and ought it not to be rectified by the rest? Is it reasonable to expect, that the disease will seize all at the same time? If it is not, ought not the sound to possess a right and power, by which they may prevent the infection from spreading? And will not *the extent* of our territory, and the *number* of states within it, vastly increase the difficulty of any political disorder diffusing its contagion, and the probability of its being repressed?[1]

---

1. See the famous argument by Publius in *The Federalist*, No. 10; and James Madison's speech of 6 June in the Federal Convention: "[W]ere we not thence admonished," Madison asked the Convention, "to enlarge the sphere as far as the nature of the Govt. would admit. This was the only defence agst. the inconveniences of democracy consistent with the democratic form of Govt." Farrand, *Records*, 1:134–35.

From the annals of mankind, these conclusions are deducible—that confederated states may act prudently and honestly, and apart foolishly and knavishly; but, that it is a defiance of all probability, to suppose, that states conjointly shall act with folly and wickedness, and yet separately with wisdom and virtue.

VIII

The proposed confederation offers to us a system of diversified representation in the legislative, executive, and judicial departments, as essentially necessary to the good government of an extensive republican empire. Every argument to recommend it, receives new force, by contemplating events, that must take place. The number of states in America will increase. If not united to the present, the consequences are evident. If united, it must be by a plan that will communicate equal liberty and assure just protection to them. These ends can never be attained, but by a close combination of the several states.

It has been asserted, that a very extensive territory cannot be ruled by a government of republican form. What is meant by this proposition? Is it intended to abolish all ideas of connection, and to precipitate us into the miseries of division, either as single states, or partial confederacies? To stupify us into despondence, that destruction may certainly seize us? The fancy of poets never feigned so dire a Metamorphosis, as is now held up to us. The Ægis of their Minerva was only said to turn men into stones. This spell is to turn "a band of brethren," into a monster, preying on itself, and preyed upon by all its enemies.

If hope is not to be abandoned, common sense teaches us to attempt the best means of preservation. This is all that men can do, and this they ought to do. Will it be said, that any kind of disunion, or a connection tending to it, is preferable to a firm union? Or, is there any charm in that despotism, which is said, to be alone competent to the rule of such an empire? There is no evidence of fact, nor any deduction of reason, that justifies the assertion. It is true, that extensive territory has in general been arbitrarily governed; and it is as true, that a number of republics, in such territory, loosely connected, must inevitably rot into despotism.

It is said—Such territory has never been governed by a confederacy of republics.[2] Granted. But, where was there ever a confederacy of republics, in such territory, united, as these states are to be by the proposed constitution? Where was there ever a confederacy, in which, the sovereignty of each state was equally represented in one legislative body, the people of each state equally represented in another, and the sovereignties and people of all the states conjointly represented, possessed such a qualified and temperating authority in making laws? Or, in which the appointment to federal offices was vested in a chief magistrate chosen as our president is to be? Or, in which, the acts of the executive department were regulated, as they are to be with us? Or, in which, the federal judges were to hold their offices independently and during good behaviour? Or, in which, the authority over the militia and troops was so distributed and controuled, as it is to be with us? Or, in which, the people were so drawn together by religion, blood, language, manners and customs, undisturbed by former feuds or prejudices? Or, in which, the affairs relating to the whole union, were to be managed by an assembly of several representative bodies, invested with different powers that became efficient only in concert, without their being embarrassed by attention to other business? Or, in which, a provision was made for the federal revenue, without recurring to coercion against states, the miserable expedient, of every other confederacy that has existed, an expedient always attended with odium, and often with a delay productive of irreparable damage? Where was there ever a confederacy, that thus adhered to the first principle in civil society; obliging by its direct authority every individual, to contribute, when the public good necessarily required it, a just proportion of aid to the support of the commonwealth protecting him—without disturbing him in the discharge of the duties owing by him to the state of which he is an inhabitant; and at the same time, so amply, so anxiously provided, for bringing the interests, and even the wishes of every sovereignty

2. Publius in *The Federalist*, No. 9, referred to this notion of an extensive republic better serving the rights of the people than a small republic as a "novel" contribution to the only recently improved science of politics.

and of every person of the union, under all their various modifications and impressions, into their full operation and efficacy in the national councils? The instance never existed. The conclusion ought not to be made. It is without premises. So far is the assertion from being true, that "a very extensive territory cannot be ruled by a government of a republican form," that such a territory cannot be well-ruled by a government of any other form.

The assertion has probably been suggested by reflections on the democracies of antiquity, without making a proper distinction between them and the democracy of The United States.

In the democracies of antiquity, the people assembled together and governed personally. This mode was incompatible with greatness of number and dispersion of habitation.

In the democracy of The United States, the people act by their representatives. This improvement collects the will of millions upon points concerning their welfare, with more advantage, than the will of hundreds could be collected under the ancient form.

There is another improvement equally deserving regard, and that is, the varied representation of sovereignties and people in the constitution now proposed.

It has been said, that this representation was a mere compromise.

It was not a mere compromise.[3] *The equal representation of each state in one branch of the legislature,* was an original substantive proposition, made in convention, very soon after the draft offered by Virginia, to which last mentioned state United America is much indebted not only in other respects, but for her merit in the origination and prosecution of this momentous business.

---

3. Strictly speaking, the notion of equal representation of each state in one branch of the legislature *was* the result of a compromise, a compromise that one might consider the essence of the statesmanship of those in Convention. Dickinson's rhetorical effort is aimed at undermining the notion that the Constitution was a "bundle of compromises" with no unifying theory of politics. In Dickinson's view such a compromise was, as he puts it, not a "*mere* compromise"; it was, rather, a prudential modification of principles after due deliberation. See Storing, "The Federal Convention of 1787: Politics, Principles, and Statesmanship," in Rossum and McDowell, eds., *The American Founding.*

The proposition was expressly made upon this principle, that a territory of such extent as that of United America, could not be safely and advantageously governed, but by a combination of republics, each retaining all the rights of supreme sovereignty, excepting such as ought to be contributed to the union; that for the securer preservation of these sovereignties, they ought to be represented in a body by themselves, and with equal suffrage; and that they would be annihilated, if both branches of the legislature were to be formed of representatives of the people, in proportion to the number of inhabitants in each state.

The principle appears to be well founded in reason, Why cannot a very extensive territory be ruled by a government of republican form? They answered, because its power must languish through distance of parts. Granted, if it be not a "body by joints and bands having nourishment ministered and knit together." If it be such a body, the objection is removed. Instead of such a perfect body, framed upon the principle that commands men to associate, and societies to confederate; that, which by communicating and extending happiness, corresponds with the gracious intentions of our maker towards us his creatures? what is proposed? Truly, that the natural legs and arms of this body should be cut off, because they are too weak, and their places supplied by strongest limbs of wood and metal.

Monarchs, it is said, are enabled to rule extensive territories, because they send viceroys to govern certain districts; and thus the reigning authority is transmitted over the whole empire. Be it so: But what are the consequences? Tyranny, while the viceroys continue in submission to their masters, and the distraction of civil war besides, when they revolt, to which they are frequently tempted by the very circumstances of their situation, as the history of such governments indisputably proves.

America is, and will be, divided into several sovereign states, each possessing every power proper for governing within its own limits for its own purposes, and also for acting as a member of the union.[4]

4. On the eve of the Federal Convention, James Madison shared his thoughts on the nature of a federal republic with George Washington: "Conceiving that an individual independence of the States is utterly irreconcileable with their aggregate sovereignty; and that a consolidation

They will be civil and military stations, conveniently planted throughout the empire, with lively and regular communications. A stroke, a touch upon any part, will be immediately felt by the whole. Rome famed for imperial arts, had a glimpse of this great truth; and endeavoured, as well as her hard-hearted policy would permit, to realize it in her *colonies*. They were miniatures of the capital: But wanted the vital principal of sovereignty, and were too small. They were melted down into, or overwhelmed by the nations around them. Were they now existing, they might be called curious automatons—something like to our living originals. These, will bear a remarkable resemblance to the mild features of patriarchal government, in which each son ruled his own household, and in other matters the whole family was directed by the common ancestor.

Will a people thus happily situated, ever desire to exchange their condition, for subjection to an absolute ruler; or can they ever look but with veneration, or act but with deference to that union, that alone can, under providence, preserve them from such subjugation?

Can any government be devised, that will be more suited to citizens, who wish for equal freedom and common prosperity; better calculated for preventing corruption of manners; for advancing the improvements that endear or adorn life; or that can be more conformed to the understanding, to the best affections, to the very nature of *man?* What harvests of happiness may grow from the seeds of liberty that are now sowing? The cultivation will indeed demand continual attention, unceasing diligence, and frequent conflict with difficulties: but, to object against the benefits offered to us by our Creator, by excepting to the terms annexed, is a crime to be equalled only by its folly.

Delightful are the prospects that will open to the view of United America—her sons well prepared to defend their own happiness, and ready

---

of the whole into one simple republic would be as inexpedient as it is unattainable, I have sought for some middle ground, which may at once support a due supremacy of the national authority, and not exclude the local authorities wherever they can be subordinately useful." Madison to Washington, 16 April 1787. See also *The Federalist,* No. 14.

to relieve the misery of others—her fleets formidable, but only to the unjust—her revenue sufficient, yet unoppressive—her commerce affluent, but not debasing—peace and plenty within her borders—and the glory that arises from a proper use of power, encircling them.

Whatever regions may be destined for servitude, let us hope, that some portions of this land may be blessed with liberty; let us be convinced, that *nothing short of such an union* as has been proposed, can preserve the blessing; and therefore let us be resolved to adopt it.

As to alterations, a little *experience* will cast more light upon the subject, than a multitude of debates. Whatever qualities are possessed by those who object, they will have the candor to confess, that they will be encountered by opponents, not in any respect inferior, and yet differing from them in judgment, upon every point they have mentioned.

Such untired industry to serve their country, did the delegates to the federal convention exert, that they not only laboured to form the best plan they could, but, *provided for making at any time amendments on the authority of the people,* without shaking the stability of the government. For this end, the Congress, whenever two-thirds of both houses shall deem it necessary, shall propose amendments to the constitution, or, on the application of the legislatures of two-thirds of the several states, *shall* call a convention for proposing amendments, which, in either case, shall be valid to all intents and purposes, as part of the constitution, when ratified by the legislatures of three-fourths of the several states, or by conventions in three-fourths thereof, as one or the other mode of ratification may be proposed by Congress.

Thus, by a gradual progress, we may from time to time *introduce every improvement in our constitution,* that shall be suitable to our situation. For this purpose, it may perhaps be advisable, for every state, as it sees occasion, to form with the utmost deliberation, drafts of alterations respectively required by them, and to enjoin their representatives, to employ every proper method to obtain a ratification.

In this way of proceeding, the undoubted sense of every state, collected in the coolest manner, not the sense of individuals, will be laid before the whole union in congress, and that body will be enabled with the clearest light that can be afforded by every part of it, and with the least occasion of irritation, to compare and weigh the sentiments of all United America; forthwith to adopt such alterations as are recommended by general unanimity; by degrees to devise modes of conciliation upon contradictory propositions; and to give the revered advice of our common country, upon those, if any such there should be, that in her judgment are inadmissible, because they are incompatible with the happiness of these states.

It cannot be with reason apprehended, that Congress will refuse to act upon any articles calculated to promote the *common* welfare, though they may be unwilling to act upon such as are designed to advance *partial* interests: but, whatever their sentiments may be, they *must* call a convention for proposing amendments, on applications of two-thirds of the legislatures of the several states.

May those good citizens, who have sometimes turned their thoughts towards a second convention, be pleased to consider, that there are men who speak as they do, yet do not mean as they do. These borrow the sanction of their respected names, to conceal desperate designs. May they also consider, whether persisting in the suggested plan, in preference to the constitutional provision, may not kindle flames of jealousy and discord, which all their abilities and virtues can never extinguish.

IX

When the sentiments of some objectors, concerning the British constitution, are considered, it is surprising, that they should apprehend so much danger to United America, as, they say, will attend the ratification of the plan proposed to us, by the late federal convention.

These gentlemen will acknowledge, that Britain has sustained many internal convulsions, and many foreign wars, with a gradual advancement in freedom, power, and prosperity. They will acknowledge, that no nation has existed that ever so perfectly united those distant extremes, private security of life, liberty, and property, with exertion of public force—so advantageously combined the various powers of militia, troops, and fleets—or so happily blended together arms, arts, science, commerce, and agriculture. From what spring has flowed this stream of happiness? The gentlemen will acknowledge, that these advantages are derived from a single democratical branch in her legislature. They will also acknowledge, that in this branch, called the house of commons, only one hundred and thirty-one are members for counties: that nearly one half of the whole house is chosen by about five thousand seven hundred persons, mostly of no property; that fifty-six members are elected by about three hundred and seventy persons, and the rest in an enormous disproportion to the numbers of inhabitants who ought to vote.

Thus are all the millions of people in that kingdom, said to be represented in the house of commons.

Let the gentlemen be so good, on a subject so familiar to them, as to make a comparison between the British constitution, and that proposed to us. Questions like these will then probably present themselves: Is there more danger to our liberty, from such a president as we are to have, than to that of Britons from an hereditary monarch with a vast revenue—absolute in the erection and disposal of offices, and in the exercise of the whole executive power—in the command of the militia, fleets, and armies, and the direction of their operations—in the establishments of fairs and markets, the regulation of weights and measures, and coining of money—who can call parliaments with a breath, and dissolve them with a nod—who can, at his will, make war, peace, and treaties irrevocably binding the nation—and who can grant pardons and titles of nobility, as it pleases him? Is there more danger to us, from twenty-six senators, or double the number, than to Britons, from an hereditary aristocratic body, consisting of many hundreds, possessed of enormous wealth in lands and money—strengthened by a host of dependants—and who, availing themselves of defects in the constitution, send many of these into the house of commons—who hold a third part of the legislative power in their own hands—and who form the highest court of judicature in the nation? Is there more danger to us, from a house of representatives, to be chosen by all the freemen of the union, every two years, than to Britons, from such a sort of representation as they have in the house of commons, the members of which, too, are chosen but every seven years? Is there more danger to us, from the intended federal officers, than to Britons, from such a monarch, aristocracy, and house of commons together? *What bodies* are there in Britain, vested with such capacities for enquiring into, checking, and regulating the conduct of national affairs, *as our sovereign states*? What proportion does the number of *free holders* in Britain bear to the number of people? And what is the proportion in United America?

If any person, after considering such questions, shall say, there will be more danger to our freedom under the proposed plan, than to that of Britons under their constitution, he must mean, that Americans are, or will be, beyond all comparison, inferior to Britons in understanding and virtue; otherwise, with a constitution and government, every branch of which is so extremely popular, they certainly might guard their rights, at least at well, as Britons can guard theirs, under such political institutions as they have; unless the person has some inclination to an opinion, that monarchy and aristocracy are favourable to the preservation of their rights. If he has, he cannot too soon recover himself. If ever monarchy or aristocracy appears in this country, it must be in the hideous form of despotism.

What an infatuated, depraved people must Americans become, if, with such unequalled advantages, committed to their trust in a manner almost miraculous, they lose their liberty? Through a single organ of representation, in the legislature only, of the kingdom just mentioned, though that organ is diseased, such portions of popular sense and integrity have been conveyed into the national councils, as have purified other parts, and preserved the whole in its present state of healthfulness. To their own vigour and attention, therefore, is that people, under providence, indebted for the blessings they enjoy. They have held, and now hold *the true balance* in their government. While they retain their enlightened spirit, they will continue to hold it; and *if they regard what they owe to others,* as well as what they owe to themselves, they will, most probably, continue to be happy.

They know, that there are powers that cannot be expressly limited, without injury to themselves; and their magnanimity scorns any fear of such powers. This magnanimity taught Charles the first, that he was but a royal servant; and this magnanimity caused James the second's army, raised, paid, and kept up by himself, to confound him with huzzas for liberty.

They ask not for compacts, of which the national welfare, and, in some cases, its existence, may demand violations. They despise such dangerous provisions against danger.

They know, that all powers whatever, even those that, according to the forms of the constitution, are irresistible and absolute, of which there are many, ought to be exercised for the public good; and that when they are used to the public detriment, they are unconstitutionally exerted.

This plain text, commented upon by their experienced intelligence, has led them safe through hazards of every kind: and they now are, what we see them. Upon the review, one is almost tempted to believe, that their insular situation, soil, climate, and some other circumstances, have compounded a peculiarity of temperature, uncommonly favourable to the union of reason and passion.

Certainly, 'tis very memorable, with what life, impartiality, and prudence, they have interposed on great occasions; have by their patriotism communicated temporary soundness to their disordered representation; and have bid public confusions to cease. Two instances out of many may suffice. The excellent William the third was distressed by a house of commons. He dissolved the parliament, and appealed to the people. They relieved him. His successor, the present king, in the like distress, made the same appeal; and received equal relief.

Thus they have acted: but Americans, who have the same blood in their veins, have, it seems, very different heads and hearts. We shall be enslaved by a president, senators, and representatives, chosen by ourselves, and continually rotating within the period of time assigned for the continuance in office of members in the house of commons? 'Tis strange: but, we are told, 'tis true. It may be so. As we have our all at stake, let us enquire, in what way this event is to be brought about. Is it to be before or after a general corruption of manners? If after, it is not worth attention. The loss of happiness then follows of course. If before, how is it to be accomplished? Will a virtuous and sensible people choose villains or fools for their officers? Or, if they should choose men of wisdom and integrity, will these lose both or either, by taking their seats? If they should, will not their places be quickly supplied by another choice? Is the like derangement again, and again, and again, to be expected? Can any man believe, that such astonishing phænomena are to be looked for? Was there ever an instance, where rulers, thus selected by the people from their own body, have, in the manner apprehended, outraged their own tender connexions, and the interests, feelings, and sentiments of their affectionate and confiding countrymen? Is such a conduct more likely to prevail in this age of mankind, than in the darker periods that have preceded? Are men more disposed now than formerly, to prefer uncertainties to certainties, things perilous and infamous to those that are safe and honorable? Can all the mysteries of such iniquity, be so wonderfully managed by treacherous rulers, that none of their enlightened constituents, nor any of their honest associates, acting with them in public bodies, shall ever be able to discover the conspiracy, till at last it shall burst with destruction to the whole federal constitution? Is it not ten thousand times less probable, that such transactions will happen, than it is, that we shall be exposed to innumerable calamities, by rejecting the plan proposed, or even by delaying to accept it?

Let us consider our affairs in another light. Our difference of government, participation in commerce, improvement in policy, and magnitude of power, can be no favourite objects of attention to the Monarchies and Sovereignties of Europe. Our loss will be their gain—our fall, their rise—our shame, their triumph. Divided, they may distract, dictate, and destroy. United, their efforts will be waves dashing themselves into foam against a rock. May our national character be—an animated moderation, that seeks only its own, and will not be satisfied with less.

To his beloved fellow-citizens of United America, the writer dedicates this imperfect testimony of his affection, with fervent prayers, for a perpetuity of freedom, virtue, piety, and felicity, to them and their posterity.

James Wilson

Oration on the Fourth of July 1788

Supplement to the *Pennsylvania Gazette*, 9 July 1788

My Friends and Fellow Citizens, *Your* candid and generous indulgence I may well bespeak, for *many* reasons. I shall mention but *one*. While I *express* it, I *feel* it, in all its force. My abilities are unequal—abilities far superior to mine would be unequal—to the occasion, on which I have the honor of being called to address you.

A people, free and enlightened, ESTABLISHING *and* RATIFYING *a system of government, which they have previously* CONSIDERED, EXAMINED *and* APPROVED! this is the spectacle, which we are assembled to celebrate; and it is the most dignified one that has yet appeared on our globe. Numerous and splended have been the triumphs of conquerors. From what causes have they originated? Of what consequences have they been productive? They have generally begun in ambition: They have generally ended in tyranny. But no thing tyrannical can participate of dignity; and to Freedom's eye, SESOSTRIS himself appears *contemptible,* even when he *treads* on the *necks of Kings.*

The Senators of Rome, seated in their curule chairs, and surrounded with all their official lustre, were an object much more respectable; and we view, without displeasure, the admiration of those untutored savages, who considered them as so many gods upon earth. But who were those Senators? They were only a *part* of a society: They were vested with only *inferior* powers.

What is the object exhibited to our contemplation? a WHOLE PEOPLE exercising its *first and greatest power*—performing an act of SOVEREIGNTY, ORIGINAL and UNLIMITED.

The scene before us is *unexampled* as well as *magnificent.* The greatest part of governments have been the deformed offspring of force and fear.

With these we deign not comparison. But there have been others who have formed bold pretentions to higher regard. You have heard of SPARTA, of ATHENS and of ROME. You have heard of their admired constitutions, and of their high prized freedom. In fancied right of these, they conceived themselves to be elevated above the rest of the human race, whom they marked with the degrading title of *Barbarians.* But did they, in all their pomp and pride of liberty, ever furnish to the astonished world an exhibition similar to that, which we now contemplate? Were their constitutions framed by those, who were appointed for that purpose, by the people? After they were framed, were they submitted to the consideration of the people? Had the people an opportunity of expressing their sentiments concerning them? Were they to *stand* or *fall* by the people's *approving or rejecting vote?* To all these questions attentive and impartial history obliges us to answer in the negative. The people were either *unfit* to be trusted; or their lawgivers were too *ambitious* to trust them.

The far-famed establishment of LYCURGUS was introduced by deception and fraud. Under the specious pretence of consulting the oracle concerning his laws, he prevailed on the SPARTANS to make a temporary experiment of them during his absence, and to swear that they would suffer no alteration of them till his return. Taking a disingenuous advantage of their scrupulous regard for their oaths, he prevented his return by a voluntary death; and in this manner endeavoured to secure a proud immortality to his system.

Even SOLON—the mild and moderating SOLON—far from considering himself as employed only to *propose* such regulations as he should think best calculated for promoting the happiness of the commonwealth, *made* and *promulgated* his laws with all the haughty airs of absolute power. On more occasions than one, we find him boasting, with much self complacency, of his extreme forbearance and condescension, because he did not establish a despotism in his own favor, and because he did not reduce his equals to the humiliating condition of his slaves.

Did NUMA submit his *institutions* to the good sense and free investigation of ROME? They were received in precious communications from the goddess EGERIA, with whose presence and regard he was supremely favored; and they were imposed on the easy faith of the citizens as the *Dictates* of an inspiration that was divine.

Such, my fellow citizens, was the origin of the most splendid establishments that have been hitherto known; and such were the arts, to which they owed their introduction and success.

What a *flattering* contrast arises from a *retrospect* of the scenes which we now *commemorate?* Delegates were *appointed* to deliberate and to propose. They *met,* and *performed* their delegated trust. The *result* of their deliberations was *laid before the people.* It was *discussed* and *scrutinized* in the *fullest, freest* and *severest* manner,—by *speaking,* by *writing* and by *printing*—by *individuals* and by *public bodies,*—by its *friends* and by its *enemies.* What was the *issue?* Most *favourable* and most *glorious* to the system. In *state* after *state,* at *time* after *time,* it was *ratified*—in some states *unanimously*—on the whole, by a large and very respectable *majority.*

It would be improper now to examine its qualities. A decent respect for those who have accepted of it will lead us to presume that it is worthy of their acceptance. The deliberate ratifications, which have taken place, at once recommend the *system,* and the *people* by whom it has been ratified.

By why—methinks I hear some one say—why is so much exultation displayed in celebrating this event? We are prepared to give the reasons of our joy. We rejoice, because, under this constitution, we hope to see *just government,* and to enjoy the *blessings* that walk in its train.

Let us begin with PEACE—the mild and modest harbinger of felicity! How seldom does the amiable wanderer chuse, for her permanent residence, the habitations of men! In their systems she sees too many arrangements, civil and ecclesiastical, inconsistent with the calmness and benignity of her temper. In the old world, how many millions of men do we behold, unprofitable to society, burthensome to industry, the props of establishments that deserve not to be supported, the causes of distrust in the times of peace,—and the instruments of destruction in the times of war? Why are they not employed in cultivating useful arts, and in forwarding public improvements? Let us indulge the pleasing expectation, that *such* will be the *operation* of *government* in the UNITED STATES. Why may we not hope, that, disentangled from the intrigues and jealousies of European politics, and unmolested with the alarm and solicitude, to which these intrigues and jealousies give birth, our councils will be directed to the encouragement, and our strength will be exerted in the cultivation of the arts of peace?

Of these, the first is AGRICULTURE. This is true in all countries. In the UNITED STATES its truth is of peculiar importance. The *subsistence* of *man,* the *materials* of *manufactures,* the *articles* of *commerce*—all spring originally from the *soil.* On *agriculture,* therefore, the *wealth of nations* is founded. Whether we consult the observations that reason will suggest, or attend to the information that history will give, we shall, in each case, be satisfied of the influence of government, good or bad, upon the state of agriculture. In a government, whose maxims are those of oppression, property is insecure. It is given, it is taken away, by caprice. Where there is no security for property, there is no encouragement for industry. Without industry, the richer the soil the more it abounds with weeds. The evidence of history warrants the truth of these general remarks. Attend to Greece; and compare her agriculture in *ancient* and in *modern* times. THEN, smiling harvests bore testimony to the bountiful boons of liberty. Now, the very earth languishes under oppression. View the *Compania* of ROME. How melancholy the prospect? Which ever way you turn your afflicted eyes, scenes of desolation crowd before them. Waste and barrenness appear around you in all their hideous forms. What is the reason? With DOUBLE *tyranny* the land is cursed. Open the *classic* page: you trace, in *chaste* description, the *beautiful* reverse of every thing you have seen. Whence proceeds the difference? When that description was made, the *force of liberty* pervaded the soil.

But is agriculture the only art, which feels the influence of government? Over MANUFACTURES and COMMERCE its power is equally prevalent. There the same causes operate; and there they produce the same effects. The *industrious village,* the *busy city,* the *crowded port*—all these are the gifts of *liberty;* and without a *good government* liberty cannot exist.

These are advantages, but these are not *all* the advantages that result from a system of good government. Agriculture, manufactures and commerce will ensure to us plenty, convenience and elegance. But is there not something still wanting to finish the man? Are *internal virtues and accomplishments* less *estimable* or less *attracting* than *external arts and ornaments?* Is the operation of government less powerful upon the *former* than upon the *latter?* By no means. Upon this, as upon a preceding topic, reason and history will concur in their information and advice. In a serene mind the SCIENCES and the VIRTUES love to dwell. But can the mind of a man be serene, when the property, liberty and subsistence of *himself,* and of *those,* for whom he feels *more* than he feels for *himself,* depends on a tyrant's nod? If the dispirited subject of oppression can, with difficulty, exert his enfeebled faculties, so far as to provide, on the incessant demands of nature, food just enough to lengthen out his wretched existence; can it be expected, that, *in such a state,* he will experience those *fine* and *vigorous movements of the soul,* without the full and free exercise of which *science* and *virtue* will *never flourish.* Look around you to the nations that now exist. View, in historic retrospect, the nations that have heretofore existed. The collected result will be an entire conviction of these all-interesting truths— *Where tyranny reins, there is the* COUNTRY *of* IGNORANCE *and* VICE—*Where* GOOD GOVERNMENT *prevails there is the* COUNTRY *of* SCIENCE *and* VIRTUE. Under a *good government,* therefore, we must look for the *accomplished man.*

But shall we confine our views *even here?* While we wish to be accomplished *men* and *citizens,* shall we wish to be *nothing more?* While we perform our duty, and promote our happiness in *this* world; shall we bestow no regards upon the *next?* Does no connexion subsist between the *two?* From *this* connexion flows the most important of all the blessings of good government. But here let us pause—*unassisted reason* can *guide* us *no farther,* she *directs* us to that HEAVEN-DESCENDED SCIENCE, by which LIFE *and* IMMORTALITY *have been brought to light.*

May we *now* say, that we have reason for our joy? But while we cherish the *delightful emotion,* let us remember those things which are *requisite* to give it *permanence* and *stability.* Shall we *lie supine,* and look, in *listless langour,* for those blessings and enjoyments, to which *exertion* is inseparably attached? If we would be *happy;* we must be *active.* The *Constitution* and our *manners* must mutually *support* and *be supported.* Even on *the* Festivity, it will not be disagreeable or incongruous to review the virtues and manners that both *justify* and *adorn* it.

FRUGALITY and TEMPERANCE first attract our attention. These simple but powerful virtues are the sole foundation, on which a good government can rest with security. They were the virtues which nursed and educated *infant* ROME, and prepared her for all her greatness. But in the giddy hour of her prosperity, she spurned from her the obscure instruments, by which it was procured; and in their place substituted *luxury* and *dissipation.* The consequence was such as might have been expected. She preserved, for some time, a gay and flourishing appearance; but the internal health and soundness of her constitution were gone. At last she fell, a victim to the poisonous draughts, which were administered by her perfidious favourites. The fate of Rome, both in her *rising* and in her *falling* state, will be the fate of every other nation that shall follow *both* parts of her example.

INDUSTRY appears next among the virtues of a good citizen. Idleness is the nurse of villains. The industrious alone constitute a nation's strength. I will not expatiate on this fruitful subject. Let one animating reflection suffice. In a *well constituted commonwealth,* the industry of every citizen extends beyond himself. A common interest pervades the society. EACH *gains from* ALL, *and* ALL *gain from* EACH. It has often been observed, that the *sciences* flourish *all together:* The remark applies *equally* to the *arts.*

Your patriot feelings attest to the truth of what I say, when, among the virtues necessary to merit and preserve the advantages of a good government, I number a *warm and uniform* ATTACHMENT *to* LIBERTY, *and to the* CONSTITUTION. The enemies of liberty are artful and insiduous. A *counterfeit* steals her *dress,* imitates her *manner,* forges her *signature,* assumes her *name.* But the real name of the *deceiver* is *Licentiousness.* Such is her effrontery, that she will charge liberty to her face with imposture; and she will, with shameless front, insist that *herself alone* is the *genuine character,* and that *herself alone* is *entitled to the respect,* which the *genuine character* deserves. With the giddy and undiscerning, on whom a deeper impression is made by dauntless impudence than by modest merit, her pretensions are often successful. *She* receives the *honors* of liberty, and *liberty herself* is treated as a *traitor* and an *usurper.* Generally, however, this bold impostor acts only a *secondary* part. Though she alone appear, upon the stage, her motions are regulated by *dark ambition,* who sits concealed behind the curtain, and who knows that *despotism,* his OTHER *favourite,* can always follow the success of *licentiousness.* Against these enemies of liberty, who act in concert, though they appear on opposite sides, the patriot citizen will keep a watchful guard.

A *good constitution* is the greatest blessing, which a society can enjoy. Need I infer, that it is the duty of every citizen to use his best and most unremitting endeavours for preserving it pure, healthful and vigorous? For the accomplishment of this great purpose, the exertions of no one citizen are unimportant. Let no one, therefore, harbour, for a moment, the mean idea, that he is and can be of no value to his country. Let the contrary manly impression animate his soul. Every one can, at *many* times, perform to the state, *useful* services; and he, who steadily pursues the road of patriotism, has the most inviting prospect of being able, at *some* times, to perform *eminent* ones.

Allow me to direct your attention, in a very particular manner, to a momentous part, which by this constitution, every citizen will frequently be called to act. All those in places of power and trust will be elected either immediately by the people; or in such a manner that their appointment will depend ultimately on such immediate election. All the *derivative* movements of *government* must spring from the *original* movement of the *people at large.* If, to *this,* they give a sufficient force and a just direction, all *the others* will be governed by its controuling power. To speak without a metaphor; if the people, at their elections, take care to chuse none but representatives that are wise and good; their representatives will take care, in their turn, to chuse or appoint none but such as are wise and good also. The remark applies to every succeeding election and appointment. Thus the characters proper for public officers will be diffused from the *immediate elections* of the people over the *remotest parts* of administration. Of what *immense consequence* is it, then, that this PRIMARY *duty* should be *faithfully* and *skillfully* discharged? On the *faithful* and *skillful* discharge of it the public happiness or infelicity, under *this* and *every other* constitution, must, in a very great measure, depend. For, believe me, no government, *even the best,* can be *happily* administered by *ignorant* or *vicious* men. You will forgive me, I am sure, for endeavouring to impress upon your minds, in the strongest manner, the importance of this great duty. It is the first *connection* in politics; and if an *error* is committed *here,* it can never be *corrected* in any *subsequent* process: The certain consequence must be *disease.* Let no one say, that he is but a *single* citizen; and that his ticket will be but *one* in the box. That *one* ticket may *turn* the election. In *battle,* every *soldier* should consider the *public safety* as depending on his *single arm.* At an *election,* every *citizen* should consider the *public happiness* as depending on his *single vote.*

A PROGRESSIVE STATE is necessary to the *happiness* and *perfection* of Man. Whatever attainments are already reached, attainments still higher should be pursued. Let us, therefore, strive with noble emulation. Let us suppose we have done *nothing,* while *any thing* yet remains to be done. Let us, with fervent zeal, press forward, and make *unceasing advances* in every thing that can SUPPORT, IMPROVE, REFINE or EMBELISH Society.

To enter into particulars under each of these heads, and to dilate them according to their importance, would be improper at *this* time. A few remarks on the *last* of them will be congenial with the entertainments of this *auspicious* day.

If we give the slightest attention to NATURE, we shall discover that with *utility she* is curious to blend *ornament.* Can *we* imitate a better pattern? Public exhibitions have been the favorite amusements of some of the wisest and most accomplished nations. GREECE, in her most shining *era,* considered her *games* as far from being the least respectable among her public establishments. The *shows* of the *Circus* evince, that, on this subject, the sentiments of GREECE were fortified by those of ROME.

Public processions may be so planned and executed, as to join *both* the properties of Nature's rule. They may *instruct* and *improve,* while they *entertain* and *please.* They may point out the *elegance* or *usefulness* of the *sciences* and the *arts.* They may preserve the *memory,* and engrave the *importance* of great *political events.* They may represent, with peculiar felicity and force, the *operation* and *effects* of great *political truths*. The *picturesque and splendid decorations around me* furnish the most *beautiful* and most *brilliant* proofs, that these remarks are FAR FROM BEING IMAGINARY.

The *commencement* of our Government has been *eminently glorious:* Let our *progress in every excellence* be *proportionably great*. It *will*, it *must* be so. What an enraptured prospect opens on the UNITED STATES! Placid HUSBANDRY walks in front, attended by the *venerable plough*. Lowing herds adorn our vallies: Bleating flocks spread o'er our hills, Verdant meadows, enameled pastures, yellow harvests, bending orchards, rise in rapid succession from east to west. PLENTY, with her *copious horn,* sits easy-smiling, and in *conscience complacency,* enjoys and presides over the scenes. COMMERCE next advances, in all her *splendid* and *embellished* forms. The rivers and lakes and seas are crouded with ships. Their shores are covered with cities. The cities are filled with inhabitants. The ARTS, decked with *elegance,* yet with *simplicity,* appear in *beautiful variety,* and *well-adjusted arrangement*. Around them are diffused, in rich abundance, the *necessaries,* the *decencies* and the *ornaments* of life. With *heartfelt contentment,* INDUSTRY beholds his *honest labors* flourishing and secure. PEACE walks *serene* and *unalarmed* over all the unmolested regions; while LIBERTY, VIRTUE and RELIGION go hand in hand harmoniously, *protecting, enlivening* and *exalting all!* HAPPY COUNTRY! MAY THY HAPPINESS BE PERPETUAL.

EPILOGUE

Benjamin Franklin

Remarks at the Closing of the Federal Convention

17 September 1787

—•—

The following remarks were recorded by James Madison at the close of the Constitutional Convention. See James Madison, *Notes of Debates in the Federal Convention of 1787* (Athens: Ohio University Press, 1966), 659. In addition, this account was also printed in the *Newport Herald* on 20 December and reprinted five times by 25 February 1788.

—•—

Whilst the last members were signing it [i.e., the Constitution] Doct.ʳ FRANK-LIN looking towards the Presidents Chair, at the back of which a rising sun happened to be painted, observed to a few members near him, that Painters had found it difficult to distinguish in their art a rising from a setting sun. I have said he, often and often in the course of the Session, and the vicisitudes of my hopes and fears as to its issue, looked at that behind the President without being able to tell whether it was rising or setting: But now at length I have the happiness to know that it is a rising and not a setting Sun.

INDEX

This book is set in Adobe Garamond. Robert Slimbach modeled his design of Claude Garamond's type on sixteenth-century original manuscripts. The companion italic was drawn from the types of Robert Granjon, a contemporary of Garamond.

This book is printed on paper that is acid-free and meets the requirements of the American National Standard for Permanence of Paper for Printed Library Materials, z39.48-1992. ∞

Book design by Louise OFarrell, Gainesville, Florida
Typography by Carlisle Communications, Ltd., Dubuque, Iowa
Printed and bound by Worzalla Publishing Co., Stevens Point, Wisconsin